IMPORTANT.

S0-AVV-008

ONLINE RESOURCES

HERE IS YOUR REGISTRATION CODE TO ACCESS
YOUR PREMIUM McGRAW-HILL ONLINE RESOURCES.

For key premium online resources you need THIS CODE to gain access. Once the code is entered, you will be able to use the Web resources for the length of your course.

If your course is using **WebCT** or **Blackboard**, you'll be able to use this code to access the McGraw-Hill content within your instructor's online course.

Access is provided if you have purchased a new book. If the registration code is missing from this book, the registration screen on our Website, and within your WebCT or Blackboard course, will tell you how to obtain your new code.

Registering for McGraw-Hill Online Resources

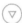

TO gain access to your McGraw-Hill web resources simply follow the steps below:

(1) USE YOUR WEB BROWSER TO GO TO: **www.mhhe.com/criticalthinking**

(2) CLICK ON **FIRST TIME USER**.

(3) ENTER THE REGISTRATION CODE* PRINTED ON THE TEAR-OFF BOOKMARK ON THE RIGHT.

(4) AFTER YOU HAVE ENTERED YOUR REGISTRATION CODE, CLICK **REGISTER**.

(5) FOLLOW THE INSTRUCTIONS TO SET-UP YOUR PERSONAL UserID AND PASSWORD.

(6) WRITE YOUR UserID AND PASSWORD DOWN FOR FUTURE REFERENCE.
KEEP IT IN A SAFE PLACE.

TO GAIN ACCESS to the McGraw-Hill content in your instructor's **WebCT** or **Blackboard** course simply log in to the course with the UserID and Password provided by your instructor. Enter the registration code exactly as it appears in the box to the right when prompted by the system. You will only need to use the code the first time you click on McGraw-Hill content.

Thank you, and welcome to your McGraw-Hill online Resources!

REGISTRATION CODE

SPN9-QO1T-3PNT-CGS8-OPGD

0-07-293714-9 T/A MOORE/PARKER: CRITICAL THINKING, 7E

Critical Thinking

Seventh Edition

Critical Thinking

BROOKE NOEL MOORE ▲ RICHARD PARKER
California State University, Chico

CHAPTER 12
with Nina Rosenstand and Anita Silvers

Boston Burr Ridge, IL Dubuque, IA Madison, WI New York
San Francisco St. Louis Bangkok Bogotá Caracas Kuala Lumpur
Lisbon London Madrid Mexico City Milan Montreal New Delhi
Santiago Seoul Singapore Sydney Taipei Toronto

Higher Education

CRITICAL THINKING, SEVENTH EDITION
Published by McGraw-Hill, a business unit of The McGraw-Hill Companies, Inc., 1221 Avenue of the Americas, New York, NY 10020. Copyright © 2004 by The McGraw-Hill Companies, Inc. All rights reserved. Previous editions © 2001, 1998, 1995, 1992, 1989, 1986 by Mayfield Publishing Company. No part of this publication may be reproduced or distributed in any form or by any means, or stored in a database or retrieval system, without the prior written consent of The McGraw-Hill Companies, Inc., including, but not limited to, any network or other electronic storage or transmission, or broadcast for distance learning.

Some ancillaries, including electronic and print components, may not be available to customers outside the United States.

2 3 4 5 6 7 8 9 0 2CUS/2CUS 0 9 8 7 6 5 4

Vice president and editor-in-chief: *Thalia Dorwick*
Publisher: *Chris Freitag*
Sponsoring editor: *Jon-David Hague*
Marketing manager: *Lisa Berry*
Production services manager: *Jennifer Mills*
Production service: *Fairplay Publishing Service*
Manuscript editor: *Joan Pendleton*
Art director: *Jeanne M. Schreiber*
Design manager: *Sharon Spurlock*
Cover designer: *Linda Robertson*
Interior designer: *Terri Wright*
Art manager: *Robin Mouat*
Photo researcher: *Connie Gardner*
Illustrators: *Jim Dandy, Lotus Art, Mitch Rigie*
Production supervisor: *Tandra Jorgensen*

The text was set in 10/12 Trump Mediaeval by Thompson Type and printed on acid-free 45# Pub Matte by Von Hoffmann, Owensville.

Cover art by Gary Overacre

The credits for this book begin on page C-1, a continuation of the copyright page.

Library of Congress Cataloging-in-Publication Data

Moore, Brooke Noel.
     Critical thinking / Brooke Noel Moore, Richard Parker. — 7th ed.
          p. cm.
     Includes index.
     ISBN 0-07-281881-6
     1. Critical thinking.   I. Parker, Richard.   II. Title.

B105.T54M66 2003
160—dc21   2003051343

INTERNATIONAL EDITION   ISBN 0-07-121491-7
Copyright © 2004. Exclusive rights by The McGraw-Hill Companies, Inc., for manufacture and export. This book cannot be re-exported from the country to which it is consigned by McGraw-Hill. The International Edition is not available in North America.

www.mhhe.com

To Alexander, Bill, and Sherry,
and also to Sydney, Darby, and Peyton Elizabeth

Contents

PART 3. Arguments

Chapter 8.   *Deductive Arguments I: Categorical Logic*   261

Chapter 9.   *Deductive Arguments II: Truth-Functional Logic*   306

Preface

Jon-David Hague, Ph.D., climbed out of his black, air-conditioned, 1995 Honda into appalling heat. "Nice place," he muttered, kicking aside an empty beer can and looking around. Dr. Hague is the new philosophy editor at McGraw-Hill, in town to hear our ideas for this edition. He was buying us breakfast at the Sin of Cortez, a Chico restaurant. We went inside and ordered Mexican food. Moore got down to business.

"Parts of the book," Moore said, "are starting to read like lectures. We want to get back to making things fun again."

Dr. Hague poured coffee and sat back in his chair. He was still wearing sunglasses.

"Surely," Parker joined in, "there's no reason this book can't be at least as enjoyable to college students as *Survivor*."

Dr. Hague frowned. "What do you have in mind?" he asked. "Are you going to talk about eating bugs?"

We assured him we'd keep it proper and decent. We planned to add new features, make organizational modifications, rewrite the denser passages, improve the content, add new exercises, and update the political context—and the Editor of Good Taste at McGraw-Hill would not flinch. Much. We spent the next three hours drinking coffee and going over specifics.

Changes in the Seventh Edition

Not every change we discussed at the Sin of Cortez was actually made; in particular, we decided not to have adopters vote on which coauthor to kick off the title page. Here are the changes that we did make.

■ *New Features*

To this edition, we have added two unusual new features:

▴ The Top Ten Fallacies of All Time (Appendix 2)
▴ The Scrapbook of Unusual Issues (Appendix 3)

"The Top Ten Fallacies of All Time" list is based on our experience during the previous six editions gathering real-life examples of fallacies to use for text illustrations and exercises. The list isn't scientifically derived, but we have a pretty good idea of which fallacies occur most often.

"The Scrapbook of Unusual Issues" is a compendium of topics to generate discussion or to adapt for homework assignments or in-class mini-writing exercises.

■ *Modified Organization*

We've modestly modified the organization of the book and now divide it into Part 1: Claims and Credibility, Part 2: Fallacies and Other Rhetorical Devices, and Part 3: Arguments.

As you can see, we devote an entire part to fallacies and other rhetorical devices. The emphasis in this edition is on traditional fallacies rather than "pseudoreasoning," although much of the change is terminological. We are also using more self-explanatory titles for fallacies. Specific content changes are noted below, where you will observe that we now cover several fallacies that were missing from previous editions.

We no longer have a separate chapter on explanations. If you used the old Chapter 7, don't worry. The essential differences between explanations and arguments are set forth in Chapter 1 (Thinking Critically: It Matters); explanations are covered in their own right in Chapter 11 (Causal Arguments). This change enabled us to devote Part 2 entirely to fallacies and other rhetorical devices. It also eliminated redundancy.

If you've devoted time in the past to the book's appendices, you should be aware that material that was in the third appendix (Some Common Patterns of Deductive Arguments) now appears in boxes in Chapters 8 and 9. Likewise, the material on conflicting claims and on analytic claims that previously was covered in the first and second appendices can be found in Chapters 8 and 9 in the first case and on our Web site in the second. One of us (Moore) doesn't assign the chapters on deductive logic (now Chapters 8 and 9) to his classes (and you needn't feel obliged to, either) and instead just goes over the commonly encountered patterns of deductive reasoning. If you are like Moore and don't try to teach deductive logic from the ground up, you may want to refer to the boxes on pages 292–293 and 329 where these patterns are displayed. (Parker, on the other hand, is a firm believer that learning the logical structure of sentences—both categorical and truth functional—is a pedagogically sound endeavor and so drives his students through Chapters 8 and 9 in a manner reminiscent of a row master with a hold full of galley slaves.)

■ *Content Changes*

In this edition, we have modified several chapters; here are the specifics.

Chapter 1, Thinking Critically: It Matters   We still cover the basics here, but we have improved the discussion of *factual* versus *nonfactual* issues and made it fit better with the section in Chapter 12 on moral reasoning. In Chapter 1, we now explain the difference between *argument* and *persuasion* and between *argument* and *explanation*. Also discussed are *subjectivism* and *relativism*.

Chapter 3, Credibility   We take a new approach to credibility in this chapter. Before, we tried to give sufficient conditions for a claim's being credible; now we discuss ways in which a claim or source can lack credibility. We include a section on advertising (found in Chapter 4 in earlier editions), and we say something about talk radio as well.

Chapter 4, Persuasion Through Rhetoric   We make a clearer distinction now between rhetoric as the venerable study of persuasive writing and rhetoric as a broad category of linguistic techniques people use when their primary objective is to influence beliefs, attitudes, and behavior. We also emphasize the distinction between logical power and psychological force.

Chapter 5, Psychological and Related Fallacies   We have substantially rewritten this chapter, placing more emphasis on fallacies than on pseudo-reasoning, covering several new fallacies, and making minor changes to terminology.

Chapter 6, More Fallacies   In this edition, we offer what we hope is a clearer explanation of the underlying mistake in all versions of ad hominem argument; we have made a few minor changes in terminology as well. The fallacies now covered in Chapters 5 and 6 are these:

the Rush Limbaugh fallacy (the "argument" from outrage)
scapegoating
scare tactics
the "argument" by force
the "argument" from pity
the "argument" from envy
apple polishing
guilt trip
wishful thinking
the peer-pressure argument
the group think fallacy
nationalism
rationalization

the "argument" from popularity
the "argument" from common practice
the "argument" from tradition
relativism
subjectivism
red herring/smokescreen
the personal attack ad hominem fallacy
the circumstantial ad hominem fallacy
the inconsistency ad hominem fallacy
poisoning the well

the genetic fallacy   the line-drawing fallacy
straw man   slippery slope
false dilemma   begging the question
the perfectionist fallacy   misplacing the burden of proof

Chapter 10, Inductive Arguments   We have revised our approach to the
relationship between analogical arguments and generalizations. The result,
with luck, is a chapter that makes sense intuitively, does not overly compli-
cate things, and is easier to teach.

Chapter 11, Causal Arguments   Several changes were made here. We added
a section on how to avoid confusing arguments with causal explanations, a
section on the ways in which causal hypotheses can be defective, and a section on explanations and excuses. Much of the latter two parts was included
in the former chapter devoted to explanations. We've also simplified the
discussion of common mistakes made in causal reasoning. Chapters 10 and
11 cover the most important inductive fallacies:

- biased sample
- hasty generalization (including appealing to anecdotal evidence
  either to establish or to rebut a generalization)
- post hoc, ergo propter hoc (and related mistakes)

Chapter 12, Moral, Legal, and Aesthetic Reasoning   The main change
here was to bring the discussion of the difference between prescriptive and
descriptive claims into conformity with what we say about it in Chapter 1.
We also try to walk readers through the important conceptual distinctions:

- factual claims versus nonfactual claims
- nonfactual claims that are value judgments versus nonfactual
  claims that are not value judgments
- moral value judgments versus nonmoral judgments

This finely tuned analysis of these important distinctions enables us to define
moral reasoning more precisely.

■ Other Changes, Including Additional Supplements

We have added new exercises and removed clunkers. Many new boxes have
been added as well and some of the old ones removed. In general, the book
has been updated to reflect the current political context.
     Also, we have added new real-life essays at the end of the book (Ap-
pendix 1) and have even included a reasonably well-argued essay you could
use as a model. Further, we offer an exercise that requires using bits and
pieces of most of the book and explains how this works. If students
asks why it is useful to study critical thinking, you could refer them to this
exercise.

In addition, we have improved our interactive student support material. Those who use this text will enjoy a full range of Internet-based services and enhancements.

- ▲ A new Online Learning Center at www.mhhe.com/criticalthinking provides interactive exercises and resources for students and instructors. It is compatible with McGraw-Hill's free PageOut course management system as well as WebCT and Blackboard, allowing instructors to create customized course Web sites.
- ▲ Packaged with each new copy of the text is a free subscription to the online resource *PowerWeb: Critical Thinking*, which contains readings from classical sources (Plato, Locke, Bacon, and more), readings on such topics as contemporary issues and perspectives, language, the media, and pseudoscience and the paranormal; and essays for critical analysis. Students can access these readings from the Online Learning Center.
- ▲ Packaged free with each new copy is also Nickolas Pappas's popular *Study Guide to Accompany Critical Thinking* on CD-ROM.

Finally, as we indicated above, we have tried to make difficult discussions more accessible and fun to read.

Distinguishing Features of This Text

We are gratified by the success of this text. Its basic features may help explain its popularity.

■ Focus

Critical thinking includes a variety of deliberative processes aimed at making wise decisions about what to believe and do, processes that center on evaluation of arguments but include much more. We believe the best way to teach critical thinking is to integrate logic, both formal and informal, with a variety of skills and topics useful in making sound decisions about claims, actions, and practices—and to make it all palatable by presenting it in real-life contexts. This book is chatty in tone—the author of another critical thinking text griped about this (his book certainly does not have the problem)—but it doesn't duck important issues.

■ Illustrations and Examples

These are taken from or designed to resemble material undergraduates will find familiar. First- and second-year university students generally enjoy the book.

■ *Boxes*

On more than one occasion, we have heard students exclaiming how much they like the boxes. We do too.

■ *Exercises*

The exercises give guided practice in applying important critical skills. There are more than a thousand in the text and many more in *The Logical Accessory* (the instructor's manual).

■ *Answers, Suggestions, and Tips*

Questions marked with a triangle in the book are answered in the answer section in the back (look for the colored page edges), and sometimes discussions that extend material in the text proper are also found there. Instructors may find the answer section useful as a direct teaching aid or as a foil for their own comments.

■ *Collaborative Exercises*

We try to involve students actively in the learning process. Several exercises require students to collaborate with one another; these exercises work pretty well. Sometimes we even use these exercises *before* explaining the material in the chapter in which they occur and before assigning the chapter as homework.

■ *Organization*

Sometimes people support what they assert by providing arguments; other times they don't. In both cases, they may try to add psychological force to what they say by using various rhetorical techniques. Logically, then, you need a critical thinking text that has three parts: one dealing with claims and credibility, another dealing with various rhetorical techniques, and a third dealing with arguments. That's how we've organized things, anyhow.

■ *Discussion of Rhetorical Devices*

Part 2 deals with a large and diversified inventory of persuasive devices, emotional appeals, and irrelevancies that we all use to add psychological power to our assertions. This part of the book helps students distinguish weak reasons from irrelevant considerations, a subtle but important distinction.

■ *Credibility*

In many cases, we must assess the credibility of sources as well as the inherent believability of what they assert. This book devotes an entire chapter (Chapter 3) to credibility, authority, and expertise.

■ *Real-Life Essays*

At the end of the book (Appendix 1) are several essays that can be used in various ways: For analysis, to provide topics for written work or in-class discussion, or as sources of additional exercises of your own design. You can read them just for amusement, too.

■ *Accommodating Alternative Teaching Strategies*

If you want to teach a traditional course in logic, you can do so using nothing more than this book. We advise first covering Chapters 1 and 7, then working through Chapters 8–11 in order. In whatever time remains, take advantage of the material in Part 2, which deals with rhetorical devices of various sorts. These devices are major players in the attempts people in the real world make to persuade each other. Adding this material to a traditional class in logic adds a powerful practical dimension to the course.

On the other hand, if you don't like to teach elementary logic, skip Chapters 8 and 9, which, we might just point out, give pretty complete treatments of categorical and truth-functional logic.

■ *Teaching Writing*

If you teach critical thinking in a basic writing course or teach basic writing in a critical-thinking course, you can adapt this book to your needs. Chapter 2 in particular is devoted to subjects related to argumentative essays.

■ *Critical Thinking Across the Disciplines*

Discussions of moral, legal, and aesthetic reasoning appear in Chapter 12.

■ *Model Essay*

In Appendix 1, we've taken an essay that deals with a controversial topic that we found in a moderately obscure magazine and edited it down to manageable length, and we offer it as an example of a fairly well-reasoned series of arguments designed to support a (probably not too popular) conclusion about the September 11, 2001, terrorist attacks. You can use it as an example of how to adduce arguments to a conclusion, or as a challenge to find rebuttals if one does not want to accept the conclusion.

■ *The Whole Enchilada Exercise*

Also in Appendix 1, this new feature illustrates how critical evaluation of a real-life issue involves skills from several chapters.

■ *A Chart of Rules of Deduction*

The rules of truth-functional deduction are gathered on one page in the form of a handy chart; we're mentioning this again, although we began doing it in the previous edition. We don't know why it took us that long to do it.

■ *Glossary*

The glossary at the end of the book defines important terms, usually correctly.

■ *The Logical Accessory (Instructor's Manual)*

The instructor's manual does not presume to guide instructors. But it does give (our) answers to the hundreds of exercises not answered in the answer section of the text. It also provides we-don't-know-how-many more examples, exercises, and test questions. We continue to include, here and there, various hints, strategies, lecture topics, tangents, and flights of fancy.

■ *Study Guide CD-ROM*

A fine student study guide, by Nickolas Pappas of the City College of New York, comes packaged with each new copy of the book. Professor Pappas has provided stimulating new exercises for each chapter that will help students master the content. We thank him profusely for his wonderful work.

■ *Essay Grading Rubric*

Grading rubrics are widely used in K–12 and are found increasingly on the college scene as well. Students like rubric-based grading. They think it reduces the subjectivity involved in evaluating essays. Our rubric is tucked into *The Logical Accessory.*

Acknowledgments

This isn't talk radio. We don't try to pin every last thing on the left or the right, on some group of poorly identified whackos, or on CNN. And we don't blame our mistakes on Jon-David Hague (our principal editor), on our fine production people, or on our excellent reviewers. We admit it, you'll just have to blame the two of us for the mistakes, as usual.

We want to thank a number of people, especially the various editors referred to above: Jon-Hyphen (as we've come to think of him); April Wells-Hayes, our meticulous production boss and den mother; Jen Mills, who oversaw the entire production process; Marty Granahan, who has the difficult job of talking people into letting us use their material just so we can criticize and poke fun at it; and our sublime copyeditor, Joan "Red Pencil" Pendleton.

Those who have advised us in the preparation of this edition or slipped us material, and to whom we are especially grateful, include

Charles Blatz, University of Toledo

K. D. Borcoman, Coastline Community College

Sandra Dwyer, Georgia State University

The Editor of Good Taste Hard at Work

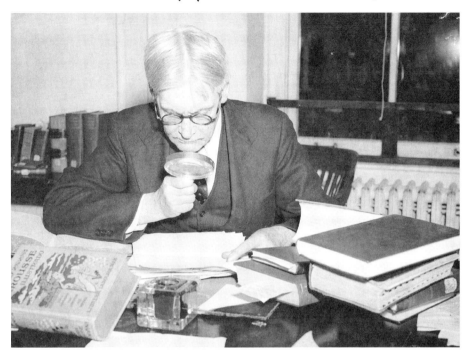

Ellery Eells, University of Wisconsin–Madison

Geoffrey Frasz, Community College of Southern Nevada

Dabney Gray, Stillman College

Steven Hoeltzel, James Madison University

Eric Parkinson, Syracuse University

James Stump, Bethel College.

We continue to be grateful for the thoughtfulness and insight of those who reviewed the first six editions and who are now too numerous to list here. They helped the book improve with each edition, and we continue to appreciate their efforts.

Special thanks are due to our colleagues at Cal State Chico, Marcel Daguerre and Anne Morrisey; Dan Barnett, Butte College; and Linda Bomstad, Cal Poly–San Luis Obispo.

Finally, we add special thanks to Alicia Alvarez Giles and Marianne Larson for their affection, patience, and support in the ways that really count.

Chapter 1

Thinking Critically: It Matters

One sunny day last spring we saw our friend Ken out mowing his lawn. Ken was in his bare feet.

"Ken," we said, "have you lost your mind?"

Ken had an answer. According to statistics, he said, the overwhelming majority of lawn-mowing accidents involve people wearing shoes. Very few accidents involve people going barefoot.

"So your chances of having an accident are statistically much greater if you wear shoes," he reasoned.

Ken is entitled to his opinion. We are all entitled to our opinions. But that doesn't mean opinions are all equally reasonable. Ken's opinion, for example—and with all due respect—could use a little fine-tuning. We humans are clever enough to send spacecraft beyond the solar system, combine genetic material so as to alter the varieties of life, and build machines that outplay grand masters at chess—yet we frequently make mistakes in logic like Ken's. Despite the impressive accomplishments of the human intellect, one frequently comes face to face with examples of faulty reasoning, error, and misjudgment. In a recent Gallup poll 18 percent of those polled thought the sun revolves around the earth. Our colleague Michael Rich discovered that over half the students in his class think the first person to walk on the moon was Lance Armstrong. As we write these words there is a story in our newspaper about one Robyn Rouse, of Columbus, Ohio, who paid $25 for a pair of green contact lenses at a grocery store to match her tennis shoes. By the next morning she had developed a serious eye infection. It's a safe bet that all of us from time to time make decisions like this—decisions that are uninformed, poorly reasoned, or otherwise defective. Occasionally such decisions are disastrous. Robyn now needs a year of treatment and a cornea transplant to save her vision.

Clear thinking requires an effort and doesn't always come naturally. But one can get better at it if one is willing to work a bit and accept guidance

Vladimir Does Not Like This Book

▲   *The title conveys the idea that Vladimir Putin dislikes this book. In fact, it's safe to say Vladimir Putin has no opinion on this book one way or the other. He does not like it, but he does not dislike it either. The title is ambiguous (discussed in Chapter 2) and could be used as innuendo (discussed in Chapter 4).*

Careful reading is important to thinking critically.

here and there. We hope this textbook, in conjunction with whatever course you may be using it in, will help you develop some of the skills required to form intelligent opinions, make good decisions, and determine the best course of action—as well as recognize when someone else's reasoning is faulty or manipulative. In short, we hope this book helps you become a more careful and critical thinker.

We hasten to caution you that thinking critically is not about attacking people. If you are reading this book for a course, chances are you will be expected to critique others' ideas, and they will be asked to critique yours. Doing this, however, doesn't mean putting people down. Every single one of us makes mistakes, and it can be useful to have others help us see them. We appreciate it when someone points out that we have a low tire or that our lawn looks bad because it lacks iron. Likewise, we can appreciate it if someone suggests that our position, theory, or idea is incomplete, unclear, insufficiently supported, or in some other way not all it could be. And when we are on the other side, we can help others see the holes in their arguments. We don't do Ken a favor by pretending his idea about mowing the lawn is a good one. Critical thinking is more about helping others than attacking them; and to the extent we are able to think critically about our own ideas, it is about helping ourselves. Our goal is knowledge and understanding, not winning or coming out on top.

So you might say this is another one of those self-help books. But unlike self-help books that tell you how to stay young or make a million dollars, this book will help you understand when books like those, and other attempts to sell you on something, have good reasoning going for them—and when they don't.

Good reasoning doesn't happen in a vacuum. When we hear somebody express an opinion, we usually already have information on the topic and can generally figure out where to find more if more is needed. Having both the desire and the ability to bring such information to bear on decisions is part of the critical-thinking process. Critical thinking involves a lot of skills: Among them are the abilities to listen and read carefully and to stay informed. Reading the *New York Times* carefully from start to finish each day for a year might do even more for your ability to think clearly than reading this book. (But it would take a lot more time.)

Basic Critical Thinking Skills

What, concretely and specifically, is critical thinking about? When we take a position on an issue, we assert or claim something. The claim and the thinking on which it is based are subject to rational evaluation. When we do that evaluating, we are thinking critically. To think critically, then, we need to know

- ▲ When someone (including ourselves) is taking a position on an issue, what that issue is, and what the person is claiming relative to that issue—that is, what the person's position is
- ▲ What considerations are relevant to that issue
- ▲ Whether the reasoning underlying the person's claims is good reasoning
- ▲ And whether, everything considered, we should accept, reject, or suspend judgment on what the person claimed

Finally,

- ▲ Doing all this requires us to be levelheaded and objective and not influenced by extraneous factors.

You can fool all of the people all of the time if the advertising budget is big enough.

—ED ROLLINS, Republican campaign adviser

Why books like this are important

These points will receive considerable coverage in this book, but we need to consider them briefly here.

Issues

Whenever we have to think critically, the first item of business is to make sure we are focusing on the correct issue. In the broadest sense, an issue is any matter of controversy or uncertainty; an issue is a point in dispute, in doubt, in question, or simply up for discussion or consideration. Should I mow the lawn barefoot? This question raises an issue. Should we get a new car? Is George W. Bush taller than his father? Are pit bulls more apt to bite than golden retrievers? Should we purchase Wal-Mart stock? As soon as we ask one of these questions, we have raised an issue. An **issue** is raised when a claim is in question. In fact, for our purposes, "question" and "issue" can be used pretty much interchangeably.

Many issues can be posed beginning with the word "whether." For example, the issues raised by the questions in the preceding paragraph can be posed as whether we should get a new car, whether George W. Bush is taller than his father, and whether pit bulls are more apt to bite than golden retrievers. But issues can be posed in other ways as well. For example, we might wonder *how many* miles per gallon a car will get, *when* the train arrived, *who* fired the fatal shot, or *what* the root causes of terrorism are. All of these become issues as soon as we consider them.

We don't need a discussion or a dispute between parties to have an issue; an issue can be raised in a single person's thoughts. Did you turn off the air conditioning before you left, you wonder? The issue here is whether you turned off the air conditioning; it's a question in your mind, so it is an issue for you.

It is common these days to call psychological problems "issues." You hear people say things like "She has an issue with this class" or "He has an issue with cats." These statements simply mean that she doesn't like this class and that cats upset him. A couple of years ago there was a popular song named "She's Got Issues," which employed the word in a similar vein. But as we use the term, an issue is never something a person *has*, and it certainly isn't something a person has *got*. There are lots of things you can do with issues—you can raise them, discuss or debate them, try to settle them, and ignore them, but one thing you can't do is simply *have* them. In this book we use "issue" the good, old-fashioned way, as what is raised when you consider whether a claim is true.

Notice also that an issue is different from a topic of conversation. Pet care can be a topic of conversation, but not an issue. How you should take care of your pet is an issue. Whether you are taking proper care of your pet is an issue. Whether dogs or cats are easier to take care of is an issue. But pet care is just a topic.

Knowing Both Sides of an Issue

According to a report in *The New Republic* magazine, written by journalist Karen Alexander, a course titled "The Politics and Poetics of Palestinian Resistance" offered in the spring of 2002 at the University of California, Berkeley, was listed in the course catalogue with this line: "Conservative thinkers are encouraged to seek other sections." The line was eventually removed.

The Roman politician and orator Cicero (106–43 B.C.E.) once advised: The person who knows only his side of an issue knows neither side. Cicero was exactly right, and his advice worth remembering.

We assume, based on the above report, that the UC Berkeley grad student who offered the course never read Cicero. He probably should have, would be our guess.

Arguments

It is all very well to take a position on a given issue, but if the issue matters to us, we want to be able to *support* our position. This is where arguments come in—they contain that support. If the issue is a simple one, like whether this key will open that lock, the argument may just be that we were able to make the relevant observations or that we have reliable information from a reasonable source. If the issue is complicated, like what causes Dutch elm disease, much more is required. Whatever the issue, arguments are what we use to resolve it, along with direct observation and information from reliable sources.

Let us define an **argument** as an attempt to support a claim or assertion by providing a reason or reasons for accepting it. The claim that is supported is called the **conclusion** of the argument, and the claim or claims that provide the support are called the **premises.** The premises, in other words, specify the reason (or reasons) for accepting the conclusion. When we offer an argument, we are reasoning.

To illustrate this familiar and important concept, suppose you see someone mowing his lawn in his bare feet. You might think to yourself,

> What the devil does that fellow think he is doing? He is going to hurt himself seriously if he doesn't watch out! I'd better tell him he should wear shoes.

You are considering the issue of whether you should warn this individual to wear shoes when he is mowing his lawn, and you have, in effect, given yourself the following argument:

> Premise: If this person doesn't wear shoes, he could be badly hurt.
> Conclusion: Therefore, I should tell him to wear shoes.

As you can see from this example, the conclusion of an argument states a position on an issue. The issue in this example is *whether* you should tell the person to wear shoes, and the conclusion of the argument is *that* you should do so.

In a moment we shall offer some advice on identifying issues and recognizing arguments, but first we need to clear up two common misconceptions about arguments.

Misconceptions About Arguments

The first misconception is that arguments are attempts to *persuade* somebody of something. Some writers even define an argument as an attempt to persuade. This definition is not as perverse as mowing the lawn in your bare feet, but it is pretty obviously incorrect. True, when you want to persuade somebody of something, you might *use* an argument. But not all arguments attempt to persuade, and many attempts to persuade do not involve argument. In fact, giving people an argument is probably one of the *least* effective methods of persuading them—which, of course, is why so few advertisers bother with arguments. (If you really want to persuade people, your best bet may simply be to flatter them or make them angry or frightened; but we shall go into this later on.)

So it is false to think all attempts to persuade are arguments. It is equally false to think that all arguments attempt to persuade. Just consider the argument in the example about the person mowing the lawn barefoot. *That* argument is not an attempt to persuade anybody of anything, although having given yourself that argument you might *then* try to persuade the person to go put on shoes. Properly understood, an argument is not an attempt to *persuade,* but an attempt to *prove* or *establish* or *support* some claim. The proper definition of an argument is that it is two or more claims, one of which, the conclusion, is supposed to follow from or be supported by the rest. An attempt to persuade is an attempt to win someone to your point of view.

The second misconception about arguments is that they are attempts to *explain.* Here again, explanation and argument are distinct entities, although at times it is easy to confuse them. An argument attempts to prove *that* some claim is true, while an explanation attempts to specify *how something works* or what *caused* it or *brought it about.* Arguing *that* a dog has fleas is quite different from explaining *how* it came to have fleas. Wondering *whether* violent crimes increased is different from wondering *what caused* violent crimes to increase. Offering an explanation of Dutch elm disease is entirely different from trying to prove that your explanation is correct. Explanations and arguments are different things. However, they are easily confused, and we will include an exercise in this chapter that should help you keep them straight.

Up a Tree

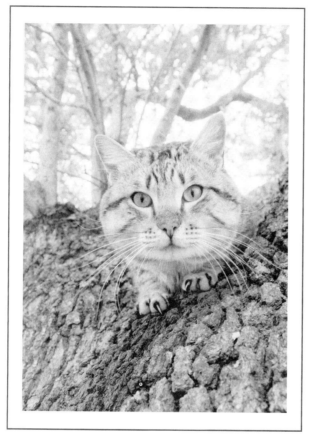

▲ *Big Boy sits atop his favorite branch in Gulfport, Miss.*
He was blown there three years ago by Hurricane Georges.

People who don't think critically get tossed around by the
winds of fate, like Big Boy here.

Recognizing Arguments

Being able to identify arguments can help you identify issues, so let's discuss arguments first and then turn to identifying issues.

An argument *always* has a conclusion. Always. Without a conclusion, a bunch of words isn't an argument. That, after all, is what an argument does: It tries to prove, establish, or confirm a claim. In other words, it sets forth a conclusion.

Fortunately, specific words and phrases often, though not always, alert us to the fact that a conclusion is about to be set forth. Take the word "therefore":

> The U.S. steel industry believes it needs government protection to be able to be competitive internationally. Therefore, the industry won't support a free trade bill.

The word "therefore" is a **conclusion indicator:** It lets an audience know that what follows (the industry won't support a free trade bill) is a conclusion.

Other fairly reliable conclusion-indicating words and phrases include

- It follows that . . .
- We may conclude that . . .
- This serves to show that . . .
- Thus . . .
- Hence, . . .
- Accordingly, . . .
- Consequently, . . .
- So . . .

An argument, then, always has a conclusion. It also always has at least one premise. Premises support the conclusion, and if you don't have support, you don't have an argument. Words and phrases that often indicate a premise is about to be stated **(premise indicators)** include

- Since . . .
- For . . .
- Because . . .
- In view of . . .
- This is implied by . . .
- Given . . .

For example, somebody says:

> It's risky to speed on I-75 in Cincinnati, since the police like to set up speed traps for folks driving up from Kentucky.

The premise of this argument is "the police like to set up speed traps for folks driving up from Kentucky." That claim is given as support for the idea that it is risky to speed on I-75 in Cincinnati. You know what the premise is because it follows the word "since."

Unfortunately, even though an argument always has a conclusion and at least one premise, the conclusion or one or more premises might be implied rather than stated overtly. For example, if François says to Desmonde:

> Des, it's a nice day, we aren't doing anything, and the car needs to be washed.

▲   *Moore and Parker's students discover they passed.*

You can be pretty sure that François is giving Desmonde an argument for the unstated conclusion that they should wash the car.

Many arguments, like François', don't contain indicator words like "therefore" and "because." This means you just have to pay attention to whether someone is trying to establish something and what he or she is trying to establish.

By the time you have finished this book, you will have had much practice in identifying arguments, premises, and conclusions.

Identifying Issues

If you listen to a group of people discussing something, at some point in the conversation you might well hear something like this:

> FIRST PERSON: "Look. The issue is whether . . ."
>
> SECOND PERSON: "No, actually, the issue is . . ."
>
> THIRD SPEAKER: "Hold on . . . what we really need to determine
>   is . . ."

And so on.

Why do people have so much trouble identifying issues? Discussions in the real world (including real-life written essays such as might be found in letters on a newspaper opinion page) are spontaneous, freewheeling, non-sequential, unorganized, haphazard, off the wall, and all over the map. Good writers and speakers certainly try to be clear about what issues they are discussing as well as about their position on them. But in free-flowing discussions and conversations (and in one person's own thinking), several issues can get attention more or less simultaneously; tangents will be followed without hesitation; irrelevancies and asides will be everywhere; and the parties to the discussion will frequently make confusing statements about what *the* issue is. Another problem is that people sometimes purposely confuse issues in order to draw attention away from a claim they don't want to deal with or to make it look as though they have proved a point when they haven't. And still a further problem is that in many conversations different speakers will address entirely different issues without realizing they're doing so. Suppose you hear:

> FIRST PERSON: School vouchers? They may be a good idea.
> They'll give parents an opportunity to get their
> kids out of bad schools. What do you think?

> SECOND PERSON: I think the people who want them are just a
> bunch of selfish zealots who want to send their
> kids to religious schools.

What is the issue here? We can't identify *the* issue. The first person's point has to do with vouchers, and the second person's point has to do with the people who want vouchers; they're talking about entirely different issues.

Let's take another example:

> MR. X: They shouldn't go building power plants right on fault zones
> like that! What's the matter with people, anyway?

> MR. Y: What's the matter with you? If it weren't for power plants,
> you wouldn't have enough light to read about faults.

These two are not addressing the same issue: Y's being right on his point won't help anyone know whether X is right on his.

So, identifying issues can be confusing. Still, it helps to remember the following two points:

First, since every argument addresses an issue, an excellent way to pin down at least some of the issues in a conversation or passage is to look for the conclusions of any arguments that have been given. Let's say a friend tells you:

> You should donate your old car to United Cerebral Palsy because doing so helps
> out a worthy cause and is tax deductible besides.

Your friend has argued you should donate your old car to United Cerebral Palsy. He or she is therefore taking a position on the issue of whether you

On Knowing What Your Great-Grandparents Knew

Having a reservoir of information in your head helps you avoid being mis-led. Here are a few things an eighth-grader was expected to know in 1895 in Kansas, along with sample questions from the final examination for that grade:

- Grammar (Sample exam question: Name and define the parts of speech.)
- Arithmetic (Sample question: Find the interest on $512.60 for 8 months and 189 days at 7 percent.)
- U.S. History (Sample question: Explain the causes and results of the Revolutionary War.)
- Orthography (Sample question: Define the following prefixes: bi, dis, mis, pre, semi, post, non, inter, mono, sup.)
- Geography (Sample questions: Name all the republics of Europe and give the capital of each. Give the inclination of the earth.)

This helps explain why our grandparents know so much.

should donate your old car to United Cerebral Palsy. The issue addressed by an argument can *always* be stated by inserting a "whether" in front of the argument's conclusion.

Second, remember that in many conversations there is no such thing as *the* issue. So, instead of trying to find out what *the* issue is, just focus on the issues that have been addressed with an argument. Look for arguments as guides to issues, because in offering a conclusion a speaker or writer is always taking a position on an issue. This strategy will not necessarily disclose what the most important issue is in a conversation or discussion, and it won't reveal every issue that has been raised because sometimes issues are raised just by asking questions. But it will at least tell you which issues are important enough to warrant somebody's providing an argument.

Factual Issues Versus Nonfactual Issues

Before we leave the subject of issues, we must call your attention to a most important distinction, the distinction between **factual** and **nonfactual issues/ questions.** Whether George W. Bush is *taller* than his father is a factual issue, but whether he is *better looking* than his father is not. Whether Dutch elm disease will spread to Oregon is a factual issue, but whether Dutch elms are the most stately trees is not. People sometimes think that only factual issues are worth discussing, but that isn't so. Is it right to run medical experiments on animals? That isn't a factual question, but it's worth discussing.

Should you contribute to the support of your aging parents? That isn't a factual question, but it is important.

People also speak of factual claims. When we take a position on a factual issue we make a **factual claim.** For example, the claim "George W. Bush is really a cleverly disguised space alien" is a factual claim. That isn't a misprint: *It is a factual claim.* It is a *false* claim, but it is indeed a factual claim, since the question of whether George W. Bush is a cleverly disguised space alien is a factual question/issue. *Saying that a claim is factual is not equivalent to saying it is true.* At the risk of being repetitious, we must emphasize: "Factual claim" does not mean "true claim." A factual claim is simply a claim, whether true or false, that states a position on a factual issue.

Obviously, then, you need to be able to tell if an issue/question is factual. *An issue is factual if there are established methods for settling it—* that is, if there are generally accepted criteria or standards on which the issue can be judged or if we can at least describe what kinds of methods and criteria would apply even though it may be impractical or impossible to actually apply them. We can determine whether George W. Bush is taller than his father by placing the two Bushes side by side and observing. We also could come up with criteria for settling whether George W. Bush is a space alien. But what could settle whether Bush Senior or Bush Junior is the better looking of the two?

Notice that, if there are no established methods for settling an issue, then, if two people disagree on that issue, there is no way to determine that either of them is mistaken. This is a mark of a nonfactual issue, since, if an issue is factual, and two people disagree about it, then at least one of them must be mistaken. Thus, if Moore and Parker disagree about whether George W. Bush is taller than his father, one of them must be mistaken. But, if they disagree about whether George W. Bush is better looking than his father, we do not insist that one of them must be mistaken. In fact, it seems odd to say that either one is "mistaken" about something like this.

So, here's how we can boil this down: There are two criteria that sort issues into the categories of factual and nonfactual: A factual issue will meet both of the following criteria:

There are established methods for settling the matter.

If two people disagree about the issue, at least one of them must be mistaken.

Any issue that fails these criteria is nonfactual.[1]

Using these two indicators of when an issue is a factual one, we see that the following questions all raise factual issues:

---

[1]It would be a mistake to think that the line between factual and nonfactual issues can be drawn with absolute clarity and distinctness. One might argue that there are some issues that might meet one of our criteria and fail the other. Difficult-to-determine cases do not affect the usefulness of the distinction, nor of this way of making it, however.

Recognizing Factual Issues

- If two people disagree on the issue, must one of them be incorrect or mistaken?
- Is there an agreed-upon method or criterion for settling the issue?

A "yes" answer to these questions indicates the issue is factual.

▲ Is there ice on the moon?

▲ Does poverty breed terrorism?

▲ Will it hurt my eyes to stick these cheapo green contact lenses in them?

▲ What time is it right now in Singapore?

▲ Hey, how much do you think we can get away with charging for plain water if we put it in a nice bottle and give it a French-sounding name?

And we see that the following questions raise nonfactual issues:

▲ Is it is okay to break a promise in order to save someone's life?

▲ Does this sweater make me look funny?

▲ Is the Italian coast as beautiful as people say?

▲ Does the death penalty give murderers what they deserve?

▲ Is it unwise to mow the lawn in your bare feet?

Some people have the idea that "factual" somehow equates to "uncontroversial," that an issue becomes "factual" when it is no longer subject to controversy. This is *not* correct. Does raising taxes cause recession? Did humans evolve from more primitive primates? Does the death penalty deter murder? These questions all raise controversial issues, but they are in each case factual issues.

Relativism and Subjectivism

Two big mistakes in thinking relate to this distinction between factual and nonfactual issues. One mistake comes from those who make the distinction, and the other from those who do not.

The first mistake is to think that, when it comes to nonfactual issues, all opinions are equally reasonable. This view is *not* correct. Whether Bill should turn down a really good job offer in North Carolina to take care of his dying father in California is an important nonfactual issue; it can be intelligently discussed and argued, and the arguments can vary in their merit. A person who argues that Bill should turn down the job offer "because the mosquitos are bad in North Carolina" has not offered as good an argument as the person who says that Bill should turn down the job offer because one's first duty is to one's parents. Chapter 12 of this text is devoted in part to moral judgments like this one, as well as to other types of nonfactual judgments; if you stick it out that far you will get guidance on why some opinions on nonfactual issues are more reasonable and rational than others.

The other mistake is made by those who fail to see a distinction between factual and nonfactual issues. One important version of this mistake is known as subjectivism, and another important version of the mistake is known as relativism. **Subjectivism** is the idea that, just as two people can both be "correct" in their opinion on a nonfactual issue, they can both be correct in their differing opinions on *factual* issues. **Relativism** is the parallel idea that two different *cultures* can be correct in their differing opinions on the same factual issue. We'd be surprised if you didn't encounter versions of subjectivism or relativism in things you read and courses you take, because both ideas are enjoying a measure of popularity these days, especially, maybe, in literature departments. But it would be unwise to take either doctrine literally. Let's say two physicians differ on whether you have cancer—a factual issue. It would be folly to suppose they might both be correct. And you can be sure that if you do have cancer, you won't be cured just by moving to a culture that hasn't heard of the disease.

Relevance, Rhetoric, and Keeping a Clear Head

Mom's opinions are bound to carry extra weight with her kids. They may even carry more weight than the opinions of someone who is better qualified on the subject at hand; after all, she is Mom. It is a fact of life that we are influenced in our thinking by considerations that, logically, are beside the point; a speaker's relationship to us is a good example of such a consideration.

Or let's say an expert is talking about the nutritional value of spinach. Let's also say he or she speaks with a refined British accent. For a lot of people the accent might lend an air of expertise to what the person says, even though a person's accent is unrelated to knowledge of nutrition or spinach.

To take an example that works in the other direction, many people attach *less* weight to what a speaker says if he or she (a) hesitates or stumbles over words, (b) is reluctant to make eye contact, (c) is perspiring or is nervous. Such behaviors may enter into our evaluation of what the person said—which, of course, is why speaking coaches encourage speakers to make eye contact and practice a smooth delivery. It can be really hard to evaluate an argument or claim objectively if the speaker exhibits mannerisms that we associate with evasiveness, insecurity, or dishonesty.

Now, one of the most serious and difficult obstacles to clear thinking is the tendency to confuse extraneous and irrelevant considerations with the

The Talk-Show Syndrome

Those of us in the lay community don't reason that way; we don't think in those terms of logic; it doesn't compute with us, that type of philosophical reasoning; we don't care.

—*Radio talk-show host BRUCE SESSIONS, summarizing his reaction to a logician giving examples of illogical arguments from Rush Limbaugh*

Our suspicions are confirmed.

merits of a claim. The examples we've given deal with such irrelevancies as a speaker's accent, dress, relationship to us, and mannerisms. Another and different obstacle is the psychological force of words, which is easy to confuse with their logical force. Consider the different impact of these two statements:

> The desperate attempts by the hawks in the Bush Administration to link Saddam Hussein to al-Qaeda only highlight the obvious fact that an invasion of Iraq has not the slightest relationship to the so-called war on terrorism.

> An invasion of Iraq is unrelated to the war on terrorism.

Logically these two statements say exactly the same thing, but the first statement has greater psychological impact. The first statement, you might say, is equivalent to the second statement with a little advertising thrown in. Being ever alert to the psychological or emotional or rhetorical force of words can help us respond objectively to assertions and not impulsively.

Earlier in this chapter, we made a distinction between argument and persuasion. Argument attempts to prove a point; persuasion attempts to win others to a point of view. It's a subtle distinction, but a very real one. Often people use argument to persuade others, and there is absolutely nothing wrong with doing that. There also is nothing wrong with being persuaded by an argument if the argument is a good one. But attempts at persuasion often rely not so much on logic as on the psychological or rhetorical power of words, and one needs to be sensitive to the psychological associations of words to avoid being manipulated. We need to avoid being seduced by the emotional coloration of the language that surrounds a claim, proposal, theory, idea, or argument. Newt Gingrich, a former Republican Congressperson and Speaker of the House, is reported to have advised Republicans to use the words "extreme," "traitor," and "treasonous" when referring to Democrats or their proposals. Words like these can inflame listeners' passions—and may make it difficult for them to evaluate ideas on their merits. Demagogues rely on the emotional associations of words to scare us, flatter us, and amuse us; to arouse jealousy, desire, and disgust; to make good things sound bad and bad things sound good; and to confuse, mislead, and

Everyone Is Entitled to His or Her Opinion

At first glance, it seems obviously true that everyone is entitled to his or her opinion; and indeed we ourselves stated this casually in the text.

But the statement requires qualification. The *police* don't force us to hold any particular opinion; and in that sense certainly everyone is entitled to his or her opinion. However, that doesn't mean that all opinions are equally intelligent, practical, or humane. Some opinions may be so bad, stupid, or dangerous that it really isn't clear that one *is* entitled to hold them. Is one entitled to the opinion that it's okay to put out a dog's eye for the fun of it? Or that Israel bombed the World Trade Center? It makes as much sense to say that someone who holds such views is entitled to an explanation of why he or she is mistaken.

The remark "Everyone is entitled to his or her opinion" is often just a conversation stopper, a way of saying "Hey, I don't want to argue about this anymore." Now certainly there are times when further discussion is useless, but that does not mean that every opinion is as good—is as "entitled" to be held—as every other. Giving equal worth to people does not require giving equal worth to their opinions.

misinform us. Critical thinking involves recognizing the rhetorical force of language and trying not to be influenced by it. This is so important that we devote three full chapters of this book to the subject.

However, you should understand that psychological and emotional coloration is also present when good and decent people state their honest opinions; persuasion is not limited to demagogues. There is nothing wrong with presenting one's views in the best and most favorable light or in trying to be as persuasive as possible. It's just that as consumers of thoughts and ideas we must refine our ability to distinguish between the thought itself and the psychological packaging in which it is given to us.

None of this should be construed as implying that critical thinking rules out feelings or emotions. Feelings and emotions can supply powerful and often perfectly safe motivations for doing things. But it is important that we also employ our ability to reason—to be swayed by good arguments and to ignore irrelevancies—if we are to live up to our potential as reasonable creatures.

Concepts and Terms

Some of the bedrock concepts in this book use a vocabulary straight from ordinary English. People have *opinions, views, thoughts, beliefs, convictions,* and *ideas,* and for our purposes these things are the same. People may also express these opinions, views, thoughts, and the like, in *statements, judgments, assertions,* or—to use our preferred word—*claims.* "Statement," "judgment," "assertion," and "claim" all mean the same for us. And, as we

Doing Things with Words

You should not get the idea from this chapter that the only important thing you can do with words is make claims or take positions on issues. You can do lots of other important things: You can hypothesize, conjecture, suppose, and propose. You can amuse or entertain. You can try to persuade others (or yourself) of something or attempt to get them (or you) to do something. We use words to pray, promise, praise, and promote; to lie, deceive, insult, and humiliate; to excuse, comfort, and let off steam; and so on indefinitely. (Sometimes we don't know *what* we are up to when we use words.) All these things are subject to critical thinking as to success, efficacy, completeness, legitimacy, authenticity, originality, clarity, and many other qualities. In this book, however, we focus primarily on claim-making and argument-presenting functions of discourse and, to a lesser extent, on hypothesizing and conjecturing functions.

Here are some examples of a few of the many different things people do with words:

Red meat is not bad for you. Now blue-green meat, that's bad for you.

—*TOMMY SMOTHERS, amusing us*

I want to rush for 1,000 or 1,500 yards, whichever comes first.

—*New Orleans Saints running back GEORGE ROGERS, expressing a desire*

I enjoyed reading your book and would look forward to reading something else you wrote if required to do so.

—*E-mail from one of our students; we'd like to think this is praise, but . . .*

Do not take this medication within two hours of eating.

—*Caution note on some gunk one of us had to drink. It's warning us, but notice that you can't tell if you're not supposed to take the medication within two hours before eating or within two hours after eating or both.*

Whenever I watch TV and see those poor starving kids all over the world, I can't help but cry. I mean, I'd love to be skinny like that but not with all those flies and death and stuff.

—*MARIAH CAREY, expressing compassion*

They know so little science that they don't realize how ridiculous they look to others.

—*MARILYN VOS SAVANT, offering her explanation of why people claim to be psychic*

It's due to the country's mixed ethnicity.

—*National Rifle Association president CHARLTON HESTON, explaining the country's high murder rate and making it clear he may not know too much about the subject*

I did not have sexual relations with that woman.

—*BILL CLINTON, telling a fib*

Osama bin Laden is either alive and well or alive and not too well or not alive.

—*Defense Secretary DONALD RUMSFELD; beats us*

have seen, whenever a claim is called into question or its truth or falsity becomes the subject of discussion, an issue has been raised, the issue of whether or not the claim is true. We use the terms "issue" and "question" pretty much interchangeably.

About truth: Philosophers wonder what sort of thing truth is and what sort of things facts are. We must leave these mysteries for your next philosophy course. In a real-life situation, when people say that a claim is true, they are often just agreeing with it. Likewise, when they say that a claim states a fact, they are often just employing an alternative method of agreeing with it. Thus, in real-life conversations, these four claims often serve the same purpose:

> A book is on the table.
> It is true that a book is on the table.
> It is a fact that a book is on the table.
> I agree; a book is on the table.

Finally, let us say something about knowledge: Maybe you wonder, when can a person be said to *know* something? For example, when can I be said to *know* that there is a book on the table? In real-life situations, you have a right to claim to know there is a book on the table if (1) you believe there is, (2) have evidence beyond a reasonable doubt there is, and (3) have no reason to think you are mistaken, such as might be the case if you hadn't slept for thirteen days.

Advice

If you sense there is more than meets the eye to thinking critically, you are on the right track. Spotting issues and arguments and evaluating arguments and claims while striving for clearheadedness isn't easy. People learn these skills through example, illustration, and informed guidance. That's where this book comes in. But if you are to improve these skills, you will have to practice. Like playing baseball or the piano, critical thinking requires constant practice if you are going to be skilled in it. We've supplied lots of exercises throughout the book and you'll find that examples of the material we cover will turn up regularly in everyday life. Put what you learn into practice—critical thinking is not just a classroom activity.

Recap

Critical thinking helps you know when someone (including yourself) is taking a position on an issue, what that issue is, and what the person is claiming relative to that issue—that is, what the person's position is. It helps you

Doubts About Rationality

These days you hear some academics express doubts about rationality. Three fairly widespread ideas are these:

- Relativists maintain one is bound by the perspective of one's own culture. They say there is no meaning in the idea of getting beyond that perspective to see which beliefs are true in some objective sense. What is true, for the relativist, is what one's culture thinks is true.

- Post-Marxist scholars, some of them anyhow, say rationality reduces to power politics. A "strong" or "valid" or "good" argument (they say) is in reality simply an argument advanced by those in society who wield the most power.

- Cognitive scientists, many of them, think reasoning involves mostly unconscious processes. Emotional disengagement, they say, is impossible.

We criticize relativism in the chapter and won't say more about it here.

Cognitive scientists are no doubt right in saying that the conclusions we come to and the opinions we hold are formed in part, or even largely, by influences of which we are not aware. Nevertheless (as we shall explore in detail in Chapter 7 and the following chapters) universally valid distinctions can be made among arguments, and there are indisputably important respects in which one argument may be said to be better than another. It may not be possible to be governed in our opinions and actions entirely by the force of good argument, but it is possible to recognize a good argument; one is rational exactly to the extent one is able to do so.

As for the idea that an argument is good or valid or strong because those in power say it is good or valid or strong, you will find an almost endless supply of examples in this book of poor, invalid, and weak arguments advanced by powerful people, and good and valid and strong arguments not endorsed at all by those in power.

know what considerations are relevant to that issue and whether the reasoning underlying the person's claim is good reasoning. It helps you determine whether, everything considered, you should accept, reject, or suspend judgment on what the person claims. These skills require you to be level-headed and objective and uninfluenced by extraneous factors.

To avoid common misconceptions and confusions connected with critical thinking, we need to remember the following:

- ▲ Issues are not psychological problems.
- ▲ Not all arguments are attempts to persuade.
- ▲ Not all attempts to persuade are arguments.
- ▲ If persuasion is an objective, other methods can work as well as or better than arguments.

- ▲ Arguments and explanations are different things.
- ▲ Factual issues and claims may or may not be controversial.
- ▲ Nonfactual issues and claims can be important, intelligently discussed, and reasonably debated.
- ▲ Not all factual claims are true.
- ▲ Subjectivism, the view that two people with conflicting opinions on a factual issue can both be correct, is a defective view.
- ▲ Relativism, the view that two different cultures can be correct in having different opinions on the same factual issue, is a defective view.
- ▲ Two statements can differ in their psychological force yet have the same content.

Exercises

The exercises in this book are designed to provide practice in critical thinking. Some can be answered directly from the pages of the text, but some will require your careful consideration. For many exercises in this book, there is no such thing as *the* correct answer, just as there is no such thing as *the* correct way to serve a tennis ball or to make lasagna. But some answers, like some tennis serves and some lasagnas, are better than others. So in many exercises, answers you give that differ from your instructor's are not necessarily incorrect. Still, your instructor's answers most likely will be rational, sound, and worth your attention. In general, his or her judgment will be very reliable. We recommend you take advantage of your instructor's experience to improve your ability to think critically.

Answers to the exercise items marked with a triangle are found in the answer section (look for the colored edges) at the back of the book. You'll also find the occasional comment, tip, suggestion, joke, or buried treasure map back there.

Exercise 1-1

Answer the questions based on your reading of Chapter 1, including the boxes.

▲ 1. What is an argument?
  2. List five fundamental critical-thinking abilities.
  3. T or F: Critical thinking provides an opportunity to attack other people.
▲ 4. Are there situations when the wisest move is to accept a claim even though we are not entirely certain it is true?
  5. What is an issue?
  6. Are topics of conversation the same as issues?

▲ 7. Are all issues posed beginning with the word "whether"?

8. T or F: Whenever a claim has been questioned, an issue has been raised.

9. Do arguments all have conclusions?

▲ 10. Can a conclusion be implied, or must it always be explicitly stated?

11. Explain the connection between an argument and an issue.

12. Are all opinions equally reasonable?

▲ 13. Are all opinions about nonfactual issues equally reasonable?

14. If one of two people disagreeing on an issue must be mistaken, then is the issue factual or nonfactual?

15. Are factual issues ever controversial?

▲ 16. T or F: All arguments are used to try to persuade someone of something.

17. T or F: All attempts to persuade someone of something are arguments.

18. Does every argument address an issue?

▲ 19. T or F: Subjectivism is the idea that two people can both be correct if they disagree on a factual issue.

▲ 20. T or F: Relativism is the idea that two cultures can both be correct if they disagree on a factual issue.

21. T or F: Explanations and arguments serve the same purpose.

22. "Therefore" and "consequently" are conclusion-indicators.

23. T or F: "Rhetorical" or "emotive force" refers to the emotional content or associations of a word or phrase.

24. T or F: The rhetorical force of language can get in the way of clear and critical thinking.

25. T or F: We should not try to put our own position on any issue in the most favorable light.

Exercise 1-2

This exercise is designed to be done as an in-class group assignment. Your instructor will indicate how he or she wants it done. On the basis of a distinction covered in this chapter, divide these items into two groups of five items each such that all the items in one group have a feature that none of the items in the second group have. Describe the feature upon which you based your classifications. Compare your results with those of a neighboring group.

1. You shouldn't buy that car because it is ugly.

2. That car is ugly, and it's expensive too.

3. Rainbows have seven different colors in them, although it's not always easy to see them all.

4. Walking is the best exercise. After all, it is less stressful on the joints than other aerobic exercises.

5. The ocean on the central coast is the most beautiful shade of sky blue. It's more green as you go north.

6. Her favorite color is yellow because it is the color of the sun.

7. Pooh is my favorite cartoon character because he has lots of personality.

8. You must turn off the lights when you leave the room. They cost a lot of money to run and you don't need them on during the day.

9. Television programs have too much violence and immoral behavior. Hundreds of killings are portrayed every month.

10. You'll be able to find a calendar on sale after the first of the year, so it is a good idea to wait until then to buy one.

Exercise 1-3

Some of these items are arguments and some are not. Can you divide them up correctly?

▲ 1. Sampras is unlikely to win the U.S. Open again this year. He has a nagging leg injury, plus he just doesn't seem to have the drive he once had.

2. Hey there, Marco!—don't go giving that cat top sirloin. What's the matter with you, you got no brains at all?

3. If you've ever met a pet bird, then you know that they are very busy creatures.

▲ 4. "'Water resistant to 100 feet,' says the front of this package for an Aqualite watch, but the fine-print warranty on the back doesn't cover 'any failure to function properly due to misuse such as water immersion.'"

Consumer Reports

5. Everybody is saying the president has made us the laughingstock of the world. What a stupid idea! He hasn't made us a laughingstock at all. There's not a bit of truth in that notion.

6. "Is the author really entitled to assert that there is a degree of unity among these essays which makes this a book rather than a congeries? I am inclined to say that he is justified in this claim, but articulating this justification is a somewhat complex task."

From a book review by Stanley Bates

▲ 7. As a long-time customer, you're already taking advantage of our money management expertise and variety of investment choices. That's a good reason for consolidating your other eligible assets into an IRA with us.

8. MOORE: Well, I see where the new chancellor wants to increase class sizes.
PARKER: Yeah, another of his bright ideas.
MOORE: Actually, I don't think it hurts to have one or two extra people in class.
PARKER: What? Of course it hurts. What are you thinking, anyway?
MOORE: Well, I just think there is good reason for increasing the class size a bit.

9. John Montgomery has been the Eastern Baseball League's best closer this season. Unfortunately, when a closer fails, as Montgomery did last night, there's usually not much chance to recover.

▲ 10. Yes, I charge a little more than other dentists. But I feel I give better service. So I think my billing practices are justified.

11. If you want to purchase the house, you must exercise your option before June 30, 2003. Otherwise, you will forfeit the option price.

Exercise 1-4 ────────────────────────────────────

Determine which of the following passages contain arguments, and, for any that do, identify the argument's conclusion. Remember that an argument occurs when one or more claims (the premises) are offered in support of a further claim (the conclusion). There aren't many hard-and-fast rules for identifying arguments, so you'll have to read closely and think carefully about some of these.

▲ 1. The *Directory of Intentional Communities* lists more than two hundred groups across the country organized around a wide variety of purposes, including environmentally aware living.

2. Carl would like to help out, but he won't be in town. So we'll have to find someone else who owns a truck.

3. In 1976, Washington, D.C., passed an ordinance prohibiting private ownership of firearms. Since then, Washington's murder rate has shot up 121 percent. Bans on firearms are clearly counterproductive.

▲ 4. Computers will never be able to converse intelligently through speech. A simple example proves that this is so. The sentences "How do you recognize speech?" and "How do you wreck a nice beach?" have entirely different meanings, but they sound similar enough that a computer could not distinguish the two.

5. Recent surveys for the National Science Foundation report that two of three adult Americans believe that alien spaceships account for UFO reports. It therefore seems likely that several million Americans may have been predisposed to accept the report on NBC's *Unsolved Mysteries* that the U.S. military recovered a UFO with alien markings.

6. "Like short-term memory, long-term memory retains information that is encoded in terms of sense modality and in terms of links with information that was learned earlier (that is, *meaning*)."

Neil R. Carlson

▲ 7. Fears that chemicals in teething rings and soft plastic toys may cause cancer may be justified. Last week, the Consumer Product Safety Commission issued a report confirming that low amounts of DEHP, known to cause liver cancer in lab animals, may be absorbed from certain infant products.

8. "It may be true that people, not guns, kill people. But people with guns kill more people than people without guns. As long as the number of lethal

weapons in the hands of the American people continues to grow, so will the murder rate."

Susan Mish'alani

9. June 1970: A Miami man gets thirty days in the stockade for wearing a flag patch on the seat of his trousers. March 2004: Miami department stores are selling boxer trunks made up to look like an American flag. Times have changed.

▲ 10. Levi's Dockers are still in style, but pleats are out.

11. There is trouble in the Middle East, there is a recession under way at home, and all the economic indicators have turned downward. It seems likely, then, that the only way the stock market can go is down.

12. Lucy is too short to reach the bottom of the sign.

▲ 13. "Can it be established that genetic humanity is sufficient for moral humanity? I think that there are very good reasons for not defining the moral community in this way."

Mary Anne Warren

14. Pornography often depicts women as servants or slaves, or as otherwise inferior to men. In light of that, it seems reasonable to expect to find more women than men who are upset by pornography.

15. "My folks, who were Russian immigrants, loved the chance to vote. That's probably why I decided that I was going to vote whenever I got the chance. I'm not sure [whom I'll vote for], but I am going to vote. And I don't understand people who don't."

Mike Wallace

▲ 16. "President Clinton's request for $1 billion to create summer jobs for low-income young people was killed in the Senate, forcing him to settle for $166.5 million. Jobs would help make them part of the real community and would represent a beacon of hope—the first step out of poverty and despair."

Christian Science Monitor

17. "Hayek argues that we cannot know enough about each person's situation to distribute to each according to his moral merit (but would justice demand we do so if we did have the knowledge?)."

Robert Nozick

18. The Great Lakes Coastal Commission should prepare regulations that are consistent with the law, obviously. We admit that isn't always easy. But there's no reason for the commission to substitute its judgment for that of the people.

▲ 19. We need to make clear that sexual preference, whether chosen or genetically determined, is a private matter. It has nothing to do with an individual's ability to make a positive contribution to society.

20. "Cinema rarely rises from a craft to an art. Usually it just manufactures sensory blizzards for persons too passive to manage the active engagement of mind that even light reading requires."

George Will

Exercise 1-5 ⎯⎯⎯⎯⎯⎯⎯⎯⎯⎯⎯⎯⎯⎯⎯⎯⎯⎯⎯⎯⎯⎯⎯⎯⎯⎯⎯⎯⎯

For each passage in this exercise, identify which of the items that follow best states the primary issue discussed in the passage. Be prepared to say why you think your choice is the correct one.

▲ 1. Let me tell you why Hank ought not to take that math course. First, it's too hard, and he'll probably flunk it. Second, he's going to spend the whole term in a state of frustration. Third, he'll probably get depressed and do poorly in all the rest of his courses.
   a. Whether Hank ought to take the math course
   b. Whether Hank would flunk the math course
   c. Whether Hank will spend the whole term in a state of frustration
   d. Whether Hank will get depressed and do poorly in all the rest of his courses

   2. The county has cut the library budget for salaried library workers, and there will not be enough volunteers to make up for the lack of paid workers. Therefore, the library will have to be open fewer hours next year.
   a. Whether the library will have to be open fewer hours next year
   b. Whether there will be enough volunteers to make up for the lack of paid workers

▲ 3. Pollution of the waters of the Everglades and of Florida Bay is due to multiple causes. These include cattle farming, dairy farming, industry, tourism, and urban development. So it is simply not so that the sugar industry is completely responsible for the pollution of these waters.
   a. Whether pollution of the waters of the Everglades and Florida Bay is due to multiple causes
   b. Whether pollution is caused by cattle farming, dairy farming, industry, tourism, and urban development
   c. Whether the sugar industry is partly responsible for the pollution of these waters
   d. Whether the sugar industry is completely responsible for the pollution of these waters

▲ 4. It's clear that the mainstream media have lost interest in classical music. For example, the NBC network used to have its own classical orchestra conducted by Arturo Toscanini, but no such orchestra exists now. One newspaper, the no-longer-existent *Washington Star,* used to have thirteen classical music reviewers—that's more than twice as many as the *New York Times* has now. H. L. Mencken and other columnists used to devote considerable space to classical music; nowadays, you almost never see it mentioned in a major column.
   a. Whether popular taste has turned away from classical music
   b. Whether newspapers are employing fewer writers on classical music
   c. Whether the mainstream media have lost interest in classical music

   5. This year's National Football League draft lists a large number of quarterbacks among its highest-ranking candidates. Furthermore, quite a number

of teams do not have a first-class quarterback. It's therefore likely that there will be an unusually large number of quarterbacks drafted early in this year's draft.
a. Whether teams without first-class quarterbacks will choose quarterbacks in the draft
b. Whether there is a large number of quarterbacks in this year's NFL draft
c. Whether an unusually large number of quarterbacks will be drafted early in this year's draft

6. An animal that will walk out into a rainstorm and stare up at the clouds until water runs into its nostrils and it drowns—well, that's what I call the world's dumbest animal. And that's exactly what young domestic turkeys do.
a. Whether young domestic turkeys will drown themselves in the rain
b. Whether any animal is dumb enough to drown itself in the rain
c. Whether young domestic turkeys are the world's dumbest animal

7. The defeat of the school voucher initiative was a bad thing for the country because now there won't be any incentive for public schools to clean up their act. Furthermore, the status quo perpetuates the private-school-for-the-rich, public-school-for-the-poor syndrome.
a. Whether there is now any incentive for public schools to clean up their act
b. Whether the defeat of the school voucher initiative was bad for the country
c. Two issues are equally stressed in the passage: whether there is now any incentive for public schools to clean up their act and whether the private-school-for-the-rich, public-school-for-the-poor syndrome will be perpetuated

8. From an editorial in a newspaper outside southern California: "The people in southern California who lost a fortune in the wildfires last year could have bought insurance that would have covered their houses and practically everything in them. And anybody with any foresight would have made sure there were no brush and no trees near the houses so that there would be a buffer zone between the house and any fire, as the Forest Service recommends. Finally, anybody living in a fire danger zone ought to know enough to have a fireproof or fire-resistant roof on the house. So, you see, most of the losses those people suffered were simply their own fault."
a. Whether there were things the fire victims could have done to prevent their losses
b. Whether insurance, fire buffer zones, and fire-resistant roofs could have prevented much of the loss
c. Whether the losses suffered by people in the fires were their own fault

9. "Whatever we believe, we think agreeable to reason, and, on that account, yield our assent to it. Whatever we disbelieve, we think contrary to reason, and, on that account, dissent from it. Reason, therefore, is allowed to be the principle by which our belief and opinions ought to be regulated."

Thomas Reid, Essays on the Active Powers of Man

a. Whether reason is the principle by which our beliefs and opinions ought to be regulated

b. Whether what we believe is agreeable to reason

c. Whether what we disbelieve is contrary to reason

d. Both b and c

10. Most people you find on university faculties are people who are interested in ideas. And the most interesting ideas are usually new ideas. So most people you find on university faculties are interested in new ideas. Therefore, you are not going to find many conservatives on university faculties, because conservatives are not usually interested in new ideas.

a. Whether conservatives are interested in new ideas

b. Whether you'll find many conservatives on university faculties

c. Whether people on university faculties are interested more in new ideas than in other ideas

d. Whether most people are correct

11. In pre–civil war Spain, the influence of the Catholic Church must have been much stronger on women than on men. You can determine this by looking at the number of religious communities, such as monasteries, nunneries, and so forth. A total of about 5,000 such communities existed in 1931; 4,000 of them were female, whereas only 1,000 of them were male. Seems to me that proves my point about the Church's influence on the sexes.

a. Whether the Catholic Church's influence was greater on women than on men in pre–civil war Spain

b. Whether the speaker's statistics really prove his point about the Church's influence

c. Whether the figures about religious communities really have anything to do with the overall influence of the Catholic Church in Spain

12. The movie *Pulp Fiction* might have been a pretty good movie without the profanity that occurred all the way through it. But without the profanity, it would not have been a believable movie. The people this movie was about just talk that way, you see. If you have them speaking Shakespearean English or middle-class suburban English, then nobody is going to pay any attention to the message of the movie because nobody will see it as realistic. It's true, of course, that, like many other movies with some offensive feature—whether it's bad language, sex, or whatever—it will never appeal to a mass audience.

a. Whether movies with offensive features can appeal to a mass audience

b. Whether *Pulp Fiction* would have been a good movie without the bad language

c. Whether *Pulp Fiction* would have been a believable movie without the bad language

d. Whether believable movies must always have an offensive feature of one kind or another

▲ 13. "From information gathered in the last three years, it has become clear that the single biggest environmental problem in the former Soviet Union—many times bigger than anything we have to contend with in the United States—is radioactive pollution from nuclear energy plants and nuclear weapons testing and production. Soviet communist leaders seemed to believe they could do anything to hasten the industrialization process and compete with Western countries, and that the land and natural resources they controlled were vast enough to suffer any abuse without serious consequence. The arrogance of the communist leaders produced a burden of misery and death that fell on the people of the region, and the scale of that burden has only recently become clear. Nuclear waste was dumped into rivers from which downstream villages drew their drinking water; the landscape is dotted with nuclear dumps which now threaten to leak into the environment; and the seas around Russia are littered with decaying hulks of nuclear submarines and rusting metal containers with tens of millions of tons of nuclear waste. The result has been radiation poisoning and its awful effects on a grand scale.

"A science advisor to former Russian President Boris Yeltsin said, 'The way we have dealt with the whole issue of nuclear power, and particularly the problem of nuclear waste, was irresponsible and immoral.'"

Adapted from the Washington Post

a. Whether communism failed to protect people from nuclear contamination as well as capitalism did
b. Whether nuclear waste problems in the former Soviet Union are much worse than had been realized until just recently
c. Whether former leaders of the Soviet Union made large-scale sacrifice of the lives and health of their people in their nuclear competition with the West
d. Whether communism, in the long run, is a much worse system than capitalism when it comes to protecting the population from harm

▲ 14. "The United States puts a greater percentage of its population in prison than any other developed country in the world. We persist in locking more and more people up despite the obvious fact that it doesn't work. Even as we build more prisons and stuff them ever more tightly, the crime rate goes up and up. But we respond: 'Since it isn't working, let's do more of it'!

"It's about time we learned that fighting criminals is not the same thing as fighting crime."

Richard Parker, radio commentary on CalNet, California Public Radio

a. Whether we build more prisons than any other country
b. Whether we imprison more people than do other countries
c. Whether reliance on imprisonment is an effective method of reducing crime
d. Whether attacking the sources of crime (poverty, lack of education, and so on) will reduce crime more than just imprisoning people who commit crimes

▲ 15. [As the Clinton administration planned to raise the fees charged for grazing animals on public land, several members of the Senate argued against the proposal.] "Senator Alan K. Simpson of Wyoming said higher prices would 'do those old cowboys in.'

"But a review of the top 500 holders of grazing permits on federal land shows that many of those 'old cowboys' are more likely to wear wingtips than boots. They include the Metropolitan Life Insurance Company, with 800,000 acres under its control, the Mormon Church, a Japanese conglomerate, the Nature Conservancy and some of the wealthiest families in the nation.

"The largest permit holders, the top 10 percent, control about half of the nation's public grazing land, according to Interior Department figures. Only 12 percent of the permit holders are listed by the government as small operators."

a. Whether Senator Simpson understands who holds grazing permits on federal land

b. Whether permits to graze on most public land are held by corporations or by individuals and families

c. Whether permits to graze on most public land are held by small operators or by large, wealthy operators

d. Whether the administration's plan to raise grazing fees is a reasonable idea

▲ 16. Letting your children surf the Net is like dropping them off downtown to spend the day doing whatever they want. They'll get in trouble.

a. Whether letting your children off downtown to spend the day doing whatever they want will lead them into trouble

b. Whether letting your children surf the Net will lead them into trouble

c. Whether restrictions should be placed on children's activities

17. When Rep. Paul McHale became the first Democrat to call for Clinton's resignation, the press pointed out that McHale wasn't running for reelection. But when Barbara Boxer, who was in a pitched battle for her Senate seat, lashed out at the president from the Senate floor, it became clear that attacking the president was politically safe.

a. Whether Barbara Boxer was fighting for her political life in California

b. Whether it was politically necessary for Barbara Boxer to attack the president

c. Whether attacking the president was politically safe

d. Whether Paul McHale's call for Clinton's resignation was sincere

18. Illinois state employees, both uniformed and non-uniformed, have been loyally, faithfully, honorably, and patiently serving the state without a contract or cost-of-living pay increase for years, despite the fact that legislators and governor have accepted hefty pay increases. All public employee unions should launch a signature-gathering initiative to place on the ballot a proposition that the Illinois constitution be amended to provide for compulsory binding arbitration for all uniformed and non-uniformed public employees, under the supervision of the state supreme court.

a. Whether Illinois state employees have been loyally, faithfully, honorably, and patiently serving the state without a contract or cost-of-living pay increase for years

b. Whether public employee unions should launch a signature-gathering initiative to place on the ballot a proposition that the Illinois constitution be amended to provide for compulsory binding arbitration for all

uniformed and non-uniformed public employees, under the supervision
of the Illinois Supreme Court

    c. Neither of the above

19. That Japan needs reform of its political institutions is hardly in doubt. The
country is experiencing the worst recession since the Second World War,
with forecasts of up to minus 3 percent growth this year. Japan is not only
the world's largest economy, but it also dominates the East Asian economic
zone, so recovery through that region depends directly on Japan. Reforms
are urgently needed to ensure this recovery will happen.

    a. Whether Japan needs reforms of its political institutions

    b. Whether Japan is experiencing its worst recession since the Second
World War

    c. Whether Japan is the world's second largest economy

    d. Whether reforms will ensure that recovery will happen

▲ 20. MOORE: So, what do you think of the governor?

    PARKER: Not much, actually.

    MOORE: What do you mean? Don't you think she's been pretty good?

    PARKER: Are you serious?

    MOORE: Well, yes. I think she's been doing a fine job.

    PARKER: Oh, come on. Weren't you complaining about her just a few
days ago?

    a. Whether Parker thinks the governor has been a good governor.

    b. Whether Moore thinks the governor has been a good governor.

    c. Whether the governor has been a good governor

    d. Whether Moore has a good argument for thinking the governor has been
a good governor

Exercise 1-6

Identify the main issue in each of the following passages.

▲ 1. Police brutality does not happen very often. Otherwise, it would not make
headlines when it does happen.

2. We have little choice but to concentrate our crime-fighting efforts on enforcement because we don't have any idea what to do about the underlying
causes of crime.

3. A lot of people think that the gender of a Supreme Court justice doesn't
make any difference. But with two women on the bench, cases dealing
with women's issues are being handled differently.

▲ 4. "The point is that the existence of an independent world explains our experiences better than any known alternative. We thus have good reason to
believe that the world—which seems independent of our minds—really is
essentially independent of our minds."

        Theodore W. Schick, Jr., and Lewis Vaughn, How to Think About Weird Things

5. Sure, some of the hotdoggers get good grades in Professor Bubacz's class. But my guess is that if Algernon takes it, all it'll get him is flunked out!

6. It is dumb to claim that sales taxes hit poor people harder than rich people. After all, the more money you have, the more you spend; and the more you spend, the more sales taxes you pay. So people with more money are always going to be paying more in sales tax than poor people.

▲ 7. If you're going to buy a computer, you might as well also sign up for some lessons on how to use the thing. After all, no computer ever did any work for its owner until its owner found out how to make it work.

8. Intravenous drug use with nonsterile needles has become one of the leading causes of the spread of AIDS. Many states passed legislation allowing officials to distribute clean needles in an effort to combat this method of infection. But in eleven states, including some of the most populous, possession of hypodermic syringes without a prescription is illegal. The laws in these foot-dragging states have to be changed if we ever hope to bring this awful epidemic to an end.

9. The best way to avoid error—that is, belief in something false—is to suspend judgment about everything except that which is absolutely certain. Because error usually leads to trouble, this shows that suspension of judgment is usually the right thing to do.

▲ 10. "[Readers] may learn something about their own relationship to the earth from a people who were true conservationists. The Indians knew that life was equated with the earth and its resources, that America was a paradise, and they could not comprehend why the intruders from the East were determined to destroy all that was Indian as well as America itself."

Dee Brown, Bury My Heart at Wounded Knee

Exercise 1-7

For each item, identify the issue that the first speaker is addressing. Are the two speakers addressing the same issue?

Example

THERESA: I think toilet paper looks better if it unwinds from the back side of the spool.

DANIEL: No way! It looks stupid that way. It should unwind from the front side of the spool.

Analysis

The issue for both Theresa and Daniel is whether the toilet paper looks better if it unwinds from the front of the spool. This issue is not a factual matter.

▲   1. MR.: Next weekend we go on Standard Time again. We'll have to set the clocks ahead.

   MRS.: It isn't next weekend; it's the weekend after. And you set the clocks back one hour, not ahead.

   2. BELIEVER: Ghosts exist. People everywhere in all cultures have believed in them. All those people couldn't be wrong.

   SKEPTIC: If ghosts exist, it's not for that reason. People once believed Earth was flat, too.

   3. SHE: You don't give me enough help around the house; you hardly ever do anything.

   HE: That's not true. I mowed the lawn on Saturday and I washed both of the cars on Sunday. What's more, I've been cleaning up after dinner almost every night and I've hauled all that stuff from the garden to the dump. So I don't see how you can say I hardly ever do anything.

   SHE: Well, you don't want to hear all that *I* do around here; your efforts are pretty puny compared to mine!

▲   4. HEEDLESS: When people complain about American intervention in places like Iraq, they tell every tinhorn dictator to go ahead and take over because America will just stand by and watch. I, for one, think people who complain like that ought to just shut up.

   CAUTIOUS: Not me. Complaining like that reminds everyone that it isn't in our best interest to get involved in extended wars abroad.

   5. ONE SPEAKER: Nothing beats summertime. It's sunny and warm, and you can wear shorts, go on picnics, take hikes, and, best of all, take in a ball game.

   ANOTHER SPEAKER: Naw, summer's hot and sticky, and there's no skiing or skating or getting warm 'round a nice cozy fire. Summer's okay—if you're a mosquito.

   6. FITNESS BUFF ONE: Look here, the speedometer cable on this exercise bike is starting to squeak. If we don't fix it, the speedometer is going to stop working.

   FITNESS BUFF TWO: What we need to do is get a new bike. This old thing is more trouble than it's worth.

   7. YOUNG GUY: Baseball players are much better now than they were forty years ago. They eat better, have better coaching, you name it.

   OLD GUY: They aren't any better at all. They just seem better because they get more publicity and play with a livelier ball.

   8. STUDENT ONE: Studying is a waste of time. Half the time, I get better grades if I don't study.

   STUDENT TWO: I'd like to hear you say that in front of your parents!

   9. PHILATELIST: Did you know that U.S. postage stamps are now being printed in Canada?

   PATRIOT: What an outrage! If there is one thing that ought to be made in the United States, it's U.S. postage stamps!

PHILATELIST: Oh, I disagree. If American printing companies can't do the work, let the Canadians have it.

10. GEORGE: I think the United States ought to pull its troops out of every country they are currently stationed in. We simply cannot afford and do not know how to police the entire globe.

   NEVILLE: Boy, there's a laugh, coming from you. You're the one who thought we should be sending more troops to Vietnam in the early seventies; you cheered the invasions of Grenada and Panama in the eighties; and you were for the action in Somalia in the nineties. It's a little too late to be handing out this isolationist stuff now, isn't it?

11. FIRST NEIGHBOR: Look here. You have no right to make so much noise at night. I have to get up early to get to work.

   SECOND NEIGHBOR: Yeah? Well, you have no right to let your idiot dog run around loose all day long.

12. STUDY PARTNER ONE: Let's knock off for a while and go get some pizza. We'll be able to function better if we have something to eat.

   STUDY PARTNER TWO: Not one of those pizzas you like! I can't stand anchovies.

13. FEMALE STUDENT: The Internet is totally overrated. It takes forever to find something you can actually use in an assignment.

   MALE STUDENT: Listen, it takes a lot longer to drive over to the library, find a place to park, and wait in line to use a terminal.

14. CITIZEN ONE: In 2004 it's going to be George W. Bush for the Republicans and John Kerry for the Democrats, what do you want to bet?

   CITIZEN TWO: I doubt it. Kerry's fading. The Democrats will find someone else.

15. CULTURALLY CHALLENGED PERSON: A concert! You think I'm gonna go to a concert when I could be home watching Monday Night Football?

   CULTURALLY CHALLENGED PERSON'S SPOUSE: Yes, if you want dinner this week.

Exercise 1-8

For each of the brief conversations that follow, identify the issue the first speaker is addressing. To what extent does the second speaker address the same issue? Does he or she miss the point? If so, might the misdirection be intentional? Some of these are best suited to class discussion.

Example

MOORE: I've seen the work of both Thomas Brothers and Vernon Construction, and I tell you Thomas Brothers does a better job.

PARKER: Listen, Thomas Brothers is the highest-priced company in the whole blasted state. If you hire them, you'll pay double for every part of the job.

Analysis

Moore thinks Thomas Brothers does better work than Vernon Construction; Parker thinks Thomas Brothers' work is overpriced. Moore's view is quite compatible with Parker's view: Thomas Brothers may indeed do the best work (i.e., Moore is right) *and* charge wildly excessive prices (i.e., Parker is right, too). However, there is an underlying issue on which Moore and Parker will almost certainly disagree: whether Thomas Brothers should be hired. They have not made this disagreement explicit yet, however.

▲ 1. URBANITE: The new requirements will force people off septic tanks and make them hook up to the city sewer. That's the only way we'll ever get the nitrates and other pollutants out of the ground water.
SUBURBANITE: You call it a requirement, but I call it an outrage! They're going to charge us from five to fifteen thousand dollars each to make the hookups! That's more than anybody in my neighborhood can afford.

2. CRITIC: I don't think it's morally proper to sell junk bonds to anybody without emphasizing the risk involved, but it's especially bad to sell them to older people who are investing their entire savings.
ENTREPRENEUR: Oh, come on. There's nothing the matter with making money.

▲ 3. ONE HAND: What with the number of handguns and armed robberies these days, it's hard to feel safe in your own home.
THE OTHER HAND: The reason you don't feel safe is that you don't have a handgun yourself. It's well known that a criminal would rather hit a house where there's no gun than a house where there is one.

4. ONE GUY: Would you look at the price they want for these recordable DVD machines? They're making a fortune in profit on every one of these things!
ANOTHER: Don't give me that. I know how big a raise you got last year—you can afford *two* of those players if you want!

▲ 5. FED-UP: This city is too cold in the winter, too hot in the summer, and too dangerous all the time. I'll be happier if I exercise my early retirement option and move to my place in Arkansas.
FRIEND: You're nuts. You've worked here so long you'll be miserable if you retire, and if you move, you'll be back in six months.

Exercise 1-9 ————————————————————

On the basis of a concept or distinction discussed in this chapter, divide the following issues into two groups, and identify the concept or distinction you used.

▲ 1. Whether George Pataki was as old when he became governor as Mario Cuomo was when he became governor.

2. Whether George Pataki is more liberal than Mario Cuomo was when Mario Cuomo was governor.

3. Whether Willie Mays hit more home runs than Mark McGwire.

▲ 4. Whether Leno tells better jokes than Letterman.

5. Whether your teacher will complain if you wear a baseball cap in class.

6. Whether your teacher should complain if you wear a baseball cap in class.

▲ 7. Whether there has ever been life on Mars.

8. Whether golf is more challenging than tennis.

9. Whether the movie scared me.

▲ 10. Whether I said the movie scared me.

11. Whether the movie is scary to lots of people.

Exercise 1-10

Decide whether each question raises a factual issue or a nonfactual issue. If some items are difficult to decide, explain why you think this is so.

▲ 1. How much does Manuel weigh?

2. Does diet soda taste more bland than regular soda?

3. Does diet soda contain less sugar than regular soda?

▲ 4. Will diet soda help you lose weight better than regular soda?

5. Is it more fun to sail on a cruise ship than to lie on the beach at Hilton Head?

6. Is it expensive to sail on a cruise ship?

▲ 7. Is there life on another planet somewhere in the universe?

8. Would most people find this bath water uncomfortably hot?

9. Is the lake too cold for swimming?

▲ 10. Is Tom Brokaw better looking than Dan Rather?

11. Is Tiger Woods a better golfer than Jack Nicklaus was?

12. Is Al Sharpton smarter than George W. Bush?

▲ 13. Is abortion immoral?

14. Is Elvis still alive?

Exercise 1-11

▲ Four of the following are factual claims, and six aren't. Can you identify them correctly?

1. Rice vinegar tastes a darn sight better than white vinegar.

2. White vinegar removes lipstick stains; rice vinegar doesn't.

3. None of the Supreme Court justices view the Constitution objectively.

4. Nine authors collaborated on that article.

5. Microsoft shares are significantly overpriced.

6. People who go to church regularly live longer than people who don't.

7. The FBI and CIA don't share information as often as they should.

8. The report stated that the FBI and CIA don't share information as often as they should.

9. Okay—enough of this logic stuff. It's Miller Time!

10. That last item is too challenging for this text.

Exercise 1-12

Sometimes factual claims contain nonfactual elements, and sometimes nonfactual claims contain factual elements. For example, here is a factual claim that contains a nonfactual element:

(A) Tom, a fine lad, is over six feet tall. (The phrase "a fine lad" is a nonfactual element.)

And here is a nonfactual claim that contains a factual element:

(B) Tom, who is over six feet tall, is a fine lad. (The clause "who is over six feet tall" is a factual element.)

Where you find factual claims in the following list, revise them so that they contain no nonfactual elements.

▲ 1. The house, an imposing two-story colonial-style building, burned to the ground.

2. Assad, who was reluctant to do so, attended the summit that took place in Qatar last March.

3. Hurricane Fran stranded 175 devastated homeowners on barrier islands.

▲ 4. The Coors Brewing Company, long a supporter of a right-wing agenda, began offering gay partners the same benefits as spouses in 1995.

5. Castellanos attended the University of North Carolina but dropped out in disgust during his final semester.

6. On August 22, the leader of a Kurdish faction wrote a desperate plea to Saddam Hussein.

▲ 7. McCovey, who at the time was overwhelmed with grief, was able to finish the assignment on time.

8. In his question, Larry King, the best interviewer in the business, probed Mr. Cheney's business contacts.

9. Senator Byrd announced his proposal to protect the pension funds of struggling workers.

▲ 10. The Reverend Jesse Jackson's provocative visit to Pakistan has been delayed due to lack of support from the Bush administration.

11. Senator Clinton gave a sharp and vigorous response to the Republican challenger.

12. This Sunday, as prescribed by the barely functioning peace accords, Bosnians are to go to the polls to elect a president.

▲ 13. For two years the rapidly expanding global computer matrix had nagged at Gates like a low-level headache.

14. Creative policies have stopped the declining enrollments at Spring Grove Community College.

15. In early 2004 the U.S. Senate tried to reach agreement on the perplexing question of how to rescue Medicare.

Exercise 1-13

Revise each of these press reports to exclude any nonfactual elements. If no such elements appear, leave the original as is.

▲ 1. OROVILLE—A judge Friday ordered an accused gunman held for trial on a felony assault charge stemming from an aborted residential robbery last month during which an Oroville bank executive was wounded.

2. WASHINGTON—As details of a remarkable week of grand jury testimony by President Clinton and a young intern filter into the public domain, Clinton apologists are unwinding a fragile string of explanations to protect him against charges of perjury and obstruction of justice.

3. LHOK SUKON, Indonesia (AP)—Human rights workers on Saturday dug up the skeletons of people whom activists believe were killed by the Indonesian military. Villagers looking on shouted slogans against former President Suharto.

▲ 4. Gunshots were fired at an apartment complex off 10th Street Friday during a "gang bang," which, according to witnesses, may have been contrived to intimidate or retaliate against rival gang members.

5. WASHINGTON—From hideouts in Afghanistan's rugged mountains, Osama bin Laden used his wealth to create cells of Muslim fighters to cleanse the country of its Soviet occupiers. Now bin Laden, who became the most significant sponsor of Islamic extremist activities in the world, is using his wealth in his war on the United States.

6. HARRISBURG, PA. (AP)—With no bathrooms or portable potties in space, NASA has relied on a brand of inexpensive, compressed adult diapers to let astronauts take care of business while they work.

▲ 7. WASHINGTON—The attorney general has launched a 90-day investigation to see if she should seek still another independent counsel, this time to check into the truthfulness of the vice president. On the face of it, suspicion arises that the investigation might be more a means of dealing with political pressure—another stalling tactic—than of enforcing the law, since the probe won't be finished until after the November elections.

8. SACRAMENTO (AP)—State senators on Thursday approved a bill by Assemblywoman Debra Bowen, D–Marina del Rey, that would give

computer owners a way to block unwanted commercial electronic mail, which is commonly known as spam.

9. WASHINGTON—Bill Clinton played kinky games with a girl in a room next to the Oval Office while dignitaries were waiting for him. Independent counsel Kenneth Starr was trying to find out whether Clinton took criminal measures to conceal this weird behavior. Clinton, of course, was merely trying to shield his "family life."

▲ 10. Prior to the 2000 national election, President George W. Bush asked whether character counts. Those who felt character was important went on to elect the feeblest intellect this nation was ever to suffer under as president.

Exercise 1-14

Which of the lettered options serves the same kind of purpose as the original remark?

Example

    Be careful! This plate is hot.

    a. Watch out. The roads are icy.

    b. Say—why don't you get lost?

Answer

    The purpose of (a) is most like the purpose of the original remark. Both are warnings.

▲ 1. I'd expect that zipper to last about a week; it's made of cheap plastic.
    a. The wrinkles on that dog make me think of an old man.
    b. Given Sydney's spending habits, I doubt Adolphus will stick with her for long.

2. If you recharge your battery, sir, it will be almost as good as new.
    a. Purchasing one CD at the regular price would entitle you to buy an unlimited number of CDs at only $4.99.
    b. I shall now serve dinner, after which you can play if you want.

3. To put out a really creative newsletter, you should get in touch with our technology people.
    a. Do unto others as you would have them do unto you.
    b. To put an end to this discussion, I'll concede your point.
    c. You'd better cut down on your smoking if you want to live longer.

▲ 4. GE's profits during the first quarter were short of GE's projections. Therefore, we can expect GE stock to fall sharply in the next day or so.
    a. Senator Torricelli apparently thinks what he does in private is nobody's business but his own.
    b. The dog is very hot. Probably he would appreciate a drink of water.
    c. The dog's coat is unusually thick. No wonder he is hot.

5. How was my date with your brother? Well . . . he has a great personality.
   a. How do I like my steak? Well, not dripping blood like this thing you just served me.
   b. How do I like the dress? Say, did you know that black is more slimming than white?

6. The wind is coming up. We'd better head for shore.
   a. They finally arrived. I guess they will order soon.
   b. We shouldn't leave yet. We just got here.

▲ 7. Ties are as wide as handkerchiefs, these days. That's why they cost so much.
   a. Belts are like suspenders. They both serve to keep your pants up.
   b. Football is like rugby. Given that, it is easy to understand why so many people get injured.

8. Daphne owns an expensive car. She must be rich.
   a. This dog has fleas. I'll bet it itches a lot.
   b. This dog has fleas. That explains why it scratches a lot.

9. Dennis's salary is going to go up. After all, he just got a promotion.
   a. Dennis's salary went up after he got a promotion.
   b. Dennis's salary won't be going up. After all, he didn't get a promotion.

▲ 10. Outlawing adult Web sites may hamper free speech, but pornography must be curbed.
   a. The grass must be mowed, even though it is hot.
   b. The grass is much too long; that means it must be mowed.

Exercise 1-15

Five of the following questions call for an explanation; five call for an argument. Identify which call for which. (It may be possible to imagine strange situations in which all ten questions call for explanations and possible to imagine other strange situations in which all ten questions might call for arguments. Don't try to imagine far-out situations like that. Try to imagine normal, everyday situations in which somebody might ask these questions.)

▲ 1. YOU TO A FRIEND: You really think the dog is overweight? What makes you so sure?

2. YOU TO A FRIEND: Hey! The dang dog got out again! How do you suppose that happened?

3. YOU TO YOUR DENTIST: Yes, yes, I know I have another cavity, but what I don't understand is why. How did I get it—too many Jolly Ranchers?

▲ 4. YOU TO YOUR DENTIST: You're saying I have another cavity? Are you certain?

5. YOU TO YOUR DOCTOR: I haven't been sleeping very well, and I wondered what might account for that.

6. YOU TO YOUR DOCTOR: Doc, I've heard really bad things about that medication. Should I be taking it?

▲   7. YOU TO A MECHANIC: This Hyundai is always giving me problems. Half the time I can't even get it in gear! What causes something like that?

8. YOU TO A MECHANIC: Well, I certainly don't dispute what you are saying, but can you tell me again why you think I need a new transmission?

9. YOU TO YOUR TEACHER: I don't understand this grade! Are you sure you didn't make a mistake?

▲ 10. YOU TO YOUR TEACHER: I understand this grade; but can you tell me how I can do better next time?

Writing Exercises

1. Turn to the "Essays for Analysis" in Appendix 1. Identify and write in your own words the principal issues in selections 3, 4, or 5. Your instructor may have other instructions in addition to (or in place of) these.

2. Do people choose which sex they are attracted to? Write a one-page answer to this question, defending your answer with at least one supporting reason. Take about ten minutes to write your answer. Do not put your name on your paper. When everyone is finished, your instructor will collect the papers and redistribute them to the class. In groups of four or five, read the papers that have been given to your group. Divide the drafts into two batches, those that contain an argument and those that do not. Your instructor will ask each group to read to the class a paper that contains an argument and a paper that does not contain an argument (assuming that each group has at least one of each). The group should be prepared to explain why they feel each paper contains or fails to contain an argument.

3. Using the issues you identified in Exercise 1 for each of the selections, choose a side on one of the issues and write a short paper supporting it.

Chapter 2

Critical Thinking and Clear Writing

There you are, with keyboard, pen, or pencil. And there it is, the enemy: a blank screen or piece of paper that you must somehow convert into an essay. If you are like many students we know, the kind of essay that causes you more trouble than any other variety is the argumentative essay, in which the purpose is to support a position on an issue. Successful essays achieve their goal by offering good arguments for their author's position. And because arguments consist of claims, a good argumentative essay contains credible claims.

In the previous chapter, we discussed claims at length and introduced the basics of argument. In this chapter, we show how to apply principles of critical thinking to essay writing: how to organize your thoughts, state your claims clearly, and avoid ineffective and counterproductive language. The chapter is not a substitute for a course in composition or writing, but it provides information that will help you write strong essays based on clearly stated arguments and reasonable claims.

As you progress through this book, you will acquire a working understanding of the various principles by which you can evaluate claims and arguments and, accordingly, argumentative essays. You can also apply these principles of critical thinking to your own writing. So working on your critical-thinking skills will help you get better at both appraising and writing argumentative essays.

The benefits work in reverse, too. You can enlist essay writing in service of critical-thinking objectives. For example, suppose you read an editorial you do not agree with. You might try drafting a response. Doing so will probably help you organize your thoughts and clarify your position; it will almost surely disclose to you considerations you had not thought of or aspects of the issue you did not perceive at first. Your thinking on the subject will probably sharpen.

Organization and Focus

A good argumentative essay must first of all be well organized. Every now and then, you encounter pieces of writing in which the words, claims, and arguments are so strangely assembled that the result is unintelligible. Let's just hope that the piece is nothing you yourself have written.

If you come across an argumentative essay that suffers from such serious organizational defects that it cannot be fully understood, then your only option is to suspend judgment on the unintelligible aspects. If, however, your own writing suffers from these defects, then you can benefit from some simple principles of good organization.

■ Principles of Organization

In an argumentative essay, the most natural and common organizational pattern is to state what you are trying to establish and then proceed to establish it by setting forth the considerations that support your position, adding explanations, illustrations, or other elaboration as needed. Here are some guidelines to help you get organized:

1. *Focus.* Make clear at the outset what issue you intend to address and what your position on the issue will be. Of course, nothing is quite so boring as an essay that begins, "In this essay I shall argue that . . ." and then goes on to itemize everything that's going to be said later. As a matter of style, you should let the reader know what to expect without using trite phrases and without going on at length.

2. *Stick to the issue.* All points you make in an essay should be connected to the issue under discussion and should always either (a) support, illustrate, explain, clarify, elaborate on, or emphasize your position on the issue or (b) serve as responses to anticipated objections. Rid the essay of irrelevancies and dangling thoughts.

Who Said What?

Can you tell which of these quotations are from students in community college and which are from the forty-third president of the United States, who happens to be a Yale graduate?

1. "Sometimes the standards of society causes people to wear a mask."
2. "Reading is the basics for all learning."
3. "I played all types of sports that was offered to children then."
4. "More and more, our imports come from overseas."
5. "Children are born as a ball of clay; to mold into what we are able, good or bad. To enhance who we are and to carry on the person we are known to be."
6. "Drug therapies are replacing a lot of medicines as we used to know it."
7. "You teach a child to read and he or her will be able to pass a literacy test."
8. "He uses an abundance of words and phrases both of which I don't believe should have."
9. ". . . if you say you're going to do something and you don't do it, that's trustworthiness."
10. "Male dominance has long been a factor in human existence since our existence."
11. "My pro-life position is I believe there's life. It's not necessarily based in religion. I think there's life there, therefore the notion of life, liberty and pursuit of happiness."

12. ". . . teaching children to read and having an education system that's responsive to the child and to the parents, as opposed to mired in a system that refuses to change, will make America what we want it to be—a literate country and hopefuller country."
13. "Men love women who can cook good."
14. "I have never really thought of myself to be very interesting as a human being or as anything else."

1, 3, 5, 8, 10, 13, and 14—Community college student; 2, 4, 6, 7, 9, 11, 12—Yale graduate

From an article by Jaime O'Neill, a member of the English faculty at Butte Community College, in *San Francisco Chronicle*, September 2, 2001.

3. *Arrange the components of the essay in a logical sequence.* This is just common sense. Make a point *before* you clarify it, for example, not the other way around. Place support for item B next to item B, not next to item F or G.

When supporting your points, bring in examples, clarification, and the like in such a way that the reader knows what you are doing. Your readers should be able to discern the relationship between any given sentence and your ultimate objective, and they should be able to move from sentence to sentence and from paragraph to paragraph without becoming lost or confused. If a reader cannot outline your essay with ease, you have not properly sequenced your material.

4. *Be complete.* You don't have to be exhaustive in your treatment of the issue; many issues are in fact much too large to be treated exhaustively in a single essay. Remember, finally, this basic principle: The more limited your topic, the easier it is to be complete in your coverage. However, do accomplish what you set out to accomplish, support fully and adequately whatever position you take on the issue, and anticipate and respond to possible objections. Also, be sure that there is closure at every level: Sentences should be complete, paragraphs should be unified wholes (and usually each should stick to a single point), and the essay should reach a conclusion. Reaching a conclusion and summarizing are not the same, incidentally. Short essays do not require summaries.

■ *Good Writing Practices*

Understanding these principles is one thing—actually employing them may be more difficult. Fortunately, five practices are almost guaranteed to improve the organization of your essay and to help you avoid other problems.

1. At some stage *after* the first draft, outline what you have written. Then make certain that the outline is logical and that every sentence in the essay fits into the outline as it should. Some writers create an informal outline before they begin, but many do not. Our advice: Just start writing and worry about outlining later.

2. Revise your work. Revising is the secret to good writing. Even major league writers revise what they write, and they revise continuously. Unless you are even more gifted than the very best professional writers, then revise, revise, revise. Don't think in terms of two or three drafts. Think in terms of *innumerable* drafts.

3. Have someone else read your essay and offer criticisms of it. Revise as required.

4. If you have trouble with grammar or punctuation, reading your essay out loud may help you detect problems that your eyes have missed.

5. After you are *completely* satisfied with your essay, put it aside. Then come back to it later for still another set of revisions.

■ *Essay Types to Avoid*

Seasoned instructors know that the first batch of essays they get from a class will most likely include several samples of each of the following types. At all costs, try to avoid these pitfalls.

▲ *The Windy Preamble.* Writers of this type of essay avoid getting to the issue and instead go on at length with introductory remarks, often about how important the issue is, how it has troubled thinkers for centuries, how opinions on the issue are many and various, and so on—and on.

▲ *The Stream-of-Consciousness Ramble.* This type of essay results when writers make no attempt to organize their thinking on the issue and instead simply list thoughts more or less in the order they come to mind.

▲ *The Knee-Jerk Reaction.* In this type of essay, writers record their first reaction to an issue without considering the issue in any depth or detail.

▲ *The Glancing Blow.* Writers of this type of essay address the issue obliquely rather than straight on. If they are supposed to evaluate the health benefits of exercise, they will discuss the health benefits of using exercise equipment. If they are supposed to consider the health benefits of using exercise equipment, they will discuss the benefits of bicycling.

▲ *Let the Reader Do the Work.* Writers of this type of essay expect the reader to follow them through non sequiturs, abrupt shifts in direction, and huge gaps in logic.

Exercise 2-1 _____

The sentences in this Associated Press health report have been scrambled. Rearrange them so that the report makes sense.

1. The men, usually strong with no known vices or ailments, die suddenly, uttering an agonizing groan, writhing and gasping before succumbing to the mysterious affliction.

2. Scores of cases have been reported in the United States during the past decade.

3. In the United States, health authorities call it "Sudden Unexplained Death Syndrome," or "SUDS."

4. Hundreds of similar deaths have been noted worldwide.

5. The phenomenon is known as "lai tai," or "nightmare death," in Thailand.

6. In the Philippines, it is called "bangungut," meaning "to rise and moan in sleep."

A "Weakest Link" Quiz for You

Here is a "Weakest Link" quiz that was circulating on the Net a while back. It's a good test of your ability to read carefully and think clearly, two key components of critical thinking.

1. You are competing in a race and overtake the runner in second place. In which position are you now?
   Answer: If you said "first," then you aren't reading carefully (or aren't thinking clearly). The correct answer, of course, is "second."
2. If you overtake the last runner, what position are you in now?
   Answer: Second to the last? Hardly. The question doesn't make sense.
3. Take 1,000. Add 40. Add another 1,000. Add 30. Add 1,000 again. Plus 20. Plus 1,000. And plus 10. What is the total?
   Answer: If you said 5,000 you weren't reading carefully. The correct answer is 4,100.
4. Marie's father has five daughters:
   1. Cha Cha
   2. Che Che
   3. Chi Chi
   4. Cho Cho
   5. ??
   What is the fifth daughter's name?
   Answer: Chu Chu? Wrong, wrong, wrong. It's Marie!

Thanks to Anne Morrissey.

7. Health officials are baffled by a syndrome that typically strikes Asian men in their 30s while they sleep.
8. Researchers cannot say what is killing SUDS victims.

Exercise 2-2

▲ The sentences in the following passage have been scrambled. Rearrange them so that the passage makes sense.

1. Weintraub's findings were based on a computer test of 1,101 doctors twenty-eight to ninety-two years old.
2. She and her colleagues found that the top ten scorers aged seventy-five to ninety-two did as well as the average of men under thirty-five.
3. "The test measures memory, attention, visual perception, calculation, and reasoning," she said.
4. "The studies also provide intriguing clues to how that happens," said Sandra Weintraub, a neuropsychologist at Harvard Medical School in Boston.

5. "The ability of some men to retain mental function might be related to their ability to produce a certain type of brain cell not present at birth," she said.

6. The studies show that some men manage to escape the trend of declining mental ability with age.

7. Many elderly men are at least as mentally able as the average young adult, according to recent studies.

Clarity in Writing

In addition to being well organized, a good argumentative essay must be clearly written. If your objective is to support your position, you must write as clearly as possible. Likewise, before you accept what someone else writes (or says), you should be sure you understand what is being expressed.

Consider these examples:

When I was in the Marine Corps, I was plainly told that many good men died in the uniform that was issued to me.

—From a letter to the editor

Not every framistan has gussets.

I am glad to be an American, and I appreciate our system of government. Also, I am for a very strong defense. However, the people protesting the war on all sides are out there because they care about life. Now we are in an awful mess. Why? We need to put ourselves in the other guy's shoes. Going out and killing the other guy may be the way to preserve your own.

—From a newspaper call-in column

Today, morals are breaking down everywhere. There are no longer any absolutes. That is why the Boy Scouts should not permit gays to be scout leaders. The Boy Scouts stand for values that never change or go out of style.

—From a student paper

I am forty-two years old and I'm conservative. I keep reading and hearing in the news that voters are in a bad mood. No, we are not. We are hopeful and up-lifted, but we are mad as hell.

—Reported by William Endicott

Legal laws are fine, but illegal ones should be changed.

—From a student paper

If openness means to "go with the flow," it is necessarily an accommodation to the present. That present is so closed to doubt about so many things impeding the progress of its principles that unqualified openness to it would mean forgetting the despised alternatives to it, knowledge of which makes us aware of what is doubtful in it.

—From ALLAN BLOOM, in The Closing of the American Mind

The first example does not mean what it first appears to mean; the second can be understood only by those familiar with framistans, whatever those are. The third example is a set of claims that individually mostly make sense—

A Little Gobbledygook from the Defense Secretary

In an Associated Press story in August 2002, Defense Secretary Donald Rumsfeld said that talk of a U.S. strike against Saddam Hussein in Iraq was hypothetical and that the president had not asked the Saudis for use of their territory. Then, in response to a question regarding King Saud's remarks about using Saudi bases, Rumsfeld responded, "The president has not proposed such a thing; therefore, I don't find it really something that has been engaged as such."

We think he just means, "it hasn't been proposed," but he wasn't quite ready to stop talking yet.

The purpose of extending the kindergarten hours is to provide a thinking meaning appropriately centered-based, academic/social program to meet the diverse needs of the kindergarten students entering at Lewis Elementary. The exposure of the students to the world, due to extended travels, has increased their student based experiences.

—From a California public school proposal for extending kindergarten hours

Maybe Bloom went to Lewis Elementary.

For more than almost half a century, the Humane Society has led the fight to protect animals.

—Humane Society solicitation sent to one of us

For how long?

but the assembled package defies comprehension. The fourth and fifth seem illogical and contradictory. (In the fourth, the second sentence asserts there are no longer any absolutes; the last sentence implies there are. In the fifth, it's hard to see how voters can be mad as hell but not in a bad mood). And the last example is nonsensical.

When we can't tell what someone else is claiming or arguing, or when someone else can't tell what we are claiming or arguing, any number of problems may be causing the difficulty. Here we consider ill-defined terms, poorly chosen words, unintentional ambiguity, vagueness, and faulty comparisons.

■ Defining Terms

Any serious attempt to support or sustain a position requires a clear statement of what is at issue. Sometimes stating what is at issue involves a careful definition of key terms.

Purposes and Types of Definitions   Definitions can serve different purposes:

- ▲ To introduce unusual or unfamiliar words, to coin new words, or to introduce a new meaning to a familiar word (these are called **stipulative definitions**)
- ▲ To explain, illustrate, or disclose important aspects of difficult concepts (**explanatory definitions**)
- ▲ To reduce vagueness and eliminate ambiguity (**precising definitions**)
- ▲ To influence the attitudes of the reader (**rhetorical definitions**)

Sometimes definitions are intended just to amuse.

Whatever their purpose, most definitions take various common forms. Three of the most common are **definition by example, definition by synonym,** and **analytical definition:**

1. *Definition by example:* pointing to, naming, or describing one or more examples of something to which the defined term

Winning the Lottery

- Each and every combination of six numbers has exactly the same chance of winning the lottery as any other combination of six numbers.
- However, the chance of drawing any sequence of six numbers (such as 1, 2, 3, 4, 5, 6 or 27, 28, 29, 30, 31, 32) is higher than drawing some particular combination of numbers.

Would you be puzzled if we told you both these assertions are correct? If you are, you didn't read the second sentence carefully. Reading carefully is a key to thinking critically.

applies. "By 'scripture' I mean books like the Bible or the Koran." "By 'temperate climate' I mean weather in an area like the mid-Atlantic states."

2. *Definition by synonym:* giving another word or phrase that means the same thing. "'Fastidious' means the same as 'fussy.'" "'Prating' is the same as 'chattering.'" "'Pulsatile' means the same as 'throbbing'"; "to be 'lubricous' is to be 'slippery.'"

3. *Analytical definition:* specifying (a) the type of thing the term applies to and (b) the differences between the things the term applies to and other things of the same type. "A mongoose is a ferret-sized mammal native to India that eats snakes and is related to civets." "A samovar is an urn with a spigot, used especially in Russia to boil water for tea."

Some terms, especially terms for abstractions (e.g., "goodness," "truth," "knowledge," "beauty") cannot be defined in any complete way, so a writer may have to settle for providing mere hints of their subtle meanings. "By 'reality' I mean the things that most of us agree have independent existence apart from our perceptions of them."

However we define a term, we should be aware that most terms convey meaning beyond the literal sense of the written or spoken words. This "meaning" is a term's **emotive, or rhetorical, force**—its tendency to elicit certain feelings or attitudes. The word "dog," for example, has the same literal meaning as "pooch," "mutt," and "cur," but all these terms differ in the attitudes they convey. Or consider the words "child," "dependent minor," "brat," and "little one." What associations do these terms have for you? When people want to manipulate the emotive force of their message, they frequently substitute euphemisms for more pointed terms. This is the origin of such substitutions as "urban camping" for "homelessness" and "food-insecure" for "starving." The emotive, or rhetorical, force of a term, which is subjective and can vary considerably from one person to another, is usually not taken to be a part of the literal meaning.

Autobiography Skewers Kansas' Sen. Bob Dole
—Headline in the *Boulder* (Colo.) *Sunday Camera* (reported by Larry Engelmann)

Say What??...

You don't have to be a national political figure to put your foot in your mouth. Ordinary folks can do it too! These are all actual examples from news programs and other published sources.

The President's energy tax won't even be noticed. Besides, it will discourage consumption.

> [Hey, if it won't be noticed, it won't discourage consumption.]

Females score lower on the SAT than males, which right there proves the tests don't show anything. They also demonstrate that teachers do a better job of teaching male students, which is just what you'd expect given the sexual bias that exists in the classroom.

> [If the SATs don't show anything, then they don't show that teachers do a better job teaching males.]

We have to liberate discussion on this campus and not be so restrained by the First Amendment.

> [Right. And we can make people free by sticking them in jail.]

Once your body gets cold, the rest of you will get cold, too.

> [On the other hand, if you can keep your body warm, the rest of you will stay warm, too.]

It's hard to support the President's invasion of Haiti when the American public is so strongly against it. And besides, he's just doing it to raise his standings in the polls.

> [Hmmm. How's it going to raise his standings if the public is so strongly against it?]

Has anyone put anything in your baggage without your knowledge?

> [Asked of a colleague by an airport security employee]

Keeping Your Word Choices Simple Good writing is often simple writing: It avoids redundancy, unnecessary complexity, and prolixity (long-windedness and wordiness). These writing characteristics often confuse readers and listeners, and they sometimes make writers (or speakers) look silly. Why write of *armed* gunmen? Gunmen are automatically armed. Why say that something is *completely* full? If it's full, it's completely full. Michael Jordan, it is often said, is a *famous* superstar. The famous part is pointless, if a person is a superstar. In fact, come to think of it, why say *super*star?

Here's another example:

They expressed their belief that at that point in time it would accord with their desire not to delay their departure.

Uh, Would You Mind Repeating That Answer?
(Gobbledygook on the Radio)

The following exchange took place during a call-in program with Dr. Laura Schlessinger (17 January 2002):

Caller: Dr. Laura, I am a Christian, and I solidly believe in Jesus as the Messiah. However, I have recently decided to familiarize myself with Judaism, Islam, etc., in order to strengthen my own commitment to Christianity. I have so often been intrigued by your decision to commit to God through Judaism. Like you, I was not raised in a seriously, genuinely religious home. Your insights would be most appreciated and welcome.

Dr. Laura: I worry that sometimes people study something else to avoid the depth of what they need to be and know right where they are.

You know, we worry a lot about that ourselves.

But all that is necessary is

They said they wanted to leave.

On the other hand, if the briefest way of making a point is to use words that a reader isn't likely to understand, it is probably better to avoid those words in favor of more familiar ones, even if it takes more of the latter to express the information. "His remarks were obfuscatory and dilatory" will be less clear to most readers than "His remarks confused the issue and were unnecessarily time-consuming." Further, because the world is a complicated place, the language we use to describe it often has to be correspondingly complicated. Sometimes it is necessary to be complicated to be clear. But, in general, simplicity is the best policy.

> *I'm for abolishing and doing away with redundancy.*
>
> —J. Curtis McKay, of the Wisconsin State Elections Board (reported by Ross and Petras)
>
> We ourselves are also for that too.

Exercise 2-3

In groups (or individually if your instructor prefers) determine what term in each of the following is being defined and whether the definition is a definition by example or by synonym or an analytical definition. If it is difficult to tell which kind of definition is present, describe the difficulty.

▲   1. A piano is a stringed instrument in which felt hammers are made to strike the strings by an arrangement of keys and levers.

2. "Decaffeinated" means without caffeine.

3. Steve Martin is my idea of a successful philosophy major.

▲ 4. The red planet is Mars.

5. "UV" refers to ultraviolet light.

6. The Cheyenne perfectly illustrate the sort of Native Americans who were plains Indians.

7. Data, in our case, is raw information collected from survey forms which is then put in tabular form and analyzed.

▲ 8. "Chiaroscuro" is just a fancy word for shading.

9. Bifocals are glasses with two different prescriptions ground into each lens, making it possible to focus at two different distances from the wearer.

10. Red is the color that we perceive when our eyes are struck by light waves of approximately seven angstroms.

▲ 11. A significant other can be taken to be a person's spouse, lover, long-term companion, or just girlfriend or boyfriend.

12. "Assessment" means evaluation.

13. A blackout is "a period of total memory loss, as one induced by an accident or prolonged alcoholic drinking." When your buddies tell you they loved your rendition of the Lambada on Madison's pool table the other night and you don't even remember being at Madison's, that is a blackout.

Adapted from the CalPoly, San Luis Obispo, Mustang Daily

14. A pearl, which is the only animal-produced gem, begins as an irritant inside an oyster. The oyster then secretes a coating of nacre around the irritating object. The result is a pearl, the size of which is determined by the number of layers with which the oyster coats the object.

15. According to my cousin, who lives in Tulsa, the phrase "bored person" refers to anybody who is between the ages of sixteen and twenty-five and lives in eastern Oklahoma.

© Grimmy Inc. Reprinted with special permission of King Features Syndicate.

■ Ambiguous Claims

A claim is an **ambiguous claim** if it can be assigned more than one meaning and if the particular meaning it should be assigned is not made clear by context. If an accountant rises from her desk on Friday afternoon and says, "My work here is finished," she might mean that she has finished the account she was working on, that her whole week's work is done and she's leaving for the weekend, or that she is fed up with her job and is leaving the company.

Sometimes an ambiguous word or phrase can make the difference in a discussion or a dispute. For example, imagine two people who are disputing whether abortion should be made illegal. Imagine that one person uses the phrase "human being" to refer to any organism that possesses a full complement of human chromosomes and the other person uses the same phrase to refer to a being recognized by statute or Supreme Court decision to have full rights as a citizen under the Constitution. There will be much wasted breath and misunderstanding until they get their two disparate definitions of this crucial phrase sorted out.

Semantic Ambiguity   A claim can be ambiguous for different reasons. Consider these claims:

1. He always lines up on the right side.

2. She is cold.

3. I know a little Greek.

4. She disputed his claim.

5. My brother doesn't use glasses.

The meanings of these claims are unclear because each claim contains an ambiguous word or phrase. For example, "claim" in (4) could mean either a statement or a claim to a gold mine; "glasses" in (5) could mean either eyeglasses or drinking glasses. A claim whose ambiguity is due to the ambiguity of a particular word or phase is called a **semantically ambiguous claim.**

The World Health Organization does not promote a drink a day for health reasons.

—*Chico Enterprise-Record*

What *do* they promote it for?

I am a marvelous housekeeper. Every time I leave a man I keep his house.

—ZSA ZSA GABOR

The Fallacy of Division in Clinton's Impeachment Trial

Assume two-thirds of a jury thinks a defendant is guilty of having lied about W, X, or Y. Which of these options logically follows?

1. Two-thirds of the jury think the defendant lied about W.
2. Two-thirds of the jury think the defendant lied about X.
3. Two-thirds of the jury think the defendant lied about Y.
4. There is at least one matter, W, X, or Y, that two-thirds of the jury think the defendant lied about.
5. None of the above.

The correct answer is 5. Two-thirds of a jury could think the defendant lied about "W, X, or Y" even though less than two-thirds thought he lied about W, and less than two-thirds thought he lied about X, and less than two-thirds thought he lied about Y!

This confusion, which is actually a subtle example of division, explained later in this chapter, was involved in one of the most important trials to ever happen in the United States, Bill Clinton's impeachment trial before the U.S. Senate.

Here's how Article I of the impeachment charges read: "William Jefferson Clinton willfully provided perjurious, false, and misleading testimony to the grand jury concerning one or more of the following: [here, four options were listed]."

Here's how the key part of Article II read: "The means used to implement this course of conduct [obstructing justice] included one or more of the following acts: [here, several options were listed]."

This presented the Clinton legal defense team with a logical dilemma. The Article I and Article II charges were both worded in such a way that, even if two-thirds of the Senate agreed that Clinton was guilty under one of these two articles of impeachment, it would not follow that there was even a single case of lying or a single case of obstructing justice that two-thirds of the Senate agreed the president committed! In other words, Clinton could have been convicted and removed from office despite not being found guilty *on any specific charge of lying or obstructing justice* by the required two-thirds of the Senate!

This, of course, explains why prosecutors normally make each crime alleged to have been committed by a defendant a separate count.

Semantic ambiguity can be eliminated by substituting an unambiguous word or phrase, such as "eyeglasses" for "glasses" in (5). Sometimes the substitution may require several extra words.

I wrote a story about a girl making lunch in a skillet.
—GARRISON KEILLOR

A big skillet, perhaps?

Syntactic Ambiguity Now consider these examples:

1. She saw the farmer with binoculars.
2. Players with beginners' skills only may use court 1.

"Grammar Does Some Work!"

Notice in a Help Wanted section of a newspaper:

Wanted. Man to take care of cow that does not smoke or drink.

If the nonsmoking and nondrinking creature is the man, the sentence should say "*who* does not smoke or drink," rather than "*that* does not smoke or drink." That the word "that" is used should tell us that it's the cow the speaker means. A little grammatical knowledge would go a long way—if the writer had any.

The Fusco Bros. © Lew Little Ent. Reprinted with permission of Universal Press Syndicate. All rights reserved.

▲ *A lot of jokes depend on ambiguity for humor. Unintentional ambiguities can make what you write sort of funny, too.*

3. People who protest often get arrested.

4. He chased the girl in his car.

5. There's somebody in the bed next to me.

In contrast with those in the preceding list, these claims are ambiguous because of their structures. Even though we understand the meaning of the phrase "with binoculars," for example, we can't tell whether it pertains to the farmer or to the subject of (1). A claim of this sort is called a **syntactically ambiguous claim.** The only way to eliminate syntactic ambiguity is to rewrite the claim.

Sometimes syntactically ambiguous claims result when we do not clearly show what a pronoun refers to. "The boys chased the girls, and they giggled a lot" is an example of this sort of ambiguity; you can't be certain whether "they" refers to the boys or to the girls. "After he removed the trash from the pool, the children played in it" is another example.

Modifying phrases can create syntactic ambiguities if we are careless with them. Consider "He brushed his teeth on the carpet." If you want to

© Grimmy Inc. Reprinted with special permission of King Features Syndicate.

avoid suggesting that a carpet might make a good toothbrush, then you should recast the sentence, perhaps as "He brushed his teeth while he was on the carpet." Or take "She wiped up the water with her younger brother." Yes, of course it is unlikely that she used her brother as a towel. But a clear writer will avoid any possibility of misunderstanding—or ridicule—by re-casting the sentence, perhaps as "She and her younger brother wiped up the water." "He was bitten while walking by a dog" should be revised either as "While he was walking, he was bitten by a dog" or as "While he was walking by a dog, he was bitten."

Grouping Ambiguity   A peculiar kind of semantic ambiguity, which we'll call **grouping ambiguity,** is illustrated by this claim:

> Secretaries make more money than physicians.

If I said anything which implies that I think that we didn't do what we should have done given the choices we faced at the time, I shouldn't have said that.

—BILL CLINTON (reported by Larry Engelmann)

Is this claim true or false? We can't say. We don't know *what* the claim is because we don't know exactly what "secretaries" and "physicians" refer to. If the claim is that secretaries *as a group* make more money than physicians make *as a group,* then the claim is true because there are many more secretaries than physicians. But if the claim is that secretaries individually make more money than physicians individually, then the claim is of course false. Whenever we refer to a collection of individuals, we must clearly show whether the reference is to the collection as a group or as individuals.

The President will keep the promises he meant to keep.

—Bill Clinton's White House sen-ior adviser, GEORGE STEPHANOPOULOS

The Fallacies of Composition and Division   Related to grouping ambigui-ties are mistakes, or **fallacies,** known as composition and division. Suppose something holds true of a group of things individually. To think it must therefore necessarily hold true of the same things as a group is to commit the **fallacy of composition.** Here are two examples of this fallacy:

Slow Recovery Likely in State

This ambiguous headline, from the *Sacramento Bee* of June 9, 2002, is subject to two interpretations, as good news and as bad news:

1. Fortunately, a recovery is likely to happen, although it will be slow.
2. Unfortunately, the recovery we're expecting will be slow.

Sampras and Agassi are the two best tennis players in the United States, so they'd make the best doubles team.

We don't spend *that* much on military salaries. After all, who ever heard of anyone getting rich in the Army? (In other words, we don't spend that much on service personnel *individually;* therefore, we don't spend much on them *as a group.*)

Conversely, to think that what holds true of a group automatically holds true of all the individuals in that group is to commit the error known as the **fallacy of division.** Here are examples:

Congress is incompetent. Therefore, Congressman Benton is incompetent.

The Eastman School of Music has an outstanding international reputation; therefore, Vladimir Peronepky, who is on the faculty of Eastman, must have a good reputation.

In the 1994 congressional elections, the voters (as a group) made it clear that they did not want a Democratic Congress. Therefore, the voters (individually) made it clear that they did not want a Democratic Congress.

The people voted for a Republican Senate.

—GEORGE BUSH

Actually, no person anywhere voted for a Republican Senate. The question "Do you want a Republican Senate?" appeared on no ballots.

Recognizing and Deciphering Ambiguity   Some claims, such as "Women can fish" and "I will put the sauce on myself," can reasonably be diagnosed as either semantically or syntactically ambiguous. So don't spend much time arguing over which category an ambiguous claim belongs to. What is important is recognizing ambiguities when you encounter them and avoiding them in your own writing.

Some ambiguous claims don't fall into any of the categories we have mentioned. For example, a claim that refers to "the fastest woman on the squad" is ambiguous if two or more women on the squad are equally fast and are faster than anyone else. "I cannot recommend him highly enough" might mean that he is even better than my highest recommendation, or it might mean that I cannot recommend him very highly at all. The ambiguity, however, is not clearly semantic or syntactic.

Often, but not nearly often enough, the context of a claim will show which possible meaning a speaker or writer intends. If a mechanic says, "Your trouble is in a cylinder," it might be unclear at first whether she means a wheel cylinder or an engine cylinder. Her meaning will probably become

More Examples of Composition and Division

Fallacy of Division

A balanced daily diet consists of the right proportion of protein, carbohydrates, and fat. Therefore, each meal should consist of the same proportion of protein, carbohydrates, and fat.

—DR. NICHOLAS PERRICONE, *author of the best-selling book,* The Wrinkle Cure

Fallacy of Composition

The Kings don't have a chance against the Lakers. The Lakers are better at every position except power forward.

—CHARLES BARKLEY

Fallacy of Division

Men are more likely than women to be involved in fatal automobile accidents. So if you are a man, you are more likely than the next woman you see to be involved in a fatal automobile accident.

—*Overheard*

We will briefly discuss the history of American Indians on this campus.

—From a flyer advertising "Conversations on Diversity" at the authors' university

Somewhere on this globe, every ten seconds, there is a woman giving birth to a child. She must be found and stopped.

—SAM LEVENSON (1911–1980)

---

clear, though, as you listen to what else she says and consider the entire context in which she is speaking.

Also, common sense often dictates which of two possible meanings a person has in mind. In the example "He brushed his teeth on the carpet," you would probably be safe to assume that "on the carpet" refers to his location and not to an unusual technique of dental hygiene. So, the claim is perhaps not truly ambiguous. But if you wish to be a clear writer (or aren't fond of people laughing at you), you should try to say exactly what you mean and not rely on common sense to make your meaning clear.

Although ambiguous claims can be a fine source of amusement, they can also furnish clever ways of duping people. In advertising, for example, a claim might make wild promises for a product when interpreted one way. But under another interpretation, it may say very little, thus giving the manufacturer a loophole against the charge of false advertising.

Unintentional ambiguity has no place in clear writing. It can defeat the purpose of communication by confusing readers, and it can sometimes make the writer look foolish. You'll find other suggestions for improving your writing elsewhere in this chapter. But we want to note here that, aside from simply learning about the problem, proofreading is probably your best guard against unintentional ambiguity. In fact, failure to proofread is a common problem with student writing. It's a good policy to read your work more than once because there are quite a few things you'll be watching for: coherence, grammar, ambiguity, word choice, vagueness, and so on. You want to make sure you find what you want and *don't* find what you *don't* want.

Waitress Sues Former Employer Over an Ambiguity!

PANAMA CITY, Fla. (AP) . . . A former Hooters waitress has sued the restaurant where she worked, saying she was promised a new Toyota for winning a beer sales contest.

Instead, she said, she won a new toy Yoda— the little green guy from the *Star Wars* movies.

Jodee Berry, 26, won a contest to see who could sell the most beer in April at the Hooters in Panama City Beach. She said the top-selling waitresses from each Hooters restaurant in the area were entered into a drawing and her name was picked.

She believed she'd won a new car.

She was blindfolded and led to the restaurant parking lot, but when her blindfold was removed she found she was the winner not of a Toyota, but a toy Yoda doll.

. . . She sued Gulf Coast Wings, Inc., owners of the restaurant, alleging breach of contract and fraudulent misrepresentation.

Her lawyer, Stephen West of Pensacola, said he was also looking at false advertising statutes.

Exercise 2-4

Rewrite the following claims to remedy problems of ambiguity. Do *not* assume that common sense by itself solves the problem. If the ambiguity is intentional, note this fact, and do not rewrite.

Example

> Former professional football player Jim Brown was accused of assaulting a thirty-three-year-old woman with a female accomplice.

Answer

> This claim is syntactically ambiguous because it isn't clear what the phrase "with a female accomplice" modifies—Brown, the woman who was attacked, or, however bizarre it might be, the attack itself (he might have thrown the accomplice at the woman). To make it clear that Brown had the accomplice, the phrase "with a female accomplice" should have come right after the word "Brown" in the original claim.

▲ 1. The Raider tackle threw a block at the Giants linebacker.

   2. Please close the door behind you.

   3. We heard that he informed you of what he said in his letter.

▲ 4. "How Therapy Can Help Torture Victims"

Headline in newspaper

   5. Charles drew his gun.

   6. They were both exposed to someone who was ill a week ago.

▲ 7. Susan has Hillary Rodham Clinton's nose.

   8. I flush the cooling system regularly and just put in new thermostats.

Watch for Weasel Numbers in Medical Studies

Ever wonder why so many medical studies discover spectacular benefits from new drugs? Maybe it's because researchers report the numbers in a way that makes them sound better than they should.

That's the concern of Dr. Jim Nuovo, professor of family and community medicine at the University of California at Davis. In a study published in the June 5 *Journal of the American Medical Assn.*, Nuovo looked at 359 studies from leading medical journals and found that only 18 of them reported results in terms of absolute risk reduction. The rest reported only relative risk reduction—which can sound far more substantial.

Here's an example from Nuovo to explain the difference: Suppose an existing drug cuts the rate of heart attacks in men to 5%. A new drug cuts that risk to 4%. In terms of relative risk that's an impressive-sounding 20% improvement. In absolute terms, however, there's only a one-percentage-point difference. The risk has gone from low to slightly lower—which doesn't sound very impressive, especially if the new drug costs 10 times as much as the existing drug.

Nuovo's point is that all of these numbers, and more, ought to be reported in every study. "There's no one number that explains everything in an article," he says. "Once you start putting things into context, you start getting a better picture." Proposed guidelines for clinical trials call for researchers to report absolute risk reduction along with relative risks, Nuovo says, but those guidelines are often ignored. Editors should require authors to follow them, he says.

Business Week, June 17, 2002, p. 85.

9. "Tuxedos Cut Ridiculously!"

An ad for formal wear, quoted by Herb Caen

▲ 10. "Police Kill 6 Coyotes After Mauling of Girl"

Headline in newspaper

11. "We promise nothing"

Aquafina advertisement

12. Former governor Pat Brown of California, viewing an area struck by a flood, is said to have remarked, "This is the greatest disaster since I was elected governor."

Quoted by Lou Cannon in the Washington Post

▲ 13. "Besides Lyme disease, two other tick-borne diseases, babesiosis and HGE, are infecting Americans in 30 states, according to recent studies. A single tick can infect people with more than one disease."

Self magazine

14. "Don't freeze your can at the game."

Commercial for Miller beer

15. Volunteer help requested: Come prepared to lift heavy equipment with construction helmet and work overalls.

▲ 16. "GE: We bring good things to life."

Television commercial

17. "Tropicana 100% Pure Florida Squeezed Orange Juice. You can't pick a better juice."

Magazine advertisement

18. "It's biodegradable! So remember, Arm and Hammer laundry detergent gets your wash as clean as can be [pause] without polluting our waters."

Television commercial

▲ 19. If you crave the taste of a real German beer, nothing is better than Dunkelbrau.

20. Independent laboratory tests prove that Houndstooth cleanser gets your bathroom cleaner than any other product.

21. We're going to look at lots this afternoon.

▲ 22. Jordan could write more profound essays.

23. "Two million times a day Americans love to eat, Rice-a-Roni—the San Francisco treat."

Advertisement

24. "New York's first commercial human sperm-bank opened Friday with semen samples from 18 men frozen in a stainless steel tank."

Strunk and White, Elements of Style

▲ 25. She was disturbed when she lay down to nap by a noisy cow.

26. "More than half of expectant mothers suffer heartburn. To minimize symptoms, suggests Donald O. Castell, M.D., of the Graduate Hospital in Philadelphia, avoid big, high-fat meals and don't lie down for three hours after eating."

Self magazine

27. "Abraham Lincoln wrote the Gettysburg address while traveling from Washington to Gettysburg on the back of an envelope."

Richard Lederer

▲ 28. "When Queen Elizabeth exposed herself before her troops, they all shouted 'harrah.'"

Richard Lederer

29. "In one of Shakespeare's famous plays, Hamlet relieves himself in a long soliloquy."

Richard Lederer

30. The two suspects fled the area before the officers' arrival in a white Ford Mustang, being driven by a third male.

31. "To travel to Canada, you will need a birth certificate or a driver's license and other photo ID."

American Automobile Association

▲ 32. "AT&T, for the life of your business."

▲ 33. The teacher of this class might have been a member of the opposite sex.

▲ 34. "Woman gets 9 years for killing 11th husband."

Headline in newspaper

35. "Average hospital costs are now an unprecedented $2,063.04 per day in California. Many primary plans don't pay 20% of that amount."

AARP Group Health Insurance Program advertisement

36. "I am a huge Mustang fan."

Ford Mustang advertisement

37. "Visitors are expected to complain at the office between the hours of 9 and 11 A.M. daily."

Sign in an Athens hotel

38. "Order your summers suit. Because is big rush we will execute customers in strict rotation."

Sign in a Rhodes tailor shop

39. "Please do not feed the animals. If you have any suitable food, give it to the guard on duty."

Sign at a Budapest zoo

40. "Our wines leave you with nothing to hope for."

From a Swiss menu

41. Our Promise—Good for life.

Cheerios

42. Thinking clearly involves hard work.

43. Cadillac—Break Through

Exercise 2-5

Determine which of the italicized expressions are ambiguous, which are more likely to refer to the members of the class taken as a group, and which are more likely to refer to the members of the class taken individually.

Example

Narcotics are habit-forming.

Answer

In this claim, *narcotics* refers to individual members of the class because it is specific narcotics that are habit-forming. (One does not ordinarily become addicted to the entire class of narcotics.)

▲ 1. *Swedes* eat millions of quarts of yogurt every day.

2. *College professors* make millions of dollars a year.

3. *Our CB radios* can be heard all across the country.

▲ 4. *Students at Pleasant Valley High School* enroll in hundreds of courses each year.

5. *Cowboys* die with their boots on.

6. The *angles of a triangle* add up to 180 degrees.

▲ 7. *The New York Giants* played mediocre football last year.

8. On our airline, *passengers* have their choice of three different meals.

9. On our airline, *passengers* flew fourteen million miles last month without incident.

▲ 10. *Hundreds of people* have ridden in that taxi.

11. *All our cars* are on sale for two hundred dollars over factory invoice.

▲ 12. *Chicagoans* drink more beer than *New Yorkers*.

13. *Power lawn mowers* produce more pollution than *motorcycles.*

14. *The Baltimore Orioles* may make it to the playoffs by the year 2000.

▲ 15. *People* are getting older.

■ *Vague Claims*

Vagueness and ambiguity are often confused. An ambiguous claim has two or more possible meanings, and the context does not make clear which meaning is intended. A **vague claim,** by contrast, has a meaning that is indistinct or imprecise.

The vagueness of a claim is a matter of degree. "He is old" is more vague than "He is at least 70," and "He is at least 70" is more vague than "He is 73 years and 225 days old."

People tend to think that vagueness is something to be avoided. What's to be avoided, however, is *an undesirable degree* of vagueness. Even though a claim may be less precise than it could be, that does not mean that it is less precise than it should be. For example, if you want to move your car and you ask the usher how long you have until the play begins, the reply "Only a minute or two" is less precise than is possible, but it is not less precise than is desirable for your purposes. You don't have time to move your car. But if you are the lead actor in the play and ask the stage manager exactly how much time you have before the curtain goes up, the same answer is probably not precise enough.

The vagueness of some claims is due to the use of "fuzzy" words, words such as "old" and "bald" and "rich," that apply to lots of borderline cases. Bill Gates, for instance, clearly is rich. But is a person who is worth a half million dollars rich? One worth a quarter million? Where does "rich" end and "well-off" begin? Notice, however, that claims with fuzzy words, like vague claims in general, are not always too vague. "Don't take a course from the bald guy in the philosophy department" may well be sufficiently precise to accomplish its intended effect, even though "bald" is not a very precise word.

Notice, too, that the absence of fuzzy words does not automatically immunize a claim from undesirable vagueness. "Maria plans to bring her sibling to class on Friday" is probably precise enough, depending on the kind

It's wonderful that we have eight-year-old boys filling sandbags with old women.

—LARRY KING, on attempts to stem Mississippi floods (reported by Larry Engelmann)

But, then, old women filled sandbags with eight-year-old boys, too.

of class we're talking about. But "Maria plans to bring her sibling to the slumber party Friday night" may not be precise enough, especially if it's your teenage daughter who is giving the slumber party and Maria's sibling is her twenty-five-year-old brother. It's not that "sibling" is particularly fuzzy; it's just that in the second of these contexts, the claim in which "sibling" appears is too imprecise for the occasion.

As should be clear by now, it makes little sense to insist that a claim be totally free of vagueness. If we had to be absolutely precise whenever we made a claim, we would say and write very little. The appropriate criticism of a claim is not that it is vague, but that it is too vague relative to what you wish to communicate or know.

■ *Claims That Make Comparisons*

Advertisers and politicians seem to be especially fond of claims like these:

Cut by up to half

Now 25 percent larger

Quietest by far

New and improved

Now better than ever

More than 20 percent richer

Such claims cry out for clarification: What does "up to half" mean? Twenty-five percent larger than what? How far is "by far"? New and improved over what? Better in what way? How much more than 20 percent? And you can ask other questions, too. Remember, though, that the amount of vagueness you can tolerate in a comparative claim depends on your interests and purposes. Knowing that attic insulation will reduce your utility bill "by 15 to 45 percent" may be all it takes for you to know that you should insulate.

Of course, some comparisons may be too vague even to be meaningful: "Have more fun in Arizona." "Gets clothes whiter than white." "Delivers more honest flavor." In other words, have fun in Arizona. Gets clothes white. Can be tasted. On the other hand, "Nothing else is a Pepsi" isn't vague; taken literally, it's necessarily true. Nothing else is a turkey, either. What the claim means, of course, is that no other soft drink tastes as good as Pepsi.

Here are some other questions to ask when you are considering claims that make comparisons:

1. *Is important information missing?* Suppose someone says that only 10 percent of child molestation cases are at the hands of alcoholics. The person might then say the statement means that alcoholics are less likely to be child molesters than are nonalcoholics because, after all, 90 percent of child molestation cases are at the hands of nonalcoholics. What's missing is important information about the percentage of the general popula-

If you are wondering about the boys, they both got gangrene and lost some legs.

—CNN anchor
ANDERSON COOPER

Makes sense, sort of, if you view the boys collectively.

Cause for Alarm?

According to the National Household Survey on Drug Abuse, cocaine use among Americans twelve to seventeen years of age increased by a whopping 166 percent between 1992 and 1995. Wow, right?

Except that the increase *in absolute terms* was a little less spectacular: In 1992, 0.3 percent of Americans aged twelve to seventeen had used cocaine; in 1995, the percentage was 0.8 percent of that population.

Be wary of comparisons expressed as percentage changes.

tion that is alcoholic. What if, say, only 3 percent of the general population is alcoholic but that 3 percent commits 10 percent of the child molestations? Then it begins to seem that alcoholics are *more* likely than others to molest children.

2. *Is the same standard of comparison being used? Are the same reporting and recording practices being used?* Check to be sure. In February 1994, the unemployment rate suddenly jumped by half a percentage point (a significant jump). Had more people been laid off? Nope. The government had simply changed the way it figured unemployment.

Here's another example. In 1993 the number of people in the United States with AIDS suddenly increased dramatically. Had a new form of the AIDS virus appeared? No; the federal government had expanded the definition of AIDS to include several new indicator conditions. Overnight, 50,000 people were considered to have AIDS who had not been so considered the day before.

3. *Are the items comparable?* Be wary of comparisons between apples and oranges. Don't place undue faith in a comparison between this April's retail business activity and last April's if Easter fell in March in one of the years or the weather was especially cold.

Or suppose someone cites statistics that show you are safer flying than driving because the accident rate for commercial airplane passengers is lower than that for car drivers. What you should note first is that the comparison is between air *passengers* and car *drivers*. A more telling comparison would be between airplane *pilots* and car drivers. And if you are considering going Greyhound, an even better comparison would be between commercial airplane pilots and commercial bus drivers. Of course, the claims about the safety of flying versus driving sometimes involve comparisons between air *passengers* and car *passengers*. But such comparisons usually still involve apples and oranges. What you really need to know is the *fatality rate* of air passengers versus that of car passengers in cars *driven by drivers who are as cautious, sober, and skilled as commercial airplane pilots.* After all, that is the kind of person who will be driving you, right?

4. *Is the comparison expressed as an average? Again, be sure important information isn't missing.* The average rainfall in Seattle is about the same as that in Kansas City. But you'll spend more time in rain gear in Seattle

There is no excuse for passing children through schools who can't read.

—GEORGE W. BUSH

Apparently, however, there is no problem with schools that don't teach grammar.

Potter's Take May Be Overhyped

Box-Office Figures Need to Be Viewed in Context

If one listens to the hype, it would seem that "Harry Potter and the Sorcerer's Stone" is destined to be the most popular and lucrative movie of all time. That's what the studio, Warner Bros., wants us to believe, and that's why box-office receipts are always touted—if not willfully distorted—for the sale of publicity and promotion.

"Harry Potter" is a smash hit, all right, but the amazing figures that attended its opening—$90 million the first weekend, $220.1 million in 17 days—don't make it the almost box-office champ. What's ignored in all the hoopla over box office are such factors as inflation, population growth and the number of movie screens at which a film opens.

When Hollywood brags about box office, it never mentions, for example, that ticket prices keep rising; that our country's population keeps growing (275 million today versus 226 million in 1980 and 131 million in 1939); or that blockbusters like "Harry Potter" open at hundreds more theaters than movies did even a decade ago.

When one considers those factors, the luster of box-office figures starts rapidly to dim. It could easily be argued that "Gone With the Wind" is the most popular film of all time, based on its huge popularity at the time of its initial release (1939) and subsequent re-releases.

During the long span of its theatrical life, "GWTW" sold 200 million movie admissions, according to Paul Dergarabedian of Exhibitor Relations, a Los Angeles-based box-office tracking firm. But with a cumulative domestic gross of $173 million, "GWTW" fell off the top 10 box-office chart years ago simply because people paid so much less to see it than they do for today's movies.

But one needn't go back 60 years to understand the misleading nature of box-office statistics. "E.T. the Extra-Terrestrial" was a huge hit when released in 1982 and remains the No. 3 box-office champ, even though its opening-weekend gross was $11.9 million.

In 2000, the average movie admission price was $5.39 (including lower rates for seniors and children), according to the National Association of Theater Owners. Dergarabedian estimates that it's climbed to $5.60 this year. Back in 1991, the average admission price was $4.21; in 1976 it was $2.13; in 1960, 69 cents; in 1949, 46 cents; and in 1939, 23 cents.

The math is simple and astonishing. With today's prices, it takes 16.1 million moviegoers to create a $90.3 million opening weekend. In 1939, it would have taken 392.6 million moviegoers to create the same number.

Here's another way of looking at the situation. If the domestic gross on "GWTW" over its entire run were adjusted for inflation, it would jump from $173 million to an estimated $1.1 billion.

Consider that "Harry Potter" opened at a record-breaking 3,672 theaters. Most of those were multiplexes, where the movie played throughout the day on multiple screens. "Harry" occupied a whopping 8,200 screens—roughly 21 percent of the nation's 37,396 total.

because it rains there twice as often as in Kansas City. If Central Valley Components, Inc., reports that average salaries of a majority of its employees have more than doubled over the past ten years, CVC still may not be a great place to work. Perhaps the increases were all due to converting the majority of employees, who worked half time, to full time and firing the rest. Comparisons that involve averages omit details that can be important, simply because they involve averages.

Remember, too, that there are different kinds of averages, or measures of central tendency, as they are also known—the mean, the median, and the mode. Consider, for instance, the average paycheck at Central Valley Components, which happens to be $41,000. That may sound generous enough.

Never try to wade a river just because it has an average depth of four feet.

—MARTIN FRIEDMAN

The wrong average can put you under.

Tom Felton and Daniel Radcliffe play rival wizards Draco Malfoy and Harry Potter in "Harry Potter and the Sorcerer's Stone."

But let's forget about inflation for a minute and ponder this question: Can "Harry Potter" top "Titanic," the current box-office champion with $600.8 million in domestic grosses, $1.2 billion in international and $1.8 billion in total receipts?

"It's too early to tell," says Dergarabedian. "It's doing extraordinarily well, and I think it's going to get a boost at Christmas. But this whole notion of surpassing 'Titanic'—that's no small feat."

Staying power is the magic potion that "Harry Potter" needs to break the record of James Cameron's Oscar-winning epic. "Titanic" took in $28.6 million its first weekend but was so durable, and generated such phenomenal repeat business, that it held the No. 1 position for 15 weeks and was still playing in some theaters a full nine months after its December 1997 release.

"It was in release for 41 weeks," says Dergarabedian. "That's amazing."

By Edward Guttmann
Chronicle Staff Writer

_____

Article from *San Francisco Chronicle*, December 24, 2001.

But that average is the **mean** (total wages divided by the number of wage earners). The **median** wage, an "average" that is the "halfway" figure (half the employees get more than the figure, and half get less), is $27,000. This average is not so impressive, at least from the perspective of a job seeker. And the **mode,** also an average, the most common rate of pay, is only $17,000. So when someone quotes "the average pay" at CVC, which average is it? At CVC a couple of executives draw fat paychecks, so the mean is a lot higher than the other two figures.

In a class of things in which there are likely to be large or dramatic variations in whatever it is that is being measured, be cautious of figures about an unspecified "average."

Misleading Averages

In 2003 George W. Bush proposed a tax cut that, he said, would give the average taxpayer $1,083.

The "average" here is the mean average. However, before you start dreaming about how to spend your $1,083, you might want to check on the modal average. Most taxpayers, according to the Urban Institute–Brookings Institution Tax Policy Center, would receive less than $100 under the Bush proposal.

Exercise 2-6

The lettered words and phrases that follow each of the following fragments vary in their precision. In each instance, determine which is the most vague and which is the most precise; then rank the remainder in order of vagueness between the two extremes. You will discover when you discuss these exercises in class that they leave some room for disagreement. Further class discussion with input from your instructor will help you and your classmates reach closer agreement about items that prove especially difficult to rank.

Example

Over the past ten years, the median income of wage earners in St. Paul
a. nearly doubled
b. increased substantially
c. increased by 85.5 percent
d. increased by more than 85 percent

Answer

Choice (b) is the most vague because it provides the least information; (c) is the most precise because it provides the most detailed figure. In between, (a) is the second most vague, followed by (d).

1. Eli and Sarah
   ▲ a. decided to sell their house and move   *precise*
   b. made plans for the future
   c. considered moving
   d. talked   *vague*
   e. discussed their future
   f. discussed selling their house

2. Manuel
   a. worked in the yard all afternoon
   b. spent the afternoon planting flowers in the yard
   c. was outside all afternoon   *vague*
   d. spent the afternoon planting salvia alongside his front sidewalk   *precise*
   e. spent the afternoon in the yard

"The Biggest Tax Increase in History"

Every presidential election seems to see somebody link the opposing candidate to "the biggest tax increase in history." What we have here, however, is an ambiguous comparison. Is the increase the biggest in *absolute dollars* or in *dollars adjusted for inflation*? And notice as well the grouping ambiguity in the claim: One and the same tax increase might not be very large as an increase in the *percentage of an individual's income* that he or she pays to taxes, and yet it might still be the largest increase in terms of the total tax revenues it produces.

3. The hurricane that struck South Carolina
   a. caused more than $20 million in property damage
   b. destroyed dozens of structures *vague*
   c. was severe and unfortunate
   d. produced no fatalities but caused $25 million in property damage *preci*

4. The recent changes in the tax code
   a. will substantially increase taxes paid by those making more than $200,000 per year
   b. will increase by 4 percent the tax rate for those making more than $200,000 per year; will leave unchanged the tax rate for people making between $40,000 and $200,000; and will decrease by 2 percent the tax rate for those making less than $40,000
   c. will make some important changes in who pays what in taxes
   d. are tougher on the rich than the provisions in the previous tax law
   e. raise rates for the wealthy and reduce them for those in the lowest brackets

5. Smedley is absent because
   a. he's not feeling well
   b. he's under the weather
   c. he has an upset stomach and a fever
   d. he's nauseated and has a fever of more than 103° *p-*
   e. he has flulike symptoms

Exercise 2-7

Which of each set of claims is vaguer, if either?

Example

   a. The trees served to make shade for the patio.
   b. He served his country proudly.

Answer

   The use of "served" in (b) is more vague than that in (a). We know exactly what the trees did; we don't know what he did.

▲ 1. a. Rooney served the church his entire life.
       b. Rooney's tennis serve is impossible to return. **ⱽ﹣**

   2. a. The window served its purpose. **ⱽ·**
       b. The window served as an escape hatch.

   3. a. Throughout their marriage, Alfredo served her dinner.
       b. Throughout their marriage, Alfredo served her well. **ⱽ﹣**

▲ 4. a. Minta turned her ankle.
       b. Minta turned to religion.

   5. a. These scales will turn on the weight of a hair.
       b. This car will turn on a dime. **ⱽ·**

   6. a. Fenner's boss turned vicious.
       b. Fenner's boss turned out to be forty-seven.

▲ 7. a. Time to turn the garden.
       b. Time to turn off the sprinkler.

   8. a. The wine turned to vinegar.
       b. The wine turned out to be vinegar.

   9. a. Harper flew around the world.
       b. Harper departed around 3:00 A.M.

▲ 10. a. Clifton turned out the light.
       b. Clifton turned out the vote.

   11. a. The glass is full to the brim.
        b. Mrs. Couch has a rather full figure.

   12. a. Kathy gave him a full report.
        b. "Oh, no, thank you! I am full."

   13. a. Oswald was dealt a full house.
        b. Oswald is not playing with a full deck.

   14. a. The pudding sat heavily on Professor Grantley's stomach.
        b. "Set the table, please."

▲ 15. a. Porker set a good example.
       b. Porker set the world record for the 100-meter dash.

Exercise 2-8

Are the italicized words or phrases in each of the following too vague given the implied context? Explain.

▲ 1. Please cook this steak *longer*. It's too rare.

   2. If you get ready for bed quickly, Mommy has a *surprise* for you.

   3. This program contains language that some viewers may find offensive. It is recommended for *mature* audiences only.

▲ 4. *Turn down the damned noise!* Some people around here want to sleep!

5. Based on our analysis of your eating habits, we recommend that you *lower* your consumption of saturated fat.

6. NOTICE: Hazard Zone. *Small* children not permitted beyond this sign.

▲ 7. SOFAS CLEANED: $48 & *up.* MUST SEE TO GIVE *EXACT* PRICES.

8. And remember, all our mufflers come with a *lifetime guarantee.*

9. CAUTION: *To avoid* unsafe levels of carbon monoxide, do not set the wick on your kerosene stove *too high.*

▲ 10. Uncooked Frosting: Combine 1 unbeaten egg white, $\frac{1}{2}$ cup corn syrup, $\frac{1}{2}$ teaspoon vanilla, and dash salt. Beat with electric mixer until of fluffy spreading consistency. Frost cake. Serve *within a few hours,* or refrigerate.

Exercise 2-9

Read the following passage, paying particular attention to the italicized words and phrases. Determine whether any of these expressions are too vague in the context in which you find them here.

> Term paper assignment: "Your paper *should be* typed, *between eight and twelve pages in length,* and double-spaced. You should *make use of* at least three *sources.* Grading will be based on *organization, use of sources, clarity of expression, quality of reasoning,* and *grammar.*
>
> A *rough draft* is due *before Thanksgiving.* The final version is due *at the end of the semester.*

Exercise 2-10

▲ Read the following passage, paying particular attention to the italicized words and phrases. All of these expressions would be too vague for use in *some* contexts; determine which are and which are not too vague in *this* context.

> In view of what can happen in twelve months to the fertilizer you apply at any one time, you can see why just one annual application may not be adequate. Here is a guide to timing the *feeding* of some of the more common types of garden flowers.
>
> Feed begonias and fuchsias *frequently* with label-recommended amounts or less frequently with *no more than half* the recommended amount. Feed roses with *label-recommended amounts* as a *new year's growth begins* and as *each bloom period ends.* Feed azaleas, camellias, rhododendrons, and *similar* plants *immediately after bloom* and again *when the nights begin cooling off.* Following these simple instructions can help your flower garden to be as attractive as it can be.

Exercise 2-11

Critique these comparisons, using the questions about comparisons discussed in the text as guides.

Example

You get much better service on Air Atlantic.

Answer

Better than on what? (One term of the comparison is not clear.)
In what way better? (The claim is much too vague to be of much use.)

▲ 1. New improved Morning Muffins! Now with 20 percent more real dairy butter!

2. The average concert musician makes less than a plumber.

3. Major league ballplayers are much better than they were thirty years ago.

▲ 4. What an arid place to live. Why, they had less rain here than in the desert.

5. On the whole, the mood of the country is more conservative than it was in the sixties.

6. Which is better for a person, coffee or tea?

▲ 7. The average GPA of graduating seniors at Ohio State is 3.25, as compared with 2.75 twenty years ago.

8. Women can tolerate more pain than men.

9. Try Duraglow with new sunscreening polymers. Reduces the harmful effect of sun on your car's finish by up to 50 percent.

▲ 10. What a brilliant season! Attendance was up 25 percent over last year.

Exercise 2-12

Critique these comparisons, using the questions discussed in the text as guides.

▲ 1. You've got to be kidding. Paltrow is much superior to Blanchett as an actor.

2. Blondes have more fun.

3. The average chimp is smarter than the average monkey.

▲ 4. The average grade given by Professor Smith is a C. So is the average grade given by Professor Algers.

5. Crime is on the increase. It's up by 160 percent over last year.

6. Classical musicians, on the average, are far more talented than rock musicians.

▲ 7. Long-distance swimming requires much more endurance than long-distance running.

8. "During the monitoring period, the amount of profanity on the networks increased by 45–47 percent over a comparable period from the preceding year. A clear trend toward hard profanity is evident."

Don Wildmon, founder of the National Federation for Decency

9. "Organizations such as EMILY's List and the Women's Campaign Fund encourage thousands of small contributors to participate, helping to offset

And While We're on the Subject of Writing . . .

Don't forget these rules of good style:

1. Avoid clichés like the plague.
2. Be more or less specific.
3. NEVER generalize.
4. The passive voice is to be ignored.
5. Never ever be redundant.
6. Exaggeration is a billion times worse than understatement.
7. Make sure verbs agrees with their subjects.
8. Why use rhetorical questions?
9. Parenthetical remarks (however relevant) are (usually) unnecessary.
10. Proofread carefully to see if you any words out.
11. And it's usually a bad idea to start a sentence with a conjunction.

This list has been making the rounds on the Internet.

the economic power of the special interests. The political system works better when individuals are encouraged to give to campaigns."

Adapted from the Los Angeles Times

▲ 10. Which is more popular, the movie *Gone With the Wind* or Bing Crosby's version of the song "White Christmas"?

Exercise 2-13

In groups, or individually if your instructor prefers, critique these comparisons, using the questions discussed in the text as guides.

▲ 1. If you worry about the stock market, you have reason. The average stock now has a price-to-earnings ratio of around 25:1.

  2. Students are much less motivated than they were when I first began teaching at this university.

  3. Offhand, I would say the country is considerably more religious than it was twenty years ago.

▲ 4. In addition, for the first time since 1960, a majority of Americans now attend church regularly.

  5. You really should switch to a high-fiber diet.

  6. Hire Ricardo. He's more knowledgeable than Annette.

▲ 7. Why did I give you a lower grade than your roommate? Her paper contained more insights than yours, that's why.

  8. Golf is a considerably more demanding sport than tennis.

Making Ambiguity Work for You

Were you ever asked to write a letter of recommendation for a friend who is, well, incompetent? If you don't want to hurt his or her feelings but also don't want to lie, Robert Thornton of Lehigh University has some ambiguous statements you can use. Here are some examples:

I most enthusiastically recommend this candidate with no qualifications whatsoever.

I am pleased to say that this candidate is a former colleague of mine.

I can assure you that no person would be better for the job.

I would urge you to waste no time in making this candidate an offer of employment.

All in all, I cannot say enough good things about this candidate or recommend the candidate too highly.

In my opinion you will be very fortunate to get this person to work for you.

9. Yes, our prices are higher than they were last year, but you get more value for your dollar.

▲ 10. So, tell me, which do you like more, fried chicken or Volkswagens?

Exercise 2-14

Find two examples of faulty comparisons, and read them to your class. Your instructor may ask other members of the class to critique them.

Persuasive Writing

The primary aim of argumentation and an argumentative essay is to establish something, to support a position on an issue. Good writers, however, write for an audience and hope that their audience will find what they write persuasive. If you are writing for an audience of people who think critically, it is helpful to adhere to these principles:

1. Confine your discussion of an opponent's point of view to issues rather than personal considerations.

2. Anticipate and discuss what opponents might say in criticism of your opinion.

3. When rebutting an opposing viewpoint, avoid being strident or insulting. Don't call opposing arguments absurd or ridiculous.

4. If an opponent's argument is good, concede that it is good.

5. If space or time is limited, be sure to concentrate on the most important considerations. Don't become obsessive about refuting every last criticism of your position.

6. Rebut objections to your position before presenting your own positive case for your side.

7. Present your strongest arguments first.

There is absolutely nothing wrong with trying to make a persuasive case for your position. However, in this book, we place more emphasis on making and recognizing good arguments than simply on devising effective techniques of persuasion. Some people can be persuaded by poor arguments and doubtful claims, and an argumentative essay can be effective as a piece of propaganda even when it is a rational and critical failure. One of the most difficult things you are called upon to do as a critical thinker is to construct and evaluate claims and arguments independently of their power to win a following. The remainder of this book—after a section on writing and diversity—is devoted to this task.

Writing in a Diverse Society

In closing a chapter that deals with writing essays, it seems appropriate to mention how important it is to avoid writing in a manner that reinforces questionable assumptions and attitudes about people's gender, ethnic background, religion, sexual orientation, physical ability or disability, or other characteristics. This isn't just a matter of ethics; it is a matter of clarity and good sense. Careless word choices relative to such characteristics not only are imprecise and inaccurate but also may be viewed as biased even if they were not intended to be, and thus they may diminish the writer's credibility. Worse, using sexist or racist language may distort the writer's own perspective and keep him or her from viewing social issues clearly and objectively.

But language isn't entirely *not* a matter of ethics, either. We are a society that aspires to be just, a society that strives not to withhold its benefits from individuals on the basis of their ethnic or racial background, skin color, religion, gender, or disability. As a people we try to end practices and change or remove institutions that are unjustly discriminatory. Some of these unfair practices and institutions are, unfortunately, embedded in our language.

Some common ways of speaking and writing, for example, assume that "normal" people are all white males. It is still common practice, for instance, to mention a person's race, gender, or ethnic background if the person is *not* a white male, and *not* to do so if the person *is*. Thus, if we are talking about a white male from Ohio, we are apt to say simply, "He is from Ohio." But if the male is Latino, we might tend to mention that fact and say, "He is a Latino from Ohio"—even when the person's ethnic background is irrele-

"Always" and "never" are two words you should always remember never to use.

—WENDELL JOHNSON

Another tip on writing.

vant to whatever we are talking about. This practice assumes that the "normal" person is not Latino and by implication insinuates that if you are, then you are "different" and a deviation from the norm, an outsider.

Of course, it may be relevant to whatever you are writing about to state that this particular man is a Latino from Ohio, and, if so, there is absolutely nothing wrong with writing "He is a Latino from Ohio."

Some language practices are particularly unfair to women. Imagine a conversation among three people, you being one of them. Imagine that the other two talk only to each other. When you speak, they listen politely; but when you are finished, they continue as though you had never spoken. Even though what you say is true and relevant to the discussion, the other two proceed as though you are invisible. Because you are not being taken seriously, you are at a considerable disadvantage. You would have reason to be unhappy.

In an analogous way, women have been far less visible in language than men and have thus been at a disadvantage. Another word for the human race is not "woman," but "man" or "mankind." The generic human has often been referred to as "he." How do you run a project? You *man* it. Who supervises the department or runs the meeting? The chair*man*. Who heads the crew? The fore*man*. Women, like men, can be supervisors, scientists, professors, lawyers, poets, and so forth. But a woman in such a profession is apt to be referred to as a "woman scientist" or "woman supervisor" or as a "lady poet" (or whatever). The implication is that in their primary signification, words like "scientist" and "supervisor" refer to men.

Picture a research scientist to yourself. Got the picture? Is it a picture of a *woman*? No? That's because the standard picture, or stereotype, of a research scientist is a picture of a man. Or, read this sentence: "Research scientists often put their work before their personal lives and neglect their husbands." Were you surprised by the last word? Again, the stereotypical picture of a research scientist is a picture of a man.

A careful and precise writer finds little need to converse in the lazy language of stereotypes, especially those that perpetuate prejudice. As long as the idea prevails that the "normal" research scientist is a man, women who are or who wish to become research scientists will tend to be thought of as out of place. So they must carry an *extra* burden, the burden of showing that they are *not* out of place. That's unfair. If you unthinkingly always write "The research scientist . . . he," you are perpetuating an image that places women at a disadvantage. Some research scientists are men, and some are women. If you wish to make a claim about male research scientists, do so. But if you wish to make a claim about research scientists in general, don't write as though they were all males.

Most often the problem of unintentional gender discrimination arises in connection with pronouns. Note how the use of "he" and "his" in the following two sentences excludes females.

As *a student* learns to read more critically, *he* usually writes more clearly, too.

What day is the day after three days before the day after tomorrow?

Complicated, but neither vague nor ambiguous

Do you have blacks, too?

—President George W. Bush, during a discussion with Brazilian President Fernando Henrique Cardoso

In fact, Brazil has more black people than does the United States.

Avoiding Sexist Language

Use the suggestions below to help keep your writing free of sexist language.

Instead of	Use
actress	actor
chairman	chair, chairperson, coordinator, director, head, leader, president, presider
congressman	congressional representative, member of Congress
fathers (of industry, and so on)	founders, innovators, pioneers, trailblazers
housewife	homemaker, woman
man (verb)	operate, serve, staff, tend, work
man (noun)	human beings, individuals, people
man and wife	husband and wife
man-hour	operator-hour, time, work-hour
mankind	human beings, humanity, humankind
manmade	artificial, fabricated, manufactured, synthetic, human-made
manpower	crew, personnel, staff, workers, workforce
newsman	journalist, newscaster, reporter
poetess	poet
policeman	police officer
repairman	repairer
spokesman	representative, spokesperson
statesmanlike	diplomatic, tactful
stewardess	flight attendant
waitress	service person, waiter
weatherman	weather reporter, weathercaster
craftsman	artisan
deliveryman	courier
foreman	supervisor; lead juror
freshman	first-year student
heroine	hero
layman	layperson

You can also refer to any of numerous reference works on bias-free language. See, for example, Marilyn Schwartz, *Guidelines for Bias-Free Writing* (Bloomington: Indiana University Press, 1995).

As *a student* learns to read more critically, *his* writing, too, usually becomes clearer.

Obviously, changing "his" and "he" to "her" and "she" would then exclude males. If the writer means to include people of both sexes, one solution is to use two pronouns: for instance, "he or she" (or "his or her").

As *a student* learns to read more critically, *she or he* usually writes more clearly, too.
As *a student* learns to read more critically, *his or her* writing, too, usually becomes clearer.

However, a usually less awkward remedy is to change from singular to plural (because plural pronouns in English do not show gender).

As *students* learn to read more critically, *they* usually write more clearly, too.
As *students* learn to read more critically, *their* writing usually becomes clearer, too.

Often the best solution of all is to rephrase the statement entirely, which is almost always possible.

Critical reading leads to clear writing.
Learning to read more critically helps students write more clearly, too.

Frequently a pronoun can simply be deleted or replaced by another word, especially "a" or "the":

The student who develops the habit of reading critically will get more out of *his* college courses.
The student who develops the habit of reading critically will get more out of college courses.
The student who develops the habit of reading critically will get more out of *a* [or *any*] college course.

The rule to follow in all cases is this: Keep writing free of *irrelevant implied evaluation* of gender, race, ethnic background, religion, or any other human attribute.

Recap

An argumentative essay is intended to support a position on some issue. Principles of critical thinking can and should be applied both to essays written by others and to those we ourselves write. Such essays must be soundly organized and clearly written and must truly support the position taken by their author.

Check Your Chart

The following are alleged to be actual notations in patients' records. Each has a flagrant ambiguity or other problem. Sometimes the problem interferes with clarity; other times it only produces amusement. Describe what is going on in each case.

- Patient has chest pain if she lies on her left side for over a year.
- She has had no rigors or shaking chills, but her husband states she was very hot in bed last night.
- The patient has been depressed ever since she began seeing me in 1983.
- I will be happy to go into her GI system; she seems ready and anxious.
- The patient is tearful and crying constantly. She also appears to be depressed.
- Discharge status: Alive but without permission. The patient will need disposition, and therefore we will get Dr. Blank to dispose of him.
- Healthy-appearing decrepit 69-year-old male, mentally alert but forgetful.
- The patient refused an autopsy.
- The patient has no past history of suicides.
- The patient expired on the floor uneventfully.
- Patient has left his white blood cells at another hospital.
- Patient was becoming more demented with urinary frequency.
- The patient's past medical history has been remarkably insignificant with only a 40-pound weight gain in the past three days.
- She slipped on the ice and apparently her legs went in separate directions in early December.
- The patient experienced sudden onset of severe shortness of breath with a picture of acute pulmonary edema at home while having sex which gradually deteriorated in the emergency room.
- The patient left the hospital feeling much better except for her original complaints.
- The patient states there is a burning pain in his penis which goes to his feet.

(These were sent around the Internet after they appeared in a column written by RICHARD LEDERER in the *Journal of Court Reporting*. Lederer is famous for his collections of remarks taken from student papers, especially papers on historical subjects.)

Writers can get into trouble in many ways, but you can avoid the most common pitfalls if you are willing to take care. To keep your essay organized, stay focused on your main points, use an outline, and be prepared to revise. To achieve clarity, be sure you clearly define new terms, terms that are especially important to your argument, or terms you are using in an un-usual way; and remember to pay attention to the emotive force of your words. Avoid redundancy and unnecessarily complex language. Watch out for ambiguous claims (claims that are insufficiently precise for the purposes at hand). Be especially careful when writing or analyzing claims that make comparisons.

It is acceptable to use persuasive techniques to support a position in an argumentative essay, but don't use them *instead* of reasonable claims and well-constructed arguments. Be careful to avoid irrelevant (and unwar-ranted) assumptions about people, including those you may overlook because they are embedded in our language.

Remember: If what you want to say is not clear to you, it certainly will remain obscure to your reader.

Having read this chapter and the chapter recap, you should begin to be able to

- ▲ Create a clear and focused organizational plan for an argumentative essay
- ▲ Define terms in your essay clearly and choose the words that best suit your purposes
- ▲ Recognize different types of ambiguity, know the uses and abuses of vagueness, and analyze comparative claims
- ▲ Make a persuasive case for your positions to an audience of people who can think critically
- ▲ Avoid sexist, racist, and other inappropriate writing practices

Additional Exercises

Exercise 2-15

Rewrite each of the following claims in gender-neutral language.

Example

We have insufficient manpower to complete the task.

Answer

We have insufficient personnel to complete the task.

▲   1. A student should choose his major with considerable care.
    2. When a student chooses his major, he must do so carefully.
    3. The true citizen understands his debt to his country.

▲ 4. If a nurse can find nothing wrong with you in her preliminary examination, she will recommend a physician to you. However, in this city the physician will wish to protect himself by having you sign a waiver.

5. You should expect to be interviewed by a personnel director. You should be cautious when talking to him.

6. The entrant must indicate that he has read the rules, that he understands them, and that he is willing to abide by them. If he has questions, then he should bring them to the attention of an official, and he will answer them.

▲ 7. A soldier should be prepared to sacrifice his life for his comrades.

8. If anyone wants a refund, he should apply at the main office and have his identification with him.

9. The person who has tried our tea knows that it will neither keep him awake nor make him jittery.

▲ 10. If any petitioner is over sixty, he (she) should have completed form E-7.

11. Not everyone has the same beliefs. One person may not wish to put himself on the line, whereas another may welcome the chance to make his view known to his friends.

12. God created man in his own image.

▲ 13. Language is nature's greatest gift to mankind.

14. Of all the animals, the most intelligent is man.

15. The common man prefers peace to war.

▲ 16. The proof must be acceptable to the rational man.

▲ 17. The Founding Fathers believed that all men are created equal.

18. Man's pursuit of happiness has led him to prefer leisure to work.

19. When the individual reaches manhood, he is able to make such decisions for himself.

▲ 20. If an athlete wants to play for the National Football League, he should have a good work ethic.

21. The new city bus service has hired several women drivers.

22. The city is also hiring firemen, policemen, and mailmen; and the city council is planning to elect a new chairman.

23. Harold Vasquez worked for City Hospital as a male nurse.

▲ 24. Most U.S. senators are men.

25. Mr. and Mrs. Macleod joined a club for men and their wives.

26. Mr. Macleod lets his wife work for the city.

▲ 27. Macleod doesn't know it, but Mrs. Macleod is a women's libber.

28. Several coeds have signed up for the seminar.

29. A judge must be sensitive to the atmosphere in his courtroom.

▲ 30. To be a good politician, you have to be a good salesman.

Exercise 2-16

▲ A riddle: A man is walking down the street one day when he suddenly recognizes an old friend whom he has not seen in years walking in his direction with a little girl. They greet each other warmly, and the friend says, "I married since I last saw you, to someone you never met, and this is my daughter, Ellen." The man says to Ellen, "You look just like your mother." How did he know that?

This riddle comes from Janice Moulton's article, "The Myth of the Neutral Man." Discuss why so many people don't get the answer to this riddle straight off.

Writing Exercises

Everyone, no matter how well he or she writes, can improve. And the best way to improve is to practice. Since finding a topic to write about is often the hardest part of a writing assignment, we're supplying three subjects for you to write about. For each—or whichever your instructor might assign—write a one- to two-page essay in which you clearly identify the issue (or issues), state your position on the issue (a hypothetical position if you don't have one), and give at least one good reason in support of your position. Try also to give at least one reason why the opposing position is wrong.

1. The exchange of dirty hypodermic needles for clean ones, or the sale of clean ones, is legal in many states. In such states, the transmission of HIV and hepatitis from dirty needles is down dramatically. But bills [in the California legislature] to legalize clean-needle exchanges have been stymied by the last two governors, who earnestly but incorrectly believed that the availability of clean needles would increase drug abuse. Our state, like every other state that has not yet done it, should immediately approve legislation to make clean needles available.

   Adapted from an editorial by Marsha N. Cohen,
   professor of law at Hastings College of Law

2. On February 11, 2003, the Eighth Circuit Court of Appeals ruled that the state of Arkansas could force death-row prisoner Charles Laverne Singleton to take antipsychotic drugs to make him sane enough to execute. Singleton was to be executed for felony capital murder but became insane while in prison. "Medicine is supposed to heal people, not prepare them for execution. A law that asks doctors to make people well so that the government can kill them is an absurd law," said David Kaczynski, the executive director of New Yorkers Against the Death Penalty.

3. Some politicians make a lot of noise about how Canadians and others pay much less for prescription drugs than Americans do. Those who are constantly pointing to the prices and the practices of other nations when it comes to pharmaceutical drugs ignore the fact that those other nations lag far behind the United States when it comes to creating new medicines.

Canada, Germany, and other countries get the benefits of American research but contribute much less than the United States does to the creation of drugs. On the surface, these countries have a good deal, but in reality everyone is worse off, because the development of new medicines is slower than it would be if worldwide prices were high enough to cover research costs.

Adapted from an editorial by Thomas Sowell,
senior fellow at the Hoover Institution

Chapter 3

Credibility

I looked the man in the eye. I found him to be very straightforward and trustworthy. We had a very good dialogue. I was able to sense his soul.

—George W. Bush, commenting on his first meeting with Russian president Vladimir Putin

The Charles Keller method of judging credibility.

W e size up people's believability, or credibility, every day. Sometimes we make mistakes.

On July 13, 2002, Charles Keller of Sacramento, California, withdrew $10,000 from his Wells Fargo savings account and gave it to two men he didn't know from Adam. The men had convinced Keller, merely by talking to him for a while, that by giving them $10,000 to demonstrate "good faith" he would receive a check for $60,000 at the end of the day. They told Mr. Keller they represented an organization that located individuals who had received large inheritances but didn't know it and were authorized to pay "finder's fees" to anyone who could help them locate the people. We don't know for sure what else they told Mr. Keller, but it is easy to imagine possibilities. Perhaps they described a neighbor of Mr. Keller as one of the people they were looking for, prompting Keller to think the finder's fee would be easy money.

It may strike you as odd that anyone at least smart enough to accumulate $10,000 in the bank would fall for such an obvious swindle. Yet people both wealthy and intelligent are conned every day. We'd bet in your own city there are intelligent people who are losing their shirt at this very moment. The problem stems not from a lack of intelligence but from other things, including perhaps wishful thinking (which we will say more about in a bit); it also stems from a failure to judge credibility correctly.

Two different things in varying degrees have or lack credibility: *claims* and *sources* (that is, *people*). Some claims lack credibility no matter who says them; other claims depend for their credibility on who says them. Do ducks quack in Morse Code? The idea would lack credibility no matter who were to express it. But the claim that ducks mate for life would depend for its credibility on who said it. It would be more believable coming from a bird expert than from our editor, for example.

Credibility is not an all-or-nothing thing, whether we are talking about claims or sources. If someone claimed that George W. Bush sends weekly bribes to the U.S. Supreme Court, his claim would be rather far-fetched. But it wouldn't be as far-fetched as the claim that George W. Bush is a space alien. A similar variability in credibility attaches to people. An individual known to lie habitually is less credible than an otherwise honest person caught lying to save someone's life. A man charged with armed robbery becomes less credible in his denial if we learn he owns a silencer and an illegal semi-automatic .40-caliber handgun with the serial numbers removed.

Now, we often judge the credibility of people on the basis of irrelevant considerations. Physical characteristics, for instance, are poor indicators of credibility or its lack. Does a person maintain eye contact? (Mr. Keller's swindlers might well have.) Is the person sweating? Does he or she laugh nervously? Does he or she shake our hand firmly? These characteristics are widely used in sizing up a person's credibility. But they are generally worthless.

Other irrelevant features we sometimes use to judge a person's credibility include gender, height, age, ethnicity, accent, and mannerisms. People also make credibility judgments on the basis of the clothes a person wears. A friend told one of us that one's sunglasses "make a statement"; maybe so, but that statement doesn't say much about credibility. A person's occupation certainly bears a relationship to his or her knowledge or abilities, but as a guide to moral character or truthfulness, it is less reliable.

Which considerations are relevant to judging someone's credibility? We shall get to these in a moment, but appearance isn't one of them. You may have the idea that you can size up a person just by looking into his or her eyes. This is a mistake. Just by looking at someone we cannot ascertain that person's truthfulness, knowledge, or character.

Of course, we sometimes get in trouble even when we accept credible claims from credible sources. Many of us rely, for example, on credible advice from qualified and honest professionals in preparing our tax returns. But qualified and honest professionals can make honest mistakes, and we can suffer the consequences. In general, however, trouble is much more likely if we accept either doubtful claims from credible sources or credible claims from doubtful sources (not to mention doubtful claims from doubtful sources). If a mechanic says we need a new transmission, the claim itself may not be suspicious—maybe the car we drive has many miles on it; maybe we neglected routine maintenance; maybe it isn't shifting smoothly. But if we find out that the mechanic has been charged with selling unneeded repairs to customers, we'd get a second opinion about our transmission.

On the other hand, if we look at Mr. Keller's case closely, it seems clear that his mistake was *not* that he did not pay close enough attention to the *swindlers'* credibility. There may well have been no detectable telltale signs that *they* were dishonest; after all, successful swindlers don't exhibit signs of dishonesty. Mr. Keller's mistake lay in accepting something the

Lovable Trickster Created a Monster with Bigfoot Hoax

Ray L. Wallace, 1918–2002 / Relatives finally fess up: Man faked famous jumbo footprints in 1958.

SEATTLE — Bigfoot is dead. Really.

"Ray L. Wallace was Bigfoot. The reality is, Bigfoot just died," said Michael Wallace about his father, who died of heart failure November 26 in a Centralia [California] nursing facility. He was 84.

The truth can finally be told, according to Mr. Wallace's family members. He orchestrated the prank that created Bigfoot in 1958.

Some experts suspected Mr. Wallace had planted the footprints that launched the term "Bigfoot." But Mr. Wallace and his family had never publicly admitted the 1958 deed until now.

"The fact is, there was no Bigfoot in popular consciousness before 1958. America got its own monster, its own Abominable Snowman, thanks to Ray Wallace," said Mark Chorvinsky, editor of *Strange* magazine and one of the leading proponents of the theory that Mr. Wallace fathered Bigfoot.

Pranks and hoaxes were just part of Mr. Wallace's nature.

"He'd been a kid all his life. He did it just for the joke, and then he was afraid to tell anybody because they'd be so mad at him," said nephew Dale Lee Wallace, who said he has the alderwood carvings of the giant humanoid feet that gave life to a worldwide phenomenon.

It was in August 1958 in Humboldt County, California, that Jerry Crew, a bulldozer operator for Wallace Construction, saw prints of huge naked feet circling and walking away from his rig.

The *Humboldt Times* in Eureka, California, ran a front-page story on the prints and coined the term "Bigfoot."

According to family members, Mr. Wallace smirked. He had asked a friend to carve the 16-inch-long feet. Then he and his brother Wilbur slipped them on and created the footprints as a prank, family members said.

His joke soon swept the country, which was fascinated by rumors of Himalayan Abominable Snowmen in the 1950s, Chorvinsky said.

"The Abominable Snowman was appropriated by Ray Wallace. It got into the press, took on a life of its own, and next thing you know there's a Bigfoot, one of the most popular monsters in the world," he said.

Mr. Wallace continued to milk the prank for years. He offered to sell a Bigfoot to Texas millionaire Tom Slick and then backed out when Slick made a serious bid. Mr. Wallace later put out a press release saying he wanted to buy a baby Bigfoot for $1 million, said Loren Coleman, who has written two books about Bigfoot. Mr. Wallace also cut a record of supposed Bigfoot sounds and printed posters of a Bigfoot sitting peacefully with other ani-

swindlers *said* that lacked credibility, such as, at the very least, "Give us $10,000 and we will give you back $60,000."

In light of these considerations a general principle emerges, to this effect:

> It is reasonable to be suspicious if a claim either lacks credibility inherently or comes from a source that lacks credibility.

Thus, we need to ask two questions: When does a *claim* lack credibility inherently—in other words, when does its content lack credibility? And when does a *source* lack credibility?

To begin with claims, the general answer is

mals, said Chorvinsky, who received several hundred pages of correspondence from Mr. Wallace.

But Mr. Wallace's chief contributions to bigfootery were films and photos he supposedly captured of the creature in the wild.

There were depictions of Bigfeet eating elk and frogs, of a Bigfoot sitting on a log, and of a Bigfoot munching on cereal.

"Ray's contribution was study into the actual behavior of Bigfoot, what it eats, how it acts," said Ray Crowe, director of the International Bigfoot Society in Hillsboro, Oregon.

Chorvinsky believes the Wallace family's admission creates profound doubts about leading evidence of Bigfoot's existence: the so-called Patterson film, the grainy celluloid images of an erect apelike creature striding away from the movie camera of rodeo rider Roger Patterson in 1967. Mr. Wallace said he told Patterson where to go—near Bluff Creek, California—to spot a Bigfoot, Chorvinsky said.

"Ray told me that the Patterson film was a hoax, and he knew who was in the suit," Chorvinsky said.

Michael Wallace said his father called the Patterson film "a fake" and said he had nothing to do with it. But he said his mother admitted she had been photographed in a Bigfoot suit. "He had several people he used in his movies," Michael Wallace said.

Mr. Wallace never received proper credit in the Bigfoot community, Chorvinsky said. "He got it off the ground, and he kept getting glossed over. He's been consistently marginalized or ignored by authors," Chorvinsky said.

Why? "Because it hurts the case for Bigfoot if you talk too much about Ray Wallace," he replied.

The Wallace family's revelation does not faze some Bigfoot experts, and the debate about Bigfoot's existence rages on.

"These rumors have been circulating for some time," said Jeff Meldrum, an associate professor of anatomy and anthropology at Idaho State University.

Meldrum said he has casts of 40 to 50 footprints that he concludes, from their anatomical features, come from authentic unknown primates.

"To suggest all these are explained by simple carved feet strapped to boots just doesn't wash," he said. Even if the Wallace family's claims are true, Meldrum added, there are historical acounts of Bigfootlike creatures going back to the 1800s. "How do you account for that?"

It's easy, replied Chorvinsky; the historical accounts were mistakes, myths, or hoaxes. "I would like to see the evidence beyond the anecdotal. Jeff Meldrum's job is to show us the beef, something beyond old newspaper articles."

As for Meldrum's claim about authentic footprints, Chorvinsky said: "Jeff Meldrum is not an expert in creating hoaxes. I was a professional magician and special-effects film director; anything can be faked."

Michael Wallace said family members knew about his father's hoax but never let on.

—Bob Young, *Seattle Times*, December 5, 2002. © 2002 Seattle Times Company. Used with permission.

✳ A claim lacks inherent credibility to the extent it conflicts with what we have observed or what we think we know—our background information—or with other credible claims.

Assessing the Content of the Claim

■ *Does the Claim Conflict with Our Personal Observations?*

Our own observations provide the most reliable source of information about the world. It is therefore only reasonable to be suspicious of any claim

What Americans Believe

According to a recent *Time*/CNN poll:

- Eighty-two percent of Americans believe in the healing power of personal prayer.
- Seventy-three percent believe that praying for someone else can help cure that person's illness.
- Seventy-seven percent believe that God sometimes intervenes to cure people who have a serious illness.

These poll results, if they reflect reality, say something about some of the claims Americans find credible. One thing that makes these high percentages interesting is that evidence of the effectiveness of prayer in healing is so difficult to document. More on that subject in Chapter 11.

that comes into conflict with what we have observed. Let's say that Parker tells Moore there will be no mail delivery today. But Moore has just a short while ago seen the mail carrier arrive and deliver the mail. Under such circumstances, obviously, neither Moore, nor you, nor anybody else needs instruction in critical thinking to decide not to accept Parker's claim. Anyone would reject it outright, in fact.

But observations are not infallible, and critical thinkers need to keep this in mind. Our observations may not be reliable if we make them when the lighting is poor or the room is noisy; when we are distracted, emotionally upset, or mentally fatigued; when our senses are impaired; or when our measuring instruments are inexact, temperamental, or inaccurate.

In addition, critical thinkers recognize that people vary in their powers of observation. Some people see and hear better than others and for this reason may be better at making observations than those whose vision or hearing is less acute. Some people have special training or experience that makes them better observers. Customs agents and professional counselors, even those who wear glasses or hearing aids, are better able than most of us to detect signs of nervousness or discomfort in people they observe. Laboratory scientists accustomed to noticing subtle changes in the properties of substances they are investigating are doubtless better than you or we at certain sorts of observations, though perhaps not at certain other sorts. In fact, some professional magicians actually prefer an audience of scientists, believing that such a group is particularly easy to fool.

Our beliefs, hopes, fears, and expectations also affect our observations. Tell someone that a house is infested with rats, and he is likely to believe he sees evidence of rats. Inform someone who believes in ghosts that a house is haunted, and she may well believe she sees evidence of ghosts. At séances staged by the Society for Psychical Research to test the observational powers of people under séance conditions, some observers insist that they see numerous phenomena that simply do not exist. Teachers who are

More on What Americans Believe

Long the most religious of the developed countries, the United States may have seen an increase in secularism in recent years. According to the Gallup Poll 2001, Americans' views of the Christian Bible have undergone substantial change in the last twenty years. The percentage who believed that the Bible is "the actual word of God" has decreased steadily since the early 1960s, from 65 percent in 1963 to 27 percent in 2001. Those who believe the Bible should not be taken literally have increased in number from 18 percent in 1963 to 49 percent in 2001. Finally, the percentage of Americans who believe the Bible is a book of fables, legends, history, and moral lessons recorded by humans has risen from 11 percent in 1963 to 20 percent in 2001.

Another survey, the *American Religious Identification Survey,* 2001, published by the Graduate Center of the City University of New York, reports that the number of Americans who claim to have no religion at all has grown from 8.16 percent in 1990 to 14.17 percent in 2001. Numbering 29.5 million, those with no religion are outnumbered only by Roman Catholics (50.9 million) and Baptists (33.8 million).

Figures reported in *Free Inquiry,* Summer 2002

told that the students in a particular class are brighter than usual are very likely to believe that the work those students produce is better than average, even when it is not.

In Chapter 5 we cover a fallacy (a fallacy is a mistake in reasoning) called *wishful thinking,* which occurs when we allow hopes and desires to influence our judgment and color our beliefs. The case of Mr. Keller, mentioned at the beginning of this chapter, more than likely involved wishful thinking: Mr. Keller must have been aware that the chances of making $50,000 by giving two strangers $10,000 are so small as to be almost nonexistent; but the thought of having or spending so much money must have blinded him to this obvious fact.

Our personal interests and biases affect our perceptions and the judgments we base on them. We overlook many of the mean and selfish actions of the people we like or love—and when we are infatuated with someone, everything that person does seems wonderful. By contrast, people we detest can hardly do anything that we don't perceive as mean and selfish. If we desperately wish for the success of a project, we are apt to see more evidence for that success than is actually present. On the other hand, if we wish for a project to fail, we are apt to exaggerate flaws that we see in it or imagine flaws that are not there at all. If a job, chore, or decision is one that we wish to avoid, we tend to draw worst-case implications from it and thus come up with reasons for not doing it. However, if we are predisposed to want to do the job or make the decision, we are more likely to focus on whatever positive consequences it might have.

"Eyewitness" Accounts

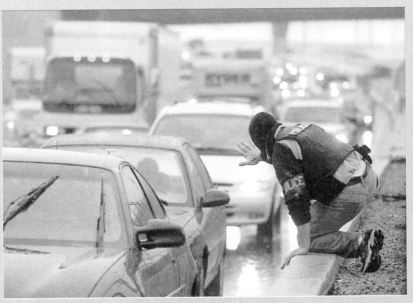

Associated Press/Rob Ostermaier

A Fairfax, Virginia, police officer signals cars after a man was shot to death October 11, 2002, at a gas station near Fredericksburg, Va. Police were looking for a white van.

When the series of sniper shootings occurred in the Washington, D.C., area during the fall of 2002, there were eyewitness reports that the perpetrators were two white men traveling in a white enclosed truck. In fact, two men who fit that description were detained and investigated by authorities. But when those doing the shootings were caught, they turned out to be two black men in a blue Chevrolet Caprice.

This is further evidence that we must be careful when deciding how much credence to put in eyewitness testimony, especially when the stakes are high. An appalling number of people have been convicted of heinous crimes by eyewitness accounts, only later to be freed from prison by conclusive DNA evidence.

Finally, the reliability of our observations is no better than the reliability of our memories, except in those cases where we have the means at our disposal to record our observations. And memory, as most of us know, can be deceptive. Critical thinkers are always alert to the possibility that what they remember having observed may not be what they did observe.

But even though firsthand observations are not infallible, they are still the best source of information we have. Any factual report that conflicts with our own direct observations is subject to serious doubt.

The Lake Wobegon Effect

In radio humorist and author Garrison Keillor's fictitious town of Lake Wobegon, "the women are strong, the men are good-looking, and all the children are above average." Thus the town lends its name to the utterly reliable tendency of people to believe that they are better than average in a host of different ways. A large majority of the population believe that they are more intelligent than average, more fair-minded, less prejudiced, and better automobile drivers.

A huge study was done not long ago by the Higher Education Research Institute at UCLA on high school seniors, with a million respondents to the survey. Seventy percent of them believed they were above average in leadership ability and only 2 percent thought they were below average. In the category of getting along with others, *fully 100 percent* of those seniors believed they were above average. What's more, in this same category 60 percent believed they were in the top 10 percent, and 25 percent believed they were in the top 1 percent!

People are more than willing to believe—it is probably safe to say *anxious* to believe—that they are better in lots of ways than the objective evidence would indicate. This tendency can make us susceptible to all kinds of trouble, from falling victim to con artists to overestimating our abilities in areas that can cost us our fortunes.

—*Adapted from* THOMAS GILOVICH, How We Know What Isn't So

■ *Does the Claim Conflict with Our Background Information?*

Factual claims must always be evaluated against our **background information**—that immense body of justified beliefs that consists of facts we learn from our own direct observations and facts we learn from others. Such information is "background" because we may not be able to specify where we learned it, unlike something we know because we witnessed it this morning. Much of our background information is well confirmed by a variety of sources. Factual claims that conflict with this store of information are usually quite properly dismissed, even if we cannot disprove them through direct observation. We immediately reject the claim "Palm trees grow in abundance near the North Pole," even though we are not in a position to confirm or disprove the statement by direct observation.

Indeed, this is an example of how we usually treat claims when we first encounter them: We begin by assigning them a certain *initial plausibility,* a rough assessment of how credible a claim seems to us. This assessment depends on how consistent the claim is with our background information—how well it "fits" with that information. If it fits very well, we give the claim a high degree of initial plausibility; we lean toward accepting it. If, however, the claim conflicts with our background information, we give it low initial plausibility and lean toward rejecting it unless very strong evidence can be produced on its behalf. The claim "More guitars

The Latest in Conspiracies!

The Internet has provided fertile ground for people—and there seem to be a lot of them—who believe that this or that or *every* aspect of our lives is controlled by someone "behind the scenes." The subjects of conspiracy theories range from the deaths of Martin Luther King, John Kennedy, and almost every other public person who has died in the last fifty years, to the worldwide domination plans of Illuminati, a small and secret group of powerful men bent on the enslavement of the planet in the name of Satan. Some of the topics we noted:

- Complete foreknowledge within the Bush administration of the 9/11 attacks
- The conspiracy to murder Princess Diana
- The secret plot to control the world's weather
- The exposé of Bill Clinton as a British secret agent
- The cover-up of the bombing at the Oklahoma City Federal Building

Discussion of such topics ranges from almost reasonable to outright loony. Running an Internet search on "conspiracies" will turn up examples from across the spectrum, more than you can look at in a lifetime!

There are three types of men in the world. One type learns from books. One type learns from observation. And one type just has to urinate on the electric fence.

—DR. LAURA
SCHLESSINGER
(reported by Larry
Englemann)

The authority of experience.

were sold in the United States last year than saxophones" fits very well with the background information most of us share, and we would hardly require detailed evidence before accepting it. However, the claim "Charlie's eighty-seven-year-old grandmother swam across Lake Michigan in the middle of winter" cannot command much initial plausibility because of the obvious way it conflicts with our background information about eighty-seven-year-old people, about Lake Michigan, about swimming in cold water, and so on. In fact, short of observing the swim ourselves, it isn't clear just what *could* persuade us to accept such a claim. And even *then* we should consider the likelihood that we're being tricked or fooled by an illusion.

Not every suspicious claim is as outrageous as the one about Charlie's nautical grandmother. Some may not have enough initial plausibility to be immediately acceptable—we may even lean toward rejecting them—but they may still be worth investigating. For example, let's say someone shows up at your door and presents you with what he says is a check for a hundred dollars from an anonymous benefactor. Before you rush right out and spend the hundred, you should, as a critical thinker, consider the possibility that somebody is playing a joke on you. However, even though it's more likely that there is a practical joke going on (practical jokes of this sort are probably more common than actual hundred-dollar surprises, after all), it's worth investigating the possibility that the gift is legitimate. A trip to your bank certainly seems in order. As in most other cases, this is a situation where nothing can take the place of investigating further and gathering more information. Then, depending on how the investigation turns out, one can hope for a reasonable

Do Your Ears Stick Straight Out?
Do You Have a Short Neck?

According to Bill Cordingley, an expert in psychographicology—that's face-reading, in case you didn't know (and we certainly didn't)—a person's facial features reveal "the whole rainbow collection" of a person's needs and abilities. Mr. Cordingley *(In Your Face: What Facial Features Reveal About People You Know and Love)* doesn't mean merely that you can infer moods from smiles and frowns. No, he means that your basic personality traits are readable from facial structures you were born with.

Do your ears stick out? You have a need to perform in public. The more they stick out, the greater the need. Is your neck short and thin? You are stubborn and dominate conversations. Large lips? You love attention. The length of your chin, location of your eyebrows, size of your ears, length of your neck, are such reliable predictors of personality that an expert can tell by looking at two people whether their relationship will succeed.

Former President Carter apparently loves attention. President Bush is an introvert (thin lips) and a control freak (small eyelids—Hey! At least they cover his eyes.)

We leave it to you to determine how credible this is. Cordingley is the former mayor of San Anselmo, California. Does that fact make this more credible?

conclusion to the matter. Unfortunately, there are no neat formulas that can resolve conflicts between what you already believe and new information. Your job as a critical thinker is to trust your background information when considering claims that conflict with that information—that is, claims with low initial plausibility—but at the same time to keep an open mind and realize that further information may cause you to give up a claim you had thought was true. It's a difficult balance, but it's worth getting right.

Finally, keep in mind that you are handicapped in evaluating a factual report on a subject in which you have no background information. This means that the broader your background information, the more likely you are to be able to evaluate any given report effectively. Without some rudimentary knowledge of economics, for example, we are in no position to evaluate claims about the dangers of a large federal deficit; unless we know what cholesterol does in the body, we cannot appreciate the benefits of low-cholesterol foods. The single most effective means of increasing your ability as a critical thinker, regardless of the subject, is to increase what you know: Read widely, converse freely, and develop an inquiring attitude! There is simply no substitute for broad, general knowledge.

The President's Own Credibility

Bush on Iraq: Is He Stretching the Facts?

WASHINGTON — President Bush, speaking to the nation this month [October 2002] about the need to challenge Saddam Hussein, warned that Iraq has a growing fleet of unmanned aircraft that could be used "for missions targeting the United States."

Associated Press/Dan Loh

President Bush speaks in Downingtown, Pa. In making his case for war with Iraq, Bush has made statements that some may find misleading. But his spokesman says his statements are "well documented and supported by the facts."

Last month, asked if there was new and conclusive evidence of Saddam's nuclear weapons capabilities, Bush cited a report by the International Atomic Energy Agency saying the Iraqis were "six months away from developing a weapon."

And last week, the president said objections by a labor union to having customs officials wear radiation detectors has the potential to delay the policy "for a long period of time."

All three assertions were powerful arguments for the actions Bush sought. And all three statements were dubious, if not wrong. Further information revealed that the aircraft lack the range to reach the United States; there was no such report by the IAEA; and the customs dispute over the detectors was resolved long ago.

By Dana Milbank
WASHINGTON POST

From the *Sacramento Bee*, Oct. 23, 2002. *Washington Post* News Service.

Assessing the Credibility of Sources

The guiding principle in evaluating claims requires that they come from credible sources. We've considered the credibility of claims as to their content. Now let's consider the credibility of sources.

A person may lack credibility in various ways, but most of them relate either to (1) his or her knowledge or to (2) his or her truthfulness, objectivity, or accuracy. If we have reason to think a source may be biased or self-serving or opinionated or conflicted about a subject, or for other reasons may not be giving us a full and complete and impartial report, then we have a reason for concern under criterion (2). We also should have concerns under criterion (2) if we have suspicions about a source's memory or ability or op-

The "Authority" of Experience

. . . a farmer never laid an egg, but he knows more about the process than hens do.

—Henry Darcy Curwen

No one knows more about this mountain than Harry. And it don't dare blow up on him. This goddamned mountain won't blow.

—Harry Truman, 83-year-old owner of a lodge near Mt. St. Helens in Washington, commenting on geologists' predictions that the volcano would erupt. (A few days later it did erupt, killing Harry Truman.)

Through their "observations," the hen and Harry know well enough what it's like to lay an egg or live near a volcano, but these observations are obviously not enough to qualify them as reliable sources about the biological and geological processes involved in egg laying and volcanic eruptions.

portunity to have made accurate observations. We shall get to questions as to a source's knowledge in a bit.

Now we can have concerns about a person's accuracy, objectivity, or truthfulness without suspecting him or her of evil intent. Generally people don't lie to one another; given an absence of a specific reason to think otherwise, it is reasonable to assume a source speaks honestly and in good conscience.

Of course, assuming that a source is honest does not require us to assume he or she cannot be mistaken. Even individuals operating in good conscience may still say things that are inaccurate, incomplete, or misleading.

For example, the reports people give one another are very frequently subject to innocent **sharpening** and **leveling**—exaggerating what the speaker thinks is the main point and dropping out or de-emphasizing details that seem peripheral. The result can be a distortion of the story.

For example, let's say you've heard reports from time to time from your college roommate about one of his or her high school friends. Based on what you have heard, you may picture this friend as very smart or exceptionally clever or unusually good-looking. This is because your roommate will probably emphasize those features he or she considers trademarks of the person. Typically, if you finally meet the friend, you may find yourself somewhat surprised by how unexceptional he or she is. The same sharpening and leveling phenomenon accounts for why we are often disappointed when we see a movie after we've heard rave reports from friends about it. By placing so much emphasis on what they liked about the movie, they have raised our expectations to a level that is hard to meet.

Why do people exaggerate this way? It's not usually dishonesty. We naturally tend to remember things that make an experience different and worth reporting and tend to report details that make stories interesting. It's always more interesting to our listeners to hear about somebody or

When the Stakes Are High

Generally speaking, it's reasonable to accept a claim from a credible source if it does not conflict with your observations, background information, or other credible claims. But if the stakes are high, it can be reasonable to hesitate.

For example, if your doctor tells you that you have a cancerous tumor on your leg and wants to amputate the leg, you'd have a claim from a credible source that meets the other requirements for credibility. We trust, however, you'd get a second opinion before rolling up your pants leg.

something that is very this or exceptionally that than to hear about someone or something that is perfectly ordinary.

Also, if we are reporting on someone we like or someone we feel indebted to (or are employed by), we may accentuate the positive and understate the negative more or less unconsciously. Of course the reverse holds true if the subject of our report is someone we dislike. This isn't dishonesty; as we mentioned earlier, it's just human nature to see mostly good in people we like or love and to perceive shortcomings in those we don't care for.

If we do have suspicions about a source's objectivity, accuracy, or veracity (truthfulness), the proper response is not to *reject* what he or she says *as false.* That would be overreacting, and is a mistake in reasoning (a fallacy). We shall discuss this in more detail in Chapter 6. The appropriate response to concerns about the objectivity, accuracy, or veracity of a source is to *suspend or reserve judgment* on what the source says.

As to a source's knowledge, just as you cannot tell merely by looking at someone whether he or she is speaking truthfully, objectively, and accurately, you can't judge his or her *knowledge* or *expertise* by looking at mere surface features. A British-sounding scientist may appear more knowledgeable than a scientist who speaks, say, with a Texas drawl, but a person's accent, height, gender, ethnicity, or clothing doesn't have much to do with a person's knowledge. In the municipal park in our town it is difficult to distinguish the people who teach at the university from the people who live in the park, based on physical appearance.

So then how do you judge a person's expertise? Education and experience are often the most important factors, followed by accomplishments, reputation, and position, in no particular order. It is not always easy to evaluate the credentials of an **expert,** and credentials vary considerably from one field to another. Still, there are some useful guidelines worth mentioning.

Education includes but is not strictly limited to formal education—the possession of degrees from established institutions of learning. (Some "doctors" of this and that received their diplomas from mail-order houses that advertise on matchbook covers. The title "doctor" is not automatically a qualification.)

A Fish Story

Randy Fite of Richards, Texas, boated three bass totaling 22 pounds, 2 ounces Wednesday to take the first-day lead at the Big K-mart BASSMaster Top 150 on Lake Champlain near Burlington, Vt. Shawn Penn of Benton, Ky., is second with 20-15. Rick Lillegard of Atkinson, N.H., had the biggest catch, a 6-pound, 4-ounce largemouth.

—USA Today, 9/16/99

We don't think so. Careful reading and a little arithmetic show that this story contains either a typographical error or something even worse, because it can't be true as it stands. Do you see why?

Experience—both the kind and the amount—is an important factor in expertise. Experience is important if it is relevant to the issue at hand, but the mere fact that someone has been on the job for a long time does not automatically make him or her good at it.

Accomplishments are an important indicator of someone's expertise but, once again, only when those accomplishments are directly related to the question at hand. A Nobel Prize winner in physics is not necessarily qualified to speak publicly about toy safety, public school education (even in science), or nuclear proliferation. The last issue may involve physics, it's true, but the political issues are the crucial ones, and they are not taught in physics labs.

A person's reputation always exists only among a particular contingent of people. You may have a strong reputation as a pool player at your local billiards emporium, but that doesn't necessarily put you in the same league as Minnesota Fats. Your friend may consider his friend Mr. Klein the greatest living expert on some particular subject, and he may be right. But you must ask yourself if your friend is in a position to evaluate Mr. Klein's credentials. Most of us have met people who were recommended as experts in some field but who turned out to know little more about that field than we ourselves knew. (Presumably in such cases those doing the recommending knew even less about the subject, or they would not have been so quickly impressed.) By and large, the kind of reputation that counts most is the one a person has among other experts in his or her field of endeavor.

The positions people hold provide an indication of how well *somebody* thinks of them. The director of an important scientific laboratory, the head of an academic department at Harvard, the author of a work consulted by other experts—in each case the position itself is substantial evidence that the individual's opinion on a relevant subject warrants serious attention.

But expertise can be bought. Recall that the last part of our principle cautions us against sources who may be biased on the subject of whatever claim we may be considering. Sometimes a person's position is an indication

Sins of Omission

The Israeli army on Monday released a Palestinian journalist employed by the Reuters news wire, five days after his arrest in the Gaza Strip, the British news agency said. Reuters photographer, Suhaib Jadallah Salem, 22, was detained on May 22 near the southern Gaza Strip border town of Rafah, from which he was planning to cross into Egypt.

—Agence France-Presse, May 27

IDF troops arrested a Reuters photographer in the Gaza Strip last Wednesday, for what military sources said were his links to terror activities. Suhaib Jadallah Salem, 22, who was intercepted while traveling to Rafah, at the southern end of the Strip, was in possession of a hand grenade when he was seized, military sources said.

—Ha'aretz, May 26

If the detail provided at the end of the second version of the story is true, then the first story creates a huge distortion by leaving it out. In either case, one or the other of these stories is extremely misleading.

From the *New Republic,* June 10, 2002, p. 9

of what his or her opinion, expert or not, is likely to be. The opinion of a lawyer retained by the National Rifle Association, offered at a hearing on firearms and urban violence, should be scrutinized much more carefully (or at least viewed with more skepticism) than that of a witness from an independent firm or agency that has no stake in the outcome of the hearings. It is too easy to lose objectivity where one's interests and concerns are at stake, even if one is *trying* to be objective.

Experts sometimes disagree, especially when the issue is complicated and many different interests are at stake. In these cases, a critical thinker is obliged to suspend judgment about which expert to endorse, unless one expert clearly represents a majority viewpoint among experts in the field or unless one expert can be established as more authoritative or less biased than the others.

Of course, majority opinions sometimes turn out to be incorrect, and even the most authoritative experts occasionally make mistakes. Thus, a claim that you accept because it represents the majority viewpoint or comes from the most authoritative expert may turn out to be thoroughly wrong. Nevertheless, take heart: At the time, you were rationally justified in accepting the majority viewpoint as the most authoritative claim. The reasonable position is one that agrees with the most authoritative opinion but allows for enough open-mindedness to change if the evidence changes.

Finally, we sometimes make the mistake of thinking that whatever qualifies someone as an expert in one field automatically qualifies that

You ain't goin' nowhere . . . son. You ought to go back to driving a truck.

—JIM DENNY, Grand Ole Opry manager, firing Elvis Presley after one performance

Blonds Have Last Laugh

It's unlikely that there was a hair of truth in a report that apparently fell into the category "too good to check."

[Recently] several British newspapers reported that the World Health Organization had found in a study that blonds would become extinct within 200 years, because blondness is a recessive gene that was dying out. The reports were repeated Friday by anchors for the ABC News program *Good Morning America,* and on Saturday by CNN.

There was only one problem, the health organization said in a statement this week: It had never reported that blonds would become extinct, and it had never done a study on the subject.

"WHO has no knowledge of how these news reports originated," the organization, a Geneva-based agency of the United Nations, announced, "but we would like to stress that we have no opinion on the future existence of blonds."

All the news reports, in Britain and the United States, cited a study from the World Health Organization—"a blondeshell study," as the *Daily Star* of London put it. But none reported any scientific details from the study or the names of the scientists who conducted it.

The British accounts were replete with the views of bleached blonds who said hairdressers would never allow blondness to become extinct, and doctors who said that rare genes would pop up to keep natural blonds from becoming an endangered species.

The big networks can be as gullible as everyone else.

From a story by Lawrence Altman in the *New York Times,* October 3, 2002.

person in other areas. Many people seem to think, for example, that business CEOs are automatically experts in economics or public policy. But even if the intelligence and skill required to become an expert in one field could enable someone to become an expert in any field—a doubtful assumption—possessing the ability to become an expert is entirely different from actually being an expert. Thus, claims put forth by experts about subjects outside their fields are not automatically more acceptable than claims put forth by nonexperts.

■ *The News Media*

The most common source of information about current events for many people is their friends and relatives, but for most of us, newspapers, newsmagazines, and the electronic media (radio, TV, and the Internet) are just as important. The Internet aside, newspapers offer the broadest coverage of general news, and radio and TV offer the most severely edited and least detailed (with the exception of extended-coverage programs and Public Broadcasting System news shows). Newsmagazines fall somewhere in the middle, although they can offer extended coverage in feature stories.

News reports, especially those that appear in major metropolitan newspapers (tabloids excepted), national newsmagazines, and television and radio news programs are generally credible sources of information. (The

Democrats have to overcome a new reality: conservative bias in the media.

—*Time* magazine, commenting on obstacles the Democratic Party faces in the 2004 election same holds true of the Internet versions of these sources.) These remarks, however, are subject to serious qualification, as we note below.

On the surface, talk radio seems to offer a wealth of information not available in news reports from conventional sources. But much of the information is based on rumor, hearsay, and gossip from heavily biased sources, and it is difficult or impossible to determine which items, if any, are legitimate. A further defect in talk radio as a source of news is that the information is almost always presented from—and colored by—a political perspective. At the same time, many talk radio hosts do scour traditional legitimate news sources for information relevant to their political agenda; and to the extent they document the source, they provide listeners with many interesting and important facts. Internet chat rooms and Web pages (excluding Web pages from major metropolitan newspapers, national newsmagazines, television networks, universities, and other reliable sources) are virtually worthless as sources of news. We'll discuss the Internet in more detail in a moment.

The breadth of coverage from major media news sources is restricted by space, by their audience's interests, and by the concerns of advertisers, pressure groups, and government officials. The accessibility of reliable reports also restricts coverage because governments, corporations, and individuals often simply withhold information.

The location, structure, and headline of a news story in both print and electronic media can be misleading about what is important or essential in the story. The selective presentation of facts is a widely used approach to persuasion in our society, not just by groups with their own agendas but by the supposedly objective news media. There is no guarantee that the media are giving us "the truth, the whole truth, and nothing but the truth." The news they present is subject to shaping by the conscious and unconscious per-

Because amazing feats are entertaining, the media often plays up amazing events for all (or more than) they are worth, distorts many not-so-amazing events to make them appear extraordinary, and sometimes even passes on complete fabrications from unreliable sources.

—THOMAS GILOVICH, *How We Know What Isn't So*, p. 100)

"*Those are the headlines, and we'll be back in a moment to blow them out of proportion.*"

spectives and purposes of publishers, editors, and owners as well as the groups mentioned above. There are several reasons for this state of affairs, and we'll look at some of the most important ones in the sections that follow.

■ Reporting the News

The popular notion of the hardworking investigative reporter who ferrets out facts, tracks down elusive sources, and badgers people for inside information is largely a creation of the moviemakers. No news service can afford to devote more than a small portion of its resources to real investigative reporting. Occasionally, this kind of reporting pays off handsomely, as was the case with Bob Woodward and Carl Bernstein's reporting of the Watergate affair in the early 1970s. The *Washington Post* won awards and sold newspapers at a remarkable rate as a result of that series of articles. But such cases are relatively rare. The great bulk of news is *given* to reporters, not dug up after weeks or days or even hours of investigation. Press conferences and press releases are the standard means of getting news from both government and private industry into the mass media. And because spokespeople in neither government nor industry are especially stupid or self-destructive, they tend to produce news items that they and the people they represent *want* to see in the media. Further, because reporters depend on sources in governmental and private institutions to pass items along, reporters who offend those sources are not likely to have them very long. A remarkable example of this interrelationship occurred over a half century ago. Walter Duranty won a Pulitzer Prize for his reporting on the Soviet Union, including his prediction that Josef Stalin would rise to power. According to Eric Newton, in *Crusaders, Scoundrels, Journalists,* "A year later, in a special report in which

Frank & Ernest reprinted by permission of Newspaper Enterprises Association, Inc.

he purposely lied, he denied the existence of a government-engineered fam-
ine that the dictator used to kill 9 million people. He wrote the story to preserve his reputation as a reporter and his access to Soviet officials."

It is important to remember that the news media in this country are
private businesses. This situation has both good and bad sides. The good
side is that the media are independent of the government, thus making it
very difficult for government officials to dictate exactly what gets printed
or broadcast. The bad side is that the media, as businesses, have to do whatever it takes to make a profit, even if this affects which items make the
headlines and which are left out entirely.

Aside from the sources of news, the media must therefore be careful
not to overly offend two other powerful constituencies: their advertisers
and their audiences. The threat of canceled advertising is difficult to ignore
when the great bulk of a business's revenues comes from advertising. (This
is true of newspapers, which receive more money from advertisers than
from those of us who purchase the papers, and of the electronic media as
well.) The other constituency, the news-reading and news-watching public,
has its own unfortunate effects on the quality of the news that is generally
available. The most important of these is the oversimplification of the information presented. Too many people would be bored by a competent explanation of the federal budget deficit or the latest crisis in the Middle East
to allow the media to offer such accounts often or in much detail without
fearing the loss of their audiences. And, in this context at least, it is not important whether American audiences are unwilling to pay attention to com-

plicated issues or whether they are simply unable to understand them. (In other contexts, however, this distinction is highly significant. Between one-third and one-half of adults in the United States would probably be unable to read and understand the page you're now reading.) Whatever the reason, it is clear that complicated issues are lost on a large percentage of American adults.

Notice the level at which television commercials and political advertisements are pitched. These products are made by highly skilled professionals, who are aware that the projection of an "image" for a candidate or a product goes much further than the coverage of facts and issues. A television network that devotes too much of its prime time to complex social issues in a nonsensationalist way will soon be looking for a new vice president for programming.

■ *Who Listens to the News?*

We come now to another problem with relying on the mass media for a real understanding of events. Much of what goes on in the world, including many of the most important events, is not only complicated but also not

Springfield, Ore., Pearl, Miss., West Paducah, Ky., Littleton, Colo., Jonesboro, Ark., Edinboro, Pa. School killings certainly appear to be on the increase. Actually, it only seems they are. According to data from the Centers for Disease Control and Prevention, school killings are actually down from the levels reached earlier in the decade and are about what they were in the 1970s.

Saran Wrap and Cancer

Did you know that food covered with Saran Wrap and then microwaved causes cancer? That's according to a study done by researchers at the University of California, Davis and reported on the Web. Except that nobody at UC Davis conducted such research. The moral: Yes, Internet information from reliable sources like universities is credible, but anyone can pretend to be a university and say anything he or she feels like. You need to stick to the official Web pages of credible sources.

And go ahead and nuke your food in Saran Wrap.

very exciting. If a television station advertised that its late news would offer extended coverage of several South American countries' threats to default on loans from United States banks, a considerable part of its audience would either go to bed early or watch reruns on another channel. And they would do so even though loans to other countries have an enormous impact upon the American economy. (How many Americans could explain the connection between Asia recovering from an economic crisis and the danger of a depressed stock market in the United States?) This story is apt to get only fifteen seconds so as not to shortchange the story of the shoot-out at the local convenience store, accompanied by some exciting film. The point is that sensational, unusual, and easily understood subjects can be counted on to receive more attention than the unexciting, the usual, and the complicated, even if the latter are much more important in the long run.

The same kind of mass preference holds for people as well as issues and events. The number of movie stars and celebrities interviewed on talk shows is wildly disproportionate to the effect these individuals have on most of our lives. But they are entertaining in ways that, say, the chairman of the Federal Reserve Board is not.

Although there is nothing wrong with entertainment and our desire to be entertained, the overindulgence of our desire to be entertained comes at the expense of our need to be informed. In the process, we become passive citizens rather than active participants in society. If we count on the media to indulge us, they will give us what we pay for.

A couple of final notes on the news media: Things have changed a lot since we wrote about this topic in the early editions of this book. Competition for readers and viewers has become fierce, and the tactics the media employ to attract an audience have begun to endanger the very idea of an independent, honest, straightforward press. Television in particular has developed new means of coming up with sensational stories, stories that may not have happened at all but for the presence of the television cameras. Here's an example of a nonstory: A film crew in Orlando, Florida, once appeared on the street in front of a house where a dead woman had been discovered. The reporter went on for some time about how police were "dumbfounded" about the cause of death of the woman inside the house and had

When the decision was made at Time *magazine to darken a cover picture of O. J. Simpson, only the lone nonwhite person in the room objected.*

—Press critic JEFF COHEN, commenting on how the lack of diversity on media staffs can affect the content of the product "put a clamp" on information about the scene. Although the story got several minutes of high-energy coverage, it turned out the woman was in her late sixties and had simply died in bed from a heart attack.

There are some programs that *look* like investigative programs but aren't. Staged dramas like *The X-Files* usually push a point of view that is more gullible than investigative. The large number of cable channels, some with twenty-four hours of news to fill, often have to scrape pretty hard to find anything newsworthy; and when nothing turns up, they may be forced to make something up—or at least make a story out of something that isn't really worth reporting.

The numerous commentators these days are paid to attract attention, not to provide factual information or insight. Thus we see a lot of "in your face" or "scream" television, where people from different parts of the political spectrum spend a half hour yelling at each other and somehow we're supposed to be better informed afterward. Our advice is to be even more skeptical of what you see on television news now than ever before; and there never was reason for too much confidence.

■ *The Internet*

An important source of information is the Internet—that amalgamation of electronic lines and connections that allows nearly anyone with a computer and a modem to link up with nearly any other similarly equipped person on the planet. Although the Internet offers great benefits, the information it provides must be evaluated with even *more* caution than information from the print media, radio, or television.

There are basically two kinds of information sources on the Internet. The first consists of commercial and institutional sources; the second, of individual and group sites on the World Wide Web. In the first category we include sources like the Lexis-Nexis facility, as well as the online services provided by newsmagazines, large electronic news organizations, and government institutions. The second category includes everything else you'll find on the Web—an amazing assortment of good information, entertainment of widely varying quality, hot tips, advertisements, come-ons, fraudulent offers, outright lies, and even the opportunity to meet the person of your dreams (or your nightmares)! (Rush Limbaugh met his current wife online, and they corresponded via e-mail for a time before meeting in person. On the other hand, in October 1996, a North Carolina man described online to a Pennsylvania woman how, if she would visit him, he would sexually torture her and then kill her. She went, and he did.)

Just as the fact that a claim appears in print or on television doesn't make it true, so it is for claims you run across online. Keep in mind that the information you get from a source is only as good as that source. The Lexis-Nexis information collection is an excellent asset for medium-depth investigation of a topic; it includes information gathered from a wide range of print sources, especially newspapers and magazines, with special collections in areas like the law. But the editorials you turn up there are no more likely to be accurate, fair-minded, or objective than the ones you read in the newspapers—which is where they first appeared anyhow. Remember also that *any* individual or group can put up a Web site. And they can say *anything* they want to on it. You have about as much reason to believe the claims you find on such sites as you would if they came from any other stranger, except you can't look this one in the eye.

FREE MONEY! If you have an e-mail account, you've probably heard from somebody in Nigeria, South Africa, or Lagos who is trying to get millions of dollars out of the country and wants your help. You will get a very large sum for furnishing your bank account number so they can temporarily put the funds there. Of course the only transfer that occurs is *out* of your account.

It takes only one in a million gullible takers to make this scheme profitable.

Advertising

> Advertising [is] the science of arresting the human intelligence long enough to get money from it.
>
> —*Stephen Leacock*

If there is anything in modern society that truly puts our sense of what is credible to the test, it's advertising. As we hope you'll agree after reading this section, skepticism is almost always the best policy when considering any kind of advertising or promotion.

Ads are used to sell many products other than toasters, television sets, and toilet tissue. They can encourage us to vote for a candidate, agree with a political proposal, take a tour, give up a bad habit, or join the army. They can also be used to make announcements (for instance, about job openings, lectures, concerts, or the recall of defective automobiles) or to create favorable climates of opinion (for example, toward labor unions or offshore oil drilling).

Advertising firms understand our fears and desires at least as well as we understand them ourselves, and they have at their disposal the expertise to exploit them.* Such firms employ trained psychologists and some of the world's most creative artists and use the most sophisticated and well-researched theories about the motivation of human behavior. Maybe most important, they can afford to spend whatever is necessary to get each detail of an advertisement exactly right. (On a per-minute basis, television ads are the most expensively produced pieces that appear on your tube.) A good ad is a work of art, a masterful blend of word and image often composed in accordance with the exacting standards of artistic and scientific genius (some ads, of course, are just plain silly). Can untrained laypeople even hope to evaluate such psychological and artistic masterpieces intelligently?

Fortunately, it is not necessary to understand the deep psychology of an advertisement to evaluate it in the way that's most important to us. When confronted with an ad, we should ask simply: Does this ad give us a good reason to buy this product? And the answer, in general terms, can be simply put: Because the only good reason to buy anything in the first place is to improve our lives, the ad justifies a purchase only if it establishes that we'd be better off with the product than without it (or that we'd be better off with the product than with the money we would trade for it).

However, do we always know when we'll be better off with a product than without it? Do we really want, or need, a bagel splitter or an exercise bike? Do people even recognize "better taste" in a cigarette? Advertisers spend vast sums creating within us new desires and fears—and hence a need to improve our lives by satisfying those desires or eliminating those fears through the purchase of advertised products. They are often successful, and we find ourselves needing something we might not have known existed before. That others can instill in us through word and image, a desire for something we did not previously desire may be a lamentable fact, but it *is* clearly a fact. Still, *we* decide what would make us better off, and *we* decide to part with our money. So it is only with reference to what in *our* view would make life better for us that we properly evaluate advertisements.

There are basically two kinds of ads: those that offer reasons and those that do not. Those that offer reasons for buying the advertised product always promise that certain hopes will be satisfied, certain needs met, or certain fears eliminated. (You'll be more accepted, have a better image, be a better parent, and so on.)

People watching a sexual program are thinking about sex, not soda pop. Violence and sex elicit very strong emotions and can interfere with memory for other things.

—Brad Bushman of Iowa State University, whose research indicated that people tend to forget the names of sponsors of violent or sexual TV shows (reported by Ellen Goodman)

---

*For an excellent treatment of this and related subjects, we recommend *Age of Propaganda: The Everyday Use and Abuse of Persuasion,* rev. ed., by Anthony R. Pratkanis and Elliot Aronson (New York: W. H. Freeman and Co., 1998).

FTC: No Miracles in Weight Loss

Marketing claims are frequently false or misleading, a study finds.

WASHINGTON — As an overweight child, Lynn McAfee scanned the ads in her mother's magazines looking for hope in the before-and-after photos of people made thin by seemingly miraculous products.

"These smiling, thin people used to be fat like me," said McAfee, 53, an advocate for overweight people. "But all I got out of those boxes and envelopes I bought in my childhood and adolescence was the sinking feeling that becoming thin like those people in the ads was hopeless."

Many people share her frustration. In a first-of-its-kind study, the Federal Trade Commission found that 55 percent of weight-loss ads make claims that are certainly false or misleading.

"There is no miracle pill that will lead to weight loss," Surgeon General Richard Carmona said at a news conference [recently] announcing the results. "Achieving and maintaining a healthy weight requires a lifelong commitment to healthful eating and adequate physical activity." . . .

FTC Chairman Timothy Muris said his agency has increased its efforts against deceptive weight-loss marketing and has prosecuted 93 fraud cases since 1990. He said the FTC will hold a public workshop on the problem in November.

Muris said the agency filed charges this month against Bio Lab, a Canadian company based in Laval, Quebec, that sells its "Quick Slim" weight-loss product in the United States. The FTC said the product, which contains a substance taken from apples, does not live up to promotions such as: "Lose up to 2 pounds daily without diet or exercise."

The company did not immediately return calls seeking comment Tuesday.

In May, the FTC sued the marketers of three electronic exercise belts—the AB Energizer, Ab Tronic and Fast Abs—accusing them of making misleading claims. Television ads showed people strapping the gadgets on their waists in search of "washboard" abs. Court injunctions took most of the ads off the air, and the cases are pending.

The FTC conducted the advertising study with the Partnership for Healthy Weight Management, a coalition that includes scientists, government agencies and legitimate weight-loss companies.

By David Ho
ASSOCIATED PRESS

"Doctor recommended."

This ambiguous ad slogan creates an illusion that many doctors, or doctors in general, recommend the product. However, a recommendation from a single doctor is all it takes to make the statement true.

Those ads that do not rely on reasons fall mainly into three categories: (1) those that bring out pleasurable *feelings* in us (e.g., through humor, glad tidings, pretty images, beautiful music, heartwarming scenes); (2) those that depict the product being used or endorsed by *people* we admire or think of ourselves as being like (sometimes these people are depicted by actors, sometimes not); and (3) those that depict the product being used in *situations* in which we would like to find ourselves. Of course, some ads go all out and incorporate elements from all three categories—and for good measure also state a reason or two why we should buy the advertised product.

Buying a product (which includes joining a group, deciding how to vote, and so forth) on the basis of reasonless ads is, with one minor exception that we'll explain shortly, never justified. Such ads tell you only that the product exists and what it looks like (and sometimes where it is available and how much it costs); if an ad tells you much more than this, then it begins to qualify as an ad that gives reasons for buying the product. Reasonless ads do tell us what the advertisers think of our values and sense of

Celebrity Endorsements We Can Live With

One of America's greatest humorists was once asked to write an endorsement for a certain brand of piano. Because he would not speak on behalf of a product he had not tried, he wrote the following:

Dear Sirs,
I guess your pianos are the best I have ever leaned against.
Yours truly,
Will Rogers

Opera singer Giovanni Martinelli, when questioned by a reporter about cigarette smoking, replied, "Tobacco, cigarettes, bah! I would not think of it!" The reporter reminded Martinelli that he had appeared in an advertisement for a particular brand of cigarette and had said that those cigarettes did not irritate his throat. "Yes, yes, of course I gave that endorsement," Martinelli said impatiently. "How could they irritate my throat? I have never smoked."

humor (not always a pleasant thing to notice, given that they have us pegged so well), but this information is irrelevant to the question of whether we should buy the product.

Ads that submit reasons for buying the product might have been treated in Part 3 of this book, which is devoted to arguments. However, so little need be said about argumentative ads that we will discuss them here. Such "promise ads," as they have been called, usually tell us more than that a certain product exists—but not much more. The promise, with rare exception, comes with no guarantees and is usually extremely vague (Gilbey's gin promises "more gin taste," Kleenex is "softer").

Such ads are a source of information about what the *sellers* of the product are willing to claim about what the product will do, how well it will do it, how it works, what it contains, how well it compares with similar products, and how much more wonderful your life will be once you've got one. However, to make an informed decision on a purchase, you almost always need to know more than the seller is willing to claim, particularly because no sellers will tell you what's wrong with their products or what's right with those of their competitors.

Further, the claims of advertisers are notorious for not only being vague but also for being ambiguous, misleading, exaggerated, and sometimes just plain false. Even if a product existed that was so good that an honest, unexaggerated, and fair description of it would justify our buying it without considering competing items (or other reports on the same item), and even if an advertisement for this product consisted of just such a description, we would still not be justified in purchasing the product on the basis of that advertisement alone. For we would be unable to tell, simply by looking at the

We are professional grade.

Meaningless but catchy slogan for GMC trucks. (We are professional grade, too.)

"Truth" vs. Cigarette Makers

Philip Morris "uncool" smoking ads may actually encourage teen smokers.

Michael Szymanczyk, chairman of Philip Morris USA, said the other day: "If you're a decent person, you don't want kids to smoke. You don't want them to do something that's going to harm them. In order for this business to exist successfully in this society, we had to accept at least some responsibility for deterring kids from smoking."

Since the sincerity of Philip Morris is forever in ashes, Szymanczyk actually meant: If you want to be seen as a decent business, you must create the illusion that you don't want to harm kids.

As Szymanczyk blathers, another barrage of evidence shows that big tobacco, whose very success depends on hiding cancer under the cowboy hats of macho men and the petite dresses of liberated women and using the imagery of mountain vistas and calm, endless ocean to dissipate fears of premature departure to eternity has—shocking!—come up mysteriously lame in deterring kids from smoking.

Researchers from the American Legacy Foundation, the public health foundation established by the 1998 tobacco settlement with the states, published a study in this month's *American Journal of Public Health* indicating that its youth antismoking campaign is far more effective at creating negative attitudes toward smoking than the efforts of Philip Morris. In some ways, the Philip Morris campaign is creating more-positive attitudes toward smoking.

The study surveyed the attitudes of more than 6,000 minors, ages 12 to 17. The American Legacy "truth" ad campaign included images of young people placing 1,200 body bags at the door of a cigarette company office building and cowboys pulling horses with body bags over the saddle. The Philip Morris "Think, don't smoke" campaign had teenagers from the beach to the basketball court saying why they do not use cigarettes.

Philip Morris had teens talking about cigarettes making you uncool, ugly or unathletic. But the commercials steered very wide from the graveyard. There were no stark, body-bag connections of cigarettes to death.

According to the American Legacy study, a majority of teenagers were aware of both campaigns, with 66 percent aware of "Think, don't smoke" and 75 percent aware of "truth." While the "truth" campaign made youth 163 percent more likely to agree that "taking a stand against smoking is important to me," the Philip Morris campaign made youth less than 10 percent more likely to agree.

While the "truth" campaign resulted in a 35 percent increase in youths agreeing that cigarette companies "deny that cigarettes cause disease," the Philip Morris campaign actually resulted in a 24 percent *decrease* in agreement. While the "truth" campaign nearly doubled the odds that youths would say "cigarette companies lie," the Philip Morris campaign resulted in virtually no change.

While the "truth" campaign resulted in no change in teens wanting to see cigarette companies go out of business, the Philip Morris campaign resulted in a 21 percent *decrease* in teens wanting big tobacco to disappear.

The authors of the American Legacy study concluded that "exposure to 'Think, don't smoke' engendered more favorable feelings toward the tobacco industry than we found among those not exposed to 'Think, don't smoke.'"

The authors said the Philip Morris campaign, with its slick studio productions built on the guaranteed failure of telling adolescents that cigarettes are "uncool" for them at the same time the company sells them with glee and glitter all over the earth, is actually meant "to buy respectability and not to prevent youth smoking."

Philip Morris boasts on its Web page that its "Think, don't smoke" campaign is working and is "measurable."

Of course, Philip Morris has done nothing so measurable as to be worthy of a medical or public health journal.

By Derrick Z. Jackson

From an op-ed piece distributed by the New York Times News Service.

advertisement, that it was uninflated, honest, fair, and not misleading. Our suspicions about advertising in general should undercut our willingness to believe in the honesty of any particular advertisement.

Thus, even advertisements that present reasons for buying an item do not by themselves justify our purchase of the item. Sometimes, of course, an advertisement can provide you with information that can clinch your decision to make a purchase. Sometimes the mere existence, availability, or affordability of a product—all information that an ad can convey—is all you need to make a decision to buy. But if the purchase is justifiable, you must have some reasons apart from those offered in the ad for making it. If, for some reason, you already know that you want or need and can afford a car with an electric motor, then an ad that informs you that a firm has begun marketing such a thing would supply you with the information you need to buy one. If you can already justify purchasing a particular brand of microwave oven but cannot find one anywhere in town, then an advertisement informing you that the local department store stocks them can clinch your decision to make the purchase.

For people on whom good fortune has smiled, those who don't care what kind of whatsit they buy, or those to whom mistaken purchases simply don't matter, all that is important is knowing that a product is available. Most of us, however, need more information than ads provide to make reasoned purchasing decisions. Of course, we all occasionally make purchases solely on the basis of advertisements, and sometimes we don't come to regret them. In such cases, though, the happy result is due as much to good luck as to the ad.

Recap

Claims lack credibility to the extent they conflict with our observations or experience or our background information, or come from sources that lack credibility. The less initial plausibility a claim has, the more extraordinary it seems, and the less it fits with our background information, the more suspicious we should be.

Doubts about sources generally fall into two categories, doubts about the source's knowledge or expertise and doubts about the source's veracity, objectivity, and accuracy. We can form reasonably reliable judgments about a person's knowledge by considering his or her education, experience, accomplishments, reputation, and position. Claims made by experts, those with special knowledge in a subject, are the most reliable, but the claims must pertain to the area of expertise and not conflict with claims made by other experts in the same area.

Major metropolitan newspapers, national newsmagazines, and network news shows are generally credible sources of news, but it is necessary to keep an open mind about what we learn from them. Skepticism is even more appropriate when we obtain information from unknown Internet sources or talk radio.

Advertising assaults us at every turn, attempting to sell us goods, services, beliefs, and attitudes. Because substantial talent and resources are employed in this effort, we need to ask ourselves constantly whether the products in question will really make the differences in our lives that their advertising claims or hints they will make. Advertisers are more concerned with selling you something than with improving your life.

Exercises

Exercise 3-1

1. The text points out that physical conditions around us can affect our observations. List at least four such conditions.

2. Our own mental state can affect our observations as well. Describe at least three of the ways this can happen, as mentioned in the text.

3. According to the text, there are two ways credibility should enter into our evaluation of a claim. What are they?

4. A claim lacks inherent credibility, according to the text, when it conflicts with what?

5. Our most reliable source of information about the world is ~~newspapers~~

6. The reliability of our observations is not better than the reliability of _____.

Exercise 3-2

List as many irrelevant factors as you can think of that people often mistake for signs of a person's truthfulness (for example, the firmness of a handshake).

Exercise 3-3

List as many irrelevant factors as you can think of that people often mistake for signs of expertise on the part of an individual (for example, appearing self-confident).

Exercise 3-4

Expertise doesn't transfer automatically from one field to another: Being an expert in one does not automatically qualify one as an expert (or even as competent) in other areas. Is it the same with dishonesty? Many people think dishonesty does transfer, that being dishonest in one area automatically discredits that person in all areas. For example, when Bill Clinton lied about having sexual encounters with his intern, some said he couldn't be trusted about anything.

If someone is known to have been dishonest about one thing, should we automatically be suspicious of his honesty regarding other things? Discuss.

Exercise 3-5

▲ In your judgment, are any of these claims less credible than others? Discuss your opinions with others in the class to see if any interesting differences in background information emerge.

1. They've taught crows how to play poker.
2. The center of Earth consists of water.
3. Ray Charles is just faking his blindness.
4. The car manufacturers already can build cars that get over 100 miles per gallon; they just won't do it because they're in cahoots with the oil industry.
5. If you force yourself to go for five days and nights without any sleep, you'll be able to get by on less than five hours of sleep a night for the rest of your life.
6. It is possible to read other people's minds through mental telepathy.
7. A diet of mushrooms and pecans supplies all necessary nutrients and will help you lose weight. Scientists don't understand why.
8. Somewhere on the planet is a person who looks exactly like you.
9. The combined wealth of the world's 225 richest people equals the total annual income of the poorest 2.5 billion people, which is nearly half the world's total population.
10. George W. Bush arranged to have the World Trade Center attacked so he could invade Afghanistan. He wants to build an oil pipeline across Afghanistan.
11. Daddy longlegs are the world's most poisonous spider, but their mouths are too small to bite.
12. Static electricity from your body can cause your gas tank to explode if you slide across your seat while fueling and then touch the gas nozzle.
13. Japanese scientists have created a device that measures the tone of a dog's bark to determine what the dog's mood is.

Exercise 3-6

Find a Web page that makes claims of dubious credibility. If your instructor's classroom has the technology, he or she will project the page for class examination.

Exercise 3-7 _____

In groups, decide which is the best answer to each question. Compare your answers with those of other groups and your instructor.

1. "SPACE ALIEN GRAVEYARD FOUND! Scientists who found an extraterrestrial cemetery in central Africa say the graveyard is at least 500 years old! 'There must be 200 bodies buried there and not a single one of them is human,' Dr. Hugo Schild, the Swiss anthropologist, told reporters." What is the appropriate reaction to this report in the *Weekly World News*?
   a. It's probably true.
   b. It almost certainly is true.
   c. We really need more information to form any judgment at all.
   d. None of these.

2. Is Elvis really dead? Howie thinks not. Reason: He knows three people who claim to have seen Elvis recently. They are certain that it is not a mere Elvis look-alike they have seen. Howie reasons that, since he has absolutely no reason to think the three would lie to him, they must be telling the truth. Elvis must really be alive, he concludes!
   Is Howie's reasoning sound? Explain.

3. VOICE ON TELEPHONE: Mr. Roberts, this is AT&T calling. Have you recently placed several long-distance calls to Lisbon, Portugal?
   MR. ROBERTS: Why, no . . .
   VOICE: This is what we expected. Mr. Roberts, I'm sorry to report that apparently someone has been using your calling card number. However, we are prepared to give you a new number, effective immediately, at no charge to you.
   MR. ROBERTS: Well, fine, I guess . . .
   VOICE: Again let me emphasize that there will be no charge for this service. Now, for authorization, just to make sure that we are calling Mr. Roberts, Mr. Roberts, please state the last four digits of your calling card number, your PIN number, please.
   Question: What should Mr. Roberts, as a critical thinker, do?

4. On Thanksgiving Day 1990, an image said by some to resemble the Virgin Mary was observed in a stained glass window of St. Dominic's Church in Colfax, California. A physicist asked to investigate said the image was caused by sunlight shining through the window and reflecting from a newly installed hanging light fixture. Others said the image was a miracle. Whose explanation is more likely true?
   a. The physicist's
   b. The others'
   c. More information is needed before we can decide which explanation is more likely.

5. It is late at night around the campfire when the campers hear the awful grunting noises in the woods around. They run for their lives! Two campers, after returning the next day, tell others they found huge footprints around

the campfire. They are convinced they were attacked by Bigfoot. Which explanation is more likely true?

a. The campers heard Bigfoot.

b. The campers heard some animal and are pushing the Bigfoot explanation to avoid being thought of as chickens, or are just making the story up for unknown reasons.

c. Given this information, we can't tell which explanation is more likely.

6. Megan's aunt says she saw a flying saucer. "I don't tell people about this," Auntie says, "because they'll think I'm making it up. But this really happened. I saw this strange light, and this, well, it wasn't a saucer, exactly, but it was round and big, and it came down and hovered just over my back fence, and my two dogs began whimpering. And then it just, whoosh! It just vanished."

   Megan knows her aunt, and Megan knows she doesn't make up stories.

a. She should believe her aunt saw a flying saucer.

b. She should believe her aunt was making the story up.

c. She should believe that her aunt may well have had some unusual experience, but it was probably not a visitation by extraterrestrial beings.

7. According to Dr. Edith Fiore, author of *The Unquiet Dead*, many of your personal problems are really the miseries of a dead soul who has possessed you sometime during your life. "Many people are possessed by earthbound spirits. These are people who have lived and died, but did not go into the afterworld at death. Instead they stayed on Earth and remained just like they were before death, with the fears, pains, weaknesses and other problems that they had when they were alive." She estimates that about 80 percent of her more than 1,000 patients are suffering from the problems brought on by being possessed by spirits of the dead. To tell if you are among the possessed, she advises that you look for such telltale symptoms as low energy levels, character shifts or mood swings, memory problems, poor concentration, weight gain with no obvious cause, and bouts of depression (especially after hospitalization). Which of these reactions is best?

a. Wow! I bet I'm possessed!

b. Well, if a doctor says it's so, it must be so.

c. If these are signs of being possessed, how come she thinks that only 80 percent of her patients are?

d. Too bad there isn't more information available, so we could form a reasonable judgment.

8.   **EOC—ENGINE OVERHAUL IN A CAN**

Developed by skilled automotive scientists after years of research and laboratory and road tests! Simply pour one can of EOC into the oil in your crankcase. EOC contains long-chain molecules and special thermoactive metallic alloys that bond with worn engine parts. NO tools needed! NO need to disassemble engine.

   Question: Reading this ad, what should you believe?

9. ANCHORAGE, Alaska (AP)—Roped to her twin sons for safety, Joni Phelps inched her way to the top of Mount McKinley. The National Park

Service says Phelps, 54, apparently is the first blind woman to scale the 20,300-foot peak.

This report is

a. Probably true

b. Probably false

c. Too sketchy; more information is needed before we can judge

Exercise 3-8

Within each group of observers, are some especially credible or especially not so?

▲ 1. Judging the relative performances of the fighters in a heavyweight boxing match.
   a. the father of one of the fighters
   b. a sportswriter for *Sports Illustrated* magazine
   c. the coach of the American Olympic boxing team
   d. the referee of the fight
   e. a professor of physical education

2. You (or your family or your class) are trying to decide whether you should buy an Apple Macintosh computer or an IBM model. You might consult
   a. a friend who owns either a Macintosh or an IBM
   b. a friend who now owns one of the machines but used to own the other
   c. a dealer for either Macintosh or IBM
   d. a computer column in a big-city newspaper
   e. reviews in computer magazines

▲ 3. The Surgical Practices Committee of Grantville Hospital has documented an unusually high number of problems in connection with tonsillectomies performed by a Dr. Choker. The committee is reviewing her surgical practices. Those present during a tonsillectomy are
   a. Dr. Choker
   b. the surgical proctor from the Surgical Practices Committee
   c. an anesthesiologist
   d. a nurse
   e. a technician

4. The mechanical condition of the used car you are thinking of buying.
   a. the used-car salesperson
   b. the former owner (who we assume is different from the salesperson)
   c. the former owner's mechanic
   d. you
   e. a mechanic from an independent garage

5. A demonstration of psychokinesis (the ability to move objects at a distance by nonphysical means).
   a. a newspaper reporter
   b. a psychologist

  c. a police detective
  d. another psychic
  e. a physicist
  f. a customs agent
  g. a magician

Exercise 3-9 _____

For each of the items below, discuss the credibility and authority of each source relative to the issue in question. Whom would you trust as most reliable on the subject?

▲ 1. Issue: Is Crixivan an effective HIV/AIDS medication?
  a. *Consumer Reports*
  b. Stadtlander Drug Company (the company that makes Crixivan)
  c. the owner of your local health food store
  d. the U.S. Food and Drug Administration
  e. your local pharmacist

▲ 2. Issue: Should possession of handguns be outlawed?
  a. a police chief
  b. a representative of the National Rifle Association
  c. a U.S. senator
  d. the father of a murder victim

▲ 3. Issue: What was the original intent of the Second Amendment to the U.S. Constitution, and does it include permission for every citizen to possess handguns?
  a. a representative of the National Rifle Association
  b. a justice of the U.S. Supreme Court
  c. a Constitutional historian
  d. a U.S. senator
  e. the President of the United States

  4. Issue: Is decreasing your intake of dietary fat and cholesterol likely to reduce the level of cholesterol in your blood?
  a. *Time* magazine
  b. *Runner's World* magazine
  c. your physician
  d. the National Institutes of Health
  e. the *New England Journal of Medicine*

  5. Issue: When does a human life begin?
  a. a lawyer
  b. a physician
  c. a philosopher
  d. a minister
  e. you

Exercise 3-10

Each of these items consists of a brief biography of a real or imagined person followed by a list of topics. On the basis of the information in the biography, discuss the credibility and authority of the person described on each of the topics listed.

▲ 1. Jeff Hilgert teaches sociology at the University of Illinois and is the director of its Population Studies Center. He is a graduate of Harvard College, where he received a B.A. in 1975, and of Harvard University, which granted him a Ph.D. in economics in 1978. He taught courses in demography as an assistant professor at UCLA until 1982; then he moved to the sociology department of the University of Nebraska, where he was associate professor and then professor. From 1987 through 1989 he served as acting chief of the Population Trends and Structure Section of the United Nations Population Division. He joined the faculty at the University of Illinois in 1989. He has written books on patterns of world urbanization, the effects of cigarette smoking on international mortality, and demographic trends in India. He is president of the Population Association of America.

Topics

   a. The effects of acid rain on humans
   b. The possible beneficial effects of requiring sociology courses for all students at the University of Illinois
   c. The possible effects of nuclear war on global climate patterns
   d. The incidence of poverty among various ethnic groups in the United States
   e. The effects of the melting of glaciers on global sea levels
   f. The change in death rate for various age groups in all Third World countries between 1970 and 1990
   g. The feasibility of a laser-based nuclear defense system
   h. Voter participation among religious sects in India
   i. Whether the winters are worse in Illinois than in Nebraska

2. Tom Pierce graduated cum laude from Cornell University with a B.S. in biology in 1973. After two years in the Peace Corps, during which he worked on public health projects in Venezuela, he joined Jeffrey Ridenour, a mechanical engineer, and the pair developed a water pump and purification system that is now used in many parts of the world for both regular water supplies and emergency use in disaster-struck areas. Pierce and Ridenour formed a company to manufacture the water systems, and it prospered as they developed smaller versions of the system for private use on boats and motor homes. In 1981, Pierce bought out his partner and expanded research and development in hydraulic systems for forcing oil out of old wells. Under contract with the federal government and several oil firms, Pierce's company was a principal designer and contractor for the Alaskan oil pipeline. He is now a consultant in numerous developing countries as well as chief executive officer and chairman of the board of his own company, and he sits on the boards of directors of several other companies.

Topics

    a. The image of the United States in Latin America
    b. The long-range effects of the Cuban revolution on South America
    c. Fixing a leaky faucet
    d. Technology in Third World countries
    e. The ecological effects of the Alaskan pipeline
    f. Negotiating a contract with the federal government
    g. Careers in biology

Exercise 3-11

Watch a debate or panel discussion (e.g., a political debate, a discussion on PBS's *NewsHour with Jim Lehrer*), and decide which participant made the better case for his or her side. When the debate is over, being honest with yourself, list as many irrelevant factors as you can that you think influenced your decision.

Exercise 3-12

From what you know about the nature of each of the following claims and its source, and given your general knowledge, assess whether the claim is one you should accept, reject, or suspend judgment on due to ambiguity, insufficient documentation, vagueness, or subjectivity (e.g., "Tom Cruise is cute"). Compare your judgment with that of your instructor.

▲ 1. "Campbell Soup is hot—and some are getting burned. Just one day after the behemoth of broth reported record profits, Campbell said it would lay off 650 U.S. workers, including 175—or 11% of the work force—at its headquarters in Camden, New Jersey."

Time

  2. [The claim to evaluate is the first one in this passage.] Jackie Haskew taught paganism and devil worship in her fourth-grade classroom in Grand Saline, Texas, at least until she was pressured into resigning by parents of her students. (According to syndicated columnist Nat Hentoff, "At the town meeting on her case, a parent said firmly that she did not want her daughter to read anything that dealt with 'death, abuse, divorce, religion, or any other issue.'")

  3. "By 1893 there were only between 300 and 1,000 buffaloes remaining in the entire country. A few years later, President Theodore Roosevelt persuaded Congress to establish a number of wildlife preserves in which the remaining buffaloes could live without danger. The numbers have increased since, nearly doubling over the past 10 years to 130,000."

Clifford May, in the New York Times Magazine

  4. Lee Harvey Oswald, acting alone, was responsible for the death of President John F. Kennedy.

Conclusion of the Warren Commission on the Assassination of President Kennedy

5. "[N]ewly released documents, including the transcripts of telephone conversations recorded by President Lyndon B. Johnson in November and December 1963, provide for the first time a detailed . . . look at why and how the seven-member Warren [Commission] was put together. Those documents, along with a review of previously released material . . . describe a process designed more to control information than to elicit and expose it."

"The Truth Was Secondary," Washington Post National Weekly Edition

6. "Short-sighted developers are determined to transform Choco [a large region of northwestern Colombia] from an undisturbed natural treasure to a polluted, industrialized growth center."

Solicitation letter from the World Wildlife Fund

7. "Frantic parents tell shocked TV audience: space aliens stole our son."

Weekly World News

▲ 8. "The manufacturer of Sudafed 12-hour capsules issued a nationwide recall of the product Sunday after two people in the state of Washington who had taken the medication died of cyanide poisoning and a third became seriously ill."

Los Angeles Times

9. "In Canada, smoking in public places, trains, planes or even automobiles is now prohibited by law or by convention. The federal government has banned smoking in all its buildings."

Reuters

10. "The list of vanishing commodities in Moscow now includes not only sausage and vodka, long rationed, but also potatoes, eggs, bread, and cigarettes."

National Geographic

11. "Maps, files and compasses were hidden in Monopoly sets and smuggled into World War II German prison camps by MI-5, Britain's counter-intelligence agency, to help British prisoners escape, according to the British manufacturer of the game."

Associated Press

▲ 12. "Cats that live indoors and use a litter box can live four to five years longer."

From an advertisement for Jonny Cat litter

13. "A case reported by Borderland Sciences Research Foundation, Vista, California, tells of a man who had attended many of the meetings where a great variety of 'dead' people came and spoke through the body mechanism of Mark Probert to the group of interested persons on a great variety of subjects with questions and answers from 'both sides.' Then this man who had attended meetings while he was in a body, did what is called 'die.' Presumably he had learned 'while in the body' what he might expect at the change of awareness called death, about which organized religion seems to know little or nothing."

George Robinson, Exploring the Riddle of Reincarnation, *undated, no publisher cited*

14. "Because of cartilage that begins to accumulate after age thirty, by the time . . . [a] man is seventy his nose has grown a half inch wider and an-

other half inch longer, his earlobes have fattened, and his ears themselves have grown a quarter inch longer. Overall, his head's circumference increases a quarter inch every decade, and not because of his brain, which is shrinking. His head is fatter apparently because, unlike most other bones in the body, the skull seems to thicken with age."

John Tierney (a staff writer for Esquire)

15. "Gardenias . . . need ample warmth, ample water, and steady feeding. Though hardy to 20°F or even lower, plants fail to grow and bloom well without summer heat."

The Sunset New Western Garden Book *(a best-selling gardening reference in the West)*

16. "Exercise will make you feel fitter, but there's no good evidence that it will make you live longer."

Dr. Jordan Tobin, National Institute on Aging

17. "Your bones are still growing until you're 35."

From a national milk ad by the National Fluid Milk Processor Promotion Board

18. "*E. coli* 0157:H7 has become common enough to be the current major cause of acute kidney failure in children." [*E. coli* is a food-borne toxin originally found in the intestines of cows.]

Robin Cook, a physician-turned-novelist. This claim was made by a fictional expert on food-borne illnesses in the novel Toxin.

19. "A woman employed as a Santa Claus at a Wal-Mart in Kentucky was fired by Wal-Mart when a child pinched her breast and complained to his mother that Santa was a woman. The woman complained to store managers."

Associated Press

▲ 20. "Bill Clinton is the biological son of Jimmy Carter."

A claim alleged to have been made in a suit alleged to have been filed in the U.S. District Court for the Southern District of New York. Reported on John E. Schwenkler's home page.

21. "The KGB forged documents to show the CIA was behind the Kennedy assassination. It also 'leaked' the information that the AIDS virus was manufactured by the CIA."

60 Minutes

Exercise 3-13

Find five advertisements that give no reasons for purchasing the products they are selling. Explain how each ad attempts to make the product seem attractive.

Exercise 3-14

Find five advertisements that give reasons for purchasing the products they are selling. Which of the reasons are promises to the purchaser? Exactly what is being promised? What is the likelihood that the product will fulfill that promise?

Exercise 3-15

Watch Fox News and CNN news programs on the same day. Compare the two on the basis of (1) the news stories covered, (2) the amount of air time given to two or three of the major stories, and (3) any difference in the slant of the presentations of a controversial story. From your reading of the chapter, how would you account for the similarities between the two in both selection and content of the stories?

Writing Exercises

1. Although millions of people have seen professional magicians like David Copperfield and Siegfried and Roy perform in person or on television, it's probably a safe assumption that almost nobody believes they accomplish their feats by means of real magical or supernatural powers—that is, that they somehow "defy" the laws of nature. But even though they've never had a personal demonstration, a significant portion of the population believe that certain psychics are able to accomplish apparent miracles by exactly such means. How might you explain this difference in belief? (Our answer is given in the *Logical Accessory* instructor's manual.)

2. In the text you were asked to consider the claim "Charlie's eighty-seven-year-old grandmother swam across Lake Michigan in the middle of winter." Because of the implausibility of such a claim—that is, because it conflicts with our background information—it is reasonable to reject it. Suppose, however, that instead of just telling us about his grandmother, Charlie brings us a photocopy depicting a page of a Chicago newspaper with a photograph of a person in a wetsuit walking up onto a beach. The caption underneath reads, "Eighty-seven-year-old Grandmother Swims Lake Michigan in January!" Based on this piece of evidence, should a critical thinker decide that the original claim is significantly more likely to be true than if it were backed up only by Charlie's word? Defend your answer.

3. Turn to the "Essays for Analysis" in Appendix 1 and assess the credibility of the author in Selection 9, "Will Ozone Blob Devour the Earth?" Based on the blurb about the author, say what you can about his likely expertise and his susceptibility to bias on the subject of the essay.

4. Are our schools doing a bad job educating our kids? Do research in the library or on the Internet to answer this question. Make a list (no more than one page long) of facts that support the claim that our schools are not doing as good a job as they should. Then list facts that support the opposite view (or that rebut the claims of those who say our schools aren't doing a good job). Again, limit yourself to one page. Cite your sources.

   Now think critically about your sources. Are any stronger or weaker than the others? Explain why on a single sheet of paper. Come prepared to read your explanation, along with your list of facts and sources, to the class.

5. Jackson says you should be skeptical of the opinion of someone who stands to profit from your accepting that opinion. Smith disagrees, pointing out that salespeople are apt to know a lot more about products of the type they sell than do most people.

   "Most salespeople are honest, and you can trust them," Smith argues. "Those who aren't don't stay in business long."

   Take about fifteen minutes to defend either Smith or Jackson in a short essay. When everyone is finished, your instructor will collect the essays and read three or more to the class to stimulate a brief discussion. After discussion, can the class come to any agreement about who is correct, Jackson or Smith?

6. Your instructor will survey the class to see how many agree with this claim: The media are biased. Then he or she will ask you to list your reasons for thinking that this claim is true. (If you do not think it is true, list reasons people might have for believing it.) After ten minutes your instructor will collect the lists of reasons and read from several of the lists. Then he or she will give you twenty minutes to defend one of these claims:
   a. The media are biased.
   b. Some of the reasons people have for believing the media are biased are not very good reasons.
   c. It is difficult to say whether the media are biased.

   At the end of the period your instructor may survey the class again to see if anyone's mind has changed, and why.

7. If you haven't done Exercise 6, your instructor will give you twenty minutes to defend an answer to the question, Are the media biased? Put your name on the back of your paper. When everyone is finished, your instructor will collect the papers and redistribute them to the class. In groups of four or five, read the papers that have been given to your group, and decide if any of them are convincing. Do not look at the names of the authors. Your instructor will ask each group to read to the class any essay that the group thinks is convincing.

Chapter 4

Persuasion Through Rhetoric

A couple of years ago, tobacco companies spent millions trying to defeat Proposition 10, an antismoking ballot initiative in California. Calling themselves "The Committee Against Unfair Taxes," they mailed out expensive glossy brochures warning voters of the perils of the initiative. They were especially anxious to inform everyone that

> The sponsors of ill-conceived Proposition 10 are perennial political activist millionaire Rob Reiner and four other Hollywood/Los Angeles millionaire social engineers who believe they know more about raising your children than you do.

This warning was accompanied by a grainy black-and-white photograph of Reiner (whom you may remember from reruns of the popular 1960s TV show *All in the Family*) that brought to mind a police mug shot.

Now, when others want us to do something or want to influence our attitudes or beliefs, they may use an argument. That is, they may offer a reason why we should or shouldn't do or believe or not believe whatever it is. They might also use threats, bribery, or even more extreme measures. But another technique is available, one used much more frequently, and it is illustrated in the statement quoted above. This technique employs the persuasive power of words, or what we have called their rhetorical force or emotive meaning—their power to express and elicit images, feelings, and emotional associations. In the next few chapters we examine some of the most common rhetorical techniques used to affect people's attitudes and opinions and behavior.

In English, **rhetoric** refers to the study of persuasive writing. As we use the term, it denotes a broad category of linguistic techniques people use when their primary objective is to influence beliefs and attitudes and behavior. Is Rob Reiner "a perennial political activist millionaire"? Or is he an "untiring advocate of social reform willing to spend his considerable fortune for just causes"? The different impressions these two descriptions create is largely due to their differing rhetorical meaning. Does Juanita "still owe over $1,000 on her credit card"? Or does Juanita "owe only a little over $1,000 on her credit card"? There's no factual difference between the two questions—only a difference in their rhetorical force. The thing to remember through these next few chapters is that rhetorical force may be psychologically effective, but by itself it establishes nothing. If we allow our attitudes and beliefs to be affected by sheer rhetoric, we fall short as critical thinkers.

Now before we get in trouble with your English teacher, let's make it clear that there is nothing wrong with trying to make your case as persuasive as possible by using well-chosen, rhetorically effective words and phrases. Good writers always do this. But we, as critical thinkers, must be able to distinguish the *argument* (if any) contained in what someone says or writes from the *rhetoric;* we must be able to distinguish the *logical* force of a set of remarks from their *psychological* force. The statement above from the tobacco companies about Rob Reiner, for example, contains *no argument whatsoever;* it just uses inflammatory rhetorical techniques aimed at getting us to vote against the antismoking initiative.

One of the things you will become aware of—as you read these pages and do the exercises and apply what you have learned to what you read and write—is that rhetoric is often mixed right in with argument. The message isn't that you should *deduct* points from an argument if it is presented in rhetorically charged language, and it isn't that you should try to get all the rhetoric out of your own writing. The message is simply that you shouldn't *add* points for rhetoric. You don't make an argument stronger by screaming it at the top of your lungs. Likewise, you don't make it stronger by adding **rhetorical devices.**

Rhetorical Devices and Techniques

Many of these rhetorical bells and whistles have names because they are so common and so well understood. Because they are used primarily to give a statement a positive or negative slant regarding a subject, they are sometimes called **slanters.** We'll describe some of the more widely used specimens.

■ *Euphemisms and Dysphemisms*

Language usually offers us a choice of words when we want to say something. Until recently, the term "used car" referred to an automobile that wasn't new, but the trend nowadays is to refer to such a car as "pre-owned." The people who sell such cars, of course, hope that the different terminology will keep potential buyers from thinking about *how* "used" the car might be—maybe it's *used up!* The car dealer's replacement term, "pre-owned," is a **euphemism**—a neutral or positive expression instead of one that carries negative associations. Euphemisms play an important role in affecting

Opponents of the estate tax, a tax imposed on inherited money, have coined a new phrase for it: the "death tax." Here is Grover Norquist, who is the head of Americans for Tax Reform in Washington, D.C., in a press release from that organization:

> Over seventy percent of Americans oppose the Death Tax, and with good reason. It is the worst form of double-taxation, where, after taxing you all your life, the government decides to take even more when you die.

"Death Tax" is a dysphemism, of course. Like many dysphemisms, it is designed to mislead the reader or listener. The estate tax is not a tax on death, but on inherited wealth, imposed on the occasion of a person's death. And the person paying the tax is not the deceased, but the inheritors, who have never paid tax on the money.

(Interestingly, the tax does not apply to the first $625,000 of a person's inheritance; and the tax rate is 37 percent of inherited wealth from $625,000 to $3 million. So the tax does not apply to all the great majority of Americans, who do not inherit that kind of money. It isn't clear that the majority of Americans *realize* that it will not apply to them, however.)

our attitudes. People may be less likely to disapprove of an assassination attempt on a foreign leader, for example, if it is referred to as "neutralization." People fighting against the government of a country can be referred to neutrally as "rebels" or "guerrillas," but a person who wants to build support for them may refer to them by the euphemism "freedom fighters." A government is likely to pay a price for initiating a "revenue enhancement," but voters will be even quicker to respond negatively to a "tax hike." The U.S. Department of Defense performs the same function it did when it was called the Department of War, but the current name makes for much better public relations.

The opposite of a euphemism is a **dysphemism.** Dysphemisms are used to produce a negative effect on a listener's or reader's attitude toward

Your Cheatin' Heart?

Here's today's timely if perhaps tasteless question: What's the difference between a rendezvous and an affair?

A rendezvous is what Bill Cosby told Dan Rather he had with the mother of the young woman who allegedly attempted to blackmail him, claiming he was her father.

A rendezvous, not an affair.

"Rendezvous" sounds so much nicer than "affair." So romantic. So pretentious. So French. . . .

An affair is middle class, guilt-ridden and furtive. A rendezvous is urbane, sophisticated and self-conscious. . . .

A rendezvous is twin martinis in the Ritz Bar.

An affair is a couple of Gallo Chardonnays after work.

A rendezvous is the back of a limousine.

An affair is the back of a minivan.

A rendezvous is Bobby Short at the Carlyle.

An affair is Kenny G, wherever. . . .

Basically, though, they boil down to much the same thing.

An affair is what you have if you can't, or won't, admit you're cheating.

A rendezvous is what you have if you can't, or won't, admit you're having an affair.

———————

From a column by DIANE WHITE

---

something or to tone down the positive associations it may have. Whereas "freedom fighter" is a euphemism for "guerrilla" or "rebel," "terrorist" is a dysphemism.

Euphemisms and dysphemisms are often used in deceptive ways or ways that at least hint at deception. All of the examples in the preceding paragraphs are examples of such uses. But euphemisms can at times be helpful and constructive. By allowing us to approach a sensitive subject indirectly— or by skirting it entirely—euphemisms can sometimes prevent hostility from bringing rational discussion to a halt. They can also be a matter of good manners: "Passed on" may be much more appropriate than "dead" if the person to whom you're speaking is recently widowed. Hence, our *purpose* for using euphemisms and dysphemisms determines whether or not those uses are legitimate.

It bears mentioning that some facts just are repellent, and for that reason even neutral reports of them sound horrible. "Lizzy killed her father with an ax" reports a horrible fact about Lizzy, but it does so using neutral language. Neutral reports of unpleasant, evil, or repellent facts do not automatically count as dysphemistic rhetoric.

The University of Washington admits that many of its faculty members suffer from what it calls "salary compression." The faculty themselves have a different word for it, as you can imagine.

—Rhetorical comparison. (And a great cartoon.)

Horsey. Reprinted with permission, Seattle Post Intelligencer.

■ Rhetorical Comparisons, Definitions, and Explanations

Definitions, explanations, and comparative claims are discussed in other chapters, but the emphasis in those discussions is on uses other than slanting. We want to remind you here that each of these can do quite a bit to prejudice an issue.

Rhetorical comparisons are used to express or influence attitudes. You might make the point that a person is of small stature by comparing her to an elf, but you could make the same point in a much less flattering way by comparing her to a gnome or a Chihuahua. You could describe the fairness of a person's complexion by comparing it to either new-fallen snow or whale blubber, but you'd better make the latter comparison out of the individual's hearing.

Rhetorical definitions smuggle prejudice of one sort or another into the meaning of a term. Abortion and associated issues are fruitful grounds for persuasive definitions. If we define "abortion" as "the murder of an unborn child," there's not much difficulty in arriving at the conclusion that abortion is morally unacceptable. Similarly, "human being" is sometimes taken to refer to any living organism (embryonic, fetal, or post-birth) that is produced by humans. By using this definition, it's easy to conclude that an

---

Whether you wish to admit it or not, when you approve, morally, of the bombing of foreign targets by U.S. military, you are approving of acts morally equivalent to the bombing in Oklahoma City.

—A rhetorical comparison by TIMOTHY MCVEIGH, Oklahoma City bomber (reported by Larry Englemann)

What Does "Rape" Mean?

In an article for Knight-Ridder Newspapers, Joanne Jacobs of the *San Jose Mercury News* disagreed markedly with the current use of the word "rape" on some university campuses. Notice how language and definition are crucial in the items she reported:

- Swarthmore College's Acquaintance Rape Prevention Workshop training manual asserts that acquaintance rape includes behavior ranging "from crimes legally defined as rape to verbal harassment and inappropriate innuendo."

- A former director of Columbia University's date-rape education program says that "every time you have an act of intercourse there must be explicit consent, and if there's not explicit consent, then it's rape."

- According to Andrea Parrot, a Cornell University psychiatry professor who's written a book on date rape, "Any sexual intercourse without mutual desire is a form of rape." It's as bad to be psychologically pressured into sexual contact by an acquaintance, writes Parrot, as to be "attacked on the streets."

Jacobs believes that defining "rape" in this way trivializes the term and is "a cruel insult to all the women who have been raped" by a man who did more than use "inappropriate innuendos." The definition of "rape" as any sex that goes farther than the woman wants, whether she made that clear or not, is "fantastically broad," she says. She also maintains that this definition makes reports of an epidemic of sexual assault on campuses highly suspect. Were the victims *raped,* she asks, or were they just *nagged*?

Others would say that use of the word "rape" for the behavior described is justified because it draws attention to the seriousness of that behavior.

Note two things: First, the definitions of "rape" given here are *precising definitions,* definitions that serve to specify the applicability of a term. But they are also disguised *rhetorical definitions* designed to influence attitudes about a variety of sexual behaviors. Second, notice that "a mere question of semantics" is sometimes a very important matter indeed.

abortion involves the taking of a human being's life and is thus a homicide. Rhetorical definitions used this way are said to "beg the question," a fault discussed in Chapter 6.

Definitions by example can also slant a discussion if the examples are prejudicially chosen. Imagine a liberal who points to a story about a conservative politician found guilty of corruption and says, "*That's* what I mean by conservative politics." Clearly, if we really want to see all sides of an issue, we must be careful to avoid definitions and examples that slant the discussion.

Sex-education classes are like in-home sales parties for abortion.

—PHYLLIS SCHLAFLY, activist

A rhetorical comparison.

▲ *Stereotypes.*

Rhetorical explanations are the same kind of slanting device, this time clothed as explanations. "He lost the fight because he's lost his nerve." Is this different from saying that he lost because he was too cautious? Maybe, but maybe not. What isn't in doubt is that the explanation is certainly more unflattering when it's put the former way.

We recently saw a good example of a rhetorical explanation in a letter to an editor:

> I am a traditional liberal who keeps asking himself, why has there been such a seismic shift in affirmative action? It used to be affirmative action stood for equal opportunity; now it means preferences and quotas. Why the change? It's because the people behind affirmative action aren't for equal rights anymore; they're for handouts.

This isn't a dispassionate scholarly explanation but a way of expressing an opinion on and trying to evoke anger at affirmative action policies.

■ *Stereotypes*

When a writer or speaker lumps a group of individuals together under one name or description, especially one that begins with the word "the" (the liberal, the Communist, the right-winger, the Jew, the Catholic, and so on), such labeling generally results in stereotyping. A **stereotype** is a thought or image about a group of people based on little or no evidence. Thinking that women are emotional, that men are insensitive, that lesbians are man haters, that southerners are bigoted, that gay men are effeminate—all count as stereotypes. Language that reduces people or things to categories can induce an audience to accept a claim unthinkingly or to make snap judgments concerning groups of individuals about whom they know little.

Some of the slanters we've already talked about can involve stereotypes. For example, if we use the dysphemism "right-wing extremist" to denigrate a political candidate, we are utilizing a negative stereotype. Com-

---

It was a reasonable proposal. That's why they rejected it.

—Former Senator BOB DOLE, explaining why the Democrats voted against a Republican proposal

A rhetorical explanation.

The ventilation fans will be taken care of in a more timely manner because we know that women love to clean.

—General YURI GLAZKOV, expressing the hope that U.S. astronaut Shannon Lucid would clean the fans when she joined the Russians on their space station.

Houston? Are you hearing this, Houston?

monly, if we link a candidate with a stereotype we like or venerate, we can create a favorable impression of the individual. "Senator Kerry addressed his opponent with all the civility of a gentleman" employs a favorable stereotype, that of a gentleman, in a persuasive comparison.

Our stereotypes come from a great many sources, many from popular literature, and are often supported by a variety of prejudices and group interests. The Native American tribes of the Great Plains were considered noble people by most whites until just before the mid–nineteenth century. But as white people grew more interested in moving them off their lands and as conflicts between the two escalated, popular literature increasingly described Native Americans as subhuman creatures. This stereotype supported the group interests of whites. Conflicts between nations usually produce derogatory stereotypes of the opposition; it is easier to destroy enemies without pangs of conscience if we think of them as less "human" than ourselves. Stereotyping becomes even easier when there are racial differences to exploit.

■ *Innuendo*

The next batch of slanting devices doesn't depend as much on emotional associations as on the manipulation of other features of language. When we communicate with one another, we automatically have certain expectations and make certain assumptions. (For example, when your instructor says, "Everybody passed the exam," she doesn't mean that everybody *in the world* passed the exam. We assume that the scope of the pronoun extends to include only those who took the exam.) These expectations and assumptions help fill in the gaps in our conversations so that we don't have to explain everything we say in minute detail. Because providing such details would be a tedious and probably impossible chore, these underlying conversational factors are crucial to the success of communication.

Consider this statement:

Ladies and gentlemen, I am proof that there is at least one candidate in this race who does not have a drinking problem.

Photographic Innuendo

In the 2002 U.S. Senate race in Montana, Republican Mike Taylor dropped out of the race at the last minute, blaming a thirty-second TV ad sponsored by the Montana Democratic Party. The Democrats, he asserted, were using a stereotype to make him look gay.

In the ad, clips show Taylor dressed in a leisure suit, rubbing lotion on another man's temples, his white shirt unbuttoned to his chest, gold necklaces dangling. (Back in the 1980s Taylor ran a beauty salon and hair-care school; the clips are from a TV show he hosted.)

Democrats denied that they were implying anything about Taylor's sexuality. The ad focused on charges that Taylor diverted federal student loans when he ran the beauty salon.

Taylor had been marketing himself as a tough Montana rancher. "The ad has destroyed the campaign," said a spokesperson for Taylor.

The city voluntarily assumed the costs of cleaning up the landfill to make it safe for developers.

—Opponents of a local housing development

The opponents neglected to mention that the law *required* the city to assume the costs. This bit of innuendo on the part of the opponents suggested, of course, that the city was in bed with the developers.

Notice that this remark does *not* say that any opponent of the speaker *does* have a drinking problem. In fact, the speaker is even allowing for the fact that other candidates may have no such problem by using the words "at least one candidate." But he has still managed to get the idea across that some opponent in the race *may* have a drinking problem. This is an example of **innuendo,** a form of suggestion.

Another example, maybe our all-time favorite, is this remark:

> I didn't say the meat was tough. I said I didn't see the horse that is usually outside.
>
> *—W. C. Fields*

As you can see, the use of innuendo enables us to insinuate something deprecatory about something or someone without actually saying it. For example, if someone asks you whether Ralph is telling the truth, you may reply, "Yes, this time," which would suggest that maybe Ralph doesn't *usually* tell the truth. Or you might say of someone, "She is competent—in many regards," which would insinuate that in some ways she is *not* competent.

Sometimes we condemn somebody with faint praise—that is, by praising a person a small amount when grander praise might be expected, we hint that praise may not really be due at all. This is a kind of innuendo. Imagine, for example, reading a letter of recommendation that says, "Ms. Flotsam has done good work for us, I suppose." Such a letter does not inspire one to want to hire Ms. Flotsam on the spot. Likewise, "She's proved to be useful so far" and "Surprisingly, she seems very astute" manage to speak more evil than good of Ms. Flotsam. Notice, though, that the literal information contained in these remarks is not negative in the least. Innuendo lies between the lines, so to speak.

Innuendo Again, This Time in the Caption

▲   *Enron's Fastow: Charged. Are Skilling and Lay Next?*
*Comment: Notice that the caption doesn't say that Skilling and Lay have been charged.
This is innuendo.*

■ *Loaded Questions*

If you overheard someone ask, "Have you always loved to gamble?" you
would naturally assume that the person being questioned did in fact love to
gamble. This assumption is independent of whether the person answered
yes or no, for it underlies the question itself. Every question rests on assumptions. Even an innocent question like "What time is it?" depends on
the assumptions that the hearer speaks English and has some means of finding out the time, for instance. A **loaded question** is less innocent, however.
It rests on one or more *unwarranted* or *unjustified* assumptions. The world's
oldest example, "Have you stopped beating your wife?" rests on the assumption that the person asked has in the past beaten his wife. If there is no reason to think that this assumption is true, then the question is a loaded one.

Innocent Until Reported Guilty

In what may be the most obvious indicator of the administration's priorities, Wen Ho Lee and Peter Lee, who reportedly passed the most clamorous secrets, are not even in jail.

—Boston University professor ANTHONY CODEVILLA, in the Washington Times, talking about the alleged passing of nuclear secrets to China

Notice how the weaseler, "reportedly," is used here. We didn't realize that people who have been *reported* to have committed crimes should be put in jail.

The loaded question is technically a form of innuendo, because it permits us to insinuate the assumption that underlies a question without coming right out and stating that assumption.

■ *Weaselers*

Overall, Dodge trucks are the most powerful.
—Ad for Dodge

Overall? What does this weaseler mean?

Weaselers are linguistic methods of hedging a bet. When inserted into a claim, they help protect it from criticism by watering it down somewhat, weakening it, and giving the claim's author a way out in case the claim is challenged.

There used to be an advertisement for a brand of sugarless gum that claimed, "Three out of four dentists surveyed recommend sugarless gum for their patients who chew gum." This claim contains two weaseling expressions. The first is the word "surveyed." Notice that the ad does not tell us the criteria for choosing the dentists who were surveyed. Were they picked at random, or were only dentists who might not be unfavorably disposed toward gum chewing surveyed? Nothing indicates that the sample of dentists surveyed even remotely represents the general population of dentists. If 99 percent of the dentists in the country disagree with the ad's claim, its authors could still say truthfully that they spoke only about those dentists surveyed, not all dentists.

The second weaseler in the advertisement appears in the last phrase of the claim: "for their patients who chew gum." Notice the ad does not claim that *any* dentist believes sugarless-gum chewing is as good for a patient's teeth as no gum chewing at all. Imagine that the actual question posed to the dentists was something like this: "If a patient of yours insisted on chewing gum, would you prefer that he or she chew sugarless gum or gum with sugar in it?" If dentists had to answer that question, they would almost certainly be in favor of sugarless gum. But this is a far cry from recommending that any person chew any kind of gum at all. The weaselers allow the advertisement to get away with what *sounds* like an unqualified recommendation for sugarless gum, when in fact nothing in the ad supports such a recommendation.

Innuendo with 𝒮𝓉𝒶𝓉𝒾𝓈𝓉𝒾𝒸𝓈

Taxpayers with incomes over $200,000 could expect on average to pay about $99,000 in taxes under Mr. Bush's plan.

—Wall Street Journal

Wow! Pity the poor taxpayer who makes over $200,000! Apparently, he or she will pay almost half of that amount in taxes.

But think again: In the words of the *New Republic* (February 3, 2003), "The *Journal*'s statistic is about as meaningful as asserting that males over the age of six have had an average of three sexual partners." Bill Gates and many others like him are among those who make over $200,000.

Let's make up a statistic. Let's say that 98 percent of American doctors believe that aspirin is a contributing cause of Reye's syndrome in children and that the other 2 percent are unconvinced. If we then claim that "some doctors are unconvinced that aspirin is related to Reye's syndrome," we cannot be held accountable for having said something false, even though our claim might be misleading to someone who did not know the complete story. The word "some" has allowed us to weasel the point.

Words that sometimes weasel—such as "perhaps," "possibly," "maybe," and "may be," among others—can be used to produce innuendo, to plant a *suggestion* without actually making a claim that a person can be held to. We can suggest that Berriault is a liar without actually saying so (and thus without making a claim that might be hard to defend) by saying that Berriault *may be* a liar. Or we can say that it is *possible* that Berriault is a liar (which is true of all of us, after all). "*Perhaps* Berriault is a liar" works nicely too. All of these are examples of weaselers used to create innuendo.

Not every use of words and phrases like these is a weaseling one, of course. Words that can weasel can also bring very important qualifications to bear on a claim. The very same word that weasels in one context may not weasel at all in another. For example, a detective considering all the possible angles on a crime who has just heard Smith's account of events may say to an associate, "Of course, it is *possible* that Smith is lying." This need not be a case of weaseling. The detective may simply be exercising due care. Other words and phrases that are sometimes used to weasel can also be used legitimately. Qualifying phrases such as "it is arguable that," "it may well be that," and so on have at least as many appropriate uses as weaseling ones. Others, such as "some would say that," are likely to be weaseling more often than not, but even they can serve an honest purpose in the right context. Our warning, then, is to be watchful when qualifying phrases turn up. Is the speaker or writer adding a reasonable qualification, insinuating a bit of innuendo, or preparing a way out? We can only warn; you need to assess the speaker, the context, and the subject to establish the grounds for the right judgment.

Great Western pays up to 12 percent more interest on checking accounts.

—Radio advertisement

Even aside from the "up to" weaseler, this ad can be deceptive about what interest rate it's promising. Unless you listen carefully, you might think Great Western is paying 12 percent on checking accounts. The presence of the word "more" changes all that, of course. If you're getting 3 percent now and Great Western gives you "up to 12 percent more" than that, they'll be giving you about 3 1/3 percent—hardly the fortune the ad seems to promise.

■ *Downplayers*

Downplaying is an attempt to make someone or something look less important or significant. Stereotypes, rhetorical comparisons, rhetorical explanations, and innuendo can all be used to downplay something. Consider this statement, for example: "Don't mind what Mr. Pierce says in class; he's a liberal." This attempt to downplay Mr. Pierce and whatever views he expresses in class makes use of a stereotype. We can also downplay by careful insertion of certain words or other devices. Let's amend the preceding example like this: "Don't mind what Mr. Pierce says in class; he's just another liberal." Notice how the phrase "just another" denigrates Mr. Pierce's status still further. Words and other devices that serve this function are known as **downplayers.**

Perhaps the words most often used as downplayers are "mere" and "merely." If Kim tells you that she has a yellow belt in the Tibetan martial art of Pujo and that her sister has a mere green belt, you would quite naturally make the assumption that a yellow belt ranks higher than a green belt. We'd probably say that Kim's use of the word "mere" gives you the *right* to make that assumption. Kim has used the word to downplay the significance of her sister's accomplishment. But notice this: It could still be that Kim's sister's belt signifies the higher rank. If called on the matter, Kim might claim that she said "mere" simply because her sister has been practicing the art for much longer and is, after all, not *that* far ahead. Whether Kim has such an out or not, she has used a downplayer to try to diminish her sister's accomplishment.

The term "so-called" is another standard downplayer. We might say, for example, that the woman who made the diagnosis is a "so-called doctor," which downplays her credentials as a physician. Quotation marks can be used to accomplish the same thing:

> She got her "degree" from a correspondence school.

Use of quotation marks as a downplayer is different from their use to indicate irony, as in this remark:

> John "borrowed" Hank's umbrella, and Hank hasn't seen it since.

The idea in the latter example isn't to downplay John's borrowing the umbrella; it's to indicate that it wasn't really a case of borrowing at all. But the use of quotation marks around the word "degree" and the use of "so-called" in the earlier examples are designed to play down the importance of their subjects. And, like "mere" and "merely," they do it in a fairly unsubtle way.

Many conjunctions—such as "nevertheless," "however," "still," and "but"—can be used to downplay claims that precede them. Such uses are more subtle than the first group of downplayers. Compare the following two versions of what is essentially the same pair of claims:

> (1) The leak at the plant was a terrible tragedy, all right; however, we must remember that such pesticide plants are an integral part of the "green revolution" that has helped to feed millions of people.

Don't Get Carried Away!

Once you're familiar with the ways slanting devices are used to try to influence us, you may be tempted to dismiss a claim or argument *just because it contains strongly slanted language.* But true claims as well as false ones, good reasoning as well as bad, can be couched in such language. Remember that the slanting *itself* gives us no reason to accept a position on an issue; that doesn't mean that there *are* no such reasons. Consider this example, written by someone opposed to using animals for laboratory research:

> It's morally wrong for a person to inflict awful pain on another sensitive creature, one that has done the first no harm. Therefore, the so-called scientists who perform their hideous and sadistic experiments on innocent animals are moral criminals just as were Hitler and his Nazi torturers.

Comment: These are strong words, and you'll find the passage contains more than one of the slanters we've discussed. But before we dismiss the passage as shrill or hysterical, it behooves us as critical thinkers to notice that it contains a piece of reasoning that may shed some light on the issue. A critical thinker who disagrees with the position taken by our speaker should do so because of a problem with the *argument* presented, not because of the strong *language* in which it is presented. (See if you can restate the reasoning in a somewhat less inflammatory way.)

(2) Although it's true that pesticide plants are an integral part of the "green revolution" that has helped to feed millions of people, it was just such a plant that developed a leak and produced a terrible tragedy.

The differences may not be as obvious as those in the cases of "mere" and "so-called," but the two versions give an indication of where their authors' sympathies lie.

The context of a claim can determine whether it downplays or not. Consider the remark "Daschle won by only six votes." The word "only" may or may not downplay Daschle's victory, depending on how thin a six-vote margin is. If ten thousand people voted and Daschle won by six, then the word "only" seems perfectly appropriate: Daschle just won by the skin of his teeth. But if the vote was in a committee of, say, twenty, then six is quite a substantial margin (it would be thirteen votes to seven, if everybody voted—almost two-to-one), and applying the word "only" to the result is clearly a slanting device designed to give Daschle's margin of victory less importance than it deserves.

As mentioned earlier, slanters really can't—and shouldn't—be avoided altogether. They can give our writing flair and interest. What *can* be avoided is being unduly swayed by slanters. Learn to appreciate the effects that subtle and not-so-subtle manipulations of language can have on you. By being

Sarcasm on the Editorial Page

Steve Benson. Reprinted by permission of United Feature Syndicate, Inc.

▲ *Background: This cartoon mocks the 1999 decision of the Kansas Board of Education to eliminate evolution as a principle of biological science. (The decision was later reversed.)*

aware, you decrease your chances of being taken in unwittingly by a clever writer or speaker.

■ Horse Laugh/Ridicule/Sarcasm

The kind of rhetorical device we call the **horse laugh** includes the use of ridicule of all kinds. Ridicule is a powerful rhetorical tool—most of us really hate being laughed at. So it's important to remember that somebody who simply gets a laugh at the expense of another person's position has not raised any objection to that position.

One may simply laugh outright at a claim ("Send aid to Russia? Har, har, har!"), laugh at another claim that reminds us of the first ("Support the Equal Rights Amendment? Sure, when the ladies start buying the drinks! Ho, ho, ho!"), tell an unrelated joke, use sarcastic language, or simply laugh at the person who is trying to make the point.

The next time you watch a debate, remember that the person who has the funniest lines and who gets the most laughs may be the person who *seems* to win the debate, but critical thinkers should be able to see the difference between argumentation on one hand and entertainment on the other. (Notice that we didn't say there's anything *wrong* with entertainment;

▲ *"Ari" refers to President George W. Bush's press secretary. Satire is a form of ridicule.*

just like most of you, we wouldn't like to spend *all* of our time watching people be serious, even if they *were* making good arguments.)

■ *Hyperbole*

Hyperbole is extravagant overstatement. A claim that exaggerates for effect is on its way to becoming hyperbole, depending on the strength of its language and the point being made. To describe a hangnail as a serious injury is hyperbole; so is using the word "fascist" to describe parents who insist that their teenager be home by midnight. Not all strong or colorful language is hyperbole, of course. "Oscar Peterson is an unbelievably inventive pianist" is a strong claim, but it is not hyperbolic—it isn't really extravagant. However, "Oscar Peterson is the most inventive musician who ever lived" goes beyond emphasis and crosses over the line into hyperbole. (How could one know that Oscar Peterson is more inventive than, say, Mozart?)

Dysphemisms often involve hyperbole. So do rhetorical comparisons. When we use the dysphemisms "traitorous" or "extremist" to describe the secretary of state's recommendations to Congress, we are indulging in hyperbole. If we say that the secretary of state is less well informed than a beet, that's hyperbole in a rhetorical comparison. In similar ways, rhetorical explanations and definitions can utilize hyperbole.

Hyperbole is also frequently used in ridicule. If it involves exaggeration, a piece of ridicule counts as hyperbole. The example above, saying that the secretary of state is less well informed than a beet, is hyperbole in a rhetorical comparison used to ridicule that official.

A claim can be hyperbolic without containing excessively emotive words or phrases. Neither the hangnail nor the Oscar Peterson examples contain such language; in fact, the word "unbelievably" is probably the most emotive word in the two claims about Peterson, and it occurs in the nonhyperbolic claim. But a claim can also be hyperbole as a result of the use of such language. "Parents who are strict about a curfew are fascists" is an example. If the word "mean" were substituted for "fascists," we might find the claim strong or somewhat exaggerated, but we would not call it hyperbole. It's when the colorfulness of language becomes *excessive*—a matter of judgment—that the claim is likely to turn into hyperbole.

Hyperbole is an obvious slanting device, but it can also have more subtle—perhaps unconscious—effects. Even if you reject the exaggeration, you may be moved in the direction of the basic claim. For example, you may reject the claim that Oscar Peterson is the most inventive musician who ever lived, but you may now believe that Oscar Peterson must certainly be an extraordinary musician—otherwise, why would someone make that exaggerated claim about him? Or suppose someone says, "Charlotte Church has the most fabulous voice of any singer around today." Even if you reject the "fabulous" part of the claim, you may still end up thinking Charlotte Church must have a pretty good voice. But be careful: Without support, you have no more reason to accept the milder claims than the wilder ones. Hyperbole can add a persuasive edge to a claim that it doesn't deserve. A hyperbolic claim is pure persuasion.

■ *Proof Surrogates*

An expression used to suggest that there is evidence or authority for a claim without actually citing such evidence or authority is a **proof surrogate.** Sometimes we can't *prove* the claim we're asserting, but we can hint that there *is* proof available, or at least evidence or authority for the claim, without committing ourselves to what that proof, evidence, or authority is. Using "informed sources say" is a favorite way of making a claim more authoritative. Who are the sources? How do we know they're informed? How does the person making the claim know they're informed? "It's obvious that" sometimes precedes a claim that isn't obvious at all. But we may keep our objections to ourselves in the belief that it's obvious to everybody but us, and we don't want to appear more dense than the next guy. "Studies show" crops up in advertising a lot. Note that this phrase tells us nothing about how many studies are involved, how good they are, who did them, or any other important information.

Here's a good example of a proof surrogate from the *Wall Street Journal:*

> We hope politicians on this side of the border are paying close attention to Canada's referendum on Quebec. . . .
>
> Canadians turned out en masse to reject the referendum. There's every reason to believe that voters in the U.S. are just as fed up with the social engineering that lumps people together as groups rather than treating them as individuals.

There *may* be "every reason to believe" that U.S. voters are fed up, but nobody has yet told us what any of those reasons are. Until we hear more evidence, our best bet is to figure that the quotation mainly reflects what the

---

A feminazi is a woman to whom the most important thing in life is seeing to it that as many abortions as possible are performed.

—RUSH LIMBAUGH

A rhetorical definition with hyperbole.

There is no other country in the Middle East except Israel that can be considered to have a stable government. . . . Is Saudi Arabia more stable? Egypt? Jordan? Kuwait? Judge for yourself!

—"Facts and Logic About the Middle East"

Proof surrogates often take the form of questions. This strategy can also be analyzed as switching the burden of proof (see Chapter 6).

writer at the *Journal* thinks is the proper attitude for U.S. voters. Without a context, such assertions are meaningless.

Remember: Proof surrogates are just that—surrogates. They are not real proof or evidence. Such proof or evidence may exist, but until it has been presented, the claim at issue remains unsupported. At best, proof surrogates suggest sloppy research; at worst, they suggest propaganda.

Recap

Speakers and writers sometimes win acceptance for a claim or influence a person's attitude or behavior without presenting reasons. We call this rhetoric. A primary means of wielding such influence is the use of rhetorical devices—words or phrases that have positive or negative emotional associations, suggest favorable or unfavorable images, or manipulate the assumptions or expectations that always underlie communication. Common rhetorical devices include euphemisms and dysphemisms; rhetorical comparisons, definitions, and explanations; stereotypes; innuendo; loaded questions; weaselers; downplayers; horse laugh, ridicule, and sarcasm; hyperbole; and proof surrogates. Such devices are often used deliberately, but subtle uses can creep into people's speech or writing even when they think they are being objective. Some such phrases, especially euphemisms and weaselers, have both valuable, nonprejudicial uses and slanting ones. Only by speaking, writing, listening, and reading carefully can we use this type of language appropriately and distinguish prejudicial from nonprejudicial uses of these devices.

Exercises

Exercise 4-7

You will want to recognize when someone is using rhetorical slanting devices to influence your attitudes and beliefs. Let's see if you can identify some of the more common devices. Select the *best* answer.

▲ 1. A question on the "North Poll," a poll associated with the Oliver North talk radio program: "Are you outraged that President Clinton may be selling burial plots in Arlington National Cemetery to big DNC donors?" In which category does this quotation most clearly fall?
   a. dysphemism
   b. stereotype
   c. weaseler/innuendo
   d. hyperbole
   e. not a slanter

2. Larry Kudlow, of *Kudlow and Cramer* on CNBC (in an *American Spectator* interview): "[Former Treasury Secretary] Bob Rubin's a smart guy, a nice man, but he hates tax cuts. To listen to Rubin on domestic issues, you could just die. He's a free-spending left-winger." Which category applies best to the last phrase of the quotation?
   a. rhetorical comparison
   b. stereotype
   c. downplayer
   d. loaded question
   e. not a slanter

3. "Making a former corporate CEO the head of the Securities and Exchange Commission is like putting a fox in charge of the henhouse." This is best seen as an example of
   a. rhetorical comparison
   b. rhetorical explanation
   c. innuendo
   d. dysphemism
   e. not a slanter

▲ 4. "Even with no sleep the night before, Margaret was beautiful the day of the ceremony." The phrase "even with no sleep the night before" is best seen as
   a. innuendo
   b. euphemism
   c. hyperbole
   d. weaseler
   e. not a slanter

5. "Right. George Bush 'won' the election in 2000, didn't he?" The use of quotation marks around "won" has the effect of a
   a. weaseler
   b. dysphemism
   c. downplayer
   d. rhetorical explanation
   e. not a slanter

6. "'Democrat' equals 'ideologically homeless ex-communist.'"

   Linda Bowles

▲ 7. The obvious truth is bilingual education has been a failure." In this statement, "the obvious truth" might best be viewed as
   a. proof surogate   *Surrogate*
   b. weaseler
   c. innuendo
   d. dysphemism
   e. not a slanter

8. After George W. Bush announced he wanted to turn a substantial portion of the federal government operation over to private companies, Bobby L. Harnage, Sr., president of the American Federation of Government Em-

ployees, said Bush had "declared all-out war on federal employees." Would
you say that the quoted passage is

   a. a rhetorical explanation

   b. a euphemism

   c. a weaseler

   d. hyperbole

   e. not a slanter

9. "You say you are in love with Oscar but are you sure he's right for you?
Isn't he a little on the mature side?" This statement contains

   a. loaded question

   b. a euphemism

   c. both a and b

   d. neither a nor b

▲ 10. "Before any more of my tax dollars go to the military, I'd like answers to
some questions, such as why are we spending billions of dollars on weapons
programs that don't work?" This statement contains an example of

   a. a downplayer

   b. a dysphemism

   c. a proof surrogate

   d. a loaded question

   e. hyperbole and a loaded question

11. "Can Governor Davis be believed when he says he will fight for the death
penalty? You be the judge." This statement contains

   a. dysphemism

   b. proof surrogate

   c. innuendo

   d. hyperbole

   e. no slanters

▲ 12. "Which is it George W. Bush lied about, whether he used cocaine, when he
used cocaine, or how much cocaine he used?" This statement contains

   a. hyperbole

   b. dysphemism

   c. loaded question

   d. proof surrogate

   e. no slanter

13. "Studies confirm what everyone knows: smaller classes make kids better
learners."

Bill Clinton

This statement contains:

   a. proof surrogate

   b. weaseler

   c. hyperbole

   d. innuendo

   e. no slanter

14. MAN SELLING HIS CAR: "True, there's a little wear and tear, but what are a few dents?" This statement contains what might best be called
    a. loaded question
    b. innuendo
    c. dysphemism
    d. euphemism

▲ 15. MAN THINKING OF BUYING THE CAR IN EXERCISE 14, TO HIS WIFE: "Okay, okay, so it's got a few miles on it. Still, it may be the only Mustang in the whole country for that price." In this item, "few" and "still" could be said to belong to the same category of slanter. (T or F)

16. In Exercise 15, "it may be" is
    a. a weaseler
    b. a proof surrogate
    c. a downplayer
    d. not a slanter

17. Still in Exercise 15, "in the whole country" is an example of
    a. innuendo
    b. hyperbole
    c. a euphemism
    d. none of these

Exercise 4-2

▲ Determine which of the numbered, italicized words and phrases are used as rhetorical devices in the following passage. If the item fits one of the text's categories of rhetorical devices, identify it as such.

> The National Rifle Association's campaign *to arm every man, woman, and child in America*[1] received a setback when the President signed the Brady Bill. But the *gun-pushers*[2] know that the bill was only *a small skirmish in a big war*[3] over guns in America. They can give up some of their more *fanatic*[4] positions on such things as *assault weapons*[5] and *cop-killer bullets*[6] and still win on the one that counts: regulation of manufacture and sale of handguns.

Exercise 4-3

▲ Follow the directions for Exercise 4-2.

> The *big money guys*[1] who have *smuggled*[2] the Rancho Vecino development onto the November ballot *will stop at nothing to have this town run just exactly as they want.*[3] *It is possible*[4] that Rancho Vecino will cause traffic congestion on the east side of town, and *it's perfectly clear that*[5] the number of houses that will be built will overload the sewer system. *But*[6] a small number of individuals have taken up the fight. *Can the developers be stopped in their desire to wreck our town?*[7]

Exercise 4-4

Follow the directions for Exercise 4-2.

> The U.S. Congress has cut off funds for the superconducting supercol-
> lider that the *scientific establishment*[1] wanted to build in Texas. The
> *alleged*[2] virtues of the supercollider proved no match for the *huge*[3]
> *cost-overruns*[4] that had piled up *like a mountain alongside a sea of red
> ink.*[5] Despite original estimates of five to six billion dollars, the latest
> figure was over eleven billion and *growing faster than weeds.*[6]

Exercise 4-5

Read the passage below and answer the questions that follow it. Your instructor may have further directions.

> Not to contribute to millennial paranoia, but we do live in strange times.
> The president is being tried over an extramarital affair.
>   I know, I know. I have heard Republican after Republican solemnly
> declaim that this is not about sex—it is about the rule of law, about the
> sanctity of oaths, about the preservation of the nation and about the re-
> tention of the very concept of virtue.
>   I have heard from Republicans that this is about absolute truth vs.
> relative truth; it is about where we went wrong in the '60s; it is about
> high crimes and misdemeanors; and it is about the law treating the
> mightiest in the land with the same impartial hand as the lowliest
> among us.
>   I have never listened to so much bilge in my life, and I have cov-
> ered the Texas Legislature for 30 years. New records for overreaching
> are set hourly.
>
> *From a column by Molly Ivins* (Fort Worth Star-Telegram)

1. What issue is the author addressing?
2. What position does the author take on that issue?
3. If the author supports this position with an argument, state that argument
   in your own words.
4. Does the author use rhetorical devices discussed in this chapter? If so, identify the main types of devices used.

Exercise 4-6

Follow the directions for Exercise 4-5, using the same list of questions.

> Schools are not a microcosm of society, any more than an eye is a mi-
> crocosm of the body. The eye is a specialized organ which does some-
> thing that no other part of the body does. That is its whole significance.
> You don't use your eyes to lift packages or steer automobiles. Special-
> ized organs have important things to do in their own specialties. So

schools, which need to stick to their special work as well, should not become social or political gadflies.

Thomas Sowell

Exercise 4-7

Follow the directions for Exercise 4-5, using the same list of questions.

"It is not the job of the state, and it is certainly not the job of the school, to tell parents when to put their children to bed," declared David Hart of the National Association of Head Teachers, responding to David Blunkett's idea that parents and teachers should draw up "contracts" (which you could be fined for breaching) about their children's behaviour, time-keeping, homework and bedtime. Teachers are apparently concerned that their five-to-eight-year-old charges are staying up too late and becoming listless truants the next day.

While I sympathise with Mr. Hart's concern about this neo-Stalinist nannying, I wonder whether it goes far enough. Is it not high time that such concepts as Bathtime, Storytime and Drinks of Water were subject to regulation as well? I for one would value some governmental guidance as to the number of humorous swimming toys (especially Hungry Hippo) allowable per gallon of water. Adopting silly voices while reading Spot's Birthday or Little Rabbit Foo-Foo aloud is something crying out for regulatory guidelines, while the right of children to demand and receive wholly unnecessary glasses of liquid after lights-out needs a Statutory Minimum Allowance.

John Walsh, The Independent

Exercise 4-8

Identify any rhetorical devices you find in the following selections, and classify those that fit the categories described in the text. For each, explain its function in the passage.

▲ 1. I trust you have seen Janet's file and have noticed the "university" she graduated from.

2. The original goal of the Milosovic government in Belgrade was ethnic cleansing in Kosovo.

3. "National Health Care: The compassion of the IRS and the efficiency of the post office, all at Pentagon prices."

From a letter to the editor, Sacramento Bee

▲ 4. Although it has always had a bad name in the United States, socialism is nothing more or less than democracy in the realm of economics.

5. We'll have to work harder to get Representative Burger reelected because of his little run-in with the law.

▲ 6. It's fair to say that, compared with most people his age, Mr. Beechler is pretty much bald.

7. During World War II, the U.S. government resettled many people of Japanese ancestry in internment camps.

▲ 8. "Overall, I think the gaming industry would be a good thing for our state."

From a letter to the editor, Plains Weekly Record

9. Morgan has decided to run for state senator. I'm sorry to hear that he's decided to become a politician.

10. I'll tell you what capitalism is: Capitalism is Charlie Manson sitting in Folsom Prison for all those murders and still making a bunch of bucks off T-shirts.

▲ 11. Clearly, Antonin Scalia is the most corrupt Supreme Court Justice in the history of the country.

12. In a February 1 article, writer Susan Beahay says Bush's abortion decision will return abortions to secrecy, risking the mother's life having a back-alley abortion. That's really juicy. The ultra-left pro-abortion crowd sure can add a little levity into a deadly serious subject.

13. It may well be that many faculty members deserve some sort of pay increase. Nevertheless, it is clearly true that others are already amply compensated.

▲ 14. I wouldn't say he copied her answers. I'd say he adjusted his own answers.

15. I love some of the bulleting and indenting features of Microsoft Word. I think it would have been a nice feature, however, if they made it possible to turn some of them off when you don't need them.

Exercise 4-9

Identify any rhetorical devices you find in the following passages, and explain their purposes. Note: Some items may contain *no* rhetorical devices.

▲ 1. "If the United States is to meet the technological challenge posed by Japan, Inc., we must rethink the way we do everything from design to manufacture to education to employee relations."

Harper's

2. According to UNICEF reports, several thousand Iraqi children died each month because of the U.N. sanctions.

3. Maybe Professor Lankirshim's research hasn't appeared in the first-class journals as recently as that of some of the other professors in his department; that doesn't necessarily mean his work is going downhill. He's still a fine teacher, if the students I've talked to are to be believed.

▲ 4. "Let's put it this way: People who make contributions to my campaign fund get access. But there's nothing wrong with constituents having access to their representatives, is there?"

Loosely paraphrased from an interview with a California state senator

5. In the 2000 presidential debates, Al Gore consistently referred to his own tax proposal as a "tax plan" and to George W. Bush's tax proposal as a "tax scheme."

6. "This healthy food provides all the necessary ingredients to help keep your bird in top health."

—Hartz Parrot Diet

▲ 7. [*Note:* Dr. Jack Kevorkian was instrumental in assisting a number of terminally ill people in committing suicide during the 1990s.] "We're opening the door to Pandora's Box if we claim that doctors can decide if it's proper for someone to die. We can't have Kevorkians running wild, dealing death to people."

Larry Bunting, assistant prosecutor, Oakland County, Michigan

8. "LOS ANGELES—Marriott Corp. struck out with patriotic food workers at Dodger Stadium when the concession-holder ordered them to keep working instead of standing respectfully during the National Anthem. . . . Concession stand manager Nick Kavadas . . . immediately objected to a Marriott representative.

"Marriott subsequently issued a second memo on the policy. It read: 'Stop all activities while the National Anthem is being played.'

"Mel Clemens, Marriott's general manager at the stadium, said the second memo clarified the first memo."

Associated Press

9. These so-called forfeiture laws are a serious abridgment of a person's constitutional rights. In some states, district attorneys' offices only have to *claim* that a person has committed a drug-related crime to seize the person's assets. So fat-cat DAs can get rich without ever getting around to proving that anybody is guilty of a crime.

▲ 10. "A few years ago, the deficit got so horrendous that even Congress was embarrassed. Faced with this problem, the lawmakers did what they do best. They passed another law."

Abe Mellinkoff, in the San Francisco Chronicle

11. "[U]mpires are baseball's designated grown-ups and, like air-traffic controllers, are paid to handle pressure."

George Will

12. "Last season should have made it clear to the moguls of baseball that something still isn't right with the game—something that transcends residual fan anger from the players' strike. Abundant evidence suggests that baseball still has a long way to go."

Stedman Graham, Inside Sports

▲ 13. "As you know, resolutions [in the California State Assembly] are about as meaningful as getting a Publishers' Clearinghouse letter saying you're a winner."

Greg Lucas, in the San Francisco Chronicle

14. The entire gain in the stock market in the first four months of the year was due to a mere fifty stocks.

15. I believe that no matter what Saddam Hussein does—including agreeing to let the inspectors back in—Bush will go to war against him. And now there's nothing to stop him. Congress has already rolled over.

16. "[Supreme Court Justice Antonin] Scalia's ideology is a bald and naked concept called 'Majoritarianism.' Only the rights of the majority are protected."

Letter to the editor of the San Luis Obispo Telegram-Tribune

17. "Mimi Rumpp stopped praying for a winning lottery ticket years ago. . . . But after a doctor told her sister Miki last year that she needed a kidney transplant, the family began praying for a donor. . . . Less than a year later, Miki has a new kidney, courtesy of a bank teller in Napa, Calif., to whom she had told her story. The teller was the donor; she was so moved by Miki's plight she had herself tested and discovered she was a perfect match. Coincidence? Luck? Divine intervention? Rumpp is sure: 'It was a miracle.'"

Newsweek

▲ 18. "We are about to witness an orgy of self-congratulation as the self-appointed environmental experts come out of their yurts, teepees, and grant-maintained academic groves to lecture us over the impending doom of the planet and agree with each other about how it is evil humanity and greedy 'big business' that is responsible for it all."

Tim Worstall, in New Times

19. "In the 1980s, Central America was awash in violence. Tens of thousands of people fled El Salvador and Guatemala as authoritarian governments seeking to stamp out leftist rebels turned to widespread arrests and death squads."

USA Today

Exercise 4-10

Discuss the following stereotypes in class. Do they invoke the same kind of images for everyone? Which are negative and which are positive? How do you think they came to be stereotypes? Is there any "truth" behind them?

1. soccer mom
2. Religious Right
3. dumb blonde
4. tax-and-spend liberal
5. homosexual agenda
6. redneck
7. radical feminist
8. contented housewife
9. computer nerd
10. tomboy
11. interior decorator
12. Washington insider
13. Earth mother
14. frat rat
15. Deadhead
16. trailer trash

Exercise 4-11

Your instructor will give you three minutes to write down as many positive and negative stereotypes as you can. Are there more positive stereotypes on your list or more negative ones? Why do you suppose that is?

Exercise 4-12

Write two brief paragraphs describing the same person, event, or situation—that is, both paragraphs should have the same informative content. The first paragraph should be written in a *purely* informative way, using language that is as neutral as possible; the second paragraph should be slanted as much as possible either positively or negatively (your choice).

Exercise 4-13

Explain the difference between a weaseler and a downplayer. Find a clear example of each in a newspaper, magazine, or other source. Next find an example of a phrase that is sometimes used as a weaseler or downplayer but that is used appropriately or neutrally in the context of your example.

Exercise 4-14

Explain how rhetorical definitions, rhetorical comparisons, and rhetorical explanations differ. Find an example of each in a newspaper, magazine, or other source.

Exercise 4-15

Look through an issue of *Time, Newsweek,* or another newsmagazine, and find a photograph that portrays its subject in an especially good or bad light—that is, one that does a nonverbal job of creating slant regarding the subject.

Exercise 4-16

In groups, invent two newspaper or magazine headlines to go with this photograph of Senator Hillary Rodham Clinton. Make one headline create a favorable impression in combination with the photo and make the other create an unfavorable impression.

Writing Exercises

1. Turn to Selection 9 in Essays for Analysis, "Will Ozone Blob Devour the Earth?" and identify as many rhetorical devices as you can find. (Your instructor may narrow the scope of the assignment to just certain paragraphs.)

2. Over the past decade, reportedly more than 2,000 illegal immigrants have died trying to cross the border into the southwestern United States. Many deaths have resulted from dehydration in the desert in the desert heat and from freezing to death on cold winter nights. A San Diego–based nonprofit humanitarian organization now leaves blankets, clothes, and water at stations throughout the desert and mountain regions for the immigrants. Should the organization do this? Its members say they are providing simple humanitarian aid, but critics accuse them of encouraging illegal activity. Take a stand on the issue and defend your position in writing. Then identify each rhetorical device you used.

3. Until recently, tiny Stratton, Ohio, had an ordinance requiring all door-to-door "canvassers" to obtain a permit from the mayor. Presumably the ordinance was intended to protect the many senior citizens of the town from harm by criminals who might try to gain entry by claiming to be conducting a survey. The ordinance was struck down by the Jehovah's Witnesses, who thought it violated their First Amendment right to free speech. The Supreme Court agreed and struck down the law in 2002. Should it have? Defend your position in a brief essay without using rhetoric. Alternatively, defend your position and use rhetorical devices, but identify each device you use.

Chapter 5

More Rhetorical Devices: Psychological and Related Fallacies

*E*very now and then we hear snatches of the syndicated national talk radio program called *Savage Nation.* The show, which also airs on MSNBC, stars Michael Savage, who has a Ph.D. in epidemiology and nutrition science from the University of California, Berkeley (according to his Web page).

Mr. Savage is perhaps the most vociferously angry of all national talk radio hosts; his opponents refer to his program as "hate radio." And it does seem undeniable that Savage's default position is outrage.

Aristotle warned against making decisions when the emotions are inflamed and cautioned us to be wary of orators who, like Mr. Savage, try to bring us to a boil with rage or stir up some powerful emotion. In this chapter we examine several rhetorical devices a speaker or writer might employ to tempt us to substitute knee-jerk emotional responses for sound judgment and careful thinking.

These devices go beyond the rhetorical coloration we talked about in the last chapter. They can be made to look like reasonable arguments containing premises and conclusions. But they don't really provide legitimate proof of what they supposedly are proving. The "reasons" they proffer for their "conclusions" do not really support those conclusions. A good argument provides a justification for accepting its conclusion. The devices in this chapter tempt us with considerations that are emotionally or psychologically linked to an issue, but they don't really support the claims they are supposed to support. They offer only *pretended* support; you might think of them as pieces of pretend reasoning, or *pseudo*reasoning.

The devices in this chapter thus all count as fallacies (a fallacy is a mistake in reasoning). The rhetorical devices we discussed in the last chapter—euphemisms, innuendo, and so forth—aren't fallacies. Of course, we commit a fallacy if we think a claim has been supported when the "support" is nothing more than rhetorically persuasive language.

People constantly accept fallacies as legitimate arguments; but the reverse mistake can also happen. We must be careful not to dismiss *legitimate* arguments as fallacies just because they *remind* us of a fallacy. Often beginning students in logic have this problem. They read about fallacies like the ones we cover here and then think they see them everywhere. These fallacies are common, but they are not everywhere; and you sometimes must consider a specimen carefully before accepting or rejecting it. The exercises at the end of the chapter will help you learn to do this, because they contain a few reasonable arguments mixed in with the fallacies.

The Rush Limbaugh Fallacy: The "Argument" from Outrage

If you tune in Mike Savage or Rush Limbaugh (who is still better known than Savage), chances are the first thing you will hear (if not a commercial) is a voice quivering with disbelief and indignation, saying something like, "It's your money . . . and the liberals want to do *what* with it? Spend it on *midnight basketball leagues*??!"

Whether the speaker is the host or someone calling in, he or she will be "mad as hell" (to borrow an expression popular in the 1980s). And the speaker wants you to be mad too—wants you to rise up in righteous indignation and *smite down* the basketball league and every other liberal proposal you run into.

Now, in case you think we are just being anti-Rush, anticonservative, or anti-Republican, we'll be getting around to the Democrats in a bit. Democrat talk-show hosts use the same techniques as Rush Limbaugh, although unfortunately for them, they aren't nearly as well known.

Surely, you might say, if someone is wasting your money, don't you have a right to be angry? The answer is "yes": Anger is not a fallacy, and sometimes it is appropriate to be angry. However, when we are angry (especially if we are in a blind rage), it's easy to become illogical in two very predictable ways. *First, we may think we have been given a reason for being angry when in fact we have not.* Is spending money on midnight basketball leagues a waste of money? Well, you need to investigate to see. If a midnight basketball league reduces crime in a neighborhood, then maybe it isn't a waste of money. It is a mistake to think that something is wrong simply because it makes us angry. Presumably we are angry because it is wrong, not the other way around.

Second, we may let the anger we feel as the result of one thing influence our evaluations of an unrelated thing. The next liberal proposal to come along must be examined on its own merits, and we shouldn't let anger over the midnight basketball leagues poison our evaluation of it. If a person, Johnson, has done something to anger us, that wouldn't be a reason for downgrading Johnson's performance on some *other* matter, nor would it be a reason for upgrading our opinion of someone else.

Rush Limbaugh Hyperventilates

Reprinted by permission of Tim Brinton.

What happens when Rush Limbaugh attacks those of us in public life is that people aren't just content to listen. People want to act because they get emotional . . . and the threats to those of us in public life go up dramatically, against us and our families, and it's very disconcerting.

—*SENATOR TOM DASCHLE (D-N.D.)*

What more do you want to do to destroy this country than what you've already tried? It is unconscionable what this man has done. This stuff gets broadcast around the world, Senator. What do you want your nickname to be? Hanoi Tom? Tokyo Tom? You sit there and pontificate on the fact that we're not winning the war on terrorism when you and your party have done nothing but try to sabotage it.

—*RUSH LIMBAUGH, responding the next day*

The **"argument" from outrage,** then, consists in inflammatory words (or thoughts) followed by a "conclusion" of some sort. It substitutes anger for reason and judgment in considering an issue. It is a favorite strategy of demagogues. In fact, it is *the* favorite strategy of demagogues. Let's say the issue is whether gay marriages should be legal. Left-of-center demagogues may wax indignantly about "narrow-minded fundamentalist bigots dictating what people can do in their bedrooms"—talk calculated to get us steamed although it really has nothing to do with the issue. On the other side, conservative demagogues may allude to gays' demanding "special rights." No-

Another Angry American

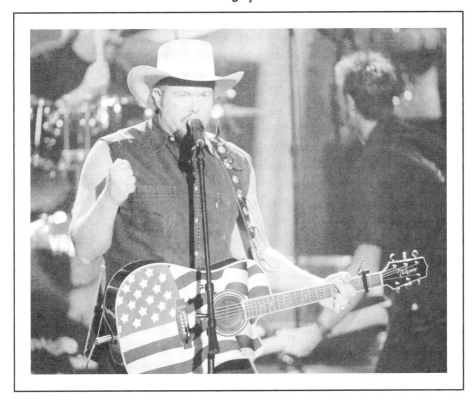

▲   *Recording artists such as Toby Keith sometimes try to boost popularity by riding the patriotism bandwagon.*

body wants someone else to get special rights, and when we hear about some-body "demanding" them, our blood pressure goes up. But wanting a right other people have is not wanting a special right; it's wanting an equal right.

A particularly dangerous type of "argument" from outrage is known as **scapegoating**—blaming a certain group of people—or even a single person (like George W. Bush or Bill Clinton) for all of life's troubles. George Wallace, the former governor of Alabama who ran for president in 1968 on a "states' rights platform" (which then was a code word for white supremacy) said he could get good old Southern boys to do anything by whooping them into a frenzy over Northern civil rights workers.

"Arguments" based on outrage are so common that the fallacy ranks high on our list of the top ten fallacies of all time, which is contained in Appendix 2. It's unfortunate they are so common—history demonstrates constantly that anger is a poor lens through which to view the world. Policies adopted in anger are seldom wise, as any parent will tell you who has laid down the law in a fit of anger.

The idea behind [talk radio] is to keep the base riled up.

—Republican political advisor Brent Lauder, explaining what talk radio is for ["the base" refers to the Republican rank and file]

Scare Tactics by Omission

The June 2002 risk assessment estimates that there would be a 95% probability that lead made airborne by the projected housing development would result in an increase of 3.7 to 4.3 μg/dL in the lead levels in children's blood.

—*From a newsletter by a group opposed to a projected housing development*

Sounds scary, all that lead going into kids' blood. However, here's what the June 2002 risk assessment really said:

The June 2002 risk assessment estimates that there would be a 95% probability that lead made airborne by the projected housing development would result in a child blood level of 3.7 to 4.3 μg/dL, well below the 10 μg/dL level of concern.

—*Office of Environmental Health Hazard Assessment*

Moral: Scare tactics can involve both distorting and omitting.

Scare Tactics

George Wallace didn't just try to anger the crowds when he told them what Northern civil rights workers were up to; he tried to *scare* them. When people become angry or afraid, they don't think clearly. They follow blindly. Demagogues like Wallace like to dangle scary scenarios in front of people.

Trying to scare people into doing something or accepting a position is using **scare tactics.** One way this might be done is the George Wallace method—dangling a frightening picture in front of someone. A simpler method might be just to threaten the person, a special case of scare tactics known as **"argument" by force.** Either way, if the idea is to get people to substitute fear for reason and judgment when taking a position on an issue, it is a fallacy. Likewise, it is a fallacy to succumb to such techniques when others use them on us.

Fear can befuddle us as easily as can anger, and the mistakes that happen are similar in both instances. Wallace's listeners may not have noticed (or not cared) that Wallace didn't actually give them *proof* that civil rights workers were doing whatever it was he portrayed them as doing; the portrayal was its own evidence, you might say. When we are befuddled with fear, we may not notice we lack evidence that the scary scenario is real. Imagine someone talking about global warming: The speaker may paint a picture so alarming we don't notice that he or she doesn't provide evidence that global warming is actually happening. Or take gay marriages again. Someone might warn us of presumably dire consequences if gay people are allowed to marry—we'll be opening "Pandora's box"; marriage will become meaningless; homosexuality will become rampant; society will collapse—but he or she may issue these warnings without providing details as to why (or how) the consequences might actually come about. The consequences are so frightening they apparently don't need proof.

Fear of one thing, X, may also affect evaluation of an unrelated thing, Y. You have your eye on a nice house and are considering buying it, and then the real estate agent frightens you by telling you the seller has received other offers and will sell soon. Some people, in this situation, might overestimate what they really can afford to pay.

To avoid translating fear of one thing into an evaluation of some unrelated thing, we need to be clear on what issues our fears are relevant to. Legitimate warnings do not involve irrelevancies and do not qualify as scare tactics. "You should be careful of that snake—it's deadly poisonous" might be a scary thing to say to someone, but we don't make a mistake in reasoning when we say it, and neither does the other person if he or she turns and runs into the house. Suppose, however, that the Michelin tire people show an ad featuring a sweet (and vulnerable) baby in a ring of automobile tires. Showing pictures of car tires around infants will produce disquieting associations in any observer, and it wouldn't be unreasonable to check our tires when we see this ad. But the issue raised by the Michelin people is whether to buy *Michelin* tires, and the fear of injuring or killing a child by driving on unsafe tires does not bear on the question of *which* tires to buy. The Michelin ad isn't a legitimate warning; it's scare tactics.

Other Fallacies Based on Emotions

Other emotions work much like anger and fear as sources of mistakes in reasoning. *Compassion,* for example, is a fine thing to have. There is absolutely nothing wrong with feeling sorry for someone. But when feeling sorry for someone drives us to a position on an unrelated matter, the result is the fallacy known as **"argument" from pity.** We have a job that needs doing; Helen can barely support her starving children and needs work desperately. But does Helen have the skills we need? We may not care if she does; and if we don't, nobody can fault us for hiring her out of compassion. But feeling sorry for Helen may lead us to misjudge her skills or overestimate her abilities, and that is a mistake in reasoning. Her skills are what they are regardless of her need. Or, suppose you need a better grade in this course to get into law school or avoid academic disqualification or whatever. If you think you *deserve* or have *earned* a better grade because you need a better grade, or you try to get your instructor to think you deserve a better grade by trying to make him or her feel sorry for you, that's the "argument" from pity. Or, if you think someone *else* deserves a better grade because of the hardships he or she (or his or her parents) suffered, that's also the "argument" from pity.

Envy and *jealousy* can also confuse our thinking. Compassion, a desirable emotion, may tempt us to emphasize a person's good points; envy and

Knee Operation Judged Useless

Fake surgery worked just as well in cases of osteoarthritis.

Here we are doing all this surgery on people and it's all a sham.

—DR. BARUCH BRODY, *Baylor College of Medicine*

Wishful thinking—allowing our desires and hopes to color our beliefs and influence our judgment—is common indeed. A powerful illustration of wishful thinking is the placebo effect, where subjects perceive improvement in a medical condition when they receive what they think is a medication but in fact is an inactive substance. Even surgical procedures, apparently, are subject to a placebo effect, judging from a study of a popular and expensive knee operation for arthritis. People who have had this procedure swear by it as significantly reducing pain. But researchers at the Houston Veterans Affairs Medical Center and Baylor College of Medicine discovered that subjects who underwent placebo (fake) surgery said exactly the same thing. Furthermore, when they tested knee functions two years after the surgery the researchers discovered that the operation doesn't improve knee functions at all.

Source: *Sacramento Bee*, July 11, 2002. From *New York Times* News Service.

jealousy tempt us to exaggerate someone's bad points. When we find fault with a person because of envy, we are guilty of the fallacy known as **"argument" from envy.** "Well, he may have a lot of money but he certainly has bad manners" would be an example of this if it is envy that prompts us to criticize him.

Pride, on the other hand, can lead us to exaggerate *our own* accomplishments and abilities and lead to our making other irrelevant judgments as well. It especially makes us vulnerable to **apple polishing.** Moore recently sat on a jury in a criminal case involving alleged prostitution and pandering at a strip club; the defendant's attorney told the members of the jury it would take *"an unusually discerning jury"* to see that the law, despite its wording, wasn't really intended to apply to someone like his client. Ultimately the jury members did find with the defense, but let us hope it wasn't because the attorney flattered their ability to discern things. Allowing praise of oneself to substitute for judgment about the truth of a claim, or trying to get others to do this, as the lawyer did, is the apple polishing fallacy.

Feelings of *guilt* work similarly. "How could you not invite Trixie to your wedding? She would never do that to you and you know she must be very hurt." The remark is intended to make someone feel sorry for Trixie, but even more fundamentally it is supposed to induce a sense of guilt. Eliciting feelings of guilt to get others to do or not do something, or to accept

Positive Outlook Won't Delay Cancer Death, Study Says

NICE, France — New research has dealt a blow to the idea that a positive outlook might improve a patient's chances of surviving cancer, scientists said Saturday.

However, experts said it is still worthwhile for patients to improve their attitude, perhaps by joining a cancer support group, because often it does make them feel better.

The findings were presented Saturday at a meeting of the European Society of Medical Oncology in Nice, France. The researchers reviewed evidence to determine whether psychologist-run support groups kept patients alive.

"There were some studies out there showing that positive-thinking type of support will not only improve your quality of life—which undoubtedly it does, I'm not questioning that—but also will prolong the lives of cancer patients," said Dr. Edzard Ernst, a professor of complementary medicine at the University of Exeter in England who led the study.

"One study from 1989 gets cited over and over and over again, and we knew there were one or two negative studies on this, too, so we decided to see if it was true," he said.

The researchers analyzed 11 studies that included a total of 1,500 patients.

"The data provided no evidence at all to show that these types of approaches prolong life in cancer patients," Ernst said.

Associated Press

More wishful thinking, apparently.

Source: *Sacramento Bee,* October 19, 2002.

the view that they should or should not do it, is popularly known as putting a **guilt trip** on someone, which is to commit a fallacy. Parents sometimes use this tactic with children when they (the parents) won't (or can't) offer a clear explanation of why something should or shouldn't be done. Certainly, if the child knowingly does something wrong, he or she should feel guilty; but whatever has been done isn't wrong *because* he or she feels guilty.

Hopes, desires, and aversions can also lead us astray logically. The fallacy known as **wishful thinking** happens when we accept or urge acceptance (or rejection) of a claim simply because it would be pleasant (or unpleasant) if it were true. Some people, for example, may believe in God simply on the basis of wishful thinking or desire for an afterlife. A smoker may refuse to acknowledge the health hazards of smoking. We've had students who are in denial about the consequences of cutting classes. The wishful thinking fallacy also underlies much of the empty rhetoric of "positive thinking"—rhetoric that claims "you are what you want to be" and other such slogans.

Most people desire to be liked or accepted by some circle of other people and are averse to having the acceptance withdrawn. A *desire for acceptance* can motivate us to accept a claim not because of its merits, but because we will gain someone's approval (or will avoid having approval withdrawn). When we do this, or try to get someone else to do it, the fallacy is the **peer**

pressure "argument." Now, obviously nobody ever said anything quite so blatant as "Ralph, this claim is true because we won't like you any more if you don't accept it." Peer pressure is often disguised or unstated, but anyone going through an American high school, where you can lose social standing merely by being seen with someone who isn't "in," knows it is a real force. Kids who feel ostracized sometimes take guns to school.

It doesn't have to be one's associates who exert peer pressure, either. In scientific experiments, people will actually revise what they say they saw if a group of strangers in the same room deny having seen the same thing.

One very common fallacy that is closely related to the peer pressure "argument" involves one's sense of *group identification,* which people experience when they are part of a group—a team, a club, a school, a gang, a state, a nation, the Elks, Wal-Mart, the U.S.A., Mauritius, you name it. Let's define the **group think fallacy** as happening when one substitutes pride of membership in a group for reason and deliberation in arriving at a position on an issue; and let's include the fallacy in our list of the top ten fallacies of all time, because it is exceedingly common. One obvious form of this fallacy involves national pride, or **nationalism**—a powerful and fierce emotion that can lead to blind endorsement of a country's policies and practices. ("My country right or wrong" explicitly discourages critical thinking and encourages blind patriotism.) Nationalism is also invoked to reject, condemn, or silence criticism of one's country as unpatriotic or treasonable (and may or may not involve an element of peer pressure). If a letter writer expresses a criticism of America on the opinion page of your local newspaper on Monday, you can bet that by the end of the week there will be a response dismissing the criticism with the "argument" that if so-and-so doesn't like it here, he or she ought to move to Russia (or Cuba or Afghanistan or Iraq).

Group think does not play cultural or political favorites, either. On the opposite side of the political spectrum are what some people call the "blame America first" folks. The group think ethic of this club includes, most importantly, automatically assuming that whatever is wrong in the world is the result of some U.S. policy. The club has no formal meetings or rules for membership, but flying an American flag would be grounds for derision and instant dismissal.

Group think "reasoning" is certainly not limited to political groups either. It occurs whenever one's affiliations are of utmost psychological importance.

Now, these various emotional fallacies, from the "argument" from outrage to the group think fallacy, all share certain properties. They often (though not always) contain assertions you might call "premises" and other assertions that you might call a "conclusion." But the "premises" don't actually *support* the "conclusion"; rather, they evoke emotions that make us want to accept the conclusion without support. So, although they can wear the clothing of *arguments,* they are really pieces of *persuasion* (Chapter 1). Whenever language is used to arouse emotions, it is wise to consider carefully whether any "conclusions" that come to mind have been supported by evidence.

Rationalizing

Let's say Mr. Smith decides to do something really nice for his wife on her birthday and buys her a new table saw. "This saw wasn't cheap," he tells her. "But you're going to be glad we have it, because it will keep me out in the garage and out of your way when you're working here in the house."

The fallacy in the reasoning in this made-up example is pretty obvious. Mr. Smith is confusing his wife's desires with his own.

When we do this, when we use a false pretext to satisfy our own desires or interests, we're guilty of **rationalizing,** a very common fallacy. It almost made our list of the top ten fallacies of all time (Appendix 2).

Now, there is nothing wrong with satisfying one's desires, at least if they don't harm someone or aren't illegal. But in this book we're talking logic, not morals. Rationalizing involves a confusion in thinking, and to the extent we wish to avoid being confused in our thinking, we should try to avoid rationalizing.

"But," you may be saying, "It is good to do nice things for other people. If you do something that helps them, or that they like, or that benefits the world, what difference does motivation make? If, for whatever reason, the table saw makes Mr. Smith's wife happy, that's what counts."

Now, there is something to be said for this argument, because it is good to make people happy. But whether Mr. Smith's wife is happy or not, there has been a confusion in his thinking, a fallacy. And it is a common fallacy indeed. Obviously most instances of rationalizing are not as blatant as Mr. Smith's, but people frequently deceive themselves as to their true motives.

Rationalizing need not be selfish, either. Let's say a former oilman is elected governor of a state that produces oil. He may act in what at some level he thinks are the best interests of his state—when in fact he is motivated by a desire to help the oil industry. (Incidentally, you can't just assume he would do this.) To the extent he is deceiving himself about his true motivation, he is rationalizing. But this isn't *selfish* rationalizing; his actions don't benefit him personally.

Rationalizing, then, involves an element of self-deception, but otherwise it isn't necessarily devious. However, some people encourage others to rationalize because they themselves stand to benefit in some way. "Hey, Smith," his buddy Jones says to him. "That's a fine idea! Really creative. Your wife will really like a saw. Maybe you could build a boat for her, and you and I could go fishing." Jones may or may not say this innocently: If he does, he too is guilty of rationalizing; if he doesn't, he's just cynical.

Everyone Knows . . .

In Chapter 4 we examined proof surrogates like "Everyone knows . . ." and "It's only common sense that. . . ." Phrases like this are used when a speaker or writer doesn't really have an argument.

An "Argument" from Unpopularity

If they're going to talk about "the facts," here's a fact: All the major religions of the world consider homosexuality wrong.

—*JANEY PARSHALL, spokesperson for the Family Research Council*

Background: Ms. Parshall is responding to a joint announcement by the American Academy of Pediatrics, the National Education Association, and the American Psychological Association that there is no support among health and mental health professional organizations for the idea that homosexuality is abnormal or mentally unhealthy.

Such phrases often appear in peer pressure "arguments" ("Pardner, in these parts everyone thinks . . .). They also are used in the group think fallacy ("As any red-blooded American patriot knows, . . .). There is, however, a third way these phrases can be used. An example would be when Robert Novak says on CNN's *Crossfire*, "Liberals are finally admitting what everyone knows, that airline safety demands compromise." Novak isn't applying or evoking peer pressure or group think; he is offering "proof" that airline safety demands compromise (and bad-mouthing liberals to boot). His proof is the fact that everyone knows it.

When we do this, when we urge someone to accept a claim (or fall prey to someone's doing it to us) simply on the grounds that all or most or some substantial number of people (other than authorities or experts, of course) believe it, we commit the fallacy known as the **"argument" from popularity.** That most people believe something is a fact is not evidence that it is a fact—most people believe in God, for example, but that isn't evidence that God exists. Likewise, if most people didn't believe in God, that wouldn't be evidence that God doesn't exist.

Most people seem to assume that bus driving and similar jobs are somehow less desirable than white-collar jobs. The widespread acceptance of this assumption creates its own momentum—that is, we tend to accept it because everybody else does, and we don't stop to think about whether it actually has anything to recommend it. For a lot of people, a job driving a bus might make for a much happier life than a job as a manager.

In *some* instances, we should point out, what people think actually *determines* what is true. The meanings of most words, for example, are determined by popular usage. In addition, it would not be fallacious to conclude that the word "ain't" is out of place in formal speech because most speakers of English believe that it is out of place in formal speech.

There are other cases where what people think is an *indication* of what is true, even if it cannot *determine* truth. If several Bostonians of your acquaintance think that it is illegal to drink beer in their public parks, then you have some reason for thinking that it's true. And if you are told by several Europeans that it is not gauche to eat with your fork in your left hand

The Great White Van

While searching for the serial sniper who terrorized the Washington, D.C., area in the fall of 2002, police encountered the suspects' blue Chevrolet Caprice several times in road checkpoints and once with the sniper asleep in the car on a side street in Baltimore. However, the vehicle did not arouse police suspicions, apparently because it did not fit the beliefs that were forming in the case. As one senior government official put it, everyone was focused on finding an angry white guy in a white van. A witness had reported seeing a white van fleeing a shooting, and then other witnesses at other shootings began to see a white van, too. (One report even turned out to have been fabricated.) One eyewitness did report seeing a fleeing Caprice, but the Caprice sighting just didn't catch on. By the end of the case the white van theory had gained so much momentum that another person who saw a Caprice didn't file a report until after the suspects were apprehended. He said he assumed the sniper's vehicle was a white van. *Time* magazine even printed a picture of the white van the police were looking for.

In Chapter 3 we pointed out that this incident shows how eyewitness accounts can be untrustworthy. Here, we see the influence of popular belief in why that's true.

in Europe, then it is not fallacious to conclude that European manners allow eating with your fork in your left hand. The situation here is one of credibility, which we discussed in Chapter 3. Natives of Boston in the first case and Europeans in the second case can be expected to know more about the two claims in question, respectively, than others know. In a watered-down sense, they are "experts" on the subjects, at least in ways that many of us are not. In general, when the "everyone" who thinks that X is true includes experts about X, then what they think is indeed a good reason to accept X.

Thus it would be incorrect to automatically label as a fallacy any instance in which a person cites people's beliefs to establish a point. (No "argument" fitting a pattern in this chapter should *unthinkingly* be dismissed.) But it is important to view such references to people's beliefs as red alerts. These are cautionary signals that warn you to look closely for genuine reasons in support of the claim asserted.

Two variations of the "argument" from popularity deserve mention: **"Argument" from common practice** consists in trying to justify or defend an *action* or *practice* (as distinguished from an assertion or claim) on the grounds that it is common. "I shouldn't get a speeding ticket because everyone drives over the limit" would be an example. "Everyone cheats on their taxes, so I don't see why I shouldn't" would be another. Now there is something to watch out for here: When a person defends an action by saying that other people do the same thing, he or she might just be requesting fair play. He or she might just be saying, in effect, "O.K., O.K., I know it's wrong, but nobody else gets punished and it would be unfair to single me out." That person isn't trying to justify the action; he or she is asking for equal treatment.

The other variant of the argument from popularity is the **"argument" from tradition,** a name that is self-explanatory. People do things because that's the way things have always been done, and they believe things because that's what people have always believed. But, logically speaking, you don't prove a claim or prove a practice is legitimate on the basis of tradition; when you try to do so, you are guilty of "argument" from tradition. The fact that it's a tradition among most American children to believe in Santa Claus, for instance, doesn't prove Santa Claus exists; and the fact it's also a tradition for most American parents to deceive their kids about Santa Claus doesn't necessarily mean it is okay for them to do so.

Relativism

We talked about relativism in Chapter 1. **Relativism** is the theory that "truth is relative" or, more precisely, this: The very same claim may be true in one culture and false in another; it all depends on what the people within the culture think. If, for example, one culture thinks flu is caused by a virus and another culture thinks flu is caused by the flu-god, then in the first culture flu is caused by a virus and in the second culture it isn't—according to a relativist. Relativists, obviously, don't think the "argument" from popularity is a fallacy. What is true *is* what people within a culture think is true, according to them. (More sophisticated versions of relativism can be found that don't sound as silly as this example; that doesn't make the basic idea any more true, as we will see in a moment.)

Now, when it comes to claims that are about moral or ethical values, such as "It is good to help others" or "Adultery is immoral," relativism has a degree of plausibility. That's because claims like these are nonfactual (see Chapter 1), and that means that if one person thinks adultery is immoral and another doesn't, we don't require one of them to be mistaken. Likewise, if one *culture* thinks adultery is immoral and the next one doesn't, we let each culture have its way on the subject. But moral relativism—the idea that the selfsame moral judgment (like "Adultery is immoral") can be true in one culture and false in another—is a difficult and controversial subject in moral philosophy, because the statement "Adultery is immoral" seems to imply that the claim holds true for people in other cultures too. We talk about moral relativism in Chapter 12, but it is primarily a subject for a course in ethics.

When it comes to *factual* claims, claims about straightforward factual matters (like "Flu is caused by a virus"), at first glance relativism seems less plausible. A factual claim, if true, seems to be true regardless of any particular culture's acceptance of it. However, relativists have sophisticated ways of defending their position. Is flu caused by a virus, as Culture A holds, or is it caused by the flu-god, as Culture B holds? Well, relativists argue, Culture A has its own standards of what counts as relevant evidence, and it has its own standards of what counts as proof; it has its own standards of what counts as true and false and its own standards of what counts as sound argument, and these standards may be different from the standards of Culture B. It is meaningless, relativists argue, to say that one culture's standards of truth and relevance and evidence and proof and argument are more correct than another's. Therefore, it is meaningless to suppose that Culture A's views on the flu are more correct than Culture B's.

This is a clever argument, but defective. The trouble is that it undermines itself. Whatever standards of correct argumentation it assumes, it "proves" that those standards are no more correct than alternative standards. It "proves," in short, that we shouldn't take it seriously.

Underneath relativism is the assumption that what is true for one person is not necessarily true for another, an assumption known as **subjectivism.** A problem with subjectivism, and any doctrine that assumes it, is that it is impossible to make any sense of it, at least when it comes to factual claims. What could it mean to think that a claim, like "The room has a window in it" or "You have type-A flu virus," could be true for Mr. Wong and not true for Ms. Mbutu? Could the room have a window if Wong believes it does and at the same time not have a window if Mbutu believes otherwise? It doesn't matter what standards of evidence each person has or what each person thinks "true" means; the room has a window or it doesn't, and if Mbutu and Wong have different opinions on the subject, one is mistaken.

The bottom line is that if we believe that a factual claim may be true for one person or culture and false for another person or culture, we make a mistake, commit a fallacy. "That may be true for you, but it is not true for me" must be understood as a short way of saying, "Maybe you accept the claim, but I don't." Alternatively, it might be interpreted as a way of saying "Let's not talk about this anymore." If others use the "true for you, not true for me" remark to insist that it's correct for you to believe a factual claim and equally correct for them to reject the very same claim, they have fallen prey to subjectivism and relativism.

Two Wrongs Make a Right

Let's say you get tired of the people upstairs stomping around late at night, and so, to retaliate, you rent a tow truck and deposit their car in the river. From an emotional standpoint, you're getting even. From a reasoning standpoint, you're committing the fallacy known as **"two wrongs make a right."** It's a fallacy because wrongful behavior on someone else's part doesn't convert wrongful behavior on your part into rightful behavior, any more than illegal behavior on someone else's part converts your illegal activity into legal activity. If an act is wrong, it is wrong. Wrong acts don't cross-pollinate such that one comes out shorn of wrongfulness.

However, there is a well-known and somewhat widely held theory known as *retributivism,* according to which it is acceptable to harm someone in return for a harm he or she has done to you. But we must distinguish legitimate punishment from illegitimate retaliation. A fallacy clearly occurs when we consider a wrong to be justification for *any* retaliatory action, as would be the case if you destroyed your neighbors' car because they made too much noise at night. It is also a fallacy when the second wrong is directed at someone who didn't do the wrong in the first place—a brother or a child of the wrongdoer, for example. And it is a fallacy to defend doing harm to another on the grounds that that individual *would* or *might* do the same to us. This would happen, for example, if we didn't return excess change to a salesclerk on the grounds that "if the situation were reversed," the clerk wouldn't have given us back the money.

On the other hand, it isn't a fallacy to defend an action on the grounds it was necessary to prevent harm from befalling oneself; bopping a mugger to prevent him from hurting you would be an instance. To take another example, near the end of World War II, the United States dropped two atomic bombs on Japanese cities, killing tens of thousands of civilians. Politicians, historians, and others have argued that the bombing was justified because it helped end the war and thus prevented more casualties from the fighting, including the deaths of more Americans. People have long disagreed on whether the argument provides *sufficient* justification for the bombings, but there is no disagreement about its being a real argument and not empty rhetoric.

Red Herring/Smokescreen

When a person brings a topic into a conversation that distracts from the original point, especially if the new topic is introduced in order to distract, the person is said to have introduced a **red herring.** (It is so called because dragging a herring across a trail will cause a dog to leave the original trail and follow the path of the herring.) In the strip-joint jury trial we mentioned earlier, the defendant was charged with pandering; but the prosecuting attorney introduced evidence that the defendant had also sold liquor to minors. That was a red herring that had nothing to do with pandering.

The difference between red herrings and their close relatives, **smokescreens,** is subtle (and really not a matter of crucial importance). Generally speaking, red herrings distract by pulling one's attention away from one topic and toward another; smokescreens tend to pile issues on or to make them extremely complicated until the original is lost in the (verbal) "smoke." When Bill Clinton had missiles fired at terrorists in Sudan, he was accused of creating a red herring to deflect public scrutiny from the Monica Lewinsky

Red Herrings in Presidential Politicking

Al Gore: I believe there are 1.4 million children in Texas who do not have health insurance; 600,000 of whom . . . were actually eligible for it, but they couldn't sign up for it because of the barriers that they had to surmount.

Jim Lehrer [Moderator]: Let's let the governor respond to that. . . . Are those numbers correct? Are his charges correct?

George W. Bush: If he's trying to allege that I'm a hard-hearted person and I don't care about children, he's absolutely wrong. We spent $4.7 billion a year in the state of Texas for uninsured people and they get health care . . . somehow the allegation that we don't care and we're going to give money for this interest or that interest and not for children in the state of Texas is totally absurd. And let me tell you who the jury is: the people of Texas. There's only been one governor ever elected to back-to-back four-year terms, and that was me.

—From the 2000 presidential debates

business. When George W. Bush talked about Iraq having missiles capable of threatening the United States, about that country's potential of having a nuclear weapon "within six months," and about similar possible Iraqi threats, he was accused of putting up a smokescreen to hide his real reasons for wanting to attack Iraq, which were said to be oil interests and his own personal desire to complete his father's unfinished business.

Let's look at another example, this one made up but fairly typical of what often happens. Let's say a reporter asks Tom Ridge (secretary of the Department of Homeland Security) whether his office has made the country substantially safer from attacks by terrorists. "I'm pleased to say," Ridge answers, "that the United States is the safest country in the world when it comes to terrorist attacks. Certainly nobody can give an absolute, one hundred percent guarantee of safety, but you are certainly safer here than in any other country of the world."

Ridge has steered clear of the original question (whether his agency had made the country safer) and is leading the reporter on a tangent, toward the comparative safety of the United States (the United States may already have been the safest country before the creation of the agency). He has dragged a red herring across the trail, so to speak.

We admit that this measure is popular. But we also urge you to note that there are so many bond issues on this ballot that the whole concept is getting ridiculous.

—A generic red herring (unclassifiable irrelevance) from a California ballot pamphlet

A Red Herring in a Letter to TIME

Time's coverage of the medical marijuana controversy was thoughtful and scrupulously researched. But what argues most persuasively for a ban on marijuana is the extraordinary threat the drug poses for adolescents. Marijuana impairs short-term memory, depletes energy and impedes acquisition of psychosocial skills. Perhaps the most chilling effect is that it retards maturation for young people. A significant number of kids who use lots of pot simply don't grow up. So it is hardly surprising that marijuana is the primary drug for more than half the youngsters in the long-term residential substance-abuse programs that Phoenix House operates throughout the country.

> —Mitchell S. Rosenthal, M.D.
> *President, Phoenix House*
> *New York City*

The issue is legalization of marijuana for *adults*; the question of what it would do to children, who presumably would be prohibited from its use, is a red herring.

Source: *Time*, November 28, 2002

Imagine the conversation continues this way:

Reporter: "Mr. Ridge, polls say about half of the public think your agency has failed to make them safer. How do you answer your critics?"

Tom Ridge: "We are making progress toward reassuring people, but quite frankly our efforts have been hampered by the tendency of the press to concentrate on the negative side of the issue."

Once again Ridge brings in a red herring to sidestep the issue raised by the reporter.

Whether a distraction or an obfuscation is a plain red herring or a smokescreen is often difficult to tell in real life, and it's better to spend your energy getting a discussion back on track rather than worrying which type you have before you.

Many of the other fallacies we have been discussing in this chapter (and will be discussing in the next chapter) qualify, in some version or other, as red herrings/smokescreens. For example, a defense attorney might talk about a defendant's miserable upbringing to steer a jury's attention away from the charges against the person; doing this would qualify as an argument from pity as well as a smokescreen/red herring. Likewise, a prosecuting attorney may try to get a jury so angry about a crime it doesn't notice the weakness of the evidence pointing to the defendant. This would be an argument from outrage—and a red herring.

To simplify things, your instructor may reserve the red herring/smokescreen categories for irrelevancies that don't qualify as one of the other

Could somebody please show me one hospital built by a dolphin? Could somebody show me one highway built by a dolphin? Could someone show me one automobile invented by a dolphin?

—Rush Limbaugh, responding to the *New York Times*' claim that dolphins' "behavior and enormous brains suggest an intelligence approaching that of human beings."

Good point. Anyone know of a hospital or highway built by Rush Limbaugh or an automobile invented by him?

fallacies mentioned in this or the next chapter. In other words, he or she may tell you that if something qualifies as, say, an argument from outrage, you should call it that rather than a red herring or smokescreen.

Recap

In a recent interview with CNN's Connie Chung (photo below), tennis champion Martina Navratilova asserted that when she left Communist Czechoslovakia for the United States she changed one system that suppresses free opinion for another. Connie Chung told Navratilova to go ahead and think that at home, but asserted that celebrities shouldn't "spill out" such thoughts in public, because "people will write it down and talk about what you said." (Chung thus ineptly confirmed the very point Navratilova was making.)

One can only speculate as to what exactly was going on in Connie Chung's head, if anything. Maybe she was worried that Navratilova's comment would make people think bad things about the United States. Maybe she thinks the tennis star's comment is unpatriotic. Maybe criticism of the United States just upsets her. Whatever her thoughts, the example nicely illustrates what we have been talking about in this chapter. Sometimes, instead of bringing forth considerations relevant to an issue, people give an unrelated "argument." Many of the fallacies we have examined are like Connie Chung's: The unrelated argument involves some kind of emotion, though it may be hard to pin down exactly what it is.

Thus we have

- ▲ "Argument" from outrage
- ▲ Scare tactics
- ▲ "Argument" by force
- ▲ "Argument" from pity
- ▲ "Argument" from envy
- ▲ Apple polishing
- ▲ Guilt trip
- ▲ Wishful thinking
- ▲ Peer pressure "argument"
- ▲ Group think fallacy
- ▲ Nationalism

Other fallacies discussed in this chapter don't invoke emotions directly, but are closely related to emotional appeals. These include

- ▲ Rationalization
- ▲ "Argument" from popularity
- ▲ "Argument" from common practices
- ▲ "Argument" from tradition
- ▲ Relativism
- ▲ Subjectivism
- ▲ Red herring/smokescreen

In all these specimens, there is something one might call a "premise" and something one might call a "conclusion," but the "premise" either fails to support the conclusion or "supports" some tangential claim. In any case a mistake in reasoning has been made, a fallacy has been committed.

Exercises

In the exercises that follow, we ask you to name fallacies, and your instructor may do the same on an exam.

Exercise 5-1

Working in groups, invent a simple, original, and clear illustration of each type of fallacy covered in this chapter. Then, in the class as a whole, select the illustrations that are clearest and most straightforward. Go over these illustrations before doing the remaining exercises in this chapter, and review them before you take a test on this material.

Exercise 5-2

Identify any instances of fallacious reasoning that occur in the following passages, either by naming them or, where you think they do not conform to any of the patterns we have described, by explaining in one or two sentences why the "argument" is irrelevant to the point at issue. (There are a few passages that contain no fallacies. Be sure you don't find one where none exist!)

▲ 1. The tax system in this country is unfair and ridiculous! Just ask anyone!

2. SHE: I think it was exceedingly boorish of you to finish off the last of their expensive truffles like that.
   HE: Bosh. They certainly would have done the same to us, if given the chance.

3. Overheard:

"Hmmmm. Nice day. Think I'll go catch some rays."

"Says here in this magazine that doing that sort of thing is guaranteed to get you a case of skin cancer."

"Yeah, I've heard that, too. I think it's a bunch of baloney, personally. If that were true, you wouldn't be able to do anything—no tubing, skiing, nothing. You wouldn't even be able to just plain lay out in the sun. Ugh!"

▲ 4. I've come before you to ask that you rehire Professor Johnson. I realize that Mr. Johnson does not have a Ph.D., and I am aware that he has yet to publish his first article. But Mr. Johnson is over forty now, and he has a wife and two high-school-aged children to support. It will be very difficult for him to find another teaching job at his age, I'm sure you will agree.

5. JUAN: But, Dad, I like Horace. Why shouldn't I room with him, anyway?

JUAN'S DAD: Because I'll cut off your allowance, that's why!

6. That snake has markings like a coral snake. Coral snakes are deadly poisonous, so you'd better leave it alone!

▲ 7. RALPH: He may have done it, but I don't hold him responsible. I'm a determinist, you know.

SHARON: What's that?

RALPH: A determinist? Someone who doesn't believe in free will. There's no free will.

SHARON: Oh. Well, I disagree.

RALPH: Why's that?

SHARON: Because. Determinism may be real for you, but it certainly isn't for me.

8. The animal rights people shouldn't pick on rodeos. If they'd come out and see the clowns put smiles on kids' faces and see horses buck off the cowboys and hear the crowd go "ooh" and "ahh" at the bull riding, why then they'd change their minds.

9. HE: Tell you what. Let's get some ice cream for a change. Sunrise Creamery has the best—let's go there.

SHE: Not that old dump! What makes you think their ice cream is so good, anyway?

HE: Because it is. Besides, that old guy who owns it never gets any business any more. Every time I go by the place I see him in there all alone, just staring out the window, waiting for a customer. He can't help it that he's in such an awful location. I'm sure he couldn't afford to move.

▲ 10. Student speaker: "Why, student fees have jumped by more than 300 percent in just two years! This is outrageous! The governor is working for a balanced budget, but it'll be on the backs of us students, the people who have the very least to spend! It seems pretty clear that these increased student fees are undermining higher education in this state. Anybody who isn't mad about this just doesn't understand the situation."

11. "Jim, I'm very disappointed you felt it necessary to talk to the media about the problems here in the department. When you join the FBI, you join a family, and you shouldn't want to embarrass your family."

12. HANK: Where I come from, there are lots of outdoor cafés and bars; people think nothing of drinking in public.
    FRANK: That may be true, but this is Salt Lake City, and they disapprove of that sort of thing very seriously around here.

▲ 13. A fictitious Western governor: "Yes, I have indeed accepted $550,000 in campaign contributions from power companies. But as I stand here before you, I can guarantee you that not one dime of that money has affected any decision I've made. I make decisions based on data, not on donors."

14. "If you ask me, you are making a mistake to break up with Rasheed. Have you forgotten how he stood by you when you needed him last year? Is this how you repay him?"

15. "What? You aren't a Cornhuskers fan? Listen, around here *everybody* is for the Huskers! This is Nebraska!"

Exercise 5-3 _____

Answer the following questions and explain your answers.

▲ 1. How relevant is the fact that a brand of toothpaste is advertised to the issue of whether to buy that brand?

2. How relevant is the fact that a brand of toothpaste *is* best-selling to the issue of whether to buy that brand?

▲ 3. How relevant is the fact that an automobile is a best-seller in its class to the issue of whether to buy that kind of automobile?

4. How relevant is the fact that a movie is a smash hit to the issue of whether to see it?

5. How relevant is the fact that a movie is a smash hit to your opinion of it?

6. How relevant is the fact that your friends like a movie to the issue of whether to see it?

▲ 7. How relevant is the fact that your friends like a movie to your opinion of it?

8. How relevant is the fact that your friends like a movie to the issue of whether to say that you like it?

9. How relevant is the fact that movie critics like a movie to the issue of whether to see it?

▲ 10. Is advertising a product as best-selling an example of the peer pressure "argument"?

Exercise 5-4

Which of the following do you believe? Which of the following do you *really* have evidence for? Which of the following do you believe on an "everyone knows" basis? Discuss your answers with other members of your class.

1. Small dogs tend to live longer than large dogs.
2. Coffee has a dehydrating effect.
3. Most people should drink at least eight glasses of water a day.
4. If you are thirsty, it means you are already dehydrated.
5. Rape is not about sex; it's about aggression.
6. Marijuana use leads to addiction to harder drugs.
7. The news media are biased.
8. You get just as much ultraviolet radiation on a cloudy day as on a sunny day.
9. If you don't let yourself get angry every now and then, your anger will build up to the exploding point.
10. Carrots make you see better.
11. Reading in poor light is bad for your eyes.
12. Sitting too close to the TV is bad for your eyes.
13. Warm milk makes you sleepy.
14. Covering your head is the most effective way of staying warm in cold weather.
15. Smoking a cigarette takes seven minutes off your life.

Exercise 5-5

For each of the passages that follow, determine whether fallacies are present and, if so, whether they fit the categories described in this chapter.

▲ 1. Boss to employee: "I'll be happy to tell you why this report needs to be finished by Friday. If it isn't ready by then, you'll be looking for another job. How's that for a reason?"

2. Mother: "I think he has earned an increase in his allowance. He doesn't have any spending money at all, and he's always having to make excuses about not being able to go out with the rest of his friends because of that."

3. Mother to father: "You know, I really believe that our third-grader's friend Joe comes from an impoverished family. He looks to me as though he doesn't get enough to eat. I think I'm going to start inviting him to have dinner at our house once or twice a week."

▲ 4. "Aw, c'mon, Jake, let's go hang out at Dave's. Don't worry about your parents; they'll get over it. You know, the one thing I really like about you is that you don't let your parents tell you what to do."

5. FIRST PERSON: You know, I might not agree with it, but I could understand it if a society decided to look down on a woman who had a child out of wedlock. But stoning to death? My God, that's barbaric and hideously immoral!
   SECOND PERSON: But remember that you come from a background much different from that of the people in that part of Nigeria. It's less immoral in that situation. Besides, in Iran stoning to death has been a common punishment for adultery under the current regime.

6. FRED: I think we should just buy the new truck and call it a business expense so we can write it off on our taxes.
   ETHEL: I don't know, Fred. That sounds like cheating to me. We wouldn't really use the truck very much in the business, you know.
   FRED: Oh, don't worry about it. This kind of thing is done all the time.

▲ 7. I'm going to use the textbook that's on reserve in the library. I'll have to spend more time on the campus, but it's sure better than shelling out over a hundred bucks for one book.

8. Imagine yourself alone beside your broken-down car at the side of a country road in the middle of the night. Few pass by and no one stops to help. Don't get caught like that—don't get caught without your Polytech cellular phone!

9. One political newcomer to another: "I tell you, Sam, you'd better change those liberal views of yours. The general slant toward conservatism is obvious. You'll be left behind unless you change your mind about some things."

▲ 10. Reporter COKIE ROBERTS: Mr. Cheney, aside from the legal issues that stem from the various United Nations resolutions, isn't there an overriding moral dimension to the suffering of so many Kurdish people in Iraq?
    DICK CHENEY: Well, we recognize that's a tragic situation, Cokie, but there are tragic situations occurring all over the world.

Adapted from an interview on National Public Radio's Morning Edition

Exercise 5-6

For each of the passages that follow, determine whether fallacies are present and, if so, whether they fit the categories described in this chapter.

▲ 1. "Grocers are concerned about *sanitation problems* from beverage residue that Proposition 11 could create. Filthy returned cans and bottles—*over 11 billion a year*—don't belong in grocery stores, where our food is stored and sold. . . . Sanitation problems in other states with similar laws have caused increased use of *chemical sprays* in grocery stores to combat rodents and insects. Vote no on 11."

Argument against Proposition 11, California ballot pamphlet

2. Overheard: "I'm not going to vote for Riordan for governor, and you shouldn't either. I lived in L.A. when Riordan was mayor, and the crime was so bad we had to leave. You couldn't walk around alone, for fear of your life, and I mean this was the middle of the day!"

3. STUDENT: I think I deserve a better grade than this on the second question.
PROF: Could be. Why do you think so?
STUDENT: You think my answer's wrong.
PROF: Well, your answer *is* wrong.
STUDENT: Maybe you think so, but I don't. You can't mark me wrong just because my answer doesn't fit your opinion.

▲ 4. C'mon, George, the river's waiting and everyone's going to be there. You want me to tell 'em you're gonna worry on Saturday about a test you don't take 'til Tuesday? What're people going to think?

5. ATTENDANT: I'm sorry, sir, but we don't allow people to top off their gas tanks here in Kansas. There's a state law against it, you know.
RICHARD: What? You've got to be kidding! I've never heard of a place that stopped people from doing that!

6. One roommate to another: "I'm telling you, Ahmed, you shouldn't take Highway 50 this weekend. In this weather, it's going to be icy and dangerous. Somebody slides off that road and gets killed nearly every winter. And you don't even have any chains for your car!"

▲ 7. That, in sum, is my proposal, ladies and gentlemen. You know that I trust and value your judgment, and I am aware I could not find a more astute panel of experts to evaluate my suggestion. Thank you.

8. JARED: In Sweden, atheists and agnostics outnumber believers 2 to 1, and in Germany, less than half the population believes in God. Here in the United States, though, over 80 percent believe in God. I wonder what makes the States so different.
ALICE: You've answered your own question. If I didn't believe in God, I'd feel like I stuck out like a sore thumb.

9. Businessman to partner: "I'm glad Brownell has some competition these days. That means when we take estimates for the new job, we can simply ignore his, no matter what it is. That'll teach him a lesson for not throwing any business our way last year."

▲ 10. One local to another: "I tell you, it's disgusting. These idiot college students come up here and live for four years—and ruin the town—and then vote on issues that affect us long after they've gone. This has got to stop! I say, let only those who have a real stake in the future of this town vote here! Transient kids shouldn't determine what's going to happen to local residents. Most of these kids come from Philadelphia . . . let them vote there."

Exercise 5-7

For each of the passages that follow, determine whether fallacies are present and, if so, whether they fit the categories described in this chapter.

▲ 1. Chair, Department of Rhetoric (to department faculty): "If you think about it, I'm certain you'll agree with me that Mary Smith is the best candidate for department secretary. I urge you to join with me in recommending her to the administration. Concerning another matter, I'm now setting up next semester's schedule, and I hope that I'll be able to give you all the classes you have requested."

2. NELLIE: I really don't see anything special about Sunquist grapefruit. They taste the same as any other grapefruit to me.
   NELLIE'S MOM: Hardly! Don't forget that your Uncle Henry owns Sunquist. If everyone buys his fruit, you may inherit a lot of money some day!

3. Letter to the editor: "It's unfortunate that there are so many short-sighted people who don't want to increase the military budget. There may be little threat from Russia these days, but they aren't the only ones we have to worry about. Most of the countries of the world are jealous of our success and would like to take what we've got for themselves. It'll be our military that keeps them from doing it."

Miltonville Gazette

▲ 4. *"Don't risk letting a fatal accident rob your family of the home they love— on the average more than 250 Americans die each day because of accidents.* What would happen to your family's home if you were one of them?
   Your home is so much more than just a place to live. It's a community you've chosen carefully . . . a neighborhood . . . a school district . . . the way of life you and your family have come to know. And you'd want your family to continue sharing its familiar comforts, even if suddenly you were no longer there. . . . Now, as a Great Western mortgage customer, you can protect the home you love. . . . Just complete the Enrollment Form enclosed for you."

Advertisement from Colonial Penn Life Insurance Company

5. "You've made your mark and your scotch says it all."

Glen Haven Reserve

6. Dear Senator Jenkins,
   I am writing to urge your support for higher salaries for state correctional facility guards. I am a clerical worker at Kingsford Prison, and I know whereof I speak. Guards work long hours, often giving up weekends, at a dangerous job. They cannot afford expensive houses or even nice clothes. Things that other state employees take for granted, like orthodontia for their children and a second car, are not possibilities on their salaries, which, incidentally, have not been raised in five years. Their dedication deserves better.
   Very truly yours, . . .

▲ 7. In *Shelley v. Kraemer,* 334 U.S.1 (1948), the "argument" was put before the Supreme Court that "state courts stand ready to enforce restrictive covenants excluding white persons from the ownership or occupancy of property covered by such agreements," and that therefore "enforcement of covenants excluding colored persons may not be deemed a denial of equal protection of the laws to the colored persons who are thereby affected."

The court decided that "this contention does not bear scrutiny." In fact, the contention seems to be an example of what form of pseudoreasoning?

8. The suggestion was once made to replace the word "manpower" in the course description of Dartmouth's Business Administration 151, Management of Human Resources, because of the sexist connotation of the word. This brought delighted responses in the press. Shouldn't they get rid of "management" in the course title, wrote someone, in favor of "personagement"? Shouldn't "human" in the title give way to "huperson," asked another? Is the course open to "freshpersons"? a third wondered. In fact, is the course open to any person? the same individual queried. "Son" is a masculine word; therefore "person" itself is sexist.

9. There are very good reasons for the death penalty. First, it serves as a deterrent to those who would commit capital offenses. Second, it is just and fair punishment for the crime committed. Third, reliable opinion polls show that over 70 percent of all Americans favor it. If so many people favor it, it has to be right.

▲ 10. Two famous political opponents are said to have had this exchange in the English Parliament:
GLADSTONE: You, sir, will either die upon the gallows or succumb to a horrible social disease!
DISRAELI: That will depend, I suppose, upon whether I embrace your principles or your mistress.

11. Frankly, I think the Salvation Army, the Red Cross, and the Wildlife Fund will put my money to better use than my niece Alison and her husband would. They've wasted most of the money I've given them. So I think I'm going to leave a substantial portion of my estate to those organizations instead of leaving it all to my spendthrift relatives.

12. "The President's prosecution of the war on terror is being handled exactly right. He wasn't elected to do nothing!"

13. Student to teacher: "I've had to miss several classes and some quizzes because of some personal matters back home. I know you have a no-make-up policy, but there was really no way I could avoid having to be out of town; it really was not my fault."

▲ 14. BUD: So here's the deal. I'll arrange to have your car "stolen," and we'll split the proceeds from selling it to a disposer. Then you file a claim with your insurance company and collect from it.
LOU: Gee, this sounds seriously illegal and dangerous.
BUD: Illegal, yeah, but do you think this is the first time an insurance company ever had this happen? Why, they actually expect it—they even budget money for exactly this sort of thing.

15. Kibitzer, discussing the job Lamar Alexander did as secretary of education: "It was absolutely clear to me that Alexander was not going to do any good for American education. He was way too involved in money-making schemes to give any attention to the job *we* were paying him for. Do you know that back before he was appointed, he and his wife invested five thou-

sand dollars in some stock deal, and four years later that stock was worth over eight hundred thousand dollars? Tell me there's nothing fishy about a deal like that!"

16. My opponent, the evolutionist, offers you a different history and a different self-image from the one I suggest. While I believe that you and I are made in the image of God and are only one step out of the Garden of Eden, he believes that you are made in the image of a monkey and are only one step out of the zoo.

▲ 17. "EPA study—Environmental Protection Agency officials have launched a new study to assess the risks of—brace yourself—taking showers. Seems someone in the EPA worries people might be injured by inhaling water vapor while taking a shower. No, we didn't make it up. It's true, according to a publication called EPA Watch.

"Doubtless, several bureaucrats will take home paychecks for months while the imagined hazard is studied. Unfortunately, there's probably a 50-50 chance someone in Washington will decide showers really are dangerous.

"Wonder if anyone at the EPA ever has studied the hazards of pouring billions of dollars into overregulation?"

Charleston *(W.Va.)* Gazette

18. "Boomers beware! The 76 million people born between 1946 and 1964 are beginning to think about retirement. They'd better listen carefully. Douglas Bernheim, an economics professor at Princeton, says current retirees were 'extraordinarily lucky' in that their home values climbed, high inflation took the sting out of their fixed-rate mortgages, and there were big increases in private and public pensions. 'The average baby boomer must triple his or her rate of savings to avoid a precipitous decline of living standards during retirement,' Bernheim said. . . .

"To be on the safe side, baby boomers should have an aggressive savings plan and not rely on government assurances of cushy retirement years. It is always best to err on the side of caution."

Charleston *(W.Va.)* Daily Mail

Writing Exercises

1. Find an example of a fallacy in a newspaper editorial or opinion magazine (substitute an example from an advertisement or a letter to the editor only as a last resort and only if your instructor permits it). Identify the issue and what side of the issue the writer supports. Explain why the passage you've chosen does not really support that position—that is, why it involves a fallacy. If the writer's claims do support some other position (possibly on a different, related issue), describe what position they do support.

2. In 1998 the police in Harris County, Texas, responded to a false report about an armed man who was going crazy. They did not find such an individual; but when they entered the home of John Geddes Lawrence, they found him

and another man, Tyron Garner, having sex. Both men were arrested and found guilty of violating a Texas law that criminalizes homosexual sex acts. The men challenged their conviction, and the case went to the United States Supreme Court in March 2003. A district attorney from the county argued, "Texas has the right to set moral standards of its people."

Do you agree or disagree with the district attorney's statement? Defend your answer in a one-page essay written in class. Your instructor will have other members of the class read your essay to see if they can find your basic argument in the midst of any rhetoric you may have used. They also will note any fallacies that you may have employed.

3. Should there be an amendment to the U.S. Constitution prohibiting desecration of the U.S. flag? In a one-page essay, defend a "yes" or "no" answer to the question. Your instructor will have other members of the class read your essay, following the instructions in Exercise 2.

Chapter 6

More Fallacies

What is the most common (and seductive) error in reasoning on the planet? You are about to find out. In this chapter we examine the infamous *argumentum ad hominem*, as well as other common fallacies.

To remind you of the overall picture, in Chapter 4 we explored ways the rhetorical content of words and phrases can be used to affect belief and attitude. In Chapter 5 we considered emotional appeals and related fallacies. The fallacies we turn to now, like the devices in the preceding chapters, can tempt us to believe something without giving us a legitimate reason for doing so.

The Ad Hominem Fallacy

The ad hominem fallacy (*argumentum ad hominem*) is the most common of all mistakes in reasoning. The fallacy rests on a confusion between the qualities of the person making a claim and the qualities of the claim itself. ("Claim" is to be understood broadly here, as including beliefs, opinions, positions, arguments, proposals and so forth.)

Parker, let us assume, is an ingenious fellow. It follows that Parker's opinion on some subject, whatever it is, is the opinion of an ingenious person. But it does not follow that Parker's *opinion itself* is ingenious. To think that it does follow would be to confuse the content of Parker's claim with Parker himself. Or let's suppose you are listening to somebody, your teacher perhaps, whom you regard as a bit strange or maybe even weird. Would it follow that the *car* your teacher drives is strange or weird? Obviously not. Likewise, it would not follow that some specific proposal that the teacher has put forth is strange or weird. A proposal made by an oddball is an oddball's proposal, but it does not follow that it is an oddball proposal. We must not confuse the qualities of the person making a claim with the qualities of the claim itself.

Now, we commit the **ad hominem** fallacy when we think that considerations about a person "refute" his or her assertions. *Ad hominem* is Latin for "to the man," indicating it is not really the subject matter that's being addressed, but the person. The most common varieties of the ad hominem fallacy are as follows.

■ *Personal Attack Ad Hominem*

"Johnson has such-and-such a negative feature; therefore, his claim (belief, opinion, theory, proposal, etc.) stands refuted." This is the formula for the **personal attack ad hominem** fallacy. The name "personal attack" is self-explanatory, because attributing a negative feature to Johnson is attacking him personally.

Now there are many negative features that we might attribute to a person: Perhaps Johnson is said to be ignorant or stupid. Maybe he is charged with being self-serving or feathering his own nest. Perhaps he is accused of being a racist or a sexist or a fascist or a cheat or of being cruel or uncaring or soft on communism or prone to kick dogs or what-have-you. The point to remember is that shortcomings in *a person* are not equivalent to shortcomings in that person's ideas, proposals, theories, opinions, claims, or arguments.

Now it is true that there are exceptional circumstances we can imagine in which some feature of a person might logically imply that what that person says is false; but these circumstances tend to be far-fetched. "Johnson's claim is false because he has been paid to lie about the matter" might qualify as an example. "Johnson's claim is false because he has been given a drug that makes him say only false things" would qualify too. But such situations are rare. True, when we have doubts about the credibility of a source, we must be careful before we accept a claim from that source. But the doubts are rarely sufficient grounds for outright rejection of the claim. No matter what claim Johnson might make and no matter what his faults might be, we are rarely justified in rejecting the claim as false simply because he has those faults.

■ *The Inconsistency Ad Hominem*

"Moore's claim is inconsistent with something else Moore has said or done; therefore, his claim (belief, opinion, theory, proposal, etc.) stands refuted." This is the formula for the **inconsistency** ad hominem, and you encounter versions of this fallacy all the time. Suppose a political commentator exclaims (as we heard Rush Limbaugh say about George W. Bush), "The president says now that he believes in global warming, but ladies and gentlemen, when the president was campaigning he scoffed at the idea." Do we have a reason here for thinking something is wrong with the president's current view? Not at all. The fact that people change their minds has no bearing on the truth of what they say either before or after.

They believe the Boy Scouts' position on homosexuality was objectionable, but they gave no heed to people's objections about using state money to fund displays about sodomy in the people's Capitol.

—California Assemblyman Bill Leonard (R-San Bernardino), criticizing the legislature for funding a gay pride display in the state's Capitol

Man! As if sodomy in the people's Capitol isn't bad enough, they have to go and fund displays about it!

Leonard's remark is an example of an inconsistency ad hominem. (It also contains a wild syntactical ambiguity, as noted above.)

Ye Olde Double Standards Argument

Beware the old "double standards" argument. It comes in various disguises. For example, in the furious discussion of whether the United States should go to war with Iraq, it surfaced in various "rebuttals" of the administration's contention that invading Iraq was justified:

- "America has supported far worse dictators than Saddam. Take the shah, for example."
- "If we are so concerned about the spread of nuclear weapons, why don't we do something about Israel?"
- "I just want to know, why don't we apply the same standard to North Korea?"
- "Twenty years ago we were supporting Saddam! You know how he got all those weapons? Most of them he bought from us."
- "Tell me this. We know for a fact that Iran is developing nuclear weapons. We also know Iran has supported terrorism. Why aren't we going to war with Iran?"

The double standard argument is actually the inconsistency ad hominem. As such, it has zero logical force either for or against doing some specific thing. That the U.S. government adhered to a double standard, if true, only proves its policies are inconsistent. It does not prove which policy is the incorrect policy.

Sometimes a person's claim seems inconsistent, not with previous statements but with that person's behavior. For example, Johnson might tell us to be more generous, when we know Johnson himself is as stingy as can be. Well, Johnson may well be a hypocrite, but we would be guilty of the inconsistency ad hominem fallacy if we regarded Johnson's stinginess or hypocrisy as grounds for rejecting what he says. This type of reasoning, where we reject what somebody says because what he or she says seems inconsistent with what he or she does, even has a Latin name: *tu quoque*, meaning "you too." This version of the inconsistency ad hominem often boils down to nothing more than saying "You too" or "You do it, too!" If a smoker urges another smoker to give up the habit, the second smoker commits the inconsistency ad hominem if she says, "Well, you do it too!"

■ Circumstantial Ad Hominem

"Parker's circumstances are such and such; therefore, his claim (belief, opinion, theory, proposal, etc.) stands refuted." This is the formula for the **circumstantial ad hominem.** An example would be "Well, you can forget about what Father Hennesy says about the dangers of abortion because Father Hennesy's a priest, and priests are required to hold such views." The speaker in this example is citing Father Hennesy's circumstances (being a

I get calls from nutso environmentalists who are filled with compassion for every snail darter that is threatened by some dam somewhere. Yet, they have no interest in the 1.5 million fetuses that are aborted every year in the United States. I love to argue with them and challenge their double standard.

—RUSH LIMBAUGH

Often an inconsistency ad hominem will accuse someone of having a double standard. Notice how this example is combined with ridicule.

There were 750,000 people in New York's Central Park recently for Earth Day. They were throwing Frisbees, flying kites, and listening to Tom Cruise talk about how we have to recycle everything and stop corporations from polluting. Excuse me.

Didn't Tom Cruise make a stock-car movie in which he destroyed thirty-five cars, burned thousands of gallons of gasoline, and wasted dozens of tires? If I were given the opportunity, I'd say to Tom Cruise, "Tom, most people don't own thirty-five cars in their life, and you just trashed thirty-five cars for a movie. Now you're telling other people not to pollute the planet? Shut up, sir."

—RUSH LIMBAUGH

An inconsistency ad hominem

priest) to "refute" Father Hennesy's opinion. This example isn't a personal attack ad hominem because the speaker may think very highly of priests in general and of Father Hennesy in particular. Clearly, though, a person could intend to issue a personal attack by mentioning circumstances that (in the opinion of the speaker) constituted a defect on the part of the person attacked. For example, consider "You can forget about what Father Hennesy says about the dangers of abortion because he is a priest and priests all have sexual hang-ups." That would qualify as both a circumstantial ad hominem (he's a priest) and a personal attack ad hominem (priests have sexual hang-ups).

■ *Poisoning the Well*

Poisoning the well can be thought of as an ad hominem in advance. If someone dumps poison down your well, you don't drink from it. Similarly, when A poisons your mind about B by relating unfavorable information about B, you may be inclined to reject what B says to you.

Well-poisoning is easier to arrange than you might think. You might suppose that to poison someone's thinking about Mrs. Jones, you would have to say or at least insinuate something deprecatory or derogatory about her. In fact, recent psycholinguistic research suggests you can poison someone's thinking about Mrs. Jones by doing just the opposite! If we don't know Mrs. Jones, even a sentence that expresses an outright denial of a connection between her and something unsavory is apt to make us form an unfavorable impression of her. Psychological studies indicate that people are more apt to form an unfavorable impression of Mrs. Jones from a sentence like "Mrs. Jones is not an ax murderer" than from a sentence like "Mrs. Jones has a sister."

Moral: Because it might be easy for others to arrange for us to have a negative impression of someone, we must be extra careful not to reject what a person says *just because* we have an unfavorable impression of the individual.

Genetic Fallacy

The **genetic fallacy** occurs when we try to "refute" a claim (or urge others to do so) on the basis of its origin or history. For example, a person might "refute" the idea that God exists on the grounds that belief in God first rose in superstitious times or on the grounds we come to believe in God to comfort ourselves in the face of death. We have heard people declare the U.S. Constitution "invalid" because it was (allegedly) drafted to protect the interests of property owners. These are examples of the genetic fallacy.

If we "refute" a proposal (or urge someone else to reject it) on the grounds it was part of the Republican (or Democratic) party platform, we commit the genetic fallacy. If we "refute" a policy (or try to get others to reject it) on the grounds that a slave-holding state in the nineteenth century originated the policy, that also would qualify. If we "rebut" (or urge others to reject) a ballot initiative on the grounds that the insurance industry or the association of trial lawyers or the American Civil Liberties Union or "Big Tobacco" or "Big Oil" or multinational corporations or the National Education Association or the National Rifle Association or the National Organization for Women proposed it or back it, we commit the fallacy. Knowing that the NRA or the NEA or NOW proposed or backs or endorses a piece of legislation may give one reason (depending on one's politics) to be suspicious of it or to have a careful look at it; but a perceived lack of merit on the part of the organization that proposed or backs or endorses a proposal is not equivalent to a lack of merit in the proposal itself. Knowing the NRA is behind a particular ballot initiative is not the same as knowing about a specific defect in the initiative itself, even if you detest the NRA.

Obviously, the genetic fallacy is similar to the ad hominem arguments we have examined. The following examples might help you see a difference between the two:

Example of (Personal Attack) Ad Hominem

The Democrats never tire of criticizing the president's war plans, but all this criticism is completely unwarranted. These people just can't get over the fact that Al Gore lost the election in 2000.

Example of Genetic Fallacy

All this criticism of the president's war plans is completely unwarranted. It all just comes from the Democrats.

Just remember what "ad hominem" means. It means "to the person." If we reject *Moore's* claim because *Moore* is, let us say, a member of the National Rifle Association, that's a (circumstantial) ad hominem. If we reject a *claim* because it originated with the National Rifle Association, that's the genetic fallacy.

Don't get into nuclear warfare with your classmates or with your instructor over whether a particular item is a genetic fallacy or this or that type of *argumentum ad hominem*. These mistakes all belong to the same family and resemble each other closely.

> *Whom are they kidding? Where are NOW's constitutional objections to the billions of dollars (including about $1 million to NOW itself) that women's groups receive under the Violence Against Women Act?*
>
> —ARMIN BROTT, issuing an ad hominem response to opposition by the National Organization for Women to a proposal to provide poor fathers with parenting and marital-skills training and classes on money management

Gender-based inconsistency ad hominem

"Positive Ad Hominem Fallacies"

An ad hominem fallacy, then, is committed if we rebut a person on the basis of considerations that, logically, apply to the person rather than to his or her claims. Strictly speaking, if we automatically transfer the positive or favorable attributes of a person to what he or she says, that's a mistake in reasoning, as well. The fact you think Moore is clever does not logically entitle you to conclude that any specific opinion of Moore's is clever. The fact that in your view the NRA represents all that is good and proper does not enable you to infer that any specific proposal from the NRA is good and

Dilbert reprinted by permission of United Features Syndicate, Inc.

▲　*A straw man generator in Dilbert's office.*

proper. Logicians did not always limit the ad hominem fallacy to cases of rebuttal, but that seems to be the usage now, and we shall follow that policy in this book. You should just remember that a parallel mistake in reasoning happens if you confuse the favorable qualities of a person with the qualities of his or her assertion.

Straw Man

Let's say Mrs. Herrington announces it is time to clean out the attic. Mr. Herrington groans and says, "What, again? Do we have to clean it out every day?"

The **straw man** fallacy happens when you "refute" a position or claim by distorting or oversimplifying or misrepresenting it. Mr. Herrington has distorted his wife's position, creating a straw man.

The straw man fallacy is very common. We can easily imagine Mrs. Herrington coming back with "Just because you think we should keep every last piece of junk forever doesn't mean I do." Now Mrs. Herrington is using a straw man herself, assuming that Mr. Herrington's position is only that they shouldn't clean out the attic right now.

The straw man fallacy is so common that it ranks next to the top on our list of the top ten fallacies of all time (see Appendix 2). One person will say he wants to eliminate the words "under God" from the Pledge of Allegiance, and his opponent will act as if he wants to eliminate the entire pledge. A conservative will oppose tightening emission standards for sulfur dioxide, and a liberal will accuse him of wanting to relax the standards. A Democratic congresswoman will say she opposes cutting taxes, and her Republican opponent will accuse her of wanting to raise taxes.

The ad hominem fallacy attempts to "refute" a claim on the basis of considerations that logically apply to its source. The straw man fallacy attempts to "refute" a claim by altering it so that it seems patently false or even ridiculous.

I'm a very controversial figure to the animal rights movement. They no doubt view me with some measure of hostility because I am constantly challenging their fundamental premise that animals are superior to human beings.

—Rush Limbaugh, setting up another straw man for the kill

False Dilemma

Suppose Mrs. Herrington in the example above says to Mr. Herrington, "Look, either we clean out the attic or all this junk will run us out of house and home. Would you prefer that?" Now Mrs. Harrington is offering Mr. Harrington a "choice": either clean out the attic or let the junk run them out of house and home. But the choice Mrs. Harrington offers is limited to just two alternatives, and there are alternatives that deserve consideration, such as doing it later or not acquiring additional junk.

The **false dilemma** fallacy occurs when you limit considerations to only two alternatives although other alternatives may be available. Like the straw man fallacy, it is encountered all the time. You say you don't want to drill for oil in the Alaskan National Wildlife Reserve? Would you prefer letting Saddam Hussein dictate the price of oil?

Or take a look at this example:

CONGRESSMAN
CLAGHORN: Guess we're going to have to cut back expenditures on social programs again this year.

YOU: Why's that?

CLAGHORN: Well, we either do that or live with this high deficit, and that's something we can't allow.

Here, Claghorn maintains that either we live with the high deficit or we cut social programs, and that therefore, because we can't live with the high deficit, we have to cut social programs. But this reasoning works only if cutting social programs is the *only* alternative to a high deficit. Of course, that is not the case (taxes might be raised or military spending cut, for example). Another example:

DANIEL: Theresa and I both endorse this idea of allowing prayer in public schools, don't we, Theresa?

THERESA: I never said any such thing!

DANIEL: Hey, I didn't know you were an atheist!

Here, Daniel's "argument" amounts to this: Either you endorse prayer in public schools, or you are an atheist; therefore, because you do not endorse school prayer, you must be an atheist. But a person does not have to be an atheist in order to feel unfavorable toward prayer in public schools. The alternatives Daniel presents, in other words, could both be false. Theresa might not be an atheist and still not endorse school prayer.

The example Daniel provides us shows how this type of fallacy and the preceding one can work together: A straw man is often used as part of a false dilemma. A person who wants us to accept X may not only ignore other alternatives besides Y but also exaggerate or distort Y. In other words,

Hot Air and Fallacies in the Pledge Debate

Comments—and some hot air—on the Federal Appeals Court ruling that the phrase "one nation under God" makes the Pledge of Allegiance unconstitutional:

> The decision is out of step with America.
>
> —GEORGE W. BUSH

Argument from popularity

> This is a case of old men . . . pushing logic to a ridiculous extreme.
>
> —GEORGE W. BUSH

Personal attack ad hominem

> Taking out the phrase "under God" at this time could be seen by Muslims as another example of godless Americanism.
>
> —RICHARD BRUCE in letter to Sacramento Bee, July 4, 2002

Scare tactics

> Only 2.5 percent of the world's population is atheist. On the other hand, a majority of the world's population—Christians, Muslims and Jews—worship the god of Abraham.
>
> —RICHARD BRUCE

Red herring

> Enough is enough. We need to put an end to judicial tyranny!
>
> —ROBERT C. BALLIET, letter in Sacramento Bee, July 4, 2002

Argument from outrage

> The judge obviously does not appreciate the heritage and legacy upon which our founding fathers built this freedom-loving land. Why not move elsewhere? Russia will embrace him.
>
> —NANCY WOODARD, letter in Sacramento Bee, July 4, 2002

Nationalism, tradition, and outrage

> The decision is just nuts.
>
> —Senate Majority Leader TOM DASCHLE

Ridicule

> Ridiculous. This decision will not sit well with the American people. The Supreme Court and Congress open each session with references to God, and the Declaration of Independence refers to God or the creator four times.
>
> —Presidential spokesperson ARI FLEISCHER

Argument from tradition

The decision is directly contrary to two centuries of American tradition.

—Attorney General JOHN ASHCROFT

Argument from tradition

An atheist lawyer. I hope his name never comes before this body for any promotion, because he will be remembered.

—Senate President Pro Tem ROBERT BYRD

Scare tactics

Our founding fathers must be spinning in their graves.

—Senator KIT BOND, R-Mo.

Argument from outrage

What is next? Will the courts now strip "so help me God" from the pledge taken by new presidents? This is the worst kind of political correctness run amok.

—Senator KIT BOND, R-Mo.

Slippery slope, ridicule, outrage, hyperbole

Will our courts, in their zeal to abolish all religious faith from public arenas, outlaw "God Bless America" too? The great strength of the United States is that we are and will continue to be, despite the liberal court's decision, one nation under God.

—ROY BLUNT, R-Mo.

More of the same

There may have been a more senseless, ridiculous decision issued by a court at some time, but I don't remember it.

—Senator JOE LIEBERMAN, D-Conn.

More ridicule

The phrase "under God" defines who we are as a nation. This nation was founded by believers in God. . . . Should we also recall all the currency so these words can be removed? The economy would go into crisis if that were to happen. No one would ever suggest such an insane thing. So why would we be forced to change the words of the P of A? Sure, the words under God were added in 1954, but they are needed. Since taking God out of our public schools and other public forums there has been a rise in crime and overall immorality. What right does the court have to keep us from expressing our beliefs in the places where our tax dollars are spent? We are citizens of this great country, too.

—MICHELLE COS, letter to Sacramento Bee, June 29, 2002

Scare tactics, begging the question, ridicule, outrage, slippery slope

▲ *Has Mom fallen for a false trilemma?*

this person leaves only *one* "reasonable" alternative because the only other one provided is really a straw man. You can also think of a false dilemma as a false dichotomy.

It might help in understanding false dilemmas to look quickly at a *real* dilemma. Consider: You know that the Smiths must heat their house in the winter. You also know that the only heating options available in their location are gas and electricity. Under these circumstances, if you find out that they do *not* have electric heat, it must indeed be true that they must use gas heat because that's the only alternative remaining. False dilemma occurs only when reasonable alternatives are ignored. In such cases, both X and Y may be false, and some other alternative may be true.

Therefore, before you accept X because some alternative, Y, is false, make certain that X and Y cannot *both* be false. Look especially for some third alternative, some way of rejecting Y without having to accept X. Example:

> MOORE: Look, Parker, you're going to have to make up your mind. Either you decide that you can afford this stereo, or you decide that you're going to do without music for a while.

Parker could reject both of Moore's alternatives (buying this stereo and going without music) because of some obvious third possibilities. One, Parker might find a less expensive stereo. Or, two, he might buy a part of this stereo now—just the CD player, amplifier, and speakers, say—and postpone until later purchase of the rest.

Before moving on, we should point out that there is more than one way to present a pair of alternatives. Aside from the obvious "either X or Y" version we've described so far, we can use the form "if not X, then Y." For instance, in the example at the beginning of the section, Congressman

Claghorn can say, "Either we cut back on expenditures, or we'll have a big deficit," but he can accomplish the same thing by saying, "If we don't cut back on expenditures, then we'll have a big deficit." These two ways of stating the dilemma are equivalent to one another. Claghorn gets the same result: After denying that we can tolerate the high deficit, he concludes that we'll have to cut back expenditures. Again, it's the artificial narrowness of the alternatives—the falsity of the claim that says "if not one, then surely the other"—that makes this a fallacy.

■ *Perfectionist Fallacy*

A particular subspecies of false dilemma and common rhetorical ploy is something we call the **perfectionist fallacy.** It comes up when a plan or policy is under consideration, and it goes like this:

> If policy X will not meet our goals as well as we'd like them met (i.e., "perfectly"), then policy X should be rejected.

This principle downgrades policy X simply because it isn't perfection. It's a version of false dilemma because it says, in effect, "Either the policy is perfect, or else we must reject it."

An excellent example of the perfectionist fallacy comes from the National Football League's experience with the instant replay rule, which allows an off-field official to review videotape of a play to determine whether the on-field official's ruling was correct. To help the replay official, tape from several angles can be viewed, and the play run in slow motion.

One of the most often heard arguments against the use of videotape replays goes like this: "It's a mistake to use replays to make calls because no matter how many cameras you have following the action on the field, you're still going to miss some calls. There's no way to see everything that's going on."

According to this type of reasoning, we should not have police unless they can prevent *every* crime or apprehend *every* criminal. You can probably think of other examples that show perfectionist reasoning to be very unreliable indeed.

■ *Line-Drawing Fallacy*

Another version of the false dilemma is called the line-drawing fallacy. An example comes from the much-publicized Los Angeles case in which four police officers were acquitted of beating a man named Rodney King. After the trial, one of the jurors indicated that an argument like the following finally convinced her and at least one other juror to vote "not guilty":

> Everybody agrees that the first time one of the officers struck King with a nightstick it did not constitute excessive force. Therefore, if we are to conclude that excessive force was indeed used, then sometime during the course of the beat-

ing (during which King was hit about fifty times) there must have been a moment—a particular blow—at which the force *became* excessive. Since there is no point at which we can determine that the use of force changed from warranted to excessive, we are forced to conclude that it did not become excessive at any time during the beating; and so the officers did not use excessive force.

[People] who are voyeurs, if they are not irredeemably sick, . . . feel ashamed at what they are witnessing.

—IRVING KRISTOL, "Pornography, Obscenity, and the Case for Censorship"

False dilemma

These jurors accepted the **line-drawing fallacy,** the fallacy of insisting that a line must be drawn at some precise point when in fact it is not necessary that such a line be drawn.

To see how this works, consider another example: Clearly, it is impossible for a person who is not rich to become rich by our giving her one dollar. But, equally clearly, if we give our lucky person fifty million dollars, one at a time (very quickly, obviously—maybe we have a machine to deal them out), she will be rich. According to the line-drawing argument, however, *if we cannot point to the precise dollar that makes her rich, then she can never get rich, no matter how much money she is given!*

The problem, of course, is that the concepts referred to by "rich" and "excessive force" (and many others) are vague concepts. We can find cases where the concepts clearly apply and cases where they clearly do not apply. But it is not at all clear exactly where the borderlines are.

Many logicians interpret line drawing as a variety of slippery slope (discussed next). The King case might be seen this way: If the first blow struck against King did not amount to excessive violence, then there's nothing in the series of blows to change that fact. So there's no excessive violence at the end of the series, either.

Our own preference is to see the line-drawing fallacy as a version of false dilemma. It presents the following alternatives: Either there is a precise place where we draw the line, or else there is no line to be drawn (no difference) between one end of the scale and the other. Either there is a certain blow at which the force used against King became excessive, or else the force never became excessive.

Again, remember that our categories of fallacy sometimes overlap. When that happens, it doesn't matter as much which way we classify a case as that we see that an error is being made.

Slippery Slope

We've all heard people make claims of this sort: "If we let X happen, the first thing you know Y will be happening." This is one form of the **slippery slope.** Such claims are fallacious when in fact there is no reason to think that X will lead to Y. Sometimes X and Y can be the same kind of thing or can bear some kind of similarity to one another, but that doesn't mean that one will inevitably lead to the other.

Opponents of handgun control sometimes use a slippery slope argument, saying that if laws to register handguns are passed, the next thing we

$8 Billion, Down the Tube!

Eight billion dollars in utility ratepayers' money and 20 years of effort will be squandered if this resolution is defeated.

—Senator FRANK MURKOWSKI, R-Alaska, using a slippery slope fallacy to argue for going forward with government plans to bury radioactive waste in Yucca Mountain, Nevada

The fact that we've spent money on it already doesn't make it a good idea.

know there will be laws to make owning any kind of gun illegal. This is fallacious if there is no reason to think that the first kind of law will make the second kind more likely. It's up to the person who offers the slippery slope claim to show *why* the first action will lead to the second.

It is also argued that one should not experiment with certain drugs because experimentation is apt to lead to serious addiction or dependence. In the case of drugs that are known to be addictive, there is no fallacy present— the likelihood of the progression is clear.

The other version of slippery slope occurs when someone claims we must continue a certain course of action simply because we have already begun that course. It was said during the Vietnam War that because the United States had already sent troops to Vietnam, it was necessary to send more troops to support the first ones. Unless there is some reason supplied to show that the first step *must* lead to the others, this is a fallacy. (Notice that it's easy to make a false dilemma out of this case as well; do you see how to do it?)

Sometimes we take the first step in a series, and then we realize that it was a mistake. To insist on taking the remainder when we could admit our mistake and retreat is to fall prey to the slippery slope fallacy. (If you insist on following one bad bet with another one, we'd like to invite you to a friendly poker game.)

The slippery slope fallacy has considerable force because *psychologically* one item does often lead to another even though *logically* it does no such thing. When we think of X, say, we may be led immediately to think of Y. But this certainly does not mean that X itself is necessarily followed by Y. Once again, to think that Y has to follow X is to engage in slippery slope thinking; to do so when there is no particular reason to think Y must follow X is to commit a slippery slope fallacy.

Misplacing the Burden of Proof

Let's say Moore asks Parker, "Say, did you know that if you rub red wine on your head your gray hair will turn dark again?"

Parker, of course, will say, "Baloney."

Let's suppose Moore then says, "Baloney? Hey, how do you know it won't work?"

Moore's question is odd, because the **burden of proof** rests on him, not on Parker. Moore has misplaced the burden of proof on Parker, and this is a mistake, a fallacy.

Misplacing the burden of proof occurs when the burden of proof is placed on the wrong side of an issue. This is a common rhetorical technique, and sometimes you have to be on your toes to spot it. People are frequently tricked into thinking they have to prove their opponent's claim is wrong, when in fact the opponent should be proving that the claim is right. For example, you often heard people trying their darnedest to prove that we shouldn't go to war with Iraq, in a context in which the burden of proof rests on those who think we should go to war.

What reasonable grounds would make us place the burden of proof more on one side of an issue than the other? There are a variety of such grounds, but they fall mainly into three categories. We can express them as a set of rules of thumb:

1. *Initial plausibility.* In Chapter 3, we said that the more a claim coincides with our background information, the greater its initial plausibility. The general rule that most often governs the placement of the burden of proof is simply this: The less initial plausibility a claim has, the greater the burden of proof we place on someone who asserts that claim. This is just good sense, of course. We are quite naturally less skeptical about the claim that Charlie's now-famous eighty-seven-year-old grandmother drove a boat across Lake Michigan than we are about the claim that she swam across Lake Michigan. Unfortunately, this rule is a rule of thumb, not a rule that can be applied precisely. We are unable to assess the specific degree of a claim's plausibility and then determine with precision just exactly how much evidence its advocates need to produce to make us willing to accept the claim. But, as a rule of thumb, the initial plausibility rule can keep us from setting the requirements unreasonably high for some claims and allowing others to slide by unchallenged when they don't deserve to.

2. *Affirmative/negative.* Other things being equal, the burden of proof falls automatically on those supporting the affirmative side of an issue rather than on those supporting the negative side. In other words, we generally want to hear reasons why something *is* the case before we require reasons why it is *not* the case. Consider this conversation:

MOORE: The car won't start.

PARKER: Yeah, I know. It's a problem with the ignition.

MOORE: What makes you think that?

PARKER: Well, why not?

▲   *Paleological misplacement of the burden of proof!*

Parker's last remark seems strange because we generally require the affirmative side to assume the burden of proof; it is Parker's job to give reasons for thinking that the problem *is* in the ignition.

This rule applies to cases of existence versus nonexistence, too. Most often, the burden of proof should fall on those who claim something exists rather than on those who claim it doesn't. There are people who believe in ghosts, not because of any evidence that there *are* ghosts, but because nobody has shown there are no such things. (When someone claims that we should believe in such-and-such because nobody has proved that it *isn't* so, we have a subtype of burden of proof known as **appeal to ignorance.**) This is a burden-of-proof fallacy because it mistakenly places the requirement of proving their position on those who do not believe in ghosts. (Of course, the first rule applies here, too, because ghosts are not part of background knowledge for most of us.)

In general, the affirmative side gets the burden of proof because it tends to be much more difficult—or at least much more inconvenient—to prove the negative side of an issue. Imagine a student who walks up to the ticket window at a football game and asks for a discounted student ticket. "Can you prove you're a student?" he is asked. "No," the student replies, "can you prove I'm not?" Well, it may be possible to prove he's not a student, but it's no easy chore, and it would be unreasonable to require it.

Incidentally, some people say it's *impossible* to "prove a negative." But difficult is not the same as impossible. And some "negatives" are even easy to prove. For example, "There are no elephants in this classroom."

3. *Special circumstances.* Sometimes getting at the truth is not the only thing we want to accomplish, and on such occasions we may purposely

Innocent Until Proved Guilty

We must point out that sometimes there are specific reasons why the burden of proof is placed entirely on one side. The obvious case in point is in criminal court, where it is the prosecution's job to prove guilt. The defense is not required to prove innocence; it must only try to keep the prosecution from succeeding in its attempt to prove guilt. We are, as we say, "innocent until proved guilty." As a matter of fact, it's possible that more trials might come to a correct conclusion (i.e., the guilty get convicted and the innocent acquitted) if the burden of proof were equally shared between prosecution and defense. But we have wisely decided that if we are to make a mistake, we would rather it be one of letting a guilty person go free than one of convicting an innocent person. Rather than being a fallacy, then, this lopsided placement of the burden of proof is how we guarantee a fundamental right: the presumption of innocence.

place the burden of proof on a particular side. Courts of law provide us with the most obvious example. Specific agreements can also move the burden of proof from where it would ordinarily fall. A contract might specify, "It will be presumed that you receive the information by the tenth of each month unless you show otherwise." In such cases, the rule governing the special circumstances should be clear and acceptable to all parties involved.

One important variety of special circumstances occurs when the stakes are especially high. For example, if you're thinking of investing your life savings in a company, you'll want to put a heavy burden of proof on the person who advocates making the investment. However, if the investment is small, one you can afford to lose, you might be willing to lay out the money even though it has not been thoroughly proved that the investment is safe. In short, it is reasonable to place a higher burden of proof on someone who advocates a policy that could be dangerous or costly if he or she is mistaken.

These three rules cover most of the ground in placing the burden of proof properly. Be careful about situations where people put the burden of proof on the side other than where our rules indicate it should fall. Take this example:

PARKER: I think we should invest more money in expanding the interstate highway system.

MOORE: I think that would be a big mistake.

PARKER: How could anybody object to more highways?

With his last remark, Parker has attempted to put the burden of proof on Moore. Such tactics can put one's opponent in a defensive position; Moore

So Much for Presumed Innocence . . .

I would rather have an innocent man executed than a guilty murderer go free.

—caller on Talk Back Live (CNN), May 2, 2000

This not uncommon thought is a bizarre false dilemma, since if the innocent man is executed, the guilty murderer *does* go free.

now has to show why we should *not* spend more on roads rather than Parker having to show why we *should* spend more. This is an inappropriate burden of proof.

You should always be suspicious when an inability to *disprove* a claim is said to show that one is mistaken in doubting the claim or in saying that it's false. It does no such thing, unless the burden was on that person to disprove the claim. Inability to disprove that there is extrasensory perception (ESP) is no reason to think that one is mistaken in doubting that ESP exists. But psychics' repeated failure to prove that ESP exists *does* weaken *their* case because the burden of proof is on them.

Begging the Question

Here's a version of a simple example of begging the question, one that's been around a long time (we'll return to it later):

> Two gold miners roll a boulder away from its resting place and find three huge gold nuggets underneath. One says to the other, "Great! That's one nugget for you and two for me," handing one nugget to his associate.
>
> "Wait a minute!" says the second miner. "Why do you get two and I get just one?"
>
> "Because I'm the leader of this operation," says the first.
>
> "What makes you the leader?" asks miner number two.
>
> "I've got twice the gold you do," answers miner number one.

This next example is as famous as the first one was silly: Some people say they can prove God exists. When asked how, they reply, "Well, the Scriptures say very clearly that God must exist." Then, when asked why we should believe the Scriptures, they answer, "The Scriptures are divinely inspired by God himself, so they must be true."

The problem with such reasoning is that the claim at issue—whether it's the case that God exists—turns out to be one of the very premises the argument is based on. If we can't trust the Scriptures, then the argument isn't any good, but the reason given for trusting the Scriptures requires the

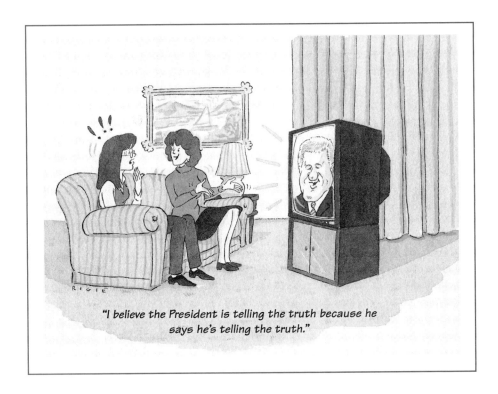

"I believe the President is telling the truth because he says he's telling the truth."

Gay marriages should not be legal because if there wasn't anything wrong with them they would already be legal, which they aren't.

—From a student essay

If you examine this "reasoning" closely, it says that gay marriages shouldn't be legal because they aren't legal. This is not quite "X is true just because X is true," but it's close. The issue is whether the law should be changed. So giving the existence of the law as a "reason" for its *not* being changed can carry no weight, logically.

existence of God, the very thing we were arguing for in the first place! Examples like this are sometimes called circular reasoning or arguing in a circle because they start from much the same place as they end up.

Rhetorical definitions can beg questions. Consider an example from an earlier chapter: If we define abortion as "the murder of innocent children," then it's obvious that abortion is morally wrong. But of course anyone who doubts that abortion is morally wrong is certainly not going to accept the definition just given. That person will most likely refuse to recognize an embryo or early-stage fetus as a "child" at all and will certainly not accept the word "murder" in the definition.

And this brings us to the real problem in cases of question begging: a misunderstanding of what premises (and definitions) it is reasonable for one's audience to accept. We are guilty of **begging the question** when we ask our audience to accept premises that are as controversial as the conclusion we're arguing for and are controversial on the same grounds. The sort of grounds on which people would disagree about the morality of abortion are much the same as those on which they would disagree about the definition of abortion above. The person making the argument has not "gone back far enough," as it were, to find common ground with the audience whom he or she wishes to convince.

Let's return to our feuding gold miners to illustrate what we're talking about. Clearly, the two disagree about who gets the gold, and, given what being the leader of the operation means, they're going to disagree just as much about that. But what if the first miner says, "Look, I picked this spot, didn't I? And we wouldn't have found anything if we'd worked where you wanted to work." If the second miner agrees, they'll have found a bit of common ground. Maybe—*maybe*—the first miner can then convince the second that this point, on which they agree, is worth considering when it comes to splitting the gold. At least there's a chance of moving the discussion forward when they proceed this way.

In fact, if you are ever to hope for any measure of success in trying to convince somebody of a claim, you should always try to argue for it based on whatever common ground you can find between the two of you. Indeed, the attempt to find common ground from which to start is what underlies the entire enterprise of rational debate.

Recap

The fallacies in this chapter, like those in Chapter 5, may resemble legitimate arguments, but none gives a reason for accepting (or rejecting) a claim. The discussions in this part of the book should help make you sensitive to the difference between relevant considerations and emotional appeals, factual irrelevancies, and other dubious argumentative tactics.

In this chapter we examined:

- Personal attack ad hominem—thinking a person's defects refute his or her beliefs

- Circumstantial ad hominem—thinking a person's circumstances refute his or her beliefs

- Inconsistency ad hominem—thinking a person's inconsistencies refute his or her beliefs

- Poisoning the well—encouraging others to dismiss what someone will say, by citing the speaker's defects, inconsistencies, circumstances, or other personal attributes

- Genetic fallacy—thinking that the origin or history of a belief refutes it

- Straw man—"rebutting" a claim by offering a distorted or exaggerated version of it

- False dilemma—an erroneous narrowing down of the range of alternatives; saying we have to accept X or Y (and omitting that we might do Z)

- Perfectionist fallacy—arguing that we either do something completely or not at all

- Line-drawing fallacy—requiring that a precise line be drawn someplace on a scale or continuum when no such precise line can be drawn; usually occurs when a vague concept is treated like a precise one

▲ Slippery slope—refusing to take the first step in a progression on unwarranted grounds that doing so will make taking the remaining steps inevitable or insisting erroneously on taking the remainder of the steps simply because the first one was taken

▲ Misplacing burden of proof—requiring the wrong side of an issue to make its case

▲ Begging the question—assuming as true the claim that is at issue and doing this as if you were giving an argument

Exercises

Exercise 6-1

Working in groups, invent a simple, original, and clear illustration of each fallacy covered in this chapter. Then in the class as a whole select the illustrations that are clearest and most straightforward. Go over these illustrations before doing the remaining exercises in this chapter, and review them before you take a test on this material.

Exercise 6-2

Identify any examples of fallacies in the following passages. Tell why you think they are present, and identify which category they belong in, if they fit any category we've described.

▲ 1. Of course Chinese green tea is good for your health. If it weren't, how could it be so beneficial to drink it?

2. Overheard: "No, I'm against this health plan business. None of the proposals are gonna fix everything, you can bet on that."

3. You have a choice: Either you let 'em out to murder and rape again and again, or you put up with a little prison overcrowding. I know what I'd choose.

▲ 4. "The legalization of drugs will not promote their use. The notion of a widespread hysteria sweeping across the nation as every man, woman, and child instantaneously becomes addicted to drugs upon their legalization is, in short, ridiculous."

From a student essay

5. Way I figure is, giving up smoking isn't gonna make me live forever, so why bother?

6. "The trouble with [syndicated columnist Joseph] Sobran's gripe about Clinton increasing the power of the federal government is that Sobran is the one who wants the government to tell women they can't have abortions."

From a newspaper call-in column

▲ 7. Aid to Russia? Gimme a break! Why should we care more about the Russians than about our own people?

8. Bush's tax cut stinks. He's just trying to please big business.

9. I believe Tim is telling the truth about his brother because he just would not lie about that sort of thing.

▲ 10. I think I was treated unfairly. I got a ticket out on McCrae Road. I was doing about sixty miles an hour, and the cop charged me with "traveling at an unsafe speed." I asked him what would have been a *safe* speed on that particular occasion—fifty? forty-five?—and he couldn't tell me. Neither could the judge. I tell you, if you don't know what speeds are unsafe, you shouldn't give tickets for "unsafe speeds."

Exercise 6-3

Classify each of the following cases of ad hominem as personal attack ad hominem, circumstantial ad hominem, inconsistency ad hominem, poisoning the well, or genetic fallacy. Identify the cases, if any, in which it might be difficult or futile to assign the item to any single one of these categories, as well as those cases, if any, where the item doesn't fit comfortably into any of these categories at all.

▲ 1. The proponents of this spend-now–pay-later boondoggle would like you to believe that this measure will cost you only one billion dollars. That's NOT TRUE. In the last general election some of these very same people argued against unneeded rail projects because they would cost taxpayers millions more in interest payments. Now they have changed their minds and are willing to encourage irresponsible borrowing. Connecticut is already awash in red ink. Vote NO.

2. Rush Limbaugh argues that the establishment clause of the First Amendment should not be stretched beyond its intended dimensions by precluding voluntary prayer in public schools. This is a peculiar argument, when you consider that Limbaugh is quite willing to stretch the Second Amendment to include the right to own assault rifles and Saturday night specials.

3. I think you can safely assume that Justice Scalia's opinions on the cases before the Supreme Court this term will be every bit as flaky as his past opinions.

▲ 4. Harvard now takes the position that its investment in urban redevelopment projects will be limited to projects that are environmentally friendly. Before you conclude that that is such a swell idea, stop and think. For a long time Harvard was one of the biggest slumlords in the country.

5. REPUBLICAN: Finally! Finally the governor is getting around to reducing taxes—as he promised. What do you think of his plan?
DEMOCRAT: Not much. He's just doing it so the Democrats won't get all the credit.

6. Dear Editor—
I read with amusement the letter by Leslie Burr titled "It's time to get tough." Did anyone else notice a little problem in her views? It seems a little odd that somebody who claims that she "loathes violence" could also say that "criminals should pay with their life." I guess consistency isn't Ms. Burr's greatest concern.

▲ 7. YOU: Look at this. It says here that white males still earn a lot more than minorities and women for doing the same job.
YOUR FRIEND: Yeah, right. Written by some woman, no doubt.

8. "Steve Thompson of the California Medical Association said document-checking might even take place in emergency rooms. That's because, while undocumented immigrants would be given emergency care, not all cases that come into emergency rooms fall under the federal definition of an emergency.
"To all those arguments initiative proponents say hogwash. They say the education and health groups opposing the initiative are interested in protecting funding they receive for providing services to the undocumented."

Article in Sacramento Bee

9. Horace, you're new to this town, and I want to warn you about the local newspaper. It's in cahoots with all them left-wing environmental nutcakes that are wrecking the economy around here. You can't believe a thing you read in it.

10. Are Moore and Parker guilty of the ad hominem fallacy or poisoning the well in their discussion of Michael Savage on p. 152?

▲ 11. Creationism cannot possibly be true. People who believe in a literal interpretation of the Bible just never outgrew the need to believe in Santa Claus.

12. "Americans spend between $28 billion and $61 billion a year in medical costs for treatment of hypertension, heart disease, cancer and other illnesses attributed to consumption of meat, says a report out today from a pro-vegetarian doctor's group.
"Dr. Neal D. Barnard, lead author of the report in the *Journal of Preventive Medicine,* and colleagues looked at studies comparing the health of vegetarians and meat eaters, then figured the cost of treating illnesses suffered by meat eaters in excess of those suffered by vegetarians. Only studies that controlled for the health effects of smoking, exercise and alcohol consumption were considered.
"The American Medical Association, in a statement from Dr. M. Roy Schwarz, charged that Barnard's group is an 'animal rights front organization' whose agenda 'definitely taints whatever unsubstantiated findings it may claim.'"

USA Today

Exercise 6-4 _____

Elegant Country Estate

- Stunning Federal-style brick home with exquisite appointments throughout
- 20 picturesque acres with lake, pasture, and woodland
- 5 bedrooms, 4.5 baths
- 5800 sq. ft. living space, 2400 sq. ft. basement
- Formal living room; banquet dining with butler's pantry; luxurious foyer, gourmet kitchen, morning room
- 3 fireplaces, 12 chandeliers

Maude and Clyde are discussing whether to buy this nice little cottage. Identify as many fallacies as you can in their conversation. Most are from this chapter, but you may see something from Chapters 4 and 5 as well.

CLYDE: Maude, look at this place! This is the house for us! Let's make an offer right now. We can afford it!

MAUDE: Oh, Clyde, be serious. That house is way beyond our means.

CLYDE: Well, I think we can afford it.

MAUDE: Honey, if we can afford it, pigs can fly.

CLYDE: Look, do you want to live in a shack? Besides, I called the real estate agent. She says it's a real steal.

MAUDE: Well, what do you expect her to say? She's looking for a commission.

CLYDE: Sometimes I don't understand you. Last week you were pushing for a really upscale place.

MAUDE: Clyde, we can't make the payments on a place like that. We couldn't even afford to heat it! And what on earth are we going to do with a lake?

CLYDE: Honey, the payments would only be around $5000 a month. How much do you think we could spend?

MAUDE: I'd say $1800.

CLYDE: Okay, how about $2050?

MAUDE: Oh, for heaven's sake! Yes, we could do $2050!

CLYDE: Well, how about $3100?

MAUDE: Oh, Clyde, what is your point?

CLYDE: So $3100 is okay? How about $3200? Stop me when I get to exactly where we can't afford it.

MAUDE: Clyde, I can't say *exactly* where it gets to be too expensive, but $5000 a month is too much.

CLYDE: Well, I think we can afford it.

MAUDE: Why?

CLYDE: Because it's within our means!

MAUDE: Clyde, you're the one who's always saying we have to cut back on our spending!

CLYDE: Yes, but this'll be a great investment!

MAUDE: And what makes you say that?

CLYDE: Because we're bound to make money on it.

MAUDE: Clyde, honey, you are going around in circles.

CLYDE: Well, can you prove we can't afford it?

MAUDE: Once we start spending money like drunken sailors, where will it end? Next we'll have to get a riding mower, then a boat for that lake, a butler for the butler's pantry—where will it end?

CLYDE: Well, we don't have to make up our minds right now. I'll call the agent and tell her we're sleeping on it.

MAUDE: Asleep and dreaming.

Exercise 6-5

In groups, vote on which option best depicts the fallacy found in each passage; then compare results with other groups in the class. *Note:* The fallacies include those found in Chapter 5 and Chapter 6.

▲ 1. The Health Editor for *USA Today* certainly seems to know what she is talking about when she recommends we take vitamins, but I happen to know she works for Tishcon, Inc., a large manufacturer of vitamin supplements.
   a. smokescreen/red herring
   b. subjectivism
   c. argument from popularity
   d. circumstantial ad hominem
   e. no fallacy

2. The president is right. People who are against attacking Iraq are unwilling to face up to the threat of terrorism.
   a. common practice
   b. peer pressure
   c. false dilemma
   d. straw man
   e. begging the question

3. Well, I for one think the position taken by our union is correct, and I'd like to remind you before you make up your mind on the matter that around here we employees have a big say in who gets rehired.
   a. wishful thinking
   b. circumstantial ad hominem
   c. scare tactics
   d. apple polishing
   e. begging the question

▲   4. On the whole, I think global warming is a farce. After all, most people think winters are getting colder, if anything. How could that many people be wrong?
   a. argument from outrage
   b. argument from popularity
   c. straw man
   d. no fallacy

5. MARCO: I think global warming is a farce.
CLAUDIA: Oh, gad. How can you say such a thing, when there is so much evidence behind the theory?
MARCO: Because. Look. If it isn't a farce, then how come the world is colder now than it used to be?
   a. begging the question
   b. subjectivism
   c. red herring
   d. circumstantial ad hominem
   e. no fallacy

6. Of course you should buy a life insurance policy! Why shouldn't you?
   a. smokescreen/red herring
   b. wishful thinking
   c. scare tactics
   d. peer pressure argument
   e. misplacing burden of proof

▲   7. My opponent, Mr. London, has charged me with having cheated on my income tax. My response is, When are we going to get this campaign out of the gutter? Isn't it time we stood up and made it clear that vilification has no place in politics?
   a. smokescreen/red herring
   b. wishful thinking
   c. argument from common practice
   d. argument from popularity
   e. circumstantial ad hominem

8. Either we impeach the man or we send a message to the kids of this country that it's all right to lie under oath. Seems like an easy choice to me.
   a. smokescreen/red herring
   b. straw man
   c. false dilemma
   d. inconsistency ad hominem
   e. none of these

9. If cigarettes aren't bad for you, then how come it's so hard on your health to smoke?
   a. circumstantial ad hominem
   b. genetic fallacy
   c. slippery slope
   d. begging the question

▲ 10. Global warming? I don't care what the scientists say. Just 'cause it's true for them doesn't make it true for me.
   a. smokescreen/red herring
   b. subjectivism
   c. argument from tradition
   d. argument from common practice

Exercise 6-6 _____

In groups, vote on which option best depicts the fallacy found in each passage, and compare results with other groups. (It is all right with us if you ask anyone who is not participating in the discussions in your group to leave.) *Note:* The fallacies include those found in Chapter 5 and Chapter 6.

▲ 1. So what if the senator accepted a little kickback money—most politicians are corrupt, after all.
   a. argument from envy
   b. argument from tradition
   c. common practice
   d. subjectivism
   e. no fallacy

2. Me? I'm going to vote with the company on this one. After all, I've been with them for fifteen years.
   a. genetic fallacy
   b. group think fallacy
   c. slippery slope
   d. no fallacy

3. Public opinion polls? They're rigged. Just ask anyone.
   a. argument from common practice
   b. guilt trip
   c. begging the question
   d. argument from popularity
   e. no fallacy

▲ 4. Hey! It can't be time for the bars to close. I'm having too much fun.
   a. false dilemma
   b. misplacing burden of proof
   c. wishful thinking
   d. argument from tradition
   e. no fallacy

5. A mural for the municipal building? Excuse me, but why should public money, *our* tax dollars, be used for a totally unnecessary thing like art? There are potholes that need fixing. Traffic signals that need to be put up. There are a *million* things that are more important. It is an *outrage,* spending taxpayers' money on unnecessary frills like art. Give me a break!
   a. inconsistency ad hominem

     b. argument from outrage
     c. slippery slope
     d. perfectionist fallacy
     e. no fallacy

6. Mathematics is more difficult than sociology, and I *really* need an easier term this fall. So I'm going to take a sociology class instead of a math class.
     a. circumstantial ad hominem
     b. argument from pity
     c. false dilemma
     d. begging the question
     e. no fallacy

▲ 7. Parker says Macs are better than PCs, but what would you expect him to say? He's owned Macs for years.
     a. personal attack ad hominem
     b. circumstantial ad hominem
     c. inconsistency ad hominem
     d. perfectionist fallacy
     e. no fallacy

8. The congressman thought the president's behavior was an impeachable offense. But that's nonsense, coming from the congressman. He had an adulterous affair himself, after all.
     a. inconsistency ad hominem
     b. poisoning the well
     c. circumstantial ad hominem
     d. genetic fallacy
     e. no fallacy

9. Your professor wants you to read Moore and Parker? Forget it. Their book is so far to the right it's falling off the shelf.
     a. poisoning the well
     b. inconsistency ad hominem
     c. misplacing burden of proof
     d. argument from tradition
     e. no fallacy

▲ 10. How do I know God exists? Hey, do you know he doesn't?
     a. perfectionist fallacy
     b. inconsistency ad hominem
     c. misplacing burden of proof
     d. slippery slope
     e. begging the question

Exercise 6-7

In groups, vote on which option best depicts the fallacy found in each passage, and compare results with other groups. *Note:* The fallacies include those found in Chapter 5 and Chapter 6.

Getting Really Worked Up over Ideas

Not long ago the editor of *Freethought Today* magazine won a court case upholding the constitutional separation of church and state. Following are a few samples of the mail she received as a result (there was much more), as they were printed in the magazine. We present them to remind you of how worked up people can get over ideas.

> Satan worshipping scum . . .
>
> If you don't like this country and what it was founded on & for *get the f—— out of it* and go straight to hell.
>
> F— you, you communist wh—.
>
> If you think that mathematical precision that governs the universe was established by random events then you truly are that class of IDIOT that cannot be aptly defined.

These remarks illustrate extreme versions of more than one rhetorical device mentioned in this part of the book. They serve as a reminder that some people become defensive and emotional when it comes to their religion. (As Richard Dawkins, professor of Public Understanding of Science at Oxford University, was prompted to remark, "A philosophical opinion about the nature of the universe, which is held by the great majority of America's top scientists and probably the elite intelligentsia generally, is so abhorrent to the American electorate that no candidate for popular election dare affirm it in public.")

—*Adapted from* Free Inquiry, *Summer 2002*

▲ 1. Laws against teenagers drinking?—They are a total waste of time, frankly. No matter how many laws we pass, there are always going to be some teens who drink.
   a. misplacing burden of proof
   b. perfectionist fallacy
   c. line-drawing fallacy
   d. no fallacy

2. Even though Sidney was old enough to buy a drink at the bar, he had no identification with him and the bartender would not serve him.
   a. perfectionist fallacy
   b. inconsistency ad hominem
   c. misplacing burden of proof
   d. slippery slope
   e. no fallacy

3. Just how much sex has to be in a movie before you call it pornographic? Seems to me the whole concept makes no sense.
   a. perfectionist fallacy

   b. line-drawing fallacy
   c. straw man
   d. slippery slope
   e. no fallacy

▲ 4. Studies confirm what everyone already knows: Smaller classes make students better learners.
   a. argument from common practice
   b. begging the question
   c. misplacing burden of proof
   d. argument from popularity
   e. no fallacy

5. The trouble with impeaching Bill Clinton is this: Going after every person who occupies the presidency will take up everyone's time and the government will never get anything else done.
   a. inconsistency ad hominem
   b. straw man
   c. group think
   d. argument from envy
   e. red herring

6. The trouble with impeaching Bill Clinton is this. If we start going after Clinton, next we'll be going after senators, representatives, governors. Pretty soon no elected official will be safe from partisan attack.
   a. inconsistency ad hominem
   b. slippery slope
   c. straw man
   d. false dilemma
   e. misplacing burden of proof

▲ 7. MR. IMHOFF: That does it. I'm cutting down on your peanut butter cookies. Those things blimp me up.
   MRS. IMHOFF: Oh, Imhoff, get real. What about all the ice cream you eat?
   a. circumstantial ad hominem
   b. subjectivism
   c. straw man
   d. slippery slope
   e. inconsistency ad hominem

8. KEN: I think I'll vote for Andrews. She's the best candidate.
   ROBERT: Why do you say she's best?
   KEN: Because she's my sister-in-law. Didn't you know that?
   a. apple polishing
   b. argument from pity
   c. scare tactics
   d. peer pressure argument
   e. none of the above

9. MOE: You going to class tomorrow?
   JOE: I s'pose. Why?

MOE: Say, don't you get tired of being a Goody Two-shoes? You must have the most perfect attendance record of anyone who ever went to this school—certainly better than the rest of us; right, guys?
a. poisoning the well
b. argument from pity
c. scare tactics
d. no fallacy
e. none of the above

▲ 10. Morgan, you're down to earth and I trust your judgment. That's why I know I can count on you to back me up at the meeting this afternoon.
a. apple polishing
b. argument from pity
c. scare tactics
d. guilt trip
e. no fallacy

11. "Do you want to sign this petition to the governor?"
"What's it about?"
"We want him to veto that handgun registration bill that's come out of the legislature."
"Oh. No, I don't think I want to sign that."
"Oh, really? So are you telling me you want to get rid of the Second Amendment?"
a. false dilemma
b. personal attack ad hominem
c. genetic fallacy
d. misplacing burden of proof
e. no fallacy

12. Outlaw gambling? Man, that's a strange idea coming from you. Aren't you the one who plays the lottery all the time?
a. inconsistency ad hominem
b. circumstantial ad hominem
c. genetic fallacy
d. scare tactics
e. no fallacy

Exercise 6-8

Most of the following passages contain fallacies from Chapter 5 or Chapter 6. Identify them where they occur and try to place them in one of the categories we have described.

▲ 1. "People in Hegins, Pennsylvania, hold an annual pigeon shoot in order to control the pigeon population and to raise money for the town. This year, the pigeon shoot was disrupted by animal rights activists who tried to release the pigeons from their cages. I can't help but think these animal rights activists are the same people who believe in controlling the human population through the use of abortion. Yet, they recoil at a similar means of controlling pigeons. What rank hypocrisy."

Rush Limbaugh

2. Dear Mr. Swanson: I realize I'm not up for a salary increase yet, but I thought it might make my review a bit more timely if I pointed out to you that I have a copy of all the recent e-mail messages between you and Ms. Flood in the purchasing department.

3. I don't care if Nike has signed up Michael Jordan, Tiger Woods, and even Santa Claus to endorse their shoes. They're a crummy company that makes a crummy product. The proof is the fact that they pay poor women a dollar sixty for a long day's work in their Vietnamese shoe factories. That's not even enough to buy a day's worth of decent meals!

▲ 4. I don't care if Nike has signed up Michael Jordan, Tiger Woods, and even Santa Claus to endorse their shoes. They're a crummy company, and I wouldn't buy their shoes no matter what the circumstance. You don't need any reason beyond the fact that they pay poor women a dollar sixty for a long day's work in their Vietnamese shoe factories. That's not even enough to buy a day's worth of decent meals!

5. JULIA: Even this long after the 2000 presidential election, I still feel sort of unsettled about it. It still feels sort of illegitimate—do you know what I mean?
   JEFF: Look, it's a done deal, and Bush is the president. Get over it!

6. POWELL FAN: Colin Powell says that diplomatic efforts to avoid war with Iraq were serious and genuine, and his word is good enough for me.
   SKEPTIC: And what makes you so sure he's telling it like it is?
   FAN: Because he's the one guy in the administration you can trust.

▲ 7. I know the repair guy in the service center screwed up my computer; he's the only one who's touched it since it was working fine last Monday.

8. If you give the cat your leftover asparagus, next thing you know you'll be feeding him your potatoes, maybe even your roast beef. Where will it all end? Pretty soon that wretched animal will be sitting up here on the table for dinner. He'll be eating us out of house and home.

9. Look, either we refrain from feeding the cat table scraps, or he'll be up here on the table with us. So don't go giving him your asparagus.

▲ 10. We have a simple choice. Saving Social Security is sure as hell a lot more important than giving people a tax cut. So write your representative now and let him or her know how you feel.

11. Let gays join the military? Give me a break. God created Adam and Eve, not Adam and Steve.

12. So my professor told me if he gave me an A for getting an 89.9 on the test, next he'd have to give people an A for getting an 89.8 on the test, and pretty soon he'd have to give everyone in the class an A. How could I argue with that?

▲ 13. Those blasted Democrats! They want to increase government spending on education again. This is the same outfit that gave us $10,000 toilets and government regulations up the wazoo.

14. All this yammering about Clinton having been a liar—spare me! Every president under the sun has lied—Reagan, Kennedy, Nixon, both Bushes, probably even Jimmy Carter.

15. Lauren did a better job than anyone else at the audition, so even if she has no experience, we've decided to give her the part in the play.

▲ 16. TERRY: I failed my test but I gave my prof this nifty argument. I said, "Look, suppose somebody did 0.0001 percent better than I, would that be a big enough difference to give him a higher grade?" And he had to say "no," so then I said, "And if someone did 0.0001 percent better than that second person, would that be a big enough difference?" And he had to say "no" to that, too, so I just kept it up, and he never could point to the place where the difference was big enough to give the other person a higher grade. He finally saw he couldn't justify giving anyone a better grade.
TERRI: Well? What happened?
TERRY: He had to fail the whole class.

17. There is an increasingly large likelihood of a war with Iraq this winter [of 2003]. It is not clear just what Saddam Hussein has in the way of nuclear, chemical, and biological weapons, but we believe he is not without some capability with weapons of those kinds. In fact, we are sure that, if it were within his capabilities at this moment, he would launch a preemptive strike against the United States. All the more reason that the United States strike first.

Loosely adapted from a conversation on NBC's Meet the Press

18. Look, maybe you think it's okay to legalize tribal casinos, but I don't. Letting every last group of people in the country open a casino is a ridiculous idea, bound to cause trouble.

▲ 19. What, you of all people complaining about violence on TV? You, with all the pro football you watch?

20. You have three Fs and a D on your exams, and your quizzes are on the borderline between passing and failing. I'm afraid you don't deserve to pass the course.

Exercise 6-9

Identify any fallacies in the following passages. Tell why you think they are present, and identify which category they belong in, if they fit any of those we've described. Instances of fallacies are all from the types found in Chapter 6.

▲ 1. Suspicious: "I would forget about whatever Moore and Parker have to say about pay for college teachers. After all, they're both professors themselves; what would you *expect* them to say?"

2. It's obvious to me that abortion is wrong—after all, everybody deserves a chance to be born.

3. Overheard: Well, I think that's too much to tip her. It's more than 15 percent. Next time it will be 20 percent, then 25 percent—where will it stop?

▲ 4. CARLOS: Four A.M.? Do we really have to start that early? Couldn't we leave a little later and get more sleep?
   JEANNE: C'mon, don't hand me that! I know you! If you want to stay in bed until noon and then drag in there in the middle of the night, then go by yourself! If we want to get there at a reasonable hour, then we have to get going early and not spend the whole day sleeping.

5. I know a lot of people don't find anything wrong with voluntary euthanasia, where a patient is allowed to make a decision to die and that wish is carried out by a doctor or someone else. What will happen, though, is that if we allow voluntary euthanasia, before you know it we'll have the patient's relatives or the doctors making the decision that the patient should be "put out of his misery."

6. "Congress was elected to make laws, not Dr. David Kessler, commissioner of the Food and Drug Administration, who convinced Clinton to have the FDA regulate nicotine. What's next? Will Dr. Kessler have Clinton regulate coffee and Coca-Cola? Will Big Macs be outlawed and overeating prohibited?"

▲ 7. Whenever legislators have the power to raise taxes, they will always find problems that seem to require for their solution doing exactly that. This is an axiom, the proof of which is that the power to tax always generates the perception on the part of those who have that power that there exist various ills the remedy for which can only lie in increased governmental spending and hence higher taxes.

8. Don't tell me I should wear my seat belt, for heaven's sake. I've seen you ride a motorcycle without a helmet!

9. People who own pit bulls show a lack of respect for their friends, their neighbors, and anybody else who might come in contact with their dogs. They don't care if their dogs chew other people up.

▲ 10. When it comes to the issue of race relations, either you're part of the solution or you're part of the problem.

11. What! So now you're telling me we should get a new car? I don't buy that at all. Didn't you claim just last month that there was nothing wrong with the Plymouth?

12. Letter to the editor: "The Supreme Court decision outlawing a moment of silence for prayer in public schools is scandalous. Evidently the American Civil Liberties Union and the other radical groups will not be satisfied until every last man, woman and child in the country is an atheist. I'm fed up."

Tri-County Observer

▲ 13. We should impeach the attorney general. Despite the fact that there have been many allegations of unethical conduct on his part, he has not done anything to demonstrate his innocence.

14. What do you mean, support Amnesty International? They only defend criminals.

15. Overheard: "Hunting immoral? Why should I believe that coming from you? You fish, don't you?"

16. "Will we have an expanding government, or will we balance the budget, cut government waste and eliminate unneeded programs?"

Newt Gingrich, in a Republican National Committee solicitation

17. "Former House Speaker Newt Gingrich, who is amazingly still welcomed on television despite his fall from power in disgrace, groused that Mondale had served on a panel recently that recommended privatizing Social Security. But don't Republicans adore this notion, even though they now call it 'private retirement investments' in deference to the idea's unpopularity?"

Political columnist Marianne Means

Exercise 6-10 ───

Identify any fallacies in the following passages. Tell why you think they are present, and identify which category they belong in, if they fit in any of those we've described.

▲ 1. Despite all the studies and the public outcry, it's still true that nobody has ever actually *seen* cigarette smoking cause a cancer. All the antismoking people can do is talk about statistics; as long as there isn't real proof, I'm not believing it.

2. There is only one way to save this country from the domination by the illegal drug establishment to which Colombia has been subjected, and that's to increase tenfold the funds we spend on drug enforcement and interdiction.

3. I believe that the great flood described in the Bible really happened. The reason is simple: Noah would not have built the ark otherwise.

▲ 4. In 1996 a University of Chicago study gave evidence that letting people carry concealed guns appears to sharply reduce murders, rapes, and other violent crimes. Gun-control backer Josh Sugarman of the Violence Policy Center commented: "Anyone who argues that these laws reduce crime either doesn't understand the nature of crime or has a preset agenda."

5. Letter to the editor: "I strongly object to the proposed sale of alcoholic beverages at County Golf Course. The idea of allowing people to drink wherever and whenever they please is positively disgraceful and can only lead to more alcoholism and all the problems it produces—drunk driving, perverted parties, and who knows what else. I'm sure General Stuart, if he were alive today to see what has become of the land he deeded to the county, would disapprove strenuously."

Tehama County Tribune

6. Letter to the editor: "I'm not against immigrants or immigration, but something has to be done soon. We've got more people already than we

can provide necessary services for, and, at the current rate, we'll have people standing on top of one another by the end of the century. Either we control these immigration policies or there won't be room for any of us to sit down."

Lake County Recorder

▲ 7. Letter to the editor: "So now we find our local crusader-for-all-that-is-right, and I am referring to Councilman Benjamin Bostell, taking up arms against the local adult bookstore. Is this the same Mr. Bostell who owns the biggest liquor store in Chilton County? Well, maybe booze isn't the same as pornography, but they're the same sort of thing. C'mon, Mr. Bostell, aren't you a little like the pot calling the kettle black?"

Chilton County Register

8. Letter to the editor: "Once again the *Courier* displays its taste for slanted journalism. Why do your editors present only one point of view?

"I am referring specifically to the editorial of May 27, regarding the death penalty. So capital punishment makes you squirm a little. What else is new? Would you prefer to have murderers and assassins wandering around scot-free? How about quoting someone who has a different point of view from your own, for a change?"

Athens Courier

9. "Clinton should have been thrown in jail for immoral behavior. Just look at all the women he has had affairs with since he left the presidency."

"Hey, wait a minute. How do you know he has had affairs since he was president?"

"Because if he didn't, then why would he be trying to cover up the fact that he did?"

▲ 10. It's practically a certainty that the government is violating the law in the arms deals with Saudi Arabians. When a reporter asked officials to describe how they were complying with the law, he was told that details about the arms sales were classified.

Exercise 6-11

Where we (Moore and Parker) teach, the city council recently debated relaxing the local noise ordinance. One student (who favored relaxation) appeared before the council and stated: "If 250 people are having fun, one person shouldn't be able to stop them."

We asked our students to state whether they agreed or disagreed with that student and to support their position with an argument. Here are some of the responses.

Divide into groups, and then identify any instances of fallacious reasoning you find in any answers, drawing from the materials in the last two chapters. Compare your results with those of other students, and see what your instructor thinks.

1. I support what the person is saying. If 250 people are having fun, one person shouldn't be able to stop them. Having parties and having a good time are a way of life for Chico State students. The areas around campus have always been this way.

2. A lot of people attend Chico State because of the social aspects. If rules are too tight, the school could lose its appeal. Without the students, local businesses would go under. Students keep the town floating. It's not just bars and liquor stores, but gas stations and grocery stores and apartment houses. This town would be like Orland.

3. If students aren't allowed to party, the college will go out of business.

4. We work hard all week long studying and going to classes. We deserve to let off steam after a hard week.

5. Noise is a fact of life around most college campuses. People should know what they are getting into before they move there. If they don't like it, they should just get earplugs or leave.

6. I agree with what the person is saying. If 250 people want to have fun, what gives one person the right to stop them?

7. I am sure many of the people who complain are the same people who used to be stumbling down Ivy Street twenty years ago doing the same thing that the current students are doing.

8. Two weeks ago I was at a party and it was only about 9:00 P.M. There were only a few people there and it was quiet. And then the police came and told us we had to break it up because a neighbor complained. Well, that neighbor is an elderly lady who would complain if you flushed the toilet. I think it's totally unreasonable.

9. Sometimes the noise level gets a little out of control, but there are other ways to go about addressing this problem. For example, if you are a neighbor and you are having a problem with the noise level, why don't you call the "party house" and let them know, instead of going way too far and calling the police?

10. I'm sure that these "narcs" have nothing else better to do than to harass the "party people."

11. You can't get rid of all the noise around a college campus no matter what you do.

12. The Chico noise ordinance was put there by the duly elected officials of the city and is the law. People do not have the right to break a law that was put in place under proper legal procedures.

13. The country runs according to majority rule. If the overwhelming majority want to party and make noise, under our form of government they should be given the freedom to do so.

14. Students make a contribution to the community, and in return they should be allowed to make noise if they want.

15. Your freedom ends at my property line.

16. A majority rule must recognize individual rights. A majority does not have the freedom to invade another person's home with anything, whether it's noise, litter, smoke, garbage, their bodies, or anything else.

Exercise 6-12

Identify any examples of fallacies in the following passages. Tell why you think these are fallacies, and identify which category they belong in, if they fit any category we've described.

▲ 1. Letter to the editor: "I would like to express my feelings on the recent conflict between county supervisor Blanche Wilder and Murdock County Sheriff Al Peters over the county budget.

"I have listened to sheriffs' radio broadcasts. Many times there have been dangerous and life-threatening situations when the sheriff's deputies' quickest possible arrival time is 20 to 30 minutes. This is to me very frightening.

"Now supervisor Wilder wants to cut two officers from the Sheriff's Department. This proposal I find ridiculous. Does she really think that Sheriff Peters can run his department with no officers? How anyone can think that a county as large as Murdock can get by with no police is beyond me. I feel this proposal would be very detrimental to the safety and protection of this county's residents."

2. Letter to the editor: "Andrea Keene's selective morality is once again showing through in her July 15 letter. This time she expresses her abhorrence of abortion. But how we see only what we choose to see! I wonder if any of the anti-abortionists have considered the widespread use of fertility drugs as the moral equivalent of abortion, and, if they have, why they haven't come out against them, too. The use of these drugs frequently results in multiple births, which leads to the death of one of the infants, often after an agonizing struggle for survival. According to the rules of the pro-lifers, isn't this murder?"

North-State Record

3. In one of her columns, Abigail Van Buren printed the letter of "I'd rather be a widow." The letter writer, a divorcée, complained about widows who said they had a hard time coping. Far better, she wrote, to be a widow than to be a divorcée, who are all "rejects" who have been "publicly dumped" and are avoided "like they have leprosy." Abby recognized the pseudo-reasoning for what it was, though she did not call it by our name. What is our name for it?

▲ 4. Overheard: "Should school kids say the Pledge of Allegiance before class? Certainly. Why shouldn't they?"

5. Letter to the editor: "Once again the Park Commission is considering closing North Park Drive for the sake of a few joggers and bicyclists. These so-called fitness enthusiasts would evidently have us give up to them for their own private use every last square inch of Walnut Grove. Then anytime anyone wanted a picnic, he would have to park at the edge of the park

and carry everything in—ice chests, chairs, maybe even grandma. I certainly hope the Commission keeps the entire park open for everyone to use."

6. "Some Christian—and other—groups are protesting against the placing, on federal property near the White House, of a set of plastic figurines representing a devout Jewish family in ancient Judaea. The protestors would of course deny that they are driven by any anti-Semitic motivation. Still, we wonder: Would they raise the same objections (of unconstitutionality, etc.) if the scene depicted a modern, secularized Gentile family?"

National Review

▲ 7. "It's stupid to keep on talking about rich people not paying their fair share of taxes while the budget is so far out of balance. Why, if we raised the tax rates on the wealthy all the way back to where they were in 1980, it would not balance the federal budget."

Radio commentary by Howard Miller

8. From a letter to the editor: "The counties of Michigan clearly need the ability to raise additional sources of revenue, not only to meet the demands of growth but also to maintain existing levels of service. For without these sources those demands will not be met, and it will be impossible to maintain services even at present levels."

9. In February 1992, a representative of the Catholic Church in Puerto Rico gave a radio interview (broadcast on National Public Radio) in which he said that the Church was against the use of condoms. Even though the rate of AIDS infection in Puerto Rico is much higher than on the U.S. mainland, the spokesman said that the Church could not support the use of condoms because they are not absolutely reliable in preventing the spread of the disease. "If you could prove that condoms were absolutely dependable in preventing a person from contracting AIDS, then the Church could support their use."

▲ 10. A 1991 book by a former member of the National Security Council indicated that supporters of Ronald Reagan may have made a deal with the Iranians who had been holding American hostages for months. The Iranians agreed not to release the hostages until after the 1980 election (in which Reagan defeated Jimmy Carter), and, it was alleged, the new administration promised to make weapons available to Iran. Here's one reaction to the announcement of the deal:

"I'm not surprised about Reagan's using trickery to get himself elected president. After all, he was nothing but an old actor, and he was used to using Hollywood trickery to fool people during his first career."

Exercise 6-13

Identify any examples of fallacies in the following passages. Tell why you think they are present, and identify which category they belong in, if they fit any category we've described.

▲ 1. The U.S. Congress considered a resolution criticizing the treatment of ethnic minorities in a Near Eastern country. When the minister of the interior was asked for his opinion of the resolution, he replied, "This is purely an internal affair in my country, and politicians in the U.S. should stay out of such affairs. If the truth be known, they should be more concerned with the plight of minority peoples in their own country. Thousands of black and Latino youngsters suffer from malnutrition in the United States. They can criticize us after they've got their own house in order."

2. It doesn't make any sense to speak of tracing an individual human life back past the moment of conception. After all, that's the beginning, and you can't go back past the beginning.

3. MOE: The death penalty is an excellent deterrent for murder.
   JOE: What makes you think so?
   MOE: Because there's no evidence that it's *not* a deterrent.
   JOE: Well, states with capital punishment have higher murder rates than states that don't have it.
   MOE: Yes, but that's only because there are so many legal technicalities standing in the way of executions that convicted people hardly ever get executed. Remove those technicalities, and the rate would be lower in those states.

▲ 4. Overheard: "The new sculpture in front of the municipal building by John Murrah is atrocious and unseemly, which is clear to anyone who hasn't forgotten Murrah's mouth in Vietnam right there along with Hayden and Fonda calling for the defeat of America. I say: Drill holes in it so it'll sink and throw it in Walnut Pond."

5. Overheard: "Once we let these uptight guardians of morality have their way and start censoring *Playboy* and *Penthouse,* the next thing you know they'll be dictating everything we can read. We'll be in fine shape when they decide that *Webster's* should be pulled from the shelves."

6. It seems the biggest problem the nuclear industry has to deal with is not a poor safety record, but a lack of education of the public on nuclear power. Thousands of people die each year from pollution generated by coal-fired plants. Yet to date, there has been no death directly caused by radiation at a commercial nuclear power plant in the United States. We have a clear choice: an old, death-dealing source of energy or a safe, clean one. Proven through the test of time, nuclear power is clearly the safest form of energy and the least detrimental to the environment. Yet it is perceived as unsafe and an environmental hazard.

▲ 7. A high school teacher once told my class that if a police state ever arose in America, it would happen because we freely handed away our civil rights in exchange for what we perceived would be security from the government. We are looking at just that in connection with the current drug crisis.

   For almost thirty years we've seen increasing tolerance, legally and socially, of drug use. Now we are faced with the very end of America as we know it, if not from the drug problem, then from the proposed solutions to it.

First, it was urine tests. Officials said that the innocent have nothing to fear. Using that logic, why not allow unannounced police searches of our homes for stolen goods? After all, the innocent would have nothing to fear.

Now we're looking at the seizure of boats and other property when even traces of drugs are found. You'd better hope some drug-using guest doesn't drop the wrong thing in your home, car, or boat.

The only alternative to declaring real war on the real enemies—the Asian and South American drug families—is to wait for that knock on the door in the middle of the night.

8. The mayor's argument is that because the developers' fee would reduce the number of building starts, ultimately the city would lose more money than it would gain through the fee. But I can't go along with that. Mayor Tower is a member of the Board of Realtors, and you know what *they* think of the fee.

9. Letter to the editor: "Next week the philosopher Tom Regan will be in town again, peddling his animal rights theory. In case you've forgotten, Regan was here about three years ago arguing against using animals in scientific experimentation. As far as I could see then and can see now, neither Regan nor anyone else has managed to come up with a good reason why animals should not be experimented on. Emotional appeals and horror stories no doubt influence many, but they shouldn't. I've always wondered what Regan would say if his children needed medical treatment that was based on animal experiments."

▲ 10. Not long before Ronald and Nancy Reagan moved out of the White House, former Chief of Staff Don Regan wrote a book in which he depicted a number of revealing inside stories about First Family goings-on. Among them was the disclosure that Nancy Reagan regularly sought the advice of a San Francisco astrologer. In response to the story, the White House spokesman at the time, Marlin Fitzwater, said, "Vindictiveness and revenge are not admirable qualities and are not worthy of comment."

Exercise 6-14

Listen to a talk-radio program (e.g., Rush Limbaugh, Michael Reagan, Michael Savage), and see how many minutes (or seconds) go by before you hear one of the following: ad hominem, straw man, ridicule, argument from outrage, or scare tactics. Report your findings to the class and describe the first item from the above list that you heard.

Exercise 6-15

Watch one of the news/public affairs programs on television (*NewsHour with Jim Lehrer, Nightline, Face the Nation*, and so on), and make a note of any examples of fallacies that occur. Explain in writing why you think the examples contain fallacious reasoning.

Alternatively, watch *Real Time* with Bill Maher. It usually doesn't take long to find a fallacy there.

Exercise 6-16

The following passages contain fallacies from both this and the preceding chapter. Identify the category in which each item belongs.

▲ 1. "I can safely say that no law, no matter how stiff the consequence is, will completely stop illegal drug use. Outlawing drugs is a waste of time."

From a student essay

2. "If we expand the commuter bus program, where is it going to end? Will we want to have a trolley system? Then a light rail system? Then expand Metrolink to our area? A city this size hardly needs and certainly cannot afford all these amenities."

From a newspaper call-in column

3. YAEKO: The character Dana Scully on *The X-Files* really provides a good role model for young women. She's a medical doctor and an FBI agent, and she's intelligent, professional, and devoted to her work.
   MICHAEL: Those shows about paranormal activities are so unrealistic. Alien abductions, government conspiracies—it's all ridiculous.

4. Overheard: "The reason I don't accept evolution is that ever since Darwin, scientists have been trying to prove that we evolved from some apelike primate ancestor. Well, they still haven't succeeded. Case closed."

▲ 5. Ladies and gentlemen, as you know, I endorsed Council Member Morrissey's bid for reelection based on his outstanding record during his first term. Because you are the movers and shakers in this community, other people place the same high value on your opinions that I do. Jim and I would feel privileged to have your support.

6. It's totally ridiculous to suppose that creationism is true. If creationism were true, then half of what we know through science would be false, which is complete nonsense.

7. KIRSTI: I counted my CDs this weekend, and out of twenty-seven, ten of them were by U2. They are such a good band! I haven't heard anything by Bono for a long time. He has such a terrific voice!
   BEN: Is he bisexual?

8. Was Gerhard a good committee chair? Well, I for one think you have to say he was excellent, especially when you consider all the abuse he put up with. Right from the start people went after him—they didn't even give him a chance to show what he could do. It was really vicious—people making fun of him right to his face. Yes, under the circumstances he has been quite effective.

▲ 9. Medical research that involves animals is completely unnecessary and a waste of money. Just think of the poor creatures! We burn and blind and torture them, and then we kill them. They don't know what is going to happen to them, but they know something is going to happen. They are scared to death. It's really an outrage.

10. Dear Editor—
    If Christians do not participate in government, only sinners will.

From a letter to the Chico Enterprise Record

11. The HMO people claim that the proposal will raise the cost of doing business in the state to such a degree that insurers will be forced to leave the state and do business elsewhere. What nonsense. Just look at what we get from these HMOs. I know people who were denied decent treatment for cancer because their HMO wouldn't approve it. There are doctors who won't recommend a procedure for their patients because they are afraid the HMO will cancel their contract. And when an HMO does cancel some doctor's contract, the patients have to find a new doctor themselves—*if* they can. Everybody has a horror story. Enough is enough.

12. HOWARD: Dad, I really appreciate your letting me borrow the Chevy. But Melanie's parents just bought her a brand new Mercedes!
    DAD: Some people just refuse to buy American!

▲ 13. [Dole campaign chairman] SCOTT REID: There is a clear pattern of campaign finance abuse by the [Clinton] administration. Indonesian business interests have steered millions into the President's campaign using a gardener as a front, and [Democratic fund-raiser] John Huang, who apparently laundered money at a fund-raiser at a Buddhist temple in California, is suddenly nowhere to be found.
    [White House Senior Adviser] GEORGE STEPHANOPOULOS: I can't let these charges go unrefuted. Dole has received millions from foreign supporters like José Fanjul, and his vice chairman for finance, Simon Fireman, had to pay the largest fine in the history of the country for massive violations of campaign-finance laws.

On NBC's Meet the Press

14. The proposal to reduce spending for the arts just doesn't make any sense. We spend a paltry $620 million for the NEA [National Endowment for the Arts], while the deficit is closing in on $200 billion. Cutting support for the arts isn't going to eliminate the deficit; that's obvious.

15. Year-round schools? I'm opposed. Once we let them do that, the next thing you know they'll be cutting into our vacation time and asking us to teach in the evenings and on the weekends and who knows where it will end. We teachers have to stand up for our rights.

▲ 16. [NBC's *Meet the Press* host] TIM RUSSERT: Mr. Perot, Bob Dole says that every vote for Ross Perot is a vote for Bill Clinton. True?
    ROSS PEROT: Of course that's not true. They've been programmed from birth to say that if they are a Republican.

17. Even if we outlaw guns we're still going to have crime and murder. So I really don't see much point in it.

From a student essay

18. Do you think affirmative action programs are still necessary in the country?
    Answers:
    a. Yes, of course. I don't see how you, a woman, can ask that question. It's obvious we have a very long way to go still.
    b. No. Because of affirmative action, my brother lost his job to a minority who had a lot less experience than he did.
    c. Yes. The people who want to end affirmative action are all white males who just want to go back to the good-old-boy system. It's always the same: Look out for number one.
    d. No. The people who want it to continue know a good deal when they see one. You think I'd want to end it if I were a minority?

Exercise 6-17

Explain in a sentence or two how each of the following passages involves a type of fallacy mentioned in either this or the preceding chapter. *Many of these examples are difficult* and should serve to illustrate how fallacies sometimes conform only loosely to the standard patterns.

▲ 1. I believe that the companies that produce passenger airliners should be more strictly supervised by the FAA. I mean, good grief, everybody knows that you can make more money by cutting corners here and there than by spending extra time and effort getting things just right, and you know there have got to be airlines that are doing exactly that.

2. From a letter to a college newspaper editor: "I really appreciated the fact that your editorial writer supports the hike in the student activity fee that has been proposed. Since the writer is a senior and won't even be here next year, he will escape having to pay the fee himself, so of course there's no downside to it as far as he's concerned. I'm against the fee, and I'll be one of those who pay it if it passes. Mine is an opinion that should count."

3. "'There's a certain sameness to the news on the Big Three [ABC, NBC, and CBS] and CNN,' says Moody, . . . who is in charge of Fox News's day-to-day editorial decisions. That's the message, Moody says, that 'America is bad, corporations are bad, animal species should be protected, and every cop is a racist killer. That's where "fair and balanced" [Fox's slogan] comes in. We don't think all corporations are bad, every forest should be saved, every government spending program is good. We're going to be more inquisitive.'"

   From an interview with John Moody, vice president for news editorial at Fox News Network, in Brill's Content *magazine*

▲ 4. During the Reagan and Bush administrations, Democratic members of Congress pointed to the two presidents' economic policies as causing huge deficits that could ultimately ruin the country's economy. President Bush dismissed such charges as "the politics of doom and gloom." "These people will find a dark cloud everywhere," he has said. Was this response fallacious reasoning?

▲ 5. "Louis Harris, one of the nation's most influential pollsters, readily admits he is in the polling business to 'have some impact with the movers and shakers of the world.' So poll questions are often worded to obtain answers that help legitimize the liberal Establishment's viewpoints."

Conservative Digest

6. "At a White House meeting in February of 1983 with Washington, D.C., anchormen, Ronald Reagan was asked to comment on 'an apparent continuing perception among a number of black leaders that the White House continues to be, if not hostile, at least not welcome to black viewpoints.' President Reagan replied as follows: 'I'm aware of all that, and it's very disturbing to me, because anyone who knows my life story knows that long before there was a thing called the civil-rights movement, I was busy on that side. As a sports announcer, I didn't have any Willie Mayses or Reggie Jacksons to talk about when I was broadcasting major league baseball. The opening line of the Spalding Baseball Guide said, "Baseball is a game for Caucasian gentlemen." And as a sports announcer I was one of a very small fraternity that used that job to editorialize against that ridiculous blocking of so many fine athletes and so many fine Americans from participating in what was called the great American game.' Reagan then went on to mention that his father refused to allow him to see *Birth of a Nation* because it was based on the Ku Klux Klan and once slept in a car during a blizzard rather than stay at a hotel that barred Jews. Reagan's 'closest teammate and buddy' was a black, he said."

James Nathan Miller, The Atlantic

7. From a letter to the editor of the *Atlantic Monthly:* "In all my reading and experience so far, I have found nothing presented by science and technology that precludes there being a spiritual element to the human being. . . . The bottom line is this: Maybe there are no angels, afterlife, UFOs, or even a God. Certainly their existence has not yet been scientifically proved. But just as certainly, their *nonexistence* remains unproved. Any reasonable person would therefore have to reserve judgment."

8. Stop blaming the developers for the fact that our town is growing! If you want someone to blame, blame the university. It brings the new people here, not the developers. Kids come here from God knows where, and lots of them like what they find and stick around. All the developers do is put roofs over those former students' heads.

▲ 9. Two favorite scientists of the Council for Tobacco Research were Carl Seltzer and Theodore Sterling. Seltzer, a biological anthropologist, believes smoking has no role in heart disease and has alleged in print that data in the huge 45-year, 10,000-person Framingham Heart Study—which found otherwise—have been distorted by anti-tobacco researchers. Framingham Director William Castelli scoffs at Seltzer's critique but says it "has had some impact in keeping the debate alive."

Sterling, a statistician, disputes the validity of population studies linking smoking to illness, arguing that their narrow focus on smoking obscures the more likely cause—occupational exposure to toxic fumes.

For both men, defying conventional wisdom has been rewarding. Seltzer says he has received "well over $1 million" from the Council for research. Sterling got $1.1 million for his Special Projects work in 1977–82, court records show.

From "How Tobacco Firms Keep Health Questions 'Open' Year After Year,"
Alix Freedman and Laurie Cohen. The article originally appeared in the
Wall Street Journal *and was reprinted in the* Sacramento Bee.

10. We have had economic sanctions in effect against China ever since the Tienanmen Square massacre. Clearly they haven't turned the Chinese leadership in Beijing into a bunch of good guys. All they've done, in fact, is cost American business a lot of money. We should get rid of the sanctions and find some other way to make them improve their human rights record.

Writing Exercises

1. Turn to any of the following selections from the Essays for Analysis in Appendix 1 and follow the instructions: 10A,B; 11A,B; 12; 14A,B; 15A,B; 16A,B; 17A,B; or 18A,B. You might also turn to Selection 19 or 20, and follow the second set of instructions of each.

2. When Marshall Gardiner married J'Noel Gardiner, he was aware that his new wife had been born a male and had recently had a sex-change operation. When Marshall Gardiner died, his wife's right to inherit half of her husband's $2.5 million estate was challenged by Marshall Gardiner's son. The son claimed the marriage was invalid under Kansas law, which declares same-sex marriages invalid, but does not address marriages involving transsexuals. The case went to the state supreme court in 2002. How should the court have ruled, in your opinion? Defend your position, using whatever rhetorical devices from Chapters 4, 5, and 6 you want. When everyone is finished, read the essays in groups looking for fallacies and other rhetorical devices. Your instructor may have groups select one essay to read to the class.

3. Should Kansas (or any other state) make same-sex marriages illegal? Take a position and defend it following the instructions for Exercise 2.

Chapter 7

The Anatomy and Varieties of Arguments

n a box back in Chapter 4, we presented this passage:

> It's morally wrong for a person to inflict awful pain on another sensitive creature, one that has done the first no harm. Therefore, the so-called scientists who perform their hideous and sadistic experiments on innocent animals are moral criminals just as were Hitler and his Nazi torturers.

The rhetorical devices used here are pretty obvious, and a person may read this passage and, especially after the comparison with Hitler and Nazi torturers, simply pass the whole thing off: "No, those scientists are not like Hitler—this person is nuts." But doing so would be a mistake, because it ignores the argument contained in the passage. Remember from Chapter 1 that an argument provides reasons (premises) in support of a conclusion. Stripped of its window dressing (mainly, the slanting devices), the argument looks like this:

1. Animals used in some experiments suffer serious pain as a result.
2. Those same animals have caused no harm (i.e., they do not deserve to suffer).
3. It is morally wrong to inflict pain upon a creature that does not deserve it.
4. Therefore, those who use animals in some experiments are committing morally wrong actions.

Now, we've laid this argument out in more detail than is probably necessary (it could be done in two steps instead of four), but we want it to be clear what is going on. If you remember the anatomy of arguments from Chapter 1,

Conclusion Indicators

When the words in the following list are used in arguments, they usually indicate that a premise has just been offered and that a conclusion is about to be presented. (The three dots represent the claim that is the conclusion.)

Thus . . .	Consequently . . .
Therefore . . .	So . . .
Hence . . .	Accordingly . . .
This shows that . . .	This implies that . . .
This suggests that . . .	This proves that . . .

Example:

Stacy drives a Porsche. This suggests that either she is rich or her parents are.

The conclusion is

Either she is rich or her parents are.

The premise is

Stacy drives a Porsche.

you'll notice that the first three claims in the argument are **premises,** and the fourth claim is the argument's **conclusion.**

This argument is actually a pretty good one. As indicated back in Chapter 1 and as we'll discuss in detail later, what this means is that the premises do in fact offer good support for the conclusion. Indeed, if all three of the premises are true, it is not going to be easy to reject the conclusion. So, if one is going to be able to reject the conclusion, it will be necessary to find something wrong with at least one of the premises. (There. We just made another argument, this time the subject was the first argument. Can you identify the premise and the conclusion of the new argument?)

Here are some further examples of arguments with the premises and conclusions identified:

[Premise] Every officer on the force has been certified, and [premise] nobody can be certified without scoring above 70 percent on the firing range. Therefore, [conclusion] every officer on the force must have scored above 70 percent on the firing range.

[Premise] Mr. Conners, the gentleman who lives on the corner, comes down this street on his morning walk every day, rain or shine. So [conclusion] something must have happened to him, because [premise] he has not shown up today.

Premise Indicators

When the words in the following list are used in arguments, they generally introduce premises. They often occur just *after* a conclusion has been given. A premise would replace the three dots in an actual argument.

Since . . .

Because . . .

For . . .

In view of . . .

This is implied by . . .

Example:

Either Stacy is rich or her parents are, since she drives a Porsche.

The premise is the claim that Stacy drives a Porsche; the conclusion is the claim that either Stacy is rich or her parents are.

Notice that sometimes the conclusion of one argument can serve as the premise of another:

[Premise] Every student who made 90 percent or better on the midterms has already been assigned a grade of A. [Premise] Since Margaret made 94 percent on her midterms, [conclusion] she already has her A.

[Premise] All those students who have been assigned A's are excused from the final exam. [Premise] Margaret got an A, so [conclusion] she is excused from the final.

The claim that Margaret has a grade of A is the conclusion in the first argument but a premise in the second.

Notice also that arguments can have unstated premises:

[Premise] You can't check books out of the library without an ID card. So [conclusion] Bill won't be able to check any books out.

The unstated premise must be "Bill has no ID card." We'll have more to say about unstated premises later.

Arguments can have unstated conclusions as well:

[Premise] The political party that best reflects mainstream opinion will win the most seats in the next election, and [premise] the Republicans certainly best reflect mainstream opinion.

The unstated conclusion is "The Republicans will win the most seats in the next election."

Don't Confuse Arguments with Explanations!

Remember from Chapter 1, you use an *argument* to show that a claim is true. You use an **explanation** to show what caused something, or what it is, or how it works, or what purpose it serves.

> The reason I believe in God is because the universe couldn't just happen by chance.

> The reason I believe in God is because my parents were devout Christians who took great pains to instill this belief in me.

These two statements have similar wording, but the first one argues God exists, the second one explains the cause of my believing in God.

Arguments and explanations often use exactly the same words, and we have to be careful not to confuse them.

Notice finally that there is a difference between **independent premises** and **dependent premises** for a conclusion.

> [Premise] Raising the speed limit will wear out the highways faster. In addition, [premise] doing so will result in more highway deaths. Therefore, [conclusion] we should not raise the speed limit.

> [Premise] Raising the speed limit will waste gas. [Premise] We don't have any gas to waste. Therefore, [conclusion] we should not raise the speed limit.

The first example gives two independent premises for the conclusion that we should not raise the speed limit (doing so would wear out the highways; doing so would waste lives). The premises are independent of one another because the falsity of one would not cancel the support the other provides for the conclusion.

But the premises in the second example (raising the speed limit will waste gas; we don't have any gas to waste) are dependent on one another. The falsity of either premise would automatically cancel the support the other provides for the conclusion that the speed limit should not be raised.

If you want, you can think of an argument with two independent premises as *two arguments for the same conclusion:*

> Raising the speed limit will wear out the highways faster. In addition, doing so will result in more highway deaths. Therefore, we should not raise the speed limit.

You can view this either as one argument with two independent premises, or as two separate arguments for one conclusion (the conclusion that we should not raise the speed limit). There are subtle theoretical differences between these views, but these differences are of little consequence to the practical task of evaluating arguments.

Exercise 7-1

Indicate which blanks would ordinarily contain premises and which would ordinarily contain conclusions.

▲ 1. ___a___, and ___b___. Therefore, ___c___.

▲ 2. ___a___. So, since ___b___, ___c___.

▲ 3. ___a___, because ___b___.

▲ 4. Since ___a___ and ___b___, ___c___.

▲ 5. ___a___. Consequently, ___b___, since ___c___ and ___d___.

Exercise 7-2

Identify the premises and conclusions in each of the following arguments.

▲ 1. Since all Communists are Marxists, all Marxists are Communists.

   2. The Lakers almost didn't beat the Kings. They'll never get past Dallas.

   3. If the butler had done it, he could not have locked the screen door. Therefore, since the door was locked, we know that the butler is in the clear.

▲ 4. That cat is used to dogs. Probably she won't be upset if you bring home a new dog for a pet.

   5. Hey, he can't be older than his mother's daughter's brother. His mother's daughter has only one brother.

   6. Moscone will never make it into the state police. They have a weight limit, and he's over it.

▲ 7. Presbyterians are not fundamentalists, but all born-again Christians are. So no born-again Christians are Presbyterians.

   8. I guess he doesn't have a thing to do. Why else would he waste his time watching daytime TV?

   9. "There are more injuries in professional football today than there were twenty years ago," he reasoned. "And if there are more injuries, then today's players suffer higher risks. And if they suffer higher risks, then they should be paid more. Consequently, I think today's players should be paid more," he concluded.

▲ 10. Let's see . . . If we've got juice at the distributor, the coil isn't defective, and if the coil isn't defective, then the problem is in the ignition switch. So the problem is in the ignition switch.

Exercise 7-3

Identify the premises and the conclusions in the following arguments.

▲ 1. The darned engine pings every time we use the regular unleaded gasoline, but it doesn't do it with super. I'd bet that there is a difference in the octane ratings between the two in spite of what my mechanic says.

2. Kera, Sherry, and Bobby were all carded at JJ's, and they all look as though they're about thirty. Chances are I'll be carded too.

3. Seventy percent of freshmen at Wharfton College come from wealthy families; therefore, probably about the same percentage of all Wharfton College students come from wealthy families.

▲ 4. When blue jays are breeding, they become very aggressive. Consequently, scrub jays, which are very similar to blue jays, can also be expected to be aggressive when they're breeding.

5. A cut in the capital gains tax will benefit wealthy people. Marietta says her family would be much better off if capital gains taxes were cut, so I'm sure her family is wealthy.

6. According to *Nature,* today's thoroughbred racehorses do not run any faster than their grandparents did. But human Olympic runners are at least 20 percent faster than their counterparts of fifty years ago. Most likely, racehorses have reached their physical limits but humans have not.

▲ 7. It's easier to train dogs than cats. That means they're smarter than cats.

8. "Let me demonstrate the principle by means of logic," the teacher said, holding up a bucket. "If this bucket has a hole in it, then it will leak. But it doesn't leak. Therefore, obviously it doesn't have a hole in it."

9. I know there's a chance this guy might be different, but the last person we hired from Alamo Polytech was a rotten engineer, and we had to fire him. Thus I'm afraid that this new candidate is somebody I just won't take a chance on.

▲ 10. If she were still interested in me, she would have called, but she didn't.

Exercise 7-4

Identify the conclusion in each of the following arguments. For any that have more than one premise, determine whether the premises provide dependent or independent reasons for the conclusion.

▲ 1. North Korea was always a much greater threat to its neighbors than Iraq. After all, North Korea has a million-man army lined up on the border ready to attack. Oh yes! They also have nuclear weapons and have said they'd use them.

2. Jim is going to ride with Mary to the party, and Sandra is going to ride with her too. So Mary won't be driving all by herself to the party.

▲ 3. Michael should go ahead and buy another car. The one he's driving is just about to fall apart, and he just got a new job and he can certainly afford another car now.

4. If Parker goes to Las Vegas, he'll wind up in a casino; and if he winds up in a casino, it's a sure thing he'll spend half the night at a craps table. So you can be sure: If Parker goes to Las Vegas, he'll spend half the night at a craps table.

5. It's going to be rainy tomorrow, and Moore doesn't like to play golf in the rain. It's going to be cold as well, and he *really* doesn't like to play when it's cold. So you can be sure Moore will be someplace other than the golf course tomorrow.

▲ 6. Hey, you're overwatering your lawn. See? There are mushrooms growing around the base of that tree—a sure sign of overwatering. Also, look at all the worms on the ground. They come up when the earth is oversaturated.

7. "Will you drive me to the airport?" she asked. "Why should I do that?" he wanted to know. "Because I'll pay you twice what it takes for gas. Besides, you said you were my friend, didn't you?"

8. If you drive too fast, you're more likely to get a ticket, and the more likely you are to get a ticket, the more likely you are to have your insurance premiums raised. So, if you drive too fast, you are more likely to have your insurance premiums raised.

▲ 9. If you drive too fast, you're more likely to get a ticket. You're also more likely to get into an accident. So you shouldn't drive too fast.

10. The war on terrorism had as its original goal the capture or elimination of Osama bin Laden. Since he's still at large, as of this point the war has not been very successful.

11. DANIEL: Where did that cat go, anyway?
THERESA: I think she ran away. Look, her food hasn't been touched in two days. Neither has her water.

▲ 12. There are several reasons why you should consider installing a solarium. First, you can still get a tax credit. Second, you can reduce your heating bill. Third, if you build it right, you can actually cool your house with it in the summer.

13. From a letter to the editor: "By trying to eliminate Charles Darwin from the curriculum, creationists are doing themselves a great disservice. When read carefully, Darwin's discoveries only support the thesis that species change, not that they evolve into new species. This is a thesis that most creationists can live with. When read carefully, Darwin actually supports the creationist point of view."

14. Editorial comment: "The Supreme Court's ruling that schools may have a moment of silence but not if it's designated for prayer is sound. Nothing stops someone from saying a silent prayer at school or anywhere else. Also, even though a moment of silence will encourage prayer, it will not favor any particular religion over any other. The ruling makes sense."

▲ 15. We must paint the house now! Here are three good reasons: (a) If we don't, then we'll have to paint it next summer; (b) if we have to paint it next summer, we'll have to cancel our trip; and (c) it's too late to cancel the trip.

Exercise 7-5

Identify the conclusion in the following arguments. For any that have more than one premise, determine whether the premises provide dependent or inde-
▲ pendent reasons for the conclusion.

1. All mammals are warm-blooded creatures, and all whales are mammals. Therefore, all whales are warm-blooded creatures.

2. Jones won't plead guilty to a misdemeanor, and if he won't plead guilty, then he will be tried on a felony charge. Therefore, he will be tried on a felony charge.

▲ 3. John is taller than Bill, and Bill is taller than Margaret. Therefore, John is taller than Margaret.

4. Rats that have been raised in enriched environments, where there are a variety of toys and puzzles, have brains that weigh more than the brains of rats raised in more barren environments. Therefore, the brains of humans will weigh more if humans are placed in intellectually stimulating environments.

5. From a letter to the editor: "In James Kilpatrick's July 7 column it was stated that Scientology's 'tenets are at least as plausible as the tenets of Southern Baptists, Roman Catholics . . . and prayer book Episcopalians.' Mr. Kilpatrick seems to think that all religions are basically the same and fraudulent. This is false. If he would compare the beliefs of Christianity with the cults he would find them very different. Also, isn't there quite a big difference between Ron Hubbard, who called himself God, and Jesus Christ, who said 'Love your enemies, bless them that curse you, do good to them that hate you'?"

6. We've interviewed two hundred professional football players, and 60 percent of them favor expanding the season to twenty games. Therefore, 60 percent of all professional football players favor expanding the season to twenty games.

7. Exercise may help chronic male smokers kick the habit, says a study published today. The researchers, based at McDuff University, put thirty young male smokers on a three-month program of vigorous exercise. One year later, only 14 percent of them still smoked, according to the report. An equivalent number of young male smokers who did not go through the exercise program were also checked after a year and it was found that 60 percent still smoked. Smokers in the exercise program began running three miles a day and gradually worked up to eight miles daily. They also spent

five and a half hours each day in modestly vigorous exercise such as soccer, basketball, biking, and swimming.

▲ 8. Letter to the editor: "I was enraged to learn that the mayor now supports the initiative for the Glen Royale subdivision. Only last year he himself proclaimed 'strong opposition' to any further development in the river basin. Besides, Glen Royale will only add to congestion, pollution, and longer lines at the grocery store, not that the grocers will mind."

9. Believe in God? Yes, of course I do. The universe couldn't have arisen by chance, could it? Besides, I read the other day that more and more physicists believe in God, based on what they're finding out about the Big Bang and all that stuff.

▲ 10. From an office memo: "I've got a good person for your opening in Accounting. Jesse Brown is his name, and he's as sharp as they come. Jesse has a solid background in bookkeeping, and he's good with computers. He's also reliable, and he'll project the right image. Best of all, he's a terrific golfer. As you might gather, I know him personally. He'll be contacting you later this week."

Exercise 7-6

Which five of the following statements are probably intended to explain the cause of something, and which five are probably intended to argue that some claim is true?

▲ 1. The reason we've had so much hot weather recently is that the jet stream is unusually far north.

2. The reason Ms. Mossbarger looks so tired is that she hasn't been able to sleep for three nights.

3. The reason it's a bad idea to mow the lawn in your bare feet is that you could be seriously injured.

▲ 4. The reason Ken mows the lawn in his bare feet is that he doesn't realize how dangerous it is.

5. You can be sure that Ryan will marry Beth. After all, he told me he would.

6. If I were you, I'd change before going into town. Those clothes look like you slept in them.

▲ 7. Overeating can cause high blood pressure.

8. Eating so much salt can cause high blood pressure, so you'd better cut back a little.

▲ 9. It's a good bet the Saddam Hussein regime wanted to build nuclear weapons, because the U.N. inspectors found devices for the enrichment of plutonium.

10. The reason Saddam wanted to build nuclear weapons was to give him the power to control neighboring Middle Eastern countries.

Good and Bad, Valid and Invalid, Strong and Weak

When we say that an argument is a **good argument,** we are saying that it gives us grounds for accepting its conclusion. "Good" and "bad" are relative terms: Arguments can be better or worse depending on the degree to which they furnish support for their conclusions.

There is more than one way in which an argument might qualify as good; before we explain them, however, we need to describe some important technical distinctions.

An argument whose premises provide absolutely conclusive support for the conclusion is "valid." In other words,

> A **valid argument** has this characteristic: It is necessary, on the assumption that the premises are true, that the conclusion be true.

This is merely a precise way of saying that the premises of a valid argument, if true, absolutely guarantee a true conclusion. Here's an example:

> [Premise] Every philosopher is a good mechanic, and [premise] Emily is a philosopher. So, [conclusion] Emily is a good mechanic.

Valid? Yes. These premises, if true, guarantee that the conclusion is true.

But notice this: Although the argument about Emily is valid, it so happens the premises aren't true. Not every philosopher is a good mechanic, and Emily is no philosopher; she's Parker's cat. So the argument is not a good one, from the standpoint of offering us justification for accepting the claim that Emily is a good mechanic. However, the argument is valid nonetheless, because the conclusion *must* follow from the premises. Thus, an argument's being valid does not depend on its premises being true. What determines whether an argument is valid is whether the conclusion *absolutely follows* from the premises. (Once again: When we say that a conclusion absolutely follows from the premises, we mean that, *if* the premises were true, the conclusion would then *have to be* true as well.) If the conclusion does absolutely follow from the premises, the argument is valid, whether or not the premises are true.

Now, a valid argument whose premises *are* true is called a "sound" argument:

> A **sound argument** has these two characteristics: It is valid, and its premises are all true.

And here is an example:

> [Premise] Some pesticides are toxic for humans, and [premise] anything that is toxic for humans is unsafe for most humans to consume. Therefore, [conclusion] some pesticides are unsafe for most humans to consume.

Abe Lincoln Knew His Logic
Validity and Soundness in the Lincoln-Douglas Debates

Here's Abraham Lincoln speaking in the fifth Lincoln-Douglas debate:

I state in syllogistic form the argument:
Nothing in the Constitution . . . can destroy a right distinctly and expressly affirmed in the Constitution.
    The right of property in a slave is distinctly and expressly affirmed in the Constitution.
    Therefore, nothing in the Constitution can destroy the right of property in a slave.

Lincoln goes on to say:

There is a fault [in the argument], but the fault is not in the reasoning; but the falsehood in fact is a fault of the premises. I believe that the right of property in a slave is *not* distinctly and expressly affirmed in the Constitution.

In other words, the argument is valid, Lincoln says, but unsound, and thus not a good argument.
    Syllogisms, by the way, are covered in Chapter 8.

This is a sound argument: It is valid, because the conclusion absolutely follows from the premises, and its premises (and hence its conclusion) are true.

It should be clear, then, that an argument can be valid without necessarily being a good argument. The argument about Emily isn't good because, even though it's valid, it doesn't justify accepting the conclusion: Its premises are false.

A sound argument, by contrast, normally does justify accepting the conclusion. We say "normally" because cases can arise in which even sound arguments aren't particularly good. Arguments that beg the question, as explained in Chapter 6, fall in this category. Or consider the argument:

If a person travels in the same direction far enough, he or she will arrive back at the place he or she started from. Therefore, if Kotar travels in the same direction far enough, he will arrive back at the place he started from.

This is a sound argument; but, if Kotar happened to live in the middle of Europe in the tenth century, it seems odd to suppose *he* would have been justified in believing that if he traveled far enough in the same direction, he would arrive back where he started.

Arguments can be useful—they can qualify as good arguments—even though we don't intend them to be valid or sound. Look at this example, in which Moore says to Parker:

Everyday English Definitions

In everyday English, "valid argument," "sound argument," and "strong argument" are used interchangeably and often just mean "good argument." Other terms people use to praise arguments include "cogent," "compelling," and "telling." Further, people often apply "valid," "sound," "cogent," and "compelling" to things other than arguments—claims, theories, and explanations, for example. So before you pounce on someone for using these words incorrectly, consider the context in which you hear them.

In everyday English, "weak argument" includes arguments that are invalid and unsound and has numerous synonyms, including "poor," "faulty," "fallacious," "specious," "unreasonable," "illogical," "stupid," and so forth.

[Premise] Every year as far back as I can remember my roses have developed mildew in the spring. [Conclusion] Therefore, my roses will develop mildew this spring, too.

This argument doesn't qualify as valid (or sound) because it is *possible* that the conclusion is false even assuming the premise is true (it might be an incredibly dry winter). Nevertheless, this isn't a bad argument. In fact, it's really quite good: It may not be absolutely impossible that Moore's roses won't get mildew this spring, but, given the premise, it is very, very likely that they will. Moore is certainly justified in believing his conclusion.

Arguments like this one, which only show that the conclusion is *probably* true, are said to be relatively *strong.* More precisely:

A **strong argument** has this distinguishing characteristic: It is *unlikely,* on the assumption that the premises are true, that the conclusion is false.

Again, notice that the premises don't actually have to be true for the argument to be strong.

When someone advances an argument like Moore's, an argument that he or she intends only to be a strong argument, it is somewhat inappropriate to discuss whether it is valid. Yes, technically, Moore's argument is invalid, but because Moore is only trying to demonstrate that the conclusion is *likely,* the criticism doesn't amount to much—he never intended that the argument be valid.

Let's summarize these various points:

1. A *good* argument justifies acceptance of the conclusion.
2. A *valid* argument has this defining characteristic: It is necessary, on the assumption that the premises are true, that the conclusion be true.

The "Science of Deduction"

Possibly the most familiar uses of the term "deduction" occur in the Sherlock Holmes stories of Arthur Conan Doyle. The most famous of these is no doubt the second chapter of *A Study in Scarlet,* which is titled "The Science of Deduction." In that chapter Dr. Watson discovers and describes Holmes's methods of observation and inference-drawing. As it turns out, Holmes engages more frequently in *inductive* inference than deductive.

When he identifies a man crossing the street below from their sitting-room window as a retired sergeant of marines, Holmes does so from such clues as an anchor tattoo on the hand and "a military carriage . . . and regulation side whiskers." Thus, he says, "There we have the marine." Notice that these facts about the man do not *absolutely guarantee* the conclusion that the man is a marine, and hence we do not have a valid deductive argument. At best, we have a strong inductive argument. (Just how strong is arguable; but never argue the point with a serious Sherlock Holmes fan.)

3. A valid argument whose premises are all true is called a *sound* argument.

4. A *strong* argument has this defining characteristic: It is unlikely, on the assumption that the premises are true, that the conclusion is false.

5. Normally, sound arguments and strong arguments with true premises are good arguments.

6. The best policy is not to speak of valid arguments as strong or weak; speak of them as sound or unsound. Likewise, the best policy is not to speak of strong or weak arguments as valid or invalid; just refer to them as strong or weak.

Finally, notice that the terms "valid" and "invalid" are absolute terms. Either an argument is valid, or it is not, and that's that. By contrast, "strong" and its opposite, "weak" (like "good" and "bad"), are relative terms. Arguments can be evaluated as stronger or weaker depending on how likely the premises show the conclusion to be.

Deduction and Induction

Philosophers have traditionally distinguished deductive arguments from inductive arguments, though the best way of defining the difference is controversial. One way to view them is to say that **deductive arguments** are those that are either valid or intended by their author to be so. **Inductive**

Deductive and Inductive; General and Specific

A lot of people, including a few authors of articles and books on logic, think it's possible to explain the difference between deductive arguments and inductive arguments by referring to whether they go from general to particular or vice versa. In the words of one such author, "Deductive arguments involve reasoning from general premises to specific conclusions, while inductive arguments involve reasoning from specific instances to general conclusions."

It's true that *many* arguments fit this scheme, but many do not. Here's an argument that is clearly deductive (and valid, in fact):

> Maria scored higher on the logic exam than Ron did, and Ron scored higher than Kenneth. So Maria must have scored higher than Kenneth.

Notice that there are no general claims at all in this argument; each one is about a specific relationship, and so it is false that all deductive arguments proceed from general claims to specific ones.

Now look at this argument:

> I've watched *The Sopranos* television show four or five times recently, and I've really liked it each time. So it's a safe bet that I'll enjoy it again when I watch it tonight.

This argument is inductive (of a type called arguments by analogy, which are described in Chapter 10), but it too contains no general claims at all; it proceeds from particular cases to a further particular case. And so it is also false that all inductive arguments proceed from specific instances to general conclusions.

arguments are neither valid nor intended to be so by their authors; nevertheless, such arguments can be quite strong.

Exercise 7-7

Fill in the blanks where called for, and answer true or false where appropriate.

1. Valid arguments are said to be strong or weak.

2. Valid arguments are always good arguments.

▲ 3. Sound arguments are _____ arguments whose premises are all _____.

4. The premises of a valid argument are never false.

5. If a valid argument has a false conclusion, then not all its premises can be true.

▲ 6. If a strong argument has a false conclusion, then not all its premises can be true.

Speaking of Holmes and Watson

Here's another item that mentions them and has (a little) to do with observation, a topic from Chapter 3.

It seems Sherlock Holmes and Dr. Watson were out on a camping trip. One night, a couple of hours after they'd gone to sleep, Holmes woke up and nudged his faithful friend.

"Watson, look up at the sky and tell me what you see."

Watson replied, "I see hundreds and hundreds of stars."

"What does that tell you?" said Holmes.

Watson pondered for a moment. "Astronomically, it tells me that there are many galaxies and potentially many, many planets similar to ours. Astrologically, I notice Saturn is in Leo. Horologically, I deduce that the time is approximately a quarter past three. Theologically, I can see that God is all powerful and we are small and insignificant. Meteorologically I suspect that we will have a beautiful day tomorrow. What does it tell you, Holmes?"

After a moment, Holmes spoke, "Watson, you idiot. Someone has stolen our tent."

7. A sound argument cannot have a false conclusion.

8. A true conclusion cannot be derived validly from false premises.

▲ 9. "Strong" and "weak" are absolute terms.

10. The following argument is valid: All swans are orange. You're a swan, so you're orange.

11. The following argument is *both* valid *and* sound: Jesse Helms is one of New York's U.S. senators, and he is a Democrat. Therefore, he is a Democrat.

12. A strong argument with true premises has a conclusion that probably is true.

Exercise 7-8

Go back to Exercises 7-2 and 7-3, and determine which arguments are valid. In the answer section at the back of the book, we have answered items 1, 4, 7, and 10 in each set.

Exercise 7-9

Given the premises, discuss whether the conclusion of each argument that follows is (a) true beyond a reasonable doubt, (b) probably true, or (c) possibly true or possibly false. You should expect disagreement on these items, but the closer your answers are to your instructor's, the better.

▲   1. The sign on the parking meter says "Out of Order," so the meter isn't working.

2. The annual rainfall in California's north valley averages twenty-three inches. So the rainfall next year will be about twenty-three inches.

3. You expect to get forty miles to the gallon in *that?* Why, that old wreck has a monster V8; besides, it's fifty years old and needs an overhaul.

4. In three of the last four presidential races, the winner of the Iowa Republican primary has not captured the Republican nomination. Therefore, the winner of the next Iowa Republican primary will not capture the Republican nomination.

▲   5. The New York steak, the Maine lobster, and the beef stroganoff at that restaurant are all exceptionally good. You can probably count on all the entrees being excellent.

6. The number of cellular telephones has increased dramatically in each of the past few years. It's a safe bet that there will be even more of them in use this coming year.

7. Since the graduates of Harvard, Yale, Princeton, and other Ivy League schools generally score higher on the Graduate Record Examination than students from Central State, it follows that the Ivy League schools do more toward educating their students than Central State does.

8. Michael Jackson has had more plastic surgery than anybody else in California. You can bet he's had more than anybody in Connecticut!

▲   9. Although Max bled profusely before he died, there was no blood on the ground where his body was found. Therefore, he was killed somewhere else and brought here after the murder.

10. When liquor was banned in 1920, hospitalizations for alcoholism and related diseases plummeted; in 1933, when Prohibition was repealed, alcohol-related illnesses rose sharply again. Legalization of cocaine, heroin, and marijuana would not curb abuse of those substances.

11. Relax. The kid's been delivering the paper for, how long? Three, four years maybe? And not once has she missed us. The paper will be here, just wait and see. She's just been delayed for some reason.

▲ 12. First, it seems clear that even if there are occasional small dips in the consumption of petroleum, the general trend shows no sign of a real permanent decrease. Second, petroleum reserves are not being discovered as fast as petroleum is currently being consumed. From these two facts we can conclude that reserves will eventually be consumed and that the world will have to do without oil.

Unstated Premises

As we've noted, arguments can have unstated premises. Suppose a husband and wife are dining out, and she says to him: "It's getting very late, so we should call for the check." For this little argument to be valid, this principle must be assumed: *"If it is getting very late, then we should call for the check."* The wife, no doubt, is assuming this principle (among many other things), and even if *she* is not assuming it, *we* must assume it if we are to credit her with a valid argument.

Most real-life arguments are like this argument in that some unstated proposition must be assumed for the argument to be valid. And it is useful to be able to specify what must be assumed for a given argument to be valid. What, for example, must be assumed for the following argument to be valid?

> Moore's dog is a bloodhound, so it has a keen sense of smell.

What must be assumed, of course, is that all bloodhounds have a keen sense of smell. We are also assuming here that we know nothing about the dog in question except that it is a bloodhound. The argument is valid if and only if we assume that all bloodhounds have a keen sense of smell. Further, since it is questionable whether *all* bloodhounds have a keen sense of smell, we see that the validity of this argument depends on a questionable assumption.

However, recall that an argument need not necessarily be valid to be a good argument. Invalid arguments may still be strong; that is, their premises may provide strong support, though less than absolutely conclusive support, for their conclusions. Let's therefore ask, Is there an unstated premise that would make the bloodhound argument a strong one? The answer is that if we plug into the argument the premise that *most* bloodhounds have a keen sense of smell, which is certainly a reasonable premise, the result is quite a strong argument:

> Moore's dog is a bloodhound.
> [Unstated: Most bloodhounds have a keen sense of smell.]
> Therefore, Moore's dog has a keen sense of smell.

If you can spot what must be assumed for an argument to be valid or to be strong, you'll be in a much better position to evaluate it. If a plausible assumption suffices to make an argument valid, then it is a good argument. If a plausible assumption can at best only make an argument strong, then it may still be a good argument, depending on how strong it is and how plausible the stated premises and unstated assumption are.

Let's consider another example:

> He's related to Edward Kennedy, so he's rich.

For the argument to be valid, one must assume that *everyone* related to Kennedy is rich, and that's not a very plausible assumption. For the argument to be strong, one must assume that *most* people related to Kennedy are rich, and although that assumption is a good bit more plausible than the first assumption, it still isn't very plausible. The most plausible relevant assumption is that *many* people related to Kennedy are rich, but with

Unstated Arguments

There aren't any. An argument can contain unstated premises or an unstated conclusion, but the argument *itself* cannot be entirely unstated. A masked bandit who waves you against a wall with a gun is not presenting you with an argument, though his actions give you a good reason for moving; if you do not want to get shot, then you need to construct an argument in your own mind—and quickly, too—with the conclusion "I'd better move" and the premise "If I don't move, I may get my head blown off."

There is no such thing, then, as an unstated argument, though an argument can have unstated premises or an unstated conclusion. Further, it isn't possible for *all* the premises in an argument to be unstated. If the bandit waves his gun and says "Better move over against that wall," he has given you a reason for moving, but he hasn't given you an argument. Maybe you think that waving a gun around *implies* a premise such as "If you don't move, I'll shoot you." But no, implication is a relationship that holds only between claims: Only a claim can imply a claim.

that assumption plugged into the argument, the argument is not particularly strong.

Another example:

It's March, so the apple trees will bloom by the end of the month.

This argument is valid only if it is assumed that the apple trees *always* bloom by the end of March. Maybe that's true where you live, but it's not true where we live. Still, where we live it's true that the apple trees *almost always* bloom by the end of March, and with this assumption plugged into the argument, the argument turns out to be pretty strong.

Identifying Unstated Premises

When someone produces an argument, it isn't productive to ask, What is this person assuming? No doubt the person is assuming many things, such as that you can hear (or read), that you understand English, that what he or she is saying is worth saying, that you aren't comatose or dead, and who knows what else. There are two better questions to ask, and the first is, "Is there a reasonable assumption I could make that would make this argument valid?" And if what you must assume for the argument to be valid isn't plausible, then you ask the second question: "Is there a reasonable assumption I could make that would make this argument strong?"

As may be clear from the preceding section, an argument can be made valid by adding to it a general claim that appropriately connects the stated premises to the conclusion and says, in effect, that if the stated premises are true, then the conclusion is true. For example, take this argument:

> It's raining, so there is a south wind.

This argument is automatically valid if you add to it the general claim "Any time it is raining, there is a south wind." (Any variation of this claim will do equally well, such as "Whenever it is raining, there is a south wind," or "Only in the presence of a south wind is there rain.") But this claim isn't particularly plausible, at least where Moore and Parker live. And thus we should modify the claim by asking the second question, "What must I assume for this argument to be strong?" When we do this, we obtain a more plausible premise: "When it rains, there is usually a south wind." This is a reasonable claim (in our neck of the woods), and including it in the argument makes the argument a strong one.

Here's another example:

> You shouldn't let her pass. After all, this is the second time you caught her cheating.

A general claim that ties the stated premise to the conclusion and yields a valid argument would be "No person caught cheating two times should be permitted to pass." We'd accept this claim and, consequently, we'd also accept the conclusion of the argument, assuming that the stated premise (that this is the second time she was caught cheating) is true.

Here's one final example:

> Yes, Stacy and Harold are on the brink of divorce. They're remodeling their house.

When we try to make the argument valid by connecting the premise to the conclusion with a general claim, we get something like "A couple that remodels their house must be on the brink of divorce." But we can suppose that nobody would seriously subscribe to such a claim. So we attempt to make the argument strong, rather than valid, by modifying the claim to "Most couples remodeling their house are on the brink of divorce." However, this claim is also implausible. The only plausible thing to say is that *some* couples who remodel are on the brink of divorce. But this claim doesn't justify a conclusion that states unqualifiedly that Stacy and Harold are on the brink of divorce.

To summarize: Formulate a general claim that connects the stated premise with the conclusion in such a way as to make the argument valid, as explained above. If that premise isn't plausible, modify or qualify it as necessary to make the argument strong. If the argument just can't be made either valid or strong except by using an implausible premise, then you really shouldn't accept the argument—or use it yourself.

In your own essays, it is good practice always to consider exactly what your readers must accept if they are to agree with your reasoning. You shouldn't require them to accept any claim that is implausible or unreasonable, whether you actually state that claim or not.

Exercise 7-10

For each passage, supply a claim that turns it into a valid argument.

Example

The fan needs oil. It's squeaking.

Claim That Makes It Valid

Whenever the fan squeaks, it needs oil.

▲ 1. Jamal is well mannered, so he had a good upbringing.

2. Bettina is pretty sharp, so she'll get a good grade in this course.

3. It must have rained lately because there are puddles everywhere.

▲ 4. He'll drive recklessly only if he's upset, and he's not upset.

5. Let's see . . . they have tons of leftovers, so their party could not have been very successful.

6. I think we can safely conclude that the battery is still in good condition. The lights are bright.

▲ 7. Either the dog has fleas, or its skin is dry. It's scratching a lot.

8. Melton was a good senator. He'd make an excellent president.

9. Gelonek doesn't own a gun. He's sure to be for gun control.

▲ 10. The Carmel poet Robinson Jeffers is one of America's most outstanding poets. His work appears in many Sierra Club publications.

Exercise 7-11

Go back to Exercise 7-10, and supply a claim that will produce a strong (but not valid) argument. In the answer section at the back of the book, we have answered items 1, 4, 7, and 10.

Example

The fan needs oil. It's squeaking.

Claim That Makes It Strong

When the fan squeaks, it usually needs oil.

Exercise 7-12

For each passage, supply a claim that turns it into a valid argument.

▲ 1. Prices in that new store around the corner are going to be high, you can bet. All they sell are genuine leather goods.

2. I had a C going into the final exam, but I don't see how I can make less than a B for the course because I managed an A on the final.

3. He's a good guitarist. He studied with Pepe Romero, you know.

▲ 4. That plant is an ornamental fruit tree. It won't ever bear edible fruit.

5. The Federal Reserve Board will make sure that inflation doesn't reach 8 percent again. Its chair is an experienced hand at monetary policy.

6. Murphy doesn't stand a chance of getting elected in this county. His liberal position on most matters is well known.

▲ 7. Jesse Ventura, the former Governor of Minnesota, was a professional wrestler. He couldn't have been a very effective governor.

8. Half the people in the front row believe in God; therefore, half the entire class believes in God.

9. Kennesaw State students are all career-oriented. I say this because every Kennesaw State student I ever met was career-oriented.

▲ 10. Population studies show that smoking causes lung cancer; therefore, if you smoke, you will get lung cancer.

Exercise 7-13

Do Exercise 7-12 again, making the arguments strong but not valid. In the answer section at the back of the book, we have answered items 1, 4, 7, and 10.

Techniques for Understanding Arguments

A good argument provides justification for accepting its conclusion. To do this, its premises must be reasonable—that is, it must be likely that they are true—and they must support the conclusion—that is, the argument must be either valid or strong. So, to evaluate an argument, we must answer these two questions:

1. Are the premises reasonable (i.e., is it likely that they are true)?
2. Do the premises support the conclusion (i.e., is the argument either valid or strong)?

Before we can proceed with the evaluation of an argument, we have to understand it. Many arguments are difficult to understand because they are

> ## *Don't Forget Fallacies*
>
> In Chapters 5 and 6 we say that people will sometimes make statements in order to establish a claim when in reality their remarks have nothing to do with the claim. For example, "Margaret's qualifications are really quite good; after all, she'd be terribly hurt to think that you didn't think highly of them." Although Margaret's disappointment would no doubt be a reason for *something* (e.g., for keeping your views to yourself), it would not be a reason for altering your opinion of her qualifications. Her feelings are, in fact, thoroughly irrelevant to her qualifications. Extraneous material of all sorts can often be eliminated as argumentative material if you ask yourself simply, "Is this really relevant to the conclusion? Does this matter to what this person is trying to establish?" If you have worked through the exercises in Chapters 5 and 6, you have already had practice in spotting irrelevances. If you haven't done these exercises, it would be useful to go back and do them now.

spoken and thus go by so quickly that we cannot be sure of the conclusion and the premises. Others are difficult to understand because they have a complicated structure. Still others are difficult to understand because they are embedded in nonargumentative material consisting of background information, prejudicial coloring, illustrations, parenthetical remarks, digressions, subsidiary points, and other window dressing. And some arguments are difficult to understand because they are confused or because the reasons they contain are so poor that we are not sure whether to regard them as reasons.

In understanding any argument, the first task is to find the conclusion—the main point or thesis of the passage. The next step is to locate the reasons that have been offered for the conclusion—that is, to find the premises. Next, we look for the reasons, if any, given for these premises. To proceed through these steps, you have to learn both to spot premises and conclusions when they occur in spoken and written passages and to understand the interrelationships among these claims—that is, the structure of the argument.

■ *Clarifying an Argument's Structure*

Let's begin with how to understand the relationships among the argumentative claims, because this problem is sometimes easiest to solve. If you are dealing with written material that you are free to mark up, one useful technique is to number the premises and conclusions and then use the numbers to lay bare the structure of the argument. Let's start with this argument as an example:

> I don't think we should get Carlos his own car. As a matter of fact, he is not responsible, because he doesn't care for his things. And anyway, we don't have

enough money for a car, since even now we have trouble making ends meet. Last week you yourself complained about our financial situation, and you never complain without really good reason.

We want to display the structure of this argument clearly. First, circle all premise and conclusion indicators. Thus:

I don't think we should get Carlos his own car. As a matter of fact, he is not responsible (because) he doesn't care for his things. And anyway, we don't have enough money for a car, (since) even now we have trouble making ends meet. Last week you yourself complained about our financial situation, and you never complain without really good reason.

Next, bracket each premise and conclusion, and number them consecutively as they appear in the argument. So what we now have is this:

① [I don't think we should get Carlos his own car.] As a matter of fact, ② [he is not responsible] because ③ [he doesn't care for his things.] And anyway, ④ [we don't have enough money for a car], since ⑤ [even now we have trouble making ends meet.] ⑥ [Last week you yourself complained about our financial situation], and ⑦ [you never complain without really good reason.]

And then we diagram the argument as follows: Using an arrow to mean "therefore" or "is intended as evidence [or as a reason or as a premise] for," the first three claims in the argument can be diagrammed as follows:

Now ⑥ and ⑦ together support ④; that is, they are *dependent* reasons for ④. To show that ⑥ and ⑦ are dependent reasons for ④, we simply draw a line under them, put a plus sign between them, and draw the arrow from the line to ④, like this:

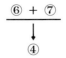

Because ⑤ and ⑥ + ⑦ are *independent* reasons for ④, we can represent the relationship between them and ④ as follows:

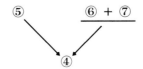

Finally, because ④ and ② are *independent* reasons for ①, the diagram of the entire argument is this:

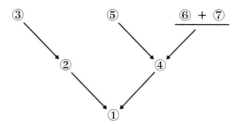

So, the conventions governing this approach to revealing argument structure are very simple: First, circle all premise- and conclusion-indicating words. Then, assuming you can identify the claims that function in the argument (a big assumption, as you will see before long), simply number them consecutively. Then display the structure of the argument using arrows for "therefore" and plus signs over a line to connect together two or more dependent premises.

Some claims, incidentally, may constitute reasons for more than one conclusion. For example:

① [Carlos continues to be irresponsible.] ② [He certainly should not have his own car], and, as far as I am concerned, ③ [he can forget about that trip to Hawaii this winter, too.]

Structure:

Frequently, too, we evaluate counterarguments to our positions. For example:

① We really should have more African Americans on the faculty. ② That is why the new diversity program ought to be approved. True, ③ it may involve an element of unfairness to whites, but ④ the benefits to society of having more black faculty outweigh the disadvantages.

Notice that claim ③ introduces a consideration that runs counter to the conclusion of the argument, which is stated in ②. We can indicate counterclaims by crossing the "therefore" arrow with lines, thus:

Beer Makes You Smarter

Can you diagram this argument from Tony Graybosch? (The answer is in the answer section at the back of the book.)

A herd of buffalo can only move as fast as the slowest buffalo and when the herd is hunted, it is the slowest and weakest ones at the back that are killed first. This natural selection is good for the herd as a whole, because the general speed and health of the whole group keeps improving by the regular attrition of the weakest members.

In much the same way, the human brain can only operate as fast as the slowest brain cells. Excessive intake of alcohol, we all know, kills brain cells; but naturally it attacks the slowest and weakest brain cells first. In this way, regular consumption of beer eliminates the weaker brain cells, making the brain a faster and more efficient machine. This shows that you always are smarter after a few beers.

This diagram indicates that item ③ has been introduced by the writer as a consideration that runs counter to ②.

Of course, one might adopt other conventions for clarifying argument structure—for example, circling the main conclusion and drawing solid lines under supporting premises and wavy lines under the premises of sub-arguments. The technique we have described is simply one way of doing it; any of several others might work as well for you. However, *no* technique for revealing argument structure will work if you cannot spot the argumentative claims in the midst of a lot of background material.

■ Distinguishing Arguments from Window Dressing

We should point out that it is not always easy to isolate the argument in a speech or a written piece. Often, speakers and writers think that because their main points are more or less clear to them, they will be equally apparent to their listeners or readers. But it doesn't always work that way.

If you are having trouble identifying a conclusion in what you hear or read, it *could* be that the passage is not an argument at all. Make sure that the passage in question is not a report, a description, an explanation, or something else altogether, rather than an argument. The key here is determining whether the speaker or writer is offering reasons intended to convince you of one or more of the claims made in the passage.

The problem could also be that the conclusion is left unstated. Sometimes it helps simply to put the argument aside and ask yourself, "What is this person trying to prove?" In any case, the first and essential step in understanding an argument is to spot the conclusion.

Stupid Liberal!

The employer introduced himself to his new gardener.
"I am a professor of logic," the employer said.
"Oh. What's that?" the gardener asked.
"I shall give you a demonstration," announced the professor. "Do you own a wheelbarrow?"
"Yes," replied the gardener.
"Then I infer you are a hard worker," the professor continued. "And from that fact I infer you have a family. And from that I infer you are conscientious and responsible. And from that I infer you are a conservative. Am I right?"
"Wow!" exclaimed the gardener. "That's right! So that's logic?"
"That's logic," preened the professor.

Later the gardener met up with one of his buddies and told him he had a job with a professor of logic.
"Logic?" his friend asked, "What's that?"
"I'll show you," the gardener said. "Do you own a wheelbarrow?"
"No."
"Stupid liberal."

If you are having difficulty identifying the *premises*, consider the possibility that you have before you a case of rhetoric (see Chapter 4). (You can't find premises in a piece of rhetoric because there *are* no premises.) You have an advantage over many students in having learned about rhetorical devices in Part 2. By this time you should be getting pretty good at recognizing them.

In the remainder of this book, we are concerned primarily with argument evaluation rather than argument clarification, so most of the arguments we present are straightforward and unconfusing; you probably won't need to use diagrams to clarify their structure. However, as you apply what you learn in this book to arguments you encounter in real life, you are apt to encounter arguments and argumentative essays whose organization is difficult to comprehend. When you do, you may find diagramming a useful technique. We also suggest that you attempt to diagram your own essays— if you find that you have difficulty, it is a good indication that you need to reorganize your essay and make the structure of your reasoning clearer.

Evaluating Arguments

Once you understand an argument, you need to evaluate it. Your mechanic can often tell if there is something wrong with your car engine simply by plugging it into a machine and reading a meter or dial. Unfortunately, you can't plug an argument into a machine. To tell if there is something wrong with an argument, you have to determine if (a) the premises support the conclusion and (b) the premises are reasonable. This may sound simple enough, but it in fact involves this entire book.

■ *Do the Premises Support the Conclusion?*

The question "Do the premises support the conclusion" means, Is the argument either (a) valid or (b) relatively strong? Do not expect to be able to answer these questions just yet, for that is what much of the remainder of this book is about.

■ *Are the Premises Reasonable?*

Any premises for which reasons have been presented in the argument are the conclusions of subarguments and should be evaluated according to the principles in Part 3. Unsupported premises should be evaluated in accordance with the guidelines and questions provided in Part 1. Let us review these guidelines in summary fashion:

1. It is reasonable to accept a premise if it comes from a credible source and does not conflict with what you have observed, your background knowledge, or other credible claims.
2. You shouldn't accept a premise that conflicts with what you have observed or otherwise have reason to believe, unless you have a very good reason for doing so.
3. You also shouldn't accept a premise that conflicts with the claims of another credible source unless the question of which source to believe has been resolved.
4. Premises that are vague, ambiguous, or otherwise unclear require clarification before acceptance.

It is reasonable to believe that baseball will still be around in thirty years, and it is also reasonable to believe that the sun will still be around in thirty years. But although it is reasonable to believe both claims, there is a greater chance that the sun will be around than that baseball will be. So we can see that, although the premises of an argument might both be reasonable, one argument might be better than another because its premises are *more* likely to be true. Comparing premises as to likelihood requires knowledge, experience, and good judgment, as well as inclination.

Alternatively, one argument might be better than another, not because its premises are more likely to be true, but because they produce a stronger argument. For example, compare these two arguments:

[Premise] Sixty percent of a random sample of two hundred residents of Minneapolis believe in God; [conclusion] therefore, approximately 60 percent of all residents of Minneapolis believe in God.

[Premise] Sixty percent of a random sample of five hundred residents of Minneapolis believe in God; [conclusion] therefore, approximately 60 percent of all residents of Minneapolis believe in God.

The second argument is a better argument because its premise provides a greater justification for believing the conclusion. Weighing the relative strengths of inductive arguments is something we'll consider in Chapters 10 and 11.

Recap

An argument consists of a conclusion and premises. Valid arguments (arguments whose conclusions absolutely follow from the premises) are either sound or unsound, depending on whether or not their premises are all true. On the other hand, conclusions of some arguments are not even intended to follow absolutely from their premises; the premises are supposed to show only that it is likely that the conclusion is true. We speak of such arguments as being to varying degrees strong or weak.

Before you can evaluate an argument, you must understand it; to do this, find the conclusion. Then locate the reasons that have been offered in support of the conclusion—these reasons are stated in the premises. One technique for clarifying the structure of a written argument—if you can identify the claims that function in the argument—is to number the claims consecutively as they are written and then use the numbers to lay out the structure of the argument.

Whatever method helps you to understand an argument, make sure that the premises are reasonable and that they support the conclusion. In Chapters 8–11, we consider more carefully when the premises of an argument do support the conclusion.

Having read this chapter and the chapter recap, you should be able to

- ▲ Explain what the parts of an argument are and identify premises and conclusions in a variety of arguments
- ▲ Discuss the distinctions among good, valid, and strong arguments and relate them to inductive and deductive arguments
- ▲ Explain what unstated premises are, and supply premises in a variety of arguments that have unstated premises making those arguments valid
- ▲ Describe techniques for understanding arguments and for evaluating arguments

Additional Exercises

Exercise 7-14

Diagram the following "arguments," using the method explained in the text.

▲ 1. ①, because ② and ③. [Assume that ② and ③ are dependent.]

2. ① and ②; therefore ③. [Assume that ① and ② are independent.]

3. Since ①, ②; and since ③, ④. And since ② and ④, ⑤. [Assume that ② and ④ are independent.]

▲ 4. ①; therefore ② and ③. But because ② and ③, ④. Consequently, ⑤. Therefore, ⑥. [Assume ② and ③ are independent.]

5. ①, ②, ③; therefore ④. ⑤, in view of ①. And ⑥, since ②. Therefore ⑦. [Assume ①, ②, and ③ are dependent.]

Exercise 7-15

Go back to Exercises 7-2, 7-3, 7-4, and 7-5, and diagram the arguments using the method explained in the text. In the answer section at the back of the book, we have answered items 1, 4, 7, and 10 in Exercises 7-2 and 7-3; items 6, 9, 12, and 15 in Exercise 7-4; and items 1, 4, 8, and 10 in Exercise 7-5.

Exercise 7-16

Diagram the arguments contained in the following passages, using the method explained in the text.

▲ 1. Dear Jim,
    Your distributor is the problem. Here's why. There's no current at the spark plugs. And if there's no current at the plugs, then either your alternator is shot or your distributor is defective. But if the problem were in the alternator, then your dash warning light would be on. So, since the light isn't on, the problem must be in the distributor. Hope this helps.
        Yours,
        Benita Autocraft

2. The federal deficit must be reduced. It has contributed to inflation, and it has hurt American exports.

3. It's high time professional boxing was outlawed. Boxing almost always leads to brain damage, and anything that does that ought to be done away with. Besides, it supports organized crime.

▲ 4. They really ought to build a new airport. It would attract more business to the area, not to mention the fact that the old airport is overcrowded and dangerous.

5. Vote for Jackson? No way. He's too radical, and he's too inexperienced, and his lack of experience would make him a dangerous council member.

Exercise 7-17

Diagram the arguments contained in the following passages, using the method explained in the text. (Your instructor may have different instructions for you to follow.)

▲ 1. Cottage cheese will help you to be slender, youthful, and more beautiful. Enjoy it often.

2. If you want to listen to loud music, do it when we are not at home. It bothers us, and we're your parents.

3. If you want to see the best version of *The Three Musketeers*, try the 1948 version. Lana Turner is luscious; Vincent Price is dastardly; Angela Lansbury is exquisitely regal; and nobody ever has or ever will portray D'Artagnan with the grace, athleticism, or skill of Gene Kelly. Rent it. It's a must.

▲ 4. From a letter to the editor: "The idea of a free press in America today is a joke. A small group of people, the nation's advertisers, control the media more effectively than if they owned it outright. Through fear of an advertising boycott they can dictate everything from programming to news report content. Politicians as well as editors shiver in their boots at the thought of such a boycott. This situation is intolerable and ought to be changed. I suggest we all listen to National Public Radio and public television."

5. Too many seniors, disabled veterans, and families with children are paying far too much of their incomes for housing. Proposition 168 will help clear the way for affordable housing construction for these groups. Proposition 168 reforms the outdated requirement for an election before affordable housing can even be approved. Requiring elections for every publicly assisted housing venture, even when there is no local opposition, is a waste of taxpayers' money. No other state constitution puts such a roadblock in front of efforts to house senior citizens and others in need. Please support Proposition 168.

6. More than forty years after President John F. Kennedy's assassination, it's no easier to accept the idea that a loser like Lee Harvey Oswald committed the crime of the century all by himself with a $12.78 mail-order rifle and a $7.17 scope. Yet even though two-thousand-plus books and films about the episode have been made, there is no credible evidence to contradict the Warren Commission finding that "the shots which killed President Kennedy and wounded Governor Connally were fired by Lee Harvey Oswald" and that "Oswald acted alone."

   After all these years, it's time to accept the conclusion. The nation pays a heavy price for chronic doubts and mistrust. Confidence in the government has declined. Participation in the voting process has steadily slid downward. The national appetite for wild theories encourages peddlers to persist. Evil is never easy to accept. In the case of JFK, the sooner we let it go, the better.

▲ 7. "Consumers ought to be concerned about the Federal Trade Commission's dropping a rule that supermarkets must actually have in stock the items they advertise for sale. While a staff analysis suggests costs of the rule outweigh the benefits to consumers, few shoppers want to return to the practices that lured them into stores only to find the advertised products they sought were not there.

"The staff study said the rule causes shoppers to pay $200 million to receive $125 million in benefits. The cost is a low estimate and the benefits a high estimate, according to the study.

"However, even those enormously big figures boil down to a few cents per shopper over a year's time. And the rule does say that when a grocer advertises a sale, the grocer must have sufficient supply of sale items on hand to meet reasonable buyer demand."

The Oregonian

8. "And we thought we'd heard it all. Now the National Rifle Association wants the U.S. Supreme Court to throw out the ban on private ownership of fully automatic machine guns.

"As the nation's cities reel under staggering murder totals, as kids use guns simply to get even after feuds, as children are gunned down by random bullets, the NRA thinks it is everybody's constitutional right to have their own personal machine gun.

"This is not exactly the weapon of choice for deer hunting or for a homeowner seeking protection. It is an ideal weapon for street gangs and drug thugs in their wars with each other and the police.

"To legalize fully automatic machine guns is to increase the mayhem that is turning this nation—particularly its large cities—into a continual war zone. Doesn't the NRA have something better to do?"

Capital Times, Madison, Wisconsin

9. From a letter to the editor: "Recently the California Highway Patrol stopped me at a drunk-drive checkpoint. Now, I don't like drunk drivers any more than anyone else. I certainly see why the police find the checkpoint system effective. But I think our right to move about freely is much more important. If the checkpoint system continues, then next there will be checkpoints for drugs, seat belts, infant car seats, drivers' licenses. We will regret it later if we allow the system to continue."

▲ 10. "Well located, sound real estate is the safest investment in the world. It is not going to disappear, as can the value of dollars put into savings accounts. Neither will real estate values be lost because of inflation. In fact, property values tend to increase at a pace at least equal to the rate of inflation. Most homes have appreciated at a rate greater than the inflation rate (due mainly to strong buyer demand and insufficient supply of newly constructed homes)."

Robert Bruss, The Smart Investor's Guide to Real Estate

11. "The constitutional guarantee of a speedy trial protects citizens from arbitrary government abuse, but it has at least one other benefit, too. It prevents crime.

"A recent Justice Department study found that more than a third of those with serious criminal records—meaning three or more felony convictions—are arrested for new offenses while free on bond awaiting federal court trial. You don't have to be a social scientist to suspect that the longer the delay, the greater the likelihood of further violations. In short, overburdened courts mean much more than justice delayed; they quite literally amount to the infliction of further injustice."

Scripps Howard Newspapers

12. "There is a prevailing school of thought and growing body of opinion that one day historians will point to a certain television show and declare: This is what life was like in small-town America in the mid-20th century.

"We like to think those future historians will be right about *The Andy Griffith Show*. It had everything, and in rerun life still does: humor, wisdom, wholesomeness and good old red-blooded American entertainment.

"That's why we are so puzzled that a group of true-blue fans of the show want to rename some suitable North Carolina town Mayberry. The group believes there ought to be a real-live city in North Carolina called Mayberry, even though everybody already knows that Mayberry was modeled on Mount Airy, sort of, since that is Sheriff Taylor's, uh, Andy Griffith's hometown.

"No, far better that the group let the whole thing drop. For one thing, we don't know of anyplace—hamlet, village, town, or city—that could properly live up to the name of Mayberry. Perhaps the best place for Mayberry to exist is right where it is—untouched, unspoiled and unsullied by the modern world. Ain't that right, Ernest T. Bass?"

Greensboro *(N.C.)* News & Record

▲ 13. As we enter a new century, about 100 million Americans are producing data on the Internet as rapidly as they consume it. Each of these users is tracked by technologies ever more able to collate essential facts about them—age, address, credit rating, marital status, etc.—in electronic form for use in commerce. One Web site, for example, promises, for the meager sum of seven dollars, to scan "over two billion records to create a single comprehensive report on an individual." It is not unreasonable, then, to believe that the combination of capitalism and technology pose a looming threat to what remains of our privacy.

Loosely adapted from Harper's

14. Having your car washed at the carwash may be the best way to go, but there are some possible drawbacks. The International Carwashing Association (ICA) has fought back against charges that automatic carwashes, in recycling wash water, actually dump the salt and dirt from one car onto the next. And that brushes and drag cloths hurt the finish. Perhaps there is some truth to these charges.

The ICA sponsored tests that supposedly demonstrated that the average home car wash is harder on a car than an automatic wash. Maybe. But what's "the average" home car wash? And you can bet that the automatic carwashes in the test were in perfect working order.

There is no way you or I can tell for certain if the filtration system and washing equipment at the automatic carwash are properly maintained. And even if they are, what happens if you follow some mud-caked pickup through the wash? Road dirt might still be caught in the bristles of the brushes or strips of fabric that are dragged over your car.

Here's my recommendation: Wash your own car.

15. Letter to the editor: "The worst disease of the next decade will be AIDS, Acquired Immune Deficiency Syndrome.

"AIDS has made facing surgery scary. In the last ten years several hundred Americans got AIDS from getting contaminated blood in surgery, and it is predicted that within a few years more hundreds of people will receive AIDS blood each year.

"Shouldn't we be tested for AIDS before we give blood? As it is now, no one can feel safe receiving blood. Because of AIDS, people are giving blood to themselves so they will be safe if they have to have blood later. We need a very sensitive test to screen AIDS donors."

North State Record

▲ 16. **Argument in Favor of Measure A**

"Measure A is consistent with the City's General Plan and City policies directing growth to the City's non-agricultural lands. A 'yes' vote on Measure A will affirm the wisdom of well-planned, orderly growth in the City of Chico by approving an amendment to the 1982 Rancho Arroyo Specific Plan. Measure A substantially reduces the amount of housing previously approved for Rancho Arroyo, increases the number of parks and amount of open space, and significantly enlarges and enhances Bidwell Park.

"A 'yes' vote will accomplish the following: • Require the development to dedicate 130.8 acres of land to Bidwell Park • Require the developer to dedicate seven park sites • Create 53 acres of landscaped corridors and greenways • Preserve existing arroyos and protect sensitive plant habitats and other environmental features • Create junior high school and church sites • Plan a series of villages within which, eventually, a total of 2,927 residential dwelling units will be developed • Plan area which will provide onsite job opportunities and retail services. . . ."

County of Butte Sample Ballot

17. **Rebuttal to Argument in Favor of Measure A**

"Villages? Can a project with 3,000 houses and 7,000 new residents really be regarded as a 'village'? The Sacramento developers pushing the Rancho Arroyo project certainly have a way with words. We urge citizens of Chico to ignore their flowery language and vote no on Measure A.

"These out-of-town developers will have you believe that their project protects agricultural land. Hogwash! Chico's Greenline protects valuable farmland. With the Greenline, there is enough land in the Chico area available for development to build 62,000 new homes. . . .

"They claim that their park dedications will reduce use of our overcrowded Bidwell Park. Don't you believe it! They want to attract 7,000 new residents to Chico by using Rancho Arroyo's proximity to Bidwell Park to outsell other local housing projects.

"The developers imply that the Rancho Arroyo project will provide a much needed school site. In fact, the developers intend to sell the site to the school district, which will pay for the site with taxpayers' money.

"Chico doesn't need the Rancho Arroyo project. Vote no on Measure A."

County of Butte Sample Ballot

18. Letter to the editor: "A relative of mine is a lawyer who recently represented a murderer who had already had a life sentence and broke out of prison and murdered someone else. I think this was a waste of the taxpayers' money to try this man again. It won't do any good. I think murderers should be executed.

"We are the most crime-ridden society in the world. Someone is murdered every 27 minutes in the U.S., and there is a rape every ten minutes and an armed robbery every 82 seconds. According to the FBI, there are 870,000 violent crimes a year, and you know the number is increasing.

"Also according to the FBI, only 10 percent of those arrested for the crimes committed are found guilty, and a large percentage are released on probation. These people are released so they can just go out and commit more crimes.

"Why are they released? In the end it is because there aren't enough prisons to house the guilty. The death sentence must be restored. This would create more room in prisons. It would also drastically reduce the number of murders. If a robber knew before he shot someone that if he was caught his own life would be taken, would he do it?

"These people deserve to die. They sacrificed their right to live when they murdered someone, maybe your mother. It's about time we stopped making it easy for criminals to kill people and get away with it."

Cascade News

▲ 19. Letter to the editor: "In regard to your editorial, 'Crime bill wastes billions,' let me set you straight. Your paper opposes mandatory life sentences for criminals convicted of three violent crimes, and you whine about how criminals' rights might be violated. Yet you also want to infringe on a citizen's right to keep and bear arms. You say you oppose life sentences for three-time losers because judges couldn't show any leniency toward the criminals no matter how trivial the crime. What is your definition of trivial, busting an innocent child's skull with a hammer?"

North State Record

▲ 20. Freedom means choice. This is a truth antiporn activists always forget when they argue for censorship. In their fervor to impose their morality, groups like Enough Is Enough cite extreme examples of pornography, such as child porn, suggesting that they are easily available in video stores.

This is not the way it is. Most of this material portrays, not actions such as this, but consensual sex between adults.

The logic used by Enough Is Enough is that if something can somehow hurt someone, it must be banned. They don't apply this logic to more harmful substances, such as alcohol or tobacco. Women and children are more adversely affected by drunken driving and secondhand smoke than by pornography. Few Americans would want to ban alcohol or tobacco even though they kill hundreds of thousands of people each year.

Writing Exercises

1. Write a one-page essay in which you determine whether, and why, it is better (you get to define "better") to look younger than your age, older than your age, or just your age. Then number the premises and conclusions in your essay and diagram it.

2. Should there be a death penalty for first-degree murder? On the top half of a sheet of paper, list considerations supporting the death penalty, and on the bottom half, list considerations opposing it. Take about ten minutes to compile your two lists. (Selection 6 in Appendix 1 may give you some ideas. Your instructor may provide extra time for you to read this selection.)

   After everyone is finished, your instructor will call on people to read their lists. He or she will then give everyone about twenty minutes to write a draft of an essay that addresses the issue, Should there be a death penalty for first-degree murder? Put your name on the back of your paper. After everyone is finished, your instructor will collect the papers and redistribute them to the class. In groups of four or five, read the papers that have been given to your group. Do not look at the names of the authors. Select the best essay in each group. Your instructor will ask each group to read the essay they have selected as best.

   As an alternative, your instructor may have each group rank-order the papers. He or she will have neighboring groups decide which of their top-ranked papers is the best. The instructor will read the papers that have been top-ranked by two (or more) groups, for discussion.

3. Follow the instructions for Exercise 2, but this time address the question, Are free-needle programs a good idea? (Selections 14A and 14B at the end of the book may give you some ideas. Your instructor may provide extra time for you to read those selections.)

4. If you have not done so already, turn to Selection 7, 12, 19, or 20 at the end of the book and follow the first set of instructions.

5. Turn to Selection 8 or 13 at the end of the book and follow the instructions.

6. Turn to Selections 10A,B; 11A,B; 14A,B; 15A,B; 16A,B; 17A,B; or 18A,B at the end of the book and discuss which side has the stronger argument and why.

Chapter 8

Deductive Arguments I: Categorical Logic

Many deductive arguments can be clarified and evaluated using techniques of categorical logic, which is a way of studying inferences that dates back to the time of Aristotle. During more than two thousand years of history, all manner of embellishments were developed and added to the basic theory, especially by monks and other scholars during the medieval period. Although some of these developments are interesting, we don't want to weight you down with lots of fine distinctions that are best appreciated by professional logicians. So we'll be content to set forth the basics of the subject in this chapter.

Categorical logic is logic based on the relations of inclusion and exclusion among classes ("categories"). Like truth-functional logic (the subject of Chapter 9), categorical logic is useful in clarifying and analyzing arguments. But this is only one reason to study the subject: There is no better way to understand the underlying logical structure of our everyday language than learning to put it into the kinds of formal terms we'll introduce in these two chapters. Just exactly what is the difference between the claim (1) "Everybody who is ineligible for physics 1A must take physical science 1" and (2) "No students who are required to take physical science 1 are eligible for physics 1A"? Here's another pair of claims: (3) "Harold won't attend the meeting unless Vanessa decides to go" and (4) "If Vanessa decides to go, then Harold will attend the meeting." You might be surprised how many college students have a very hard time trying to determine whether the claims in each pair say the same thing. In this chapter and the next, we'll show you a foolproof method for determining how to unravel the logical implications of such claims and for seeing how any two such claims relate to one another. [Incidentally, claims (1) and (2) do not say the same thing at all, and neither do (3) and (4).] If you're signing a lease or entering into a contract of any kind, it pays to be able to figure out just what is being said in it and what is not; people who have trouble with claims like those just stated are at risk when there is more at stake.

Studying categorical and truth-functional logic can teach us to become more careful and precise in our own thinking. Getting comfortable with this type of thinking can be helpful in general, but for those who will some-day be applying to law school, medical school, or graduate school, it has the added advantage that many admittance exams for such programs deal with the kinds of reasoning discussed in this chapter.

Let's start by looking at the four basic kinds of claims on which categorical logic is based.

Categorical Claims

A **categorical claim** says something about classes (or "categories") of things. Our interest lies in categorical claims of certain standard forms. A **standard-form categorical claim** is a claim that results from putting names or de-scriptions of classes into the blanks of the following structures:

A: All _____ are _____.
(*Example:* All Presbyterians are Christians.)

E: All _____ are _____.
(*Example:* No Muslims are Christians.)

I: Some _____ are _____.
(*Example:* Some Christians are Arabs.)

O: Some _____ are not _____.
(*Example:* Some Muslims are not Sunnis.)

The phrases that go in the blanks are **terms;** the one that goes into the first blank is the **subject term** of the claim, and the one that goes into the second blank is the **predicate term.** Thus, "Christians" is the predicate term of the first example above and the subject term of the third example. In many of the examples and explanations that follow, we'll use the letters S and P (for "subject" and "predicate") to stand for terms in categorical claims. And we'll talk about the subject and predicate *classes,* which are just the classes that the terms refer to.

But first a caution: Only nouns and noun phrases will work as terms. An adjective alone, such as "red," won't do. "All fire engines are red" does *not* produce a standard-form categorical claim because "red" is not a noun or noun phrase. To see that it is not, try switching the places of the terms: "All red are fire engines." This doesn't make sense, right? But "red vehicles" (or even "red things") will do because "All red vehicles are fire engines" makes sense (even though it's false).

Looking back at the standard-form structures given above, notice that each one has a letter to its left. These are the traditional names of the four types of standard-form categorical claims. The claim "All Presbyterians are

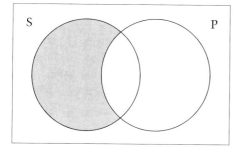

FIGURE 1   A-claim: All S are P.

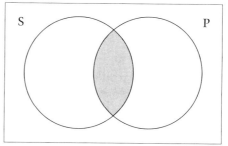

FIGURE 2   E-claim: No S are P.

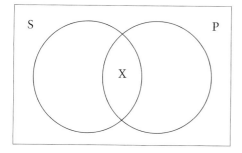

FIGURE 3   I-claim: Some S are P.

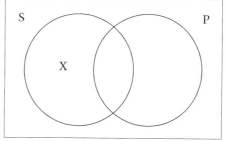

FIGURE 4   O-claim; Some S are not P.

Christians" is an A-claim, and so are "All idolators are heathens," "All people born between 1946 and 1964 are baby boomers," and any other claim of the form "All S are P." The same is true for the other three letters and the other three kinds of claims.

■ *Venn Diagrams*

Each of the standard forms has its own graphic illustration in a **Venn diagram,** as shown in Figures 1 through 4. Named after British logician John Venn, these diagrams exactly represent the four standard-form categorical claim types. In the diagrams, the circles represent the classes named by the terms, shaded areas represent areas that are empty, and areas containing Xs represent areas that are not empty—that contain at least one item. An area that is blank is one that the claim says nothing about; it may be occupied, or it may be empty.*

Notice that in the diagram for the A-claim, the area that would contain any members of the S class that were not members of the P class is shaded—that is, it is empty. Thus, that diagram represents the claim "All S are P," since there is no S left that isn't P. Similarly, in the diagram for the

---

*There is one exception to this, but we needn't worry about it for a few pages yet.

E-claim, the area where S and P overlap is empty; any S that is also a P has been eliminated. Hence: "No S are P."

For our purposes in this chapter, the word "some" means "at least one." So, the third diagram represents the fact that at least one S is a P, and the X in the area where the two classes overlap shows that at least one thing inhabits this area. Finally, the last diagram shows an X in the area of the S circle that is outside the P circle, representing the existence of at least one S that is not a P.

We'll try to keep technical jargon to a minimum, but here's some terminology we'll need: The two claim types that *include* one class or part of one class within another, the A-claims and I-claims, are **affirmative claims;** the two that *exclude* one class or part of one class from another, the E-claims and O-claims, are **negative claims.**

Although there are only four standard-form claim types, it's remarkable how versatile they are. A large portion of what we want to say can be rewritten, or "translated," into one or another of them. Because this task is sometimes easier said than done, we'd best spend a little while making sure we understand how to do it. And we warn you in advance: A lot of standard form translations are not very pretty—but it's accuracy we seek here, not style.

■ *Translation into Standard Form*

The main idea is to take an ordinary claim and turn it into a standard-form categorical claim that is exactly equivalent. We'll say that two claims are **equivalent claims** if, and only if, they would be true in all and exactly the same circumstances—that is, under no circumstances could one of them be true and the other false. (You can think of such claims as "saying the same thing," more or less.)

Lots of ordinary claims in English are easy to translate into standard form. A claim of the sort "Every X is a Y," for example, more or less automatically turns into the standard-form A-claim "All Xs are Ys." And it's easy to produce the proper term to turn "Minors are not eligible" into the E-claim "No minors are eligible people."

All standard-form claims are in the present tense, but even so we can use them to talk about the past. For example, we can translate "There were creatures weighing more than four tons that lived in North America" as "Some creatures that lived in North America are creatures that weighed more than four tons."

What about a claim like "Only sophomores are eligible candidates"? It's good to have a strategy for attacking such translation problems. First, identify the terms. In this case, the two classes in question are "sophomores" and "eligible candidates." Now, which do we have on our hands, an A-, E-, I-, or O-claim? Generally speaking, nothing but a careful reading can serve to answer this question. So, you'll need to think hard about just what relation between classes is being expressed and then decide how that relation is best turned into a standard form. Fortunately, we can provide some rules of thumb that help in certain frequently encountered problems, in-

© 2003 by Sidney Harris. Reprinted with permission.

▲ *Aristotle was interested in a lot of subjects besides logic—practically everything, in fact. Fortunately for his reputation, these remarks (which he did* make!*) are not typical of him.*

cluding one that applies to our current example. If you're like most people, you don't have too much trouble seeing that our claim is an A-claim, but *which* A-claim? There are two possibilities:

All sophomores are eligible candidates

and

All eligible candidates are sophomores.

If we make the wrong choice, we can change the meaning of the claim significantly. (Notice that "All sophomores are students" is very different from "All students are sophomores.") In the present case, notice that we are saying something about *every* eligible candidate—namely, that he or she must be a sophomore. (*Only* sophomores are eligible—i.e., no one else is eligible.) In an A-claim, the class so restricted is always the subject class. So, this claim should be translated into

All eligible candidates are sophomores.

In fact, *all claims of the sort "Only Xs are Ys" should be translated as "All Ys are Xs."*

But there are other claims in which the word "only" plays a crucial role and which have to be treated differently. Consider, for example, this claim: "The only people admitted are people over twenty-one." In this case, a restriction is being put on the class of people admitted; we're saying that *nobody else is admitted* except those over twenty-one. Therefore, "people admitted" is the subject class: "All people admitted are people over twenty-one." And, in fact, *all claims of the sort "The only Xs are Ys" should be translated as "All Xs are Ys."*

The two rules of thumb that govern most translations of claims that hinge on the word "only" are these:

The word "only," used by itself, introduces the *predicate* term of an A-claim.

The phrase "the only" introduces the *subject* term of an A-claim.

Note that, in accordance with these rules, we would translate both of these claims

Only matinees are half-price shows

and

Matinees are the only half-price shows

as

All half-price shows are matinees.

The kind of thing a claim directly concerns is not always obvious. For example, if you think for a moment about the claim "I always get nervous when I take logic exams," you'll see that it's a claim about *times.* It's about getting nervous and about logic exams indirectly, of course, but it pertains directly to times or occasions. The proper translation of the example is "All times I take logic exams are times I get nervous." Notice that the word "whenever" is often a clue that you're talking about times or occasions, as well as an indication that you're going to have an A-claim or an E-claim. "Wherever" works the same way for places: "He makes trouble wherever he goes" should be translated as "All places he goes are places he makes trouble."

There are two other sorts of claims that are a bit tricky to translate into standard form. The first is a claim about a single individual, such as "Aristotle is a logician." It's clear that this claim specifies a class, "logicians," and places Aristotle as a member of that class. The problem is that categorical claims are always about *two* classes, and Aristotle isn't a class. (We certainly couldn't talk about *some* of Aristotle being a logician.) What we want to do is treat such claims as if they were about classes with exactly one member—in the present case, Aristotle. One way to do this is to use the term "people

The Most Versatile Word in English

Question:

There's only one word that can be placed successfully in any of the 10 numbered positions in this sentence to produce 10 sentences of different meaning (each sentence has 10 words): (1) *I* (2) *helped* (3) *my* (4) *dog* (5) *carry* (6) *my* (7) *husband's* (8) *slippers* (9) *yesterday* (10). What is that word?

—GLORIA J., Salt Lake City, Utah

Answer:

The word is "only," which makes the following 10 sentences:

1. Only *I* helped my dog carry my husband's slippers yesterday.
   (Usually the cat helps too, but she was busy with a mouse.)
2. I only *helped* my dog carry my husband's slippers yesterday.
   (The dog wanted me to carry them all by myself, but I refused.)
3. I helped only *my* dog carry my husband's slippers yesterday.
   (I was too busy to help my neighbor's dog when he carried them.)
4. I helped my only *dog* carry my husband's slippers yesterday.
   (I considered getting another dog, but the cat disapproved.)
5. I helped my dog only *carry* my husband's slippers yesterday.
   (I didn't help the dog eat them; I usually let the cat do that.)
6. I helped my dog carry only *my* husband's slippers yesterday.
   (My dog and I didn't have time to help my neighbor's husband.)
7. I helped my dog carry my only *husband's* slippers yesterday.
   (I considered getting another husband, but one is enough.)
8. I helped my dog carry my husband's only *slippers* yesterday.
   (My husband had two pairs of slippers, but the cat ate one pair.)
9. I helped my dog carry my husband's slippers only *yesterday.*
   (And now the dog wants help again; I wish he'd ask the cat.)
10. I helped my dog carry my husband's slippers yesterday only.
    (And believe me, once was enough—the slippers tasted *terrible.*)

—MARILYN VOS SAVANT, *author of the "Ask Marilyn" column (Reprinted with permission from* Parade *and Marilyn vos Savant. Copyright © 1994, 1996.)*

who are identical with Aristotle," which of course has only Aristotle as a member. (Everybody is identical with himself or herself, and nobody else is.) The important thing to remember about such claims can be summarized in the following rule of thumb:

> Claims about single individuals should be treated as A-claims or E-claims.

"Aristotle is a logician" can therefore be translated into "All people identical with Aristotle are logicians," an A-claim. Similarly, "Aristotle is not left-handed" becomes the E-claim "No people identical with Aristotle are left-handed people." (Your instructor may prefer to leave the claim in its original form and simply *treat* it as an A-claim or an E-claim. This avoids the awkward "people identical with Aristotle" wording and is certainly okay with us.)

It isn't just people that crop up in individual claims. Often this kind of treatment is called for when we're talking about objects, occasions, places, and other kinds of things. For example, the preferred translation of "St. Louis is on the Mississippi" is "All cities identical with St. Louis are cities on the Mississippi."

Other claims that cause translation difficulty contain what are called *mass nouns.* Consider this example: "Boiled okra is too ugly to eat." This claim is about a *kind of stuff.* The best way to deal with it is to treat it as a claim about *examples* of this kind of stuff. The present example translates into an A-claim about *all* examples of the stuff in question: "All examples of boiled okra are things that are too ugly to eat." An example such as "Most boiled okra is too ugly to eat" translates into the I-claim "Some examples of boiled okra are things that are too ugly to eat."

As we noted, it's not possible to give rules or hints about every kind of problem you might run into when translating claims into standard-form categorical versions. Only practice and discussion can bring you to the point where you can handle this part of the material with confidence. The best thing to do now is to turn to some exercises.

Exercise 8-1

Translate each of the following into a standard-form claim. Make sure that each answer follows the exact form of an A-, E-, I-, or O-claim and that each term you use is a noun or noun phrase that refers to a class of things. Remember that you're trying to produce a claim that's equivalent to the one given; it doesn't matter whether the given claim is actually true.

▲ 1. Every salamander is a lizard.

   2. Not every lizard is a salamander.

   3. Only reptiles can be lizards.

▲ 4. Snakes are the only members of the suborder Ophidia.

   5. The only members of the suborder Ophidia are snakes.

   6. None of the burrowing snakes is poisonous.

▲ 7. Anything that's an alligator is a reptile.

   8. Anything that qualifies as a frog qualifies as an amphibian.

   9. There are frogs wherever there are snakes.

▲ 10. Wherever there are snakes, there are frogs.

  11. Whenever the frog population decreases, the snake population decreases.

12. Nobody arrived except the cheerleaders.

▲ 13. Except for vice presidents, nobody got raises.

14. Unless people arrived early, they couldn't get seats.

15. Home movies are often as boring as dirt.

▲ 16. Socrates is a Greek.

17. The bank robber is not Jane's fiancé.

18. If an automobile was built before 1950, it's an antique.

▲ 19. Salt is a meat preservative.

20. Most corn does not make good popcorn.

Exercise 8-2

Follow the instructions given in the preceding exercise.

▲ 1. Students who wrote poor exams didn't get admitted to the program.

2. None of my students is failing.

3. If you live in the dorms, you can't own a car.

▲ 4. There are a few right-handed first basemen.

5. People make faces every time Joan sings.

6. The only tests George fails are the ones he takes.

▲ 7. Nobody passed who didn't make at least 50 percent.

8. You can't be a member unless you're over fifty.

9. Nobody catches on without studying.

▲ 10. I've had days like this before.

11. Roofers aren't millionaires.

12. Not one part of Michael Jackson's face is original equipment.

▲ 13. A few holidays fall on Saturday.

14. Only outlaws own guns.

15. You have nothing to lose but your chains.

▲ 16. Unless you pass this test you won't pass the course.

17. If you cheat, your prof will make you sorry.

18. If you cheat, your friends couldn't care less.

▲ 19. Only when you've paid the fee will they let you enroll.

20. Nobody plays who isn't in full uniform.

■ The Square of Opposition

Two categorical claims *correspond* to each other if they have the same subject term and the same predicate term. So, "All Methodists are Christians"

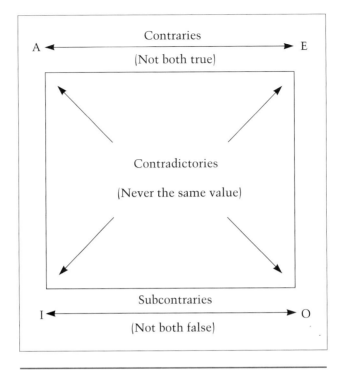

FIGURE 5 The square of opposition.

corresponds to "Some Methodists are Christians": In both claims, "Methodists" is the subject term, and "Christians" is the predicate term. Notice, though, that "Some Christians are not Methodists" does *not* correspond to either of the other two; it has the same terms but in different places.

We can now exhibit the logical relationships between corresponding A-, E-, I-, and O-claims. The **square of opposition,** in Figure 5, does this very concisely. The A- and E-claims, across the top of the square from each other, are **contrary claims**—they can both be false, but they cannot both be true. The I- and O-claims, across the bottom of the square from each other, are **subcontrary claims**—they can both be true, but they cannot both be false. The A- and O-claims and the E- and I-claims, which are at opposite diagonal corners from each other, respectively, are **contradictory claims**—they never have the same truth values.

Notice that these logical relationships are reflected on the Venn diagrams for the claims (see Figures 1 through 4). The diagrams for corresponding A- and O-claims say exactly opposite things about the left-hand area of the diagram, namely, that the area *has* something in it and that it *doesn't*; those for corresponding E- and I-claims do the same about the center area. Clearly, exactly one claim of each pair is true no matter what—either the relevant area is empty, or it isn't.

The diagrams show clearly how both subcontraries can be true: There's no conflict in putting X's in both left and center areas. In fact, it's possible to diagram an A-claim and the corresponding E-claim on the same diagram; we just have to shade out the entire subject class circle. This amounts to saying that *both* an A-claim and its corresponding E-claim can be true *as long as there are no members of the subject class.* We get an analogous result for subcontraries: They can both be false as long as the subject class is empty.* We can easily avoid this result by making an assumption: When making inferences from one contrary (or subcontrary) to another, we'll assume that the classes we're talking about are not entirely empty. On this assumption, the A-claim or the corresponding E-claim (or both) must be false, and the I-claim or the corresponding O-claim (or both) must be true.

If we have the truth value of one categorical claim, we can often deduce the truth values of the other three corresponding claims by using the square of opposition. For instance, if we hear "All aluminum cans are recyclable items," we can immediately infer that its contradictory, "Some aluminum cans are not recyclable items," is false; the corresponding E-claim, "No aluminum cans are recyclable items," is also false because it is the contrary of the original A-claim and cannot be true if the A-claim is true. The corresponding I-claim, "Some aluminum cans are recyclable items," must be true because we just determined that *its* contradictory, the E-claim, is false.

However, we cannot *always* determine the truth values of the remaining three standard-form categorical claims. For example, if we know only that the A-claim is false, all we can infer is the truth value (true) of the corresponding O-claim. Nothing follows about either the E- or the I-claim. Because the A- and the E-claim can both be false, knowing that the A-claim is false does not tell us anything about the E-claim—it can still be either true or false. And if the E-claim remains undetermined, then so must its contradictory, the I-claim.

So here are the limits on what can be inferred from the square of opposition: Beginning with a *true* claim at the top of the square (either A or E), we can infer the truth values of all three of the remaining claims. The same is true if we begin with a *false* claim at the bottom of the square (either I or O): We can still deduce the truth values of the other three. But if we begin with a false claim at the top of the square or a true claim at the bottom, all we can determine is the truth value of the contradictory of the claim in hand.

---

*It is quite possible to interpret categorical claims this way. By allowing both the A- and the E-claims to be true and both the I- and the O-claims to be false, this interpretation reduces the square to contradiction alone. We're going to interpret the claims differently; however, at the level at which we're operating, it seems much more natural to see "All Cs are Ds" as conflicting with "No Cs are Ds."

Exercise 8-3

Translate the following into standard-form claims, and determine the three corresponding standard-form claims. Then, assuming the truth value in parentheses for the given claim, determine the truth values of as many of the other three as you can.

Example

> Most snakes are harmless. (True)
>
> Translation (I-claim): Some snakes are harmless creatures. (True)
> Corresponding A-claim: All snakes are harmless creatures. (Undetermined)
> Corresponding E-claim: No snakes are harmless creatures. (False)
> Corresponding O-claim: Some snakes are not harmless creatures. (Undetermined)

▲ 1. Not all anniversaries are happy occasions. (True)

2. There's no such thing as a completely harmless drug. (True)

3. There have been such things as just wars. (True)

▲ 4. There are allergies that can kill you. (True)

5. Woodpeckers sing really well. (False)

6. Mockingbirds can't sing. (False)

7. Some herbs are medicinal. (False)

8. Logic exercises are easy. (False)

Three Categorical Operations

The square of opposition allows us to make inferences from one claim to another, as you were doing in the last exercise. We can think of these inferences as simple valid arguments, because that's exactly what they are. We'll turn next to three operations that can be performed on standard-form categorical claims. They, too, will allow us to make simple valid arguments and, in combination with the square, some not-quite-so-simple valid arguments.

■ Conversion

You find the **converse** of a standard-form claim by switching the positions of the subject and predicate terms. The E- and I-claims, but not the A- and O-claims, contain just the same information as their converses; that is,

> All E- and I-claims, but not A- and O-claims, are equivalent to their converses.

Each member of the following pairs is the converse of the other:

E: No Norwegians are Slavs.
   No Slavs are Norwegians.

I: Some state capitals are large cities.
   Some large cities are state capitals.

Notice that the claims that are equivalent to their converses are those with symmetrical Venn diagrams.

■ *Obversion*

To discuss the next two operations, we need a couple of auxiliary notions. First, there's the notion of a *universe of discourse.* With rare exceptions, we make claims within contexts that limit the scope of the terms we use. For example, if your instructor walks into class and says, "Everybody passed the last exam," the word "everybody" does not include everybody in the world. Your instructor is not claiming, for example, that your mother and the President of the United States passed the exam. There is an unstated but obvious restriction to a smaller universe of people—in this case, the people in your class who *took* the exam. Now, for every class within a universe of discourse, there is a *complementary class* that contains everything in the universe of discourse that is *not* in the first class. Terms that name complementary classes are complementary terms. So "students" and "non-students" are **complementary terms.** Indeed, putting the prefix "non" in front of a term is often the easiest way to produce its complement. Some terms require different treatment, though. The complement of "people who took the exam" is probably best stated as "people who did not take the exam" because the universe is pretty clearly restricted to people in such a case. (We wouldn't expect, for example, the complement of "people who took the exam" to include *everything* that didn't take the exam, including your shoes and socks!)

Now, we can get on with it: To find the **obverse** of a claim, (a) change it from affirmative to negative, or vice versa (i.e., go horizontally across the square—an A-claim becomes an E-claim; an O-claim becomes an I-claim, and so on); then (b) replace the predicate term with its complementary term.

> All categorical claims of all four types, A, E, I, and O, are equivalent to their obverses.

Here are some examples; each claim is the obverse of the other member of the pair:

A: All Presbyterians are Christians.
   No Presbyterians are non-Christians.

E: No fish are mammals.
   All fish are nonmammals.

"You should say what you mean," the March Hare went on.

"I do," Alice hastily replied; "at least—at least I mean what I say—that's the same thing, you know."

"Not the same thing a bit!" said the Hatter. "Why, you might just as well say that 'I see what I eat' is the same thing as 'I eat what I see!'"

—LEWIS CARROLL, *Alice's Adventures in Wonderland*

The Mad Hatter is teaching Alice *not* to convert A-claims.

Venn Diagrams for the Three Operations

One way to see which operations work for which types of claim is to put them on Venn diagrams. Here's a regular diagram, which is all we need to explain *conversion:*

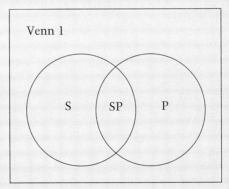

Venn 1

Imagine an I-claim, Some S are P, diagrammed on the above. It would have an X in the central area labeled SP, where S and P overlap. But its converse, Some P are S, would also have an X in that area, since that's where P and S overlap. So, the symmetry of the diagram shows that conversion works for I-claims. The same situation holds for E-claims, except we're shading the central area in both cases rather than placing Xs.

Now, let's imagine an A-claim, All S are P, the diagram for which requires us to shade all the subject term that's not included in the predicate term—i.e., the leftmost area above. But its converse, All P are S, would require that we shade out the *rightmost* area of the diagram, since the subject term is now over there on the right. So the claims with asymmetrical diagrams cannot be validly converted.

We need a somewhat more complicated diagram to explain the other two operations. Let's use a rectangular box to represent the universe of discourse (see text for an explanation) within which our classes and their complements fall. Then we'll label S all the areas that would contain Ss, P the areas where we'd find Ps, S̄ anywhere we would *not* find Ss, and P̄ any-

I: Some citizens are voters.
    Some citizens are not nonvoters.

O: Some contestants are not winners.
    Some contestants are nonwinners.

■ *Contraposition*

You find the **contrapositive** of a categorical claim by (a) switching the places of the subject and predicate terms, just as in conversion, and (b) replacing both terms with complementary terms. Each of the following is the contrapositive of the other member of the pair:

where we would *not* find Ps. Here's the result (make sure you understand what's going on here—it's not all that complicated):

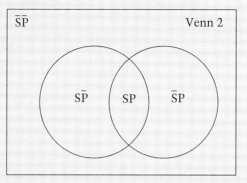

Now let's look at *obversion.* Imagine an A-claim, All S are P, diagrammed on the above. We'd shade out the area labeled S$\bar{P}$, wouldn't we? (All the subject class that's not part of the predicate class.) Now consider its obverse, "No S are $\bar{P}$." Since it's an E-claim, we shade where the subject and predicate overlap. And that turns out to be exactly the same area we shaded out for it's obverse! So these two are equivalent: They produce the same diagram. If you check, you'll find you get the same result for each of the other three types of claim, since obversion is valid for all four types.

Finally, we'll see how *contraposition* works out on the diagram. The A-claim, All S are P, once again is made true by shading out the S$\bar{P}$ area of the diagram. But now consider this claim's contrapositive, All $\bar{P}$ are $\bar{S}$. Shading out all the subject class that's outside the predicate class produces the same diagram as the original, thus showing that they are equivalent. Try diagramming an O-claim and it's contrapositive, and you'll find yourself putting an X in exactly the same area for each.

But if you diagram an I-claim, Some S are P, putting an X in the central SP area, and then diagram its contrapositive, Some $\bar{P}$ are $\bar{S}$, you'll find that the X would have to go entirely outside both circles, since that's the only place $\bar{P}$ and $\bar{S}$ overlap! Clearly, this says something different from the original I-claim. You'll find a similarly weird result if you consider an E-claim, since contraposition does *not* work for either I- or E-claims.

A: All Mongolians are Muslims.
    All non-Muslims are non-Mongolians.

O: Some citizens are not voters.
    Some nonvoters are not noncitizens.

All A- and O-claims, but not E- and I-claims, are equivalent to their contrapositives.

The operations of conversion, obversion, and contraposition are important to much of what comes later, so make sure you can do them correctly and that you know which claims are equivalent to the results.

Exercise 8-4

Find the claim described, and determine whether it is equivalent to the claim you began with.

▲ 1. Find the contrapositive of "No Sunnis are Christians."

2. Find the obverse of "Some Arabs are Christians."

3. Find the obverse of "All Sunnis are Muslims."

▲ 4. Find the converse of "Some Kurds are not Christians."

5. Find the converse of "No Hindus are Muslims."

6. Find the contrapositive of "Some Indians are not Hindus."

▲ 7. Find the converse of "All Shiites are Muslims."

8. Find the contrapositive of "All Catholics are Christians."

9. Find the converse of "All Protestants are Christians."

▲ 10. Find the obverse of "No Muslims are Christians."

Exercise 8-5

Follow the directions given in the preceding exercise.

▲ 1. Find the obverse of "Some students who scored well on the exam are students who wrote poor essays."

2. Find the obverse of "No students who wrote poor essays are students who were admitted to the program."

3. Find the contrapositive of "Some students who were admitted to the program are not students who scored well on the exam."

▲ 4. Find the contrapositive of "No students who did not score well on the exam are students who were admitted to the program."

5. Find the contrapositive of "All students who were admitted to the program are students who wrote good essays."

6. Find the obverse of "No students of mine are unregistered students."

▲ 7. Find the contrapositive of "All people who live in the dorms are people whose automobile ownership is restricted."

8. Find the contrapositive of "All commuters are people whose automobile ownership is unrestricted."

9. Find the contrapositive of "Some students with short-term memory problems are students who do poorly in history classes."

▲ 10. Find the obverse of "No first basemen are right-handed people."

Exercise 8-6

For each of the following, find the claim that is described.

Two Common Mistakes

Some of the nuts and bolts on the imported Fords are metric; therefore, some are not.
Some of the nuts and bolts on the imported Fords are not metric; therefore, some are.

It's common for a person to make an inference from "Some As are Bs" to Some As are not Bs," as the first sentence above specifies. But this is a mistake; it's an invalid inference. One might try to defend the mistake by saying, Look, if *all* As are Bs, why not just say so? By not saying so, you're implying that some As are *not* Bs, aren't you? Nope, in fact you're not. One reason we might say "Some As are Bs" is because we only *know* about some As; we may not know whether all of them are Bs.

The same kind of account, naturally, works for going the other way, as in the sentence above.

Example

Find the contrary of the contrapositive of "All Greeks are Europeans."
First, find the contrapositive of the original claim. It is "All non-Europeans are non-Greeks." Now, find the contrary of that. Going across the top of the square (from an A-claim to an E-claim), you get "No non-Europeans are non-Greeks."

1. Find the contradictory of the converse of "No clarinets are percussion instruments."

▲ 2. Find the contradictory of the obverse of "Some encyclopedias are definitive works."

3. Find the contrapositive of the subcontrary of "Some English people are Celts."

▲ 4. Find the contrary of the contradictory of "Some sailboats are not sloops."

5. Find the obverse of the converse of "No sharks are freshwater fish."

Exercise 8-7

For each of the numbered claims below, determine which of the lettered claims that follow are equivalent. You may use letters more than once if necessary. (Hint: This is a lot easier to do after all the claims are translated, a fact that indicates at least one advantage to putting claims into standard form.)

1. Some people who have not been tested can give blood.

▲ 2. People who have not been tested cannot give blood.

3. Nobody who has been tested can give blood.

▲ 4. Nobody can give blood except those who have been tested.
   a. Some people who have been tested cannot give blood.

    b. Not everybody who can give blood has been tested.
    c. Only people who have been tested can give blood.
    d. Some people who cannot give blood are people who have been tested.
    e. If a person has been tested, then he or she cannot give blood.

Exercise 8-8

Try to make the claims in the following pairs correspond to each other—that is, arrange them so that they have the same subject and the same predicate terms. Use only those operations that produce equivalent claims; for example, don't convert A- or O-claims in the process of trying to make the claims correspond. You can work on either member of the pair or both. (The main reason for practicing on these is to make the problems in the next two exercises easier to do.)

Example

    a. Some students are not unemployed people.
    b. All employed people are students.

These two claims can be made to correspond by obverting claim (a) and then converting the result (which is legitimate because the claim has been turned into an I-claim before conversion). We wind up with "Some employed people are students," which corresponds to (b).

▲   1. a. Some Slavs are non-Europeans.
      b. No Slavs are Europeans.

   2. a. All Europeans are Westerners.
      b. Some non-Westerners are non-Europeans.

   3. a. All Greeks are Europeans.
      b. Some non-Europeans are Greeks.

▲   4. a. No members of the club are people who took the exam.
      b. Some people who did not take the exam are members of the club.

   5. a. All people who are not members of the club are people who took the exam.
      b. Some people who did not take the exam are members of the club.

   6. a. Some cheeses are not products high in cholesterol.
      b. No cheeses are products that are not high in cholesterol.

▲   7. a. All people who arrived late are people who will be allowed to perform.
      b. Some of the people who did not arrive late will not be allowed to perform.

   8. a. No nonparticipants are people with name tags.
      b. Some of the people with name tags are participants.

   9. a. Some perennials are plants that grow from tubers.
      b. Some plants that do not grow from tubers are perennials.

One More Time

If this is true:

>   Some people who work in the casino are not members of the tribe.

Doesn't this next claim have to be true too?

>   Some members of the tribe are not people who work in the casino.

Nope. Wrong again. The O-claim, however much it might remind us of its converse, says something quite different from it and cannot be inferred from it.

▲ 10. a. Some decks that play digital tape are not devices equipped for radical oversampling.
  b. All devices that are equipped for radical oversampling are decks that will not play digital tape.

Exercise 8-9

Which of the following arguments is valid? (Remember, an argument is valid when the truth of its premises guarantees the truth of its conclusion.)

▲ 1. Whenever the battery is dead, the screen goes blank; that means, of course, that whenever the screen goes blank, the battery is dead.

  2. For a while there, some students were desperate for good grades, which meant some weren't, right?

  3. Some players in the last election weren't members of the Reform Party. Obviously, therefore, some members of the Reform Party weren't players in the last election.

▲ 4. Since some of the students who failed the exam were students who didn't attend the review session, it must be that some students who weren't at the session failed the exam.

  5. None of the people who arrived late were people who got good seats, so none of the good seats were occupied by latecomers.

  6. Everybody who arrived on time was given a box lunch, so the people who did not get a box lunch were those who didn't get there on time.

▲ 7. None of the people who gave blood are people who were tested, so everybody who gave blood must have been untested.

  8. Some of the people who were not tested are people who were allowed to give blood, from which it follows that some of the people who were *not* allowed to give blood must have been people who were tested.

9. Everybody who was in uniform was able to play, so nobody who was out of uniform must have been able to play.

▲ 10. Not everybody in uniform was allowed to play, so some people who were not allowed to play must not have been people in uniform.

Exercise 8-10 ⎯⎯⎯⎯⎯⎯⎯⎯⎯⎯⎯⎯⎯⎯⎯⎯⎯⎯⎯⎯

For each pair of claims, assume that the first has the truth value given in parentheses. Using the operations of conversion, obversion, and contraposition along with the square of opposition, decide whether the second claim is true, false, or remains undetermined.

Example

a. No aardvarks are nonmammals. (True)

b. Some aardvarks are not mammals.

Claim (a) can be obverted to "All aardvarks are mammals." Because all categorical claims are equivalent to their obverses, the truth of this claim follows from that of (a). Because this claim is the contradictory of claim (b), it follows that claim (b) must be false.

Note: If we had been unable to make the two claims correspond without performing an illegitimate operation (such as converting an A-claim), then the answer is automatically *undetermined.*

▲ 1. a. No mosquitoes are poisonous creatures. (True)
    b. Some poisonous creatures are mosquitoes.

2. a. Some students are not ineligible candidates. (True)
    b. No eligible candidates are students.

▲ 3. a. Some sound arguments are not invalid arguments. (True)
    b. All valid arguments are unsound arguments.

4. a. Some residents are nonvoters. (False)
    b. No voters are residents.

▲ 5. a. Some automobile plants are not productive factories. (True)
    b. All unproductive factories are automobile plants.

Many of the following will have to be rewritten as standard-form categorical claims before they can be answered.

6. a. Most opera singers take voice lessons their whole lives. (True)
    b. Some opera singers do not take voice lessons their whole lives.

7. a. The hero gets killed in some of Gary Brodnax's novels. (False)
    b. The hero does not get killed in some of Gary Brodnax's novels.

8. a. None of the boxes in the last shipment are unopened. (True)
    b. Some of the opened boxes are not boxes in the last shipment.

▲ 9. a. Not everybody who is enrolled in the class will get a grade. (True)
       b. Some people who will not get a grade are enrolled in the class.

   10. a. Persimmons are always astringent when they have not been left to
          ripen. (True)
       b. Some persimmons that have been left to ripen are not astringent.

Categorical Syllogisms

A **syllogism** is a two-premise deductive argument. A **categorical syllogism** (in standard form) is a syllogism whose every claim is a standard-form categorical claim and in which three terms each occur exactly twice in exactly two of the claims. Study the following example:

> All Americans are consumers.
> Some consumers are not Democrats.
> Therefore, some Americans are not Democrats.

Notice how each of the three terms "Americans," "consumers," and "Democrats" occurs exactly twice in exactly two different claims. The *terms of a syllogism* are sometimes given the following labels:

> *Major term:* the term that occurs as a predicate term of the syllogism's conclusion

> *Minor term:* the term that occurs as the subject term of the syllogism's conclusion

> *Middle term:* the term that occurs in both of the premises but not at all in the conclusion

The most frequently used symbols for these three terms are *P* for major term, *S* for minor term, and *M* for middle term. We use these symbols throughout to simplify the discussion.

In a categorical syllogism, each of the premises states a relationship between the middle term and one of the other terms, as shown in Figure 6. If both premises do their jobs correctly—that is, if the proper connections between S and P are established via the middle term, M—then the relationship between S and P stated by the conclusion will have to follow—that is, the argument is valid.

In case you're not clear about the concept of validity, remember: An argument is valid if, and only if, it is not possible for its premises to be true while its conclusion is false. This is just another way of saying that *were* the premises of a valid argument true (whether they are in fact true or false), then

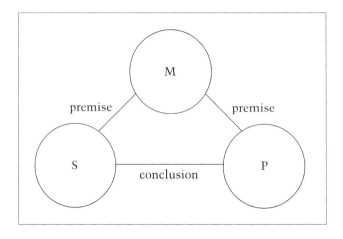

FIGURE 6   Relationship of terms in categorical syllogisms.

the truth of the conclusion would be guaranteed. In a moment we'll begin developing the first of two methods for assessing the validity of syllogisms.

First, though, let's look at some candidates for syllogisms. In fact, only one of the following qualifies as a categorical syllogism. Can you identify which one? What is wrong with the other two?

1. All cats are mammals.
    Not all cats are domestic.
    Therefore, not all mammals are domestic.

2. All valid arguments are good arguments.
    Some valid arguments are boring arguments.
    Therefore, some good arguments are boring arguments.

3. Some people on the committee are not students.
    All people on the committee are local people.
    Therefore, some local people are nonstudents.

We hope it was fairly obvious that the second argument is the only proper syllogism. The first example has a couple of things wrong with it: Neither the second premise nor the conclusion is in standard form—no standard-form categorical claim begins with the word "not"—and the predicate term must be a noun or noun phrase. The second premise can be translated into "Some cats are not domestic creatures" and the conclusion into "Some mammals are not domestic creatures," and the result is a syllogism. The third argument is okay up to the conclusion, which contains a term that does not occur anywhere in the premises: "nonstudents." However, because "nonstudents" is the complement of "students," this argument can be turned into a proper syllogism by obverting the conclusion, producing "Some local people are not students."

© 2003 by Sidney Harris. Reprinted with permission.

Once you're able to recognize syllogisms, it's time to learn how to determine their validity. We'll turn now to our first method, the Venn diagram test.

■ The Venn Diagram Method of Testing for Validity

Diagramming a syllogism requires three overlapping circles, one representing each class named by a term in the argument. To be systematic, in our diagrams we put the minor term on the left, the major term on the right, and the middle term in the middle, but lowered a bit. We will diagram the following syllogism step by step:

> No Republicans are collectivists.
> All socialists are collectivists.
> Therefore, no socialists are Republicans.

In this example, "socialists" is the minor term, "Republicans" is the major term, and "collectivists" is the middle term. See Figure 7 for the three circles required, labeled appropriately.

We fill in this diagram by diagramming the premises of the argument just as we diagrammed the A-, E-, I-, and O-claims earlier. The premises in the above example are diagrammed like this: First: No Republicans are

Paradoxes

The first claim in this box is false.

If the preceding claim is true, then it must be false, right? But if it's false, then what it says is true. So, if it's true, it's false, and if it's false, it's true. Which is it?

This is an example of a liar paradox. Logicians do not agree about what to say about this type of problem. Neither do we. (Although the most frequently said thing about such paradoxes is that they show you can't let a claim refer to itself.)

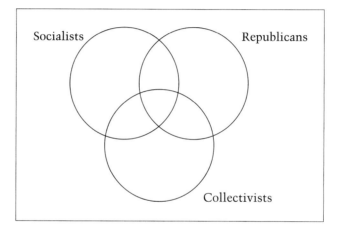

FIGURE 7   Before either premise has been diagrammed.

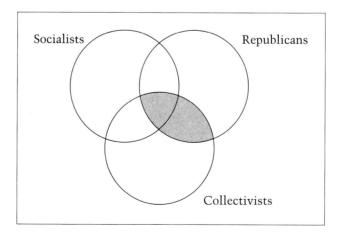

FIGURE 8   One premise diagrammed.

© Dan Piraro. Reprinted with special permission of King Features Syndicate.

collectivists (Figure 8). Notice that in this figure we have shaded the entire area where the Republican and collectivist circles overlap.

Second: All socialists are collectivists (Figure 9). Because diagramming the premises resulted in the shading of the entire area where the socialist and Republican circles overlap, and because that is exactly what we would do to diagram the syllogism's conclusion, we can conclude that the syllogism is valid. In general, a syllogism is valid if and only if diagramming the premises automatically produces a correct diagram of the conclusion.* (The one exception is discussed later.)

---

*It might be helpful for some students to produce *two* diagrams, one for the premises of the argument and one for the conclusion. The two can then be compared: Any area of the conclusion diagram that is shaded must also be shaded in the premises diagram, and any area of the conclusion diagram that has an X must also have one in the premises diagram. If both of these conditions are met, the argument is valid. (Thanks to Professor Ellery Eells of the University of Wisconsin, Madison, for the suggestion.)

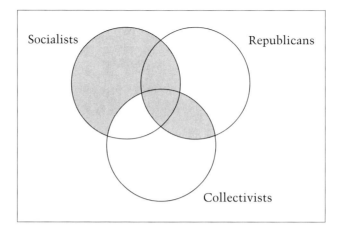

FIGURE 9   Both premises diagrammed.

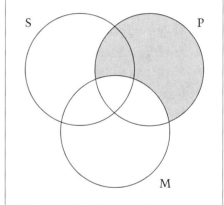

FIGURE 10   **FIGURE 11**

When one of the premises of a syllogism is an I- or O-premise, there can be a problem about where to put the required X. The following example presents such a problem (see Figure 10 for the diagram). Note in the diagram that we have numbered the different areas in order to refer to them easily.

Some S are not M.
All P are M.
Some S are not P.

(The horizontal line separates the premises from the conclusion.)

An X in either area 1 or area 2 of Figure 10 makes the claim "Some S are not M" true, because an inhabitant of either area is an S but not an M. How do we determine which area should get the X? In some cases, the de-

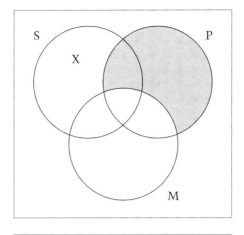

FIGURE 12

cision can be made for us: *When one premise is an A- or E-premise and the other is an I- or O-premise, diagram the A- or E-premise first.* (Always shade before putting in Xs.) Refer to Figure 11 to see what happens with the current example when we follow this rule.

Once the A-claim has been diagrammed, there is no longer a choice about where to put the X—it has to go in area 1. Hence, the completed diagram for this argument looks like Figure 12. And from this diagram we can read the conclusion "Some S are not P," which tells us that the argument is valid.

In some syllogisms, the rule just explained does not help. For example,

All P are M.
Some S are M.
Some S are P.

A syllogism like this one still leaves us in doubt about where to put the X, even after we have diagrammed the A-premise (Figure 13): Should the X go in area 4 or 5? When such a question remains unresolved, here is the rule to follow: *An X that can go in either of two areas goes on the line separating the areas,* as in Figure 14.

In essence, an X on a line indicates that the X belongs in one or the other of the two areas, maybe both, but we don't know which. When the time comes to see whether the diagram yields the conclusion, we look to see whether there is an X *entirely* within the appropriate area. In the current example, we would need an X entirely within the area where S and P overlap; because there is no such X, the argument is invalid. An X *partly* within the appropriate area fails to establish the conclusion.

Please notice this about Venn diagrams: When both premises of a syllogism are A- or E-claims and the conclusion is an I- or O-claim, diagramming the premises cannot possibly yield a diagram of the conclusion (because

FIGURE 13

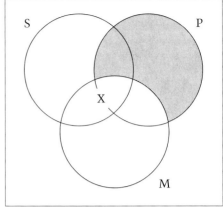

FIGURE 14

A- and E-claims produce only shading, and I- and O-claims require an X to be read from the diagram). In such a case, remember our assumption that every class we are dealing with has at least one member. This assumption justifies our looking at the diagram and determining whether any circle has all but one of its areas shaded out. *If any circle has only one area remaining unshaded, an X should be put in that area.* This is the case because any member of that class has to be in that remaining area. Sometimes placing the X in this way will enable us to read the conclusion, in which case the argument is valid (on the assumption that the relevant class is not empty); sometimes placing the X will not enable us to read the conclusion, in which case the argument is invalid, with or without any assumptions about the existence of a member within the class.

■ *Categorical Syllogisms with Unstated Premises*

Many "real-life" categorical syllogisms have unstated premises. For example, suppose somebody says:

> You shouldn't give chicken bones to dogs. They could choke on them.

The speaker's argument rests on the unstated premise that you shouldn't give dogs things they could choke on. In other words, the argument, when fully spelled out, is this:

> All chicken bones are things dogs could choke on.
> [No things dogs could choke on are things you should give dogs.]
> Therefore, no chicken bones are things you should give dogs.

The unstated premise appears in brackets.

Our Coach, the Expletive

A few years ago, exasperated with his team's losing, former coach Dick Motta of the Sacramento Kings threatened to trade his star player, Wayman Tisdale, because Motta doubted Tisdale's ability to be a leader.

"You almost have to be a bad guy to be a great leader in this league," Motta said. "Very few guys can do it. There's no way Wayman Tisdale is ever going to be a bad guy."

You can put this argument into standard form, can't you?

Motta also said, "The great ones turn into pieces of [expletive] when they assume leadership. Wayman is a preacher's son. He's not going to be an [expletive]."

Same type of argument, right? Roughly:

All great leaders are pieces of expletive.
Tisdale is not a piece of expletive.
Therefore, Tisdale is not a great leader.

(When he was told what Motta said about him, Tisdale said he thought Motta should know, since Motta was a leader: All great leaders are pieces of expletive; Motta is a great leader; therefore, Motta is a piece of expletive.)

To take another example:

Driving around in an old car is dumb, since it might break down in a dangerous place.

Here the speaker's argument rests on the unstated premise that it's dumb to risk a dangerous breakdown. In other words, when fully spelled out, the argument is this:

All examples of driving around in an old car are examples of risking dangerous breakdown.
[All examples of risking dangerous breakdown are examples of being dumb.]
Therefore, all examples of driving around in an old car are examples of being dumb.

When you hear (or give) an argument that looks like a categorical syllogism that has only one stated premise, usually a second premise has been assumed and not stated. Ordinarily this unstated premise remains unstated because the speaker thinks it is too obvious to bother stating. The unstated premises in the arguments above are good examples: "You shouldn't give dogs things they could choke on," and "It is dumb to risk a dangerous breakdown."

When you encounter (or give) what looks like a categorical syllogism that is missing a premise, ask: Is there a reasonable assumption I could make that would make this argument valid? We covered this question of unstated premises in more detail on pages 241–245, and you might want to look there for more information on the subject.

At the end of this chapter, we have included a few exercises that involve missing premises.

■ *Real-Life Syllogisms*

We'll end this section with a word of advice. Before you use a Venn diagram or the rules method for determining the validity of real-life arguments, it helps to use a letter to abbreviate each category mentioned in the argument. This is mainly just a matter of convenience: It is easier to write down letters than to write down long phrases.

Take the first "real-life" categorical syllogisms given above:

> You shouldn't give chicken bones to dogs because they could choke on them.

The argument spelled out, once again, is this:

> All chicken bones are things dogs could choke on.
> [No things dogs could choke on are things you should give dogs.]
> Therefore, no chicken bones are things you should give dogs.

Abbreviating each of the three categories with a letter, we get

> C = chicken bones; D = things dogs could choke on; and S = things you should give dogs.

Then, the argument is

> All C are D
> [No D are S]
> Therefore, no C are S.

Likewise, the second argument was this:

> Driving around in an old car is dumb, since it might break down in a dangerous place.

When fully spelled out, the argument is

> All examples of driving around in an old car are examples of risking dangerous breakdown.
> [All examples of risking dangerous breakdown are examples of being dumb.]
> Therefore, all examples of driving around in an old car are examples of being dumb.

Abbreviating each of the three categories, we get

> D = examples of driving around in an old car; R = examples of risking danger-
> ous breakdown; S = examples of being dumb.

Then, the argument is

> All D are R
> [All R are S]
> Therefore, all D are S.

A final tip: Take the time to write down your abbreviation key clearly.

Exercise 8-11

Use the diagram method to determine which of the following syllogisms are valid and which are invalid.

▲ 1. All paperbacks are books that use glue in their spines.
    No books that use glue in their spines are books that are sewn in signatures.
    No books that are sewn in signatures are paperbacks.

   2. All sound arguments are valid arguments.
    Some valid arguments are not interesting arguments.
    Some sound arguments are not interesting arguments.

   3. All topologists are mathematicians.
    Some topologists are not statisticians.
    Some mathematicians are not statisticians.

▲ 4. Every time Louis is tired he's edgy. He's edgy today, so he must be tired today.

   5. Every voter is a citizen, but some citizens are not residents. Therefore, some voters are not residents.

   6. All the dominant seventh chords are in the mixolydian mode, and no mixolydian chords use the major scale. So no chords that use the major scale are dominant sevenths.

▲ 7. All halyards are lines that attach to sails. Painters do not attach to sails, so they must not be halyards.

   8. Only systems with removable disks can give you unlimited storage capacity of a practical sort. Standard hard disks never have removable disks, so they can't give you practical, unlimited storage capacity.

   9. All citizens are residents. So, since no noncitizens are voters, all voters must be residents.

▲ 10. No citizens are nonresidents, and all voters are citizens. So all residents must be nonvoters.

Brodie!

"Otterhounds are friendly, are fond of other dogs, bark a lot, and like to chase cats."

"That describes Brodie exactly! He must be an otterhound."

Not so fast, dog lover. The argument seems to be

All otterhounds are friendly, fond of other dogs, and like to chase cats.
Brodie is friendly, fond of other dogs, and likes to chase cats.
Therefore, Brodie is an otterhound.

This argument has the form

All As are X
All Bs are X.
Therefore, all Bs are As.

If you use techniques described in this chapter, you will see that arguments with this form are invalid. If you just stumbled on this box or your instructor referred you to it, common sense should tell you the same. It's like arguing "All graduates of Harvard are warm-blooded, and Brodie is warm-blooded;" therefore, Brodie is a graduate of Harvard."

Moral: Be on the watch for arguments like the one above. They aren't uncommon. Plus, see the next box, "Additional Common Invalid Argument Forms."

Exercise 8-12

Put the following arguments in standard form (you may have to use the obversion, conversion, or contraposition operations to accomplish this); then determine whether the arguments are valid by means of diagrams.

▲ 1. No blank disks contain any data, although some blank disks are formatted. Therefore, some formatted disks do not contain any data.

2. All ears of corn with white tassels are unripe, but some ears are ripe even though their kernels are not full-sized. Therefore, some ears with full-sized kernels are not ears with white tassels.

3. Prescription drugs should never be taken without a doctor's order. So no over-the-counter drugs are prescription drugs, because all over-the-counter drugs can be taken without a doctor's order.

▲ 4. All tobacco products are damaging to people's health, but some of them are addictive substances. Some addictive substances, therefore, are damaging to people's health.

5. A few compact disc players use 24× sampling, so some of them must cost at least a hundred dollars, because you can't buy any machine with 24× sampling for less than a hundred dollars.

6. Everything that Pete won at the carnival must be junk. I know that Pete won everything that Bob won, and all the stuff that Bob won is junk.

▲ 7. Only people who hold stock in the company may vote, so Mr. Hansen must not hold any stock in the company, because I know he was not allowed to vote.

8. No off-road vehicles are allowed in the unimproved portion of the park, but some off-road vehicles are not four-wheel-drive. So some four-wheel-drive vehicles are allowed in the unimproved part of the park.

9. Some of the people affected by the new drainage tax are residents of the county, and many residents of the county are already paying the sewer tax. So it must be that some people paying the sewer tax are affected by the new drainage tax, too.

▲ 10. No argument with false premises is sound, but some of them are valid. So some unsound arguments must be valid.

■ *The Rules Method of Testing for Validity*

The diagram method of testing syllogisms for validity is intuitive, but there is a faster method that makes use of three simple rules. These rules are based on two ideas, the first of which has been mentioned already: affirmative and negative categorical claims. (Remember, the A- and I-claims are affirmative; the E- and O-claims are negative.) The other idea is that of *distribution*.

A-claim: All Ⓢ are Ⓟ.
E-claim: No Ⓢ are Ⓟ.
I-claim: Some Ⓢ are Ⓟ.
O-claim: Some Ⓢ are not Ⓟ.

FIGURE 15 Distributed terms.

Terms that occur in categorical claims are either distributed or undistributed: Either the claim says something about every member of the class the term names, or it does not.* Three of the standard-form claims distribute one or more of their terms. In Figure 15, the circled letters stand for distributed terms, and the uncircled ones stand for undistributed terms. As the figure shows, the A-claim distributes its subject term, the O-claim distributes its predicate term, the E-claim distributes both, and the I-claim distributes neither.

We can now state the three *rules of the syllogism.* A syllogism is valid if and only if all of these conditions are met:

1. **The number of negative claims in the premises must be the same as the number of negative claims in the conclusion.** (Because the conclusion is always one claim, this implies that no valid syllogism has two negative premises.)

2. **At least one premise must distribute the middle term.**

3. **Any term that is distributed in the conclusion of the syllogism must be distributed in its premises.**

These rules are easy to remember, and with a bit of practice, you can use them to determine quickly whether a syllogism is valid.

Which of the rules is broken in this example?

All pianists are keyboard players.
Some keyboard players are not percussionists.
Some pianists are not percussionists.

---

*The above is a rough-and-ready definition of distribution. If you'd like a more technical version, here's one: A term is *distributed* in a claim if, and only if, on the assumption that the claim is true, the class named by the term can be replaced by *any* subset of that class without producing a false claim. Example: In the claim "All senators are politicians," the term "senators" is distributed because, assuming the claim is true, you can substitute *any* subset of senators (Democratic ones, Republican ones, tall ones, short ones . . .) and the result must also be true. "Politicians" is not distributed: The original claim could be true while "All senators are honest politicians" was false.

© 2003 by Sidney Harris. Reprinted with permission.

▲   *Nope. 'Fraid it's none of the above. Is it clear what error our logician is making?*

The term "keyboard players" is the middle term, and it is undistributed in both premises. The first premise, an A-claim, does not distribute its predicate term; the second premise, an O-claim, does not distribute its subject term. So this syllogism breaks rule 2.

Another example:

> No dogs up for adoption at the animal shelter are pedigreed dogs.
> Some pedigreed dogs are expensive dogs.
> _____
> Some dogs up for adoption at the animal shelter are expensive dogs.

This syllogism breaks rule 1 because it has a negative premise but no negative conclusion.

A last example:

> No mercantilists are large landowners.
> All mercantilists are creditors.
> _____
> No creditors are large landowners.

The minor term, "creditors," is distributed in the conclusion (because it's the subject term of an E-claim) but not in the premises (where it's the predicate term of an A-claim). So this syllogism breaks rule 3.

Recap

In this chapter, we have developed the basics of categorical logic. There are four types of standard-form categorical claims (A: "All S are P"; E: "No S are P"; I: "Some S are P"; and O: "Some S are not P"). These can be represented by Venn diagrams. Translation of ordinary English claims into standard-form categorical ones is made somewhat easier by a few rules of thumb: "Only" introduces a predicate term; "the only" introduces a subject term; "whenever" means we're probably talking about times or occasions; "wherever" means we're probably talking about places. Claims about individuals should be treated as A- or E-claims.

The square of opposition displays the relations of contradiction, contrariety, and subcontrariety among corresponding standard-form claims. Conversion, obversion, and contraposition are three operations that can be performed on categorical claims—depending on the kind of claim on which you perform the operation, the result can be an equivalent claim.

Categorical syllogisms are standardized deductive arguments. We can test them for validity by two methods, one of which relies on Venn diagrams and one of which relies on rules about affirmative/negative claims and about the distribution of terms.

Having read this chapter and the chapter recap, you should be able to

- ▲ Define categorical logic and explain the four kinds of standard-form categorical claims
- ▲ Diagram standard-form categorical claims using Venn diagrams and translate claims into equivalent claims
- ▲ Exhibit the logical relationships among corresponding claims and determine the truth value of those claims using the square of opposition
- ▲ Make inferences about claims using the operations conversion, obversion, and contraposition
- ▲ Explain categorical syllogisms and determine their validity using both the diagram method and the rules method

Additional Exercises

Exercise 8-13

In each of the following items, identify whether A, B, or C is the middle term.

▲ 1. All A are B.
    <u>All A are C.</u>
    All B are C.

2. All B are C.
   No C are D.
   No B are D.

3. Some C are not D.
   All C are A.
   Some D are not A.

▲ 4. Some A are not B.
   Some B are C.
   Some C are not A.

5. No C are A.
   Some B are A.
   Some C are not B.

Exercise 8-14

Which terms are distributed in each of the following?

▲ 1. All A are B.
   (a.) A only
   b. B only
   c. Both A and B
   d. Neither A nor B

2. No A are B.
   a. A only
   b. B only
   (c.) Both A and B
   d. Neither A nor B

3. Some A are B.
   a. A only
   b. B only
   c. Both A and B
   (d.) Neither A nor B

▲ 4. Some A are not B.
   a. A only
   (b.) B only
   c. Both A and B
   d. Neither A nor B

Exercise 8-15

How many negative claims appear in the premises of each of the following arguments? (In other words, how many of the premises are negative?) Your options are 0, 1, or 2.

▲ 1. All A are B.
   All A are C.
   Therefore, all B are C.

2. All B are C.
   No C are D.
   Therefore, no B are D.

3. Some C are not D.
   All C are A.
   Therefore, some D are not A.

▲ 4. Some A are not B.
   Some B are C.
   Therefore, some C are not A.

5. No A are B.
   Some B are not C.
   Some A are C.

Exercise 8-16

Which rules (if any) are broken in each of the following? Select from these options:

   a. Breaks rule 1 only

   b. Breaks rule 2 only

   c. Breaks rule 3 only

   d. Breaks more than one rule

   e. Breaks no rule

▲ 1. All A are B.
   All A are C.
   Therefore, all B are C.

2. All B are C.
   No C are D.
   Therefore, no B are D.

3. Some C are not D.
   All C are A.
   Therefore, some D are A.

▲ 4. Some A are not B.
   Some B are C.
   Therefore, some C are not A.

5. Some A are C.
   Some C are B.
   Therefore, some A are B.

6. Some carbostats are framistans.
   No framistans are arbuckles.
   Some arbuckles are not carbostats.

▲ 7. All framistans are veeblefetzers.
   <u>Some veeblefetzers are carbostats.</u>
   Some framistans are carbostats.

   8. No arbuckles are framistans.
   <u>All arbuckles are carbostats.</u>
   No framistans are carbostats.

   9. All members of the class are registered students.
   <u>Some registered students are not people taking fifteen units.</u>
   Some members of the class are not people taking fifteen units.

▲ 10. All qualified mechanics are people familiar with hydraulics.
   <u>No unschooled people are people familiar with hydraulics.</u>
   No qualified mechanics are unschooled people.

Exercise 8-17

Which rules (if any) are broken in each of the following?

   Note: If an argument breaks a rule, *which* rule is broken depends on how you translate the claims in the argument. For example, the claim "Dogs shouldn't be given chicken bones" could be translated as an *E-claim:* "No dogs are animals that should be given chicken bones." But it also could be translated as an *A-claim:* "All dogs are animals that shouldn't be given chicken bones." If the original claim appeared in an invalid argument, one rule would be broken if you translated it as the E-claim. A different rule would be broken if you translated it as the A-claim.

▲ 1. All tigers are ferocious creatures. Some ferocious creatures are zoo animals. Therefore, some zoo animals are tigers. (For this and the following items, it will help if you abbreviate each category with a letter. For example, let T = tigers, F = ferocious creatures, and Z = zoo animals.)

   2. Some pedestrians are not jaywalkers. Therefore, some jaywalkers are not gardeners, since no gardeners are pedestrians.

   3. Because all shrubs are ornamental plants, it follows that no ornamental plants are cacti, since no cacti qualify as shrubs.

▲ 4. Weightlifters aren't really athletes. Athletics requires the use of motor skills; and few, if any, weightlifters use motor skills.

   5. The trick to finding syllogisms is to think categorically, as well as to focus on the key argument in a passage. For example, some passages contain a good bit of rhetoric, and some passages that do this make it hard to spot syllogisms, with the result that it is hard to spot syllogisms in some passages.

   6. Every broadcast network has seen its share of the television audience decline during the past six years. But not every media outlet that has a decline in television audience share has lost money. So not every broadcast network has lost money.

▲ 7. Many students lift papers off the Internet, and this fact is discouraging to teachers. However, it must be noted that students who do this are only cheating themselves, and anyone who cheats himself or herself loses in the long run. Therefore, lifting papers off the Internet is a losing proposition in the long run.

8. When he was Speaker of the House, Mr. Newt Gingrich could be counted on to advance Republican causes. At the time, nobody who would do that could be accused of being soft on crime, which explains why at the time Gingrich could hardly be accused of being soft on crime.

9. It would be in everyone's interest to amend the Constitution to permit school prayer. And it is obviously in everyone's interest to promote religious freedom. It should be no surprise, then, that amending the Constitution to permit school prayer will promote religious freedom.

▲ 10. If you want to stay out all night dancing, it is fine with me. Just don't cry about it if you don't get good grades. Dancing isn't a total waste of time, but dancing the whole night certainly is. There are only so many hours in a day, and wasting time is bound to affect your grades negatively. So, fine, stay out dancing all night. It's your choice. But you have to expect your grades to suffer.

Exercise 8-18

Refer back to Exercises 8-11 and 8-12 and check the arguments for validity using the rules. We recommend abbreviating each category with a letter.

Once again, remember: If an argument breaks a rule, *which* rule is broken depends on how you translate the claims in the argument. For example, the claim "Dogs shouldn't be given chicken bones" could be translated as an E-claim: "No dogs are animals that should be given chicken bones." But it also could be translated as an A-claim (the obverse of the other version): "All dogs are animals that shouldn't be given chicken bones." If the original claim appeared in an invalid argument, one rule would be broken if you translated it as an E-claim. A different rule would be broken if you translated it as an A-claim.

Answers to 2, 5, 7, and 8 are given in the answer section.

Exercise 8-19

For each of the following items: Abbreviate each category with a letter, then translate the argument into standard form using the abbreviations. Then test the argument for validity using either the diagram method or the rules method.

Note: For many of these items it can be difficult to translate the arguments into standard form.

▲ 1. Some athletes are not baseball players, and some baseball players are not basketball players. Therefore, some athletes are not basketball players.

2. Rats are disease-carrying pests, and as such should be eradicated, because such pests should all be eradicated.

▲ 3. This is not the best of all possible worlds, because the best of all possible worlds would not contain mosquitoes, and *this* world contains plenty of mosquitoes!

4. From time to time, the police have to break up parties here on campus, since some campus parties get out of control, and when a party gets out of control, well, you know what the police have to do.

5. I know that all fundamentalist Christians are evangelicals, and I'm pretty sure that all revivalists are also evangelicals. So, if I'm right, at least some fundamentalist Christians must be revivalists.

▲ 6. "Their new lawn furniture certainly looks cheap to me," she said. "It's made of plastic, and plastic furniture just looks cheap."

7. None of our intramural sports are sports played in the Olympics, and some of the intercollegiate sports are not Olympic sports either. So some of the intercollegiate sports are also intramural sports.

8. The moas were all Dinornithidae, and no moas exist anymore. So there aren't any more Dinornithidae.

▲ 9. Everybody on the district tax roll is a citizen, and all eligible voters are also citizens. So everybody on the district tax roll is an eligible voter.

10. Any piece of software that is in the public domain may be copied without permission or fee. But that cannot be done in the case of software under copyright. So software under copyright must not be in the public domain.

11. None of the countries that have been living under dictatorships for these past few decades are familiar with the social requirements of a strong democracy—things like widespread education and a willingness to abide by majority vote. Consequently, none of these countries will make a successful quick transition to democracy, since countries where the above-mentioned requirements are unfamiliar simply can't make such a transition.

▲ 12. Trust Senator Cobweb to vote with the governor on the new tax legislation. Cobweb is a liberal, and liberals just cannot pass up an opportunity to raise taxes.

13. Investor-held utilities should not be allowed to raise rates, since all public utilities should be allowed to raise rates, and public utilities are not investor-held.

14. Masterpieces are no longer recorded on cassettes. This is because masterpieces belong to the classical repertoire, and classical music is no longer recorded on cassettes.

15. It isn't important to learn chemistry, since it isn't very useful, and there isn't much point in learning something that isn't useful.

16. Stockholders' information about a company's worth must come from the managers of that company, but in a buy-out, the managers of the company are the very ones who are trying to buy the stock from the stockholders. So,

ironically, in a buy-out situation, stockholders must get their information about how much a company is worth from the very people who are trying to buy their stock.

▲ 17. All of the networks devoted considerable attention to reporting poll results during the last election, but many of those poll results were not especially newsworthy. So the networks have to admit that some unnewsworthy items received quite a bit of their attention.

▲ 18. If a person doesn't understand that the earth goes around the sun once a year, then that person can't understand what causes winter and summer. Strange as it may seem, then, there are many American adults who don't know what causes winter and summer, because a survey a year or so ago showed that many such adults don't know that the earth goes around the sun.

19. Congress seems ready to impose trade sanctions on China, and perhaps it should. China's leaders cruelly cling to power. They flout American interests in their actions in Tibet, in their human-rights violations, in their weapons sales, and in their questionable trade practices. Any country with a record like this deserves sanctions.

▲ 20. Since 1973, when the U.S. Supreme Court decided *Miller v. California*, no work can be banned as obscene unless it contains sexual depictions that are "patently offensive" to "contemporary community standards" and unless the work as a whole possesses no "serious literary, artistic, political or scientific value." As loose as this standard may seem when compared with earlier tests of obscenity, the pornographic novels of "Madame Toulouse" (a pseudonym, of course) can still be banned. They would offend the contemporary standards of *any* community, and to claim any literary, artistic, political, or scientific value for them would be a real joke.

21. All creationists are religious, and all fundamentalists are religious, so all creationists are fundamentalists.

22. Every sportscaster is an athlete, and no athlete is a college professor. Therefore, no sportscasters are college professors.

23. Anyone who voted for the Democrats favors expansion of medical services for the needy. So, the people who voted for the Democrats all favor higher taxes, since anyone who wants to expand medical services must favor higher taxes.

24. All cave dwellers lived before the invention of the radio, and no one alive today is a cave dweller. Thus, no person who lived before the invention of the radio is alive today.

25. Conservationists don't vote for Republicans, and all environmentalists are conservationists. Thus, environmentalists don't vote for Republicans. (Hint: Remember, the order of the premises can be reversed.)

26. Since all philosophers are skeptics, it follows that no theologian is a skeptic, since no philosophers are theologians. (Hint: Don't forget to convert, if necessary—and if permissible!)

27. Each philosopher is a skeptic, and no philosopher is a theologian. Therefore, no skeptic is a theologian. (Hint: Remember, you can convert some claims about classes.)

28. Peddlers are salesmen, and confidence men are, too. So, peddlers are confidence men.

29. Should drug addicts be treated as criminals? Well, addicts are all excluded from the class of decent people, yet all criminals belong to that class. Accordingly, no addicts are criminals.

30. Critical thinkers recognize invalid syllogisms: therefore, critical thinkers are logicians, since logicians can spot invalid syllogisms, too.

31. The Mohawk Indians are Algonquin, and so are the Cheyenne. So, the Mohawks are really just Cheyenne.

32. Idiots would support the measure, but no one else would. Whatever else you may think of the school board, you can't say they are idiots. [Therefore . . .]

Exercise 8-20

This exercise is a little different, and you may need to work one or more such items in class in order to get the hang of them. Your job is to try to prove each of the following claims about syllogisms true or false. You may need to produce a general argument—that is, to show that *every* syllogism that does *this* must also do *that*—or you may need to produce a counterexample, that is, an example that proves the claim in question false. The definition of categorical syllogism and the rules of the syllogism are of crucial importance in working these examples.

▲ 1. Every valid syllogism must have at least one A- or E-claim for a premise.

2. Every valid syllogism with an E-claim for a premise must have an E-claim for a conclusion.

3. Every valid syllogism with an E-claim for a conclusion must have an E-claim for a premise.

▲ 4. It's possible for a syllogism to break two of the rules of the syllogism.

5. No syllogism can break three of the rules of the syllogism.

Exercise 8-21

The following is an anonymous statement of opinion that appeared in a newspaper call-in column.

> This is in response to the person who called in that we should provide a shelter for the homeless, because I think that is wrong. These people make the downtown area unsafe because they have nothing to lose by robbing, mugging, etc. The young boy killed by the horseshoe pits was attacked by some of these bums, assuming that witnesses really saw

people who were homeless, which no doubt they did, since the so-called homeless all wear that old worn-out hippie gear, just like the people they saw. They also lower property values. And don't tell me they are down and out because they can't find work. The work is there if they look for it. They choose for themselves how to live, since if they didn't choose, who did?

A lot of things might be said in criticism of this tirade, but what we want you to notice is the breakdown of logic. The piece contains, in fact, a gross logic error, which we ask you to make the focus of a critical essay. Your audience is the other members of your class; that is, you are writing for an audience of critical thinkers.

Exercise 8-22

Pornography violates women's rights. It carries a demeaning message about a woman's worth and purpose and promotes genuine violence. This is indeed a violation of women's civil rights and justifies the Minneapolis City Council in attempting to ban pornography.

This letter to the editor is, in effect, two syllogisms. The conclusion of the first is that pornography violates women's rights. This conclusion also functions as a premise in the second syllogism, which has as its own conclusion the claim that the Minneapolis City Council is justified in attempting to ban pornography. Both syllogisms have unstated premises. Translate the entire argument into standard-form syllogisms, supplying missing premises, and determine whether the reasoning is valid.

Exercise 8-23

Each of the following arguments contains an unstated premise, which, together with the stated premise, makes the argument in question valid. Your job is to identify this unstated premise, abbreviate each category with a letter, and put the argument in standard form.

▲ 1. Ladybugs eat aphids; therefore, they are good to have in your garden.

2. CEOs have lots of responsibility; therefore, they should be paid a lot.

3. Anyone who understands how a computer program works knows how important logic is. Therefore, anyone who understands how a computer program works understands how important unambiguous writing is.

▲ 4. Self-tapping screws are a boon to the construction industry. They make it possible to screw things without drilling pilot holes.

5. No baseball player smokes anymore. Baseball players all know that smoking hampers athletic performance.

6. You really ought to give up jogging. It is harmful to your health.

7. Camping isn't much fun. It requires sleeping on the hard ground and getting lots of bug bites.

8. Having too much coffee makes you sleep poorly. That's why you shouldn't do it.

9. Do you have writer's block? No problem. You can always hire a secretary.

10. "You think those marks were left by a—snake? That's totally crazy. Snakes don't leave footprints."

Writing Exercises

1. Should dogs be used in medical experiments, given that they seem to have the capacity to experience fear and feel pain? Write a short paper defending a negative answer to this question, taking about five minutes to do so. When you have finished, exchange your argument with a friend and rewrite each other's argument as a categorical syllogism or a combination of categorical syllogisms. Remember that people often leave premises unstated.

2. Follow the instructions for Exercise 1, but this time defend the position that it is not wrong to use dogs in medical experiments.

3. Turn to Selection 7 in Appendix 1 and follow the second set of instructions.

4. Turn to Selection 14A, 14B, 15A, 15B, 16A, or 16B and follow the second alternative assignment.

Chapter 9

Deductive Arguments II: Truth-Functional Logic

*T*he earliest development of truth-functional logic took place among the Stoics, who flourished from about the third century B.C.E. until the second century C.E. But it was in the late nineteenth and twentieth centuries that the real power of **truth-functional logic** (known also as *propositional* or *sentential logic*) became apparent.

The "logic of sentences" is one of the bases on which modern symbolic logic rests, and as such it is important in such intellectual areas as set theory and the foundations of mathematics. It is also the model for electrical circuits of the sort that are the basis of digital computing. But truth-functional logic is also a useful tool in the analysis of arguments.

The study of truth-functional logic can benefit you in several ways. For one thing, you'll learn something about the structure of language that you wouldn't learn any other way. For another, you'll get a sense of what it's like to work with a very precise, nonmathematical system of symbols that is nevertheless very accessible to nearly any student willing to invest a modest amount of effort. The model of precision and clarity that such systems provide can serve you well when you communicate with others in ordinary language.

If you're not comfortable working with symbols, the upcoming sections on truth-functional arguments and deductions might look intimidating. But they are not as forbidding as they may appear. We presume that the whole matter of a symbolic system is unfamiliar to you, so we'll start from absolute scratch. Keep in mind, though, that everything builds on what goes before. It's important to master each concept as it's explained and not fall behind. Catching up can be very difficult. If you find yourself having difficulty with a section or a concept, put in some extra effort to master it before moving ahead. It will be worth it in the end.

Truth Tables and the Truth-Functional Symbols

Our "logical vocabulary" will consist of claim variables and truth-functional symbols. Before we consider the real heart of the subject, truth tables and the symbols that represent them, let's first clarify the use of letters of the alphabet to symbolize terms and claims.

■ *Claim Variables*

In Chapter 8, we used uppercase letters to stand for terms in categorical claims. Here we use uppercase letters to stand for claims. Our main interest is now in the way that words such as "not," "and," "or," and so on affect claims and link them together to produce compound claims out of simpler ones. So don't confuse the Ps and Qs, called **claim variables,** that appear in this chapter with the term variables used in Chapter 8.*

■ *Truth Tables*

Let's now consider truth tables and symbols. In truth-functional logic, any given claim, P, is either true or false. The following little table, called a **truth table,** displays both possible truth values for P:

P
—
T
F

Whichever truth value the claim P might have, its negation or contradictory, which we'll symbolize ~P, will have the other. Here, then, is the truth table for **negation:**

P	~P
T	F
F	T

The left-hand column of this table sets out both possible truth values for P, and the right-hand column sets out the truth values for ~P based on

---

*It is customary to use one kind of symbol, usually lowercase letters or Greek letters, as *claim variables* and plain or italicized uppercase letters for *specific claims.* Although this use has some technical advantages and makes possible a certain theoretical neatness, students often find it confusing. Therefore, we'll use uppercase letters for both variables and specific claims and simply make it clear which way we're using the letters.

P's values. This is a way of defining the negation sign, ~, in front of the P. The symbol means "change the truth value from T to F or from F to T, depending on P's values." Because it's handy to have a name for negations that you can say aloud, we read ~P as "not-P." So, if P were "Parker is at home," then ~P would be "It is not the case that Parker is at home," or, more simply, "Parker is not at home." In a moment we'll define other symbols by means of truth tables, so make sure you understand how this one works.

Because any given claim is either true or false, two claims, P and Q, must both be true, both be false, or have opposite truth values, for a total of four possible combinations. Here are the possibilities in truth-table form:

P	Q
T	T
T	F
F	T
F	F

A **conjunction** is a compound claim made from two simpler claims, called *conjuncts. A conjunction is true if and only if both of the simpler claims that make it up (its conjuncts) are true.* An example of a conjunction is the claim "Parker is at home and Moore is at work." We'll express the conjunction of P and Q by connecting them with an ampersand (&). The truth table for conjunctions looks like this:

P	Q	P & Q
T	T	T
T	F	F
F	T	F
F	F	F

P & Q is true in the first row only, where both P and Q are true. Notice that the "truth conditions" in this row match those required in the italicized statement above.

Here's another way to remember how conjunctions work: If either part of a conjunction is false, the conjunction itself is false. Notice finally that although the word "and" is the closest representative in English to our ampersand symbol, there are other words that are correctly symbolized by the ampersand: "but" and "while," for instance, as well as phrases such as "even though." So, if we let P stand for "Parsons is in class" and Q stand for "Quincy is absent," then we should represent "Parsons is in class even though Quincy is absent" by P & Q. The reason is that the compound claim is true only in one case: where both parts are true. And that's all it takes to require an ampersand to represent the connecting word or phrase.

A **disjunction** is another compound claim made up of two simpler claims, called *disjuncts. A disjunction is false if and only if both of its dis-*

© 2003 by Sidney Harris. Reprinted by permission.

juncts are false. Here's an example of a disjunction: "Either Parker is at home or Moore is at work." We'll use the symbol ∨ ("wedge") to represent disjunction when we symbolize claims—as indicated in the example, the closest word in English to this symbol is "or." The truth table for disjunctions is this:

P	Q	P ∨ Q
T	T	T
T	F	T
F	T	T
F	F	F

Notice here that a disjunction is false only in the last row, where both of its disjuncts are false. In all other cases a disjunction is true.

The third kind of compound claim made from two simpler claims is the **conditional claim.** In ordinary English, the most common way of stating conditionals is by means of the words "if . . . then . . . ," as in the example "If Parker is at home, then Moore is at work."

We'll use an arrow to symbolize conditionals: P→Q. The first claim in a conditional, the P in the symbolization, is the **antecedent,** and the second—Q in this case—is the **consequent.** *A conditional claim is false if and only if its antecedent is true and its consequent is false.* The truth table for conditionals looks like this:

P	Q	P→Q
T	T	T
T	F	F
F	T	T
F	F	T

Only in the second row, where the antecedent P is true and the consequent Q is false, does the conditional turn out to be false. In all other cases it is true.

Of the four types of truth-functional claims—negation, conjunction, disjunction, and conditional—the conditional typically gives students the most trouble. Let's have a closer look at it by considering an example that may shed light on how and why conditionals work. Let's say that Moore promises you that, if his paycheck arrives this morning, he'll buy you lunch. So now we can consider the conditional,

If Moore's paycheck arrives this morning, then Moore will buy you lunch.

We can symbolize this using P (for the claim about the paycheck) and L (for the claim about lunch): P→L. Now let's try to see why the truth table above fits this claim.

The easiest way to see this is by asking yourself what it would take for Moore to break his promise. A moment's thought should make this clear: Two things have to happen before we can say that Moore has fibbed to you. The first is that his paycheck must arrive this morning. (After all, he didn't say what he was going to do if his paycheck *didn't* arrive, did he?) Then, it being true that his paycheck arrives, he must then *not* buy you lunch. Together, these two items make it clear that Moore's original promise was false. Notice: Under no other circumstances would we say that Moore broke his promise. And *that* is why the truth table has a conditional false in one and only one case, namely, where the antecedent is true and the consequent is false. Basic information about all four symbols is summarized in Figure 1.

Our truth-functional symbols can work in combination. Consider, for example, the claim "If Paula doesn't go to work, then Quincy will have to work a double shift." We'll represent the two simple claims in the obvious way, as follows:

Negation (~)	Conjunction (&)
Truth table:	Truth table:
P ~P T F F T	P Q (P & Q) T T T T F F F T F F F F
Closest English counterparts: "not," or "it is not the case that"	Closest English counterparts: "and," "but," "while"
Disjunction (∨)	Conditional (→)
Truth table:	Truth table:
P Q (P ∨ Q) T T T T F T F T T F F F	P Q (P →Q) T T T T F F F T T F F T
Closest English counterparts:"or," "unless"	Closest English counterparts: "if . . . . then," "provided that"

FIGURE 1 The Four Basic Truth-Functional Symbols

P = Paula goes to work.
Q = Quincy has to work a double shift.

And we can symbolize the entire claim like this:

~P→Q

Here is a truth table for this symbolization:

P	Q	~P	~P→Q
T	T	F	T
T	F	F	T
F	T	T	T
F	F	T	F

Notice that the symbolized claim ~P→Q is false in the *last* row of this table. That's because here and only here the antecedent, ~P, is true and its consequent, Q, is false. Notice that we work from the simplest parts to the most complex: The truth value of P in a given row determines the truth value of ~P, and that truth value in turn, along with the one for Q, determines the truth value of ~P→Q.

Consider another combination: "If Paula goes to work, then Quincy and Rogers will get a day off." This claim is symbolized this way:

P→(Q & R)

This symbolization requires parentheses in order to prevent confusion with (P→Q) & R, which symbolizes a different claim and has a different truth table. Our claim is a conditional with a conjunction for a consequent, whereas (P→Q) & R is a conjunction with a conditional as one of the conjuncts. The parentheses are what make this clear.

You need to know a few principles to produce the truth table for the symbolized claim P→(Q & R). First you have to know how to set up all the possible combinations of true and false for the three simple claims P, Q, and R. In claims with only one letter, there were two possibilities, T and F. In claims with two letters, there were four possibilities. *Every time we add another letter, the number of possible combinations of T and F doubles, and so, therefore, does the number of rows in our truth table.* The formula for determining the number of rows in a truth table for a compound claim is $r = 2^n$, where r is the number of rows in the table and n is the number of letters in the symbolization. Because the claim we are interested in has three letters, our truth table will have eight rows, one for each possible combination of T and F for P, Q, and R. Here's how we do it:

P	Q	R
T	T	T
T	T	F
T	F	T
T	F	F
F	T	T
F	T	F
F	F	T
F	F	F

The systematic way to construct such a table is to alternate Ts and Fs in the right-hand column, then alternate *pairs* of Ts and *pairs* of Fs in the next column to the left, then sets of *four* Ts and sets of *four* Fs in the next, and so forth. The leftmost column will always wind up being half Ts and half Fs.

The second thing we have to know is that the truth value of a compound claim in any particular case (i.e., any row of its truth table) depends entirely upon the truth values of its parts; and if these parts are themselves compound, their truth values depend upon those of their parts; and so on, until we get down to letters standing alone. The columns under the letters, which you have just learned to construct, will then tell us what we need to know. Let's build a truth table for P→(Q & R) and see how this works.

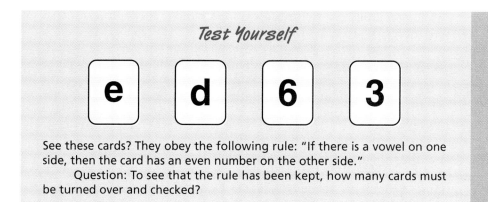

See these cards? They obey the following rule: "If there is a vowel on one side, then the card has an even number on the other side."

   Question: To see that the rule has been kept, how many cards must be turned over and checked?

—————

P.S. Most university students flunk this simple test of critical thinking.

P	Q	R	Q & R	P→(Q & R)
T	T	T	T	T
T	T	F	F	F
T	F	T	F	F
T	F	F	F	F
F	T	T	T	T
F	T	F	F	T
F	F	T	F	T
F	F	F	F	T

The three columns at the left, under P, Q, and R, are our *reference columns,* set up just as we discussed above. They determine what goes on in the rest of the table. From the second and third columns, under the Q and the R, we can fill in the column under Q & R. Notice that this column contains a T only in the first and fifth rows, where both Q and R are true. Next, from the column under the P and the one under Q & R, we can fill in the last column, which is the one for the entire symbolized claim. It contains Fs in only rows two, three, and four, which are the only ones where its antecedent is true and its consequent is false.

   What our table gives us is a *truth-functional analysis* of our original claim. Such an analysis displays the compound claim's truth value, based on the truth values of its simpler parts.

   If you've followed everything so far without problems, that's great. If you've not yet understood the basic truth table idea, however, as well as the truth tables for the truth-functional symbols, then by all means stop now and go back over this material. You should also understand how to build a truth table for symbolizations consisting of three or more letters. What comes later builds on this foundation, and like any construction project, without a strong foundation the whole thing collapses.

A final note before we turn to tips for symbolizing compound claims: Two claims are **truth-functionally equivalent** if they have exactly the same truth table—that is, if the Ts and Fs in the column under one claim are in the same arrangement as those in the column under the other. Generally speaking, when two claims are equivalent, one can be used in place of another—truth-functionally, they each imply the other.*

■ *Symbolizing Compound Claims*

Most of the things we can do with symbolized claims are pretty straightforward; that is, if you learn the techniques, you can apply them in a relatively clear-cut way. What's less clear-cut is how to symbolize a claim in the first place. We'll cover a few tips for symbolization in this section and then give you a chance to practice with some exercises.

Remember, when you symbolize a claim, you're displaying its truth-functional structure. The idea is to produce a version that will be truth-functionally equivalent to the original informal claim—that is, one that will be true under all the same circumstances as the original and false under all the same circumstances. Let's go through some examples that illustrate some standard symbolization problems.

"If" and "Only If"   In symbolizing truth-functional claims, as in translating categorical claims in Chapter 8, nothing can take the place of a careful reading of what the claim in question says. It always comes down to a matter of exercising careful judgment. Nonetheless, there are some tips we can give you that should make the job a little easier.

Of all the basic truth-functional types of claim, the conditional is probably the most difficult for students to symbolize correctly. There are so many ways to make these claims in ordinary English that it's not easy to keep track. Fortunately, the phrases "if" and "only if" account for a large number of conditionals, so you'll have a head start if you understand their uses. Here are some rules of thumb to remember:

1. The word "if," used alone, introduces the antecedent of a conditional.
2. The phrase "only if" introduces the consequent of a conditional.

---

*The exceptions to this remark are due to *non*-truth-functional nuances that claims sometimes have. Most compound claims of the form P & Q, for example, are interchangeable with what are called their commutations, Q & P. That is, it doesn't matter which conjunct comes first. (Note that this is also true of disjunctions but *not* of conditionals.) But at times "and" has more than a truth-functional meaning, and in such cases which conjunct comes first can make a difference. In "Daniel got on the train and bought his ticket," the word "and" would ordinarily mean "and then." So "Daniel bought his ticket and got on the train" turns out to be a different claim from the previous one; it says that he did the two things in a different order from that stated in the first claim. This temporal-ordering sense of "and" is part of the word's occasional non-truth-functional meaning.

Truth-Functional Trickery

Using what you know about truth-functional logic, can you identify how the sender of this encouraging-looking notice can defend the claim (because it *is* true) even though the receiver is not really going to win one nickel?

You Have Absolutely Won

$1,000,000.00

If you follow the instructions inside
and return the winning number!

Answer: Because there is not going to be any winning number inside (there are usually several *losing* numbers, in case that makes you feel better), the conjunction "You follow the instructions inside and [you] return the winning number" is going to be false, even if you do follow the instructions inside. Therefore, because this conjunction is the antecedent of the whole conditional claim, the conditional claim turns out to be true.

Of course, uncritical readers will take the antecedent to be saying something like "If you follow the instructions inside *by returning the winning number inside* (as if there were a winning number inside). These are the people who may wind up sending their own money to the mailer.

To put it another way: It's not the location of the part in a conditional that tells us whether it is the antecedent or the consequent; it's the logical words that identify it. Consider this example:

> Moore will get wet *if* Parker capsizes the boat.

The "Parker" part of the claim is the antecedent, even though it comes *after* the "Moore" part. It's as though the claim had said,

> If Parker capsizes the boat, Moore will get wet.

We would symbolize this claim as $P \rightarrow M$. Once again, it's the word "if" that tells us what the antecedent is.

> Parker will beat Moore at 9-ball *only if* Moore has a bad day.

This claim is different. In this case, the "Parker" part is the antecedent because "only if" introduces the consequent of a conditional. This is truth-functionally the same as

> If Parker beats Moore at 9-ball (P), then Moore had (or must have had) a bad day (B).

Hell Hath Enlarged Herself

The fearful, and unbelieving, and the abominable, and murderers, and whoremongers, and sorcerers, and idolators, and all liars, shall have their part in the lake which burneth with fire and brimstone.

—*Revelation 21:8*

This came to us in a brochure from a religious sect offering salvation for the believer. Notice, though, that the passage from the Bible doesn't say that, if you believe, you won't go to hell. It says, if you don't believe, you will go to hell.

Using the letters indicated in parentheses, we'd symbolize this as

$P \rightarrow B$

Don't worry about the grammatical tenses; we'll adjust those in whatever way necessary so that the claims make sense. We can use "if" in front of a conditional's antecedent, or we can use "only if" in front of its consequent; we produce exactly equivalent claims in the two cases. As in the case with "if," it doesn't matter where the "only if" part of the claim occurs. The part of this claim that's about Moore is the consequent, even though it occurs at the beginning of this version:

Only if Moore has a bad day will Parker beat him at 9-ball.

Exercise 9-1

Symbolize the following using the claim variables P and Q. (You can ignore differences in past, present, and future tense.)

▲ 1. If Quincy learns to symbolize, Paula will be amazed.

▲ 2. Paula will teach him if Quincy pays her a big fee.

▲ 3. Paula will teach him only if Quincy pays her a big fee.

▲ 4. Only if Paula helps him will Quincy pass the course.

▲ 5. Quincy will pass if and only if Paula helps him.

Claim 5 in the preceding exercise introduces a new wrinkle, the phrase "if and only if." Remembering our rules of thumb about how "if" and "only if" operate separately, it shouldn't surprise us that "if and only if" makes both antecedent and consequent out of the claim it introduces. We can make P both antecedent and consequent this way:

$(P \rightarrow Q) \& (Q \rightarrow P)$

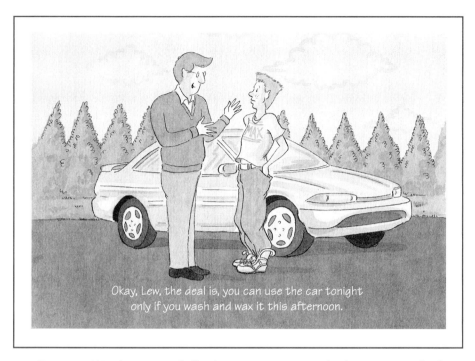

Okay, Lew, the deal is, you can use the car tonight
only if you wash and wax it this afternoon.

▲ *Comment: We often use "only if" when we mean to state both necessary and sufficient conditions, even though, literally speaking, it produces only the former. If Lew
were a critical thinker, he'd check this deal more carefully before getting out the hose
and bucket.*

There are other ways to produce conditionals, of course. In one of its
senses, the word "provided" (and the phrase "provided that") works like the
word "if" in introducing the antecedent of a conditional. "Moore will buy
the car, provided the seller throws in a ton of spare parts" is equivalent to the
same expression with the word "if" in place of "provided."

Necessary and Sufficient Conditions   Conditional claims are sometimes
spelled out in terms of necessary and sufficient conditions. Consider this
example:

The presence of oxygen is a necessary condition for combustion.

This tells us that we can't have combustion without oxygen, or "If we have
combustion (C), then we must have oxygen (O)." Notice that the necessary
condition becomes the consequent of a conditional: $C \rightarrow O$.

A sufficient condition *guarantees* whatever it is a sufficient condition
for. Being born in the United States is a sufficient condition for U.S. citizen-
ship—that's *all* one needs to be a U.S. citizen. Sufficient conditions are expressed as the antecedents of conditional claims, so we would say, "If John
was born in the United States (B), then John is a U.S. citizen (C)": $B \rightarrow C$.

Another "If" and "Only if" Confusion

Do you want to install and run News Menu 3.0 distributed by MSNBC Interactive News LLC? Caution: MSNBC Interactive News LLC asserts that this content is safe. You should install/view this content if you trust MSNBC Interactive News LLC to make that assertion.

—*Download caution on the MSNBC Web site*

Presumably they mean not "if" but "only if." Do you see why? In any case, this caution contains one heck of a weaseler (Chapter 4).

You should also notice the connection between "if" and "only if" on the one hand and necessary and sufficient conditions on the other. The word "if," by itself, introduces a sufficient condition; the phrase "only if" introduces a necessary condition. So the claim "X is a necessary condition for Y" would be symbolized "Y→X."

From time to time, one thing will be both a necessary and a sufficient condition for something else. For example, if Jean's payment of her dues to the National Truth-Functional Logic Society (NTFLS) guaranteed her continued membership (making such payment a sufficient condition) and there was no way for her to continue membership *without* paying her dues (making payment a necessary condition as well), then we could express such a situation as "Jean will remain a member of the NTFLS (M) if and only if she pays her dues (D)": (M→D) & (D→M).

We often play fast and loose with how we state necessary and sufficient conditions. A parent tells his daughter, "You can watch television only if you clean your room." Now, the youngster would ordinarily take cleaning her room as both a necessary and a sufficient condition for being allowed to watch television, and probably that's what a parent would intend by those words. But notice that the parent actually stated only a necessary condition; technically, he would not be going back on what he said if room cleaning turned out not to be sufficient for television privileges. Of course he'd better be prepared for more than a logic lesson from his daughter in such a case, and most of us would be on her side in the dispute. But, literally, it's the necessary condition that the phrase "only if" introduces, not the sufficient condition.

"Unless"   Consider the claim "Paula will foreclose unless Quincy pays up." Asked to symbolize this, we might come up with ~Q→P because the original claim is equivalent to "If Quincy doesn't pay up, then Paula will foreclose." But there's an even simpler way to do it. Ask yourself, what is the truth table for ~Q→P? If you've gained familiarity with the basic truth tables by this time, you realize that it's the same as the table for P ∨ Q. And, as a matter of fact, you can treat the word "unless" exactly like the word "or" and symbolize it with a "∨."

Playoff Logic

Following is an excerpt from an Ira Miller piece in the sports pages of the *San Francisco Chronicle* in which he sets up the Oakland Raiders' possibilities leading up to the 2002 Superbowl. When you're setting out lots of possible combinations of events, and drawing conclusions about what happens in which case, you are nearly bound to use some truth-functional logic. (You could arrange these things in terms of categorical logic, but the results would look very bizarre.)

Just for fun, symbolize the three sentences we've put in bold type. Use the following symbol dictionary. (Symbolizations are given in the answer section in the back of the book.)

B = The Raiders get a bye. (A bye is the ability to skip a game.)

C = The Raiders win one more game.

J = Raiders beat the Jets.

L = Jets (New York) lose to Buffalo next Sunday.

D = Raiders beat Denver.

F = Raiders finish 11–5.

A = The AFC East winner is 11–5.

N = New England wins the AFC East.

W = The Dolphins lose this week.

This has been such a wacky, unpredictable NFL season that something like this almost figured: Suddenly, the New York Jets are a much more important opponent for the Raiders than the Denver Broncos.

In fact, the Raiders' game on Sunday at Denver might have no bearing at all on whether they get a first-round bye in the playoffs.

Here's why: **(1) For the Raiders to earn that elusive bye** (forget home-field advantage; as a practical matter, it belongs to Pittsburgh), **they must win at least one more game, and it must be against the Jets, unless New York loses at home to Buffalo next Sunday.**

Because the Jets-Bills game will be over when the Raiders begin their game at Denver, they will know where they stand.

Basically, this is the deal for the Raiders. **(2) If they win both of their remaining games—at Denver, home vs. the Jets—and finish 12–4, they get a bye. But if they finish 11–5, and the AFC East winner also is 11–5, which is likely, they get a bye only if New England wins the AFC East.**

For the record, **(3) there is one combination that could clinch a bye for the Raiders this week: if the Dolphins and Jets lose and the Raiders beat Denver.**

At the moment, the Patriots are 10–5 and the Jets and Miami both are 9–5. The Raiders are the only opponent with a winning record remaining for any of those three teams. New England has a bye, then plays at 1–13 Carolina. The Jets play 2–12 Buffalo at home before coming to Oakland. Fast-fading Miami has two home games remaining, against 7–7 Atlanta and then Buffalo.

—San Francisco Chronicle, *December 25, 2001*

"Either..." Sometimes we need to know exactly where a disjunction begins; it's the job of the word "either" to show us. Compare the claims

> Either P and Q or R

and

> P and either Q or R.

These two claims say different things and have different truth tables, but the only difference between them is the location of the word "either"; without that word, the claim would be completely ambiguous. "Either" tells us that the disjunction begins with P in the first claim and Q in the second claim. So we would symbolize the first (P & Q) ∨ R and the second P & (Q ∨ R).

The word "if" does much the same job for conditionals as "either" does for disjunctions. Notice the difference between

> P and if Q then R

and

> If P and Q then R.

"If" tells us that the antecedent begins with Q in the first example and with P in the second. Hence, the second must have P & Q for the antecedent of its symbolization.

In general, the trick to symbolizing a claim correctly is to pay careful attention to exactly what the claim says—and this often means asking yourself just exactly what would make this claim false (or true). Then try to come up with a symbolization that says the same thing—that is false (or true) in exactly the same circumstances. There's no substitute for practice, so here's an exercise to work on.

Exercise 9-2

When we symbolize a claim, we're displaying its truth-functional structure. Show that you can figure out the structures of the following claims by symbolizing them. Use these letters for the first ten items:

> P = Parsons objects.
> Q = Quincy turns (or will turn) the radio down.
> R = Rachel closes (or will close) her door.

Use the symbols ~, &, ∨, and →. We suggest that, at least at first, you make symbolization a two-stage process: First, replace simple parts of claims with letters; then, replace logical words with logical symbols, and add parentheses as required. We'll do an example in two stages to show you what we mean.

Example

If Parsons objects, then Quincy will turn the radio down but Rachel will not close her door.

Stage 1: If P, then Q but ~R.
Stage 2: P→(Q & ~R)

▲ 1. If Parsons objects then Quincy will turn the radio down, and Rachel will close her door.

▲ 2. If Parsons objects, then Quincy will turn the radio down and Rachel will close her door.

3. If Parsons objects and Quincy turns the radio down then Rachel will close her door.

4. Parsons objects and if Quincy turns the radio down Rachel will close her door.

▲ 5. If Parsons objects then if Quincy turns the radio down Rachel will close her door.

6. If Parsons objects Quincy turns the radio down, and if Rachel closes her door Quincy turns the radio down.

7. Quincy turns the radio down if either Parsons objects or Rachel closes her door.

8. Either Parsons objects or, if Quincy turns the radio down, then Rachel will close her door.

9. If either Parsons objects or Quincy turns the radio down then Rachel will close her door.

10. If Parsons objects then either Quincy will turn the radio down or Rachel will close her door.

For the next ten items, use the following letters:

C = My car runs well.
S = I will sell my car.
F = I will have my car fixed.

▲ 11. If my car doesn't run well, then I will sell it.

▲ 12. It's not true that if my car runs well, then I will sell it.

13. I will sell my car only if it doesn't run well.

14. I won't sell my car unless it doesn't run well.

15. I will have my car fixed unless it runs well.

▲ 16. I will sell my car, but only if it doesn't run well.

17. Provided my car runs well, I won't sell it.

18. My car's running well is a sufficient condition for my not having it fixed.

19. My car's not running well is a necessary condition for my having it fixed.

▲ 20. I will neither have my car fixed nor sell it.

Exercise 9-3 _____

Construct truth tables for the symbolizations you produced for Exercise 9-2. Determine whether any of them are truth-functionally equivalent to any others. (Answers to items 1, 5, and 12 are provided in the answer section at the end of the book.)

Truth-Functional Arguments

Categorical syllogisms (discussed in Chapter 8) have a total of 256 forms. A truth-functional argument, by contrast, can take any of an infinite number of forms. Nevertheless, we have methods for testing for validity that are flexible enough to encompass every truth-functional argument. In the remainder of this chapter, we'll look at three of them: the truth-table method, the short truth-table method, and the method of deduction.

Before doing anything else, though, let's quickly review the concept of validity. An argument is *valid*, you'll recall, if and only if the truth of the premises guarantees the truth of the conclusion—that is, if the premises were true, the conclusion could not then be false. (In logic, remember, it doesn't matter whether the premises are *actually* true.)

The *truth-table test for validity* requires familiarity with the truth tables for the four truth-functional symbols, so go back and check yourself on those if you think you may not understand them clearly. Here's how the method works: We present all of the possible circumstances for an argument by building a truth table for it; then we simply look to see if there are any circumstances in which the premises are all true and the conclusion false. If there are such circumstances—one row of the truth table is all that's required—then the argument is invalid.

Let's look at a simple example. Let P and Q represent any two claims. Now look at the following symbolized argument:

$P \rightarrow Q$
$\sim P$
Therefore, $\sim Q$

We can construct a truth table for this argument by including a column for each premise and one for the conclusion:

P	Q	~P	P→Q	~Q
T	T	F	T	F
T	F	F	F	T
F	T	T	T	F
F	F	T	T	T

A Real-Life Example

Sometimes it takes effort to see the truth-functional logic in a passage. To illustrate, consider the letter to Marilyn vos Savant in the column printed below:

If homosexuality is a product of nature and not chosen, are fewer homosexuals being born every year? As homosexuality becomes more acceptable, it seems logical that passing genetic material to offspring should be declining.

—*WES ALEXANDER, Lilburn, Ga.*

We don't know how many gay people there were in the past any more than we know how many gay people there are now. Estimates of today's gay population range from 1% to 10%, but we don't know whether the number is up, down or stable.

The genetic situation is also unknown. For example, genes can be passed on by people who are themselves unaffected by them. And gay people could be born that way for reasons other than strictly genetic ones: Conditions during pregnancy play an important role in the development of the unborn baby.

Even the social situation is unclear. Gay people may want to have families as much (or as little) as straight people do. After all, when heterosexual couples make love, they usually aren't trying to conceive. A desire for a heterosexual relationship is definitely not the same thing as a desire to become a parent.

Anyway, population is determined by women—heterosexual *and* homosexual. A gay woman is just as capable of having a baby and, if she wants to be a mother, that's what she'll do. And like a straight woman, she has a choice of straight and gay partners. The main difference is that she's less likely to live with him afterward. Either way, the population statistics are unaffected.

Can you see that the letter has this form?

H = Homosexuality is becoming more acceptable
P = Homosexuality is a product of nature and not chosen
F = Fewer homosexuals are born every year

H
H → (P → F)
~F
/ ∴ ~P

Be sure to notice which premises Ask Marilyn disputes (and why).

The first two columns are reference columns; they list truth values for the letters that appear in the argument. The third and fourth columns appear under the two premises of the argument, and the fifth column is for the conclusion. Note that in the third row of the table, both premises are true and the conclusion is false. This tells us that it is possible for the premises of this argument to be true while the conclusion is false; thus, the argument is invalid. Because it doesn't matter what claims P and Q might stand for, the same is true for *every* argument of this pattern. Here's an example of such an argument:

> If the Saints beat the Forty-Niners, then the Giants will make the playoffs. But the Saints won't beat the Forty-Niners. So the Giants won't make the playoffs.

Using S for "The Saints beat (or will beat) the Forty-Niners," and G for "The Giants make (or will make) the playoffs," we can symbolize the argument like this:

$$S \rightarrow G$$
$$\underline{\sim S}$$
$$\sim G$$

The first premise is a conditional, and the other premise is the negation of the antecedent of that conditional. The conclusion is the negation of the conditional's consequent. It has exactly the same structure as the argument for which we just did the truth table; accordingly, it too is invalid.

Let's do another simple one:

> We're going to have large masses of arctic air (A) flowing into the Midwest unless the jet stream (J) moves south. Unfortunately, there's no chance of the jet stream's moving south. So you can bet there'll be arctic air flowing into the Midwest.

Symbolization gives us

$$A \vee J$$
$$\underline{\sim J}$$
$$A$$

Here's a truth table for the argument:

1 A	2 J	3 A ∨ J	4 ~J
T	T	T	F
T	F	T	T
F	T	T	F
F	F	F	T

Note that the first premise is represented in column 3 of the table, the second premise in column 4, and the conclusion in one of the reference columns, column 1. Now, let's recall what we're up to. We want to know whether this argument is valid—that is to say, is it possible for the premises to be true and the conclusion false? If there is such a possibility, it will turn up in the truth table because, remember, the truth table represents every possible situation with respect to the claims A and J. We find that the premises are both true in only one row, the second, and when we check the conclusion, A, we find it is true in that row. Thus, there is *no* row in which the premises are true and the conclusion false. So the argument is valid.

Here's an example of a rather more complicated argument:

> If Scarlet is guilty of the crime, then Ms. White must have left the back door unlocked and the colonel must have retired before ten o'clock. However, either Ms. White did not leave the back door unlocked, or the colonel did not retire before ten. Therefore, Scarlet is not guilty of the crime.

Let's assign some letters to the simple claims so that we can show this argument's pattern.

S = Scarlet is guilty of the crime.
W = Ms. White left the back door unlocked.
C = The colonel retired before ten o'clock.

Now we symbolize the argument to display this pattern:

$$S \rightarrow (W \mathbin{\&} C)$$
$$\underline{\sim W \lor \sim C}$$
$$\sim S$$

Let's think our way through this argument. As you read, refer back to the symbolized version above. Notice that the first premise is a conditional, with "Scarlet is guilty of the crime" as antecedent and a conjunction as consequent. In order for that conjunction to be true, both "Ms. White left the back door unlocked" and "The colonel retired before ten o'clock" have to be true, as you'll recall from the truth table for conjunctions. Now look at the second premise. It is a disjunction that tells us *either* Ms. White did not leave the back door unlocked *or* the colonel did not retire before ten. But if either or both of those disjuncts are true, at least one of the claims in our earlier conjunction is false. So it cannot be that *both* parts of the conjunction are true. This means the conjunction symbolized by W & C must be false. And so the consequent of the first premise is false. How can the entire premise be true, in that case? The only way is for the antecedent to be false as well. And that means that the conclusion, "Scarlet is not guilty of the crime," must be true.

All of this reasoning (and considerably more that we don't require) is implicit in the following truth table for the argument:

If Saddam doesn't back down, the U.S. should launch an air strike. He backed down. Therefore, we shouldn't launch a strike.

—WILLIAM COHEN, Secretary of Defense

Whoops, a mistake in logic.

Rule 1

Hitler was clearly intent on taking over the world. Mr. Buchanan thinks we should have stood by silently watching, and so, no, I would not say he belongs in the Republican Party.

The remark by Senator John McCain of Arizona is actually Rule 1 (page 331) with an unstated premise, in effect:

[If Mr. Buchanan thinks we should have stood by silently watching, then Mr. Buchanan does not belong in the Republican Party.]
Mr. Buchanan thinks we should have stood by silently watching.
Therefore, Mr. Buchanan does not belong in the Republican Party.

1 S	2 W	3 C	4 ~W	5 ~C	6 W & C	7 S →(W & C)	8 ~W ∨ ~C	9 ~S
T	T	T	F	F	T	T	F	F
T	T	F	F	T	F	F	T	F
T	F	T	T	F	F	F	T	F
T	F	F	T	T	F	F	T	F
F	T	T	F	F	T	T	F	T
F	T	F	F	T	F	T	T	T
F	F	T	T	F	F	T	T	T
F	F	F	T	T	F	T	T	T

We've numbered the columns at the top to make reference somewhat easier. The first three are our reference columns, columns 7 and 8 are for the premises of the argument, and column 9 is for the argument's conclusion. The remainder—4, 5, and 6—are for parts of some of the other symbolized claims; they could be left out if we desired, but they make filling in columns 7 and 8 a bit easier.

Once the table is filled in, evaluating the argument is easy. Just look to see whether there is any row in which the premises are true and the conclusion is false. One such row is enough to demonstrate the invalidity of the argument.

In the present case, we find that both premises are true only in the last three rows of the table. And in those rows, the conclusion is also true. So there is no set of circumstances—no row of the table—in which both premises are true and the conclusion is false. Therefore, the argument is valid.

Although filling out a complete truth table always produces the correct answer regarding a truth-functional argument's validity, it can be quite a tedious chore—in fact, life is much too short to spend much of it filling in truth tables. Fortunately, there are shorter and more manageable ways of finding such an answer. The easiest systematic way to determine the validity or invalidity of truth-functional arguments is the *short truth-table method*. Here's the idea behind it: Because, if an argument is invalid, there has to be at least one row in the argument's truth table where the premises are true and the conclusion is false, we'll look directly for such a row. Consider this symbolized argument:

P→Q
~Q→R
――――
~P→R

We begin by looking at the conclusion. Because it's a conditional, it can be made false only one way, by making its antecedent true and its consequent false. So we do that, by making P false and R false.

Can we now make both premises true? Yes, as it turns out, by making Q true. This case,

P	Q	R
F	T	F

makes both premises true and the conclusion false and thus proves the argument invalid. What we've done is produce the relevant row of the truth table without bothering to produce all the rest. Had the argument been valid, we would not have been able to produce such a row.

Here's how the method works with a valid argument. Consider this example:

(P ∨ Q)→R
S→Q
――――
S→R

The only way to make the conclusion false is to make S true and R false. So we do that:

P	Q	R	S
		F	T

Now, with S true, the second premise requires that we make Q true. So we do that next:

P	Q	R	S
	T	F	T

But now, there is no way at all to make the first premise true, because P ∨ Q is going to be true (because Q is true) and R is already false. Because there is no other way to make the conclusion false and the second premise true and because this way fails to make the first premise true, we can conclude that the argument is *valid.*

In some cases, there may be more than one way to make the conclusion false. Here's a symbolized example:

P & (Q ∨ R)
R → S
P → T
———————
S & T

Because the conclusion is a conjunction, it is false if either or both of its conjuncts are false, which means we could begin by making S true and T false, S false and T true, or both S and T false. This is trouble we'd like to avoid if possible, so let's see if there's someplace else we can begin making our assignment. (Remember: The idea is to try to assign true and false to the letters so as to make the premises true and the conclusion false. If we can do it, the argument is invalid.)

In this example, to make the first premise true, we *must* assign true to the letter P. Why? Because the premise is a conjunction and both of its parts must be true for the whole thing to be true. That's what we're looking for: places where we are *forced* to make an assignment of true or false to one or more letters. Then we make those assignments and see where they lead us. In this case, once we've made P true, we see that, to make the third premise true, we are forced to make T true (because a true antecedent and a false consequent would make the premise false, and we're trying to make our premises true).

After making T true, we see that, to make the conclusion false, S must be false. So we make that assignment. At this point we're nearly done, needing only assignments for Q and R.

P	Q	R	S	T
T			F	T

Are there any other assignments that we're forced to make? Yes: We must make R false to make the second premise true. Once we've done that, we see that Q must be true to preserve the truth of the first premise. And that completes the assignment:

P	Q	R	S	T
T	T	F	F	T

This is one row in the truth table for this argument—the only row, as it turned out—in which all the premises are true and the conclusion is false; thus, it is the row that proves the argument invalid.

Some Common Truth-Functional Argument Patterns

Some truth-functional patterns are so built into our thinking process that they almost operate at a subverbal level. But, rather than trust our subverbal skills, whatever those might be, let's identify three common patterns that are perfectly valid—their conclusions follow with certainty from their premises—and three invalid imposters—each of the imposters bears a resemblance to one of the good guys. We'll set them up in pairs:

Valid Argument Forms

In this case, the premises guarantee the conclusion.

1. Modus ponens (or affirming the antecedent)

   If P, then Q

   P

   _____

   Q

2. Modus tollens (or denying the consequent)

   If P, then Q

   Not-Q

   _____

   Not-P

3. Chain argument

   If P, then Q

   If Q, then R

   _____

   If P, then R

Invalid Argument Forms

Here, the premises can be true while the conclusion is false.

1-A. Affirming the consequent

   If P, then Q

   Q

   _____

   P

2-A. Denying the antecedent

   If P, then Q

   Not-P

   _____

   Not-Q

3-A. Undistributed middle (truth-functional version)

   If P, then Q

   If R, then Q

   _____

   If P, then R

In the preceding example, there was a premise that forced us to begin with a particular assignment to a letter. Sometimes neither the conclusion nor any of the premises forces an assignment on us. In that case we must use trial and error: Begin with one assignment that makes the conclusion false (or some premise true) and see if it will work. If not, try another assignment. If all fail, then the argument is valid.

Often, several rows of a truth table will make the premises true and the conclusion false; any one of them is all it takes to prove invalidity. Don't get the mistaken idea that, just because the premises are all true in one row and so is the conclusion, the conclusion follows from the premises—that is, that the argument must be valid. To be valid, the conclusion must be true in *every* row in which all the premises are true.

To review: Try to assign Ts and Fs to the letters in the symbolization so that all premises come out true and the conclusion comes out false. There may be more than one way to do it; any of them will do to prove the argument invalid. If it is impossible to make the premises and conclusion come out this way, the argument is valid.

Exercise 9-4

Construct full truth tables or use the short truth-table method to determine which of the following arguments are valid.

▲ 1. P ∨ ~Q
   ~Q
   ―――
   ~P

   2. P → Q
   ~Q
   ―――
   ~P

   3. ~ (P ∨ Q)
   R → P
   ―――
   ~R

▲ 4. P → (Q → R)
   ~ (P → Q)
   ―――――
   R

   5. P ∨ (Q → R)
   Q & ~R
   ―――――
   ~P

   6. (P → Q) ∨ (R → Q)
   P & (~P → ~R)
   ―――――――
   Q

▲ 7. (P & R) → Q
   ~Q
   ―――――
   ~P

   8. P & (~Q → ~P)
   R → ~Q
   ―――――
   ~R

   9. L ∨ ~J
   R → J
   ―――
   L → ~R

  10. ~F ∨ (G & H)
   P → F
   ―――――
   ~H → ~P

Exercise 9-5

Use either the long or short truth-table method to determine which of the following arguments are valid.

▲ 1. K → (L & G)
   M → (J & K)
   B & M
   ―――
   B & G

▲ 2. L ∨ (W → S)
    P ∨ ~S
    ~L → W
    ──────────
    P

▲ 3. M & P
    R → ~P
    F ∨ R
    G → M
    ──────────
    G & F

▲ 4. (D & G) → H
    M & (H → P)
    M → G
    ──────────
    D & P

▲ 5. R → S
    (S & B) → T
    T → E
    ──────────
    (R ∨ B) → E

Deductions

The next method we'll look at is less useful for proving an argument *invalid* than the truth-table methods, but it has some advantages in proving that an argument is valid. The method is that of **deduction.**

When we use this method, we actually deduce (or "derive") the conclusion from the premises by means of a series of basic truth-functionally valid argument patterns. This is a lot like "thinking through" the argument, taking one step at a time to see how, once we've assumed the truth of the premises, we eventually arrive at the conclusion. We'll consider some extended examples showing how the method works as we explain the first few basic argument patterns. We'll refer to these patterns as truth-functional rules because they govern what steps we're allowed to take in getting from the premises to the conclusion. (Your instructor may ask that you simply learn some or all of the basic valid argument patterns. It's a good idea to be able to identify these patterns whether you go on to construct deductions from them or not.)

■ Group I Rules: Elementary Valid Argument Patterns

This first group of rules should be learned before you go on to the Group II rules. Study them until you can work Exercise 9-6 with confidence.

Rule 1: Modus ponens (MP), also known as affirming the antecedent   Any argument of the pattern

$$P \rightarrow Q$$
$$\underline{P}$$
$$Q$$

is valid. If you have a conditional among the premises and if the antecedent of that conditional occurs as another premise, then by **modus ponens** the consequent of the conditional follows from those two premises. The claims involved do not have to be simple letters standing alone—it would have made no difference if, in place of P, we had had something more complicated, such as (P ∨ R), as long as that compound claim appeared everywhere that P appears in the pattern above. For example:

1. (P ∨ R)→Q   Premise
2. P ∨ R   Premise
3. Q   From the premises, by modus ponens

The idea, once again, is that if you have *any conditional whatsoever* on a line of your deduction and if you have the antecedent of that conditional on some other line, you can write down the consequent of the conditional on your new line.

If the consequent of the conditional is the conclusion of the argument, then the deduction is finished—the conclusion has been established. If it is not the conclusion of the argument you're working on, the consequent of the conditional can be listed just as if it were another premise to use in deducing the conclusion you're after. An example:

1. P→R
2. R→S
3. P   Therefore, S

We've numbered the three premises of the argument and set its conclusion off to the side. (Hereafter we'll use a slash and three dots [/∴] in place of "therefore" to indicate the conclusion.) Now, notice that line 1 is a conditional, and line 3 is its antecedent. Modus ponens allows us to write down the consequent of line 1 as a new line in our deduction:

4. R   1, 3, MP

At the right we've noted the abbreviation for the rule we used and the lines the rule required. These notes are called the *annotation* for the deduction. We can now make use of this new line in the deduction to get the conclusion we were originally after, namely, S.

5. S   2, 4, MP

Again, we used modus ponens, this time on lines 2 and 4. The same explanation as that for deriving line 4 from lines 1 and 3 applies here.

THE BORN LOSER reprinted by permission of Newspaper Enterprise Association, Inc.

Notice that the modus ponens rule and all other Group I rules can be used only on whole lines. This means that you can't find the items you need for MP as *parts* of a line, as in the following:

$$P \lor (Q \to R)$$
$$\frac{Q}{P \lor R} \qquad \text{(erroneous!)}$$

This is *not* a legitimate use of MP. We do have a conditional as *part* of the first line, and the second line is indeed the antecedent of that conditional. But the rule cannot be applied to parts of lines. The conditional required by rule MP must take up the entire line, as in the following:

$$P \to (Q \lor R)$$
$$\frac{P}{Q \lor R}$$

Rule 2: Modus tollens (MT), also known as denying the consequent   The **modus tollens** pattern is this:

$$P \to Q$$
$$\frac{\sim Q}{\sim P}$$

If you have a conditional claim as one premise and if one of your other premises is the negation of the consequent of that conditional, you can write down the negation of the conditional's antecedent as a new line in your deduction. Here's a deduction that uses both of the first two rules:

```
1. (P & Q)→R
2. S
3. S→~R          /∴~(P & Q)
4. ~R            2, 3, MP
5. ~(P & Q)      1, 4, MT
```

In this deduction we derived line 4 from lines 2 and 3 by modus ponens, and then 4 and 1 gave us line 5, which is what we were after, by modus tollens. The fact that the antecedent of line 1 is itself a compound claim, (P & Q), is not important; our line 5 is the antecedent of the conditional with a negation sign in front of it, and that's all that counts.

Rule 3: Chain argument (CA)

$$\frac{\begin{array}{c} P \to Q \\ Q \to R \end{array}}{P \to R}$$

The **chain argument** rule allows you to derive a conditional from two you already have, provided the antecedent of one of your conditionals is the same as the consequent of the other.

Rule 4: Disjunctive argument (DA)

$$\frac{\begin{array}{c} P \vee Q \\ \sim P \end{array}}{Q} \qquad \frac{\begin{array}{c} P \vee Q \\ \sim Q \end{array}}{P}$$

From a disjunction and the negation of one disjunct, the other disjunct may be derived.

Rule 5: Simplification (SIM)   This one is obvious, but we need it for obvious reasons:

$$\frac{P \& Q}{P} \qquad \frac{P \& Q}{Q}$$

If the conjunction is true, then of course the conjuncts must all be true. You can pull out one conjunct from any conjunction and make it the new line in your deduction.

If the Dollar Falls . . .

The valid argument patterns are in fact fairly common. Here's one in an article in *Time* as to why a weakening dollar is a threat to the stock market:

> Why should we care? . . . If the dollar continues to drop, investors may be tempted to move their cash to currencies on the upswing. That would drive the U.S. market lower. . . . Because foreigners hold almost 40% of U.S. Treasury securities, any pullout would risk a spike in interest rates that would ultimately slaughter the . . . market.

The chain argument here is reasonably obvious. In effect: If the dollar falls, then investors move their cash to currencies on the upswing. If investors move their cash to currencies on the upswing, then the U.S. market goes lower. If the U.S. market goes lower, then interest rates on U.S. Treasury securities rise. If interest rates on U.S. Treasury securities rise, then the . . . market dies. [Therefore, if the dollar falls, then the . . . market dies.]

Rule 6: Conjunction (CONJ)

P
Q
―――
P & Q

This rule allows you to put any two lines of a deduction together in the form of a conjunction.

Rule 7: Addition (ADD)

$$\frac{P}{P \lor Q} \qquad \frac{Q}{P \lor Q}$$

Clearly, no matter what claims P and Q might be, if P is true then *either* P or Q must be true. The truth of one disjunct is all it takes to make the whole disjunction true.

Rule 8: Constructive dilemma (CD)

P → Q
R → S
P ∨ R
―――
Q ∨ S

The disjunction of the antecedents of any two conditionals allows the derivation of the disjunction of their consequents.

Rule 9: Destructive dilemma (DD)

$$P \rightarrow Q$$
$$R \rightarrow S$$
$$\underline{\sim Q \lor \sim S}$$
$$\sim P \lor \sim R$$

The disjunction of the negations of the consequents of two conditionals allows the derivation of the disjunction of the negations of their antecedents. (Refer to the pattern above as you read this, and it will make a lot more sense.)

Exercise 9-6

For each of the following groups of symbolized claims, identify which of the Group I rules was used to derive the last line.

▲ 1. P→(Q & R)
     (Q & R)→(S ∨ T)
     P→(S ∨ T)

▲ 2. (P & S) ∨ (T→R)
     ~(P & S)
     T→R

▲ 3. P ∨ (Q & R)
     (Q & R)→S
     P→T
     S ∨ T

▲ 4. (P ∨ R)→Q
     ~Q
     ~(P ∨ R)

▲ 5. (Q→T)→S
     ~S ∨ ~P
     R→P
     ~(Q→T) ∨ ~R

Exercise 9-7

Construct deductions for each of the following using the Group I rules. Each can be done in just a step or two (except number 10, which takes more).

▲ 1. 1. R→P
     2. Q→R   / ∴ Q→P

  2. 1. P→S
     2. P ∨ Q
     3. Q→R   / ∴ S ∨ R

God and Evil

An age-old argument that God is either not all powerful or not all good goes like this:

> If God is all powerful, then he would be able to abolish evil.
> If God is all good, then he would not allow evil to be.
> Either God is not able to abolish evil, or God allows evil to be.
> Therefore, either God is not all powerful, or God is not all good.

This argument, you can see, is just an instance of Rule 9 (see page 336).

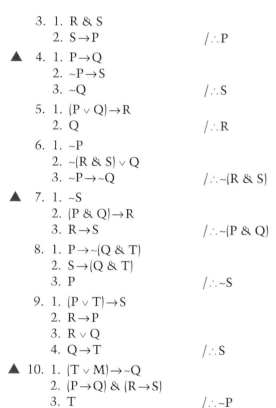

   3. 1. R & S
      2. S→P   /∴P

▲ 4. 1. P→Q
      2. ~P→S
      3. ~Q   /∴S

   5. 1. (P ∨ Q)→R
      2. Q   /∴R

   6. 1. ~P
      2. ~(R & S) ∨ Q
      3. ~P→~Q   /∴~(R & S)

▲ 7. 1. ~S
      2. (P & Q)→R
      3. R→S   /∴~(P & Q)

   8. 1. P→~(Q & T)
      2. S→(Q & T)
      3. P   /∴~S

   9. 1. (P ∨ T)→S
      2. R→P
      3. R ∨ Q
      4. Q→T   /∴S

▲ 10. 1. (T ∨ M)→~Q
      2. (P→Q) & (R→S)
      3. T   /∴~P

■ Group II Rules: Truth-Functional Equivalences

A claim or part of a claim may be replaced by any claim or part of a claim to which it is equivalent by one of the following equivalence rules. Don't despair if this sounds complicated. The way such replacement works will become clear after a few examples.

There are a few differences between these rules about equivalences and the Group I rules. First, these rules allow us to go two ways instead of one—from either claim to its equivalent. Second, these rules allow us to re-place part of a claim with an equivalent part, rather than having to deal with entire lines of a deduction all at once. In the examples that follow the first few rules, watch for both of these differences.

We'll use a double-headed arrow (↔) to indicate the equivalence of two claims.

Rule 10: Double negation (DN)

$$P \leftrightarrow {\sim}{\sim}P$$

This rule allows you to add or remove two negation signs in front of any claim, whether simple or compound. For example, this rule allows the derivation of either of the following from the other

$$P \rightarrow (Q \vee R) \qquad P \rightarrow {\sim}{\sim}(Q \vee R)$$

because the rule guarantees that (Q ∨ R) and its double negation, ~~(Q ∨ R), are equivalent. This in turn guarantees that P→(Q ∨ R) and P→~~(Q ∨ R) are equivalent, and hence that each implies the other.

Here's an example of DN at work:

1. P ∨ ~(Q→R)
2. (Q→R)   / ∴ P
3. ~~(Q→R)   2, DN
4. P   1, 3, DA

Rule 11: Commutation (COM)

$$(P \mathbin{\&} Q) \leftrightarrow (Q \mathbin{\&} P)$$
$$(P \vee Q) \leftrightarrow (Q \vee P)$$

This rule simply allows any conjunction or disjunction to be "turned around," so that the conjuncts or disjuncts occur in reverse order. Here's an example:

$$P \rightarrow (Q \vee R) \qquad P \rightarrow (R \vee Q)$$

Notice that commutation is used on *part* of the claim—just the consequent.

Rule 12: Implication (IMPL)   This rule allows us to change a conditional into a disjunction and vice versa.

$$(P \rightarrow Q) \leftrightarrow ({\sim}P \vee Q)$$

Notice that the antecedent always becomes the negated disjunct, or vice versa, depending on which way you're going. Another example:

$$(P \vee Q) \rightarrow R \leftrightarrow {\sim}(P \vee Q) \vee R$$

Rule 13: Contraposition (CONTR)   This rule may remind you of the categorical operation of contraposition (see Chapter 8)—this rule is its truth-functional version.

$$(P \rightarrow Q) \leftrightarrow (\sim Q \rightarrow \sim P)$$

This rule allows us to exchange the places of a conditional's antecedent and consequent, but only by putting on or taking off a negation sign in front of each. Here's another example:

$$(P \& Q) \rightarrow (P \vee Q) \leftrightarrow \sim (P \vee Q) \rightarrow \sim (P \& Q)$$

Sometimes you want to perform contraposition on a symbolization that doesn't fit either side of the equivalence because it has a negation sign in front of either the antecedent or the consequent but not both. You can do what you want in such cases, but it takes two steps, one applying double negation and one applying contraposition. Here's an example:

$(P \vee Q) \rightarrow \sim R$
$\sim \sim (P \vee Q) \rightarrow \sim R$ Double negation
$R \rightarrow \sim (P \vee Q)$ Contraposition

Your instructor may allow you to combine these steps (and refer to both DN and CONTR in your annotation).

Rule 14: DeMorgan's Laws (DEM)

$\sim (P \& Q) \leftrightarrow (\sim P \vee \sim Q)$
$\sim (P \vee Q) \leftrightarrow (\sim P \& \sim Q)$

Notice that when the negation sign is "moved inside" the parentheses, the "&" changes into a "$\vee$," or vice versa. It's important not to confuse the use of the negation sign in DeMorgan's Laws with that of the minus sign in algebra. Notice that when you take $\sim (P \vee Q)$ and "move the negation sign in," you do *not* get $(\sim P \vee \sim Q)$. The wedge must be changed to an ampersand or vice versa whenever DEM is used. You can think of $\sim (P \vee Q)$ and $(\sim P \& \sim Q)$ as saying "neither P nor Q," and you can think of $\sim (P \& Q)$ and $(\sim P \vee \sim Q)$ as saying "not both P and Q."

Rule 15: Exportation (EXP)

$$[P \rightarrow (Q \rightarrow R)] \leftrightarrow [(P \& Q) \rightarrow R]$$

Square brackets are used exactly as parentheses are. In English, the exportation rule says that "If P, then if Q, then R" is equivalent to "If both P and Q, then R." (The commas are optional in both claims.) If you look back to Exercise 9-2, items 3 and 5 (page 321), you'll notice that, according to the exportation rule, each of these can replace the other.

Rule 16: Association (ASSOC)

[P & (Q & R)] ↔ [(P & Q) & R]
[P ∨ (Q ∨ R)] ↔ [(P ∨ Q) ∨ R]

Association simply tells us that, when we have three items joined together with wedges or with ampersands, it doesn't matter which ones we group together. If we have a long disjunction with more than two disjuncts, it still requires only one of them to be true for the entire disjunction to be true; if it's a conjunction, then all the conjuncts have to be true, no matter how many of them there are, in order for the entire conjunction to be true. Your instructor may allow you to drop parentheses in such symbolizations, but if you're developing these rules as a formal system, he or she may not.

Rule 17: Distribution (DIST)   This rule allows us to "spread a conjunct across a disjunction" or to "spread a disjunct across a conjunction." In the first example below, look at the left-hand side of the equivalence. The P, which is conjoined with a disjunction, is picked up and dropped (distributed) across the disjunction by being conjoined with each part. (This is easier to understand if you see it done on a chalkboard than by trying to figure it out from the page in front of you.) The two versions of the rule, like those of DEM, allow us to do exactly with the wedge what we're allowed to do with the ampersand.

[P & (Q ∨ R)] ↔ [(P & Q) ∨ (P & R)]
[P ∨ (Q & R)] ↔ [(P ∨ Q) & (P ∨ R)]

Rule 18: Tautology (TAUT)

(P ∨ P) ↔ P
(P & P) ↔ P

This rule allows a few obvious steps; they are sometimes necessary to "clean up" a deduction.

Figure 2 shows some deductions that use rules from both Group I and Group II. Look at them carefully, covering up the lines with a piece of paper and uncovering them one at a time as you progress. This gives you a chance to figure out what you might do before you see the answer. In any case, make sure you understand how each line was achieved before going on. If necessary, look up the rule used to make sure you understand it.

The first example is long, but fairly simple. Length is not always proportional to difficulty.

1. P→(Q→R)
2. (T→P) & (S→Q)
3. T & S   /∴R
4. T→P   2, SIM

Group I

1. Modus ponens (MP) $\quad$ P → Q $\quad$ P $\quad$ Q	2. Modus tollens (MT) $\quad$ P → Q $\quad$ ~Q $\quad$ ~P	3. Chain argument (CA) $\quad$ P → Q $\quad$ Q → R $\quad$ P → R
4. Disjunctive $\quad$ argument (DA) $\quad$ P v Q $\quad$ P v Q $\quad$ ~P $\qquad$ ~Q $\quad$ Q $\qquad\quad$ P	5. Simplification (SIM) $\quad$ P & Q $\quad$ P & Q $\quad$ P $\qquad\quad$ Q	6. Conjunction (CONJ) $\quad$ P $\quad$ Q $\quad$ P & Q
7. Addition (ADD) $\quad$ P $\qquad\quad$ Q $\quad$ P v Q $\quad$ P v Q	8. Constructive $\quad$ dilemma (CD) $\quad$ P → Q $\quad$ R → S $\quad$ P v R $\quad$ Q v S	9. Destructive dilemma (DD) $\quad$ P → Q $\quad$ R → S $\quad$ ~Q v ~S $\quad$ ~P v ~R

Group II

10. Double negation (DN) $\quad$ P ⟷ ~~P	11. Commutation (COM) $\quad$ (P & Q) ⟷ (Q & P) $\quad$ (P v Q) ⟷ (Q v P)	12. Implication (IMPL) $\quad$ (P → Q) ⟷ (~P v Q)
13. Contraposition (CONTR) $\quad$ (P → Q) ⟷ (~Q → ~P)	14. DeMorgan's Laws (DEM) $\quad$ ~(P v Q) ⟷ (~P & ~Q) $\quad$ ~(P & Q) ⟷ (~P v ~Q)	15. Exportation (EXPORT) [P → (Q → R)] ⟷ [(P & Q) → R]
16. Association (ASSOC) [P & (Q & R)] ⟷ [(P & Q) & R] [P v (Q v R)] ⟷ [(P v Q) v R]	17. Distribution (DIST) [P & (Q v R)] ⟷ [(P & Q) v (P & R)] [P v (Q & R)] ⟷ [(P v Q) & (P v R)]	18. Tautology (TAUT) $\quad$ (P v P) ⟷ P $\quad$ (P & P) ⟷ P

FIGURE 2   Truth-Functional Rules for Deductions

5.	S → Q	2, SIM
6.	T	3, SIM
7.	S	3, SIM
8.	P	4, 6, MP
9.	Q	5, 7, MP
10.	P & Q	8, 9, CONJ
11.	(P & Q) → R	1, EXP
12.	R	10, 11, MP

It's often difficult to tell how to proceed when you first look at a deduction problem. One strategy is to work backward. Look at what you want to get, look at what you have, and see what you would need in order to get what you want. Then determine where you would get *that*, and so on. We'll explain in terms of the following problem.

1. P→(Q & R)
2. S→~Q
3. S   / ∴ ~P

4. ~Q   2, 3, MP
5. ~Q ∨ ~R   4, ADD
6. ~(Q & R)   5, DEM
7. ~P   1, 6, MT

We began by wanting ~P as our conclusion. If we're familiar with modus tollens, it's clear from line 1 that we can get ~P if we can get the negation of line 1's consequent, which would be ~(Q & R). That in turn is the same as ~Q ∨ ~R, which we can get if we can get either ~Q or ~R. So now we're looking for someplace in the first three premises where we can get ~Q. That's easy: from lines 2 and 3, by modus ponens. A little practice and you'll be surprised how easy these strategies are to work, at least *most* of the time!

Exercise 9-8

The annotations that explain how each line was derived have been left off the following deductions. For each line, supply the rule used and the numbers of any earlier lines the rule requires.

▲ 1.   1. P→Q   (Premise)
        2. R→S   (Premise)
        3. Q→~S   (Premise) / ∴ P→~R
        4. P→~S
        5. ~S→~R
        6. P→~R

   2.   1. ~P   (Premise)
        2. (Q→R) & (R→Q)   (Premise)
        3. R ∨ P   (Premise) / ∴ Q
        4. R
        5. R→Q
        6. Q

   3.   1. P→Q   (Premise)
        2. R→(~S ∨ T)   (Premise)
        3. ~P→R   (Premise) / ∴ (~Q & S)→T

    4. ~Q→~P
    5. ~Q→R
    6. ~Q→(~S ∨ T)
    7. ~Q→(S→T)
    8. (~Q & S)→T

▲ 4. 1. (P & Q)→T   (Premise)
     2. P   (Premise)
     3. ~Q→~P   (Premise) /∴ T
     4. P→Q
     5. Q
     6. P & Q
     7. T

  5. 1. ~(S ∨ R)   (Premise)
     2. P→S   (Premise)
     3. T→(P ∨ R)   (Premise) /∴ ~T
     4. ~S & ~R
     5. ~S
     6. ~P
     7. ~R
     8. ~P & ~R
     9. ~(P ∨ R)
    10. ~T

Exercise 9-9

Derive the indicated conclusions from the premises supplied.

▲ 1. 1. P & Q
    2. P→R   /∴ R

▲ 2. 1. R→S
    2. ~P ∨ R   /∴ P→S

  3. 1. P ∨ Q
    2. R & ~Q   /∴ P

▲ 4. 1. ~P ∨ (~Q ∨ R)
    2. P   /∴ Q→R

  5. 1. T ∨ P
    2. P→S   /∴ ~T→S

  6. 1. Q ∨ ~S
    2. Q→P   /∴ S→P

  7. 1. ~S ∨ ~R
    2. P→(S & R)   /∴ ~P

▲ 8. 1. ~Q & (~S & ~T)
    2. P→(Q ∨ S)   /∴ ~P

9. 1. P ∨ (S & R)
    2. T→(~P & ~R)   /∴~T
10. 1. (S & P)→R
    2. S   /∴P→R

Exercise 9-10

Derive the indicated conclusions from the premises supplied.

▲ 1. 1. P→R
       2. R→Q   /∴~P ∨ Q

   2. 1. ~P ∨ S
       2. ~T→~S   /∴P→T

   3. 1. F→R
       2. L→S
       3. ~C
       4. (R & S)→C   /∴~F ∨ ~L

▲ 4. 1. P ∨ (Q & R)
       2. (P ∨ Q)→S   /∴S

   5. 1. (S & R)→P
       2. (R→P)→W
       3. S   /∴W

   6. 1. ~L→(~P→M)
       2. ~(P ∨ L)   /∴M

▲ 7. 1. (M ∨ R) & P
       2. ~S→~P
       3. S→~M   /∴R

   8. 1. Q→L
       2. P→M
       3. R ∨ P
       4. R→(Q & S)   /∴~M→L

   9. 1. Q→S
       2. P→(S & L)
       3. ~P→Q
       4. S→R   /∴R & S

▲ 10. 1. P ∨ (R & Q)
       2. R→~P
       3. Q→T   /∴R→T

■ Conditional Proof

Conditional proof (CP) is both a rule and a strategy for constructing a deduction. It is based on the following idea: Let's say we want to produce a deduction for a conditional claim, P→Q. If we produce such a deduction, what have we proved? We've proved the equivalent of "If P were true, then Q would be true." One way to do this is simply to *assume* that P is true (that is, to add it as an additional premise) and then to prove that, on that assumption, Q has to be true. If we can do that—prove Q after assuming P—then we'll have proved that if P then Q, or P→Q. Let's look at an example of how to do this; then we'll explain it again.

Here is the way we'll use CP as a new rule: Simply write down the antecedent of whatever conditional we want to prove, drawing a circle around the number of that step in the deduction; in the annotation, write "CP Premise" for that step. Here's what it looks like:

1. P ∨ (Q→R)   Premise
2. Q   Premise   /∴ ~P→R
③ ~P   CP Premise

Then, after we've proved what we want—the consequent of the conditional—in the next step, we write the full conditional down. Then we draw a line in the margin to the left of the deduction from the premise with the circled number to the number of the line we deduced from it. (See below for an example.) In the annotation for the last line in the process, list *all the steps from the circled number to the one with the conditional's consequent,* and give CP as the rule. Drawing the line that connects our earlier CP premise with the step we derived from it indicates we've stopped making the assumption that the premise, which is now the antecedent of our conditional in our last step, is true. This is known as *discharging the premise.* Here's how the whole thing looks:

1. P ∨ (Q→R)   Premise
2. Q   Premise   /∴ ~P→R
③ ~P   CP Premise
4. Q→R   1, 3, DA
5. R   2, 4, MP
6. ~P→R   3–5, CP

Here's the promised second explanation. Look at the example. Think of the conclusion as saying that, given the two original premises, *if we had ~P, we could get R.* One way to find out if this is so is to *give ourselves ~P* and then see if we can get R. In step 3, we do exactly that: We give ourselves ~P. Now, by circling the number, we indicate that *this is a premise we've given ourselves* (our "CP premise") and therefore that it's one we'll have to get rid of before we're done. (We can't be allowed to invent, use, and keep just any old premises we like—we could prove *anything* if we could do that.) But once we've given ourselves ~P, getting R turns out to be easy! Steps 4 and 5 are pretty obvious, aren't they? (If not, you need more practice with the other rules.) In steps 3 through 5 what we've actually proved is that *if we had ~P,* then we could get R. So we're justified in writing down step 6 because that's exactly what step 6 says: If ~P, then R.

Once we've got our conditional, ~P→R, we're no longer dependent on the CP premise, so we draw our line in the left margin from the last step that depended on the CP premise back to the premise itself. We *discharge* the premise.

Here are some very important restrictions on the CP rule:

1. CP can be used only to produce a conditional claim: After we discharge a CP premise, the very next step must be a conditional with the preceding step as consequent and the CP premise as antecedent. [Remember that lots of claims are equivalent to conditional claims. For example, to get (~P ∨ Q), just prove (P→Q), and then use IMPL.]

2. If more than one use is made of CP at a time—that is, if more than one CP premise is brought in—they must be discharged in exactly the reverse order from that in which they were assumed. This means that the lines that run from different CP premises must not cross each other. See examples below.

3. Once a CP premise has been discharged, no steps derived from it—those steps encompassed by the line drawn in the left margin—may be used in the deduction. (They depend on the CP premise, you see, and it's been discharged.)

4. All CP premises must be discharged.

This sounds a lot more complicated than it actually is. Refer back to these restrictions on CP as you go through the examples, and they will make a good deal more sense.

Here's an example of CP in which two additional premises are assumed and discharged in reverse order.

```
 1. P→[Q ∨ (R & S)]      Premise
 2. (~Q→S)→T             Premise        /∴ P→T
 3. P                     CP Premise
 4. Q ∨ (R & S)          1, 3, MP
 5. ~Q                    CP Premise
 6. R & S                4, 5, DA
 7. S                        6, SIM
 8. ~Q→S                  5–7, CP
 9. T                     2, 8, MP
10. P→T                   3–9, CP
```

Notice that the additional premise added at step 5 is discharged when step 8 is completed, and the premise at step 3 is discharged when step 10 is completed. Once again: Whenever you discharge a premise, you must make that premise the antecedent of the next step in your deduction. (You might try the preceding deduction without using CP; doing so will help you appreciate having the rule, however hard to learn it may seem at the moment. Using CP makes many deductions shorter, easier, or both.

Here are three more examples of the correct use of CP:

```
 1. (R→~P)→S              Premise
 2. S→(T ∨ Q)             Premise        /∴ ~(R & P)→(T ∨ Q)
 3. ~(R & P)              CP Premise
 4. ~R ∨ ~P               3, DEM
 5. R→~P                  4, IMPL
 6. S                     1, 5, MP
 7. (T ∨ Q)               2, 6, MP
 8. ~(R & P)→(T ∨ Q)   3–7, CP
```

In this case, one use of CP follows another:

```
 1. (P ∨ Q)→R                    Premise
 2. (S ∨ T)→U                    Premise        /∴ (~R→~P) & (~U→~T)
 3. ~R                           CP Premise
 4. ~(P ∨ Q)                     1, 3, MT
 5. ~P & ~Q                      4, DEM
 6. ~P                           5, SIM
 7. ~R→~P                        3–6, CP
 8. ~U                           CP Premise
 9. ~(S ∨ T)                     2, 8, MT
10. ~S & ~T                      9, DEM
11. ~T                           10, SIM
12. ~U→~T                        8–11, CP
13. (~R→~P) & (~U→~T)   7, 12, CONJ
```

In this case, one use of CP occurs "inside" another:

```
 1. R→(S & Q)                    Premise
 2. P→M                          Premise
 3. S→(Q→~M)                     Premise
 4. (J ∨ T)→B                    Premise        /∴ R→(J→(B & ~P))
 5. R                            CP Premise
 6. J                            CP Premise
 7. J ∨ T                        6, ADD
 8. B                            4, 7, MP
 9. (S & Q)                      1, 5, MP
10. (S & Q)→~M                   3, EXP
11. ~M                           9, 10, MP
12. ~P                           2, 11, MT
13. B & ~P                       8, 12, CONJ
14. J→(B & ~P)                   6–13, CP
15. R→(J→(B & ~P))              5–14, CP
```

Before ending this section on deductions, we should point out that our system of truth-functional logic has a couple of properties that are of great theoretical interest: It is both sound and complete. To say that a logic system is sound (in the sense most important to us here) is to say that *every deduction that can be constructed using the rules of the system constitutes a valid argument.* Another way to say this is that no deduction or string of deductions allows us to begin with true sentences and wind up with false ones.

To say that our system is complete is to say that *for every truth-functionally valid argument that there is (or even could be), there is a deduction in our system of rules that allows us to deduce the conclusion of that argument from its premises.* That is, if conclusion C really does follow validly from premises P and Q, then we know for certain that it is possible to construct a deduction beginning with just P and Q and ending with C.

We could have produced a system that is both sound and complete and that had many fewer rules than our system has. However, in such systems, deductions tend to be very difficult to construct. Although our system is burdened with a fairly large number of rules, once you learn them, producing proofs is not too difficult. So, in a way, every system of logic is a trade-off of a sort. You can make the system small and elegant but difficult to use, or you can make it larger and less elegant but more efficient in actual use. (The smaller systems are more efficient for some purposes, but those purposes are quite different from ours in this book.)

Recap

This chapter has been concerned with the truth-functional structures of claims and arguments. These structures result from the logical connections between claims, connections that are represented in English by words such as "and," "or," "if . . . then," and so forth.

Truth-functional connections are explained by truth tables, which display the conditions under which a claim is true and those under which it is false. Truth tables are used to define truth-functional symbols, which stand for logical connections between claims in symbolizations. To symbolize a claim is simply to reduce it to its truth-functional structure.

To evaluate truth-functional arguments—which are just arguments that depend on truth-functional connections for their validity—we learned first about the full truth-table method. This method requires that we set out a truth table for an argument and then check to see whether there are circumstances in which the premises are true and the conclusion false. In the short truth-table method, we look directly for such rows: If we find one, the argument is invalid; if we don't, it is valid.

We can improve our efficiency in determining the validity of many truth-functional arguments by learning to recognize certain elementary valid argument patterns. These patterns can be linked up to produce deductions, which are sequences of valid truth-functional inferences.

Additional Exercises

Exercise 9-11

Display the truth-functional structure of the following claims by symbolizing them. Use the letters indicated.

   D = We do something to reduce the deficit.
   B = The balance of payments gets worse.
   C = There is (or will be) a financial crisis.

▲ 1. The balance of payments will not get worse if we do something to reduce the deficit.

2. There will be no financial crisis unless the balance of payments gets worse.

3. Either the balance of payments will get worse or, if no action is taken on the deficit, there will be a financial crisis.

▲ 4. The balance of payments will get worse only if we don't do something to reduce the deficit.

5. Action cannot be taken on the deficit if there's a financial crisis.

6. I can tell you about whether we'll do something to reduce the deficit and whether our balance of payments will get worse: Neither one will happen.

▲ 7. In order for there to be a financial crisis, the balance of payments will have to get worse and there will have to be no action taken to reduce the deficit.

8. We can avoid a financial crisis only by taking action on the deficit and keeping the balance of payments from getting worse.

9. The *only* thing that can prevent a financial crisis is our doing something to reduce the deficit.

Exercise 9-12

For each of the numbered claims below, there is exactly one lettered claim that is equivalent. Identify the equivalent claim for each item. (Some lettered claims are equivalent to more than one numbered claim, so it will be necessary to use some letters more than once.)

▲ 1. Oil prices will drop if the OPEC countries increase their production.

2. Oil prices will drop only if the OPEC countries increase their production.

3. Neither will oil prices drop nor will the OPEC countries increase their production.

▲ 4. Oil prices cannot drop unless the OPEC countries increase their production.

5. The only thing that can prevent oil prices dropping is the OPEC countries' increasing their production.

6. A drop in oil prices is necessary for the OPEC countries to increase their production.

▲ 7. All it takes for the OPEC countries to increase their production is a drop in oil prices.

8. The OPEC countries will not increase their production while oil prices drop; each possibility excludes the other.

a. It's not the case that oil prices will drop, and it's not the case that the OPEC countries will increase their production.

b. If OPEC countries increase their production, then oil prices will drop.

c. Only if OPEC countries increase their production will oil prices drop.

d. Either the OPEC countries will not increase their production, or oil prices will not drop.

e. If the OPEC countries do not increase production, then oil prices will drop.

Exercise 9-13

Construct deductions for each of the following. (Try these first without using conditional proof.)

▲ 1. 1. P
2. Q & R
3. (Q & P)→S   /∴ S

2. 1. (P ∨ Q) & R
2. (R & P)→S
3. (Q & R)→S   /∴ S

3. 1. P→(Q→~R)
2. (~R→S) ∨ T
3. ~T & P   /∴ Q→S

▲ 4. 1. P ∨ Q
2. (Q ∨ U)→(P→T)
3. ~P
4. (~P ∨ R)→(Q→S)   /∴ T ∨ S

5. 1. (P→Q) & R
2. ~S
3. S ∨ (Q→S)   /∴ P→T

6. 1. P→(Q & R)
2. R→(Q→S)   /∴ P→S

▲ 7. 1. P→Q   /∴P→(Q ∨ R)
    8. 1. ~P ∨ ~Q
        2. (Q→S)→R   /∴P→R
    9. 1. S
        2. P→(Q & R)
        3. Q→~S   /∴~P
▲ 10. 1. (S→Q)→~R
        2. (P→Q)→R   /∴~Q

Exercise 9-14

Use the rule of conditional proof to construct deductions for each of the
following.

▲ 1. 1. P→Q
        2. P→R   /∴P→(Q & R)
    2. 1. P→Q
        2. R→Q   /∴(P ∨ R)→Q
    3. 1. P→(Q→R)   /∴(P→Q)→(P→R)
▲ 4. 1. P→(Q ∨ R)
        2. T→(S & ~R)   /∴(P & T)→Q
    5. 1. ~P→(~Q→~R)
        2. ~(R & ~P)→~S   /∴S→Q
    6. 1. P→(Q→R)
        2. (T→S) & (R→T)   /∴P→(Q→S)
▲ 7. 1. P ∨ (Q & R)
        2. T→~(P ∨ U)
        3. S→(Q→~R)   /∴~S ∨ ~T
    8. 1. (P ∨ Q)→R
        2. (P→S)→T   /∴R ∨ T
    9. 1. P→~Q
        2. ~R→(S & Q)   /∴P→R
▲ 10. 1. (P & Q) ∨ R
        2. ~R ∨ Q   /∴P→Q

Exercise 9-15

Display the truth-functional form of the following arguments by symbolizing
them; then use the truth-table method, the short truth-table method, or the
method of deduction to prove them valid or invalid. Use the letters provided.
(We've used underscores in the example and in the first two problems to help
you connect the letters with the proper claims.)

Example

> If M̲aria does not g̲o to the movies, then she will h̲elp Bob with his logic
> homework. Bob will f̲ail the course unless Maria h̲elps him with his
> logic homework. Therefore, if M̲aria goes to the movies, Bob will f̲ail
> the course. (M, H, F)

Symbolization

> 1. ~M→H   (Premise)
> 2. ~H→F   (Premise)   /∴ M→F

Truth Table

M	H	F	~M	~H	~M→H	~H→F	M→F
T	T	T	F	F	T	T	T
T	T	F	F	F	T	T	F

We need to go only as far as the second row of the table, since both premises
come out true and the conclusion comes out false in that row.

▲ 1. If it's c̲old, Dale's motorcycle won't s̲tart. If Dale is not l̲ate for work, then
his motorcycle must have s̲tarted. Therefore, if it's c̲old, Dale is l̲ate for
work. (C, S, L)

2. If profits depend on u̲nsound environmental practices, then either the quality of the environment will deteriorate, or profits will d̲rop. Jobs will be
plentiful only if profits do not drop. So, either jobs will not be plentiful, or
the quality of the environment will deteriorate. (U, Q, D, J)

3. The new road will not be built unless the planning commission approves
the funds. But the planning commission's approval of the funds will come
only if the environmental impact report is positive, and it can't be positive
if the road will ruin Mill Creek. So, unless they find a way for the road not
to ruin Mill Creek, it won't be built. (R, A, E, M)

▲ 4. The message will not be understood unless the code is broken. The killer
will not be caught if the message is not understood. Either the code will be
broken, or Holmes's plan will fail. But Holmes's plan will not fail if he is
given enough time. Therefore, if Holmes is given enough time, the killer
will be caught. (M, C, K, H, T)

5. If the senator votes against this bill, then he is opposed to penalties against
tax evaders. Also, if the senator is a tax evader himself, then he is opposed
to penalties against tax evaders. Therefore, if the senator votes against this
bill, he is a tax evader himself. (V, O, T)

6. If you had gone to class, taken good notes, and studied the text, you'd have
done well on the exam. And, if you'd done well on the exam, you'd have
passed the course. Since you did not pass the course and you did go to class,
you must not have taken good notes and not studied the text.

▲   7. Either John will go to class, or he'll miss the review session. If John misses the review session, he'll foul up the exam. If he goes to class, however, he'll miss his ride home for the weekend. So John's either going to miss his ride home or foul up the exam.

8. If the government's position on fighting crime is correct, then if more people are locked up, then the crime rate should drop. But the crime rate has not dropped despite the fact that we've been locking up record numbers of people. It follows that the government's position on fighting crime is not correct.

9. The creation story in the Book of Genesis is compatible with the theory of evolution, but only if the creation story is not taken literally. If, as most scientists think, there is plenty of evidence for the theory of evolution, the Genesis story cannot be true if it is not compatible with evolution theory. Therefore, if the Genesis story is taken literally, it cannot be true.

▲ 10. The creation story in the Book of Genesis is compatible with the theory of evolution, but only if the creation story is not taken literally. If there is plenty of evidence for the theory of evolution, which there is, the Genesis story cannot be true if it is not compatible with evolution theory. Therefore, if the Genesis story is taken literally, it cannot be true.

11. If there was no murder committed, then the victim must have been killed by the horse. But the victim could have been killed by the horse only if he, the victim, was trying to injure the horse before the race; and, in that case, there certainly was a crime committed. So, if there was no murder, there was still a crime committed.

12. Holmes cannot catch the train unless he gets to Charing Cross Station by noon; and if he misses the train, Watson will be in danger. Because Moriarty has thugs watching the station, Holmes can get there by noon only if he goes in disguise. So, unless Holmes goes in disguise, Watson will be in danger.

▲ 13. It's not fair to smoke around nonsmokers if secondhand cigarette smoke really is harmful. If secondhand smoke were not harmful, the American Lung Association would not be telling us that it is. But they are telling us that it's harmful. That's enough to conclude that it's not fair to smoke around nonsmokers.

14. If Jane does any of the following, she's got an eating disorder: If she goes on eating binges for no apparent reason, if she looks forward to times when she can eat alone, or if she eats sensibly in front of others and makes up for it when she's alone. Jane does in fact go on eating binges for no apparent reason. So it's clear that she has an eating disorder.

15. The number of business majors increased markedly during the past decade; and if you see that happening, you know that younger people have developed a greater interest in money. Such an interest, unfortunately, means that greed has become a significant motivating force in our society; and

if greed has become such a force, charity will have become insignificant. We can predict that charity will not be seen as a significant feature of this past decade.

Exercise 9-16 ————————————————————

Use the box on page 329 to determine which of the following are valid arguments.

1. If Bobo is smart, then he can do tricks. However, Bobo is not smart. So he cannot do tricks.

2. If God is always on America's side, then America wouldn't have lost any wars. America has lost wars. Therefore, God is not always on America's side.

3. If your theory is correct, then light passing Jupiter will be bent. Light passing Jupiter is bent. Therefore, your theory is correct.

4. Moore eats carrots and broccoli for lunch, and if he does that, he probably is very hungry by dinner time. Conclusion: Moore is very hungry by dinner time.

5. If you value your feet, you won't mow the lawn in your bare feet. Therefore, since you do mow the lawn in your bare feet, we can conclude that you don't value your feet.

6. If Bobo is smart, then he can do tricks; and he can do tricks. Therefore, he is smart.

7. If Charles walked through the rose garden, then he would have mud on his shoes. We can deduce, therefore, that he did walk through the rose garden, because he has mud on his shoes.

8. If it rained earlier, then the sidewalks would still be wet. We can deduce, therefore, that it did rain earlier, because the sidewalks are still wet.

9. If you are pregnant, then you are a woman. We can deduce, therefore, that you are pregnant, because you are a woman.

10. If this stuff is on the final, I will get an A in the class because I really understand it! Further, the teacher told me that this stuff will be on the final, so I know it will be there. Therefore, I know I will get an A in the class.

11. If side A has an even number, then side B has an odd number, but side A does not have an even number. Therefore, side B does not have an odd number.

12. If side A has an even number, then side B has an odd number, and side B does have an odd number. Therefore, side A has an even number.

13. If the theory is correct, then we would have observed squigglyitis in the specimen. However, we know the theory is not correct. Therefore, we did not observe squigglyitis in the specimen.

14. If the theory is correct, then we would have observed dilation in the specimen. Therefore, since we did not observe dilation in the specimen, we know the theory is not correct.

15. If we observe dilation in the specimen, then we know the theory is correct. We observed dilation—so the theory is correct.

16. If the comet approached within 1 billion miles of the earth, there would have been numerous sightings of it. There weren't numerous sightings. So it did not approach within 1 billion miles.

17. If Baffin Island is larger than Sumatra, then two of the five largest islands in the world are in the Arctic Ocean. And Baffin Island, as it turns out, is about 2 percent larger than Sumatra. Therefore, the Arctic Ocean contains two of the world's largest islands.

18. If the danger of range fires is greater this year than last, then state and federal officials will hire a greater number of firefighters to cope with the danger. Since more firefighters are already being hired this year than were hired all last year, we can be sure that the danger of fires has increased this year.

19. If Jack Davis robbed the Central Pacific Express in 1870, then the authorities imprisoned the right person. But the authorities did not imprison the right person. Therefore, it must have not been Jack Davis who robbed the Central Pacific Express in 1870.

20. If the recent tax cuts had been self-financing, then there would have been no substantial increase in the federal deficit. But they turned out not to be self-financing. Therefore, there will be a substantial increase in the federal deficit.

21. The public did not react favorably to the majority of policies recommended by President Ronald Reagan during his second term. But if his electoral landslide in 1984 had been a mandate for more conservative policies, the public would have reacted favorably to most of those he recommended after the election. Therefore, the 1984 vote was not considered a mandate for more conservative policies.

22. Alexander will finish his book by tomorrow afternoon only if he is an accomplished speed reader. Fortunately for him, he is quite accomplished at speed reading. Therefore, he will get his book finished by tomorrow afternoon.

23. If higher education were living up to its responsibilities, the five best-selling magazines on American campuses would not be *Cosmopolitan, People, Playboy, Glamour,* and *Vogue.* But those are exactly the magazines that sell best in the nation's college bookstores. Higher education, we can conclude, is failing in at least some of its responsibilities.

24. Broc Glover was considered sure to win if he had no bad luck in the early part of the race. But we've learned that he has had the bad luck to be involved in a crash right after the start, so we're expecting another driver to be the winner.

25. If Boris is really a spy for the KGB, then he has been lying through his teeth about his business in this country. But we can expose his true occupation if he's been lying like that. So, I'm confident that if we can expose his true occupation, we can show that he's really a KGB spy.

26. The alternator is not working properly if the ammeter shows a negative reading. The current reading of the ammeter is negative. So, the alternator is not working properly.

27. Fewer than 2 percent of the employees of New York City's Transit Authority are accountable to management. If such a small number of employees are accountable to the management of the organization, no improvement in the system's efficiency can be expected in the near future. So, we cannot expect any such improvements any time soon.

28. If Charles did not pay his taxes, then he did not receive a refund. Thus, he did not pay his taxes, since he did not receive a refund.

29. If they wanted to go to the party, then they would have called by now. But they haven't, so they didn't.

30. "You'll get an A in the class," she predicted.
    "What makes you say that?" he asked.
    "Because," she said, "if you get an A, then you're smart, and you *are* smart."

31. If Florin arrived home by eight, she received the call from her attorney. But she did not get home by eight, so she must have missed her attorney's call.

32. The acid rain problem will be solved, but only if the administration stops talking and starts acting. So far, however, all we've had from the president is words. Words are cheap. Action is what counts. The problem will not be remedied, at least not while this administration is in office.

Writing Exercises

1. a. In a one-page essay, evaluate the soundness of the argument in the box on page 337. Alternatively, in a one-page essay evaluate the soundness of the argument in the letter to Ask Marilyn (page 323). Write your name on the back of your paper.
   b. When everyone is finished, your instructor will collect the papers and redistribute them to the class. In groups of four or five, read the papers that have been given to your group and select the best one. The instructor will select one group's top-rated paper to read to the class for discussion.

2. Take about fifteen minutes to write an essay responding to the paper the instructor has read to the class in Exercise 1. When everyone is finished, the members of each group will read each other's responses and select the best one to share with the class.

Inductive Arguments

*I*n July 2002, George Kapidian, of New Braunfels, Texas, lost his new home in a devastating flood. After four days of violent thunderstorms around San Antonio, the Guadalupe River rose twenty feet—flooding Mr. Kapidian's house and destroying everything in it. Seven people died in the raging floodwaters.

Seventy-two-year-old Mr. Kapidian should have known better. He was aware that the area was subject to flooding; in fact, his house was built on the foundation of a house washed away by a flood just three years earlier. But when he bought the house he reasoned, "What are the odds it would happen again?"

People often think this way, and the old saying "lightning never strikes twice in the same place" would seem to confirm their reasoning—if it were true. But it isn't true, and this kind of thinking can lead to some very bad conclusions indeed. Mr. Kapidian's reasoning would lead us to go swimming at a beach where someone was recently mauled by a shark because, after all, "What are the odds it would happen again?" Well, in truth, the odds are much greater that it will happen again at *this* beach than at a beach where there has been no recent shark attack. And in the original case, the Guadalupe River's having flooded in that spot on earlier occasions made it *more* likely that it would flood there again, not less likely.

When we extend what we have already observed to things or situations we have not observed, we are reasoning inductively; we are producing inductive arguments. This chapter is all about making and evaluating such arguments. Mr. Kapidian's problem was that his inductive reasoning was improper. His part of Texas had been subject to floods in past years; if he had properly extended that information to future years, he would not have been surprised to see flooding again.

We can sketch a general formula that practically all inductive arguments fit, some maybe a little more obviously than others. Here is the formula followed by a bit of explanation:

Lightning never strikes the same place twice.

Do you believe this? Try the idea out on someone who works at a fire lookout on a mountaintop in thunderstorms.

Premise: X has properties a, b, and c.
Premise: Y has properties a, b, and c.
Premise: X has further property p.
Conclusion: Y also has property p.

X is something we know some things about—namely, that it has properties a, b, c, and p. Y is something we know less about—only that it has properties a, b, and c. We don't *know* whether it has property p, but we make an inference that it does, because X has that property and Y is like X in several other ways. We are counting on the fact that if Y is like X in *some* ways we know about (a, b, and c), this makes it to some degree likely that Y is like X in some *further* way that we don't know about (i.e., in having p). Indeed, this last sentence sums up the most fundamental principle of inductive arguments. We could put it another way by saying that a number of similarities make *further* similarities likely. You can probably find other ways to formulate this general principle yourself. In what follows, we'll use X and Y to indicate which items fit which part of the formula above.

Moore knows several people with Harley-Davidson motorcycles, and they all leak oil. He wouldn't be surprised to learn, therefore, that the Harley that Parker just bought leaks oil. Why does he think so? Because he draws an inference from the Harley-Davidsons he knows about (Xs, more than one of them in this case) to the one Parker just bought (Y), reckoning that what's true of the ones he knows is likely to be true of the one he just learned about.

Your neighbor's new dog barks at you when you take out the trash on Monday, Tuesday, and Wednesday; you expect the dog to bark at you when you take out the trash on Thursday. You are arguing inductively from what happened when you took out the trash on Monday, Tuesday, and Wednesday (Xs) to what will happen when you take out the trash on Thursday (Y).

The peaches you bought at the A&P Market looked okay but were mushy; you don't buy any more of that batch because you think the other peaches in the batch will be mushy as well. Here again you are making an inductive inference—you are extending what you know about the peaches you bought (Xs) to the rest of the peaches in that particular batch (Ys).

It is common to describe inductive arguments as arguments in which the premises, if true, are claimed to support some degree of *probability* for the conclusion's truth, but not its *certainty*. In none of the arguments above do the facts we know guarantee the truth of the conclusion we draw, but they do make it *more likely* that that conclusion is true. We'll adopt the following as a working characterization of inductive arguments:

An **inductive argument** is an argument the premises of which are intended to provide some degree of *probability* for the truth of the conclusion.*

---

*A somewhat more precise way to put this: An inductive argument is one for which it is claimed that the conclusion has a greater likelihood of being true if its premises are all true than if its premises are not all true.

Remember that this distinguishes such arguments from deductive ones, since the link between the premises and conclusion of the latter is one of certainty, not probability: If the premises are true in a valid deductive argument, the conclusion cannot fail to be true. In a good inductive argument, the conclusion can still fail to be true, but it is less likely to be so.

Inductive arguments give us a way of extending our belief from things we know about to things unknown. Throughout our discussion, we'll use the term **sample** to refer to an item or items we believe something about, and we'll use the term **target** (or **target class** or **target population**) to refer to an item or group of items to which we wish to extend our belief. The feature we know about in the sample and we extend to the target object (or target class) is the **feature** (or **property**) **in question.** Referring back to our formula at the beginning of this section, X is our sample, Y is our target, and p is our property in question.

Applying the same terminology to the peach example, our *sample* is the peaches we bought, the *target class* is the entire batch of peaches, and the *property in question* is being mushy. Are you catching on to the terminology?

In the dog example, our sample is the three previous occurrences of taking out the trash (we already believe the dog barked on those occasions), the target is the next occurrence of taking out the trash (we're reasoning that the dog will bark on this further occasion), and the property in question is the dog's barking when this further deed is done.

And in the motorcycle example, the sample consists of the Harleys that Moore knew about previously, the target is Parker's recently acquired bike, and the property in question is that of leaking oil. Make sure you understand this terminology or most of the rest of the chapter is going to be hard to follow. It isn't as complicated as it might sound at first.

Analogical Arguments and Generalizations

Remember that the target in an argument can be either an entire class (or "population")* of objects, events, occasions, and the like, or it can be just a single such item. Notice also that sometimes the members of the sample are *drawn from* the target (when it is an entire class), and sometimes they are not. For instance, in the example about peaches, the members of the sample (the peaches you bought at the A&P) are also members of the target class (the entire batch of A&P peaches). In the barking-dog example, the members of the sample (Monday's, Tuesday's, and Wednesday's trash haulings) are *not* drawn from the target (Thursday's trash hauling). It is common to divide inductive arguments into categories, and the differences we've just been describing characterize the two main such categories: **inductive generalizations** and **analogical arguments** (or **arguments by analogy**). Ordinarily, arguments by analogy have one thing or event for a target while generalizations always have

---

*The terms "class" and "population" are used interchangeably in this discussion.

Analogical Arguments and Generalizations

Let's take a closer look at the relationship between analogical arguments and generalizations. Consider an analogical argument such as the following:

> We observe that, in a sample of ten American cities of over 750,000 population, every one of them has a public rail transportation system. We also observe that San Francisco is like the cities in the sample in lots of ways (geography, tax base, etc.) We then draw the conclusion that San Francisco probably also has a public rail transportation system.

This is purely inductive argument. Now let's look at another way of reaching the same conclusion from the same premises.

> (A) We make the first observation we made previously, that every one of a sample of ten American cities of over 750,000 population has a public rail system. Since our sample is representative of American cities over three-quarters of a million in general, we go on to generalize that, probably, *all* American cities over 750,000 population have rail transportation systems.
> (B) We then construct another argument, from the premise that all American cities over 750,000 population probably have rail transportations systems to the conclusion that San Francisco, an American city, probably has a rail transportation system.

In this argument scenario, there are two separate arguments: argument A is inductive, and argument B is deductive. Notice that both argument scenarios produce the conclusion that San Francisco's rail system is probable. It should be obvious why in the first scenario; in the second, part A, being inductive, only establishes its conclusion with probability. Therefore, since no deductive argument can provide more certainty for its conclusion than is present for its premises, the final conclusion of B is also merely probable.

So, although analogical argument proceeds by a more direct route to its conclusion, there is always a side trip possible via a generalization to an entire class followed by a return trip to the conclusion by means of a deductive argument.

a class of things or events. In all cases, generalizations have their samples drawn from the target class, while this is never true of arguments by analogy.* (So, the example above about peaches is a generalization; the other examples are arguments by analogy.) Fortunately, although they differ in these ways, the two kinds of arguments both follow the same principles and are evaluated on similar criteria. Thus we will be able to treat them similarly and

---

*Since we do not have a target class in an argument by analogy, the "sample" cannot be a sample of such a class. So we'll just say that the "sample" in such arguments is an item or a group of items from which we are attempting to draw an inference about the target object. This preserves the parallel with generalizations.

will point out any differences that are necessary as we go along. So far, once again, the principal difference is that, in a generalization, the sample is drawn from the target class; in an analogical argument, the sample and the target are distinct—one is not a part of the other. (As mentioned, generalizations always have a class as a target and analogical arguments usually have a single object or just a few objects, but there are exceptions to this way of distinguishing between them.) For an interesting aspect of the relationship between analogical arguments and generalizations, see the box opposite.

Principles of Constructing and Evaluating Inductive Arguments

The most important principle of good inductive reasoning is that the item or items from which we are arguing—our sample—must be similar to the item or items we are arguing to—our target. Let's put that in boldface:

> **The more like one another our sample and target are, the stronger our argument; the less alike they are, the weaker the argument.**

The more Parker's Harley-Davidson is like the others Moore knows (e.g., similar in model, in age, in maintenance history), the more likely it is to leak oil like the others. The more Thursday's trash hauling is like the previous three days' (e.g., done at the same time of day, with the same amount of noise, and with nobody having shot the dog in the meantime), the more likely it is to provoke the neighbor's dog to bark as it did on the earlier occasions.

Exactly the same principle holds when we are generalizing to an entire class of things (as distinct from arguing by analogy from one item to another). When we generalize from the peaches we bought to the *entire* batch of peaches they came from, we don't want our sample peaches to be atypical for that batch of peaches—we want them to be as much like the rest of the batch as possible. When speaking of the similarity between sample and target class of an inductive generalization, the word that is most often used is "representativeness." This word, though awkward to say, is important. We can characterize it and its opposite, "bias," in the following way: The more an inductive argument's sample is similar to its target in all relevant respects, the more **representative** the sample is said to be. (We'll give another definition below, one that applies especially to formal generalizations, but which is essentially the same as this one.) A sample that is significantly different from the target in one or more relevant respects is said to be a **biased sample.**

One special circumstance arises when we don't know whether the target in an analogical argument has a particular relevant feature. For example, what if we don't know whether Parker's Harley is a flathead or a knucklehead or has some other type of engine configuration? In that case, Parker's cycle is more likely to resemble some members of the sample if the latter

Typical Sample Cases: Deduction in Disguise

Let's say you want to know whether gold is denser than lead. To find out, you take exactly one cubic centimeter of gold and the same volume of lead, and you place them on the two sides of a balance scale. The weighing shows that the cubic centimeter of gold is heavier than the lead (in fact, the weight of the lead is about 59 percent of that of the gold). You then conclude that, as a matter of fact, gold in general is more dense than lead—that is, that *every instance* of gold is more dense than *every instance* of lead.

Are you committing the fallacy of hasty generalization by basing your conclusion on only one case? No, of course not. The reason is that you can safely assume that every instance of gold is similar in density to every other instance of gold and that instances of lead are likewise similar with regard to properties like density, because gold and lead are elements.

Reasoning such as this is often made out to be a peculiar kind of inductive argument, one where a little sample goes a long way, as it were. In fact, though, arguments like this are really *deductive* arguments in disguise. The assumption that makes the argument inductively strong (namely, that in the matter of density, gold is all alike and so is lead) also makes the argument deductively valid! The argument turns out to be this:

General assumption: All gold is alike with regard to density, and so is all lead.

Result of weighing: This gold is denser than this lead.

Conclusion: Gold is denser than lead.

---

contains a variety of engine types. In such cases, *variety* in the sample strengthens the argument. So, if we don't know whether our target has some property, we're better off if some of our sample have it and some don't. (This is no different from how we treat generalizations: Our generalization about peaches is stronger if the sample contains peaches from the top, bottom, and middle of the container.) Of course, if we *do* know that the target has a certain property, then the more of the sample that have it, the better.

The second principle governing inductive arguments is about the number of items in the sample, and we may as well put that in boldface too:

In general, the larger the sample the better—that is, the stronger the argument.

The more peaches in our sample, the more confidence we are entitled to feel in extending our observations about those peaches to the rest of the peaches in the batch. The more times an area has flooded in the past, the more insurance we should buy. The more times the dog has barked at us, the more we should expect it to bark at us tomorrow. The more leaky Harleys we know about, the more we ought to consider buying Parker a bag of kitty litter for his garage floor.

The two principles work together, but the first is more important. Everything else being equal, the most important thing is for the items in the sample to be similar to the target—to the items we are arguing to. We can't argue very well even from a huge sample if the items in that sample are different in some significant way from those we are arguing to. On the other hand, a sample consisting of just a single item can warrant a generalization to an entire class if that item is sufficiently similar to the other items in the class. If one copy of a book has a misprint on page 327, then it is extremely likely that every other copy of the book from that printing has a similar misprint. (If we know that all the items in a target class are exactly similar, then we get a different kind of situation. See the box titled "Typical Sample Cases: Deduction in Disguise.")

However, if the items in the class of things we are concerned about are not known to be homogeneous or are known to be nonhomogeneous, then we cannot get away with a small sample. For example, to draw conclusions about the political views of, say, Canadian truck drivers, we'd need a sample large enough to represent the diverse array of personalities, socioeconomic levels, educational background, life experiences, and so forth, that are found in such a large and nonhomogeneous population. How this is accomplished will be explained in the following section.

Formal and Informal Inductive Arguments

Before we go on, we need to separate two "levels" of inductive argumentation. The first level, and the one that concerns most of us most of the time, is that of everyday, informal arguments. We encounter both generalizations and arguments by analogy at this level, and, if you pay close attention, you'll discover that you are making inferences like these practically all the time. They are integral to our rational process, with many such inferences occurring at a subargumentative level—that is, we don't reach the point of putting our thinking into words (which, you might recall, is a necessary condition of making an argument).

The second level is that of what we might call "scientific" or "formal" argumentation. At this level we find generalizations in the form of public opinion polls, ratings for television and radio stations, and research surveys of all sorts. We also find scientific studies undertaken to discover what causes what, but that's the subject of the next chapter.

There are a couple of obvious differences between formal and informal arguments. First, most formal arguments turn out to be generalizations. You could certainly produce a formal, scientifically controlled argument by analogy, but you just won't happen upon one in your everyday life very often. Second, formal arguments require an attention to detail—including reliance on some moderately sophisticated mathematics—that is usually impossible to achieve and generally not necessary in their informal counterparts. But, as we're going to see, however different they may look, arguments at both levels depend entirely on exactly the same general principles. A long and complicated statistical study of the population decline of spotted owls and a quick inference about whether to return to a restaurant you tried last week are measured against the very same general criteria.

So here's our plan: We're going to make an excursus into formal arguments, explaining how several concepts operate at that level as we trace an example from beginning to end. It may get a little technical along the way, but it isn't really complicated. After the formal treatment, we'll show how the principles at that level have corresponding versions at the informal level and how we apply them to our everyday reasoning.

Example of a Formal Generalization: A Political Poll

Imagine that you graduate from college one of these days. (We're serious.) You take a position at a survey research firm that does political polling. Your first job is to manage a poll commissioned by a potential candidate for the presidency—say, Jeb Bush, who figures that it's his time to be president, his father and older brother having already had their turn. Bush wants to know whether the Republican voters of New Hampshire would vote for him rather than, say, John McCain in the presidential primary in that state. Your job is to produce a reasonably accurate assessment of public opinion on the issue at the lowest reasonable cost.

Of course, the most accurate way to settle the issue would be to ask all the Republican voters of New Hampshire. But that would be excessively expensive. So you will have to make do with asking a sample of those voters and extending the knowledge gained thereby to a conclusion about the whole class. How well that knowledge will extend to the whole class depends on how good a job you do. The two most important decisions you have to make are these: How will you select the sample so that it is representative of the entire target class of voters? How large will the sample need to be in order to adequately represent that class?

Clearly, it would be a mistake to let the Republicans on the faculty at the University of New Hampshire be the sample, even if doing so would produce a sample of the right size. It would be a mistake because those faculty at UNH are very likely *not* to represent the entire target class. Indeed, they are too different in too many relevant ways from many, many members of the target class. Which brings us to the question, Just what does it mean for a sample to be representative of a target? In a nutshell, we can say that *a sample is representative of a target class if, and only if, it possesses all the relevant features of the target class in proportions similar to those of the target class.* We should add that a feature is said to be relevant when it is likely that its presence or absence would affect the presence or absence of the property in question. The following should make this clear.

Let's ask ourselves whether there are features of the Republican UNH faculty that are not features of the entire target class. Sure there are: For example, there is a much higher percentage of advanced degrees among the former than among the latter. Now we ask ourselves, Is the possession of advanced degrees relevant to the property in question (which, you'll recall, is the likelihood of voting for Jeb Bush rather than John McCain)? It is very likely that the level of one's education affects the way a person votes, which means that this feature is relevant. Notice that this doesn't mean that *every* highly educated voter must vote differently from every less educated voter, only that the former *tend* to vote in certain ways somewhat more frequently than the latter.

So, by possessing relevant properties that make them different from the target class, the UNH faculty members can't form the sample you want for your survey—they would give you a very biased sample indeed.

Notice also that we don't have to know with absolute certainty that higher levels of education have significant effects on the way a person votes; we only need a strong suspicion. The general rule is, If we're not sure whether a feature is relevant, the safe path is to presume that it *is* relevant. It's a matter of being safe rather than sorry.

You now have a problem: How are you going to find a group that will share relevant features with the entire target class? Setting out to construct such a group (which, as we'll see in the next chapter, actually has to be done sometimes) is a real chore. For starters, we don't usually know what all the relevant features are—Does the age of a Republican in New Hampshire help determine how he or she votes? Probably. Does being left-handed? Probably not. What about being a commuter versus working at home? Who knows? And, even if we knew what all the relevant features are, it would still be a big job getting our sample to exhibit them in just the proportions in which they occur in the target class.

Fortunately for you and the job at hand, there is a method that solves the problem we've been describing. You've probably already figured out what it is: a randomly selected sample. A **random selection process** gives every member of the target class an equal chance of becoming a member of the sample. If we randomly select our sample from the target population, we should, within certain limits, get a sample that possesses all the characteristics of the target class in proportions more or less similar to those found in the target class. We should point out that, as a practical matter, coming up with actual procedures for getting a random selection process can be a difficult problem; statisticians often have to settle for something that works only *pretty* well because it's affordable. Another word on that in a few moments.

> Some people use statistics like a drunk uses a lamp post, more for support than illumination.

Random Variation: Problems and Solutions

A lot of people misunderstand what random selection is all about in cases like the ones we're discussing. They often think that randomness is the goal of the process. And indeed it is *a* goal, but it is merely the means by which we try to achieve the *real* goal, which is representativeness. Fortunately, randomness does a pretty good job of helping us reach this goal; unfortunately, it doesn't do a perfect job. In fact, any given randomly selected sample from a target class might misrepresent that target to some extent or other. That is, there's nothing in a sample, even if it is perfectly random, that *guarantees* that it will be representative.

What does this mean for our need to come up with an answer to the question "How many New Hampshire Republican voters would prefer to vote for Bush over McCain?" It means we have to build some "wiggle room" into the answer. Fortunately, there are some perfectly reasonable ways to do that.

For one thing, nobody would expect you and your firm to be able to determine *exactly, to the precise number,* how many voters would prefer Bush. If you can get reasonably close, you'll have done a good job. So, you want to be able to tell the Bush people, "approximately such-and-such percent" prefer one candidate to the other, or "about so-and-so percent" prefer him. Giving yourself this wiggle room is known as providing an "error margin." An **error margin** is a range of percentage points within which an answer is claimed to fall (rather than a precise percentage point or even fraction of a percentage point). The idea is the same here as in the situation where a potential automobile buyer asks a salesman about a car's gas mileage: The salesman should only have to say *approximately* what mileage can be expected, not *exactly* how many miles per gallon one will get. Of course, if the error margin is too big, the survey is useless. If you have to tell the Bush campaign that somewhere between 10 and 90 percent of New Hampshire Republican voters prefer Bush, you haven't given them much for their money, have you? We'll return to this in a moment.

The second way to make the argument provided by the survey a reasonable one is to allow that there is *some* chance that it might be wrong. Indeed, it would be a rare argument where a person is extending knowledge about a known thing to claims about an unknown thing and where the person would be willing to bet his or her life on the outcome. We don't usually bet the farm unless we *know* we're right. What you want to do here is identify a "confidence level" for your argument. A **confidence level** is a measure of the argument's strength; the higher the confidence level, the more likely the argument's conclusion is to be true. So, we can say that it is "very likely" that such and such a percentage of voters prefer Bush, or we can actually quantify mathematically what percentage of likelihood the conclusion has.

Given that the sample of a survey is randomly selected from the target class, the error margin of the generalization's conclusion and the argument's confidence level are determined entirely by the size of the sample. Here's the principle:

> As the sample size of a generalization gets larger, either the error margin becomes more narrow, or the confidence level of the argument becomes greater, or a combination of both.

Notice that this principle relates three variables—sample size, confidence level, and error margin—and shows how they are interdependent. It's very important that you understand how these three factors relate to one another.

The Great Slip-Up of 1948

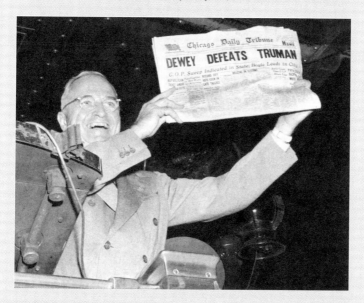

Because of a strike, the *Chicago Daily Tribune* had to go to press earlier than usual the night of the 1948 presidential election. So they relied on some early returns, some "expert" opinion, and public opinion polls to decide on the famous "Dewey Defeats Truman" headline. But the polls were not sufficiently accurate, as Truman edged Dewey in a narrow upset victory.

Okay. We've determined that your sample of voters in the New Hampshire primary needs to be randomly selected—we're going to leave it to you to determine how to do that, but we'll warn you to be careful: You don't want to make the mistake the *Chicago Daily Tribune* made. (See the box above.)

Sample Size

By the end of the last section, we had come back around to the topic of **sample size,** and now it's time to deal with it. When it comes to surveys of the sort we're talking about, the question "How many individuals does the sample need to contain?" has a neat, short answer: somewhere between 1,000 and 1,500. You may find it interesting that, no matter what the survey is about, it usually requires between 1,000 and 1,500 in the sample regardless of whether the target class is Republican primary voters in New Hampshire, voters of all parties in New England, citizens of the United States, or human beings on the entire planet. In short, as long as we're not talking about very small target classes (which we can safely ignore, since generalizations like

TABLE 10-1   **Approximate Error Margins for Random Samples of Various Sizes**

Confidence level of 95 percent in all cases.

Sample Size	Error Margin (%)	Corresponding Range (Percentage Points)
10	±30	60
25	±22	44
50	±14	28
100	±10	20
250	±6	12
500	±4	8
1,000	±3	6
1,500	±2	4

The error margin decreases rapidly as the sample size begins to increase, but this decrease slows markedly as the sample gets larger. It is usually pointless to increase the sample beyond 1,500 unless there are special requirements of precision or confidence level.

(We presume, both here and in the text, that the target population is large—that is, 10,000 or larger. When the target is small, there is a correction factor that can be applied to determine the appropriate error margin. But most reported polls have large enough targets that we need not concern ourselves with the calculation methods for correcting the error margin here.)

these don't apply to them), the size of the target is not relevant to the size of the sample required. The reason for this will become clear in what follows.

We are not going to discuss the mathematics that lie behind the facts we're describing here, but they are among the most basic mathematics in this field—you can trust them. They guarantee the details that you'll find in Table 10-1, which you should look at now. Notice that the column on the left represents a series of increasing sample sizes. In the second column, we find the error margins that correspond to the various sample sizes expressed as "plus or minus x percentage points." This expression is the means by which statisticians express the amount of "wiggle room" an argument requires for its conclusion. The third column just shows the range of percentage points that the error margin produces.

The two most important things to notice about Table 10-1 are, first, that the error margin narrows very quickly as the size of the sample increases from 10 to 25 and then to 50, but as we go down the columns the narrowing of the error margin slows down. So, by the time we get to a sample size of 500, with an error margin of plus or minus 4 percent, we have to *double* the sample to 1,000 in order to decrease the error margin by one percentage point, to plus or minus 3 percent. It takes another 500 added to the sample to get it down one more percentage point. (These error margins are approximate; they've been rounded off for convenience's sake.) In order to get the error margin down to, say, 1 percent or less, we have to vastly increase the size of the sample, and for most practical purposes, the gain in a more precise conclusion (one with a narrow error margin) is outweighed by the difficulty and expense of having to add so many new members to the sample. And this explains the claim made above that we very seldom go beyond 1,000 to 1,500 members of a sample—because the trouble of increasing a sample beyond that is hardly worth the modest decrease produced in the error margin.

Now, throughout the preceding paragraphs, we've been making a presumption about confidence levels. We've been presuming that the people who hired you, the Bush campaign, would be satisfied with a 95 percent confidence level for the survey. We chose this figure because it is the standard of the polling industry—if a confidence level is not mentioned in a professionally done poll, the assumption is that it is 95 percent. This means simply that one can be 95 percent sure that the conclusion of the argument does indeed follow from the premises—in other words, that we can have considerable confidence in the conclusion.* If we have a smaller sample, we will, of course, have a lower confidence level or a larger error margin. On the other hand, if it is important to have a confidence level higher than 95 percent, then we need a larger sample, if the error margin is not to be affected.

In general, professional surveying and polling organizations have settled on the 95 percent figure for a standard level of confidence and an error margin of around 3 percentage points. And thus the figure of 1,000 or a little over is the standard sample size for most professionally done scientific polls.

This brings us to the second thing—or, actually, things—you should remember about Table 10.1. You should make a mental note of the three or four lines near the bottom of the table so that, if you run across a survey with a suspiciously small sample, you'll know what kind of error margins it would be reasonable—or unreasonable—to claim for it. We recently saw in a golf magazine that approximately 200 golfers had been surveyed about something or other and that less than half of them, 45 percent, in fact, had agreed with the poll question. Does this mean that less than half of all golfers can be expected to agree with the poll question? Not at all. If it has the usual confidence level, a sample of 200 must have an error margin of around plus or minus 8 percent, which means it may be that as many as 53 percent—a majority—actually agree with the poll question.

Informal Inductive Arguments

Most of the inductive arguments we have to deal with in everyday life—both generalizations and arguments by analogy—are most definitely *not* of the formal, scientific variety we've been talking about in the last few pages. The most important difference between formal or scientific inductive arguments

---

*If you held our feet to the fire about this, we'd have to say that the *real* meaning of a 95 percent confidence level is that an average of 95 out of every 100 random samples from this target class will have the property in question within the range of the error margin. But this translates into practical terms in the way we've put it in the text.

on one hand and informal, everyday arguments on the other is that the latter do not make use of randomly selected samples. In everyday inductive reasoning, we make use of whatever is at hand—the Harleys Moore is familiar with, the peaches you bought at the A&P this morning, and the like. For this reason, it should be obvious, we cannot make the kinds of calculations that make formal arguments precise.

■ *Informal Error Margins: "Cautious" Conclusions*

But many of the concepts and principles we've described in connection with formal arguments do have their place in their everyday counterparts—they just take a more easygoing form. We probably wouldn't say to a colleague, "Based on my experience in freshman courses, I'd conclude that the grade point for the freshman class is 2.1036." And we're not likely to say to a fishing partner, "Ed, I've looked at the Fish and Game Department statistics, and your chance of catching a fish in that lake that weighs more than three pounds is 12 percent, plus or minus 3 percent." Ed would probably throw us out of the boat. We'd actually say something like, "I'd conclude that the freshman grade point is somewhere around a two-point," or "You're not likely to catch a three-pounder in that lake." These are informal ways of providing error margins for our inferences. Increasing the informal "error margins" in everyday arguments makes the conclusion more cautious.

■ *Informal Confidence Levels: Hedging Our Bets*

In informal arguments we also set informal confidence levels (as distinct from informal error margins) by adjusting the cautiousness of the conclusion. For example, it's more cautious to conclude "there's a good chance" the Yankees will win the pennant than to conclude "You can be pretty sure" the Yankees will win the pennant. "There's a good chance" and "You can be pretty sure" are informal ways of expressing our "confidence level." Obviously, the informal "confidence level" or "error margin" for our conclusion should be appropriate for the premises of our argument. If the Yankees have won only 40 games, we must be more cautious in concluding they will win the pennant than if they won over a hundred.

■ *Summing Up: Evaluating Inductive Generalizations and Analogical Arguments*

When all is said and done, the issue of whether we have a strong inductive generalization (or analogical argument) or a weak one, or something in between, can be reduced to three key questions:

1. **Are the sample and the target sufficiently alike?** If it's a generalization we have before us, this can be stated in terms of representativeness: Does the sample adequately represent the target class? If

we're looking at an argument by analogy, the question is simply,
Do members of the sample adequately resemble the target item in
relevant respects?

If sample and target are alike with regard to features that are relevant to the
property in question, then the argument will be strong; it will be weaker to
the extent they are unlike regarding these features. Notice that a significant difference with respect to only one relevant feature is all it takes to
ruin an otherwise good inductive argument. If, in our A&P example, the
peaches in the sample had all come from the bottom layer of the container,
this would make a big difference in the strength of the argument. If the argument is a formal generalization, the best we can do is to make sure the
sample was drawn from the target class by a random process.

2. **Is the sample of sufficient size?**

In a formal argument, we've seen that the size of the sample determines the
calculated confidence level and error margin. In informal arguments, the
general rule is, The bigger the sample, the better (given the same degree of
caution in the conclusion). It is possible, as we've indicated, to get a pretty
good argument from a small sample—as small as one single item, in fact.
But this can occur only when we know that the sample item or items are
very, very similar to the target item or to all the members of the target class.
It's also helpful in such cases if we can stand a fairly large error margin. To
illustrate, consider this example: Let's say that Moore owns a five-year-old
Toyota Camry, and he recommends a similar car to Parker when the latter
decides he needs to buy one. Parker finds one that is the same year and model
as Moore's; it has approximately the same number of miles on it; it has been
driven and maintained in similar fashion, and the various fittings—transmission, air conditioning, etc.—are also similar. Parker asks Moore what kind
of gas mileage his car gets, and Moore says he averages 30 miles to the gallon.
Now, on the assumption that Parker's driving habits are similar to Moore's,[*]
it would be a pretty safe bet that Parker will get *fairly similar* mileage. If
Parker were to conclude that he'll get, say, between 25 and 35 miles per gallon, we'd say he had a very strong argument. It's a high probability that his
mileage will fall somewhere within this substantial range. Were he to conclude that he'll probably average between 28 and 32 mpg, he'd still have a
pretty good case, but considerably less strong than when he adopted the
wider error margin—the more cautious conclusion.
These considerations about Moore's gas mileage point to the third key
question about inductive generalizations and analogical arguments:

3. **Is the cautiousness of the conclusion appropriate for the premises?**

---

[*]They aren't.

Cautious conclusions are easier to support than incautious conclusions. If, to revert to an earlier example, the Yankees have won 50 percent of their games so far, we need to be more cautious before we bet on their winning their next game than we would if they've won 66 percent. In short, we shouldn't go out on a limb with our conclusion, unless we have a nice, sturdy trunk (premise) to support us. To say that the conclusion of an inductive generalization or analogical argument is not sufficiently cautious is just a way of saying that it is not a strong argument.

Fallacies

Given what we've been discussing in the previous sections, learning about inductive argument fallacies will amount to little more than learning a little terminology. There are two main categories of fallacy. The first of these is biased sample (sometimes called "biased generalization" when it occurs in that type of argument and "biased analogy" when it appears in an analogical argument). A **biased sample** occurs when the sample is not sufficiently similar to the target; if the argument is a generalization, this means the sample is not *representative* of the target. Let's say that, for whatever reason, Moore knows quite a number of people who own Harleys. But all of those machines are older models, built when Harley-Davidson was owned by an organization different from the one that now owns it, and built to a design different from the more recently manufactured machine that Parker is buying. In this case, even if Moore's sample is sufficiently large (even if it contained hundreds and hundreds of such motorcycles!), the argument would be a very poor one: The sample is simply biased—it is too different from the target in ways that are highly relevant to the property of leaking oil.*

If we jump to a conclusion from a sample that is too small, we are guilty of the fallacy of **hasty conclusion** (or, if the argument is a generalization, **hasty generalization**). If Moore knew of one Harley-Davidson motorcycle, and from the fact that it leaked oil he concluded that Parker's Harley (never mind the entire class of Harleys!) would leak oil, he'd be guilty of hasty conclusion (or, in the case of the entire class, of hasty generalization). On the other hand, if he knew of fifteen or twenty people who owned Harleys of a considerable variety of types, he'd have a much stronger argument, and we wouldn't accuse him of committing any such fallacy.

Within the category of the hasty conclusion/generalization fallacy, a couple of special subspecies bear mention. The first and best known of these is the **fallacy of anecdotal evidence.** The fallacy has this name because it always consists in taking a story about one case (or, sometimes, more than one, but always a very small number) and drawing an unwarranted conclusion from it. If a student is considering taking a philosophy course at our

---

*Something like this is actually true, if we understand recent Harley-Davidson history correctly.

Who Do You Trust?

- When it comes to deciding which kind of car to buy, which do you trust more—the reports of a few friends or the results of a survey based on a large sample?
- When it comes to deciding whether an over-the-counter cold remedy (e.g., vitamin C) works, which do you trust more—a large clinical study or the reports of a few friends?

Many people trust the reports of friends over more reliable statistical information. We hope you aren't among 'em. (According to R. E. Nisbett and L. Ross, *Human Inference: Strategies and Shortcomings of Human Social Judgment* [Englewood Cliffs, N.J.: Prentice Hall, 1980], people tend to be insensitive to sample size when evaluating some product, being swayed more by the judgments of a few friends than by the results of a survey based on a large sample.)

university, and in conversation with another student she hears, "You'd better be careful, because philosophy courses are *hard*, I'm seriously telling you. I know what I'm talking about too, because I took a course from Dr. Moore last term and it was *way hard!*" If, on the basis of this conversation, our student decides that all philosophy courses are difficult and therefore she won't take one, she's guilty of the fallacy of anecdotal evidence. She's jumped to a conclusion from the story (the anecdote) her friend told her and simply doesn't have enough evidence to reach that conclusion.

Before completing this section, we should add that most samples that are too small are also biased. Indeed, small size is one typical source of biased samples, and this is more true as one finds more variety in the target class. However, when a sample is too small, we'll apply the hasty conclusion label to it, and we'll reserve the biased sample label for arguments whose samples are biased, however large they might be.

Polls: Problems and Pitfalls

One of the most frequently encountered uses of inductive arguments is in polls, especially public opinion polls (and most especially in election years). We explained many of the concepts that are important in conducting and reporting polls a bit earlier in the chapter, but it's time now to look at a couple of the problems that crop up in this important use of inductive argumentation.

We should emphasize first that a properly conducted and accurately reported poll can be a very reliable source of information. But we hasten to add that a lot of polls that you hear or read about are *not* properly done and

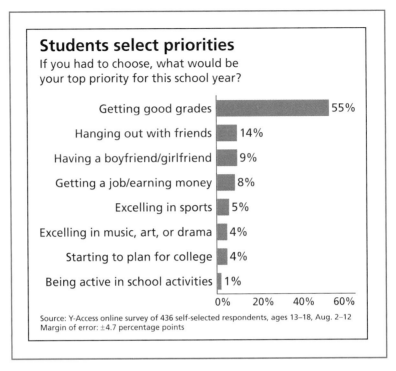

Students select priorities
If you had to choose, what would be
your top priority for this school year?

Priority	Percentage
Getting good grades	55%
Hanging out with friends	14%
Having a boyfriend/girlfriend	9%
Getting a job/earning money	8%
Excelling in sports	5%
Excelling in music, art, or drama	4%
Starting to plan for college	4%
Being active in school activities	1%

Source: Y-Access online survey of 436 self-selected respondents, ages 13–18, Aug. 2–12
Margin of error: ±4.7 percentage points

▲   *Comment: A good example of a worthless poll . . .*

often the people who report on the results cannot tell the difference between a good poll and a bad one. We can't go into every possible way a poll can fail, but in what follows we'll take notice of two of the most common ones.

■ *Self-Selected Samples*

Recall that a generalization from a sample is only as good as the representativeness of the sample. Therefore, keep this in mind: *No poll should be trusted if the members of the sample are there by their own choice.* When a television station asks its viewers to call in to express an opinion on some subject, the results tell us very, very little about what the entire population thinks about that subject. There are all kinds of differences possible—indeed, likely—between the people who call in and the population in general. The same goes for polls conducted by mail-in responses. One of the most massive polls ever processed—and one of the most heavily flawed, we should add—was done in 1993. The political organization of H. Ross Perot, a very wealthy businessman who ran for president as a member of the Reform Party, paid for a poll that was conducted by means of the magazine *TV Guide.* People were asked to answer questions posed in the magazine, then tear out or reproduce the pages and send them in for processing. There were other things wrong with this poll, and we'll get to some of them in a minute, but you've already heard all you need to know to discount any results that it produced. In such polls, the sample consists only of people who have strong enough feelings on the issues to respond and who have the time to go to the trouble of doing it. Such a situation almost guarantees that the sample will have views that are significantly different from those of the target population as a whole.

Another example, just for fun: A few years ago the late Abigail Van Buren ("Dear Abby") asked her female readers to write in answering the question "Which do you like more, tender cuddling or 'the act' (sex)?" More of her responders preferred cuddling, it turned out, and when she published this fact it provoked another columnist, Mike Royko, to ask his male readers which *they* liked better, tender cuddling or bowling. Royko's responders preferred bowling. Although both surveys were good fun, neither of them could be taken to reflect accurately the views of either columnist's readership, let alone society in general.

It should go without saying that person-on-the-street interviews (which have become extremely popular in our neck of the woods) should be utterly discounted as indications of popular opinion. They include small samples, almost always biased because, among other reasons, the interviews are usually conducted at a single location and include only people willing to stick their faces in front of a camera. You should read these interviews as fun, not as a reflection of the views of the general public.

■ *Slanted Questions*

A major source of unreliability in polling practices is the wording of the questions that are asked. It is possible to ask nearly any question of importance in many different ways. Consider this pair of questions:

▲ Do you think the school board should agree to teachers' demands for higher pay?

▲ Do you think it is reasonable for local public school teachers to seek pay raises?

These questions ask essentially the same thing, but you would be smart to expect more negative answers to the first version than to the second. The context in which a question is asked can be important too. Imagine a question asking about approval of pay raises for public school teachers, but imagine it coming after one or the other of the following questions:

▲ Are you aware that teachers in this district have not had a salary increase for the past six years?

▲ Are you aware that the school district is facing a budget shortfall for the coming fiscal year?

We'd expect the approval of raises would fare better when asked after the first of these questions than after the second.

Studies indicate that more brunettes than blondes or redheads have high-paying corporate jobs.

—From a letter in the *San Francisco Chronicle*

Is this evidence of discrimination against blondes and redheads, as the writer of the letter thought?

Nope; there are more brunettes to begin with. We'd be suspicious if *fewer* brunettes had high-paying corporate jobs.

We might add that the inclusion of slanted questions is not always accidental. Oftentimes a group or an organization will want to produce results that are slanted in their direction, and so they will include questions that are designed to do exactly that. This is an exercise in deception, of course, but unfortunately it is more widespread than we'd wish.

Have a look at the box ("Ask Us No [Loaded] Questions . . . ") and you'll see how one large, very expensive poll can contain most of the errors we've been discussing.

Playing by the Numbers

What if your instructor were to flip a coin ten times, and it came up heads seven times out of that ten? Would this make you think your teacher is a wizard or a sleight-of-hand artist? Of course not. There's nothing unusual in the coin coming up heads seven times out of ten, despite the fact that we all know the chance of heads in a fair coin flip is 50-50 (or 1 in 2, or, as the statisticians put it, 0.5). But what if your instructor were to get heads 70 percent of the time after flipping the coin a *hundred* times? This would be much more unexpected, and if he or she were to flip the coin a *thousand* times and get 70 percent heads—well, the whole class should leave right now for Las Vegas, where your instructor will make you all rich.

Why is 70 percent heads so unsurprising in the first case and so nearly miraculous in the last? The answer lies in what we call the **law of large numbers,** which says,

> The larger the number of chance-determined repetitious events considered, the closer the alternatives will approach predictable ratios.

This is not as complicated as it sounds; metaphorically, it just says that large numbers "behave" better than small numbers. Here's the idea: Because a single fair coin flip (i.e., no weighted coin, no prestidigitation) has a 50 percent chance of coming up heads, we say that the **predictable ratio** of heads to tails is 50 percent. The law of large numbers says that the more flips you include, the closer to 50 percent the heads-to-tails ratio will get.

The reason smaller numbers don't fit the percentages as well as bigger ones is that any given flip or short series of flips can produce nearly any kind of result. There's nothing unusual about several heads in a row or several tails—in fact, if you flip a thousand times, you'll probably get several "streaks" of heads and tails (and a sore thumb, too). Such streaks will balance each other out in a series of a thousand flips, but even a short streak can skew a small series of flips. The idea is that when we deal with small numbers, every number counts for a very large number of percentage points. Just two extra cases of heads can produce a 70:30 ratio in ten flips, a ratio that would be astounding in a large number of flips.

Ask Us No [Loaded] Questions; We'll Tell You No Lies

In the spring of 1993, H. Ross Perot did a nationwide survey that received a lot of publicity. But a survey is only as good as the questions it asks, and loaded questions can produce a biased result. *Time* and CNN hired the Yankelovich Partners survey research firm to ask a split random sample of Americans two versions of the questions; the first was Perot's original version, the second was a rewritten version produced by the Yankelovich firm. Here is what happened for three of the topics covered.

Question 1

PEROT VERSION: "Do you believe that for every dollar of tax increase there should be two dollars in spending cuts with the savings earmarked for deficit and debt reduction?"

YANKELOVICH VERSION: "Would you favor or oppose a proposal to cut spending by two dollars for every dollar in new taxes, with the savings earmarked for deficit reduction, even if that meant cuts in domestic programs like Medicare and education?"

RESULTS: Perot version: 67 percent yes; 18 percent no
Yankelovich version: 33 percent in favor; 61 percent opposed

Question 2

PEROT VERSION: "Should the President have the Line Item Veto to eliminate waste?"

YANKELOVICH VERSION: "Should the President have the Line Item Veto, or not?"

RESULTS: Perot version: 71 percent in favor; 16 percent opposed
Yankelovich version: 57 percent in favor; 21 percent opposed

Question 3

PEROT VERSION: "Should laws be passed to eliminate all possibilities of special interests giving huge sums of money to candidates?"

YANKELOVICH VERSION: "Should laws be passed to prohibit interest groups from contributing to campaigns, or do groups have a right to contribute to the candidate they support?"

RESULTS: Perot version: 80 percent yes; 17 percent no
Yankelovich version: 40 percent for prohibition; 55 percent for right to contribute

The law of large numbers operates in many circumstances. It is the reason we need a minimum sample size even when our method of choosing a sample is entirely random. To infer a generalization with any confidence, we need a sample of a certain size before we can trust the numbers

Welcome to Saint Simpson's

There are many ways that statistical reports can be misleading. The following illustrates one of the stranger ways, known to statisticians as "Simpson's Paradox":

Let's say you need a fairly complicated but still routine operation, and you have to pick one of the two local hospitals, Mercy or Saint Simpson's, for the surgery. You decide to pick the safer of the two, based on their records for patient survival during surgery. You get the numbers: Mercy has 2,100 surgery patients in a year, of which 63 die—a 3 percent death rate. Saint Simpson's has 800 surgery patients, of whom 16 die—a 2 percent death rate. You decide it's safer to have your operation done at Saint Simpson's.

The fact is, you could actually be *more* likely to die at Saint Simpson's than at Mercy Hospital, despite the former hospital's lower death rate for surgery patients. But you would have no way of knowing this without learning some more information. In particular, you need to know how the total figures break down into smaller, highly significant categories.

Consider the categories of high-risk patients (older patients, victims of trauma) and low-risk patients (e.g., those who arrive in good condition for elective surgery). Saint Simpson's may have the better looking overall record, not because it performs better, but because *Saint Simpson's gets a higher proportion of low-risk patients than does Mercy.* Let's say Mercy had a death rate of 3.8 percent among 1,500 high-risk patients, whereas Saint Simpson's, with 200 high-risk patients, had a death rate of 4 percent. Mercy and Saint Simpson's each had 600 low-risk patients, with a 1 percent death rate at Mercy and a 1.3 percent rate at Saint Simpson's.

So, as it turns out, it's a safer bet going to Mercy Hospital whether you're high risk or low, even though Saint Simpson's has the lower overall death rate.

The moral of the story is to be cautious about accepting the interpretation that is attached to a set of figures, especially if they lump together several categories of the thing being studied.

—Adapted from a story in the Washington Post, *which quoted extensively from* DAVID S. MOORE, *professor of statistics at Purdue University*

Almost no one in Las Vegas believes the gambler's fallacy is in fact a fallacy.

—From an anonymous reviewer of this book

to "behave" as they should. Smaller samples increase the likelihood of random sampling error.

The law of large numbers also keeps knowledgeable gamblers and gambling establishments in business. They know that if they make a bet that gives them even a modest advantage in terms of a predictable ratio, then all they have to do is make the bet often enough (or, more frequently, have some chump make the opposing bet against them often enough) and they will come out winners.

Let's consider an example. A person who plays roulette in an American casino gives away an advantage to the house of a little over 5 percent. The odds of winning are 1 in 38 (because there are slots for thirty-six numbers plus a zero and a double-zero), but when the player wins, the house pays

Reverse Gambler's Fallacy

If you want to get tails, your chances are greater if you flip after there's been a run of heads, right? Well, no—that's the gambler's fallacy.

And if you *don't* want to get tails, you are better off if you flip *before* there's been a run of heads—Whoops! That's the gambler's fallacy in reverse.

off only at the rate of 1 in 36 (as if there were no zeros). Now, this advantage to the house doesn't mean you might not walk up to a table and bet on your birthday and win four times in a row. But the law of large numbers says that if you pull up a chair and play long enough, eventually the house will win it all back—and the rent money, too.

A final note while we're speaking about gambling. There is a famous error known as the **gambler's fallacy,** and it is as seductive as it is simple. Let's say that you're flipping a coin, and it comes up heads four times in a row. You succumb to the gambler's fallacy if you think that the odds of its coming up heads the next time are anything except 50 percent. It's true that the odds of a coin coming up heads five times in a row are small—only a little over 3 in 100—but once it has come up heads four times in a row, the odds are still 50-50 that it will come up heads the next time. Past performance may give you a clue about a horse race, but not about a coin flip (or any other event with a predictable ratio).

Recap

Inductive arguments include inductive generalizations, analogical arguments, and a third kind we'll discuss in the next chapter.

Inductive generalizations are made when we infer that an entire class or population of things (a target class or population) has a property or feature (the property or feature in question) because a sample of those things has that property or feature. Analogical arguments are made when we infer that some specific thing or things have a property or feature because some other similar things have that property or feature. We can evaluate generalizations and analogical arguments by considering three questions:

1. Are the sample and the target sufficiently alike? If we're considering a generalization, this is the same as asking if the sample is representative of the target class. If it's an analogical argument we have before us, it's simply a matter of whether the sample and target item are sufficiently similar in relevant respects.

2. Is the sample of sufficient size?

3. Is the cautiousness of the conclusion appropriate for the premises?

Which Is More Likely?

Which is more likely to have a week in which over 60 percent of new babies are boys—a large hospital or small hospital? If you thought it was a large hospital, you need to reread the section on the law of large numbers. (The example is from R. E. Nisbett and L. Ross, *Human Inference: Strategies and Shortcomings of Human Social Judgment.* Englewood Cliffs, N.J.:Prentice Hall, 1980.)

Several fallacies occur regularly when people use inductive arguments like the ones described in this chapter. We discussed biased sample (when the sample is not sufficiently representative), hasty conclusion or hasty generalization (when the sample is not big enough to warrant confidence in the conclusion), and anecdotal evidence (a version of hasty conclusion in which a single story or anecdote—or at most a very small number of such stories—is taken to support a conclusion that is actually unwarranted; this is often used to "refute" a larger body of statistical evidence).

Finally, we learned that the law of large numbers governs statistically predictable outcomes of events—the longer you play against the house, the more odds will favor it in precisely predictable ways. (Stay away from bets in the center of the craps table.)

Exercises

Exercise 10-1

In groups (or individually, if the instructor prefers), decide whether each of the following comments is (a) an analogical argument or (b) an analogy that isn't in an argument.

▲ 1. These shrubs look rather similar to privet. I bet they keep their leaves in the winter, just like privet.

2. Working in this office is just about exactly as much fun as driving in Florida without air conditioning.

3. The last version of Word was filled with bugs; that's why I know the new version will be the same way.

▲ 4. If you ask me, Dr. Walker has as much personality as a piece of paving concrete.

5. I hate math, and soon as I saw all those formulas and junk, I knew I'd hate this symbolic logic stuff too.

6. Your new boyfriend has been married five times?! Say—do you seriously think it'll work out better the next time?

▲   7. Too much sun will make your face all wrinkly; I suppose it would have that effect on your hands, too.

8. A CEO who had sex with an intern would be fired on the spot. A senior officer who slept with a recruit would be court-martialed. That's why Bill Clinton should not have been acquitted by the Senate.

9. I go, "Mom, don't buy me any more Levi's"; and she's like, "What?" So I told her, "They're for people your age," and she's like, "Well, I'll just give them to your sister"; and so I told her you're just like me and you won't want them either.

▲ 10. Here, you can use your screwdriver just like a chisel, if you want. Just give it a good whack with this hammer.

11. In elections during economic hard times, the party out of the White House has always made major gains in the Congress. That's why we can expect the president's party to suffer losses in the next election.

12. "Those thinkers in whom all stars move in cyclic orbits are not the most profound. Whoever looks into himself as into vast space and carries galaxies in himself, also knows how irregular all galaxies are; they lead into the chaos and labyrinth of existence."

Friedrich Nietzsche

▲ 13. "Religion . . . is the *opium* of the people. To abolish religion as the *illusory* happiness of the people is to demand their *real* happiness."

Karl Marx

14. "Publishing is to thinking as the maternity ward is to the first kiss."

Friedrich Von Schlegel

15. She's not particularly good at tennis, so I doubt she'd be good at racquetball.

▲ 16. "A book is like a mirror. If an ape looks in, a saint won't look out."

Ludwig Wittgenstein

17. As odd as it sounds, historically the stock market goes up when there is bad news on unemployment, and the latest statistics show the unemployment rate is skyrocketing. This could be a good time to buy stocks.

18. I never met anyone from North Carolina who didn't have an accent thicker than molasses.

▲ 19. Yamaha makes great motorcycles, so I'll bet their pianos are pretty good, too.

20. The last time we played Brazil in soccer we got run through the washer and hung out to dry.

Exercise 10-2

In groups (or individually if the instructor prefers), decide whether each of the following is (a) an analogical argument or (b) an inductive generalization.

▲   1. Paulette, Georgette, Babette, and Brigitte are all Miami University English majors, and they are all atheists. Therefore, probably all the English majors at Miami University are atheists.

2. Paulette, Georgette, Babette, and Brigitte are all Miami University English majors, and they are all atheists. Therefore Janette, who is a Miami University English major, probably is also an atheist.

3. Gustavo likes all the business courses he has taken at Harvard to date. Therefore, he'll probably like all the business courses he takes at Harvard.

▲ 4. Gustavo likes all the business courses he has taken at Harvard to date. Therefore, he'll probably like the next business course he takes at Harvard.

5. Gustavo likes all the business courses he has taken at Harvard to date. Therefore, his brother, Sergio, who also attends Harvard, will probably like all the business courses he takes there, too.

6. Forty percent of Moore's 8:00 A.M. class are atheists. Therefore, 40 percent of all Moore's students are atheists.

▲ 7. Forty percent of Parker's 8:00 A.M. class are atheists. Therefore, probably 40 percent of Parker's 9:00 A.M. class are atheists.

8. Forty percent of Moore's 8:00 A.M. class are atheists. Therefore, probably 40 percent of all the students at Moore's university are atheists.

9. Bill Clinton lied to the American public about his relationship with Monica Lewinsky; therefore, he probably lied to the American public about Iraq, too.

▲ 10. Bill Clinton lied to the American public about his relationship with Monica Lewinsky; therefore, he probably lied to the American public about most things.

Exercise 10-3

In groups (or individually, if the instructor prefers), decide whether each of the following is (a) an analogical argument or (b) an inductive generalization.

▲ 1. With seven out of the last nine El Niños, we saw below-average rainfall across the northern United States and southern Canada. Therefore, chances are we'll see the same with the next El Niño.

2. I've been to at least twenty Disney movies in my lifetime, and not one of them has been especially violent. I guess the Disney people just don't make violent movies.

3. Most of my professors wear glasses; it's a good bet most professors everywhere do the same.

▲ 4. Seems like the Christmas decorations go up a little earlier each year. I bet next year they're up by Halloween.

5. The conservatives I've met dislike Colin Powell. Based on that, I'd say most conservatives feel the same way.

6. FIRST PROF: I can tell after just one test exactly what a student's final grade will be.

SECOND PROF: How many tests do you give, just a couple?

FIRST PROF: As a matter of fact, I give a test every week of the semester.

▲ 7. MRS. BRUDER: Bruder! Bruder! Guess what! The music department is selling two of their grand pianos!

MR. BRUDER: Well, let's check it out, but remember the last pianos they sold were way overpriced. Probably it'll be the same this time.

8. A 60 percent approval rating? Those polls are rigged by the liberal media. Most of the people I know say the man ought to be impeached.

9. The New England Patriots have won six of their last seven home games. They're playing at home on Sunday. Don't bet against them.

▲ 10. You're going out with a Georgette? Well, don't expect much because I've known three Georgettes and all of them have been stuck up, spoiled yuckheads. I'll bet this one will be a yuckhead, too.

Exercise 10-4

Go through the preceding exercise and for each item identify (1) the sample, (2) the target or target class (population), and (3) the feature (property) in question.

Exercise 10-5

In groups (or individually, if the instructor prefers), determine in which of the following inductive generalizations or analogical arguments the sample, the target or target class, or feature (property) in question is excessively vague or ambiguous.

▲ 1. The tests in this class are going to be hard, judging from the first midterm.

2. Judging from my experience, technical people are exceedingly difficult to communicate with sometimes.

3. The transmissions in 1999 Chrysler minivans tend to fail prematurely, if my Voyager is any indication.

▲ 4. Women can tolerate more stress than can men. My husband even freaks when the newspaper is a little late.

5. Movies are much too graphic these days. Just go to one—you'll see what I mean.

6. Violent scenes in the current batch of movies carry a message that degrades women. Just go see any of the movies playing downtown right now.

▲ 7. You'll need to get better clothing than that if you're going to Iowa. In my experience, the weather there sucks much of the year.

8. Entertainment is much too expensive these days, judging from the cost of movies.

9. Art majors sure are weird! I roomed with one, once. Man.

▲ 10. Artsy people bug me. They're all like, aaargh, you know what I mean?

11. The French just don't like Americans. Why, in Paris, they won't give you the time of day.

12. All the research suggests introverts are likely to be well-versed in computer skills.

▲ 13. Suspicious people tend to be quite unhappy, judging from what I've seen.

Exercise 10-6

How well does the sample in each of the following arguments represent the target or target class? In groups (or individually), choose from the following options:

a. Very well

b. Pretty well

c. Not very well

d. Very poorly

▲ 1. The coffee in that pot is lousy—I just had a cup.

2. The coffee at that restaurant is lousy—I just had a cup.

3. The food in that restaurant is lousy—I just ate there.

▲ 4. This student doesn't write very well, judging from how poorly she wrote on the first paper.

5. Terrence didn't treat her very well on their first date; I can't imagine he will treat her better next time.

6. I expect I'll have trouble sleeping after this huge feast. Whenever I go to bed on a full stomach, I never sleep very well.

▲ 7. Lupe's sister and mother both have high blood pressure; chances are Lupe does too.

8. Every movie Courtney Cox Arquette has been in has been great! I bet her next movie will be great, too!

▲ 9. Women don't play trombones; leastwise, I never heard of one who did.

10. I'm sure Blue Cross will cover that procedure because I have Blue Cross and they covered it for me.

11. Cocker spaniels are nice dogs, but they eat like pigs. When I was a kid, we had this little cocker that ate more than a big collie we had.

▲ 12. Cadillacs are nice cars, but they are gas hogs. When I was a kid, we owned this Cadillac that got around ten miles per gallon.

13. Cockatoos are great birds, but they squawk. A lot. Had one when I was a kid, and even the neighbors complained, it was so raucous.

14. The parties at the university always turn into drunken brawls. Why, just last week the police had to go out and break up a huge party at Fifth and Ivy.

Exercise 10-7 _____

Arrange the alternative conclusions of the following arguments in order of increasing cautiousness and then compare your rankings with those of three or four classmates. Some options are pretty close to being tied. Don't get in feuds with classmates or the teacher over close calls.

▲ 1. Not once this century has this city gone Republican in a presidential election. Therefore . . .
   a. I wouldn't count on it happening this time.
   b. it won't happen this time.
   c. in all likelihood it won't happen this time.
   d. there's no chance whatsoever it will happen this time.
   e. it would be surprising if it happened this time.
   f. I'll be a donkey's uncle if it happens this time.

2. Byron doesn't know how to play poker, so . . .
   a. he sure as heck doesn't know how to play blackjack.
   b. it's doubtful he knows how to play blackjack.
   c. there's a possibility he doesn't know how to play blackjack.
   d. don't bet on him knowing how to play blackjack.
   e. you're nuts if you think he knows how to play blackjack.

3. Every time I've used the Beltway, the traffic has been heavy, so I figure that . . .
   a. the traffic is almost always heavy on the Beltway.
   b. frequently the traffic on the Beltway is heavy.
   c. as a rule, the traffic on the Beltway is heavy.
   d. the traffic on the Beltway can be heavy at times.
   e. the traffic on the Beltway is invariably heavy.
   f. typically, the traffic on the Beltway is heavy.
   g. the traffic on the Beltway is likely to be heavy most of the time.

Exercise 10-8 _____

In which of the following arguments is the conclusion insufficiently cautious or overly cautious or neither, given the premises? After you have decided, compare your results with those of three or four classmates.

▲ 1. We spent a day on the Farallon Islands last June, and was it ever foggy and cold! So dress warmly when you go there this June. Based on our experience, it is 100 percent certain to be foggy and cold.

2. We've visited the Farallon Islands on five different days, two during the summer and one each during fall, winter, and spring. It's been foggy and cold every time we've been there. So dress warmly when you go there. Based on our experience, there is an excellent chance it will be foggy and cold whenever you go.

3. We've visited the Farallon Islands on five different days, all in June. It's been foggy and cold every time we've been there. So dress warmly when you go there in June. Based on our experience, it could well be foggy and cold.

▲ 4. We've visited the Farallon Islands on five different days, all in June. It's been foggy and cold every time we've been there. So dress warmly when you go there in June. Based on our experience, there is a small chance it will be foggy and cold.

5. We've visited the Farallon Islands on five different days, all in January. It's been foggy and cold every time we've been there. So dress warmly when you go there in June. Based on our experience, it almost certainly will be foggy and cold.

Exercise 10-9

For the past four years, Clifford has gone on a hundred-mile bicycle ride on the Fourth of July. He has always become too exhausted to finish the entire hundred miles. He decides to try the ride once again, but thinks, "Well, I probably won't finish it this year, either, but no point in not trying."

▲ 1. Does the conclusion as expressed seem appropriately cautious given the size of the sample and its similarity to the target?

2. Suppose the past rides were done in a variety of different weather conditions. With this change, would the argument be stronger than the original, weaker, or about the same?

3. Suppose that Clifford is going to ride the same bike this year that he's ridden in all the previous rides. Does this make the argument stronger than the original version, weaker, or neither?

▲ 4. Suppose the past rides were all done on the same bike, but that bike is not the bike Clifford will ride this year. Does this make the argument stronger than the original version, weaker, or neither?

5. Suppose Clifford hasn't yet decided what kind of bike to ride in this year's ride. Now, is the argument made stronger or weaker or neither if the past rides were done on a variety of different kinds of bike (e.g., road bikes, mountain bikes, racing bikes, etc.)?

6. Suppose the past rides were all done on flat ground and this year's ride will also be on flat ground. Does this make the argument stronger than the original version, weaker, or neither?

7. Suppose the past rides were all done on flat ground and this year's ride will be done in hilly territory. Does this make the argument stronger than the original version, weaker, or neither?

▲ 8. Suppose Clifford doesn't know what kind of territory this year's ride will cover. Is his argument made stronger or weaker or neither if the past rides were done on a variety of kinds of territory?

9. Suppose the past rides were all done in hilly territory and this year's ride will be done on flat ground. Does this make the argument stronger than the original version, weaker, or neither?

▲ 10. In answering the preceding item, did you take into consideration information you have about bike riding in different kinds of terrain or did you consider only the criteria for evaluating inductive arguments in general?

Exercise 10-10

During three earlier years Kirk has tried to grow artichokes in his backyard garden, and each time his crop has been ruined by mildew. Billie prods him to try one more time, and he agrees to do so, though he secretly thinks: "This is probably a waste of time. Mildew is likely to ruin this crop, too." (Note: To say that the new information warrants a more cautious conclusion is the same as saying the new information makes the argument weaker. Similarly for "less cautious" and "stronger.")

▲ 1. Suppose this year Kirk plants the artichokes in a new location. Does this information warrant a more cautious conclusion or less cautious conclusion than the original?

2. Suppose on the past three occasions Kirk planted his artichokes at different times of the growing season. Does this information warrant a more cautious conclusion or less cautious conclusion than the original?

3. Suppose this year Billie plants marigolds near the artichokes. Does this information warrant a more cautious conclusion or less cautious conclusion than the original?

▲ 4. Suppose the past three years were unusually cool. Does this information warrant a more cautious conclusion or less cautious conclusion than the original?

5. Suppose only two of the three earlier crops were ruined by mildew. Does this information warrant a more cautious conclusion or less cautious conclusion than the original?

6. Suppose one of the earlier crops grew during a dry year, one during a wet year, and one during an average year. Does this information warrant a more cautious conclusion or less cautious conclusion than the original?

▲ 7. Suppose this year, unlike the preceding three, there is a solar eclipse. Does this information warrant a more cautious conclusion or less cautious conclusion than the original?

8. Suppose this year Kirk fertilizes with lawn clippings for the first time. Does this information warrant a more cautious conclusion or less cautious conclusion than the original?

9. Suppose this year Billie and Kirk acquire a large dog. Does this information warrant a more cautious conclusion or less cautious conclusion than the original?

▲ 10. Suppose this year Kirk installs a drip irrigation system. Does this information warrant a more cautious conclusion or less cautious conclusion than the original?

Exercise 10-11

Every student I've met from Ohio State believes in God. My conclusion is that most of the students from Ohio State believe in God.

▲ 1. Suppose (as is the case) that Ohio State has no admission requirements pertaining to religious beliefs. Suppose further the students in the sample were all interviewed as they left a local church after Sunday services. Does this supposition warrant a more cautious conclusion or less cautious conclusion than the original?

2. Suppose all those interviewed were first-year students. Does this supposition warrant a more cautious conclusion or less cautious conclusion than the original?

3. Suppose all students interviewed were on the Ohio State football team. Does this supposition warrant a more cautious conclusion or less cautious conclusion than the original?

▲ 4. Suppose the speaker selected all the students interviewed by picking every tenth name on an alphabetical list of students' names. Does this supposition warrant a more cautious conclusion or less cautious conclusion than the original?

5. Suppose the students interviewed all responded to a questionnaire published in the campus newspaper titled "Survey of Student Religious Beliefs." Does this supposition warrant a more cautious conclusion or less cautious conclusion than the original?

6. Suppose the students interviewed were selected at random from the record office's list of registered automobile owners. Does this supposition warrant a more cautious conclusion or less cautious conclusion than the original?

Exercise 10-12

Read the passage below, and answer the questions that follow.

> In the Georgia State University History Department, students are invited to submit written evaluations of their instructors to the department's personnel committee, which uses those evaluations to help determine whether history instructors should be recommended for retention and promotion. In his three history classes, Professor Ludlum has a total of one hundred students. Six students turned in written evaluations of Professor Ludlum; four of these evaluations were negative, and two were positive. Professor Hitchcock, who sits on the History Department Personnel Committee, argued against recommending Ludlum for promotion. "If a majority of the students who bothered to evaluate Ludlum find him lacking," he stated, "then it's clear to me that a majority of all his students find him lacking."

▲ 1. What is the sample in Professor Hitchcock's reasoning?

2. What is the target or target class?

3. What is the property in question?

▲ 4. Is this an analogical argument or a generalization?

5. Are there possibly important differences between the sample and the target (or target class) that should reduce our confidence in Professor Hitchcock's conclusion?

▲ 6. Is the sample random?

7. How about the size of Professor Hitchcock's sample? Is it large enough to help ensure that the sample and target or target classes won't be too dissimilar?

▲ 8. Based on the analysis of Professor Hitchcock's reasoning that you have just completed in the foregoing questions, how strong is his reasoning?

Exercise 10-13

George's class is doing a survey of student opinion on social life and drinking. One of the questions is "Do you believe that students who are members of fraternities and sororities drink more alcohol than students who are not members of such organizations?" Let's say that George would wager a large sum on a bet only if he had a 95 percent chance of winning. Answer the following questions for him. (Use Table 10-1 on page 368 to help you with this exercise.)

▲ 1. Exactly 60 percent of a random sample of 250 students at George's college believe that students in fraternities and sororities drink more than others. Should George bet that exactly 60 percent of the student population hold the same belief?

2. Should he bet that *at least* 60 percent hold that belief?

3. Should he bet that *no more than* 66 percent hold the belief?

▲ 4. According to the text, the largest number that he can safely bet hold the belief mentioned is _____ percent.

5. Let's change the story a bit. Let's make the sample size 100 and once again say exactly 60 percent of it hold the belief in question. Should George bet that at least 55 percent of the total student population hold the belief?

6. Should he bet that at least 50 percent of the total hold it?

▲ 7. It is safe for George to bet that no more than _____ percent of the total population share the belief in question. What's the smallest number that can be placed in the blank?

Exercise 10-14

Critically analyze these arguments by analogy. Do this by specifying what things are compared in the analogy and then identifying important relevant dissimilarities between these things. If any of the arguments seem pretty strong— that is, if the dissimilarities are not relevant or particularly important—say so.

Example

> Earth and Venus are twin planets; both have atmospheres that protect them from the harsh environment of outer space, both are about the same size and exert similar gravitational force, both have seasons, both have days and nights, and there are other similarities. Earth has life; therefore, Venus may well have life, too.

Analysis

1. The terms of the analogy are Earth and Venus.
2. Important relevant dissimilarities are that Venus's atmosphere is composed of 96 percent carbon dioxide, whereas Earth's contains about 0.03 percent. Also, the surface temperature of Venus is higher than the boiling point of lead.

▲ 1. Tiger Woods began playing golf at the age of two, and look what he's accomplished. I'm going to start golf lessons for my two-year-old, too, by golly.

2. A household that doesn't balance its budget is just asking for trouble. It's the same with the federal government. Balance the federal budget, or watch out.

3. Saccharin has been determined to cause cancer in rats; in similar doses, it's likely to do so in humans as well.

▲ 4. Senator Clinton has been an excellent senator for New York; therefore, she would make an excellent president.

5. Ross Perot really knows how to run a business; therefore, he'd have made an excellent president.

6. There's no way I can actually feel other people's pain or experience their fear or anxiety. Nevertheless, I can be quite sure other people experience these things because they behave as I do when I experience them. Therefore, I can be equally sure animals experience these things when they behave in a similar fashion.

▲ 7. Bush has an 80 percent approval rating in Georgia. It's safe to assume he is equally popular in Massachusetts.

8. Suppose you had never seen a clock before and one day you found one lying on the ground somewhere. You'd be certain it had been made by an intelligent being who was up to the task of creating such a thing. Now think of the Earth. It displays a far more complex design than a clock. It is safe to conclude that it, too, just like a clock, is the product of an intelligent creator, and one up to such a momentous task as creating a world. This is a very good reason to think that God exists.

9. Trying to appease Adolf Hitler was totally counterproductive; trying to appease Saddam Hussein would likely have had similar results.

▲ 10. The Barneses are traveling to Europe for a year and decide to find a student to house-sit for them. They settle on Warren because he is neat and tidy in his appearance. "If he takes such good care of his personal appearance," Mrs. Burns thinks, "he's likely to take good care of our house, too."

11. Abortion consists in killing a living person. If abortion is wrong, therefore so is capital punishment.

Exercise 10-15

Identify any fallacies that are present in the following passages:

▲ 1. From a letter to the editor: "I read with great interest the May 23 article on the study of atheists in federal prisons, according to which most of these atheists identify themselves as socialists, communists, or anarchists. That most atheists, along with all their other shortcomings, turn out to be political wackos surprises yours truly not one bit."

2. I ordered a packet of seeds from Hansen Seed Company last year, and only half of them germinated. I'll bet you get only half the plants you're expecting from the order you just sent them.

3. My cousin has a Dodge truck that he drives around on the ranch and back and forth to town as well. It now has 120,000 miles on it without any major overhaul. I've started to believe the commercials: Dodge does build tough trucks!

▲ 4. Drug abuse among professional athletes is a serious and widespread problem. Three players from a single team admitted last week that they had used cocaine.

5. Most Americans favor a national lottery to reduce the federal debt. In a poll taken in Las Vegas, more than 80 percent said they favored such a lottery.

6. I think collies are one of the easiest breeds of dog to train. I had one when I was young, and she was really easy to teach. Of course, if you need more evidence, there's Lassie.

7. From a letter to the editor: "Last week, members of the Animal Liberation Front stole several hours of videotapes of experiments done to animals at the University of Pennsylvania's Head Injury Clinical Research Center. According to reliable reports, one of the tapes shows baboons having their brains damaged by a piston device that smashed into their skulls with incredible force. The anesthetic given the baboons was allegedly insufficient to prevent serious pain. Given that this is what animal research is all about, Secretary of Health and Human Services Margaret Heckler acted quite properly in halting federal funding for the project. Federal funding for animal research ought to be halted, it seems to me, in the light of these atrocities."

▲ 8. Overheard: "You're not going to take a course from Harris, are you? I know at least three people who say he's terrible. All three flunked his course, as a matter of fact."

9. A majority of Ohio citizens consider the problem of air pollution critical. According to a survey taken in Cleveland, more than half the respondents identified air pollution as the most pressing of seven environmental issues and as having either "great" or "very great" importance.

▲ 10. Comment: What are we getting for the billions we spend on these new weapons? Absolutely nothing. Just look at the Apache helicopter. I read where they can't fly one of them for more than ten hours without grounding it for major repairs.

11. The IRS isn't interested in going after the big corporations, just middle-class taxpayers like you and me. I was audited last year, and I know several people who have been audited. You ever hear of ExxonMobil getting nailed?

12. I am totally outraged by the ethics of our elected representatives. Just look around: Bill Clinton accepted illegal campaign donations; Newt Gingrich was fined $300,000 for misusing money. I tell you, they are all just a bunch of crooks.

▲ 13. When he was president, Ronald Reagan occasionally would wave a copy of the "Help Wanted" section of some newspaper to demonstrate that U.S. unemployment wasn't really so bad. What was the fallacy in this "argument"?

Exercise 10-16

1. In the text, it is said that a person playing roulette has a disadvantage of about 5 percent compared with the house. Explain what this means.

2. Choose two or three other gambling bets for which you can calculate or look up the odds against the bettor. (Stick with games of pure chance; those that can involve a bit of skill, such as twenty-one—also known as black-jack—are much more difficult to deal with.) Determine which bet gives the house the smallest advantage.

3. Choose a state lottery and determine the odds against winning for a given ticket. Can you determine what kind of advantage the "house" has in such a gamble?

Exercise 10-17

1. Explain in your own words what the law of large numbers says.

2. "Over the long term, human births will approximate 50 percent males and 50 percent females." Is this a reasonable application of the law of large numbers? What facts can you think of that are relevant to determining whether this is a reasonable application of the law?

3. A person is betting on flips of a coin. He always bets on heads. After he loses three in a row, you hear him say, "Okay, I'm due for one now!" as he raises his bet. Write a brief note in which you give him some friendly advice.

Writing Exercises

1. Which of the following general claims do you accept? Select one that you accept and write a one-page essay presenting evidence (giving arguments) for the claim. When you are finished, write down on a separate piece of paper a number between 1 and 10 that indicates how strong you think your overall "proof" of the general claim is, with 10 = very strong and 1 = very weak. Take about two minutes to complete your essay. Write your name on the back of your paper.

   General claims:

   You get what you pay for.
   Nice guys finish last.
   Everything else being equal, men prefer blondes.
   Women are more gentle and nurturing than men.
   Politicians are untrustworthy.
   Government intrudes into our private lives/business affairs too much.
   Too many welfare recipients don't deserve assistance.
   College teachers are liberals.
   Jocks are dumb.
   The superwealthy pay less in taxes than they should.

2. When everyone is finished, the instructor will collect the papers and redistribute them to the class. In groups of four or five, read the papers and assign a number from 1 to 10 to each one (10 = very strong; 1 = very weak). When all groups are finished, return the papers to their authors. When you get your paper back, compare the number you assigned to your work with the number the group assigned to it. The instructor may ask volunteers to defend their own judgment of their work against the judgment of the group. Do you think there is as much evidence for the claim you selected as you did when you argued for it initially?

Chapter 11

Causal Arguments

A few months ago Uncle Pete (an actual uncle of one of your authors) came down with pneumonia. His condition was life-threatening. Aunt Clara prayed for Pete—and, we are happy to report, Uncle Pete recovered. Did Aunt Clara's prayers help? Aunt Clara is certain they did. ("Can you prove they didn't?" she asks.) Pete's doctor is keeping his thoughts to himself.

We don't know whether Aunt Clara's prayers helped Uncle Pete—and, in fact, neither does Aunt Clara. We know only that Aunt Clara prayed and then Uncle Pete recovered. Knowing that, however, is not the same as knowing that the prayers had anything at all to do with the recovery.

Thinking that X being followed by Y means that X caused Y is a common mistake in reasoning. It's known as the **post hoc fallacy** and is one of the most common mistakes people make.

"Post hoc fallacy" is short for the Latin phrase *post hoc, ergo propter hoc*, which translates as "After that, therefore because of that," or to put it a bit more loosely, "This thing happened right after that other thing, so this thing was caused by that other thing." Whenever we reason this way, we make that mistake. Uncle Pete's cure happened when, or just after, Aunt Clara prayed; therefore the praying caused the cure—this is post hoc reasoning.

That this kind of reasoning is a mistake should be obvious. Moore's birthday happened just before Parker's, but Moore's birthday didn't cause Parker's.

On the other hand, suppose Howard topples over with a heart attack immediately after sprinting up two flights of stairs. Doesn't the fact that the heart attack came on the heels of the sprint suggest the one thing caused the other? The answer is no. After all, the heart attack also came on the heels of Howard's sweating heavily, and it would be peculiar to suppose on these grounds that his sweating caused his heart attack. Something else obviously needs to be considered before we can say that the sprinting caused the heart attack. What other things? To answer this, we need to look at the principles involved when we reason our way to a statement about cause and effect.

Informal Causal Reasoning

A **causal claim** (or **cause-and-effect claim**) states or suggests the presence (or absence) of causation. An example is worth several words, so here are examples of causal claims:

- Aunt Clara's praying helped Uncle Pete recover from pneumonia.
- At high concentrations, some enzymes damage healthy tissue.
- Pressing the two surfaces together produced a permanent bond.
- Dnase significantly improves lung function.
- Vitamin C does not cure colds.
- Fertilizing with Scott's didn't do anything for my lawn.
- Sprinting caused Howard to have a heart attack.

A statement to the effect that X causes or caused Y can, of course, be offered as a hypothesis rather than as a claim: A **hypothesis** is a supposition offered as a starting point for further investigation. When you hypothesize, you aren't actually claiming something, you are conjecturing (which is a rather fancy way to say you're making a guess). However, the reasoning that supports a claim and the reasoning that tests a hypothesis is the same, so, for practical purposes we can treat causal claims and **causal hypotheses** as the same kind of thing.

Two Basic Patterns of Causal Reasoning

When we assert (or hypothesize) that one thing causes or caused another, our reasoning often will rely on either (or some combination) of two distinct patterns of inference: relevant-difference reasoning and common-thread reasoning.

■ Relevant-Difference Reasoning

If your prized azaleas aren't doing well this year, and you want to know why, you will ask yourself, What else is different this year? If a single relevant difference stands out about this year's azaleas (in addition to their not doing well), you naturally suspect it had something to do with the poor bloom. For example, if this year was hotter and drier than previous years, you would

The Spotted Owl

After logging in old-growth forests was halted in the Pacific Northwest to save the spotted owl, the general economy in that area went into a dramatic tailspin. To conclude from this fact that the measures taken to save the spotted owl *caused* the economic decline is to be guilty of *post hoc* reasoning. To have caused the economic decline, these measures would have to have been the *only relevant thing to happen before the decline.* (In fact, the most severe economic recession since the Great Depression also happened at the same time, throughout the American economy. Maybe the attempt to save the spotted owl caused that, too.)

naturally suspect that the hot, dry weather was involved causally with the poor bloom.

In other words, if an effect is present in one situation and it isn't present in other, similar, situations, we try to find the **relevant difference** between the situation in which the effect is present and the situations in which it isn't. If we find a relevant difference, we suspect that it caused (or was a part of the cause of) the effect we are interested in.

If, for example, the cancer rate in one neighborhood is higher than in others, you want to know what's different about that neighborhood. Is there a former toxic dump nearby? Are chemical solutions present for some reason? If so, we will think that the dump or solutions have something to do with the high cancer rate. If you wake up one morning with a splitting headache and you remember having done something different the night before (reading for several hours in poor light, for example), you will suspect that this variation in behavior caused the headache.

It isn't just bad effects we are interested in. If somebody who hasn't been especially friendly starts going out of his way to be nice, you might wonder what caused the change. Again, you consider what's different about this situation that would explain why Trent, or whoever it is, suddenly wants to be friendly. Did you just get promoted and are now Trent's supervisor? You might well suspect that fact had something to do with the change.

In each instance, an effect has occurred that didn't occur in other, similar, situations. *If there is some important relevant difference between this situation, in which the effect occurred, and the other situations, in which it didn't, we suspect that difference played a causal role in the effect we are concerned about.* The fact that Howard had a heart attack after sprinting up two flights of stairs doesn't give us a real reason for suspecting the sprinting caused the heart attack. If we have legitimate grounds for that suspicion, it is that the sprinting is the only difference between this occasion, on which Howard had a heart attack, and other occasions, on which he did not. Likewise, the fact that Pete recovered after Aunt Clara prayed does not in itself show that her praying played a part in his recovery. You need to know that her praying was the only relevant difference between the time when he was sick and the time when he was well.

■ *Common-Thread Reasoning*

Now, a different pattern of reasoning is illustrated by considering what happens when you have *multiple* occurrences of some effect. For example, what happens when a group of people all come down with the same mysterious health symptoms such as those that accompany SARS? The first thing health officials do is look for a **common thread** among the victims. Did they all breathe the same air? Were they all present in the same location? Is there some person they all contacted? Common threads are immediately suspicious as possible causes of the illness.

Or let's suppose some years your azaleas bloom prolifically and other years they don't. You will look for a common thread among the years they bloom well (or among the years they don't). For example, if, whenever they bloomed well you always pruned in the fall rather than the winter, you'd suspect time of pruning might have something to do with quality of bloom.

Or let's suppose every Saturday evening during the summer the mosquitoes in the backyard are present in hideous numbers but on other evenings they aren't. What is it about Saturday evening? you should wonder. What do Saturday evenings have in common that might be relevant to mosquitoes? For example, do you mow the grass every Saturday in the early evening? If so, you should suspect that is the explanation.

Common-thread reasoning and relevant-difference reasoning are similar, so let's summarize them abstractly:

> **RELEVANT-DIFFERENCE REASONING:**
>
> If an effect is present in one situation but not present in other similar situations, any relevant differences between the situation where the effect is present and the other situations where it isn't are suspicious as the cause (or part of it) of the effect in question.

> **COMMON-THREAD REASONING**
>
> If an effect is present in multiple situations, any common thread that unites those situations in which the effect is present are suspicious as the cause (or part of it) of the effect in question.

Common-thread reasoning is best suited as a method for forming hypotheses to be tested in some other way, usually involving relevant-difference reasoning. That's because the multiple occurrences of the effect could always have resulted from different causes. In other words, coincidence may have

"Teen Smoking Surge Reported After Joe Camel's 1988 Debut"

So said the Associated Press headline that accompanied this graphic. The article, however, stated that the Centers for Disease Control *attributed* the surge in part to kid-friendly cartoon advertising like the Joe Camel ads. It also noted that then-president Clinton had blamed the increase on the Joe Camel ad campaign.

It is true that the CDC studies showed that the rate for beginning smokers had been *declining* steadily for over a decade before it started increasing again in 1988. It is also true that *something* caused the rate to start increasing again, beginning in 1988. And finally, it is true that R. J. Reynolds introduced *Joe Camel* in its advertising for Camel cigarettes in 1988.

But *this* information, while suspicious, does not show that the increase was *caused*, even in part, *by* the ad campaign. For example, reportedly there was a notable increase in the appearance of cigarette smoking in movies beginning about then, too. As it stands, this is *post hoc, ergo propter hoc.*

Rise in youth smoking
The incidence of youths becoming regular smokers jumped 50 percent between 1988 and 1996. A look at the rate of youths who started smoking daily, age 12–17:

Per 1,000 non-smoking youths*

80	1996:
75	**77.0**
70	1988:
65	**51.2**
60	
55	
50	

1988 '90 '92 '94 '96

*Considered non-smokers at start of year
Source: Centers for Disease Control and Prevention

---

played a role—maybe Sally got sick for one reason, Tony got sick for an entirely unrelated reason, Cisco for some third reason, and so forth. Also, multiple occurrences of an effect are likely to have many other things in common besides whatever it was that caused them—for example, Tony and Sally and Cisco might all be friends, might have traveled together in the same car, and so on.

Relevant-difference reasoning, on the other hand, can be reasonably conclusive—at least in experimental conditions. If a piece of litmus paper turns red when you dip it in a liquid, it is safe to think the liquid caused the alteration. That's because the litmus paper prior to dipping and the litmus paper during dipping were exactly the same, except for the liquid. This may sound like post hoc reasoning, but it isn't: The reason for saying the liquid caused the litmus paper to turn red isn't just that it turned red after touching the liquid. The reason is that touching the liquid was the only relevant difference that could explain the paper's turning red.

Even apart from carefully controlled experimental conditions, relevant-difference reasoning yields conclusions that are certain by everyday standards of rigor. If the car won't start immediately after you installed a new electrical

According to a report in the Journal of the American Medical Association, infants who are breastfed have higher IQs later in life.

—On the other hand, maybe parents with higher IQs are more aware of the health advantages of breastfeeding and as a result are more likely to breastfeed their children.

device, and you are sure the before-installation and after-installation conditions are the same except for the device and the failure to start, you are right to think the device or its installation is the problem.

Common Mistakes in Informal Causal Reasoning

When we use relevant-difference or common-thread reasoning, we can make mistakes. Those that follow are pretty common. The strength of the reasoning depends on the extent to which we can eliminate these mistakes. Post hoc reasoning essentially involves a failure to eliminate the following mistakes.

- ▲ *We can overlook alternative common threads or differences.* Let's say the azaleas don't bloom well this spring. Well, we failed to fertilize the azaleas last winter; but we must be careful not to focus just on that and, as a result, overlook other relevant differences— for example, the fact that we also failed to prune them last winter.

- ▲ *We can focus on irrelevant differences or common threads.* What if, this year, we read two new books on ornamental horticulture? This is a difference between this year and previous years all right, but it isn't a *relevant* difference if we don't actually *do* anything different to our azaleas. Just *reading* about them plays no role in whether or not they bloom. What do we mean when we say a difference or thread is relevant? We mean it is not unreasonable to suppose the difference might have caused the feature in question. Obviously, the more you know about a subject, the better able you are to say whether a given difference is relevant. If you knew nothing about anything, then you would have no idea what is relevant and what isn't.

- ▲ *We can overlook the possibility that causation is the reverse of what has been asserted.* Did his fall cause the rope to break? Or did the rope's breaking cause his fall? Does your back ache because of your poor posture? Or is your poor posture the result of your aching back?

- ▲ *We can overlook the possibility that the stated cause and the stated effect are both effects of some third, underlying cause.* For example: Did Sarah become nauseated because of the hot peppers she ate? Maybe, but if Sarah is pregnant, maybe *that* caused her to want hot peppers and also caused her to be nauseated.

- ▲ *We can fail to consider the possibility of coincidence.* This is especially likely in common-thread reasoning. For example, if your throat, head, and chest all hurt, it is reasonable to look for a common thread. But possibly the pains result from separate and unrelated

See What Happens If You Watch the Tube?

Recent research indicates that people who watch several hours of TV each day, as compared with those who don't watch very much, express more racially prejudiced attitudes, perceive women as having more limited abilities and interests than men, overestimate the prevalence of violence in society, and underestimate the number of old people. Does this suggest to you that these attitudes and misconceptions are the *result* of watching a lot of TV, that TV *causes* people to have these attitudes and misconceptions? If so, that's fine. But remembering not to overlook possible underlying common causes should lead you to contemplate another idea. It's possible that what accounts for these attitudes and misconceptions isn't too much TV, but rather *ignorance*, and that ignorance is also what makes some people happy spending hours in front of the tube. An underlying common cause?

causes: In other words, possibly there is no relevant common thread. Coincidences happen all the time, and they are frequently taken as cause and effect when they are nothing of the sort.

If we fail to take these possibilities into consideration, we are apt to be left thinking A caused B merely because A happened before B. In other words, if we don't consider these possibilities, we are likely to commit the post hoc fallacy.

Exercise 11-1

Which of the following are causal claims (hypotheses)?

▲ 1. Webber's being healthy is probably what made the Kings so much better this year.

2. Dress more warmly! It's windy out there.

3. Gilbert's disposition has deteriorated since he and his wife separated; it isn't just coincidence.

▲ 4. When Senator Lott praised Strom Thurman, that forced some conservatives to call for his resignation.

5. Getting that new trumpet player certainly improved the brass section.

6. When men wear a swimsuit, they have difficulty doing math problems.

▲ 7. Despite all the injuries, the Dolphins manage to keep winning. It must have something to do with their positive attitude.

8. Too little sleep will slow down your reaction time.

9. Women are worse drivers than men.

Carrots Can Kill!
A few orange and green ruminations about life, death and vegetables from the Miner Institute, Chazy, New York

Nearly all sick people have eaten carrots. Obviously, the effects are cumulative.

An estimated 99.9 percent of all people who die from cancer have eaten carrots.

Another 99.9 percent of people involved in auto accidents ate carrots within 60 days before the accident.

Some 93.1 percent of juvenile delinquents come from homes where carrots are served frequently.

Among the people born in 1839 who later dined on carrots, there has been a 100 percent mortality rate.

All carrot eaters born between 1900 and 1910 have wrinkled skin, brittle bones, few teeth, and failing eyesight . . . if the perils of carrot consumption have not already caused their deaths.

—Priorities *magazine, Summer 1990*

What errors in causal reasoning can you find in these "arguments"?

▲ 10. Randomized clinical trials produce unbiased data on the benefits of drugs.

11. The batteries in that flashlight are completely dead.

12. The reason that flashlight won't work is that the batteries are completely dead.

▲ 13. Believe me, the batteries in that flashlight are dead. Try it, and you'll see it doesn't work.

14. Sandra's true reason for running for treasurer is she likes all the attention.

15. Aunt Clara thinks her prayers cured Uncle Pete.

▲ 16. The risk of having a heart attack is 33 percent higher in the winter than in the summer, even in Los Angeles.

Exercise 11-2

What is the cause and what is the effect in each of the following?

▲ 1. The cat won't eat, so Mrs. Quibblebuck searches her mind for a reason. "Now, could it be," she thinks, "that I haven't heard mice scratching around in the attic lately?" "That's the explanation," she concludes.

2. Each time one of the burglaries occurred, observers noticed a red Mustang in the vicinity. The police, of course, suspect the occupants as being responsible.

The Great 9/11 Mystery

How could all these facts be mere coincidence?

- The day was 9/11 (9 plus 1 plus 1 equals 11).
- American Airlines Flight 11 was the first to hit the World Trade Center.
- 92 people were on board (9 plus 1 plus 1 equals 11).
- September 11 is the 254th day of the year (2 plus 5 plus 4 equals 11).
- "New York City" has 11 letters in it.
- "The Pentagon" has 11 letters in it.
- "Saudi Arabia" (where most of the 9/11 terrorists were from) has 11 letters in it.
- "Afghanistan" has 11 letters in it.
- And get this: Within eleven months of September 11, 2001, eleven men, all connected to bioterror and germ warfare, died in strange and violent circumstances: One suffocated; another was stabbed, another hit by a car; another shot dead by a fake pizza delivery boy; one was killed in an airplane crash; one died from a stroke while being mugged; and the rest met similar ends.

Could this possibly be coincidence? What are the odds against all these things happening and being connected by the number 11?

Well if you think these events must somehow be causally interconnected, you'd have a lot of company. But it wouldn't include mathematicians—or us. Why not? In a world where so many things happen, strange and

3. Violette is a strong Cowboys fan. Because of her work schedule, however, she has been able to watch their games only twice this season, and they lost both times. She resolves not to watch any more. "It's bad luck," she decides.

▲ 4. Giving the little guy more water could have prevented him from getting dehydrated, said Ms. Delacruz.

5. OAXACA, Mexico (AP)—Considered by many to be Mexico's culinary capital, this city took on McDonald's and won, keeping the hamburger giant out of its colonial plaza by passing around tamales in protest.

6. Eating fish or seafood at least once a week lowers the risk of developing dementia, researchers have found.

▲ 7. It has long puzzled researchers why people cannot detect their own bad breath. One theory is that people get used to the odor.

8. Researchers based at McDuff University put thirty young male smokers on a three-month program of vigorous exercise. One year later, only 14 percent of them still smoked. An equivalent number of young male smokers who

Touchstone Pictures/Frank Masi

In the movie *Signs*, Mel Gibson is worried about the dark secrets of the universe.

seemingly improbable coincidences are bound to happen every second of every day.

Not convinced? Ask each of your classmates to think of as many events or things connected with the 9/11 attack that involve the number 11. Give each person a week to work on this. We'll bet the collected list of "suspicious" coincidences is very long.

As for the men connected with bioterrorism and germ warfare, you might be interested to know that the American Society for Microbiology alone has 41,000 members, and the total number of people "connected" in some way or other with bioterrorism and germ warfare would be indefinitely larger than that. We'd bet our royalties that in the eleven months following September 11, a lot more than just eleven people connected with bioterrorism and germ warfare died mysteriously and/or violently.

Lisa Belkin of the *New York Times Magazine* wrote an article on this subject (August 18, 2002), from which we learned about the coincidences mentioned above.

Incidentally, "Moore/Parker" has eleven letters.

did not go through the exercise program were also checked after a year, and it was found that 60 percent still smoked. The experiment is regarded as supporting the theory that exercise helps chronic male smokers kick the habit.

9. The stronger the muscles, the greater the load they take off the joint, thus limiting damage to the cartilage, which explains why leg exercise helps prevent osteoarthritis.

▲ 10. Many judges in Oregon will not process shoplifting, trespassing, and small-claims charges. This saves the state a lot of money in court expenses.

Exercise 11-3

Identify each reasoning pattern as (a) relevant-difference reasoning or (b) common-thread reasoning.

▲ 1. Pat never had trouble playing that passage before. I wonder what the problem is. It must have something to do with the piano she just bought.

Coincidence

One of your authors has a son whose birthday is exactly six months from that of his mother. Is this relationship of birthdays a coincidence or evidence of some "deeper" mother-son connection? Well, regardless of what the fortune-tellers might say about it, it's coincidence, of course. It would be silly to wonder whether these dates are a "sign" of some other connection between the two people. But coincidences are taken as such signs all the time. People who trade in conspiracy theories and prophecy depend on our willingness to place unwarranted weight on coincidence.

But think for a minute about what makes a coincidence. It is nothing but an event or, more usually, a combination of events, that we take to be unlikely—events that "beat the odds." For example, the odds of the birthdays described above being the case for any two randomly chosen people are very small (1 in 365). But notice: For any two people, *whatever* the relation between their birthdays, the odds of their being related in exactly that way are also very small! (In fact, ignoring leap years, the odds are 1 in 365 against it.) Indeed, no matter what combination of events happens, the odds of exactly that combination of events happening is likely to be very small. So, when we think about it that way, most *everything* is a coincidence! Which amounts to saying that nothing is more coincidental than most other things.

Of course, we are able to identify and characterize some combinations of events, and we don't readily do that for others. Having birthdays exactly six months apart is easier to characterize than having them, say, 80 days apart. For no good reason, we find it easier to attribute significance to the former than to the latter. But, as far as odds are concerned, one is just as unlikely as the other.

The point here is just that, given the extraordinary number of things that happen every day, it would be amazing if some combination of them, unlikely as it may be, didn't occasionally get our attention. In the words of mathematician John Allen Paulos, "In reality, the most astonishingly incredible coincidence imaginable would be the complete absence of all coincidences."

2. Sometimes the fishing is pretty good around here; sometimes it isn't. When I try to pin down why, it seems like the only variable is the wind. Strange as it sounds, the fish just don't bite when it's windy.

3. The price of gas has gone up more than 40 cents a gallon in the past three or four weeks. It all started when they had that fire down there in that refinery in Texas. Must have really depleted supplies somehow.

▲ 4. You know, it has occurred to me, whenever we have great roses like this, it's always after a long period of cloudy weather. I'll bet they don't like direct sun.

5. All of a sudden he's all "Let's go to Beano's for a change." Right. Am I supposed to think it's just coincidence his old girlfriend started working there?

6. You really want to know what gets into me and makes me be so angry? It's you! You and your stupid habit of never lifting up the toilet seat.

▲ 7. Why in heck am I so tired today? Must be all the studying I did last night. Thinking takes a lot of energy.

8. The computer isn't working again. Every time it happens the dang kids have been playing with it. Why can't they just use the computers they have down at school?

9. What makes your dog run away from time to time? I bet it has to do with that garbage you feed him. You want him to stay home? Feed him a better brand of dog food.

▲ 10. I'll tell you what caused all these cases of kids taking guns to school and shooting people. Every single one of those kids liked to play violent videogames, that's what caused it.

11. Gag! What did you do to this coffee, anyway—put Ajax in it?

12. Can you beat that? I set this battery on the garage floor last night and this morning it was dead. I guess the old saying about cement draining a battery is still true.

▲ 13. Clinton was impeached. Then his standing went up in the opinion polls. Just goes to show: No publicity is bad publicity.

14. Why did the dog yelp? Are you serious? You'd yelp if someone stomped on your foot, too.

15. Dennis certainly seems more at peace with himself these days. I guess starting up psychotherapy was good for him.

▲ 16. Every time we have people over, the next morning the bird is all squawky and grumpy. The only thing I can figure is it must not get enough sleep when people are over in the evening.

17. The lawn mower started up just fine last week, and now it won't start at all. Could the fact I let it stand out in the rain have something to do with it?

18. Every time Moore plays soccer, his foot starts to hurt. It also hurts right after he goes jogging. But when he bicycles, or uses an elliptical trainer, he doesn't have a problem. He decides to avoid exercise that involves pounding his feet on the ground.

▲ 19. You know, all of a sudden she's been, like, cool toward me? A bit, you know, icy? I don't think she liked it when I told her I was going to start playing poker with you guys again.

20. Your Chevy Suburban is hard to start. My Chevy Suburban starts right up. You always use Chevron gas; I use Texaco. You'd better switch to Texaco.

Exercise 11-4

Identify the numbered items as A, B, or C, where

A = possible coincidence

B = possible reversed causation

C = possibly a case in which the stated cause and stated effect both result from some third thing, an underlying cause

▲ 1. Whenever I mow the lawn I end up sneezing a lot more than usual. Must be gas fumes from the mower.

2. Maybe the reason he's sick is all the aspirin he's taking.

3. The only thing that could possibly account for Clark and his two brothers all having winning lottery tickets is that all three had been blessed by the Reverend Dim Dome just the day before. I'm signing up for the Reverend's brotherhood.

▲ 4. What else could cause the leaves to turn yellow in the fall? It's got to be the cold weather!

5. Perhaps Jason is nearsighted because he reads so many books.

6. First, Rodrigo gets a large inheritance. Then Charles meets the girl of his dreams. And Amanda gets the job she was hoping for. What did they all have in common? They all thought positively. It can work for you, too.

▲ 7. It's common knowledge that osteoarthritis of the knee causes weakness in the quadriceps.

8. Ever since the country lost its moral direction, the crime rate has gone through the ceiling. What more proof do you need that the cause of sky-rocketing crime is the breakdown in traditional family values?

9. Wow! Is Johnson hot or what? After that rocky start, he has struck out the last nine batters to face him. That's what happens when ol' Randy gets his confidence up.

▲ 10. Research demonstrates that people who eat fish are smarter. I'm going to increase my intake.

11. What a night! All those dogs barking made the coyotes yap, and nobody could get any sleep.

12. Isn't it amazing how when the leaves drop off in the winter, it makes the branches brittle?

▲ 13. What explains all the violence in society today? TV. Just look at all the violence they show these days.

14. On Monday, Mr. O'Toole came down with a cold. That afternoon, Mrs. O'Toole caught it. Later that evening, their daughter caught it, too.

15. Retail sales are down this year. That's because unemployment is so high.

16. Yes, they're saying electric blankets aren't really a health threat, but I know better. A friend had cancer and know what? He slept with an electric blanket.

17. At finals time, the bearded man on the front campus offers prayers in return for food. Donald is thinking, "Sure. Why not?—can't hurt anything." He approaches the bearded man with a tidbit. Later: The bearded man prays. Donald passes his finals. To skeptical friends: "Hey, you never know. I'll take all the help I can get."

18. It is an unusually warm evening, and the birds are singing with exceptional vigor. "Hot weather does make a bird sing," Uncle Irv observes.

▲ 19. Why did Uncle Ted live such a long time? A good attitude, that's why.

20. Studies demonstrate that people who are insecure about their relationships with their partners have a notable lack of ability to empathize with others. That's why we recommend that partners receive empathy training before they get married.

21. Lack of self-confidence can be difficult to explain, but common sense suggests that stuttering is among the causes, judging from how often the two things go together.

▲ 22. When I went to Munich last summer I went to this movie, and who was there? This guy I went to school with and hadn't seen in 15 years! No way that could be coincidence!

23. It's odd. I've seen a huge number of snails this year, and the roses have mildew. Don't know which caused which, but one of them obviously caused the other.

24. Her boyfriend is in a bad mood, you say? I'll bet it's because she's trying just a bit too hard to leash him. Probably gets on his nerves.

▲ 25. Many people note that top executives wear expensive clothes and drive nice cars. They do the same, thinking these things must be a key to success.

26. ". . . and let's not underestimate the importance of that home field advantage, guys."
    "Right, Dan. Six of the last seven teams that had the home field advantage went on to win the Super Bowl."

27. On your trip across the country, you note that the traffic is awful at the first intersection you come to in Jersey. "They certainly didn't do anyone a favor by putting a traffic light at this place," you reflect. "Look at all the congestion it caused."

Causation in Populations

Many causal claims do not apply in any straightforward way to individuals but rather apply to populations.* The claim "Drinking causes cancer of the mouth," for example, should not be interpreted as meaning that drinking

---

*For our analysis of causal factors in populations, we are indebted to Ronald N. Giere, *Understanding Scientific Reasoning*, 3d ed. (Fort Worth: Holt, Rinehart, and Winston, 1991).

Let's say increased TV watching does correlate with increased incidence of violent behavior. Maybe watching TV leads to the violent behavior—but, equally as likely, maybe both are a result of an underlying psychological cause (whatever causes kids to act violently also causes them to like to watch violent behavior). Or maybe kids who act violently become more interested in looking at violence (in the same way that signing up for a sport may heighten one's interest in watching the sport on TV).

Correlations, like the one reported in this graphic, do not establish causation. Thinking they do is a type of post hoc reasoning.

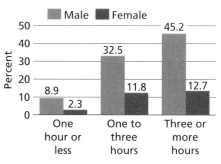

Television's effect on kids

Adolescents who watch more television are more prone to violent behavior later in life, a new study shows.

Percent of kids who acted aggressively at ages 16 or 20, based on number of hours of TV watched daily at age 14:

Note: The study was conducted over a 17-year interval with 707 individuals.

Source: *Science* Magazine

Associated Press

will cause mouth cancer for any given individual, or even that drinking will cause mouth cancer for the majority of individuals. The claim is that drinking is a *causal factor* for mouth cancer—that is, there would be more cases of mouth cancer if everyone drank than if no one did. And so it is with other claims about causation in populations: To say that X causes Y in population P is to say that there would be more cases of Y in population P if every member of P were exposed to X than if no member of P were exposed to X.

The evidence on which such claims may be soundly based comes principally from three kinds of investigations or "arguments" All are applications of relevant-difference reasoning, which we explained in the previous section.

The basic idea behind these investigations is this. Suppose someone wants to know if port wine applied to bald men's heads promotes hair growth. How would you find out? You would round up a group of bald men and divide them into two subgroups. On the heads of the men in one subgroup. you'd apply port wine. If the men in both subgroups are the same in all respects except for the port wine applied to the heads of the men in the one subgroup (a big "if"), then if the men in that subgroup sprout hair, you conclude that the port wine caused the hair growth, because it, the port wine, is the only relevant difference between the two groups.

With that as background, let's look at these types of investigations just a bit more closely.

■ *Controlled Cause-to-Effect Experiments*

In **controlled cause-to-effect experiments,** a random sample of a target population is itself randomly divided into two groups: (1) an experimental group, all of whose members are exposed to a suspected causal factor, C (e.g., exposure of the skin to nicotine), and (2) a control group, whose members are all treated exactly as the members of the experimental group, except that they are not exposed to C. Both groups are then compared with respect to frequency of some effect, E (e.g., skin cancer). If the difference, d, in the frequency of E in the two groups is sufficiently large, then C may justifiably be said to cause E in the population.

This probably sounds complicated, but the principles involved are matters of common sense. You have two groups that are essentially alike, except that the members of one group are exposed to the suspected causal agent. If the effect is then found to be sufficiently more frequent in that group, you conclude that the suspected causal agent does indeed cause the effect in question.

Familiarizing yourself with these concepts and abbreviations will help you understand cause-to-effect experiments:

> **experimental group**—the sample of the target population whose members are all exposed to the suspected causal agent
>
> **control group**—the sample of the target population whose members are treated exactly as the members of the experimental group are except that they are not exposed to the suspected causal agent
>
> C—the suspected causal agent
>
> E—the effect whose cause is being investigated
>
> d—the difference in the frequency of this effect in the experimental group and in the control group

Let us suppose that the frequency of the effect in the experimental group is found to be greater than in the control group. *How much greater* must the frequency of the effect in the experimental group be for us to say that the suspected causal agent actually is a causal factor? That is, how great must d be for us to believe that C is really a causal factor for E? After all, even if nicotine does *not* cause skin cancer, the frequency of skin cancer found in the experimental group *might* exceed the frequency found in the control group because of some chance occurrence.

Suppose that there are one hundred individuals in our experimental group and the same number in our control group, and suppose that d was greater than 13 percentage points—that is, suppose the frequency of skin cancer in the experimental group exceeded the frequency in the control group by more than 13 percentage points. Could that result be due merely to chance? Yes, but there is a 95 percent probability that it was *not* due to chance. If the frequency of skin cancer in the experimental group were to

Hey, Couch Potato—Read This!

You sometimes hear people say they avoid exercise because they know of someone who had a heart attack while working out. We trust you now recognize such reasoning as *post hoc:* To show that Uncle Ned's heart attack was caused by lifting weights, or whatever, you have to do more than show that the one thing happened and then the other thing happened.

There is a further problem here. To wonder whether strenuous exercise causes heart attacks is to wonder whether such exercise is a **causal factor** for heart attacks. And you can't really answer such questions by appealing to specific incidents, as we explain in the text. To think that you can show that something is (or isn't) a causal factor in a population by referring to isolated, specific events is to appeal illegitimately to anecdotal evidence, as we discuss at the end of this chapter.

(For the record: According to research published in the *New England Journal of Medicine* at the end of 1993, males who undertake heavy physical exertion increase their risk of a heart attack by around 100 times *if* they are habitually sedentary—out of shape. For those who do exercise regularly, strenuous exertion doesn't increase their risk of heart attack.)

exceed the frequency in the control group by more than 13 percentage points (given one hundred members in each group), then this finding would be *statistically significant at the .05 level,* which simply means that we could say with a 95 percent degree of confidence that nicotine is a cause of skin cancer. If we were content to speak with less confidence, or if our samples were larger, then the difference in the frequency of skin cancer between the experimental group and control group would not have to be as great to qualify as statistically significant.

Thus, saying that the difference in frequency of the effect between the experimental and control groups is **statistically significant** at some level (e.g., .05) simply means that it would be unreasonable to attribute this difference in frequency to chance. Just how unreasonable it would be depends on what level is cited. If no level is cited—as in reports of controlled experiments that stipulate only that the findings are "significant"—it is customary to assume that the results were significant at the .05 level, which simply means that the result could have arisen by chance in about five cases out of one hundred. Recall from Chapter 10 that we referred to a 95 percent confidence level, which is another way of saying we have the kind of probability found in a .05 significance level.

Media reports of controlled experiments usually state or clearly imply whether the difference in frequency of the effect found in the experimental and control groups is significant. However, if, as occasionally happens, there is a question about whether the results are statistically significant (i.e., are unlikely to have arisen by chance), it is important not to assume uncritically or automatically either of the following:

If you look at the new cases of death from AIDS, the fastest growing category could be ladies over the age of 70. If last year one woman over 70 died from AIDS and this year two do, you get a 100 percent increase in AIDS deaths for that category.

—JOHN ALLEN PAULOS

Percentage increases from a small baseline can be misleading.

E-Commerce: The Buyer Wins

Will the Net pull prices ever lower?

Theoretically, Internet retailing is supposed to be a positive sum game that allows consumers to win via easy access to price and product information and retailers to gain by obtaining detailed information on buyers' needs, tastes, and price sensitivity. If a new study on life insurance costs by Jeffrey R. Brown of Harvard University and Austan Goolsbee of the University of Chicago is any indication, however, it's consumers who really come out ahead.

The two economists noticed that the average prices of term life insurance, which had been edging down in response to falling mortality rates during the 1990s, suddenly fell sharply in 1996 and 1997. Meanwhile, a growing number of Web sites had begun offering price quotes from a variety of companies to potential buyers of term life insurance.

To see whether there was a connection, the authors matched highly detailed data from 1992 to 1997 on household Internet usage in the 50 states with similar data on the cost of term life insurance policies purchased by households over the same period. (The first set of data came from Forrester Research, the second from LIMRA International, a life insurance trade group.)

The results are striking. Among households of different age groups in different states, the study shows a strong correlation between rising Net usage and falling costs of term insurance. By contrast, costs of whole life insurance, for which online quotes were unavailable, hardly changed. The authors estimate that each 10% increase in the share of individuals in a group (say, those age 30–34 in Utah, 40–44 in Texas) using the Net reduced the group's average term insurance costs by 3% to 5%. By 1997, annual nationwide savings to consumers totaled $115 million to $215 million.

Thus, the Internet—by enabling people to comparison shop without having to first contact a variety of insurance agents—apparently drove insurance prices down not only for Web surfers but for their neighbors as well. And that was in a period in which Net usage was relatively low by today's standards.

For buyers, of course, this picture spells good news, suggesting that markets will become increasingly competitive as more and more people log on and search for low prices. Sellers both online and offline, however, are likely to find their profit margins under chronic pressure—forcing them to engage in continual cost-cutting. "That's a lesson the stock market finally appears to be learning," says Goolsbee.

By Gene Koretz

Source: Business Week, January 8, 2001.

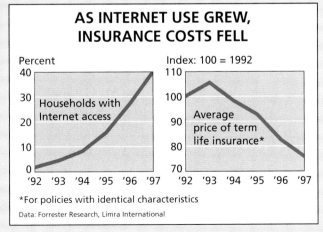

AS INTERNET USE GREW, INSURANCE COSTS FELL

Percent — Households with Internet access

Index: 100 = 1992 — Average price of term life insurance*

*For policies with identical characteristics

Data: Forrester Research, Limra International

Caution! These graphs show only correlation, not cause and effect!

TABLE 11-1   Approximate Statistically Significant *d*'s at .05 Level

Number in Experimental Group (with Similarly Sized Control Group)	Approximate Figure That d Must Exceed to Be Statistically Significant (in Percentage Points)
10	40
25	27
50	19
100	13
250	8
500	6
1,000	4
1,500	3

1. *That the sample is large enough to guarantee significance.* A large sample is no guarantee that the difference (*d*) in the frequency of the effect in the experimental group and in the control group is statistically significant. (However, the larger the sample, the smaller *d*—expressed as a difference in percentage points—need be to count as significant.) People are sometimes overly impressed by the mere size of a study.

2. *That the difference in frequency is great enough to guarantee significance.* The fact that there seems to be a pronounced difference in the frequency of the effect in the experimental group and in the control group is no guarantee that the difference is statistically significant. If the sample size is small enough, it may not be. If there are fifty rats in an experimental group and fifty more in a control group, then even if the frequency of skin cancer found in the experimental group exceeds the frequency of skin cancer found in the control group by as much as 18 percentage points, this finding would not be statistically significant (at the .05 level). If each group contained a thousand rats, a difference in frequency of 3 points would not qualify as significant. (And remember that a 3-point difference can be referred to as a "whopping" 50 percent difference if it is the difference between 6 points and 3 points.) Unless you have some knowledge of statistics, it is probably best not to assume that findings are statistically significant unless it is clearly stated or implied that they are.

Nevertheless, it may be helpful to you to have some rough idea of when a difference in frequency of effect in the experimental and control groups may be said to be statistically significant at the .05 level. Table 11-1 provides some examples.

Suppose there are ten individuals each in the randomly selected experimental and control groups. To be statistically significant at the .05 level, the difference between experimental and control group in frequency of the

Cigarettes, Cancer, and the Genetic-Factors Argument

For years the tobacco industry challenged the data showing that smoking causes lung cancer. The industry argued that certain unknown genetic factors (1) predispose some people to get cancer and also (2) predispose those same people to smoke.

The tobacco people are just doing what critical thinkers should do, looking for a common underlying cause for two phenomena that seem on the face of things to be related directly by cause and effect. However, they have never found any such common cause, and the claim that there *might be* one is not equivalent to the claim that there *is* one. Further, even if the industry theory is correct, that wouldn't diminish the other risks involved in smoking.

We should point out, however, that scientists have recently discovered that a chemical found in cigarette smoke damages a gene, known as p53, that acts to suppress the runaway growth of cells that lead to tumors. Researchers regard the discovery as finding the exact mechanism of causation of cancer by cigarette smoke; the discovery seems to put the whole issue of whether cigarettes cause cancer beyond much doubt.

effect must exceed 40 percentage points. If there are twenty-five people in each group, then d must exceed 27 points to be statistically significant, and so forth.

Even if it is clear in a controlled experiment that d is significant, there are a few more considerations to keep in mind when reviewing reports of experimental findings. First, the results of controlled experiments are often extended analogically from the target population (e.g., rats) to another population (e.g., humans). Such analogical extensions should be evaluated in accordance with the criteria for analogical arguments discussed in the previous chapter. In particular, before accepting such extensions of the findings, you should consider carefully whether there are important relevant differences between the target population in the experiment and the population to which the results of the experiment are analogically extended.

Second, it is important in controlled experiments that the sample from which the experimental and control groups are formed be representative of the target population, and thus it is essential that the sample be taken at random. Further, because the experimental and control groups should be as similar as possible, it is important that the assignment of subjects to these groups also be a random process. In reputable scientific experiments it is safe to assume that randomization has been so employed, but one must be suspicious of informal "experiments" in which no mention of randomization is made.

And while we're talking about reputable sources, remember that any outfit can call itself the "Cambridge Institute for Psychological Studies" and publish its reports in its own "journal." Organizations with prestigious-sounding place names (Princeton, Berkeley, Palo Alto, Bethesda, and so on), proper names (Fulbright, Columbia, and so on), or concepts (institute, academy, research, advanced studies) *could* consist of little more than a couple of university dropouts with a dubious theory and an axe to grind.

■ *Nonexperimental Cause-to-Effect Studies*

A **nonexperimental cause-to-effect study** (or argument) is another type of study designed to test whether something is a causal factor for a given effect. In this type of study, members of a target population (say, humans) who have not yet shown evidence of the suspected effect E (e.g., cancer of the colon) are divided into two groups that are alike in all respects except one. The difference is that members of one group, the experimental group, have all been exposed to the suspected cause C (fatty diets, for example), whereas the members of the other group, the control group, have not. Such studies differ from controlled experiments in that the members of the experimental group are not exposed to the suspected causal agent *by the investigators*—clearly, one limit of experimental studies is that investigators can't purposely expose human subjects to potentially dangerous agents. Eventually, just as in the controlled experiment, experimental and control groups are both compared with respect to the frequency of E. If the frequency in the experimental group exceeds the frequency in the control group by a statistically significant margin, we may conclude that C is the cause of E in the target population.

In reports of nonexperimental cause-to-effect studies, as in reports of controlled experiments, if it is not stated or clearly implied that the findings are significant, do not assume that they are merely because either (1) the samples are large or (2) the difference in the frequency of the effect in absolute terms or percentages is striking.

Likewise, (3) if a causal relationship found to hold in the target population on the basis of such a study is extended analogically to other populations, you should evaluate this analogical extension very carefully, especially with respect to any relevant differences between the target population and the analogical population.

And, finally, (4) note the following important difference between controlled experiments and nonexperimental cause-to-effect studies: In a *controlled* experiment, the subjects are assigned to experimental and control groups by a random process, after which the experimental subjects are exposed to C. This randomization ensures that experimental and control groups will be alike except for the suspected causal agent that the experimental group is then exposed to. But in the *nonexperimental* study, the experimental group (which is still so called even though no experiment is performed) is composed of randomly selected individuals who have already been exposed to the suspected causal agent or who say they were. And the individuals who have already been exposed to C (or who say they were) may differ from the rest of the target population in some respect in addition to having been exposed to C. For example, there is a positive correlation between having a fatty diet and drinking alcoholic beverages. Thus, an experimental group

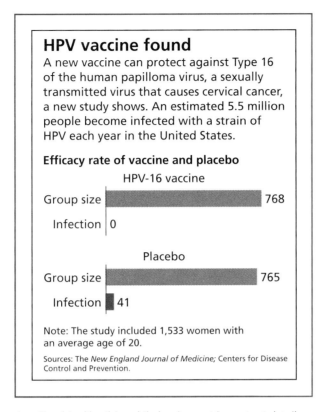

HPV vaccine found

A new vaccine can protect against Type 16 of the human papilloma virus, a sexually transmitted virus that causes cervical cancer, a new study shows. An estimated 5.5 million people become infected with a strain of HPV each year in the United States.

Efficacy rate of vaccine and placebo

HPV-16 vaccine

Group size ▮ 768

Infection | 0

Placebo

Group size ▮ 765

Infection ▮ 41

Note: The study included 1,533 women with an average age of 20.

Sources: The *New England Journal of Medicine;* Centers for Disease Control and Prevention.

▲   Graphics like this, while leaving out important details, help readers understand cause-and-effect investigations.

composed by random means from those in the general population who have fatty diets would include more than its fair share of drinkers. Consequently, the high rate of colon cancer observed in this experimental group might be due in part to the effects of drinking.

It is important, then, that the process by which the individuals in the general population "self-select" themselves (regarding their exposure to C) not be biased in any way related to the effect. In good studies, any factors that might bias the experimental group are controlled by one means or another. Often, for example, the control group is not randomly selected, but rather is selected to match the experimental group for any other relevant factors. Thus, in a study that seeks to relate fatty diets to cancer of the colon, an experimenter will make certain that the same percentage of drinkers is found in the control group as in the experimental group.

Nonexperimental studies of the variety explained here and in the next section are *inherently* weaker than controlled experiments as arguments for causal claims. Because we do not have complete knowledge of what factors are causally related to what other factors, it is impossible to say for certain that all possibly relevant variables in such studies have been

Learning Australian, Lesson 42:
That's Australian for "Another Round!"

Long-term heavy drinkers are not damaging their mental faculties, contrary to previous suggestions, despite consuming the equivalent of eight pints of beer a day, researchers say.

Drinkers scored just as well on psychological and intellectual tests and showed no more signs of brain shrinkage than non-drinkers or those who consumed alcohol only in moderation.

A number of studies have suggested that heavy long-term alcohol use can cause brain damage, including a type of alcohol-induced dementia.

However, researchers from Australia say they can find no evidence that persistent lifelong consumption of alcohol is related to cognitive functioning in men in their 70s.

The researchers, from the Australian National University, Canberra, and the Center for Education and Research on Aging in Sydney, looked at 209 men with an average age of 73 who were veterans of World War II. They were given 18 tests to measure intellectual function, as well as scans for brain atrophy.

The daily alcohol consumption of the men [averaged two and one-half pints of beer and went as high as eight pints].

—CHRIS MIHILL, *Scripps Howard News Service*

We'd look for confirmation of these results before we'd recommend regular trips to the pub. Notice that this study ignores *other* problems caused by alcohol.

controlled. It is good policy to imagine what characteristics those who have been exposed to the suspected causal agent might have and contemplate whether any of these factors may be related to the effect. If you can think of any relevant variables that have not been controlled, you should have doubts about any causal claim that is made on the basis of such studies.

■ *Nonexperimental Effect-to-Cause Studies*

A **nonexperimental effect-to-cause study** is a third type of study designed to test whether something is a causal factor for a given effect. In this type of study, the "experimental group," whose members already display the *effect* being investigated, E (e.g., cancer of the mouth), is compared with a control group none of whose members have E, and the frequency of the suspected cause, C (e.g., using chewing tobacco), is measured. If the frequency of C in the experimental group significantly exceeds its frequency in the control group, then C may be said to cause E in the target population.

Cautionary remarks from the discussion of nonexperimental cause-to-effect studies apply equally to nonexperimental effect-to-cause studies. That is, if it isn't clear that the findings are significant, don't assume that they are merely because (1) the samples seem large or (2) the difference in the frequency expressed in absolute terms seems striking; and (3) evaluate carefully analogical extensions of the results to other populations.

Notice further that (4) the subjects in the experimental group may differ in some important way (in addition to showing the effect) from the rest of the target population. Thus, for instance, former smokers are more likely than others to use chewing tobacco and are also more likely to get mouth cancer. If you sample randomly from a group of victims of mouth cancer, therefore, you are likely to produce more ex-smokers in your sample than occur in the general population. The result is that you are likely to discover more chewing-tobacco users in the sample, even if chewing tobacco plays no role whatsoever in causing cancer of the mouth. Any factor that might bias the experimental group in such studies should be controlled. If, in evaluating such a study, you can think of any factor that has not been controlled, you can regard the study as having failed to demonstrate causation.

Notice, finally, that (5) effect-to-cause studies show only the probable frequency of the cause, not the effect, and thus provide no grounds for estimating the percentage of the target population that would be affected if everyone in it were exposed to the cause.

Appeal to Anecdotal Evidence

In Chapter 10, we discussed the mistake of trying to reach a conclusion by citing one or two examples—i.e., by appealing to anecdotes. There is another type of appeal to anecdotal evidence that relates to causal arguments, as distinct from generalizations: trying to either prove or disprove that X is a causal factor for Y by citing an example or two of an X that did (or didn't) cause a Y. Arguing that red wine prevents colds because we know someone who drinks red wine and never catches cold would be an instance of this type of weak argument. It would be similarly weak to argue that red wine doesn't prevent colds because we've never observed that effect in us. Those who submit that smoking doesn't cause cancer because they know a smoker who lived to ninety-eight and died of old age are guilty of the causal type of anecdotal argument.

To establish that X is a causal factor for Y, we have to show that there would be more cases of Y if everyone did X than if no one did, and you can't really show this—or demonstrate that X isn't a causal factor for Y—by citing an example or two. Isolated incidents can reasonably serve to raise suspicions about causal factors, but that is all.

One of the most common mistakes made in everyday reasoning is to appeal to anecdotal evidence in one or the other of the ways discussed here and in Chapter 10. And now that you know what is involved in saying that something is a causal factor, you know why you can't establish this sort of causal claim by appealing to an anecdote.

Weird Science

Here are some of the criticisms made by research authorities who, in the June 5 *Journal of the American Medical Association,* reviewed the quality of current medical research literature.

- Studies often fail to put results in the context of previous studies.
- Authors of studies do not adequately address legitimate scientific criticism after publication, and journal editors do not require them to do so.
- Study collaborators frequently disagree about their study's conclusions, and the published reports often fail to represent the full range of authors' opinions.
- Guidelines showing how results ought to be reported are often ignored or badly applied.

As indicated, these criticisms were part of an assessment of current literature in medical research. It was found that research reported in company-funded studies was often inaccurate, incomplete, or otherwise misleading in ways that favored the drug companies.

—————
Source: *Business Week,* June 24, 2002.

Exercise 11-5

Identify each of the following as (a) a claim about causation between specific occurrences, (b) a claim about causal factors in populations, or (c) neither of these.

▲ 1. The hibiscus died while we were away. There must have been a frost.

2. Carlos isn't as fast as he used to be; that's what old age will do.

3. Kent's college education helped him get a high-paying job.

▲ 4. The most frequently stolen utility vehicle is a 2000 Jeep Wrangler.

5. Vitamin C prevents colds.

6. The man who put this town on the map was Dr. Jaime Diaz.

▲ 7. The high reading on the thermometer resulted from two causes: This thermometer was located lower to the ground than at other stations, and its shelter was too small, so the ventilation was inadequate.

8. Oily smoke in the exhaust was caused by worn rings.

9. The initial tests indicate that caffeine has toxic effects in humans.

▲ 10. Neonatal sepsis is usually fatal among newborns.

11. WIN 51,711 halted development of paralysis in mice that had recently been infected with polio-2.

12. A stuck hatch cover on *Spacelab* blocked a French ultraviolet camera from conducting a sky survey of celestial objects.

13. An experimental drug has shown broad antiviral effects on a large number of the picornaviruses against which it has been tested.

▲ 14. Investigation revealed the problem was a short-circuited power supply.

15. Arteriovenous malformations—distortions of the capillaries connecting an arteriole and a small vein in the brain—can bleed, causing severe headaches, seizures, and even death.

16. Because of all the guns that its citizens own, the United States has never been invaded.

▲ 17. According to two reports in the *New England Journal of Medicine,* oil from fish can prevent heart disease.

18. The most important cause in the growing problem of illiteracy is television.

19. "Raymond the Wolf passed away in his sleep one night from natural causes; his heart stopped beating when the three men who slipped into his bedroom stuck knives in it."

> *Jimmy Breslin,* The Gang That Couldn't Shoot Straight

▲ 20. The dramatic increases in atmospheric CO_2, produced by the burning of fossil fuels, are warming the planet and will eventually alter the climate.

Exercise 11-6

Go to Church and Live Longer

According to Bill Scanlon, a reporter for the Scripps Howard News Service, researchers from the University of Colorado, the University of Texas, and Florida State University determined that twenty-year-olds who attend church at least once a week for a lifetime live on the average seven years longer than twenty-year-olds who never attend. The data came from a 1987 National Health Interview Survey that asked 28,000 people their income, age, church-attendance patterns, and other questions. The research focused on 2,000 of those surveyed who subsequently died between 1987 and 1995.

Propose two different causal hypotheses to explain these findings.

Hypothesis One:

What data would you need to have greater confidence in this hypothesis?

Hypothesis Two:

What data would you need to have greater confidence in this hypothesis?

Other Hypotheses:

What data would you need to have greater confidence in these hypotheses?

Auberry Drive Cancer Toll at 7

A new state review will try to see if more than coincidence is at work.

Another two related cancers on Auberry Drive have surfaced, bringing to seven the number of similarly stricken children and adults within one square mile just north of Elk Grove.

The news reinforces some residents' suspicions that they are witnessing a disease cluster perpetuated by some unknown toxic exposure.

"It's no surprise to me," said Dee Lewis, a nearby resident who has been investigating possible environmental links for the past three years.

At The Bee's request, state officials on Wednesday agreed to re-evaluate the area's cancer incidence to determine whether the concentration is more than a coincidence.

Rosemary Cress, an epidemiologist with the state-run California Cancer Registry, has concluded from earlier statistical analyses that the area's incidence of childhood leukemia is not outside the range of chance. She does not expect further analyses to change the conclusion.

By Chris Bowman

The incidence of cancer will be higher on some streets in a community than on others simply due to chance. But as a matter of psychology, it may be difficult to accept that fact if you live on one of the streets that has a high incidence of cancer.

Source: Sacramento Bee/Mitchell Brooks

Exercise 11-7

> There is no single event, activity, decision, law, judgment, in this period of time that I call the "three strikes" era—other than "three strikes"—that could explain the tremendous acceleration in the drop in crime.
>
> *Dan Lungren, former California Attorney General, who helped draft*
> *California's Three Strikes law*

Under this law, conviction for a third felony carried with it a mandatory sentence of twenty-five years to life. Although the crime rate in California had been falling before the law took effect in 1994, it reportedly fell even faster after the law was enacted, and California's crime rate dropped to levels not seen since the 1960s.

Provide two reasonable alternative hypotheses to explain the acceleration of the drop in the crime rate in California. What data would you need to be convinced that Lungren's hypothesis is the best?

Exercise 11-8

Suppose a university teacher wants to know whether or not requiring attendance improves student learning. How could she find out? In groups (or individually if the instructor prefers), describe an experiment that an instructor might actually use. Groups may then compare proposals to see who has the best idea.

Exercise 11-9

For each of the following investigations:

a. Identify the causal hypothesis at issue.

b. Identify what kind of investigation it is.

c. Describe the control and experimental groups.

d. State the difference in effect (or cause) between control and experimental groups.

e. Identify any problems in either the investigation or in the report of it, including but not necessarily limited to uncontrolled variables.

f. State the conclusion you think is warranted by the report.

▲ 1. Scientists have learned that people who drink wine weekly or monthly are less likely to develop dementia, including Alzheimer's disease. (Daily wine drinking, however, seems to produce no protective effect.) The lead researcher was Dr. Thomas Truelsen, of the Institute of Preventive Medicine at Kommunehospitalet in Copenhagen. The researchers identified the drinking patterns of 1,709 people in Copenhagen in the 1970s and then assessed them for dementia in the 1990s, when they were aged 65 or older. When they were assessed two decades later, 83 of the participants developed dementia. People who drank beer regularly were at an increased risk of developing dementia.

Adapted from BBC News *(online), November 12, 2002*

2. Learning music can help children do better at math. Gordon Shaw of the University of California, Irvine, and Frances Rauscher at the University of Wisconsin compared three groups of second-graders: 26 received piano instruction plus practice with a math videogame, 29 received extra English lessons plus the game, and 28 got no special lessons. After four months the piano kids scored 15 to 41 percent higher on a test of ratios and fractions than the other participants.

Adapted from Sharon Begley, Newsweek, *July 24, 2000*

3. The Carolina Abecedarian Project [A-B-C-D, get it?] selected participants from families thought to be at risk for producing mildly retarded children. These families were all on welfare, and most were headed by a single mother, who had scored well below average on a standardized IQ test (obtaining IQs of 70 to 85). The project began when the participating children were 6 to 12 weeks old, and continued for the next 5 years. Half of the

participants were randomly assigned to take part in a special day-care program designed to promote intellectual development. The program ran from 7:15 to 5:15 for 5 days a week for 50 weeks each year until the child entered school. The other children received the same dietary supplements, social services, and pediatric care, but did not attend day-care. Over the next 21 years, the two groups were given IQ tests and tests of academic achievement. The day-care program participants began to outperform their counterparts on IQ tests starting at 18 months and maintained this IQ advantage through age 21. They also outperformed the others in all areas of academic achievement from the third year of school onward.

Adapted from Developmental Psychology, *6th ed., David R. Schaffer*

▲ 4. Research at the University of Pennsylvania and the Children's Hospital of Philadelphia indicates that children who sleep in a dimly lighted room until age two may be up to five times more likely to develop myopia (nearsightedness) when they grow up.

The researchers asked the parents of children who had been patients at the researchers' eye clinic to recall the lighting conditions in the children's bedroom from birth to age two.

Of a total of 172 children who slept in darkness, 10 percent were nearsighted. Of a total of 232 who slept with a night light, 34 percent were nearsighted. Of a total of 75 who slept with a lamp on, 55 percent were nearsighted.

The lead ophthalmologist, Dr. Graham E. Quinn, said that, "just as the body needs to rest, this suggests that the eyes need a period of darkness."

Adapted from an AP report by Joseph B. Verrengia

5. You want to find out if the coffee grounds that remain suspended as sediment in French press, espresso, and Turkish and Greek coffee can cause headaches.

You divide fifty volunteers into two groups and feed both groups a pudding at the same time every day. However, one group mixes eight grams of finely pulverized used coffee grounds into the pudding before eating it (that's equivalent to the sediment in about one and a half liters of Turkish coffee). Within three weeks, you find that 50 percent of the group that has eaten grounds have had headaches; only 27 percent of the other group have experienced a headache. You conclude that coffee grounds may indeed cause headaches and try to get a grant for further studies. (This is a fictitious experiment.)

6. Do you enjoy spicy Indian and Asian curries? That bright yellow-orange color is due to curcumin, an ingredient in the spice turmeric. An experiment conducted by Bandaru S. Reddy of the American Health Foundation in Valhalla, New York, and reported in *Cancer Research,* suggests that curcumin might suppress the development of colon cancer

Places where turmeric is widely used have a low incidence of colon cancer, so the research team decided to investigate. They administered a powerful colon carcinogen to sixty-six rats, and then added curcumin at the rate of 2,000 parts per million to the diet of thirty of them. At the end of a year, 81 percent of the rats eating regular rat food had developed cancerous tumors, compared with only 47 percent of those that dined on the curcumin-enhanced diet. In addition, 38 percent of the tumors in rats eating regular food were invasive, and that was almost twice the rate in rodents eating curcumin-treated chow.

Adapted from Science News

▲ 7. Does jogging keep you healthy? Two independent researchers interested in whether exercise prevents colds interviewed twenty volunteers about the frequency with which they caught colds. The volunteers, none of whom exercised regularly, were then divided into two groups of ten, and one group participated in a six-month regimen of jogging three miles every other day. At the end of the six months the frequency of colds among the joggers was compared both with that of the nonjoggers (group A) and with that of the joggers prior to the experiment (group B). It was found that, compared with the nonjoggers, the joggers had 25 percent fewer colds. The record of colds among the joggers also declined in comparison with their own record prior to the exercise program.

8. "In the fifty-seven-month study, whose participants were all male physicians, 104 of those who took aspirin had heart attacks, as compared with 189 heart attacks in those who took only a sugar pill. This means ordinary aspirin reduced the heart attack risk for healthy men by 47 percent. At least seven long-term studies of more than 11,000 heart attack victims have shown that one-half or one aspirin per day can reduce the risk of a second attack by up to 20 percent."

Adapted from the Los Angeles Times

9. "Although cigarette ads sometimes suggest that smoking is 'macho,' new studies indicate that smoking can increase the risk of impotence. In a study of 116 men with impotence caused by vascular problems, done at the University of Pretoria, South Africa, 108 were smokers. Two independent studies, one done by the Centre d'Etudes et de Recherches di l'Impuissance in Paris, and reported in the British medical journal *Lancet,* and the other done by Queen's University and Kingston General Hospital in Ontario, found that almost two-thirds of impotent men smoked.

"To test whether smoking has an immediate effect on sexual response, a group of researchers from Southern Illinois and Florida State universities fitted 42 male smokers with a device that measures the speed of arousal. The men were divided into three groups, one group given high-nicotine cigarettes, one group cigarettes low in nicotine, and one group mints. After smoking one cigarette or eating a mint, each man was placed in a private room and shown a two-minute erotic film while his sexual response was monitored. Then he waited ten minutes, smoked two more cigarettes or ate another mint, and watched a different erotic film, again being monitored.

"The results: Men who smoked high-nicotine cigarettes had slower arousal than those who smoked low-nicotine cigarettes or ate mints."

Adapted from Reader's Digest

10. "A study published in the July 27 *Journal of the American Medical Association* indicates that taking androgen (a male sex hormone) in high doses

for four weeks can have important effects on the high density lipoproteins (HDLs) in the blood, which are believed to protect against the clogging of vessels that supply the heart. Ben F. Hurley, an exercise physiologist from the University of Maryland in College Park who conducted the study at Washington University, monitored the levels of HDL in the blood of sixteen healthy, well-conditioned men in their early thirties who were taking androgens as part of their training program with heavy weights. Prior to use of the hormone, all had normal levels of HDLs. After four weeks of self-prescribed and self-administered use of these steroids the levels dropped by about 60 percent.

"Hurley is cautious in interpreting the data. 'You can't say that low HDL levels mean that a specified person is going to have a heart attack at an earlier age. All you can say is that it increases their risk for heart disease.'"

D. Franklin, Science News

11. "New studies reported in the *Journal of the American Medical Association* indicate that vasectomy is safe. A group headed by Frank Massey of UCLA paired 10,500 vasectomized men with a like number of men who had not had the operation. The average follow-up time was 7.9 years, and 2,300 pairs were followed for more than a decade. The researchers reported that, aside from inflammation in the testes, the incidence of diseases for vasectomized men was similar to that in their paired controls.

"A second study done under federal sponsorship at the Battelle Human Affairs Research Centers in Seattle compared heart disease in 1,400 vasectomized men and 3,600 men who had not had the operation. Over an average follow-up time of fifteen years, the incidence of heart diseases was the same among men in both groups."

Edward Edelson, New York Daily News; *reprinted in* Reader's Digest

12. "A new study shows that the incidence of cancer tumors in rats exposed to high doses of X-rays dropped dramatically when the food intake of the rats was cut by more than half. Dr. Ludwik Gross of the Veterans Administration Medical Center noted that this study is the first to demonstrate that radiation-induced tumors can be prevented by restricting diet.

"The experimenters exposed a strain of laboratory rats to a dose of X-rays that produced tumors in 100 percent of the rats allowed to eat their fill—about five or six pellets of rat food a day.

"When the same dose of X-rays was given to rats limited to two pellets of food a day, only nine of 29 females and one of 15 males developed tumors, the researchers reported.

"The weight of the rats on the reduced diet fell by about one-half, but they remained healthy and outlived their counterparts who died of cancer, Gross said. He noted that the restricted diet also reduced the occurrence of benign tumors. There is no evidence that restriction of food intake will slow the growth of tumors that have already formed in animals, he said."

Paul Raeburn, Sacramento Bee

13. "Encephalitis, or sleeping sickness, has declined greatly in California during the past thirty years because more people are staying inside during

prime mosquito-biting hours—7 P.M. to 10 P.M., researchers said. Paul M. Gahlinger of San Jose State University and William C. Reeves of the School of Public Health at UC Berkeley conducted the study. 'People who watch television on warm summer evenings with their air conditioners on are less likely to be exposed during the peak biting period of mosquitoes that carry encephalitis,' Reeves said.

"The researchers found that those counties in California's Central Valley with the highest television ownership had the lowest encephalitis rates for census years. Of 379 Kern County residents interviewed by telephone, 79 percent said they used their air conditioners every evening and 63 percent said they watched television four or more evenings a week during the summer.

"The percentage of residents who spend more time indoors now because of air conditioning than in 1950 more than doubled, from 26 percent to 54 percent, the researchers said."

Associated Press, Enterprise-Record *(Chico, California)*

▲ 14. "A study released last week indicated that Type A individuals, who are characteristically impatient, competitive, insecure and short-tempered, can halve their chances of having a heart attack by changing their behavior with the help of psychological counseling.

"In 1978, scientists at Mt. Zion Hospital and Medical Center in San Francisco and Stanford University School of Education began their study of 862 predominantly male heart attack victims. Of this number, 592 received group counseling to ease their Type A behavior and improve their self-esteem. After three years, only 7 percent had another heart attack, compared with 13 percent of a matched group of 270 subjects who received only cardiological advice. Among 328 men who continued with the counseling for the full three years, 79 percent reduced their Type A behavior. About half of the comparison group was similarly able to slow down and cope better with stress.

"This is the first evidence 'that a modification program aimed at Type A behavior actually helps to reduce coronary disease,' says Redford Williams of Duke University, an investigator of Type A behavior."

Science News

Exercise 11-10

Here's a news report on the costs of drug abuse that appeared during the administration of George H. W. Bush. See if you can find any flaws in the reasoning by which the figures were reached.

J. Michael Walsh, an officer of the National Institute on Drug Abuse, has testified that the "cost of drug abuse to U.S. industry" was nearly $50 billion a year, according to "conservative estimates." President Bush has rounded this figure upward to "anywhere from $60 billion to $100 billion." This figure would seem to be a difficult one to determine. Here's how Walsh arrived at it. After a survey of 3,700 households, a NIDA

The Wrong Initials Can Shorten Your Life

Researchers at the University of California, San Diego, looking at twenty-seven years of California death certificates, found that men with "indisputably positive" initials like JOY and WOW and ACE and GOD and WIN and VIP lived 4.48 years longer than a control group of men with neutral initials and ambiguous initials, like DAM and WET and RAY and SUN, that had both positive and negative interpretation. Further, men with "plainly negative" initials like ASS or DUD died on average 2.8 years earlier than did the men in the control group.

As an exercise, propose an explanation for these findings that isn't defective in terms of the criteria discussed in this chapter. Explain how you would test the explanation.

contractor analyzed the data and found that the household income of adults who had *ever* smoked marijuana daily for a month [or at least twenty out of thirty days] was 28 percent less than the income of those who hadn't. The analysts called this difference "reduced productivity due to daily marijuana use." They calculated the total "loss," when extrapolated to the general population, at $26 billion. Adding the estimated costs of drug-related crimes, accidents, and medical care produced a grand total of $47 billion for "costs to society of drug abuse."

Doubtful Causal Claims/Hypotheses

Lets say you have trouble sleeping at night and go to the doctor to find out what's wrong. He runs several tests on you and then informs you that, at long last, he has an explanation.

"The cause of your not sleeping," he announces, "is insomnia."

Here you wouldn't need to know what your doctor's reasoning was. His explanation is *inherently* defective. Some causal claims and hypotheses are like that. They suffer from inherent difficulties, problems that lie within the claim itself.

Here are some common defects of this nature.

1. **Circularity:** A causal claim might be circular. This happens when the "cause" merely restates the effect. When your doctor says you can't sleep because of insomnia, his claim is circular. Insomnia just *is* not sleeping. "She has trouble writing because she has writer's block" would be another example of circular causal explanation. Having trouble writing and having writer's block amount to the same thing. A circular causal claim cannot teach you anything new about causes and effects (although it might teach you a new *name* for an effect).

Keeping Secrets

THE FAR SIDE® BY GARY LARSON

© 1984 FarWorks, Inc. All Rights Reserved/Dist. by Creators Syndicate

The Far Side® by Gary Larson © 1984 FarWorks, Inc. All Rights Reserved. Used with permission.

▲   *If somebody told you that cows stand up and talk to each other, you'd say he or she was nuts, right? After all, nobody has ever seen cows doing that. But suppose the person were to respond by telling you that cows stand up only when nobody can see them? Or suppose a psychic were to explain that his or her psychic abilities disappear when threatened or contaminated by the skepticism of an investigating scientist.*

What's wrong with those explanations? Read the rest of the chapter to find out.

2. **Nontestability:** "AIDS is God's punishment for evil." The problem with this assertion, quite obviously, lies in the fact you cannot test whether it is true. There is no way to detect when the hand of God is present and when it isn't. "You can't sleep because you are possessed" would be another example of a nontestable claim.

Now, one does have to bear in mind that being *difficult* to test is *not* necessarily a defect in a causal hypothesis. Scientific hypotheses can be enormously difficult to test. The problem is with claims for which a test is *unimaginable,* like the examples above.

3. **Excessive vagueness:** "The reason Nasim has trouble in his relationships? Bad karma." The trouble with this claim is that "bad karma" is too vague: What does "bad karma" include, and what does it exclude? A similar problem of vagueness would arise if someone tried to attribute Nasim's difficulty to his having "impure thoughts." ("Trouble in his relationships" is pretty vague as well, but if we know Nasim and the speaker we might have an idea what the phrase refers to.)   These two claims about Nasim are also untestable; indeed, in general, if a claim is too vague, we won't know exactly how to go about testing it. But not all untestable claims are too vague: "An invisible gremlin inside your car's engine explains why it misses occasionally" is untestable, but not especially vague.

4. A claim might also involve **unnecessary assumptions.** The assertion above about an invisible gremlin causing the engine to miss does that, since there are *other* explanations for the car's missing that do *not* assume gremlins. Similarly, you sometimes hear déjà vu explained as being caused by memories from previous lives. But that claim, as well as being untestable, requires assuming past lives, which isn't necessary since déjà vu experiences can be induced by electric stimulation of areas within the brain.

5. A similar problem is that a causal claim or hypothesis might **conflict with well-established theory.** For example, an explanation of a person's height as due to something the person did in a past life conflicts with genetic theory. Now, that an assertion conflicts with a well-established theory is not necessarily a *fatal* flaw, because theoretical advances often involve rejecting ideas that once counted as well-established. The theory of continental drift, for example, conflicted with other geological principles. Likewise, the theories of Einstein and other twentieth-century physicists conflicted with Newtonian physics. But evidence was required to establish the new ideas. If a proffered explanation conflicts with well-established theory, we have good reasons to look for an alternative account and to demand powerful evidence of its truth. Also, the fact that there are many examples in which well-established theory is later rejected is itself no evidence at all of the truth of any specific causal claim.

Exercise 11-11

Use letter grades (A, B, C, etc., with pluses and minuses if you wish) to evaluate each of the following explanations as to its degree of testability, its freedom from vagueness, and its noncircularity. ("A, A, A," for example, would indicate an explanation that was clearly testable, contained little or no vagueness, and was not at all circular.)

Indians Flock to See Statues "Drink" Milk

NEW DELHI, India — Millions rushed to Hindu temples across India on Thursday after reports of a miracle—the statues of one of their gods were drinking milk.

The faithful—bearing milk in everything from earthen and steel pots to tumblers and jugs—converged on temples that had reproductions of the elephant-headed Lord Ganesha.

"It is a miracle," said A. K. Tiwari, a priest at a temple in Southern New Delhi.

Scientists dismissed that explanation, saying the offered milk trickled down the granite or marble idols in a thin film that was not easily visible.

Crowds thronged temples in dozens of cities, including New Delhi, Bombay, Calcutta and Madras.

Police and paramilitary soldiers were called out to guard temples across India. In the northern town of Jamshedpur, police waved bamboo canes to control a crowd of 500 that tried to storm a temple.

Tiwari, the priest, said the excitement began early Thursday when a devotee dreamed that the deity wanted milk. When the man, who wasn't identified, held a spoonful of milk near the statue's trunk, the milk disappeared.

Word spread quickly, and people began lining up at temples as early as 4 a.m.

The faithful dismissed suggestions of a hoax.

"It cannot be a hoax. Where would all the milk being offered go? It is such a small idol, it can't take in so much," said Parmesh Soti, a business executive who stood in line. "The gods have come down to Earth to solve our problems."

So widespread were the reports of a miracle that the federal Department of Science and Technology was asked to investigate.

Their scientists offered milk mixed with colored pigment to an idol in a New Delhi temple. Although it disappeared from the spoon, it soon coated the idol. The scientists credited the "miracle" to surface tension, saying molecules of milk were pulled from the spoon by the texture of the statues.

Associated Press, in The Sacramento Bee

▲ 1. What causes your engine to miss whenever you accelerate? Perhaps a spark plug is firing sporadically.

2. Antonio certainly had a run of hard luck—but then I warned him not to throw out that chain letter he got.

3. Divine intervention can cure cancer.

▲ 4. Having someone pray for you can cure cancer.

5. Having your mother pray for you brings good luck.

6. Good luck is the result of being very fortunate.

▲ 7. Why did Claudia catch a cold? She's just prone to that sort of thing, obviously.

8. Agassi won the match simply because he wanted it more than Sampras.

9. Tuck can play high notes so well because he has an excellent command of the upper register.

10. Parker's trip to Spain last year is the reason his Spanish is not quite as bad as it used to be.

Exercise 11-12

Use the criteria discussed in the text to evaluate the following causal explanations. The criteria, once again, are

> Testability
> Noncircularity
> Freedom from excessive vagueness
> Freedom from conflict with well-established theory

▲ 1. The reason he has blue eyes is that he acquired them in a previous incarnation.

2. The Pacers did much better in the second half of the game. That's because they gained momentum.

3. "Men are biologically weaker than women and that's why they don't live as long, a leading expert declares."

Weekly World News

▲ 4. PARKER: Gad, there are a lot of lawyers in this country today.
MOORE: That's because there are so many lawsuits that there's a huge demand for lawyers.

5. Why did he come down with the flu? He's just prone to that sort of thing, I guess.

6. If God had meant for people to fly, he'd have given them wings.

▲ 7. Alcoholics find it so difficult to give up drinking because they have become physiologically and psychologically addicted to it.

8. Alcoholics find it so difficult to give up drinking because they have no willpower.

9. The reason the latest episode of *The Rings* was a box-office hit is that Roger Ebert, one of the most influential movie critics, gave it a good review.

▲ 10. According to some psychologists, we catch colds because we want to. Most of the time we are not aware of this desire, which may, therefore, be said to be subconscious. Viruses are present when we have a cold, but unless we desire to catch cold, the viruses do not affect us.

11. Why does she sleep so late? I guess she's just one of those people who have a hard time waking up in the morning.

12. I wonder what made me choose Budweiser. Maybe I've been subjected to subliminal advertising.

▲ 13. The area along this part of the coast is especially subject to mudslides because of the type of soil that's found on the slopes and because there is not enough mature vegetation to provide stability with root systems.

14. How did he win the lottery twice? I'd have to say he's psychic.

15. "Parapsychologist Susan Blackmore failed to find evidence of ESP in numerous experiments over more than a decade. *Fate* magazine's consulting editor D. Scott Rogo explained her negative results as follows: 'In the course of my conversations with Blackmore I have come to suspect that

When Is Affirmative Action Not Affirmative Action?

A letter-writer to the "Ask Marilyn" column in *Parade* magazine mentions a case worth your attention:

    The writer, Christopher McLaughlin, of Orange Park, Florida, reported a company that opened a factory generating 70 white-collar jobs and 385 blue-collar jobs.

    For the 70 white-collar positions, 200 males and 200 females applied; 15 percent of the males were hired, and 20 percent of the females were hired.

    For the 385 blue-collar jobs, 400 males applied and 100 females applied; 75 percent of the males were hired, and 85 percent of the females were hired.

    In short, the percentage of female applicants hired was greater than the percentage of male applicants hired in both categories. A victory for women, yes?

    Nope—at least not according to the Equal Employment Opportunity Commission. The EEOC calculated that a female applying for a job at the factory had a 59 percent chance of being denied employment, whereas a male applicant had only a 45 percent chance of not being hired. So the company actually discriminated against women, the EEOC said.

    Here's why: When you consider *total* applications, out of 600 male applicants, 330 were hired, and out of 300 female applicants, 125 were hired. That means that 55 percent of the male applicants—but only 41 percent of the female applicants—were hired.

    (This case should remind you of the Saint Simpson's example in Chapter 10—see the box on page 378.)

she resists—at a deeply unconscious level—the idea that psychic phenomena exist. . . . *If* Blackmore is ever fortunate enough to witness a poltergeist or see some other striking display of psychic phenomena, I am willing to bet that her experimental results will be more positive.'"

The Skeptical Inquirer

16. According to a report by Scotty Paul, writing in *Weekly World News,* thousands of tourists who defied an ancient curse and took home souvenir chunks of lava rock from Hawaii's Volcanoes National Park have felt the bitter wrath of a vengeful volcano goddess. The curse explains why a Michigan man tumbled to his death down a stairway and why a Canadian tourist died in a head-on auto accident, as well as why a Massachusetts widow lost her life savings in the stock market. The three suffered their misfortunes after taking lava rocks from the volcano and defying the curse of Madame Pele, the volcano goddess.

▲ 17. Why is there so much violence these days? Rap music, that's why. That and the fact that there's so much violence on TV and in the movies.

18. The reason I got into so much trouble as a kid is that my father became a heavy drinker.

19. In their book *The Gulf Breeze Sightings: The Most Astounding Multiple Sightings of UFOs in U.S. History,* authors Ed and Frances Walters provide photographs of UFOs. According to the *Pensacola News Journal,* the man who now lives in the house the Walters family occupied at the time they photographed the UFOs discovered a flying saucer hidden under some insulation in the attic of the garage. With this model, news photographers were able to create photos of "UFOs" that looked like the Walterses' photos. Walters denies the model was his, but the paper in which it was wrapped contains part of a house plan Walters drew up (Walters is a building contractor). Walters says that model was planted by someone who wished to discredit him.

A Gulf Breeze youngster named Tom Smith also has come forth, admitting that he and Walters's son helped produce the fake saucer photos. He has five UFO photos of his own to substantiate his claim. Walters says Smith's photos are genuine. Which of the two explanations given for the original UFO photos is more plausible, and why? (This report is from *The Skeptical Inquirer.*)

▲ 20. According to mathematician and science writer Martin Gardner, in Shivpuri, a village near Poona, India, there is a large stone ball weighing about 140 pounds in front of a mausoleum containing the remains of Kamarali Darvesh, a Muslim saint. It is possible for five men to stand around the ball and touch it with a forefinger at spots on or below the ball's equator. After they recite in unison "Kamarali Darvesh," an attendant gives a signal, and the ball slowly rises. The explanation of this phenomenon, according to devout Muslims, is that it is a miracle of Allah's.

Causal Explanations and Arguments

Recently we complained to a friend about the paint on a Chevy truck one of us owns.

"What's wrong with it?" he asked.

"It's peeling all over the place," we said.

"Why's it doing that?" he asked.

"That's what we would like to know," we said.

Our friend wasn't confused about this conversation. He understood clearly what it was we wanted to know: We wanted an *explanation* of why the paint on the truck was peeling. We wanted to know what caused it to peel.

Although our friend wasn't confused, causal explanations—explanations of the causes of something—are often confused with arguments, mainly because they involve some of the same words and phrases. But arguing and explaining are different enterprises. They respond to different questions. If someone questions *whether* the paint is peeling, he needs an argument that it either is or isn't. The question of what caused it to peel, on the other hand, assumes that it is peeling and just asks why.

People shouldn't get causal explanations confused with arguments because, with the exception of one complication we shall get to in a second, it is easy to tell them apart. A causal explanation is a causal claim or hypothesis, and as such it asserts or implies cause and effect. A few examples make this clear. The items on the left all assert cause and effect. Those on the right do not—they are arguments.

CAUSAL CLAIM/EXPLANATION	ARGUMENT
The reason Republicans are fiscally conservative is that big business gives a lot of money to fiscal conservatives.	The reason you should vote for Republicans is that they are fiscally conservative.
Dennis didn't live up to expectations; that's why they fired him.	I heard that Dennis didn't live up to expectations; that's why I am pretty sure they will fire him.
The water in the eastern Pacific was 5 degrees above normal in 2002, making 2002 a wetter year across the southern tier of states.	The water in the eastern Pacific was 5 degrees above normal in to assume 2002 was a wetter year across the southern tier of states.

So, the moral is obvious. Don't be fooled by superficial similarities. Causal explanations can look superficially like arguments, but they assert cause and effect. Arguments try to prove that something is the case.

The only complication is that, unfortunately, *sometimes causal explanations are used as premises in arguments.* For example, you might explain *what caused* the carburetor on a lawn mower to be gummed up to prove (argue) *that* the carburetor is gummed up. A Ford ad might explain *what causes* Ford trucks to be best-sellers in order to prove (argue) *that* they are great trucks. Your doctor might explain what caused you to get scarlet fever in order to prove (argue) that what you have is indeed scarlet fever.

Consider the following additional example:

> You won't be able to see the comet from here tonight. The reason is that we're too close to the lights of the city to see anything that faint in the sky.

The speaker explains what it is that *will cause* you to not be able to see the comet from here; but it is very likely that he or she wants to provide you with evidence that you won't be able to see the comet from here. In that case, he or she is using this causal explanation to *argue* that you won't be able to see the comet from here tonight.

The moral is simple: Causal explanations can function as premises of arguments.

■ Explanations and Excuses

Let's suppose you are late to class—maybe you had a flat tire or your battery was dead. You don't want the professor to mark you down, so you explain why you are late. This is a causal explanation used as an argument; you are arguing that, since your lateness was caused by a flat tire (or whatever), *there-*

Study Backs an Old Idea about Crime

Target petty offenses to prevent serious ones, the theory goes.

Maybe you know about the Broken Windows theory of law enforcement. According to that theory, graffiti, petty vandalism, and other misdemeanor crimes in a neighborhood lead to more serious crime problems; and curtailing blight in a neighborhood prevents it from descending into a world of burglary, drugs, car theft, and violent crimes. Mayor Rudolph Giuliani vigorously subscribed to this theory during his term in office, during which New York City became a cleaner, safer place.

However, the theory had apparently not had much statistical support until an analysis of crime rates for all California counties from 1989 to 2000, by the California Institute for County Government, disclosed that the rate of arrests for serious property crimes indeed fell (overall by 3.6 percent) as the ratio for misdemeanor arrests increased. In some counties, where efforts were made to streamline prosecution for petty crimes, the decline in serious crimes was quite dramatic.

This makes sense, because some people who commit petty crimes also commit more serious crimes, and locking them up automatically reduces the number of serious crimes. But the findings (or at least the newspaper reports of them) leave room for skepticism as to the Broken Windows idea. One, the reduction in the rate of serious crimes might be the cause rather than the effect of an increase in petty crime arrest. The study was limited to property crimes like burglary and auto theft, which may well have declined anyway in this period of relative prosperity, thus increasing enforcement opportunities for misdemeanors. Two, apparently the crime rates were the averages for the counties, which gives rural counties disproportionate weight in the final results. In rural counties, even a small increase or decrease in absolute numbers can produce dramatic percentage shifts.

The most you can say is that the findings at least don't contradict the Broken Windows theory.

Source: *Sacramento Bee*, August 12, 2002.

fore you should be excused for being late. When we try to justify or defend or excuse something we (or someone else) did, we sometimes explain its causes. Imagine David is caught stealing a loaf of bread; he then explains to the authorities that he needed the bread to feed his children. David is attempting to argue that his behavior should be excused, and his explanation of what caused him to steal the bread provides grounds for his argument.

Not every attempt to explain behavior is an attempt to excuse or defend the behavior. After the September 11 suicide attacks on the World Trade Center, speakers on some university campuses offered explanations of the causes of the attacks. In some cases they were accused of trying to excuse the attacks, and perhaps some of them were trying to do that. But others weren't trying to excuse the attacks; they were simply trying to explain their causes. The distinction was lost on some people; attempts to explain the causes of the attacks were frequently condemned as traitorous. (In fact, one of our own colleagues who tried to express his views about the geopolitical causes of the attacks made the national news and was promptly invited by Rush Limbaugh to move to Afghanistan.)

If you assume without thinking about it that anyone who tries to explain the causes of bad behavior is trying to excuse it, you commit a fallacy. (Remember from Chapter 2 that a fallacy is a mistake in reasoning.) This fallacy, which we shall call **confusing explanations and excuses,** is common. For example, someone may try to explain why many Germans adopted the vicious anti-Semitic views of the Nazi party during the 1930s. The speaker may point out that the German economy was in a mess, that the country still suffered from terms imposed on it at the end of World War I, and, furthermore, that people often look for scapegoats on whom they can blame their troubles. These remarks may help us understand why the German people were easily led into anti-Semitism, but an uncritical listener may believe that the speaker is trying to muster sympathy for those people and their actions. As a matter of fact, just such an explanation was given by Phillipp Jenniger in the German parliament on the fiftieth anniversary of the *Kristallnacht,* a night when Nazis attacked Jewish neighborhoods and shops. Many of Jenniger's fellow Germans misunderstood his account, thinking it was designed to make excuses for the Nazis' actions. But it does not follow that a person proposing explanations has any sympathy at all for the views or actions being explained.

To sum things up, sometimes we explain the causes of something that sounds bad in order to excuse it; but sometimes such explanations are simply used to explain. Causal explanations can be entirely neutral with regard to approval or disapproval of an action. If we fail to see the difference between explaining behavior and excusing it, we may stifle attempts to explain it. The speaker may worry that we will think he or she is defending the bad behavior. This would be unfortunate because, lacking an explanation for such behavior, we may be hampered in our attempts to discourage it.

Recap

When we reason about cause and effect in informal, real-life situations, we often (but not always) want to know what caused some effect that interests us. It is never legitimate to conclude that one thing caused another just because the two things occurred around the same time—this is the *post hoc* fallacy. Instead, we must use either relevant-difference reasoning or common-thread reasoning. However, we must be careful not to focus on irrelevant differences or common threads, and we must not overlook alternative relevant common threads and differences. In addition, we should consider the possibilities that causation is the reverse of what we suspect and that the effect and suspected cause are both the effects of some third, underlying cause. Further, we must consider whether the effect and suspected cause are connected merely through coincidence.

We establish that something is a causal factor in a population on the basis of cause-to-effect experimentation or on the basis of cause-to-effect or effect-to-cause studies. We cannot establish causation on the basis of an example or two that looks like cause and effect.

Causal claims can suffer from inherent defects, most notably circularity, nontestability, excessive vagueness, dependence on unnecessary assumptions, or conflict with well-established theory.

Despite superficial similarities in phrasing, causal claims and arguments respond to different questions. A complication is that causal claims can be used as premises of arguments. Sometimes arguments that use causal claims in this way attempt to excuse something, but it is a mistake to think that they all do.

Additional Exercises

Exercise 11-13

In twenty-five words or less, argue *that* a lot of kids cheat in high school. Then, again in twenty-five words or less, explain *why* a lot of kids cheat in high school. You may be asked by your instructor to read your response. The idea here is to make sure you understand the difference between an argument and an explanation.

Exercise 11-14

In this exercise, five items are best seen as arguments and five are best seen as explanations. Sort the items into the proper categories.

1. I got sick because I didn't get enough rest over the weekend.
2. You shouldn't buy that computer because it doesn't have very much memory.
3. The president should resign because foreign leaders are going to lose faith in his leadership skills.
4. Pine trees are called "evergreens" because they don't lose their leaves in the fall.
5. You are making a mistake to wear that outfit because it makes you look too old.
6. Stephanie won't wear outfits like that because she thinks they are tacky.
7. Used couches are so plentiful here because the students give them away at the end of each school year.

8. If I were you, I wouldn't open up a furniture store in this town, because students give good furniture away at the end of each school year.

9. Freestone peaches are better than clingstone, because they are easier to eat and have a crisper texture.

10. The sky appears blue because of the way light reflects off the atmosphere.

Exercise 11-15

In this exercise there are ten items. Four are arguments and seven are explanations. That adds up to eleven, and that's because one explanation is used to justify or excuse behavior. Determine which items fall into which categories.

▲ 1. Collins is absent again today because she's ill.

2. I told you Collins was ill. Just look at her color.

3. Did Bobbie have a good time last night? Are you kidding? She had a *great* time! She stayed up all night, she had such a good time.

▲ 4. The reason Collins was ill is that she ate and drank more than she should have.

5. For a while there, Jazzercise was really popular. But you don't hear much about it anymore. That's probably because rock makes you feel more like moving than jazz. Jazz just makes you feel like moving into another room.

6. How come light beer has fewer calories than real beer? It has less alcohol, that's why.

▲ 7. The senator's popularity goes up and down, up and down. That's because somctimes he says things that make sense, and other times he says things that are totally outrageous.

8. VIKKI: Say, remember the California Raisins? Whatever happened to them, anyway?
   NIKKI: They faded. I guess people got tired of them or something.

9. Programs of preferential treatment may seem unfair to white males, but a certain amount of unfairness to individuals can be tolerated for the sake of the common good. Therefore, such programs are ethically justified.

▲ 10. I'm telling him, "Let's book!" and he's like, "Relax, dude," and since it's his wheel, what can I do? That's why we're late, man.

Exercise 11-16

Which of the following are arguments and which are explanations? Do any of the arguments use explanations to justify or excuse behavior?

▲ 1. What a winter! And to think it's all just because there's a bunch of cold water off the California coast.

2. Hmmmm. I'm pretty sure you have the flu. You can tell because if you had a cold you wouldn't have aches and a fever. Aches and fever are a sure sign you have the flu.

3. You know, it occurs to me the reason the band sounded so bad is the new director. They haven't had time to get used to him or something.

▲ 4. For a while there it seemed like every male under thirty was shaving his head. It was probably the Michael Jordan influence.

▲ 5. Believe it or not, couples who regard each other as relatively equal are more likely to suffer from high blood pressure than are couples who perceive one or the other as dominant. This is an excellent reason for marrying someone you think is beneath (or above) you.

6. Believe it or not, couples who regard each other as relatively equal are more likely to suffer from high blood pressure than are couples who perceive one or the other as dominant. The reason seems to be that couples who see their partners as relatively equal tend to argue more often and more vigorously, pushing up blood pressure.

Exercise 11-17

Which of the following explanations is used to argue that a certain behavior is or was justified or should be excused, and which isn't?

▲ 1. You don't believe me when I say sometimes you can see Pluto with the naked eye? Just think of how the solar system works. The planets all orbit around the sun, and at a certain point, Pluto's orbit gets very close to Earth's orbit.

▲ 2. Yes, yes, I know Susan never goes out, but you can hardly blame her. She thinks it is important to study, and she may be right.

▲ 3. Harold didn't return the book when it was due, but he couldn't help it. Somebody broke into his car and stole his backpack, and the book was in it.

4. Maria really does have perfect pitch. See, her parents were both musicians, and perfect pitch is hereditary. She inherited it from them.

5. It takes time and effort to write decent essays. If you doubt it, just let me tell you what all is involved. You have to pick a topic. You have to think about the audience. You have to organize things and compose an outline. And you have to write about 50 million drafts.

6. Believe it or not, in Germany, it is illegal to name a child "Osama bin Laden." Maybe you think no government has the right to tell someone they can't name their kid what they want; but the way the Germans look at it, the government should protect children, and children with names like "Osama bin Laden" could be picked on at school.

7. "I'm really sorry our dogs made so much noise last night. They thought someone was trying to break into the house, and it took a long time for us to quiet them down."

8. Well, ordinarily I wouldn't be happy if I saw someone cutting down trees in his yard, but those trees are diseased and constantly losing branches. He's doing the right thing to take them out.

9. Sanctions against South Africa are usually cited as bringing down apartheid, but the real explanation was the diplomatic isolation and the threat from guerrillas in neighboring countries.

10. Why in heck would anyone plant zucchini when they could be growing something good like tomatoes or eggplant? The only reason I can see is she must be nuts.

Exercise 11-18

Several of these items seem clearly to be arguments. Among these arguments are three explanations used to argue something. Of these, one is used to justify someone's behavior. Identify which of the items fall into these three categories, and then state what the remaining three items are.

1. If you ask a person to pick a number between 12 and 5, he'll probably say 7. That's because his brain automatically subtracts 5 from 12.

2. Ask a person to name a vegetable, and the first thing to come to mind is a carrot. Don't believe me? Ask someone.

3. To be acid-free, take Pepcid AC.

4. Why, just look at all the dog hair on this keyboard. Where do you let your dog sleep, anyway? No wonder your computer isn't working right.

5. On September 19, Mike Tyson will make the holy trek to Las Vegas, to ask the Nevada Athletic Commission to reinstate his boxing license, and chances are they will. Why would they do that for a man who bit another boxer, attacked a sixty-two-year-old man, and kicked another older man in the groin? The answer can be stated in a sentence: Vegas likes big money.

6. Feet hurt? Really hurt? Chances are you have weak or fallen arches.

7. "Let me explain to you why you know the public opinion polls are all rigged. Everybody I know hates Clinton, and if you listen to talk radio you can tell that most people agree with us."

Adapted from a newspaper call-in column

8. Linda takes care of two youngsters, puts in a forty-hour week at her job, is troop leader for the local chapter of the Girl Scouts, serves half a day each week as a teacher's aide, and is almost finished with a book on time management. So it shouldn't surprise you that she hasn't been able to come out to the coast for a visit lately.

9. I believe God exists because my parents brought me up that way.

10. I believe God exists because there obviously had to be a first cause for everything, and that first cause was God.

Exercise 11-19 _____

For each of the following passages, determine whether the writer or speaker is most likely presenting an argument or an explanation, or both. Determine also whether any argument present attempts to justify an action or practice. If more information about the context is needed to answer, or if your answer assumes some unusual context for the passage, explain.

▲ 1. I can't understand how the garage got this cluttered. Must be we just never throw anything away.

2. When the sun reaches its equinox, it is directly over the equator, a fact that explains why the days are exactly the same length every place on the globe at that time.

3. Awww, don't get on her, Mom. The reason she didn't rake the leaves is that her stomach began hurting. She *had* to go lie down.

▲ 4. Watch out! Parker's giving a test today. I saw him carrying a big manila folder into the classroom.

5. Moore gave a test on Friday because he wanted to surprise everyone.

6. They get so many fires in southern California in the fall because that's when you get the Santa Ana winds, which blow in from the desert and make everything hot and extremely dry.

7. LATE SLEEPER: Those idiot garbage collectors. Why do they have to make so much noise so early in the morning, anyway?
   EARLY RISER: Give 'em a break. They gotta make noise when they work, and they gotta start work early to get done on time.

▲ 8. HOSTESS: You know, I really think you should shave. The company's coming in less than an hour and you look like a hairy pig.
   HOST: Hey, I told you! I can't shave because my razor is broken. What am I supposed to do, shave with my pocket knife?

9. So you actually believe he knows the names of the people in the audience because God tells him? Here's how he really does it. He's got a wireless radio receiver in his ear, okay? And the people fill out prayer cards before the show. Then his wife collects them and radios the details to him during the show.

▲ 10. Let me explain to you why that was a great movie. The acting was good, the story was interesting, the photography was a knockout, and the ending was a killer.

11. Harold must be rich. Just look at the car he's driving.

▲ 12. I agree that the water contamination around here is getting worse and worse. It's because we've allowed people to install septic systems whenever and wherever they want.

13. "I could never endure to shake hands with Mr. Slope. A cold, clammy perspiration always exudes from him, the small drops are ever to be seen standing on his brow, and his friendly grasp is unpleasant."

Anthony Trollope, Barchester Towers

14. I know you think I wasted my vote by voting for Ralph Nader in the 2000 election, but that isn't so. I didn't approve of either of the main candidates, and if I'd voted for one of them and he had won, then my vote would have counted as an endorsement of him and his views. I don't want to add my endorsement to what I think are bad policies.

▲ 15. It could be that you're unable to sleep because of all that coffee you drink in the evening.

16. The coffee I drink in the evening can't be why I'm not sleeping, because I drink only decaffeinated coffee.

17. Of *course* the real estate industry depends on tax benefits. Just look at how hard the real estate lobby fought to preserve those benefits.

▲ 18. Although the computer case is double-insulated, the pins in the cable connections are not insulated at all. In fact, they are connected directly to the logic board inside the machine. So, if you are carrying a charge of static electricity and you touch those connector pins, you can fry the logic circuits of your computer.

19. The orange is sour because it didn't have a chance to ripen properly.

20. "In 1970 Chrysler abandoned reverse-thread lug bolts on the left-hand side of its cars and trucks. One of those engineers must have realized, after about fifty years of close observation, that sure enough, none of the wheels were falling off the competition's cars, which had your ordinary, right-hand wheel fastenings."

John Jerome, Truck

▲ 21. "Economically, women are substantially worse off than men. They do not receive any pay for the work that is done in the home. As members of the labor force their wages are significantly lower than those paid to men, even when they are engaged in similar work and have similar educational backgrounds."

Richard Wasserstrom, "On Racism and Sexism," in Today's Moral Problems

22. Some people think that Iowa has too much influence in determining who becomes a leading presidential candidate, but I don't agree. Having early caucuses in a relatively small state makes it possible for a person to begin a run at the presidency without spending millions and millions of dollars. And it may as well be Iowa as any other state.

23. "The handsome physical setting of Los Angeles is more threatened than the settings of most of the world's major cities. All the region's residents are affected by the ever-present threat of earthquakes, foul-smelling and chemical-laden tap water, and the potential for water shortages by the year 2000."

Charles Lockwood and Christopher Leinberger, "Los Angeles Comes of Age," in the Atlantic Monthly

24. She appears hard-hearted, but in reality she is not. She maintains strict discipline because she believes that if her children learn self-discipline, in the long run they will lead happier, more productive lives.

▲ 25. Letter to the editor: "Many people are under the impression that the Humane Society is an animal rights organization. Let me correct this misconception. Our purpose is that of an animal welfare organization. Animal rights groups have some excellent ideas but they are too broad of scope for us. We focus our attention on the care and welfare of the animals in our community. It is our primary purpose to provide humane care for homeless and owner-surrendered animals. However, we are against mistreatment of animals and we assist the State Humane Officer who investigates cases of animal abuse."

▲ 26. "American Airlines, United Airlines and TWA confirmed [before September 11, 2001] to the *Los Angeles Times* that some of their crews bypass passenger metal detectors. They said their current security procedures are effective and argued that switching to metal detectors would be costly and inefficient. Furthermore, they said, their security policies have been approved by the Federal Aviation Administration."

Los Angeles Times

Exercise 11-20

Which of the following items is an explanation used as an argument? Remember, trying to justify behavior is giving an argument.

▲ 1. The reason the door keeps banging is that the windows are open on the south side of the house and there is a strong south breeze.

2. Moore always starts his class exactly on the hour, because he has a lot to cover, and he can't afford to waste time.

3. Moore always starts his class exactly on the hour. Don't believe me? Just ask anyone.

▲ 4. The Rotary Club provides free dinners on Thanksgiving, the reason being that they want to help the poor.

5. So you think the lawn mower won't start because it's too old? Here's what's really going on. We let gas sit in the carburetor all winter and it gums up the works—that's why it won't start. It has nothing to do with its being too old.

6. "If slavery had been put to a vote, slavery never would have been overturned. We don't accept that you can put civil rights to a vote in a sexist and racist society."

Heather Bergman, member of the Coalition to Defend Affirmative Action by Any Means Necessary

▲ 7. Rejecting a last-minute bid by Democrats to give President Clinton's lawyers a few days for review, House Republican leaders on Thursday arranged to make public today 445 pages of Independent Counsel Kenneth Starr's report on possible impeachable offenses by the president. It may seem as if the Republicans are seeking to embarrass the president as much as they can, but in fact they called for the release because they feel the public deserves to know as soon as possible why Starr believes he has credible evidence that Clinton committed several crimes.

8. The share of public-school budgets devoted to regular education plummeted from 80 percent in 1967 to less than 59 percent in 1996. The rest goes to students with special needs. This at least partially accounts for declines in test scores among America's average students.

9. Just as Mary Shelley's Frankenstein monster fascinated us, computer viruses have come to do the same because they are much like a man-made life-form. Because of this fascination, you'll see more and more viruses turn up in hoaxes, urban legends, television shows, and movies.

Adapted from Scientific American

▲ 10. It is becoming more and more clear that child molestation is passed down from one generation to another. What isn't clear is whether the tendency is actually an inherited trait or whether a young child's being molested by a parent psychologically conditions the child to be a molester when he becomes an adult. Either way, it looks as though a child with a molester for a parent is not the same as the rest of us; he has something to overcome that we don't, and it may be impossible for us to understand what a difficult problem he may have in avoiding the forbidden behavior.

Exercise 11-21

According to statistics from the Department of Transportation (reported by John Lang of the Scripps Howard News Service), in 1996 men accounted for a little more than 50 percent of licensed drivers and women for a little more than 49 percent. But according to these 1996 statistics, 41,010 male drivers were involved in fatal crashes, as opposed to only 14,145 female drivers. (This works out to about 74 percent male.) Of the drivers killed in those crashes, it was 17,822 male and 6,632 female. (This works out to about 73 percent male.)

Also, according to DOT statistics, in 1996, 86 percent of the people killed while pedaling a bicycle were men.

Which of the following conclusions can you derive from this information? (Assume all the conclusions pertain to 1996.)

1. Men were more likely than women to be involved in a fatal automobile crash.
2. If an automobile crash involved a fatality, it was more likely to have been a man than a woman.
3. Your brother was more likely to have been involved in a fatal automobile crash than your sister.
4. If your sibling was involved in a fatal automobile crash, it's more likely a brother than a sister.
5. Male drivers were more likely than females drivers to be killed in an automobile crash.
6. Men were less skilled than women at avoiding fatal automobile crashes.
7. Men were less able than women to avoid fatal automobile crashes.

8. Men were more likely than women to be killed while pedaling a bicycle.

9. If someone you know was killed while pedaling a bicycle, chances are the victim was a male.

10. If someone you know was killed in a traffic accident, it is more likely it was a bicycle accident than an auto accident.

Exercise 11-22

Men are involved in far more fatal automobile crashes than are women. List as many plausible explanations for this as you can.

Exercise 11-23

Let's say you randomly divide 700 men in the early stages of prostate cancer into two groups. The men in one group have their prostate removed surgically; those in the other group are simply watched to let the disease take its course. Researchers did this to 700 Scandinavian men and reported the results in the *New England Journal of Medicine* in fall 2002. As it turns out, 16 of those who underwent surgery died from prostate cancer, as compared with 31 of those who did not undergo surgery. On the face of it, these figures suggest your chances of not dying from prostate cancer are better if you have surgery. But put on your thinking caps and answer the following questions.

1. Suppose that despite these findings, there was no statistically significant difference in how long the men in each group lived. What would that suggest?

2. The follow-up comparison lasted six years. Suppose that after ten years the death rates from prostate cancer were the same for the two groups. What would that suggest?

3. Suppose Scandinavian men are not screened for prostate cancer as aggressively as American men and tend to be older when they get their first diagnosis.

4. Suppose Scandinavian men are screened more aggressively for prostate cancer than are American men and tend to be younger when they get their first diagnosis.

Here, as elsewhere, you need to know the whole picture to make a judgment. How old were the men to begin with? If they were relatively young men, how long did the study last? Was there a difference in how long the men in the two groups lived? (Note that prostate removal has risks and sometimes produces important negative side effects.)

Writing Exercises

1. How might one determine experimentally whether or not gender-based or ethnicity-based discrimination occurs in hiring? (Differences in unemploy-

Are Women Less Competitive?

Studies uncover a striking pattern

Although women have made huge strides in catching up with men in the workplace, a gender gap persists both in wages and levels of advancement. Commonly cited explanations for this gap range from charges of sex discrimination to claims that women are more sensitive than men to work-family conflicts and thus less inclined to make sacrifices for their careers.

Now, however, two new studies by economists Uri Gneezy of the University of Chicago and Aldo Rustichini of the University of Minnesota suggest that another factor may be at work: a deeply ingrained difference in the way men and women react to competition that manifests itself even at an early age.

The first study focused on short races run by some 140 9- and 10-year-old boys and girls in a physical education class. At that age, there was no significant difference between the average speeds of boys and girls when each child ran the course alone. But when pairs of children with similar initial speeds ran the race again, things changed. Boys' speeds increased appreciably when running against either a boy or a girl, but more so when paired with a girl. Girls

showed no increase when running against a boy and even ran a bit more slowly when paired with a girl.

The second study, by Gneezy, Rustichini, and Muriel Niederle of Stanford University, involved several hundred students at an elite Israeli technical university. Groups of six students were paid to solve simple maze problems on a computer. In some groups, subjects were paid 50¢ for each problem they solved during the experiment. In others, only the person solving the most problems got rewarded—but at the rate of $3 for each maze solved.

Regardless of the sexual makeup of the groups, men and women, on average, did equally well when students were paid for their own performance. But when only the top student was paid, average male performance rose sharply—by about 50%—while female performance remained the same.

The authors conclude that females tend to be far less responsive to competition than males—a tendency with important implications for women and business. It may hurt women in highly competitive labor markets, for example, and hamper efficient job placement—especially for positions in which competitiveness is not a useful trait.

That's something companies with highly competitive atmospheres may need to consider, says Rustichini. If they don't, the results could be "both a subtle bias against women and, in many cases, foregone worker productivity."

By Gene Koretz

Let's Race: Boys' speeds went up.

Source: Business Week, December 9, 2002.

ment rates can be powerful evidence, but it is not experimental.) See if you can design an experiment, and describe it in a brief essay.

2. Are women less competitive than men? In a brief essay, (a) explain what you think the investigations in the box show, if anything; or (b) set forth alternative explanations for the results; or (c) describe what implications you think these investigations have.

Prayer Heals!

A study by Duke University researchers found that angioplasty patients with acute heart ailments who were prayed for by seven religious groups did 50 to 100 percent better while in the hospital than patients who received no prayers.

The researchers divided 150 patients at the Durham Veterans Affairs medical center into five 30-person groups. All groups received traditional medical treatment.

The control group received only the traditional medical treatment. Three groups received nontraditional therapies: stress relaxation, guided imagery, or touch therapy. The names of the remaining group were sent to seven different prayer groups, which prayed for all 30 patients by name.

Neither the patients nor the hospital staff knew the treatment assignment of the control group or the group whose members were prayed for.

The researchers, Dr. Mitch Krucoff, a Duke cardiologist, and nurse Suzanne Crater, developed statistical measures using EEG monitoring heart rate, blood pressure, and clinical outcomes to examine the effectiveness of the four different treatments.

In addition to the improvements recorded in those who received prayers, the patients who received the other nontraditional treatments did 30 to 50 percent better than the control group.

"If people are seeking to put themselves into the right relationship with God, which is what prayer is, then you would expect it to have some beneficial effects," said Dr. Geoffrey Wainwright, a professor at the Duke University School of Divinity.

—Adapted from an *Associated Press* report written by Scott Mooneyham

3. Carefully read the story about prayer in the box and note what conclusions you think would most likely be drawn from it by most readers. Then determine how well those conclusions are actually supported by the evidence as described in the account. Identify any problems of vagueness or any other lack of clarity, missing information, and so forth.

4. Which of the following causal hypotheses do you accept? Select one that you accept and write a one-page essay presenting evidence (giving arguments) for the claim. When you are finished, write down on a separate piece of paper a number between 1 and 10 that indicates how strong you think your overall "proof" of the claim is, with 10 = very strong and 1 = very weak. Take about ten minutes to complete your essay. Write your name on the back of your paper.

Causal hypotheses:

Pot leads to heroin/crack addiction.
The death penalty is a deterrent to murder.
The death penalty is not a deterrent to murder.
Chocolate causes acne.
Welfare makes people lazy.
Spare the rod and spoil the child.
People think better after a few beers.
Pornography contributes to violence against women.
If you want to get someone to like you, play hard to get.
Vitamin C prevents colds.
Rap music (TV, the movies) contributes to the crime problem.

When everyone is finished, the instructor will collect the papers and redistribute them to the class. In groups of four or five, read the papers and assign a number from 1 to 10 to each one (10 = very strong; 1 = very weak). When all groups are finished, return the papers to their authors. When you get your paper back, compare the number you assigned to your work with the number the group assigned to it. The instructor may ask volunteers to defend their own judgment of their work against the judgment of the group. Do you think there is as much evidence for the claim you selected as you did when you argued for it initially?

Chapter 12

Moral, Legal, and Aesthetic Reasoning

with Nina Rosenstand and Anita Silvers

*I*n early winter 2003, our friend Elliott Howard was offered a position as the manager of a country club near Winston-Salem, North Carolina.* For Elliott, this was the chance of a lifetime. Unfortunately, there was a problem. Elliott's father, who lived near Elliott in California, was old and had non-Hodgkins lymphoma. It was vital that Elliott live close by to care for him.

This presented a dilemma. On the one hand, Elliott's father depended on Elliott. On the other, Elliott knew he would not get another chance like this. He was getting on in years himself, and the job offer had come to him only through an unusual chain of events, one that would not likely ever be repeated.

Elliott attempted to find a way to accept the position and still provide for his father. Unfortunately, this turned out not to be possible. In the end, Elliott was faced with this hard choice: He could take the job, or he could take care of his father, but he could not do both.

Finally, reluctantly, Elliott turned down the job offer.

From time to time we all face tough moral decisions like this. Sometimes we must weigh our own interests against our responsibilities to people we love. Sometimes we face moral dilemmas of a different sort. When he was governor of Texas, George W. Bush had to decide whether to bestow clemency on Karla Faye Tucker, a woman whose life had undergone a transformation in prison and whose execution many people believed to be unwarranted. A mother may have to determine whether her daughter's birthday takes precedence over a professional responsibility. It can be excruciating to decide whether a dear pet's time has finally come.

When we think abstractly, we might have the idea that morality is a mere matter of personal opinion and that moral issues offer little room for reasoning. But when we are confronted with a real moral dilemma, we see

*We have altered the circumstances slightly and changed our friend's name to protect his identity.

instantly that this view is not correct. We reason about moral issues. We consider options, weigh consequences, think about what is right and wrong and why. Some considerations are more important than others, and some arguments are better than others. If Elliott decided what to do by flipping a coin, we would think there was something wrong with him.

In the first part of this chapter, we want to look at the basic concepts and principles that are always involved in moral reasoning.

Factual Issues and Nonfactual Issues

Think back to Chapter 1 again, or reread pages 11–13; better yet, do both. There we called your attention to the distinction between factual issues and claims and nonfactual issues and claims. You take a position on a factual issue by making a factual claim. And there are two ways of telling whether an issue is factual. If, when two people take opposite positions on an issue, it is necessary that one of them be mistaken, the issue is factual. Alternatively, if methods or criteria can be described for settling an issue, it is factual.

Thus, the claims in the left column are factual claims (that is, a person making them is taking a position on a factual issue). The claims in the right column are not.

CLAIMS

Factual Claims	*Nonfactual Claims*
1. Gina is twenty-seven.	1. Gina is mature for her age.
2. Karl Rove is the president's campaign adviser.	2. Karl Rove has excellent people skills.
3. The third *Rings* movie lasts over three hours.	3. The third *Rings* movie is tedious and boring.
4. Senator Kennedy did not graduate from Harvard.	4. Senator Kennedy is generous and kind.
5. Anyone under eighteen is still legally a child.	5. Anyone under eighteen is too inexperienced to make wise decisions.

Now, at this point we must subdivide the category of nonfactual issues/claims. First, there are nonfactual issues/claims that express values and those that do not. You may well have heard the expression "value judgment": That's a widely used name for a claim that expresses a value, and we shall use that term as well.*

---

*Philosophers often use the term "prescriptive claims" interchangeably with value judgment, and your instructor may wish to do so as well.

NONFACTUAL CLAIMS

Nonfactual Claims That Are Value Judgments	*Nonfactual Claims That Are Not Value Judgments*
1. Gina shouldn't ask people for money.	1. Gina has unusually dainty features.
2. Karl Rove ought to spend more time with his family.	2. Karl Rove looks a lot like Santa Claus.
3. The third *Rings* movie is better than the first.	3. The third *Rings* movie is scarier than the first.
4. Senator Kennedy is an excellent cellist.	4. Senator Kennedy is a tough-minded advocate of civil liberties.
5. Children should be taught to appreciate music.	5. Children are avid learners.

And we need to make one further distinction, this one between value judgments that assign moral values to something and value judgments that do not. For example, if you assert that one should not permit dogs to suffer needlessly, you are assigning a (negative) moral value to dogs' being allowed to suffer needlessly. If you assert that dogs make wonderful companions for old people, you are assigning a (positive) nonmoral value to dogs. Thus:

VALUE JUDGMENTS

Moral Value Judgments	*Nonmoral Value Judgments*
1. Gina is a really good person.	1. Gina has beautiful eyes.
2. Karl Rove frequently deceives other people.	2. Karl Rove dresses very well.
3. The third *Rings* movie is a very bad influence on people's behavior.	3. The third *Rings* movie has some of the best special effects of any movie made this year.
4. It was wrong of Senator Kennedy to have withheld information.	4. It was terrible timing for Senator Kennedy to have been involved in the trouble during the election.
5. Sam's son was responsible for the bullying incident at school.	5. Children are responsible for decisions made about many families' vacations.

Now we can bring into clear focus what moral reasoning is all about. *Moral reasoning is distinguished from other kinds of reasoning by the fact that the conclusions it tries to reach are moral value judgments.*

Typically, moral value judgments employ such words as "good," "bad," "right," "wrong," "ought," "should," "proper," and "justified." But one must also bear in mind that, although these words often signal a moral evaluation, they do not always do so. For example, if you tell somebody she ought to keep her promises, that's a moral value judgment. If you tell her she ought to keep her knees bent when skiing, you are assigning a positive value to her keeping her knees bent when skiing, but not a moral value.

Before continuing, do these exercises to help clarify these various important distinctions.

Exercise 12-1

Determine which of the following are factual claims and which are nonfactual claims.

▲ 1. Lizards make fine pets.
   2. You can get a clothes rack at True Value for less than $15.00.
   3. The last haircut I got at Supercuts was just totally awful.
▲ 4. It was a great year for regional politics.
   5. Key officials of the Department of Defense are producing their own unverified intelligence reports about an arms buildup.
   6. Texas leads the nation in accidental deaths caused by police chases.
▲ 7. Napoleon Bonaparte was the greatest military leader of modern times.
   8. Racial segregation is immoral anytime anywhere.
   9. President Bush is deploying a "missile defense" that hasn't been adequately tested.
▲ 10. Air consists mainly of nitrogen and oxygen.

Exercise 12-2

Determine which of the following nonfactual claims are value judgments and which are not.

▲ 1. T-shirts made by Fruit of the Loom are soft and luxurious.
   2. Rumsfeld is not nearly as detailed in reports to the press as is Powell.
   3. The Pentagon was not nearly as supportive of a war as it should have been.
▲ 4. Tens of billions of dollars have been wasted on worthless public transportation schemes.
   5. Atlanta is sultry in the summer.
   6. Religious school teachers are stricter than their nonreligious counterparts.
▲ 7. Six Flags has the scariest rides in the state.
   8. The politician with the best sense of humor? That would have to have been Bob Dole.
   9. Eugene is not nearly as happy as his wife, Polly.
  10. Polly is more selfish than she should be.

Exercise 12-3 _____

Determine which of the following value judgments are moral value judgments and which are not.

▲   1. Marina's car puts out horrible smoke; for the sake of us all, she should get it tuned up.

  2. After the surgery, Nicky's eyesight improved considerably.

  3. Ms. Beeson ought not to have embezzled money from the bank.

▲   4. Violence is always wrong.

  5. Matthew ought to wear that sweater more often; it looks great on him.

  6. Sandy, you are one of the laziest people I know!

▲   7. My computer software is really good; it even corrects my grammar.

  8. "Little Lisa has been very good tonight," said the babysitter.

  9. Judge Ramesh is quite well-informed.

▲ 10. Judge Ramesh's decision gave each party exactly what it deserved.

  11. The editor couldn't use my illustrations; she said they were not particularly interesting.

  12. Wow. That was a tasty meal!

  13. The last set of essays was much better than the first set.

  14. Do unto others as you would have them do unto you.

  15. People who live in glass houses shouldn't throw stones.

  16. You really shouldn't make so much noise when the people upstairs are trying to sleep.

  17. It is unfair the way Professor Smith asks questions no normal person can answer.

  18. "Allegro" means fast, but not that fast!

  19. Being in touch with God gives your life meaning and value.

  20. Thou shalt not kill.

■ *Getting an "Ought" from an "Is": Factual Premises*
and Moral Value Judgments

It has been said that no claim about plain fact—that is, no factual claim—can imply a claim that attributes a moral value or a moral obligation. In other words, we cannot legitimately infer what *ought (morally) to be* the case from a claim about what *is* the case. Using the terminology from the previous section, we can put it this way: No value judgment can follow from a set of purely factual premises. For example, consider the following argument:

  1a. Mr. Jones is the father of a young child. Therefore, Mr. Jones ought to contribute to his child's support.

We hear such claims often in the context of everyday life, and we are often persuaded by such conclusions. But we should beware, for the conclusion doesn't follow from the premise; it is, in other words, a **non sequitur.** Jumping to such conclusions is a common phenomenon that philosophers generally refer to as the **naturalistic fallacy.** Let us take a closer look. The premise of this argument states a (nonmoral) fact, but the conclusion is an "ought" claim that prescribes a moral obligation for Mr. Jones. As the philosopher David Hume pointed out, there is nothing in a purely factual statement that implies a moral duty—the concept of duty is added to the statement by our sense of right and wrong.

However, this seems to lead to an unacceptable situation, for shouldn't we, on the basis of facts and statistics, be able to make policies about social and moral issues? If we know that child abuse is likely to create a new generation of adults who will also practice child abuse, shouldn't we then have the right to state that "child abuse should be prevented by all means" without being accused of committing a non sequitur? The answer is that of course facts and statistics can be used to formulate social and moral policies, but not the facts and statistics *by themselves:* We must add a premise to make the argument valid. In this case the premise is the moral statement that "child abuse is wrong." Adding this statement may seem trivial, and you may object that this evaluation is already given with the word "abuse," but the fact is that our moral sense, whether it is based on feelings or reasoning or both, is what allows us to proceed from a set of facts to a conclusion about what ought to be done. Let us return to Mr. Jones:

> 1b. Premise: Mr. Jones is the father of a young child.
>
> Premise: Parents ought to contribute to the support of their young children.
>
> Conclusion: Therefore, Mr. Jones ought to contribute to his child's support.

The result is now a valid deductive argument. Now, in a real-life dispute about whether Mr. Jones has an obligation toward his child, an argument like example 1b is not likely to convince anyone that Mr. Jones has this obligation if he or she doesn't agree with the premise that parents should take care of their children. But the fact that the argument is valid does help clarify matters. It may be an undisputed fact that Jones is a parent, but it may not be as undisputed that parents ought to take care of their young children under all circumstances. In other words, if you disagree with the conclusion, you need not start disagreeing with the factual claim of the first premise, but you can enter into a discussion about the truth of the second premise. It is important to be able to enter into such discussions apart from the case of Mr. Jones, for otherwise it would be too easy for us to let our thinking be prejudiced by the facts presented in the first premise.

Let us consider a few additional examples:

> 2a. Sophie promised to pay Jennifer five dollars today. So Sophie ought to pay Jennifer five dollars today.

It is perfectly natural to want to see this as a convincing argument as it stands. But, in keeping with our strategy, we require that an "ought" claim be explicitly stated in the premises. In this case, what would you say is the missing premise? The most obvious way of putting it is "One ought to keep one's promises." If we add the required premise we get this:

> 2b. Sophie promised to pay Jennifer five dollars today. One ought to keep one's promises. So Sophie ought to pay Jennifer five dollars today.

If it seems to you that the second premise is not really necessary in order for the conclusion to follow, that is probably because you accept that making a promise involves a moral duty to keep the promise. In that case, the second premise would just be true by definition, but even so, there is no harm in stating it. And suppose it is *not* true by definition? Not all implicit moral evaluations are; and if they are not, then adding the premise is absolutely necessary in order for the argument to be valid. Consider this example:

> 3a. It is natural for women to have children. Therefore, women ought to have children, and those who try to avoid having children are unnatural.

The trouble with this argument is the concept of "natural," a very ambiguous word. There are several hidden assumptions behind this argument, and one of these—which we'll call the missing premise here—is the following: "What is natural is morally good, and going against nature is evil." We might also say, "What is natural reveals God's intentions with his creation, and if one goes against God's intentions, one is evil (or sinful)." This also explains the concept of "unnatural," for although "natural" in the premise looks completely descriptive, "unnatural" in the conclusion has a judgmental slant. If we add the missing premise, the argument will look like this:

> 3b. It is natural for women to have children. What is natural is morally good, and going against nature is evil. Therefore, women ought to have children, and those who try to avoid having children are evil.

Now the argument is valid, but you may not want to agree with the conclusion. If so, although in some sense it is, overall, "natural" for females to have offspring, you may want to dispute the premise that what is natural is always morally good. After all, many "natural" things, such as leaving severely disabled individuals to fend for themselves or scratching oneself in public, are considered unacceptable in our culture.

Whether an "ought" claim can ever follow directly from an "is" claim has been a controversial issue among philosophers; some point out that a statement such as "An open flame can burn you, so stay away from the campfire" makes an unproblematic transition from an "is" to an "ought"; other philosophers point out that there is a hidden premise that is taken for granted: that getting burned is bad because it hurts.

Exercise 12-4 _____

In each of the following passages, a moral principle must be added as an extra premise to make the argument valid. Supply the missing principle.

Example

> Mrs. Montez's new refrigerator was delivered yesterday, and it stopped working altogether. She has followed the directions carefully but still can't make it work. The people she bought it from should either come out and make it work or replace it with another one.

Principle

> People should make certain that the things they sell are in proper working order.

1. After borrowing Morey's car, Leo had an accident and crumpled a fender. So, Leo ought to pay whatever expenses were involved in getting Morey's car fixed.

▲ 2. When Sarah bought the lawn mower from Jean, she promised to pay another fifty dollars on the first of the month. Since it is now the first, Sarah should pay Jean the money.

3. Kevin worked on his sister's car all weekend. The least she could do is let him borrow the car for his job interview next Thursday.

4. Harold is obligated to supply ten cords of firewood to the lodge by the beginning of October, since he signed a contract guaranteeing delivery of the wood by that date.

▲ 5. Since it was revealed yesterday on the 11:00 news that Mayor Ahearn has been taking bribes, he should step down any day now.

6. As a political candidate, Ms. Havenhurst promised to put an end to crime in the inner city. Now that she is in office, we'd like to see some results.

▲ 7. Since he has committed his third felony, he should automatically go to prison for twenty-five years.

▲ 8. Laura's priest has advised Laura and her husband not to sign up for the in vitro fertilization program at the hospital because such treatments are unnatural.

9. Ali has been working overtime a lot lately, so he should receive a bonus.

10. It is true there are more voters in the northern part of the state. But that shouldn't allow the north to dictate to the south.

■ *Consistency and Fairness*

A common mistake made in moral reasoning is inconsistency—treating cases that are similar as if they weren't that way. For example, suppose Moore announces on the first day of class that the final in the class will be optional "except," he says, pointing at some person at random, "for the young woman there in the third row. For you," he says, "the final is mandatory."

The problem is that Moore is treating a student who is similar to the rest of the class as if she were different. And the student will want to know, of course, why she has been singled out: "What's so different about me?" she will wonder (as she drops the course).

A similar sort of problem occurs if Moore gives two students the same grade despite the fact that one student did far better in the course than the other. Treating dissimilar cases as if they were similar isn't inconsistent; it just involves a failure to make relevant discriminations.

As you have probably foreseen by now, when we treat people inconsistently, the result is often *unfair*. It is unfair to the woman in the third row to require her alone to take the final; alternatively, it would be unfair to the rest of the class to make the final mandatory for them and to make it optional for the woman in the third row. From the perspective of critical thinking, what is so troubling about unfairness is that it is illogical. It is like saying "All Xs are Y" and then adding, "Some Xs are not Y."

This doesn't mean, of course, that if you have been treating people unfairly, you should *continue* to treat them unfairly on the grounds that it would be inconsistent for you to change your policy. There is nothing illogical in saying, in effect, "I treated the Xs I encountered to date wrongly, but now I will not treat the Xs I encounter wrongly." People sometimes adhere to a bad policy simply on the grounds that it would be inconsistent of them to change, but there is no basis in logic for this idea.

Not all cases of inconsistency result in unfairness. For example, let's imagine that Harlan approved of the war in Iraq and opposed the war in Vietnam but is unable to point out any relevant differences between the two cases. This isn't a matter of unfairness, exactly; it's just inconsistency on Harlan's part.

When are two or more cases sufficiently similar to warrant our calling somebody inconsistent who treats them as if they were different? The answer is that there is no hard-and-fast rule. The point to keep in mind, however, is that the burden of proof is on the person who appears inconsistent to show that he or she is not treating similar cases dissimilarly. If, when challenged, Harlan cannot *tell* us what's different about Vietnam and Iraq that justifies his difference in attitude between the two, then we are justified in regarding him as inconsistent.

Imagine that Carol is a salesperson who treats black customers and white customers differently: She is, let us imagine, much more polite to customers of her own racial group (we needn't worry about which group that is). Can Carol explain to us what is so different about black and white customers that would justify her treating them differently? If not, we are justified in regarding her practices as inconsistent.

Suppose, however, that Carol thinks that skin color itself is a difference between blacks and whites relevant to how people should be treated, and she charges us with failing to make relevant discriminations. Here it would be easy for us to point out to Carol that skin color is an immutable characteristic of birth like height or eye color; does Carol adjust her civility to people depending on those characteristics?

It isn't difficult to perceive the inconsistency on the part of a salesperson who is more polite to customers of one group; but other cases are far tougher, and many are such that reasonable people will disagree about their proper assessment. Is a person inconsistent who approves of abortion but not capital punishment? Is a person inconsistent who, on the one hand, believes that the states should be free to reduce spending on welfare but, on the other, does not think that the states should be able to eliminate ceilings on punitive damages in tort cases? No harm is done in asking "What's the difference?" and because much headway can be made in a discussion by doing so, it seems wise to ask.

In Chapter 6, we talked about the inconsistency ad hominem, a fallacy we commit when we think we rebut the content of what someone says by pointing out inconsistency on his or her part. Now, let's say Ramesh tells us it is wrong to hunt, and then we find out Ramesh likes to fish. And let's say that, when we press Ramesh, he cannot think of any relevant moral difference between the two activities. Then he is being inconsistent. But that does not mean that it is right to hunt; nor does it mean that it is wrong to fish. An inconsistency ad hominem occurs if we say something like "Ramesh, you are mistaken when you say it is wrong to hunt, because you yourself fish." It is not an inconsistency ad hominem to say "Ramesh, you are being inconsistent. You must change your position either on the hunting or on the fishing."

Similarly, let's suppose Professor Moore gives Howard an A and gives James a C, but cannot think of any differences between their performance in his course. It would be the inconsistency ad hominem if we said "Moore, James does not deserve a C, because you gave Howard an A." Likewise, it would be the inconsistency ad hominem if we said "Moore, Howard does not deserve an A, because you gave James a C." But it is *not* illogical for us to say "Moore, you are being inconsistent. You have misgraded one of these students."

Exercise 12-5

Answer the question or respond to the statement that concludes each item.

▲ 1. Tory thinks that women should have the same rights as men. However, he also thinks that although a man should have the right to marry a woman, a woman should not have the right to marry a woman. Is Tory being consistent in his views?

▲ 2. At Shelley's university, the minimum GPA requirement for admission is relaxed for 6 percent of the incoming students. About half of those allowed to attend the university under one of its special admissions programs are affirmative action students—women and members of minorities. The other half are athletes, children of alumni, and talented art students. Shelley is opposed to special admissions programs for affirmative action students. She is not opposed to special admissions programs for art students, athletes, and children of alumni. Is Shelley consistent?

▲ 3. Marin does not approve of abortion because the Bible says explicitly, "Thou shalt not kill." "'Thou shalt not kill' means thou shalt not kill," he says. Marin does, however, approve of capital punishment. Is Marin consistent?

4. Koko believes that adults should have the unrestricted right to read whatever material they want to read, but she does not believe that her seventeen-year-old daughter Gina should have the unrestricted right to read whatever she wants to read. Is Koko consistent?

5. Jack maintains that the purpose of marriage is procreation. On these grounds he opposes same-sex marriages. "Gays can't create children," he explains. However, he does not oppose marriages between heterosexual partners who cannot have children due to age or medical reasons. "It's not the same," he says. Is Jack being consistent?

6. Alisha thinks the idea of outlawing cigarettes is ridiculous. "Give me a break," she says. "If you want to screw up your health with cigarettes, that's your own business." However, Alisha does not approve the legalization of marijuana. "Hel-loh-o," she says. "Marijuana is a *drug,* and the last thing we need is more druggies." Is Alisha being consistent?

7. California's Proposition 209 amends the California state constitution to prohibit "discrimination or preferential treatment" in state hiring based on race, gender, or ethnicity. Opponents say that Proposition 209 singles out women and members of racial and ethnic minorities for unequal treatment. Their argument is that Proposition 209 makes it impossible for members of these groups to obtain redress for past discrimination through preferential treatment, whereas members of other groups who may have suffered past discrimination (gays, for example, or members of religious groups) are not similarly restricted from seeking redress. Evaluate this argument.

▲ 8. Harold prides himself on being a liberal. He is delighted when a federal court issues a preliminary ruling that California's Proposition 209 (see previous item) is unconstitutional. "It makes no difference that a majority of California voters approved the measure," Harold argues. "If it is unconstitutional, then it is unconstitutional." However, California voters also recently passed an initiative that permits physicians to prescribe marijuana, and Harold is livid when the U.S. Attorney General says that the federal government will ignore the California statute and will use federal law to prosecute any physician who prescribes marijuana. Is Harold consistent?

9. Graybosch is of the opinion that we should not perform medical experiments on people against their will, but he has no problem with medical experiments being done on dogs. His wife disagrees. She sees no relevant difference between the two cases.

"What, no difference between people and dogs?" Graybosch asks.

"There are differences, but no differences that are relevant to the issue," Graybosch's wife responds. "Dogs feel pain and experience fear just as much as people."

Is Graybosch's wife correct?

10. Mr. Bork is startled when a friend tells him he should contribute to the welfare of others' children as much as to his own.

"Why on earth should I do that?" Mr. Bork asks his friend.

"Because," his friend responds, "there is no relevant difference between the two cases. The fact that your children are yours does not mean that there is something different about them that gives them a greater entitlement to happiness than anyone else's children."

How should Mr. Bork respond?

11. The university wants to raise the requirements for tenure. Professor Peterson, who doesn't have tenure, says that doing so is unfair to her. She argues that those who received tenure before she did weren't required to meet such exacting standards; therefore, neither should she. Is she correct?

12. Reverend Heintz has no objection to same-sex marriages, but is opposed to polygamous marriages. Is there a relevant difference between the two cases, or is Reverend Heintz being inconsistent?

■ *Major Perspectives in Moral Reasoning*

Moral reasoning usually takes place within one or more frameworks or perspectives. Here we present some of the perspectives that have been especially influential in Western moral thought.

Relativism   A popular view of ethics, especially perhaps among undergraduates taking a first course in philosophy, is **moral relativism,** which we'll define as the idea that what is right and wrong depends on and is determined by one's group or culture.

A mistake sometimes made in moral reasoning is to confuse the following two claims:

1. What is *believed* to be right and wrong may differ from group to group, society to society, or culture to culture.
2. What *is* right and wrong may differ from group to group, society to society, or culture to culture.

The second claim, but not the first, is moral relativism. Please read the two claims carefully. They are so similar it takes a moment to see they are actually quite different. But they are different. The first claim is incontestable; the second claim is controversial and problematic. It may well have been the majority belief in ancient Greece that there was nothing wrong with slavery. But that does not mean that at that time there was nothing wrong with slavery.

Another popular moral perspective is an extreme form of relativism known as **subjectivism,** according to which what is right and wrong is just a matter of subjective opinion. The theory often loses its appeal when some of its implications are noticed. For example, what if Parker thinks that it is right for a person to do X, and Moore thinks that it is wrong for a person to do X? Is it right or wrong for a person to do X? Subjectivism seems to place its adherents in a logically untenable situation.

Subjectivists sometimes think they avoid problems by saying something like "Well, it's right for Parker to do X, but wrong for Moore to do it." However, let's suppose that X in this case is torturing a pet. Would we wish to say, "Well, because Parker doesn't think there is anything wrong with torturing a pet, then there isn't anything wrong with *his* doing it"?

Relativism and subjectivism were popular among cultural anthropologists in the 1920s and still have popular appeal. But neither has won widespread acceptance among moral philosophers.

Utilitarianism   The perspective we call **utilitarianism** rests on the idea that if an individual can feel pleasure and pain, then he or she deserves moral consideration. (This broad criterion has led many utilitarians to include animals in their considerations.) The theory is based on one principle, the **principle of utility:** Maximize happiness and minimize unhappiness. This means that the utilitarian is concerned with the *consequences* of actions and decisions. If an act will produce more happiness than will the alternatives, the act is the right one to do; if it will produce less happiness, it would be morally wrong to do it in place of one of its alternatives.

Many of us use a pro-and-con list of consequences as a guideline when considering what course of action to take. Let's assume you have to decide whether to go home for Thanksgiving or to spend the long weekend writing a term paper that is due. Your family is expecting you, and they will be disappointed if you don't come home. However, their disappointment will be lessened by their knowing that your studies are important to you. On the other hand, if you stay to finish the paper, you will miss seeing your friends at home. But if you go home, you will not finish the paper on time, and your final grade may be adversely affected. As a utilitarian, you try to weigh the consequences of the alternatives on everyone's happiness. You also have to factor in how *certain* the outcomes of each alternative are with respect to happiness, assigning relatively more weight to relatively more certain positive outcomes. Because you can generally be more certain of the effect of an act on your own happiness and on the happiness of others you know well, it is often morally proper to favor that act that best promotes your own or their happiness. Of course, you must not use this as an excuse to be entirely self-serving: Your own happiness isn't more important morally than another's. The best course of action morally is not always the one that best promotes your own happiness.

In sum, utilitarians weigh the consequences of the alternatives, pro and con, and then choose the alternative that maximizes happiness. One of the original and most profound intellects behind utilitarianism, Jeremy

Bentham (1748–1832), even went so far as to devise a *hedonistic calculus*—a method of assigning actual numerical values to pleasures and pains based on their intensity, certainty, duration, and so forth. Other utilitarians think that some pleasures are of a higher quality (e.g., reading Shakespeare is of a higher quality than watching Daffy Duck). Although there are other important issues in utilitarianism, the basic idea involves weighing the consequences of possible actions in terms of happiness. Utilitarianism has considerable popular appeal, and real-life moral reasoning is often utilitarian to a considerable extent.

Nevertheless, some aspects of the theory are problematic. Typically, when we deliberate whether or not to do something, we don't always take into consideration just the effect of the action on happiness. For example, other people have *rights* that we sometimes take into account. We would not make someone in our family a slave even if the happiness produced for the family by doing so outweighed the unhappiness it created for the slave. We also consider our *duties* and *obligations*. We think it is our duty to return a loan to someone even if we are still short on cash and the other person doesn't need the money and doesn't even remember having loaned it to us. If we make a date and then want to break it because we've met the love of our life, we think twice about standing up our original date, even if we believe that our overall happiness will far outweigh the temporary unhappiness of our date. To many, the moral obligation of a promise cannot be ignored for the sake of the overall happiness that might result from breaking it.

In estimating the moral worth of what people do, utilitarianism also seems to discount people's *intentions*. Suppose a mugger attacks somebody just as a huge flower pot falls from a balcony above. The mugger happens to push the individual the instant before the flower pot lands on the exact spot where the victim had been standing. The mugger has saved the victim's life, as it turns out. But would we say that the mugger did a morally good deed just because his action had a happy result? According to utilitarianism we would, assuming the net result of the action was more happiness than would otherwise have been the case. So utilitarianism doesn't seem to be the complete story in moral reasoning.

Duty Theory/Deontologism   Immanuel Kant (1724–1804), who witnessed the beginning phases of the utilitarian philosophy, found that philosophy deficient because of its neglect, among other things, of moral duty. Kant's theory is a version of what is called **duty theory,** or **deontologism.**

Kant acknowledged that our lives are full of imperatives based on our own situations and our objectives. If we want to advance at work, then it is imperative that we keep our promises; if we are concerned about our friends' happiness, then it is imperative that we not talk about them behind their backs. But this type of **hypothetical imperative,** which tells us we ought to do (or ought not to do) something in order to achieve such and such a result, is not a *moral* imperative, Kant argued. Keeping a promise so we'll get a solid reputation is neither morally praiseworthy nor morally blameworthy, he said. For our act to be *morally* praiseworthy, it must be done, not

Acts and Rules

Let's say you are thinking of cheating on a test. It isn't inconceivable that the sum total of happiness in the world would be increased by this single *act* of cheating. But it also isn't inconceivable that if the *principle* involved were adopted widely, the sum total of happiness would be decreased.

This raises an interesting question: When calculating happiness outcomes, should we contemplate happiness outcomes of the particular *act* in question? Or should we contemplate happiness outcomes of adoption of the *principle* involved in the act?

Clearly there are difficult issues here. Accordingly, some philosophers have made a distinction between "act utilitarianism," which evaluates the moral worth of an act on the happiness it would produce, and "rule utilitarianism," which evaluates the moral worth of an act on the happiness that would be produced by adoption of the principle it exemplifies. (A possible middle ground might be to attempt to factor in, as a part of the happiness outcomes of a particular act, the likelihood that doing it will contribute to a general adoption of the principle involved. This is often what we do when we ask, "But what if everyone did this?")

for the sake of some objective, but simply because *it is right.* Our action of keeping our promise is morally praiseworthy, he said, only if we do it simply because it is right to keep our promises. A moral imperative is unconditional or **categorical;** it prescribes an action, not for the sake of some result, but simply because that action is our moral duty.

It follows from this philosophy that when it comes to evaluating an action morally, what counts is not the result or consequences of the action, as utilitarianism maintains, but the intention from which it is done. And the morally best intention, indeed in Kant's opinion the *only* truly morally praiseworthy intention, is that according to which you do something just because it is your moral duty.

But what makes something our moral duty? Some deontologists ground duty in human nature; others ground it in reason; in Western culture, of course, many believe moral duty is set by God. How can we tell what our duty is? Some believe our duty is to be found by consulting conscience; others believe that it is just self-evident or is clear to moral intuition. Those who maintain that human moral duties are established by God usually derive their specific understanding of these duties through interpretations of religious texts such as the Bible, though there is disagreement over what the correct interpretation is and even over who should do the interpreting.

Kant answered the question, How can we tell what our moral duty is? as follows: Suppose you are considering some course of action—say, whether to borrow some money you need very badly. But suppose that you know you can't pay back the loan. Is it morally permissible for you to borrow money under such circumstances? Kant said to do this: First, find the *maxim* (prin-

Inmate Who Got New Heart While Still in Prison Dies

A California prison inmate believed to be the first in the nation to receive a heart transplant while incarcerated has died, officials said Tuesday.

Department of Corrections spokesman Russ Heimerich said the inmate, whose identity has been withheld, died late Monday at Stanford University Medical Center.

Heimerich said the exact cause of death was still undetermined, "but it looks like his body was rejecting the heart" he received in an expensive and controversial taxpayer-financed operation in January.

Officials estimated the surgery and subsequent care—including the $12,500 a day it cost to keep him in the Stanford facility after he was admitted Nov. 23—have cost more than $1.25 million. Heimerich said that figure does not include transportation, medication or providing round-the-clock security while the inmate was in the hospital.

"It could easily reach $2 million when it's all added in," Heimerich said.

The prisoner was a 32-year-old two-time felon serving a 14-year sentence for robbing a Los Angeles convenience store in 1996. He was eligible for parole in October 2008.

He became the center of a national controversy after The Bee disclosed the surgery, which also took place at Stanford.

The operation raised questions about whether there should be limits on the kinds of medical care to which prison inmates are entitled.

At the time of the transplant, prison officials said they were required under numerous court orders, including a 1976 U.S. Supreme Court decision, to provide necessary health care to all inmates.

The decision to provide the inmate, who had longtime heart problems caused by a viral infection, with a new heart was made by a medical panel at Stanford. The surgery was performed on a day when at least 500 other Californians were waiting for similar operations.

But medical professionals and organ transplant centers said they can make decisions about who gets organs and who doesn't based only on medical protocols and not social factors.

While the first of its kind, the transplant is not likely to be the last. As California's prison population ages, authorities are concerned the cost of inmate health care will soar far above last fiscal year's $663 million.

Compounding the problem, Heimerich said, is that many inmate patients don't follow doctor's orders. He said the heart recipient apparently did not follow all of the medical recommendations, although it wasn't clear his failure to do so played a role in his death.

"We can treat them," Heimerich said, "but we can't baby-sit them."

By Steve Wiegand
BEE STAFF WRITER

Comment: Such cases involve legal reasoning (see next section of this chapter) as well as moral reasoning. The position taken here by medical professionals is duty theory; they are explicitly ruling out utilitarian considerations in deciding whom to give transplants to.

Source: The *Sacramento Bee*, December 17, 2002.

ciple of action) involved in what you want to do. In the case in question, the maxim is "Every time I'm in need of money, I'll go to my friends and promise I'll pay it back, even if I know I can't." Next, ask yourself, "Could I want this maxim to be a *universal* law or rule, one that everyone should follow?" This process of *universalization* is the feature that lets you judge whether something would work as a moral law, according to Kant. Could you make it a universal law that it is okay for everybody to lie about paying back loans? Hardly: If everyone adopted this principle, then there would be no such thing as loan making. In short, the universalization of your principle undermines the very principle that is universalized. If everyone adopted the principle, then nobody could possibly follow it. The universalization of your principle is illogical, so it is your duty to pay back loans.

As you can see, the results of acting according to Kant's theory can be radically different from the results of acting according to utilitarianism. Utilitarianism would condone borrowing money with no intention of repaying it, assuming that doing so would produce more happiness than would be produced by not doing so. But Kant's theory would not condone it.

Kant also noted that if you were to borrow a friend's money with no intention of repaying it, you would be treating your friend merely as a means to an end. If you examine cases like this, in which you use other people as mere tools for your own objectives, then, Kant said, you will find in each case a transgression of moral duty, a principle of action that cannot be universalized. Thus, he warned us, it is our moral duty never to treat someone else *merely* as a tool, as means to an end. Of course Kant did not mean that Moore cannot ask Parker for help on some project; doing so would not be a case of Moore's using Parker *merely* as a tool.

Kant's theory of the moral necessity of never treating other people as mere tools can be modified to support the ideas that people have rights and that treatment of others must always involve fair play. Regardless of whether you subscribe to Kant's version of duty theory, the chances are that your own moral deliberations are more than just strictly utilitarian and may well involve considerations of what you take to be other moral requirements, including your duties and the rights of others.

Divine Command Theory   Those who believe moral duty is set by an authority of some sort subscribe to "command" duty theory. (Some authorities view Kant's duty theory as a version of command duty theory, with the authority for Kant being *reason.*) In our culture, probably the most popular version of command duty theory is that according to which our moral duty is set by God; it thus is known as **divine command theory.** As noted above, those who hold this view generally derive their understanding of God's commandments by interpretation of religious texts like the Bible. How, for example, is "Thou shalt not kill" to be understood? Should it be understood as prohibiting capital punishment, or killing in self-defense, or killing in wartime? Does it cover abortion? There is obviously room for disagreement here; likewise, there is room for disagreement over who is to do the interpreting, whether it is to be oneself, or one's minister, or the head of one's church, or whoever.

A philosophical difficulty in divine command theory lies in the question, Is God *justified* in decreeing an act to be right, or is his decree simply arbitrarily? On the one hand, we don't want to say that God hands down rules arbitrarily; yet the first alternative seems to imply that there is some stan-

I'm not guilty of murder. I'm guilty of obeying the laws of the Creator.

—BENJAMIN MAT-
THEW WILLIAMS,
who committed
suicide while
awaiting sentenc-
ing for having
murdered a gay
couple

dard of rightness and wrongness *above* or *apart* from God, in terms of which God finds the justification for his edicts.

Virtue Ethics   Utilitarianism and duty theory, as well as most other classical approaches to moral theory, focus on the question of what to do. For that reason they are commonly referred to as ethics of conduct. However, another approach was predominant in classical Greek thinking and has regained popularity in recent years. That approach, known as **virtue ethics,** focuses not on *what to do,* but on *how to be;* in other words, the moral issue is not one of single actions or types of actions but of developing a *good character.*

The ancient Greeks believed it was supremely important for a person to achieve psychological and physical balance; and to do that, the person needed to develop a consistently good character. A person out of balance will not be able to assess a situation properly and will tend to overreact or not react strongly enough; moreover, such a person will not know his or her proper limits. People who recognize their own qualifications and limitations and who are capable of reacting to the right degree, at the right time, toward the right person, and for the right reason are virtuous persons. They understand the value of the idea of moderation: not too much and not too little, but in each case a response that is just right.

Aristotle (384–322 B.C.E.) regarded virtue as a trait, like wisdom, justice, or courage, that we acquire when we use our capacity to reason to moderate our impulses and appetites. The largest part of Aristotle's major ethical writing, the *Nicomachean Ethics,* is devoted to analysis of specific moral virtues as means between extremes (for example, courage is the mean between fearing everything and fearing nothing). He also emphasized that virtue is a matter of habit; it is a trait, a way of living.

Virtue ethics is not an abstruse ethical theory. Many of us (fortunately) wish to be (or become) persons of good character. And as a practical matter, when we are deliberating a course of action, our approach often is to consider what someone whose character we admire would do in the circumstances.

Still, it is possible that virtue theory alone cannot answer all moral questions. Each of us may face moral dilemmas of such a nature that it simply isn't clear what course of action is required by someone of good character.

■ *Moral Deliberation*

Before you began this chapter, you may have assumed that moral discussion is merely an exchange of personal opinion or feeling, one that reserves no place for reason or critical thinking. But moral discussion usually assumes some sort of perspective like those we have mentioned here. Actually, in real life, moral reasoning is often a mixture of perspectives, a blend of utilitarian considerations weighted somewhat toward one's own happiness, modified by ideas about duties, rights, and obligations, and mixed often with a thought, perhaps guilty, about what the ideally virtuous person (a parent, a teacher) would do in similar circumstances. It also sometimes

Why Moral Problems Seem Unresolvable

Differences of opinion over ethical issues sometimes seem irreconcilable. Yet this fact often strikes thoughtful people as amazing, because ethical opponents often share a great deal of common ground. For example, pro-life and pro-choice adherents agree on the sanctity of human life. So why in the world can't they resolve their differences? Likewise, those who favor affirmative action and those who agree that racism and sexism still exist and are wrong and need to be eradicated—why on earth can't they resolve their differences?

The answer, in some cases, comes down to a difference in moral perspective. Take affirmative action. Those who favor affirmative action often operate within a utilitarian perspective: They assume that whether a policy should be adopted depends on whether adopting the policy will produce more happiness than will not adopting it. From this perspective, if policies of affirmative action produce more happiness over the long run, then they should be adopted—end of discussion. But those who oppose affirmative action (on grounds other than blatant racism) do so because they believe deontologism trumps utilitarianism. From the deontologist perspective, even if affirmative action policies would produce more happiness in the long run, if they involve even temporarily using some people as a means to that objective, then they are wrong—end of discussion.

In other disputes the root difference lies elsewhere. Pro-life and pro-choice adherents often both are deontologists and agree, for example, that in the absence of a powerful justification, it is wrong to take a human life. They may disagree, however, either as to what counts as a human life or as to what counts as a powerful justification. This difference, then, comes down to a difference in basic definitions—which fact, incidentally, illustrates how silly it can be to dismiss a discussion as "mere semantics."

involves mistakes—factual and nonfactual claims may be confused, inconsistencies may occur, inductive arguments may be weak or deductive arguments may be invalid, fallacious reasoning may be present, and so forth.

We can make headway in our own thinking about moral issues by trying to get clear on what perspective, if any, we are assuming. For example, suppose we are thinking about the death penalty. Our first thought might be that society is much better off if murderers are executed. Are we then assuming a utilitarian perspective? Asking ourselves this question might lead us to consider whether there are *limits* on what we would do for the common good—for example, would we be willing to risk sacrificing an innocent person? It might also lead us to consider how we might *establish* whether society is better off if murderers are executed—if we are utilitarians, then ultimately we will have to establish this if our reasoning is to be compelling.

Or suppose we have seen a friend cheating on an exam. Should we report it to the teacher? Whatever our inclination, it may be wise to consider our perspective. Are we viewing things from a utilitarian perspective? That is, are we assuming that it would promote the most happiness overall to report our friend? Or do we simply believe that it is our duty to report him or her, come what may? Would a virtuous person report the person? Each of these questions will tend to focus our attention on a particular set of considerations—those that are the most relevant to our way of thinking.

It may occur to you to wonder at this point if there is any reason for choosing among perspectives. The answer to this question is yes: Adherents of these positions, philosophers such as those we mentioned, offer grounding or support for their perspectives in theories about human nature, the natural universe, the nature of morality, and other things. In other words, they have *arguments* to support their views. If you are interested, we recommend a course in ethics.

Exercise 12-6

1. Roy needs to sell his car, but he doesn't have money to spend on repairs. He plans to sell the vehicle to a private party without mentioning that the rear brakes are worn. Evaluate Roy's plan of action from a Kantian perspective—that is, can the maxim of Roy's plan be universalized?

2. Defend affirmative action from a utilitarian perspective.

3. Criticize affirmative action from a Kantian perspective. (Hint: Consider Kant's theory that people must never be treated as means only.)

4. Criticize or defend medical experimentation on animals from a utilitarian perspective.

5. Criticize or defend medical experimentation on animals from a divine command perspective.

6. A company has the policy of not promoting women to be vice presidents. What might be said about this policy from the perspective of virtue ethics?

7. What might be said about the policy mentioned in item 6 from the perspective of utilitarianism?

8. Evaluate bisexuality (in humans) from a divine command perspective.

9. In your opinion, would the virtuous person, the person of the best moral character, condemn, approve, or be indifferent to bisexuality?

10. "We can't condemn the founding fathers for owning slaves; people didn't think there was anything wrong with it at the time." Comment on this remark from the standpoint of duty theory.

11. "Let's have some fun and see how your parrot looks without any feathers." (The example is from philosopher Joseph Grcic.) Which of the following perspectives seems best equipped to condemn this suggestion?
    a. utilitarianism
    b. Kantian duty theory
    c. divine command theory
    d. virtue ethics
    e. relativism

12. "Might makes right." Could a utilitarian accept this? Could a virtue ethicist? Could Kant? Could a relativist? Could someone who subscribes to divine command theory?

Exercise 12-7

> This is Darwin's natural selection at its very best. The highest bidder gets youth and beauty.

These are the words of fashion photographer Ron Harris, who auctioned the ova of fashion models via the Internet. The model got the full bid price, and the Web site took a commission of an additional 20 percent. The bid price included no medical costs, though it listed specialists who were willing to perform the procedure. Harris, who created the video "The 20 Minute Workout," said the egg auction gave people the chance of reproducing beautiful children who would have an advantage in society. Critics, however, were numerous. "It screams of unethical behavior," one said. "It is acceptable for an infertile couple to choose an egg donor and compensate her for her time, inconvenience and discomfort," he said. "But this is something else entirely. Among other things, what happens to the child if he or she turns out to be unattractive?"

Discuss the (moral) pros and cons of this issue for five or ten minutes in groups. Then take a written stand on the question "Should human eggs be auctioned to the highest bidder?" When you are finished, discuss which moral perspective seems to be the one in which you are operating.

Exercise 12-8

> Jesus wants to be our best friend. . . . If we let him direct our lives, he will give us the desires of our heart . . . we must yield to God and let him direct our future plans.

Selection 12 in Appendix 1 concerns a student who was denied permission to deliver a valedictorian speech at his public high school graduation that contained this statement.

The principal held that religious points of view cannot be presented at an event sponsored by a publicly funded agency. If the student had given his speech, the principal said, it would be as if the school had condoned the strong religious message the words contained.

The student, on the other hand, said he should be free to express his opinions and beliefs in a graduation speech. He said:

> I would not object if a Buddhist student gave a graduation speech and thanked Buddha, or a graduation speaker thanked Satan and urged people to follow Satan's example. Our country was founded on godly principles. God is on all of our money. It's pretty absurd that you can't even mention God at a graduation.

Should the student have been denied permission to include the statement we've quoted in his graduation speech? Think about the issue for a few minutes and then discuss it in groups of four or five for another five or ten minutes. After that, take a position on the issue and, on a piece of paper, defend the position with the best argument you can think of. Groups should then decide which moral perspective or combination of moral perspectives your defense seems to adopt.

Legal Reasoning

When we think about arguments and disputes, the first image to come to most minds is probably that of an attorney arguing a case in a court of law. Although it's true that lawyers require a solid understanding of factual matters related to their cases and of psychological considerations as well, especially where juries are involved, it is still safe to say that a lawyer's stock-in-trade is argument. Lawyers are successful—in large part—to the extent that they can produce evidence in support of the conclusion that most benefits their client—in other words, their success depends on how well they can put premises and conclusions together into convincing arguments.

■ *Legal Reasoning and Moral Reasoning Compared*

There are some obvious similarities between moral and legal claims. For example, they are both often prescriptive—they tell us what we should do. Both play a role in guiding our conduct, but legal prescriptions carry the weight of society behind them in a way that moral prescriptions do not: We can be punished if we fail to follow the former. In terms of specific actions, it's obvious that the class of illegal activities and the class of immoral activities greatly overlap. Indeed, a society whose moral and legal codes were greatly at odds would be very difficult to understand.

In our own society, we use the term "morals offenses" for a certain class of crimes (usually related to sexual practices), but in reality, most of the crimes we list in our penal codes are also offenses against morality: murder, robbery, theft, rape, and so on. There are exceptions both ways. Lying is almost always considered immoral, but it is illegal only in certain circumstances—under oath or in a contract, for example. On the other hand, there are many laws that have little or nothing to do with morality: laws that govern whether two people are married, laws that determine how far back from the street you must build your house, laws that require us to drive on the right side of the road, and so on. (It may be morally wrong to endanger others by driving on the wrong side of the road, but it is of no moral consequence whether the *correct* side is the right or the left. Hence, the actual content of the law is morally neutral.)

■ *Two Types of Legal Studies: Justifying Laws and Interpreting Laws*

Two principal kinds of questions are asked in legal studies. (Such studies, incidentally, are known variously as "jurisprudence" and "philosophy of law.") The first kind of question asks what the law *should be* and what procedures for making law should be adopted; the second kind asks what the law *is* and how it should be applied. Typically, philosophers are more interested in the former type of question and practicing attorneys in the latter.

By and large, reasoning about the first kind of question differs very little from moral reasoning as described in the first part of this chapter. The difference is simply that the focus is on justifying *laws* rather than on justifying moral statements or principles. We are often most interested in the justification of laws when those laws forbid us from doing something we might otherwise want to do or when they require us to do something we might otherwise want not to do. Justifications are simply arguments that try to establish the goodness, value, or acceptability of something. Here, they are used to try to answer the question, What should the law be?

Consider whether a law that forbids doing X should be enacted by your state legislature.* Typically, there are four main grounds on which a supporter of a law can base his or her justification. The first is simply that doing X is immoral. The claim that the law should make illegal anything that is immoral is the basis of the position known as **legal moralism.** One might use such a basis for justifying laws forbidding murder, assault, or unorthodox sexual practices. For a legal moralist, the kinds of arguments designed to show that an action is immoral are directly relevant to the question of whether the action should be illegal.

The next ground on which a law can be justified is probably the one that most people think of first. It is very closely associated with John Stuart Mill (1806–1873) and is known as the **harm principle:** The only legitimate basis for forbidding X is that doing X causes harm to others. Notice that the harm principle states not just that harm to others is a good ground for forbidding an activity, but that it is the *only* ground. (In terms of the way we formulated such claims in Chapter 9, on truth-functional logic, the principle would be stated, "It is legitimate to forbid doing X *if and only if* doing X causes harm to others.") A person who defends this principle and who wants to enact a law forbidding X will present evidence that doing X does indeed cause harm to others. Her arguments could resemble any of the types covered in earlier chapters.

A third ground on which our hypothetical law might be based is legal paternalism. **Legal paternalism** is the view that laws can be justified if they prevent a person from doing harm to him- or herself; that is, they forbid or make it impossible to do X, *for a person's own good.* Examples include laws

---

*The example here is of a criminal law—part of a penal code designed to require and forbid certain behaviors and to punish offenders. The situation is a little different in civil law, a main goal of which is to shift the burden of a wrongful harm (a "tort") from the person on whom it falls to another, more suitable person—usually the one who caused the harm.

that require that seat belts be worn while riding in automobiles and that helmets be worn while riding on motorcycles.

The last of the usual bases for justifying criminal laws is that some behavior is generally found offensive. The **offense principle** says that a law forbidding X can be justifiable if X causes great offense to others. Laws forbidding burning of the flag are often justified on this ground.

The second question mentioned earlier—What *is* the law and how should it be applied?—may be more straightforward than the first question, but it can still be very complicated. We needn't go into great detail here about why this is the case, but an example will provide an indication. Back in Chapter 2 we discussed vague concepts, and we found that it is impossible to rid our talk entirely of vagueness. Here's an example from the law. Let's suppose that a city ordinance forbids vehicles on the paths in the city park. Clearly, a person violates the law if he or she drives a truck or a car down the paths. But what about a motorbike? A bicycle? A go-cart? A child's pedal car? Just what counts as a vehicle and what does not? This is the kind of issue that must often be decided in court because—not surprisingly—the governing body writing the law could not foresee all the possible items that might, in somebody's mind, count as a vehicle.

The process of narrowing down when a law applies and when it does not, then, is another kind of reasoning problem that occurs in connection with the law.

■ *The Role of Precedent in Legal Reasoning*

Generally speaking, legal reasoning is like other reasoning insofar as it makes use of the same kinds of arguments: They are deductive or inductive; if the former, they can be valid or invalid; if the latter, they can range from strong to weak. The difference between legal and other types of reasoning is mainly in the subject matter to which the argumentative techniques are applied, a taste of which we have sampled in the preceding paragraphs.

There is one kind of argument that occupies a special place in reasoning about legal matters, however: the **appeal to precedent.** This is the practice in the law of using a case that has already been decided as an authoritative guide in deciding a new case that is similar. The appeal to precedent is a variety of argument by analogy in which the current case is said to be sufficiently like the previous case to warrant deciding it in the same way. The general principle of treating like cases alike, discussed in the previous section on moral reasoning, applies here for exactly the same reasons. It would be illogical—and most would say, in some cases at least, unfair or immoral—to treat similar cases in different ways. The Latin name for the principle of appeal to precedent is ***stare decisis*** ("don't change settled decisions," more or less). Using terminology that was applied in the Chapter 10 discussion of analogical argument, we'd say that the earlier, already settled case is the sample, the current case is the target, and the property in question is the way in which the first case was decided. If the target case is sufficiently like the sample case, then, according to the principle of *stare decisis,* it should be decided the same way. Arguments in such situations, naturally, tend to focus on whether the current case really is like the precedent in enough relevant respects. Aside from the fact that such disputes sometimes have more significant consequences for the parties involved, they are not importantly different from those over analogies in other subject matters.

Exercise 12-9

For each of the following kinds of laws, pick at least one of the four grounds for justification discussed in the text—legal moralism, the harm principle, legal paternalism, and the offense principle—and construct an argument designed to justify the law. You may not agree either with the law or with the argument; the exercise is to see if you can connect the law to the (allegedly) justifying principle. For many laws, there is more than one kind of justification possible, so there can be more than one good answer for many of these.

▲   1. Laws against shoplifting
▲   2. Laws against forgery
    3. Laws against suicide
▲   4. Laws against spitting on the sidewalk
    5. Laws against driving under the influence of drugs or alcohol
▲   6. Laws against adultery
    7. Laws against marriage between two people of the same sex
    8. Laws that require people to have licenses before they practice medicine
    9. Laws that require drivers of cars to have driver's licenses
▲ 10. Laws against desecrating a corpse
   11. Laws against trespassing
   12. Laws against torturing your pet (even though it may be legal to kill your pet, if it is done humanely)

Exercise 12-10

This exercise is for class discussion or a short writing assignment. In the text, "Vehicles are prohibited on the paths in the park" was used as an example of a law that might require clarification. Decide whether the law should be interpreted to forbid motorcycles, bicycles, children's pedal cars, and battery-powered remote-control cars. On what grounds are you deciding each of these cases?

Exercise 12-11

The U.S. Supreme Court came to a decision not long ago about the proper application of the word "use." Briefly, the case in point was about a man named

John Angus Smith, who traded a handgun for cocaine. The law under which Smith was charged provided for a much more severe penalty—known as an enhanced penalty—if a gun was used in a drug-related crime than if no gun was involved. (In this case, the enhanced penalty was a mandatory thirty-year sentence; the "unenhanced" penalty was five years.) Justice Antonin Scalia argued that Smith's penalty should not be enhanced because he did not use the gun in the way the writers of the law had in mind; he did not use it *as a gun.* Justice Sandra Day O'Connor argued that the law only requires the *use* of a gun, not any particular *kind* of use. If you were a judge, would you vote with Scalia or with O'Connor? Construct an argument in support of your position. (The decision of the court is given in the answer section at the back of the book.)

Aesthetic Reasoning

Like moral and legal thinking, aesthetic thinking relies on a conceptual framework that integrates fact and value. Judgments about beauty and art—even judgments about whether something is a work of art or just an everyday object—appeal to principles that identify sources of aesthetic or artistic value. So when you make such a judgment, you are invoking aesthetic concepts, even if you have not made them explicit to yourself or to others.

■ *Eight Aesthetic Principles*

Here are some of the aesthetic principles that most commonly support or influence artistic creation and critical judgment about art. The first three identify value in art with an object's ability to fulfill certain cultural or social functions.

1. *Objects are aesthetically valuable if they are meaningful or teach us truths.* For example, Aristotle says that tragic plays teach us general truths about the human condition in a dramatic way that cannot be matched by real-life experience. Many people believe art shows us truths that are usually hidden from us by the practical concerns of daily life.

2. *Objects are aesthetically valuable if they have the capacity to convey values or beliefs that are central to the cultures or traditions in which they originate or that are important to the artists who made them.* For example, John Milton's poem *Paradise Lost* expresses the seventeenth-century Puritan view of the relationship between human beings and God.

3. *Objects are aesthetically valuable if they have the capacity to help bring about social or political change.* For instance, Abraham Lincoln commented that Harriet Beecher Stowe's *Uncle Tom's Cabin* contributed to the antislavery movement, which resulted in the Civil War.

Another group of principles identifies aesthetic value with objects' capacities to produce certain subjective—that is, psychological—states in persons who experience or appreciate them. Here are some of the most common or influential principles of the second group:

4. *Objects are aesthetically valuable if they have the capacity to produce pleasure in those who experience or appreciate them.* For instance, the nineteenth-century German philosopher Friedrich Nietzsche identifies one kind of aesthetic value with the capacity to create a feeling of ecstatic bonding in audiences.

5. *Objects are aesthetically valuable if they have the capacity to produce certain emotions we value, at least when the emotion is brought about by art rather than life.* In the *Poetics*, Aristotle observes that we welcome the feelings of fear created in us by frightening dramas, whereas in everyday life fear is an experience we would rather avoid. The psychoanalyst Sigmund Freud offers another version of this principle: While we enjoy art, we permit ourselves to have feelings so subversive that we have to repress them to function in everyday life.

6. *Objects are aesthetically valuable if they have the capacity to produce special nonemotional experiences, such as a feeling of autonomy or the willing suspension of disbelief.* This principle is the proposal of the nineteenth-century English poet Samuel Taylor Coleridge. One of art's values, he believes, is its ability to stimulate our power to exercise our imaginations and consequently to free ourselves from thinking that is too narrowly practical.

Notice that principles 4 through 6 resemble the first three in that they identify aesthetic value with the capacity to fulfill a function. According to these last three, the specified function is to create some kind of subjective or inner state in audiences; according to the first three, however, art's function is to achieve such objective outcomes as conveying information or knowledge or preserving or changing culture or society. But there are yet other influential aesthetic principles that do not characterize art in terms of capacities for performing functions. According to one commonly held principle, art objects attain aesthetic value by virtue of their possessing a certain special aesthetic property or certain special formal configurations:

7. *Objects are aesthetically valuable if they possess a special aesthetic property or exhibit a special aesthetic form.* Sometimes this aesthetic property is called "beauty," and sometimes it is given another name. For instance, the early-twentieth-century art critic Clive Bell insists that good art is valuable for its own sake, not because it fulfills any function. To know whether a work is good aesthetically, he urges, one need only look at it or listen to it to see or hear whether it has "significant form." "Significant form" is valuable for itself, not for any function it performs.

Finally, one familiar principle insists that no reasons can be given to support judgments about art. Properly speaking, those who adhere to this principle think that to approve or disapprove of art is to express an unreasoned preference rather than to render judgment. This principle may be stated as follows:

8. *No reasoned argument can conclude that objects are aesthetically valuable or valueless.* This principle is expressed in the Latin saying *"De gustibus non est disputandum,"* or "Tastes can't be disputed."

The principles summarized here by no means exhaust the important views about aesthetic value, nor are they complete expositions of the views they represent. Historically, views about the nature of art have proven relatively fluid, for they must be responsive to the dynamics of technological and cultural change. Moreover, even though the number of familiar conceptions of aesthetic value is limited, there are many alternative ways of stating these that combine the thoughts behind them in somewhat different ways.

Consequently, to attempt to label each principle with a name invites confusion. For example, let's consider whether any of the principles might be designated *formalism,* which is an important school or style of art. Although the seventh principle explicitly ascribes aesthetic value to a work's form as opposed to its function, the formal properties of artworks also figure as valuable, although only as means to more valuable ends, in certain formulations of the first six principles. For instance, some scholars, critics, and artists think certain formal patterns in works of art can evoke corresponding emotions, social patterns, or pleasures in audiences—for example, slow music full of minor chords is commonly said to make people feel sad.

You should understand that all of the principles presented here merely serve as a basic framework within which you can explore critical thinking about art. If you are interested in the arts, you will very likely want to develop a more complex and sophisticated conceptual framework to enrich your thinking about this subject.

> The story is told of the American tourist in Paris who told Pablo Picasso that he didn't like modern paintings because they weren't realistic. Picasso made no immediate reply. A few minutes later the tourist showed him a snapshot of his house.
>
> "My goodness," said Picasso, "is it really as small as that?"
>
> —JACOB BRAUDE

■ *Using Aesthetic Principles to Judge Aesthetic Value*

The first thing to notice about the aesthetic principles we've just discussed is that some are compatible with each other. Thus, a reasonable thinker can appeal to more than one in reaching a verdict about the aesthetic value of an object. For instance, a consistent thinker can use both the first and the fifth principle in evaluating a tragic drama. Aristotle does just this in his *Poetics.* He tells us that tragedies are good art when they both convey general truths about the human condition and help their audiences purge themselves of the pity and fear they feel when they face the truth about human limitations. A play that presents a general truth without eliciting the proper catharsis (release of emotion) in the audience, or a play that provokes tragic emotions unaccompanied by recognition of a general truth, is not as valuable as a play that does both.

However, some of these principles cannot be used together consistently to judge aesthetic value. These bear the same relationship to each other as do contrary claims (recall the square of opposition in Chapter 8). They cannot both be true, although both might be false. For instance, the principle that art is valuable in itself, by virtue of its form or formal configuration (not because it serves some function), and the principle that art is valuable because it serves a social or political function cannot be used consistently together. You might have noticed also that the eighth principle contradicts the others; that is, the first seven principles all specify kinds of reasons for guiding and supporting our appreciation of art, but the last principle denies that there can be any such good reasons.

Finally, it is important to understand that the same principle can generate both positive and negative evaluations, depending on whether the work in question meets or fails to meet the standard expressed in the principle. For example, the fourth principle, which we might call aesthetic hedonism, generates positive evaluations of works that produce pleasure but negative evaluations of works that leave their audiences in pain or displeased.

Exercise 12-12

Suppose that the two statements in each of the following pairs both appear in a review of the same work of art. Identify which of the eight aesthetic principles each statement in the pair appeals to. Then state whether the principles are compatible (that is, they do not contradict each other) and thus form the basis for a consistent critical review or whether they contradict each other and cannot both be used in a consistent review.

▲ 1. a. Last weekend's performance of the Wagnerian operatic cycle was superb; the music surged through the audience, forging a joyous communal bond.
   b. Smith's forceful singing and acting in the role of Siegfried left no doubt why Wagner's vision of heroic morality was attractive to his Teutonic contemporaries.

2. a. Leni Riefenstahl's film *Triumph of the Will* proved to be effective art because it convinced its audiences that the Nazi party would improve the German way of life.
   b. Despite its overtly racist message, *Triumph of the Will* is great art, for films should be judged on the basis of their visual coherence and not in terms of their moral impact.

3. a. All lovers of art should condemn Jackson Pollock's meaningless abstract expressionist splatter paintings.
   b. These paintings create neither sadness nor joy; those who view them feel nothing, neither love nor hate nor any of the other passions that great art evokes.

▲ 4. a. Laurence Olivier's film production of *Hamlet* has merit because he allows us to experience the impact of the incestuous love that a son can feel for his mother.

▲ *Pablo Picasso,* Guernica

    b. Nevertheless, Olivier's *Hamlet* is flawed because it introduces a dimension inconceivable to an Elizabethan playwright.

5. a. There is no point arguing about or giving reasons for verdicts about art, because each person's tastes or responses are so personal.
    b. Those who condemn sexually explicit performance art do not recognize that art is valuable to the extent it permits us to feel liberated and free of convention.

■ *Evaluating Aesthetic Criticism: Relevance and Truth*

Is any evaluation of a work of art as good as any other in creating a critical treatment of that work? The answer is no, for two reasons: (1) the principles of art one adopts function as a conceptual framework that distinguishes relevant from irrelevant reasons; (2) even a relevant reason is useless if it is not true of the work to which it is applied.

    Let's consider the first reason. What would convince you of the value of a work if you accepted principles 4 through 6—all of which maintain that aesthetic value resides in the subjective responses art evokes in its audiences? In this case, you are likely to be drawn to see Picasso's *Guernica* if you are told that it has the power to make its viewers experience the horrors of war; but you would not be attracted by learning, instead, that *Guernica* explores the relationship of two- and three-dimensional spatial concepts. Suppose you reject principles 1 through 3, which conceive of aesthetic value in terms of the work's capacity to perform an objective, cognitive, moral, social, or political function. The fact that Picasso was a Communist will strike you as irrelevant to appreciating *Guernica* unless you accept one or more of the first three principles.

    To illustrate the second reason, look at the nearby reproduction of *Guernica.* Suppose a critic writes, "By giving his figures fishlike appearances and showing them serenely floating through a watery environment,

The aim of art is to represent not the outward appearance of things, but their inward significance.

—ARISTOTLE

Picasso makes us feel that humans will survive under any conditions." But no figures in *Guernica* look anything like fish; moreover, they are surrounded by fire, not water, and they are twisted with anguish rather than serene. So, this critic's reasons are no good. Because they are not true of the work, they cannot guide us in perceiving features that enhance our appreciation. A similar problem occurs if reasons are implausible. For instance, an interpretation of *Guernica* as a depiction of the Last Supper is implausible, because we cannot recognize the usual signs of this theme, the twelve disciples and Christ at a table (or at least at a meal), in the far fewer figures of the painting.

Exercise 12-13

State whether each of the reasons below is relevant according to any one of the aesthetic principles. If the reason is relevant, identify the principle that makes it so. If no principle makes the reason relevant, state that it is irrelevant.

▲ 1. Raphael's carefully balanced pyramidal compositions give his paintings of the Madonna such beautiful form that they have aesthetic value for Christian and atheist alike.

2. By grouping his figures so that they compose a triangle or pyramid, Raphael directs the viewer's eye upward to heaven and thereby teaches us about the close connection between motherhood and God.

3. The melody from the chorus "For unto Us a Child Is Born" in Handel's *Messiah* was originally composed by Handel for an erotic love song. Consequently, it evokes erotic responses which distract and detract from the devotional feeling audiences are supposed to experience when they hear *Messiah* performed.

▲ 4. Vincent van Gogh tells us that he uses clashing reds and greens in *The Night Café* to help us see his vision of "the terrible passions of humanity"; it is the intensity with which he conveys his views of the ugliness of human life that makes his work so illuminating.

5. The critics who ignored van Gogh's painting during his lifetime were seriously mistaken; by damaging his self-esteem, they drove him to suicide.

6. Moreover, these critics misjudged the aesthetic value of his art, as evidenced by the fact that his paintings now sell for as much as $80 million.

▲ 7. By showing a naked woman picnicking with fully clothed men in *Déjeuner sur l'herbe*, Édouard Manet treats women as objects and impedes their efforts to throw off patriarchal domination.

Exercise 12-14

June the chimp has been very sad and lonely, so the zoo director gives her some paper, paints, and brushes to keep her busy. Look at the photograph of the chim-

▲   *June the chimpanzee*

▲   *June's painting*

panzee painting and at the photograph of the chimpanzee's painting. Does June's work have aesthetic value? Use each of the eight principles to formulate one reason for or against attributing aesthetic value to June's work. You should end up with eight reasons, one appealing to each principle.

■ *Why Reason Aesthetically?*

The various aesthetic principles we've introduced are among those most commonly found, either explicitly or implicitly, in discussions about art. Moreover, they have influenced both the creation of art and the selection of art for both private and public enjoyment. But where do these principles come from? There is much debate about this; to understand it, we can draw on notions about definition (introduced in Chapter 2) as well as the discussion of generalizations (Chapter 10).

Some people think that aesthetic principles are simply elaborate definitions of our concepts of art or aesthetic value. Let's explain this point. We use definitions to identify things; for example, by definition we look for three sides and three angles to identify a geometric figure as a triangle. Similarly, we can say that aesthetic principles are definitions; that is, these principles provide an aesthetic vocabulary to direct us in recognizing an object's aesthetic value.

If aesthetic principles are true by definition, then learning to judge art is learning the language of art. But because artists strive for originality, we are constantly faced with talking about innovative objects to which the critic's familiar vocabulary does not quite do justice. This aspect of art challenges even the most sophisticated critic to continually extend the aesthetic vocabulary.

Others think that aesthetic principles are generalizations that summarize what is true of objects treated as valuable art. Here, the argument is by analogy from a sample class to a target population. Thus, someone might hold that all or most of the tragic plays we know that are aesthetically valuable have had something important to say about the human condition; for this reason, we can expect this to be true of any member of the class of tragic plays we have not yet evaluated. Or, also by inductive analogy, musical compositions that are valued so highly that they continue to be performed throughout the centuries all make us feel some specific emotion, such as joy or sadness; so we can predict that a newly composed piece will be similarly highly valued if it also evokes a strong, clear emotion. Of course, such arguments are weakened to the extent that the target object differs from the objects in the sample class. Because there is a drive for originality in art, newly created works may diverge so sharply from previous samples that arguments by analogy sometimes prove too weak.

It is sometimes suggested that these two accounts of the source of aesthetic principles really reinforce each other: Our definitions reflect to some extent our past experience of the properties or capacities typical of valuable art, and our past experience is constrained to some extent by our definitions. But if art changes, of what use are principles, whether analytic or inductive, in guiding us to make aesthetic judgments and—even more difficult—in fostering agreement about these judgments?

At the very least, these principles have an emotive force that guides us in perceiving art. You will remember that emotive force (discussed briefly in Chapter 2) is a dimension of language that permits the words we use to do something more than convey information. In discussion about art, the words that constitute reasons can have an emotive force directing our attention to particular aspects of a work. If the critic can describe these aspects accurately and persuasively, it is thought, the audience will focus on these aspects and experience a favorable (or unfavorable) response similar to the critic's. If a critic's reasons are too vague or are not true of the work to which they are applied, they are unlikely to bring the audience into agreement with the critic.

The principles of art, then, serve as guides for identifying appropriate categories of favorable or unfavorable response, but the reasons falling into these categories are what bring about agreement. They are useful both in developing our own appreciation of a work of art and in persuading others. The reasons must be accurately and informatively descriptive of the objects to which they are applied. The reasons enable us (1) to select a particular way of viewing, listening, reading, or otherwise perceiving the object and (2) to recommend, guide, or prescribe that the object be viewed, heard, or read in this way.

So, aesthetic reasons contain descriptions that prompt ways of perceiving aspects of an object. These prescribed ways of seeing evoke favorable (or unfavorable) responses or experiences. For instance, suppose a critic states that van Gogh's brush strokes in *Starry Night* are dynamic and his colors intense. This positive critical reason prescribes that people focus on these features when they look at the painting. The expectation is that persons whose vision is swept into the movement of van Gogh's painted sky and pierced by the presence of his painted stars will, by virtue of focusing on these formal properties, enjoy a positive response to the painting.

To learn to give reasons and form assessments about art, practice applying these principles as you look, listen, or read. Consider what aspects of a painting, musical performance, poem, or other work each principle directs you to contemplate. It is also important to expand your aesthetic vocabulary so that you have words to describe what you see, hear, or otherwise sense in a work. As you do so, you will be developing your own aesthetic expertise. And, because your reasons will be structured by aesthetic principles others also accept, you will find that rational reflection on art tends to expand both the scope and volume of your agreement with others about aesthetic judgments.

Recap

Reasoning about morality is distinguished from reasoning about matters of fact only in that the former always involves claims that express moral values. Such claims are moral value judgments. Claims about matters of fact, by contrast, are factual because they describe what is believed to be the case. Certain words—especially "ought," "should," "right," and "wrong"—are used in value judgments in a moral sense, although these terms can also be used in a nonmoral sense.

A conclusion containing a value judgment can't be reached solely from premises that are purely factual; in other words, you can't get an "ought" from an "is." To be valid, an argument that has a value-expressing conclusion—that is, a moral argument—must also have a value-expressing premise. Although such premises often remain unstated, we need to state them deliberately to avoid assuming that the value somehow can be derived from a factual premise. Then, in case we disagree with the moral conclusion but can't dispute the factual premise, we can point to the value-expressing premise as the point with which we disagree.

People are sometimes inconsistent in their moral views: They treat similar cases as if the cases were different even when they cannot tell us what is importantly different about them. When two or more cases that are being treated differently seem similar, the burden of proof is on the person who is treating them differently to explain what is different about them.

Moral reasoning is usually conducted within a perspective or framework. In this chapter we considered relativism, subjectivism, utilitarianism, Kantian duty theory, divine command theory, and virtue ethics. Often, different perspectives converge to produce similar solutions to a moral issue;

on other occasions they diverge. Keeping in mind our own perspective can help focus our own moral deliberations on relevant considerations.

There are similarities between the subjects of moral reasoning and legal reasoning, especially in that they both are often prescriptive. Legal studies are devoted to problems like that of justifying laws that prescribe conduct; we looked at legal moralism, the harm principle, legal paternalism, and the offense principle as grounds for such justification. Problems in determining just when and where a law applies often require making vague claims specific.

Precedent is a kind of analogical argument by means of which current cases are settled in accordance with guidelines set by cases decided previously. Whether a precedent governs in a given case is decided on grounds similar to those of any other analogical argument.

To reason aesthetically is to make judgments within a conceptual framework that integrates facts and values. Aesthetic value is often identified as the capacity to fulfill a function, such as to create pleasure or promote social change. Alternatively, aesthetic value is defined in terms of a special aesthetic property or form found in works of art. Still another view treats aesthetic judgments as expressions of tastes. Reasoned argument about aesthetic value helps us to see, hear, or otherwise perceive art in changed or expanded ways and to enhance our appreciation of art. A critic who gives reasons in support of an aesthetic verdict forges agreement by getting others to share perceptions of the work. The greater the extent to which we share such aesthetic perceptions, the more we can reach agreement about aesthetic value.

Additional Exercises

Exercise 12-15

State whether the following reasons are (a) helpful in focusing perception to elicit a favorable response, (b) helpful in focusing perception to elicit an unfavorable response, (c) too vague to focus perception, (d) false or implausible and therefore unable to focus perception, or (e) irrelevant to focusing perception. The information you need is contained in the reasons, so try to visualize or imagine what the work is like from what is said. All of these are paraphrases of testimony given at a hearing in 1985 about a proposal to remove *Tilted Arc,* an immense abstract sculpture, from a plaza in front of a federal office building.

▲ 1. Richard Serra's *Tilted Arc* is a curved slab of welded steel 12 feet high, 120 feet long, weighing over 73 tons, covered completely with a natural oxide coating. The sculpture arcs through the plaza. By coming to terms with its harshly intrusive disruption of space, we can learn much about how the nature of the spaces we inhabit affects our social relations.

▲ *Richard Serra,* Tilted Arc

2. Richard Serra is one of our leading artists, and his work commands very high prices. The government has a responsibility to the financial community. It is bad business to destroy this work because you would be destroying property.

3. *Tilted Arc*'s very tilt and rust remind us that the gleaming and heartless steel and glass structures of the state apparatus can one day pass away. It therefore creates an unconscious sense of freedom and hope.

▲ 4. *Tilted Arc* looks like a discarded piece of crooked or bent metal; there's no more meaning in having it in the middle of the plaza than in putting an old bicycle that got run over by a car there.

5. *Tilted Arc* launches through space in a thrilling and powerful acutely arched curve.

6. *Tilted Arc* is big and rusty.

▲ 7. Because of its size, thrusting shape, and implacably uniform rusting surface, *Tilted Arc* makes us feel hopeless, trapped, and sad. This sculpture would be interesting if we could visit it when we had time to explore these feelings, but it is too depressing to face every day on our way to work.

8. Serra's erotically realistic, precise rendering of the female figure in *Tilted Arc* exhibits how appealingly he can portray the soft circularity of a woman's breast.

9. *Tilted Arc* is sort of red; it probably isn't blue.

▲ *Artemisia Gentileschi,* Judith

Exercise 12-16 _____

The artist Artemisia Gentileschi was very successful in her own time. Success came despite the trauma of her early life, when she figured as the victim in a notorious rape trial. But after she died, her work fell into obscurity; it was neither shown in major museums nor written about in art-history books. Recently, feminist scholars have revived interest in her work by connecting the style and/or theme of such paintings as her *Judith* with her rape and with feelings or issues of importance to women. But other scholars have pointed out that both her subject matter and her treatment of it are conventionally found as well in the work of male painters of the Caravaggist school, with which she is identified. Based on this information, and using one or more of the aesthetic principles described in this chapter, write an essay arguing either that the painting *Judith* has aesthetic value worthy of our attention or that it should continue to be ignored.

Writing Exercises

1. In the movie *Priest*, the father of a young girl admits to the local priest—in the confessional—that he has molested his daughter. However, the man lacks remorse and gives every indication that he will continue to abuse the girl. For the priest to inform the girl's mother or the authorities would be for him to violate the sanctity of the confessional, but to not inform anyone would subject the girl to further abuse. What should the priest do? Take about fifteen minutes to do the following:

   a. List the probable consequences of the courses of action available to the priest.

   b. List any duties or rights or other considerations that bear on the issue.

   When fifteen minutes are up, share your ideas with the class.

   Now take about twenty minutes to write an essay in which you do the following:

   a. State the issue.

   b. Take a stand on the issue.

   c. Defend your stand.

   d. Rebut counterarguments to your position.

   When you are finished, write down on a separate piece of paper a number between 1 and 10 that indicates how strong you think your argument is (10 = very strong; 1 = very weak). Write your name on the back of your paper.

   When everyone is finished, the instructor will collect the papers and redistribute them to the class. In groups of four or five, read the papers and assign a number from 1 to 10 to each one (10 = very strong; 1 = very weak). When all groups are finished, return the papers to their authors. When you get your paper back, compare the number you assigned to your work with the number the group assigned it. The instructor may ask volunteers to defend their own judgment of their work against the judgment of the group. Do you think there is as much evidence for your position as you did at the beginning of the period?

2. Follow the same procedure as above to address one of the following issues:

   a. A friend cheats in the classes he has with you. You know he'd just laugh if you voiced any concern. Should you mention it to your instructor?

   b. You see a friend stealing something valuable. Even though you tell your friend that you don't approve, she keeps the item. What should you do?

   c. Your best friend's fiancé has just propositioned you for sex. Should you tell your friend?

   d. Your parents think you should major in marketing or some other practical field. You want to major in literature. Your parents pay the bills. What should you do?

Essays for Analysis (and a Few Other Items)

THREE STRIKES AND THE WHOLE ENCHILADA

In this first selection, we've taken a real-life case of some importance and identified how various sections of the book bear on the issue and various aspects of the controversy that surround it. As we said at the beginning, this material is not designed to operate just in the classroom.

As you no doubt know, several states have "three strikes" laws, which call for life terms for a criminal convicted of any felony—if the criminal already has two prior felony convictions that resulted from serious or violent crime.

Have such laws helped to reduce crime in the states that have them? This is a factual question (Chapter 1), a question of causation (Chapter 11). How might the issue be resolved?

In California, Frank Zimring, a University of California, Berkeley, law professor, analyzed the records of 3,500 criminal defendants in Los Angeles, San Diego, and San Francisco before and after California's law was enacted. Zimring found no evidence the law was a deterrent to crime. For our purposes we do not need to go into the details of the study.

People Against Crime, an organization that favors tougher penalties for criminals, denounced the study as "so much more left-wing propaganda coming out of a notoriously liberal university."

This charge is an ad hominem fallacy (Chapter 6). But is it nevertheless a reasonable challenge to Zimring's credibility that warrants not outright rejection of the study but suspension of judgment about its findings (Chapter 3)? The answer is no. Stripped of its rhetoric (Chapter 4), the charge is only that the author of the study is a professor at Berkeley; and that charge gives no reason to suspect bias on his part.

Other criticisms of the study were reported in the news. A spokesperson for the California secretary of state said, "When you see the crime rate going down 38 percent since three strikes you can't say it doesn't work."

This remark is an example of the fallacy "post hoc, ergo propter hoc," discussed in Chapter 11. In fact, that's being charitable. According to Zimring's research, the crime rate had been declining at the same rate before the law was passed.

The same spokesperson also criticized the Zimring study for ignoring the number of parolees leaving the state (to avoid getting a third strike, presumably). This is a red herring (Chapter 5). If the decline in the crime rate was unaffected after the law passed, as the Zimring study reportedly learned, then the law had no effect regardless of what parolees did or did not do.

The spokesperson also said, "Clearly when people are committing 20 to 25 crimes a year, the year they are taken off the street, that's 20 to 25 crimes that aren't going to happen." This too is a red herring (Chapter 5): If the decline in the crime rate remained the same before and after the "three strikes" law, then that's the end of the story. The criticism assumes criminals will continue to commit crimes at the same rate if there is no mandatory life sentence for a third felony. It therefore also begs the question (Chapter 6)—it assumes the law works in order to prove the law works. You will also have noticed the proof surrogate "clearly" (Chapter 4) in the criticism.

One might, of course, maintain that without the law the crime rate would have *stopped* declining, which would mean that the law had an effect after all. But the burden of proof (Chapter 6) is not on Zimring to *disprove* the possibility that the crime rate would have stopped declining if the law had not been passed.

A critic might also say that Zimring's study was conducted too soon after the law for the effects of the law to show up. This is another red herring (Chapter 5). It is not a weakness in the study that it failed to find an effect that might show up at a *later* time.

Selection 2

CONTROLLING IRRATIONAL FEARS AFTER 9/11

We present this selection as an example of a fairly well-reasoned argumentative essay. There is more here than arguments—there's some window dressing and you'll probably find some slanters here and there as well. You should go through the selection and identify the issues, the positions taken on those issues, and the arguments offered in support of those arguments. Are any arguments from opposing points of view considered? What is your final assessment of the essay?

The terrorist attacks of September 11, 2001, produced a response among American officials, the media, and the public that is probably matched only by the attack on Pearl Harbor in 1941. Since it is the very nature of terrorism not only to cause immediate damage but also to strike fear in the hearts of the population under attack, one might say that the terrorists were extraordinarily successful, not just as a result of their own efforts but also in consequence of the American reaction. In this essay, I shall argue that this reaction was irrational to a great extent and that to that extent Americans unwittingly cooperated with the terrorists in achieving a major goal: spreading fear and thus disrupting lives. In other words, we could have reacted more rationally and as a result produced less disruption in the lives of our citizens.

There are several reasons why one might say that a huge reaction to the 9/11 attacks was justified. The first is simply the large number of lives that were lost. In the absence of a shooting war, that 2,800 Americans should die from the same cause strikes us as extraordinary indeed. But does the sheer size of the loss of life warrant the reaction we saw? Clearly sheer numbers do not always impress us. It is unlikely, for example, that many Americans remember that, earlier in 2001, an earthquake in Gujarat, India, killed approximately 20,000 people. One might explain the difference in reaction by saying that we naturally respond more strongly to the deaths of Americans closer to home than to those of others halfway around the world. But then consider the fact that, every *month* during 2001 more Americans were killed in automobile crashes than were killed on 9/11 (and it has continued every month since as well). Since the victims of car accidents come from every geographical area and every social stratum, one can say that those deaths are even "closer to home" than the deaths that occurred in New York, Washington, and Pennsylvania. It may be harder to identify with an earthquake victim in Asia than with a 9/11 victim, but this cannot be said for the victims of fatal automobile accidents.

One might say that it was the *malice* of the perpetrators that makes the 9/11 deaths so noteworthy, but surely there is plenty of malice present in the 15,000 homicides that occur every year in the United States. And while we have passed strict laws favoring prosecution of murderers, we do not see the huge and expensive shift in priorities that has followed the 9/11 attacks.

It seems clear, at least, that sheer numbers cannot explain the response to 9/11. If more reasons were needed, we might consider that the *actual total* of the number of 9/11 deaths seemed of little consequence in post-attack reports. Immediately after the attacks, the estimated death toll was about 6,500. Several weeks later it was clear that fewer than half that many had actually died, but was there a great sigh of relief when it was learned that over 3,000 people who were believed to have died were still alive? Not at all. In fact, well after it was confirmed that no more than 3,000 people had died, Secretary of Defense Donald Rumsfeld still talked about "over 5,000" deaths on 9/11. So the actual number seems to be of less consequence than one might have believed.

We should remember that fear and outrage at the attacks are only the beginning of the country's response to 9/11. We now have a new cabinet-level Department of Homeland Security; billions have been spent on beefing up

Note: This essay borrows very heavily from "A Skeptical Look at September 11th", an article in the *Skeptical Inquirer* of September/October 2002 by Clark R. Chapman and Alan W. Harris. Rather than clutter the essay with numerous references, we simply refer the reader to the original, longer piece.

security and in tracking terrorists and potential terrorists; billions more have been spent supporting airlines whose revenues took a nosedive after the attacks; the Congress was pulled away from other important business; the National Guard was called out to patrol the nation's airports; air travelers have been subjected to time-consuming and expensive security measures; you can probably think of a half-dozen other items to add to this list.

It is probable that a great lot of this trouble and expense is unwarranted. We think that random searches of luggage of elderly ladies getting on airplanes in Laramie, Wyoming, for example, is more effective as a way of annoying elderly ladies than of stopping terrorism.

If we had been able to treat the terrorist attacks of 9/11 in a way similar to how we treat the carnage on the nation's highways—by implementing practices and requirements that are directly related to results (as in the case of speed limits, safety belts, and the like, which took decades to accomplish in the cause of auto safety)— rather than by throwing the nation into a near panic and using the resulting fears to justify expensive but not necessarily effective or even relevant measures.

But we focused on 9/11 because of its terrorist nature and because of the spectacular film that was shown over and over on television, imprinting forever the horrific images of the airliner's collision with the World Trade Center and the subsequent collapse of the two towers. The media's instant obsession with the case is understandable, even if it is out of proportion to the actual damage, as awful as it was, when we compare the actual loss to the loss from automobile accidents.

Finally, our point is that marginal or even completely ineffective expenditures and disruptive practices have taken our time, attention, and national treasure away from other matters with more promise of making the country a better place. We seem to have all begun to think of ourselves as terrorist targets, but, in fact, reason tells us we are in much greater danger from our friends and neighbors behind the wheels of their cars.

The remainder of the essays in this section are here for analysis and evaluation. Your instructor will probably have specific directions if he or she assigns them, but at a minimum, they offer an opportunity to identify issues, separate arguments from other elements, identify premises and conclusions, evaluate the likely truth of the premises and the strength of the arguments, look for unstated assumptions or omitted premises, and lots of other stuff besides. We offer sample directions for many of the pieces.

Selection 3

EXCERPTS FROM FEDERAL COURT RULING
ON THE PLEDGE OF ALLEGIANCE

The following are excerpts from the ruling yesterday by a three-judge federal appeals court panel in San Francisco that reciting the Pledge of

Allegiance in public schools is unconstitutional because it includes the phrase "one nation under God." The vote was 2 to 1. Judge Alfred T. Goodwin wrote the majority opinion, in which Judge Stephen Reinhardt joined. Judge Ferdinand F. Fernandez wrote a dissent.

From the Opinion by Judge Goodwin

In the context of the pledge, the statement that the United States is a nation "under God" is an endorsement of religion. It is a profession of a religious belief, namely, a belief in monotheism. The recitation that ours is a nation "under God" is not a mere acknowledgment that many Americans believe in a deity. Nor is it merely descriptive of the undeniable historical significance of religion in the founding of the republic. Rather, the phrase "one nation under God" in the context of the pledge is normative. To recite the pledge is not to describe the United States; instead, it is to swear allegiance to the values for which the flag stands: unity, indivisibility, liberty, justice, and—since 1954— monotheism. The text of the official pledge, codified in federal law, impermissibly takes a position with respect to the purely religious question of the existence and identity of god. A profession that we are a nation "under God" is identical, for Establishment Clause purposes, to a profession that we are a nation "under Jesus," a nation "under Vishnu," a nation "under Zeus," or a nation "under no god," because none of these professions can be neutral with respect to religion. "The government must pursue a course of complete neutrality toward religion." Furthermore, the school district's practice of teacher-led recitation of the pledge aims to inculcate in students a respect for the ideals set forth in the pledge, and thus amounts to state endorsements of these ideals. Although students cannot be forced to participate in recitation of the pledge, the school district is nonetheless conveying a message of state endorsement of a religious belief when it requires public school teachers to recite, and lead the recitation, of the current form of the pledge. . . . 1

   The pledge, as currently codified, is an impermissible government endorsement of religion because it sends a message to unbelievers "that they are outsiders, not full members of the political community, and an accompanying message to adherents that they are insiders, favored members of the political community." 2

From the Dissent by Judge Fernandez

We are asked to hold that inclusion of the phrase "under God" in this nation's Pledge of Allegiance violates the religion clauses of the Constitution of the United States. We should do no such thing. We should, instead, recognize that those clauses were not designed to drive religious expression out of public thought; they were written to avoid discrimination. We can run through the litany of tests and concepts which have floated to the surface from time to time. Were we to do so, the one that appeals most to me, the one I think to be correct, is the concept that what the religion clauses of the First Amendment require is neutrality; that those clauses are, in effect, an early kind of equal 3 protection provision and assure that government will neither discriminate for nor discriminate against religion or religions. But, legal world abstractions and ruminations aside, when all is said and done, the danger that "under God" in our Pledge of Allegiance will tend to bring about a theocracy or suppress somebody's belief is so miniscule as to be de minimis. The danger that phrase presents to our First Amendment freedoms is picayune at most.

Selection 4

GAYS' IMPACT ON MARRIAGE UNDERESTIMATED

Jeff Jacoby

1   It was a year ago last month that the Vermont law authorizing same-sex civil unions—a marriage by another name—took effect, and the *New York Times* marked the anniversary with a story July 25. "Quiet Anniversary for Civil Unions," the double headline announced. "Ceremonies for Gay Couples Have Blended Into Vermont Life." It was an upbeat report, and its message was clear: Civil unions are working just fine.

2   The story noted in passing that most Vermonters oppose the law. Presumably, they have reasons for not wanting legal recognition conferred on homosexual couples, but the *Times* had not room to mention them. It did have room, though, to dismiss those reasons—whatever they might be—as meritless: "The sky has not fallen," Gov. Howard Dean said, "and the institution of marriage has not collapsed. None of the dire predictions have come true. . . . There was a big rhubarb, a lot of fear-mongering, and now people realize there was nothing to be afraid of."

3   In the *Wall Street Journal* two days later, much the same point was made by Jonathan Rauch, the esteemed Washington journalist and vice president of the Independent Gay Forum. Opponents of same-sex marriage, he wrote, worry "that unyoking marriage from its traditional male-female definition will destroy or severely weaken it. But this is an empirical proposition, and there is reason to doubt it. Opponents of same-sex marriage have done a poor job of explaining why the health of heterosexual marriage depends on the exclusion of a small number of homosexuals."

4   The assertion that same-sex marriage will not damage traditional family life is rarely challenged, as Rep. Barney Frank, D-Mass., said during the 1996 congressional debate over the Defense of Marriage Act.

5   "I have asked and I have asked and I have asked, and I guess I will die . . . unanswered," Frank taunted. "How does the fact that I love another man and live in a committed relationship with him threaten your marriage? Are your relations with your spouses of such fragility that the fact that I have a committed, loving relationship with another man jeopardizes them?"

6   When another congressman replied that legitimizing gay unions "threatens the institution of marriage," Frank said, "That argument ought to be made by someone in an institution because it has no logical basis whatsoever."

But Frank's sarcasm, Rauch's doubts and Dean's reassurances notwithstanding, the threat posed by the same-sex unions to traditional marriage and family life is all too real. Marriage is harmed by anything that diminishes its privileged status. It is weakened by anything that erodes the social sanctions that Judeo-Christian culture developed over the centuries for channeling men's naturally unruly sexuality into a monogamous, lasting, and domestic relationship with one woman. For proof, just look around. 7

Over the past 40 years, marriage has suffered one blow after another. The sexual revolution and the pill made it much easier for men to enjoy women sexually without having to marry them. Legalized abortion reduced pressure on men to marry women they impregnated and reduced the need for women to wait for lasting love. The widespread acceptance of unmarried cohabitation—which used to be disdained as "shacking up"—diminished marrage further. Why get married if intimate companionship can be had without public vows and ceremony? 8

The rise of the welfare state with its subsidies for single mothers subverted marriage by sending the unmistakable message that husbands were no longer essential for family life. And the rapid spread of no-fault divorce detached marriage from any assumption of permanence. Where couples were once expected to stay married "for as long as you both shall live"—and therefore to put effort into making their marriage work—the expectation today is that they will remain together only "for as long as you both shall love." 9

If we now redefine marriage so it includes the union of two men or two women, we will be taking this bad situation and making it even worse. 10

No doubt the acceptance of same-sex marriage would remove whatever stigma homosexuality still bears, a goal many people would welcome. But it would do so at a severe cost to the most basic institution of our society. For all the assaults marriage has taken, its fundamental purpose endures: to uphold and encourage the union of a man and a woman, the framework that is the healthiest and safest for the rearing of children. If marriage stops meaning even that, it will stop meaning anything at all. 11

Selection 5

BUSH'S ENVIRONMENTAL RECORD

Bob Herbert

Bob Herbert is a *New York Times* columnist.

Do you remember the character "Pig-Pen" in the "Peanuts" cartoons? He was always covered with dirt and grime. He was cute, but he was a walking sludge heap, filthy and proud of it. He once told Charlie Brown, "I have affixed to me the dirt and dust of countless ages. Who am I to disturb history?" 1

For me, Pig-Pen's attitude embodies President Bush's approach to the   2
environment.

We've been trashing, soiling, even destroying the wonders of nature for   3
countless ages. Why stop now? Who is Bush to step in and curb this venerable orgy of pollution, this grand tradition of fouling our own nest?

Oh, the skies may once have been clear and the waters sparkling and   4
clean. But you can't have that and progress too. Can you?

Last week we learned that the Bush administration plans to cut fund-   5
ing for the cleanup of 33 toxic waste sites in 18 states. As the *New York
Times'* Katharine Seelye reported, this means "that work is likely to grind
to a halt on some of the most seriously polluted sites in the country."

The cuts were ordered because the Superfund toxic waste cleanup is run-   6
ning out of money. Rather than showing the leadership necessary to replenish
the fund, the president plans to reduce its payouts by cleaning up fewer sites.

Pig-Pen would have been proud.   7

This is not a minor matter. The sites targeted by the Superfund pro-   8
gram are horribly polluted, in many cases with cancer-causing substances.
Millions of Americans live within a few miles of these sites.

The Superfund decision is the kind of environmental move we've come   9
to expect from the Bush administration. Mother Nature has been known to
tremble at the sound of the president's approaching footsteps. He's an environmental disaster zone.

In February, a top enforcement official at the Environmental Protection   10
Agency, Eric Schaeffer, quit because of Bush administration policies that he
said undermined the agency's efforts to crack down on industrial polluters.

Schaeffer said he felt he was "fighting a White House that seems deter-   11
mined to weaken the rules we are trying to enforce."

That, of course, is exactly what this White House is doing.   12

Within weeks of Schaeffer's resignation came official word that the ad-   13
ministration was relaxing the air quality regulations that applied to older
coal-fired power plants, a step backward that delighted the administration's
industrial pals.

During this same period the president broke his campaign promise to   14
regulate the industrial emissions of carbon dioxide, a move that, among
other things, would have helped in the fight to slow the increase in global
warming. Bush has also turned his back on the Kyoto Protocol, which
would require industrial nations to reduce their emissions of carbon dioxide and other greenhouse gases.

The president was even disdainful of his own administration's report   15
on global warming, which acknowledged that the U.S. would experience
far-reaching and, in some cases, devastating environmental consequences
as a result of the climate change.

The president's views on global warming seem aligned with those of   16
the muddle-headed conservative groups in Texas that have been forcing
rewrites in textbooks to fit their political and spiritual agendas. In one
environmental science textbook, the following was added: "In the past,
Earth has been much warmer than it is now, and fossils of sea creatures

show us that the sea level was much higher than it is today. So does it really matter if the world gets warmer?"

Sen. Joseph Lieberman, not exactly a left-winger on the environment or anything else, gave a speech in California in February in which he assailed the president's lack of leadership on global warming and other environmental issues. He characterized the president's energy policy as "mired in crude oil" and said Bush had been "AWOL in the war against environmental pollution."   17

Several states, fed up with Bush's capitulation to industry on these matters, have moved on their own to protect the environment and develop more progressive energy policies.   18

Simply stated, the president has behaved irresponsibly toward the environment and shows no sign of changing his ways.   19

You could laugh at Pig-Pen. He was just a comic strip character. But Bush is no joke. His trashing of the environment is a deadly serious matter.   20

Selection 6

DEATH PENALTY HAS NO PLACE IN U.S.

Cynthia Tucker

Many Americans will applaud the decision of a Jasper, Texas, jury to condemn John William King to die. They will argue that the death penalty is exactly what King deserves for chaining James Byrd Jr. to the back of a pickup truck and dragging him until his body was torn apart—his head and right arm here, his torso there.   1

If there is to be capital punishment in this country, isn't this just the sort of case that demands it? King is the epitome of cold-blooded evil, a man who bragged about his noxious racism and attempted to win converts to his views. He believed he would be a hero after Byrd's death. He has proved himself capable of the sort of stomach-churning cruelty that most of us would like to believe is outside the realm of human behavior.   2

Besides, there is the matter of balancing the books. King is a white man who (with the help of accomplices, apparently) killed a black man. For centuries, the criminal justice system saw black lives as so slight, so insignificant, that those who took a black life rarely got the death penalty. Isn't it a matter of fairness, of equity, of progress, that King should be put to death?   3

No. Even though King is evil. Even though he is utterly without remorse. Even though he is clearly guilty. (After the prosecution mounted a case for five days, King's lawyers mounted a defense of only one hour. The jury of 11 whites and one black then deliberated only two and half hours to determine King's guilt.)   4

This is no brief for King, who would probably chain me to the back of a pickup truck as quickly as he did Byrd. This is a plea for America, which is strong enough, just enough and merciful enough to have put aside, by now, the thirst for vengeance.   5

The question is not, Does John William King deserve the death penalty? 6
The question is, Does America deserve the death penalty?

Capital punishment serves no good purpose. It does not deter crime. If it 7
did, this country would be blessedly crime-free. It does not apply equally to all.
King notwithstanding, the denizens of death row are disproportionately blacks
and Latinos who have killed whites. It remains true that the lives of blacks and
Latinos count for less, that their killers are less likely to be sentenced to die.

Death row also counts among its inmates a high quotient of those who 8
are poor, dumb and marginalized. Those criminals blessed with education,
status and connections can usually escape capital punishment:

Last Tuesday, William Lumpkin, an attorney in Augusta, Ga., was 9
found guilty of capital murder in the death of real estate agent Stan White,
who owned the title to Lumpkin's home and was about to evict him. Lumpkin beat White to death with a sandbag and dumped the body in the Savan-
nah River. But Lumpkin descends from Georgia gentry; one ancestor was a
state Supreme Court justice. He was sentenced to life in prison.

Worse than those inequities, capital punishment is sometimes visited 10
upon the innocent. Lawrence C. Marshall, a law professor at Northwestern
University, is director of the National Conference on Wrongful Convictions
and the Death Penalty. Since 1972, he says, 78 innocent people have been
released from death row.

It does not strain the imagination to think that maybe, just maybe, the 11
system did not catch all of its errors and some of those who were wrongly convicted have already been sent to their deaths. How many? There is no way to
know, but even one is too many. The execution of even one innocent man puts
us law-abiding citizens uncomfortably close to the level of a John William King.

Selection 7

Instructions: Identify the main issue in this essay and the author's position
on this issue. Then state in your own words three arguments given by the
author in support of his position.

As an additional exercise, show how at least two of these arguments
can be treated as categorical syllogisms (Chapter 8), as truth-functional
arguments (Chapter 9), or as common deductive argument patterns.

HETERO BY CHOICE?

A radio commentary by Richard Parker

For a while there, everybody who could get near a microphone was claiming 1
that only he or she and his or her group, party, faction, religion, or militia
stood for real American family values.

Now, it was seldom made clear just what those values were supposed 2
to be. I have a notion that if [my son] Alex and I were to go out and knock

over a few gas stations and convenience stores, the mere fact that we did it together would make it count as somebody's family values.

For some, the phrase "family values" never amounted to more than a euphemism for gay-bashing. I remember a [few] years ago, during the loudest squawking about values, when a reporter asked Dan Quayle whether he believed that a gay person's homosexuality was a matter of his or her psychological makeup or whether it was a matter of choice. He answered that he believed it was mainly a matter of choice. Two weeks later, Barbara Bush was quoted as saying that sexual orientation is mainly a matter of choice. Since then, it's turned up frequently.   3

It seems to me that people who make such a remark are either being remarkably cynical (if they don't really believe it themselves) or remarkably fatuous (if they do believe it).   4

If it were *true* that a person's sexual preference were a matter of choice, then it must have happened that each of us, somewhere back along the way, *decided* what our sexual preference would be. Now, if we'd made such decisions, you'd think that somebody would remember doing it, but nobody does.   5

In my case, I just woke up one morning when I was a kid and discovered that girls were important to me in a way that boys were not. I certainly didn't sit down and *decide* that it was girls who were going to make me anxious, excited, terror-struck, panicky, and inclined to act like an idiot.   6

Now, if the people who claim to hold the "choice" view were right, it must mean that gay people have always chosen—they've *decided*—to have the sexual orientation they have. Can you imagine a person, back in the '50s, say, who would *choose* to have to put up with all the stuff gay people had to put up with back then? It's bad enough now, but only the mad or the criminally uninformed would have *chosen* such a life back then.   7

(Actually, it seems clear to me that the whole idea of a preference rules out the notion of choice. I choose to eat chocolate rather than vanilla, but I don't choose to *prefer* chocolate to vanilla. One simply discovers what one prefers.)   8

If it's clear that people don't consciously choose their sexual preferences, why would anybody make such claims? I can think of a cynical reason: It only makes sense to condemn someone for something they choose, not for things they can't do anything about.   9

Is it just a coincidence that people who claim we choose our sexual preferences are often the same people who demonize homosexuals? No, of course not. In fact, their cart comes before their horse: They are damned sure going to condemn gay people, and so, since you can only condemn someone for voluntary actions, it *must* be that one's sexuality is a voluntary choice. Bingo! Consistent logic. Mean, vicious, and mistaken. But consistent.   10

Selection 8

In a brief essay, argue for whether Bonnie and Clyde should receive the same or different punishment.

BONNIE AND CLYDE

Bonnie and Clyde are both driving on roads near a mountain community in   1
northern California. Both are driving recklessly—much faster than the
posted speed limit. Each of them has a passenger in the car.

At a sharp and very dangerous curve, Bonnie loses control of her car and   2
crashes into some nearby trees; only moments later, on another dangerous
section of road, Clyde's car goes into a skid, leaving the road and rolling
over several times down an embankment.

As a result of their accidents, Bonnie and Clyde are bruised and shaken,   3
but not seriously hurt. However, both of their passengers are hurt badly and
require medical attention. Passersby call an ambulance from the next town,
and soon it arrives, taking the injured passengers to the only medical facility in the area.

A neurosurgeon who is on duty examines both passengers when they   4
arrive at the medical center. She determines that both have suffered serious
head injuries and require immediate cranial surgery if they are to survive.
However, she is the only person available who is competent to perform the
surgery, and she cannot operate on both patients at once. Not knowing what
to do, she tries to find someone to call for advice. But she can reach nobody.
So she flips a coin.

As a result of the coin flip, the surgeon operates on Bonnie's passenger   5
and leaves Clyde's passenger in the care of two medical technicians. The
latter do the best they can, but Clyde's passenger dies. Because of the attention of the physician, Bonnie's passenger survives and, in time, makes a
complete recovery.

Selection 9

Identify rhetorical devices, including slanters and fallacious reasoning, and
evaluate the credibility and potential bias of the author.

WILL OZONE BLOB DEVOUR THE EARTH?

Edward C. Krug

At the time this essay was first published, Edward C. Krug was director
of environmental projects for CFACT, Committee For A Constructive
Tomorrow, a group based in Washington, D.C., that promotes free-market
solutions to current environmental concerns.

The great and good protectors of the environment are hailing the latest bit   1
of science-by-press-release.

Simultaneously staged with the announcement that the National Aero-   2
nautics and Space Administration (NASA) and the National Oceanic and

Atmospheric Administration have begun studying the possible development of an ozone hole over the Northern Hemisphere, the [first] Bush administration, Greenpeace, Sen. Al Gore (D-Tenn.), and others proclaimed that this "discovery" justifies the banning of all human-made substances that contain chlorine and bromine. Chlorine and bromine, by the way, are common elements also found in seawater, in plants, and in you and me.

3   I've been asked why I, a scientist, would dare question all this concern for the environment. The answer: Real science operates quite differently from what passes for environmental "science" these days.

4   Take physics, for example. Cold-fusion scientists were vilified by the scientific community a few years ago for their violation of scientific ethics when they went to the media with their supposed findings before their articles had been peer-reviewed.

5   The release of such unproven scientific findings is materially and sociologically devastating. It is highly misleading and causes the misallocation of limited social resources. It also undermines the very process of science and the public's faith in the objectivity of science.

6   The science of physics, which stones to death false prophets and therefore produces new miracles every day, operates in a way exactly the opposite of the new environmental "science," which stones to death the real prophets and therefore produces new scandals every day.

7   The Feb. 3 NASA press release on the new ozone hole over the Northern Hemisphere is being widely lauded. But there has been no peer review of the data. Indeed, peer review cannot even begin until after the end of March, because all the data have not yet been collected.

8   Even so, the details of the press release give pause. It states that according to ozone hole theory, we could have been losing 1 percent to 2 percent of our ozone per day in mid-January. But this appears not to have happened. Furthermore, it notes that we have information on only about half of the theoretically relevant chemical processes in the atmosphere, and only about 30 percent of the theoretically relevant range of altitude.

9   Why couldn't NASA obey the time-honored ethics of science and wait until sometime after March to make its findings known?

10   For the same reason that biologist Paul Ehrlich in 1968 dared anybody to prove wrong his theory that the world would run out of food in 1977. And for the same reason that the Environmental Protection Agency Administrator William Reilly announced last April that unpublished NASA satellite data would show ozone depletion had speeded up to twice its previous rate. By the time 1977 rolled around and people were still eating food, and by the time NASA finally published its satellite data showing that ozone is increasing (not decreasing), nobody cared anymore.

11   Environmentalists also abuse the scientific method. In real science, one must prove the positive, not the negative. If a hypothesis cannot explain all the data, it gets thrown out. In the new environmental "science," by contrast, utterances of doom are automatically assumed to be correct. And it is assumed that society must act on them, unless someone can prove the environmental fantasy has absolutely no possibility of ever coming true.

Since it is logically impossible to prove the negative, environmentalists 12
have a sweet racket going: We must subordinate ourselves to their will lest
their horrible predictions come to pass.

These are also the rules for the "space invaders" game. In this game, 13
the leader says we face dreadful danger from hostile invaders from space.
Since it is impossible to prove there is no alien life in the universe, we are
forced to make the leader emperor of Earth so that he or she can save us all
from this potential horror.

One might wish that NASA played "space invaders" instead of issuing 14
"ozone-blob-that-may-swallow-Earth" press releases into the real world.

Selections 10A and 10B

Evaluate the arguments on both sides. Who has the stronger arguments,
and why? Make certain your response does not rest too heavily on rhetorical devices. As an alternative assignment, determine which author relies
more heavily on rhetorical devices to persuade the audience.

EQUAL TREATMENT IS REAL ISSUE—NOT MARRIAGE

USA Today

Our view: The fact is that marriage is already a messy entanglement of
church and state.

With shouting about "gay marriage" headed for a new decibel level . . . 1
chances for an amicable resolution seem bleak.

Traditionalists see the issue in private, religious terms, and with legis- 2
lators in many states mobilizing around their cause, they're in no mood to
compromise. They say marriage, by common definition, involves a man
and a woman. And for most people, it's just that. In polls, two-thirds of the
public supports the status quo.

But looking through the lenses of history and law, as judges must, mar- 3
riage is far from a private religious matter. So much so that short of a constitutional amendment, compromise is inevitable.

Not only does the state issue marriage licenses and authorize its offi- 4
cers to perform a civil version of the rite, it gives married couples privileged
treatment under law.

For example, when one spouse dies the house and other property held 5
jointly transfer easily for the other's continued use and enjoyment. The survivor gets a share of continuing Social Security and other benefits. Joint
health and property insurance continues automatically.

If there's no will, the law protects the bereaved's right to inherit. There's 6
no question of who gets to make funeral arrangements and provide for
the corpse.

It's the normal order of things, even for households that may have ex- 7
isted for only the briefest time, or for couples who may be long estranged
though not divorced.

But some couples next door—even devoted couples of 20 or 30 years' 8
standing—don't have those rights and can't get them because of their sex.

Support for marriage is justified as important to <u>community stability</u>, 9
and it undoubtedly is. But when it translates into <u>economic and legal dis-</u>
<u>crimination</u> against couples who may be similarly committed to each other,
that <u>should be disturbing.</u>

The U.S. Constitution says every person is entitled to equal protection 10
under law. Some state constitutions go farther, specifically prohibiting sexual discrimination. . . .

Ironically, people who oppose gay marriages on religious grounds would 11
have their way but for the fact that marriage has evolved as a messy entanglement of church and state. To millions, marriage is a sacrament, and the
notion that the state would license or regulate a sacrament ought to be an
outrage. Imagine the uproar if a state legislature tried to license baptisms or
communions, and wrote into law who could be baptized or who could receive bread and wine. Or worse yet gave tax breaks to those who followed
those practices.

Short of getting out of the marriage business altogether, which isn't 12
likely to happen, the state must figure a way to <u>avoid discrimination.</u> The
hundreds of employers now extending workplace benefits to unmarried but
committed couples and the handful of municipalities offering informal "domestic partner" status may be pointing in the right direction.

The need is <u>not necessarily to redefine marriage but to assure equal</u> 13
<u>treatment under the law.</u>

GAY MARRIAGE "UNNATURAL"

The Rev. Louis P. Sheldon

*The Rev. Louis P. Sheldon is chairman of the Traditional Values Coali-
tion, a California-based organization of some 32,000 churches.*

Opposing view: Opinion polls show that nearly 80% of Americans
don't accept "homosexual marriage."

In everything which has been written and said about . . . homosexual 1
marriage . . . , the most fundamental but important point has been over-
looked. [Marriage is both culturally and physiologically compatible but claim
so-called homosexual marriage is neither culturally nor physiologically
possible.] 2

Homosexuality is not generational. The family tree that starts with a
homosexual union never grows beyond a sapling. Without the cooperation
of a third party, the homosexual marriage is a dead-end street. In cyber language, the marriage is not programmed properly and there are hardware
problems as well.

. . . Across America, "rights" are being created and bestowed routinely by judges indifferent to the wishes and values of their communities. This new wave of judicial tyranny confers special rights upon whichever group can cry the shrillest claim of victimhood. 3

genetic or not?

At the core of the effort of homosexuals to legitimize their behavior is the debate over whether or not homosexuality is some genetic or inherited trait or whether it is a chosen behavior. The activists argue that they are a minority and homosexuality is an immutable characteristic. 4

never been proven

But no school of medicine, medical journal or professional organization such as the American Psychological Association or the American Psychiatric Association has ever recognized the claim that homosexuality is genetic, hormonal or biological. 5

While homosexuals are few in number, activists claim they represent about 10% of the population. More reliable estimates suggest about 1% of Americans are homosexual. They also are the wealthiest, most educated and most traveled demographic group measured today. Per capita income for the average homosexual is nearly twice that for the average American. They are the most advantaged group in America. 6

Homosexuality is a behavior-based life-style. No other group of Americans have ever claimed special rights and privileges based solely on their choice of sexual behavior, and the 1986 Supreme Court decision of Bowers vs. Hardwick said sodomy is not a constitutionally protected right. 7

When the state enacts a new policy, it must be reflected in its public school curriculum. Textbook committees and boards of education will ensure that all of that flows into the classroom. American families do not want the "normalcy" of homosexual marriage taught to their children. 8

Churches may not be forced to perform homosexual weddings but individual churches that resist may be subjected to civil suit for sexual discrimination. Resistance may be used as a basis for denying them access to federal, state or local government programs. In the Archdiocese of New York, Catholic churches were singled out by the city and denied reimbursement given to every other church for providing emergency shelter to the city's homeless. The reason cited was Catholic opposition to homosexual "rights" ordinances. 9

Whatever the pronouncements of the . . . nation's highest court, Americans know that "homosexual marriage" is an oxymoron. Calling a homosexual relationship a marriage won't make it so. There is no use of rhetoric that can sanitize it beyond what it is: unnatural and against our country's most basic standards. Every reputable public opinion poll demonstrates that nearly 8 of every 10 Americans don't accept the pretense of "homosexual marriage." 10

Selections 11A and 11B

Evaluate the arguments on both sides. Who has the stronger arguments, and why? Make certain your response does not rest too heavily on rhetorical devices.

Alternative assignment: Determine which author relies more heavily on rhetorical devices to persuade his or her audience.

LATEST RULING IS GOOD SCOUT MODEL

USA Today

Groups that take in public funds can't shut out minorities.

1 The Boy Scouts still don't get it. They want all the perquisites and support due a welcoming, public-service organization—while retaining a '50s-style right to discriminate against minorities.

2 Fortunately, most similar organizations understand by now that it's wrong to invite the public in, use taxpayer-financed facilities and then claim the right to act like a small and sectarian private club.

3 The Scouts, virtually alone, still want it both ways. And they're vowing to go to the U.S. Supreme Court in defense of their hypocrisy.

4 The national Scout bureaucracy professes shock at the New Jersey Supreme Court's decision this week in favor of a highly honored Scout who was expelled by the organization for being gay.

5 The reason ought to be obvious: The Scouts solicit and get generous public support in troop sponsorship, free space for their activities and cash contributions. And they attempt, nonselectively, to bring in almost every pre-teen in pants. Therefore they are subject to New Jersey's law barring discrimination on the basis of race, religion or sexual orientation.

6 Their claim to "freedom of association" smacks of what the Jaycees argued in the Supreme Court in 1984 in defense of barring women—and lost. It's what Rotary clubs argued in 1987—and lost. It's what businessmen's clubs argued in 1988—and lost.

7 The argument is embarrassingly similar to that used by the white-supremacist defenders of racial segregation as a way of life in the 1950s and '60s.

8 Civil rights watchdogs say the Scouts are about the last national organization to make such a claim. Others, including Jaycees and Rotary, say they are stronger for having abandoned their former discriminatory practices.

9 Unfortunately, the Scouts' arguments have worked in states with weaker anti-discrimination laws or more pliable courts. California's Supreme Court even found a tortuous distinction between the Boys Clubs, covered by that state's law, and the Scouts, who aren't. The ayatollahs of California Scouting were permitted to kick out otherwise model Scouts who made the mistake of being honest about their religious uncertainties or sexual makeup.

10 The reaction has been a backlash: In California, Illinois, Maine and elsewhere, some governments, local charities and corporations are unwilling to fund and sponsor Scout programs because the Scouts insist on discriminating. And more lawsuits are soaking up Scout funds.

The Scouts' lofty objectives and 80-year record of success with nearly 100 million boys are commendable. The Scout Law soundly directs a Scout to "seek to understand others," to "treat others as he wants to be treated." 11

The bosses of Scouting—and their apologists—ought to reread that good advice. 12

DECISION ASSAULTS FREEDOM

Larry P. Arnn

Larry P. Arnn is president of the Claremont Institute in California.

Opposing view: The organization has the right to select its associates.

Since 1911, Boy Scouts have been required to swear: "On my honor I will do my best to do my duty to God and country and to obey the Scout Law; To help other people at all times; To keep myself physically strong, mentally awake, and morally straight." This oath has shaped the character and habits of generations of young men. 1

In New Jersey, the Boy Scout oath and the principles behind it are effectively voided. The state's Supreme Court ruled that the Scouts must re-admit James Dale, a scoutmaster who revealed his homosexuality in 1990. 2

The court said that the Scouts' decision to expel Dale was "based on little more than prejudice" and was "not justified by the need to preserve the organization's expressive rights." 3

Nonsense. The court's decision [tramples] on the rights of privacy, free association, and religious liberty to promote homosexuality as a civil right. The implications go far beyond the Boy Scouts. 4

Under American civil rights law, once a group becomes a protected minority, a myriad of constitutional forces is called to its defense. If homosexuality is granted this special status, it will affect every family in the land. 5

Furthermore, the court said that the Scouts are a "place of public accommodation" because they have a broad-based membership and work closely with other public service groups. But the Boy Scouts do not hang a sign that says all may enter. As the name implies, they are looking first of all for boys. More specifically, boys who will promise to follow the creed that makes scouting what it is. We can change that only by destroying scouting. 6

The rights of the Boy Scouts, not James Dale, are being violated. Each of us has under the Constitution the right to associate with whom we please. That means necessarily the right not to associate, too. If that right cannot be protected here, it cannot be protected anywhere. Indeed, churches will be next. 7

This case likely will go to the U.S. Supreme Court. But maybe the next president will sign a Defense of the Boy Scouts Act. We must hope for that, and also for a good decision from the U.S. Supreme Court. 8

Determine whether this essay contains an argument and, if it does, what it is.

Alternative assignment: Identify rhetorical devices, including slanters and fallacious reasoning.

IS GOD PART OF INTEGRITY?

Editorial from *Enterprise Record,* Chico, California

What Oroville High School was trying to do last Friday night, said Superintendent Barry Kayrell, was "maintain the integrity of the ceremony."   1

The ceremony was graduation for approximately 200 graduates.   2

The way to maintain "integrity," as it turned out, was to ban the words "God" and "Jesus Christ."   3

The result was a perfect example of out-of-control interpretation of the separation of church and state.   4

The high school's action in the name of "integrity" needlessly disrupted the entire proceeding as almost the entire graduating class streamed out of their seats in support of Chris Niemeyer, an exemplary student who had been selected co-valedictorian but was barred from speaking because he wanted to acknowledge his belief in God and Jesus Christ.   5

The speech, said Kayrell, "was more of a testimonial."   6

It was preaching, added OHS principal Larry Payne.   7

"I truly believe in the separation (of church and state)," explained Kayrell.   8

It was a complicated story that led to last Friday night.   9

Niemeyer and fellow senior Ferin Cole had prepared their speeches ahead of time and presented them to school officials. Cole, who plans to attend Moody Bible College, had been asked to deliver the invocation.   10

Both mentioned God and Jesus Christ. Both were told that was unacceptable.   11

Both filed a last-minute action in federal court, challenging the school's censorship. At a hearing Friday, just hours before graduation, a judge refused to overrule the school on such short notice. The suit, however, continues, and the judge acknowledged it will involve sorting out complex constitutional questions.   12

Defeated in court, Niemeyer and Cole met with school officials to see what could be salvaged.   13

Both agreed to remove references to the deity, but Cole wanted to mention why, in an invocation—by definition a prayer—he was not allowed to refer to God. That was nixed, and Cole simply bowed out.   14

Niemeyer was supposed to deliver his revised draft to Payne by 5 P.M.   15

He missed the deadline, but brought the draft with him to the ceremony.   16

When it was his turn to speak, Niemeyer came forward, but Payne instead skipped over the program listing for the valedictory address and   17 announced a song. The two debated the question on stage as the audience and graduates-to-be looked on.

Finally turned away, Niemeyer left the stage, tears of frustration on his cheeks, and his classmates ran to his side in a dramatic show of support.   18

You might say they were inspired by integrity.   19

The object of the First Amendment to the U.S. Constitution is to bar government-enforced religion. It was not designed to obliterate belief in God.   20

To stretch that command to denying a student the right to acknowledge what has spurred him on to the honor he has won is a bitter perversion.   21

That would apply whether the student was Islamic, Buddhist or any belief—atheist included. There is room, it would seem, for diversity in valedictory speeches, too.   22

Not at Oroville High School. There God and integrity don't mix.   23

It's spectacles like that played out last Friday night that have prompted Congress to consider a constitutional amendment aimed at curbing such misguided excess.   24

Earlier in the week it drew a majority vote in House, but fell short of the two-thirds margin needed.   25

Maybe such actions as witnessed locally can push it over the top.   26

Selection 13

Identify the conclusion of the article. How many arguments are given for it?

SHORTEN FEDERAL JAIL TIME

From the *Washington Post*

Don Edwards

> U.S. Rep. Don Edwards, D-Calif., was chairman of the House Judiciary Subcommittee on Civil and Constitutional Rights.

A debate is raging in the federal judiciary about whether the number of federal judges should be increased. This question should not be decided by Congress until it straightens out the mess it has made of the courts' jurisdiction.   1

Beginning in 1981, with the highly publicized "War on Crime," Congress has swamped the federal courts with thousands of criminal cases, many unsuited for the federal judiciary. The result is that civil cases are neglected and our federal prisons are bulging with prisoners, many of whom should not be there at all.   2

In its effort to be tough on drug offenders and other criminals, Congress enacted mandatory minimum laws that require judges to impose a certain sentence on the offender regardless of the person's background and the   3 nature of the crime. The statutes now number over 100, with many more proposed. Not only must we not enact new ones, but Congress should repeal the ones now on the books for the following reasons:

- The federal prison population has tripled since 1980 and is projected to quintuple by the year 2000. Three-quarters of new arrivals are drug offenders; by 1996, these offenders will comprise two-thirds of the prison population. Ninety-one percent of mandatory minimum sentences are imposed on nonviolent first-time offenders.

- To accommodate this influx of new prisoners, we opened 29 new federal prisons between 1979 and 1990. They cost $1.7 billion to maintain, and each new cell cost $50,000. With the continued precipitous increase in population, by 2002 we will be spending $2.8 billion annually.

  If we had instead sentenced these inmates to an alternative to prison, such as probation or a halfway house, we could have saved $384 million in 1992 and, projections show, an astounding $438 million in 1993. The Bureau of Prisons says that the recidivism rate for offenders sentenced to alternatives is extremely low—only 14 percent.

- Because of mandatory sentencing laws, federal district judges have no discretion in sentencing. They must send offenders to prison for long terms. Between 1984, when mandatory minimums were first enacted, and 1991, the sentence length for a nonviolent offender increased an average of 48 months. Ironically, mandatory sentencing laws often mean that nonviolent offenders receive longer sentences than violent offenders.

- We are filling our prisons with nonviolent, first-time offenders while dangerous and violent criminals often avoid mandatory minimum sentences.

- Morale in the federal judiciary is often low. The Judicial Conference, representing all federal judges, has come out against mandatory minimum sentences, and two senior judges recently announced publicly that they would no longer preside over drug trials because of these inequities. . . .

We must reverse the congressional policies that have created this mind-   4
less mandatory minimum sentencing, which overcrowds our federal prisons. At $30,000 per year to maintain these inmates, we not only cannot afford to implement these senseless policies, but we are creating a criminal training ground for first-time nonviolent offenders who might otherwise be turned into law-abiding citizens.

Selections 14A and 14B

Evaluate the arguments on both sides. Who has the stronger arguments, and why?

Alternative assignment: Identify rhetorical devices and determine which author relies more heavily on such devices.

Second alternative assignment: In each of the two essays, find four arguments that can be treated as categorical syllogisms. Set up a key, letting a letter stand for a relevant category. Be sure you identify the category in plain English. Then circle all and only the distributed terms. Then state whether each syllogism is valid, identifying rules broken by any syllogisms that are not.

CLEAN NEEDLES BENEFIT SOCIETY

USA Today

Our view: Needle exchanges prove effective as AIDS counterattack. They warrant wider use and federal backing.

Nothing gets knees jerking and fingers wagging like free needle-exchange programs. But strong evidence is emerging that they're working.   1

The 37 cities trying needle exchanges are accumulating impressive data that they are an effective tool against spread of an epidemic now in its 13th year.   2

- In Hartford, Conn., demand for needles has quadrupled expectations—32,000 in nine months. And free needles hit a targeted population: 55% of used needles show traces of AIDS virus.
- In San Francisco, almost half the addicts opt for clean needles.
- In New Haven, new HIV infections are down 33% for addicts in exchanges.

Promising evidence. And what of fears that needle exchanges increase addiction? The National Commission on AIDS found no evidence. Neither do new studies in the *Journal of the American Medical Association*.   3

Logic and research tell us no one's saying, "Hey, they're giving away free, clean hypodermic needles! I think I'll become a drug addict!"   4

Get real. Needle exchange is a soundly based counterattack against an epidemic. As the federal Centers for Disease Control puts it, "Removing contaminated syringes from circulation is analogous to removing mosquitoes."   5

Addicts know shared needles are HIV transmitters. Evidence shows drug users will seek out clean needles to cut chances of almost certain death from AIDS.   6

Needle exchanges neither cure addiction nor cave in to the drug scourge. They're a sound, effective line of defense in a population at high risk. (Some 28% of AIDS cases are IV drug users.) And AIDS treatment costs taxpayers far more than the price of a few needles.   7

It's time for policymakers to disperse the fog of rhetoric, hyperbole and scare tactics and widen the program to attract more of the nation's 1.2 million IV drug users.   8

We're a pragmatic society. We like things that work. Needle exchanges   9
have proven their benefit. They should be encouraged and expanded.

PROGRAMS DON'T MAKE SENSE

Peter B. Gemma Jr.

Opposing view: It's just plain stupid for government to sponsor dangerous, illegal behavior.

If the Clinton administration initiated a program that offered free tires to   1
drivers who habitually and dangerously broke speed limits—to help them
avoid fatal accidents from blowouts—taxpayers would be furious. Spending
government money to distribute free needles to junkies, in an attempt to
help them avoid HIV infections, is an equally volatile and stupid policy.

It's wrong to attempt to ease one crisis by reinforcing another.   2

It's wrong to tolerate a contradictory policy that spends people's hard-   3
earned money to facilitate deviant behavior.

And it's wrong to try to save drug abusers from HIV infection by per-   4
petuating their pain and suffering.

Taxpayers expect higher health-care standards from President Clinton's   5
public-policy "experts."

Inconclusive data on experimental needle-distribution programs is no   6
excuse to weaken federal substance-abuse laws. No government bureaucrat
can refute the fact that fresh, free needles make it easier to inject illegal
drugs because their use results in less pain and scarring.

Underwriting dangerous, criminal behavior is illogical: If you subsidize   7
something, you'll get more of it. In a Hartford, Conn., needle-distribution
program, for example, drug addicts are demanding taxpayer-funded needles
at four times the expected rate. Although there may not yet be evidence of
increased substance abuse, there is obviously no incentive in such schemes
to help drug-addiction victims get cured.

Inconsistency and incompetence will undermine the public's confi-   8
dence in government health-care initiatives regarding drug abuse and the
AIDS epidemic. The Clinton administration proposal of giving away needles hurts far more people than [it is] intended to help.

Selections 15A and 15B

Evaluate the arguments on both sides. Who has the stronger arguments,
and why?

Alternative assignment: Identify rhetorical devices and determine
which author relies more heavily on them.

Second alternative assignment: In the first essay, find as many arguments as you can that can be treated as categorical syllogisms. Set up a key,

letting a letter stand for a relevant category. Be sure you identify the category in plain English. Then circle all and only the distributed terms. Then state whether each syllogism is valid, identifying rules broken by any syllogisms that are not.

MAKE FAST FOOD SMOKE-FREE

USA Today

Our view: The only thing smoking in fast-food restaurants should be the speed of the service.

Starting in June, if you go to Arby's, you may get more than a break from burgers. You could get a break from tobacco smoke, too.   1

The roast-beef-sandwich chain on Tuesday moved to the head of a stampede by fast-food restaurants to limit smoking.   2

Last year, McDonald's began experimenting with 40 smokeless restaurants. Wendy's and other fast-food chains also have restaurants that bar smoking.   3

But Arby's is the first major chain to heed a call from an 18-member state attorneys general task force for a comprehensive smoking ban in fast-food restaurants. It will bar smoking in all its 257 corporate-owned restaurants and urge its 500 franchisees to do the same in their 2,000 restaurants.   4

Other restaurants, and not just the fast-food places, should fall in line.   5

The reason is simple: Smoke in restaurants is twice as bad as in a smoker's home or most other workplaces, a recent report to the *Journal of the American Medical Association* found.   6

Fast-food restaurants have an even greater need to clear the air. A quarter of their customers and 40% of their workers are under 18.   7

Secondhand smoke is a class A carcinogen. It is blamed for killing an estimated 44,000 people a year. And its toxins especially threaten youngsters' health.   8

The Environmental Protection Agency estimates that secondhand smoke causes up to 1 million asthma attacks and 300,000 respiratory infections that lead to 15,000 hospitalizations among children each year.   9

All restaurants should protect their workers and customers. If they won't, then local and state governments should do so by banning smoking in them, as Los Angeles has.   10

A person's right to a quick cigarette ends when it threatens the health of innocent bystanders, and even more so when many of them are youngsters.   11

They deserve a real break—a meal in a smoke-free environment that doesn't threaten their health.   12

DON'T OVERREACT TO SMOKE

Brennan M. Dawson

Opposing view: With non-smoking sections available, and visits brief, what's the problem?

If the attorneys general from a handful of states—those charged with upholding the law—were to hold a forum in Washington, you might expect
them to be tackling what polls say is the No. 1 public issue: crime.   1

Not these folks. They're worried someone might be smoking in the smoking section of a fast-food restaurant. And, there might be children in the non-
smoking section. Thus, they say, fast-food chains should ban all smoking.   2

Some would argue that this raises serious questions about priorities.
But it may be worth debating, since this is supposed to be about protecting
children. Everyone is (and should be) concerned with children's health and
well-being.   3

But what are we protecting them from—the potential that a whiff of
smoke may drift from the smoking section to the non-smoking section during the average 20-minute visit for a quick burger?   4

Anyone knowledgeable would tell you that none of the available studies can reasonably be interpreted to suggest that incidental exposure of a
child to smoking in public places such as restaurants is a problem. After
all, with the almost universal availability of non-smoking sections, parents
have the option of keeping their kids out of the smoking section.   5

A recent study published in the *American Journal of Public Health* reported that the separate smoking sections in restaurants do a good job of
minimizing exposure to tobacco smoke. According to the figures cited, customers would have to spend about 800 consecutive hours in the restaurants
to be exposed to the nicotine equivalent of one cigarette.   6

That would represent about 2,400 fast-food meals. Under those conditions, most parents would worry about something other than smoking.   7

Selections 16A and 16B

Evaluate the arguments on both sides. Who has the stronger arguments,
and why?

Alternative assignment: Identify rhetorical devices and determine
which author relies more heavily on them.

Second alternative assignment: In each of the two essays, find as many
arguments as you can that can be treated as categorical syllogisms. Set up a
key, letting a letter stand for a relevant category. Be sure you identify the
category in plain English. Then circle all and only the distributed terms.
Then state whether each syllogism is valid, identifying rules broken by any
syllogisms that are not.

BUYING NOTES MAKES SENSE AT LOST-IN-CROWD CAMPUSES

USA Today

Our view: Monster universities and phantom professors have only
themselves to blame for note-selling.

Higher education got a message last week from a jury in Gainesville, Fla.: Its customers, the students across the nation, deserve better service.   1

The jury found entrepreneurs are free to sell notes from college professors' lectures. And Ken Brickman is an example of good, old free enterprise, even if his services encourage students to skip class.   2

Brickman is a businessman who pays students to take notes in classes at the University of Florida. From a storefront a block off campus, he resells the notes to other students with a markup.   3

Professors and deans bemoan Brickman's lack of morals. They even use the word "cheating." They'd be more credible if their complaints—and the university's legal resources—were directed equally at Brickman's competitor in the note-selling business a few blocks away.   4

The difference: The competition pays professors for their notes; Brickman pays students. Morals are absent, it seems, only when professors aren't getting their cut.   5

The deeper issue is why Brickman has found a lucrative market. It's easy to say that uninspired students would rather read someone else's notes than spend time in class, but that's not the point.   6

Why are students uninspired? Why are they required to learn in auditorium-size classes where personal attention is non-existent, taking attendance impossible, and students can "cut" an entire semester with no one noticing?   7

Why are students increasingly subjected to teaching assistants—graduate students who know little more than they—who control classes while professors are off writing articles for esoteric journals that not even their peers will read?   8

Why are there not more professors—every former student can remember one—who transmit knowledge of and enthusiasm for a subject with a fluency and flair that make students eager to show up? No one would prefer to stay away and buy that professor's notes.   9

The debate over professorial priorities—students vs. research—is old. But so long as students come in second, they'll have good reasons to go to Ken Brickman for their notes.   10

BUYING OR SELLING NOTES IS WRONG

Opposing view: Note-buyers may think they're winners, but they lose out on what learning is all about.*

It's tough being a college student. Tuition costs and fees are skyrocketing. Classes are too large. Many professors rarely even see their students, let alone know their names or recognize their faces. The pressure for grades is intense. Competition for a job after graduation is keen.   1

---

*The author of the companion piece to the *USA Today* editorial on this subject would not give us permission to reproduce her essay in a critical thinking text, so we wrote this item ourselves.

But that's no excuse for buying the notes to a teacher's course. What 2
goes around comes around. Students who buy someone else's notes are only
cheating themselves—by not engaging in the learning process to the fullest
extent. They aren't learning how to take notes. Or how to listen. Or how to
put what someone is saying into their own words.

What happens if the notes are inaccurate? Will a commercial note-taker 3
guarantee the notes? Would you want to take a test using someone else's
notes?

Besides, what the professor says is her own property. It is the result of 4
hard work on her part. A professor's lectures are often her principal means
of livelihood. Nobody but the professor herself has the right to sell her property. Buying the notes to her lectures without her permission is just like
selling a book that she wrote and keeping the money for yourself.

And buying the notes from someone who is selling them without the 5
teacher's permission is the same as receiving stolen goods.

And that's assuming that there will be anyone out there to buy the 6
notes in the first place. After all, most students will want to take notes for
themselves, because they know that is their only guarantee of accuracy.
People who think they can get rich selling the notes to someone's lectures
should take a course in critical thinking.

The pressure for good grades doesn't justify buying or selling the notes 7
to a professor's lectures without her permission. If you can't go to class,
you shouldn't even be in college in the first place. Why come to school if
you don't want to learn?

Selections 17A and 17B

Evaluate the arguments on both sides. Who has the stronger arguments,
and why?

Alternative assignment: Identify rhetorical devices and determine
which author relies more heavily on them.

NEXT, COMPREHENSIVE REFORM OF GUN LAWS

USA Today

Our view: Waiting periods and weapon bans are welcome controls, but
they're just the start of what's needed.

The gun lobby got sucker-punched by the U.S. Senate last weekend. It 1
couldn't happen to a more deserving bunch.

For seven years, gun advocates have thwarted the supersensible Brady 2
bill, which calls for a national waiting period on handgun purchases.
Through a mix of political intimidation, political contributions and perverse constitutional reasoning, gun lobbyists were able to convince Congress to ignore the nine out of 10 Americans who support that idea.

But suddenly, after two days of filibuster, the Senate abruptly adopted the Brady bill. The House has already acted, so all that remains is to do some slight tinkering in a House-Senate conference, and then it's off to the White House for President Clinton's signature. 3

That's not the end of welcome gun control news, though. As part of the anti-crime bill adopted last week, the Senate agreed to ban the manufacture and sale of 19 types of assault-style semiautomatic weapons. Although these weapons constitute fewer than 1% of all guns in private hands, they figure in nearly 10% of all crime. The bill also bans some types of ammunition and restricts gun sales to, and ownership by, juveniles. 4

These ideas are worthy, but they can't do the whole job. Waiting periods and background checks keep criminals from buying guns from legal dealers. Banning certain types of anti-personnel weapons and ammunition will keep those guns and bullets from growing more common and commonly lethal. 5

Yet the wash of guns and gun violence demands much, much more. The judicial ability to process firearm-related crimes with certainty and speed is part of the solution. But even more so is the adoption of laws that permit gun licensing, gun registration and firearm training and education. 6

After years of denying the popular mood, Congress appears ready to honor it. That merits applause. But its new laws are just a start. Without truly comprehensive controls, the nationwide slick of gun carnage is bound to continue its bloody, inexorable creep. 7

GUN LAWS ARE NO ANSWER

Alan M. Gottlieb

Opposing view: Disarming the law-abiding populace won't stop crime. Restore gun owners' rights.

Every time another gun control law is passed, violent crime goes up, not down, and the gun-ban crowd starts to yelp for more anti-gun laws. 1

So it's no surprise that the gun-banners are already snapping at the heels of our Bill of Rights. 2

They turn a blind eye to the fact that California, with a 15-day waiting period, experienced a 19% increase in violent crime and a 20% increase in homicide between 1987 and 1991. And that a 1989 ban on "assault weapons" in that state has also resulted in increased violent crime. 3

In Illinois, after a 30-day waiting period was installed, that state experienced a 31% increase in violent crime and a 36% increase in the homicide rate. 4

And, a handgun ban in Washington, D.C., has made it the murder capital of the world! 5

The results are in. Gun control makes the streets safe for violent criminals. It disarms their victims—you and me. The people's right to protect themselves should be restored, not restricted. 6

Case in point: Bonnie Elmasri of Wisconsin, who was being stalked by her estranged husband despite a court restraining order, was killed along 7 with her two children while she waited for the handgun she purchased under that state's gun-waiting-period law.

Bonnie and her children are dead because of gun control laws, as are thousands of other victims each year.   8

Anybody who believes that disarming the law-abiding populace will help reduce crime has rocks in the head.   9

The next time a violent criminal attacks you, you can roll up your copy of USA TODAY and defend yourself with it. It may be all you'll have left for self-protection.   10

Selections 18A and 18B

Evaluate the arguments on both sides. Who has the stronger arguments, and why?

Alternative assignment: Identify rhetorical devices and determine which author relies more heavily on them.

HOW CAN SCHOOL PRAYER POSSIBLY HURT? HERE'S HOW

USA Today

Our view: Mississippi case shows how people's rights can be trampled by so-called "voluntary prayer."

What harm is there in voluntary prayer in school?   1

That's the question . . . House Speaker Newt Gingrich and others pose in their crusade to restore prayer to the classroom. They argue that a constitutional amendment to "protect" so-called voluntary school prayer could improve morals and at worst do no harm.   2

Well, a mother's lawsuit filed Monday against Pontotoc County, Miss., schools says otherwise. It shows government-sponsored voluntary prayer in school threatens religious liberty.   3

All the mother, Lisa Herdahl, wants is that her six children get their religious instruction at home and at their Pentecostal church, not at school.   4

But their school hasn't made that easy. Prayers by students go out over the public address system every day. And a Bible study class is taught at every grade.   5

School officials argue that since no one is ordered to recite a prayer or attend the class, everything is voluntary.   6

But to Herdahl's 7-year-old son, it doesn't seem that way. She says he was nicknamed "football head" by other students after a teacher told him to wear headphones so he wouldn't have to listen to the "voluntary" prayers.   7

And she says her 11-year-old son was branded a "devil worshiper" after a teacher told students he could leave a Bible class because he didn't believe in God.   8

Indeed, Herdahl's children have suffered exactly the kind of coercion to 9
conform that the Supreme Court found intolerable when it banned state-written prayers in 1962 and outlawed Alabama's moment of silence for meditation or voluntary prayer in 1985.

As the court noted in those cases, when government—including 10
schools—strays from neutrality in religious matters, it pits one religion against another. And youngsters especially can feel pressured to submit to a majority's views.

That's why a constitutional amendment to protect "voluntary prayer" 11
in school is so dangerous.

Students don't need an amendment to pray in school now. They have 12
that right. And they can share their religious beliefs. They've formed more than 12,000 Bible clubs nationwide that meet in schools now, only not during class time.

For the Herdahls, who refused to conform to others' beliefs, state-sponsored 13
voluntary prayer and religious studies have made school a nightmare.

For the nation, a constitutional amendment endorsing such ugly activities could make religious freedom a joke. 14

WE NEED MORE PRAYER

Armstrong Williams

Armstrong Williams is a Washington, D.C.–based business executive, talk-show host, and author of The Conscience of a Black Conservative.

Opposing view: The tyranny of the minority was never envisioned by the nation's Founding Fathers.

The furor aroused by . . . Newt Gingrich's remarks about renewing school 1
prayer illustrates how deep cultural divisions in American society really are.

A few moments of prayer in schools seems a small thing—harmless 2
enough, almost to the point of insignificance. Yet it has provoked an impassioned firestorm of debate about the dangers of imposing viewpoints and the potential for emotionally distressing non-religious children.

The Constitution's framers were wary of a "tyranny of the majority," 3
and so they imposed restraints on the legislature. They never foresaw, nor would they have believed, the tyranny of the minority made possible through an activist judiciary changing legal precedents by reinterpreting the Constitution.

The American ideal of tolerance has been betrayed by its use in directly 4
attacking the deeply held convictions of millions of Americans.

The fact that this country was once unashamedly Christian did not 5
mean that it was necessarily intolerant of other views—at least not nearly so intolerant of them as our rigid secular orthodoxy is toward all religious expression. Through the agency of the courts, a few disgruntled malcontents have managed to impose their secular/humanist minority views on the majority.

But it has not always been so.   6

The confidence with which some maintain that school prayer is mani-   7
festly unconstitutional belies an ignorance of our nation's history. America
was founded by religious men and women who brought their religious beliefs and expressions with them into public life.

It was in 1962 that an activist Supreme Court ruled that denomination-   8
ally neutral school prayer was judged to violate the establishment clause of
the First Amendment. Since then, the "wall of separation" between church
and state has rapidly become a prison wall for religious practice.

The drive to protect the delicate sensibilities of American children from   9
the ravages of prayer is particularly ironic when our public schools have become condom clearinghouses that teach explicit sex.

The real heart of the school prayer issue is the role of religion in our   10
public life.

Selection 19

Summarize the author's argument or arguments, if any.
    Alternative assignment: Identify rhetorical devices, if any.

PLANET OF THE WHITE GUYS

Barbara Ehrenreich

On the planet inhabited by the anti–affirmative action activists, the only   1
form of discrimination left is the kind that operates against white males.
There, in the name of redressing ancient wrongs, white men are routinely
shoved aside to make room for less qualified women and minorities. These
favored ones have no problems at all—except for that niggling worry that
their colleagues see them as underqualified "affirmative-action babies."
Maybe there was once an evil called racism in this charmed place—30 or
300 years ago, that is—but it's been replaced by affirmative action.

Now I agree that discrimination is an ugly thing no matter who's at the   2
receiving end, and that it may be worth reviewing affirmative action . . . to
see whether it's been fairly applied. People should not be made to suffer for
the wicked things perpetrated by their ancestors or by those who merely
looked like them. Competent white men should be hired over less competent women and minorities; otherwise, sooner or later, the trains won't run
on time and the planes will fall down from the sky.

But it would be a shame to sidestep the undeniable persistence of   3
racism in the workplace and just about everywhere else. Consider the recent lesson from Rutgers University. Here we have a perfectly nice liberal
fellow, a college president with a record of responsiveness to minority concerns. He opens his mouth to talk about minority test scores, and then—
like a Tourette's syndrome victim in the grip of a seizure—he comes out

with the words "genetic hereditary background." Translated from the academese: minorities are dumb, and they're dumb because they're born that way.

Can we be honest here? I've been around white folks most of my life—from left-wingers to right-wingers, from crude-mouthed louts to prissy-minded élitists—and I've heard enough to know that *The Bell Curve* is just a long-winded version of what an awful lot of white people actually believe. Take a look, for example, at a survey reported by the National Opinion Research Center in 1991, which found a majority of whites asserting that minorities are lazier, more violence-prone and less intelligent than whites. Even among the politically correct, the standard praise word for a minority person is "articulate," as if to say, "Isn't it amazing how well he can speak!"

Prejudice of the quiet, subliminal kind doesn't flow from the same place as hate. All you have to do to be infected is look around: at the top of the power hierarchy—filling more than 90% of top corporate-leadership slots and a grossly disproportionate share of managerial and professional positions—you see white men. Meanwhile, you tend to find minorities clustered in the kind of menial roles—busing dishes, unloading trucks—that our parents warned were waiting for us too if we didn't get our homework done.

So what is the brain to make of this data? It does what brains are designed to do: it simplifies and serves up the quickie generalizations that are meant to guide us through a complex world. Thus when we see a black colleague, who may be an engineer or a judge, the brain, in its innocence, announces helpfully, "Janitor-type approaching, wearing a suit."

Maybe it's easier for a woman to acknowledge this because subliminal prejudice hurts women too. Studies have shown, for example, that people are more likely to find an article convincing if it is signed by "Bob Someone" instead of, say, "Barbara Someone." It's just the brain's little habit of parceling reality into tidy equations, such as female = probable fluffhead. The truth is that each of us carries around an image of competence in our mind, and its face is neither female nor black. Hence our readiness to believe, whenever we hear of a white male losing out to a minority or a woman, that the white guy was actually more qualified. In Jesse Helms' winning 1990 campaign commercial, a white man crumples up a rejection letter, while the voice-over reminds him that he was "the best-qualified." But was he? Is he always? And why don't we ever hear a white guy worry out loud that his colleagues suspect he got the job—as white men have for centuries—in part because he's male and white?

It's a measure of the ambient racism that we find it so hard to believe that affirmative action may actually be doing something right: ensuring that the best guy gets the job, regardless of that guy's race or sex. Eventually, when the occupational hierarchy is so thoroughly integrated that it no longer makes sense for our subconscious minds to invest the notion of competence with a particular skin color or type of genitalia, affirmative action can indeed be cast aside like training wheels.

Meanwhile, aggrieved white men can console themselves with the gains their wives have made. Numerically speaking, white women are the biggest beneficiaries of affirmative action, and because white women tend to marry white men, it follows that white men are, numerically speaking, among the top beneficiaries too. On this planet, Bob Dole and Pat Buchanan may not have been able to figure that out yet, but most white guys, I like to think, are plenty smart enough.

Selection 20

Summarize the author's argument or arguments, if any.
> Alternative assignment: Identify rhetorical devices, if any.

DO WOMEN REALLY NEED AFFIRMATIVE ACTION?

Joanne Jacobs

Joanne Jacobs is a columnist for the *San Jose Mercury News.*

I was an affirmative action hire, back in 1978. As a result, I became the first woman on my newspaper's editorial board. Was I qualified? I certainly didn't have much experience. My boss took a chance on me. I like to think it paid off for him, as well as for me. 1

At any rate, I made the editorial board safe for women, who now make up half the editorial pages staff. 2

Defenders of affirmative action have a new strategy: Consider the ladies. Recently, a liberal coalition kicked off a campaign to cast affirmative action as a gender issue rather than a racial issue. Affirmative action is essential for women's advancement, argued feminist leaders. "Women will not quietly accept a rollback of our rights that have been part of the American scene for over a generation," said Katherine Spillar of the Feminist Majority. 3

It's a smart, though doomed, strategy. 4

The smart part is that women (if not feminists) are a majority of the population. If women were persuaded that affirmative action guarantees not only our benefits but also our "rights," public thinking would shift dramatically. 5

Poll data suggest that the majority of Americans accept preferences for women in jobs and college admissions; most are deeply hostile to preferences for minority group members. 6

The doomed part is that most white women don't think they'd lose their rights or their jobs if affirmative action ceased to exist; some are concerned about the job prospects of their white male husbands. 7

Affirmative action used to mean reaching out to people excluded from opportunities by overt discrimination or old-boy networks, giving everyone a chance to compete fairly. Now it means judging members of previously excluded groups by different, generally lower, standards than others. 8

Are women less able to compete [today] because of past discrimination? 9
Certainly not women under the age of 45.

In the past, affirmative action helped women—especially educated, 10
middle-class women—enter occupations previously reserved for men. Some
argue that affirmative action primarily benefited white women who were
most prepared to take advantage of opportunities, and most likely to have
connections to powerful men.

Certainly, it appears that affirmative action has done most for those 11
who needed it least. It has opened doors; it has not built ladders.

While women haven't achieved parity in income or in top executive 12
ranks or in all careers, affirmative action can provide little help in achieving those goals in the future.

In education, affirmative action already is passé. Women don't need to 13
be judged by different standards to get into college, and they're not. Females
earn higher high school grades than males, and are more likely to attend
college.

Women are underrepresented in the mathematical sciences and in engi- 14
neering studies. An affirmative action program that admitted calculus-
deficient women to physics class would do them no favor. The solution is
not changing the standards; it's persuading more girls to take more math in
high school.

Women do worry about workplace equity, but here too affirmative ac- 15
tion isn't likely to play much of a role. The much-discussed "glass ceiling"
for women in business is related to two factors: family and calculus.

Women are more likely than men to put family needs ahead of career 16
advancement. These choices have consequences. Women who work more
at home don't get to be CEO.

Selection 21

WANT BETTER SCHOOLS? SUPPORT TEACHERS

Dean Simpson Jr.

Dean Simpson Jr. is a journalist and English teacher at Mount Whitney
High School in Visalia.

In the education business we have a saying—you get what you get. That 1
means we teachers deal with everyone who comes through the schoolhouse
door and do our best to send them out at the end of their term as educated,
productive citizens. We don't always succeed, but overall I think we do a
pretty good job, particularly considering the circumstances.

So it really aggravated me when my local newspaper, the *Visalia Times-* 2
Delta, ran an editorial the essence of which was that teachers need to quit
complaining about things we can't control, "a diverse population, poorly

prepared students, television, parents who don't want to be involved and per-pupil spending," and focus on what we can control, "more rigorous course offerings, return to heavy concentration of reading and writing, longer school sessions and updated curriculum." Unfortunately, such admonitions seem to be on the lips of every legislator and a good many citizens in California today.

The implication is that teachers are a bunch of crybabies for complaining about conditions. Has it ever occurred to anyone that education is the only industry that cannot control the raw materials with which it works? No other industry is accused of whining if it advocates and lobbies for better conditions within its business.   3

If US Steel receives a shipment of substandard pig iron from a supplier, no one accuses it of whining when it sends it back. If Ford Motor Co. is sent a batch of defective tires, it's not expected to refabricate them. It sends them back. In education—we get what we get.   4

Imagine the newspaper has 10 openings to fill and must hire the first 10 people who walk through the door. A blind man running the press? Non-English speakers writing and editing copy? Editors who have no concept of personnel management? Advertising sales people with no communication skills? And you'd better be able to show an increase in profit and decline in the number of errors in the copy. After all, standards must be raised and met. Oh, and there's no money for additional training.   5

Now let's take a look at some of the things teachers are told we need to do to improve education, which will apparently overcome all the problems in the schools today. The first need supposedly is for more rigorous course offerings.   6

From kindergarten up, the curriculum is more rigorous than it has ever been. When I attended kindergarten in 1951, children learned "socialization," finger-painting and maybe their ABCs. Now they learn to read and write and do addition and subtraction up to 10s and sometimes beyond. Kindergartners also learn geometric shapes and handle thought problems using, among other things, simple graphs.   7

All the math I needed for admission to college in 1964 was geometry. Now students must have Algebra II and trigonometry to have much of a chance of college acceptance.   8

Advanced Placement classes—high school classes where students may earn college credit after completing the course and passing a rigorous test— didn't exist when I graduated. Today, virtually every high school in California offers these.   9

As far as the need for a heavy concentration on reading and writing, my students not only read a lot, I also expect them to interpret what they read. No fill-in-the-bubbles tests. They dig into what they've read, understand it, apply it to their lives and write about what they learn from the literature and its application in the world. None of these skills, unfortunately, show up on standardized tests.   10

Freshman enter my journalism class as experienced writers having written much more, and with greater depth of thought, than was expected of my generation until we entered college.   11

The next element that supposedly would make "for better trained, bet- 12
ter educated students" is "longer school sessions." I'm not sure whether
that refers to a longer school day or longer school year, but it doesn't really
matter. If it's a longer school day, we must do away with all school sports,
as they do in other countries. Those who wish can play club sports—for a
fee. Other electives and extracurricular activities? Gone. We can't cherry
pick here. We either do it as it's done in Europe and Japan, or we don't.

Is a longer school year the goal? Why? I know the Japanese have a longer 13
school year, and they score better on standardized tests, too. But if those
schools are so far superior to ours, why are their students, and students
from nearly every country in the world, clamoring to get into our universities? And why are our high school graduates able to compete successfully
with those foreign students at our universities?

A graduate from Redwood, one of our Central Valley high schools, re- 14
ceived a Nobel Prize last year. If foreign schools are so great, why is the
United States, with its allegedly awful schools, so far ahead in technology,
industrial production and every other category worth mentioning?

As far as updating curriculum, can anyone update his home or business 15
without money? Textbooks cost money. Lab materials, technology, and
continuing education and training for teachers cost money. Show me the
money or shut up and get out of the way.

What we need in education is support. If we set standards—and we've 16
actually been fighting for high standards for a long time—parents and community members must help us enforce them, not just by paying lip service,
but by feeling real pain when necessary. Standards are inherently hard to
reach and not everyone will reach them, at least not easily. We in education have been doing our part for years. Remember CLAS and CAP tests?
Educators didn't dump them in the trash can. Politicians and the public did.

Instead of accusing us of being whiners, see us as advocates for im- 17
provement of all conditions that contribute to educational success for all
children. Help us by addressing the social problems we can't control and
we'll continue to improve the conditions we can.

---

*This article appeared in the *Sacramento Bee,* October 30, 1999.

The Top Ten Fallacies of All Time

First, we should say that we are not exactly reporting on a scientific study of reasoning errors. Far from it. We're simply listing for you what we think, based on our experience, are the top ten fallacies that crop up in spoken and written discourse. While we're disclaiming, we should point out that some of the items on our list are not really *errors* of reasoning, but *failures to reason at all.* We've included a remark or two for each, but we remind you that all of them are discussed at greater length in the text.

Ad Hominem/Genetic Fallacy   If it operated no place but in politics, ad hominem would still be among the most ubiquitous examples of flawed thinking. While the fact that a claim came from a prominent Democrat or Republican might be reason to suspect that it is political spin, we constantly see people refuse even to consider—and sometimes even to hear—claims from a political perspective not their own.

But what goes in politics also goes in other arenas. Adversaries in practically every field of endeavor put less, or no, stock in their opponents' claims. We've seen this happen in disputes between physical scientists and behavioral scientists, between factions of a single academic department and between members of the same family. If they're the enemy, they cannot be right.

Wishful Thinking   It may surprise some that this category makes the list, but in observing people's behavior, we've come to think that they frequently put a lot more trust in what they *want* to be true than in what they have sufficient evidence for. Advertising, our beliefs about famous people, and many other aspects of life play upon this tendency. How frequently do we see people buy products that claim they'll make them younger-looking or more attractive only to see no results? And then those same people will buy the next product that comes along, possibly with the same ingredients but with a bigger advertising budget or better-looking models. We can't explain this in any other way except the triumph of wishful thinking.

Neither of your authors is sure about capital punishment. But we'd seriously consider an exception for people who invent scams based on wishful thinking and milk elderly people out of money they've spent their lives saving up.

"Argument" from Popularity   Operating in conjunction with wishful thinking, appeal to the authority of one's peers and predecessors accounts for a great proportion of the belief in the supernatural aspects of the world's religions down through history. This alone is sufficient to place it prominently on the list.

If a person thought that none of her peers believed in miracles, and she had never witnessed anything firsthand herself that she considered miraculous, what are the chances that she would believe in miracles in general? We believe it is very slight. But most people (well over half of Americans) do believe in miracles, and we're pretty sure such a belief rests at least in substantial part on the fact that most of one's peers share the belief.

Hasty Conclusion   The human mind is quick to notice connections between and among things, events, people, and such. Often, its ability to latch on to similarities is a matter of survival. ("A snake like that bit Oog the other day, and he died. I'm leaving this one alone.") But connections that we make "naturally" need to be sifted through our reasoning faculty. ("When I dreamed that it would rain on Easter, it did. Last night I dreamed the stock market would go up . . . I think I'll add to the portfolio.") We must learn to distinguish psychological connections from logical ones and real causes from coincidence.

Some related fallacies fall under this headline: One is the mistake of making generalizations from evidence that is merely anecdotal. We are very quick to conclude that our own experience or that of our friends is sufficient to arrive at a conclusion about the entire world. But the fact that your friend had no trouble quitting smoking is no reason to think that others won't.

A second variation is drawing conclusions (or generalizing) based on a bad analogy. The fact that two (or more) things are alike in *some* way is not all by itself a reason to think they're alike in some other way. Analogous items have to be very carefully scrutinized for relevant similarities and dissimilarities before we can draw conclusions about one from the other.

A final variety of the hasty conclusion fallacy, and a sad one, is the way the public (following the media) jump to conclusions about a person's guilt when in fact the person has merely been mentioned as a possible suspect. Examples range from the famous Sam Shepard case (on which the TV series and movie titled *The Fugitive* were based) to the case of Richard Jewell, who was actually a hero in the bomb incident at the 1996 Atlanta Olympics—he spotted the fateful knapsack and warned people away from what turned out to be a pipe bomb, but later his name was leaked as a suspect.

Although he was soon cleared by the authorities, the stigma of suspicion stuck to him and he was hounded for months at ball games and other events. His hopes for a career in law enforcement went down the drain. This, and similar stories, are the result of a public that makes up its mind on the basis of mere slivers of information.

"Argument" from Outrage   This category makes the list because of the increase in polarizing political discourse. The mere mention of Bill Clinton (on one hand) or George Bush (on the other) has the power to raise the blood pressure of large numbers of citizens. Animosity and bile have taken over from the presentation and evaluation of evidence, with the result that national political discussion has been on a downward trend for over a generation. We attribute at least part of the decline to the electronic media. Radio and television, although they had the potential to raise the level of public discourse, have had the opposite effect. ("Television is a medium," said Ernie Kovacs, "because it is neither rare nor well done.") Many television shows where politics are "discussed" have turned into shouting matches in which several morons compete for the loudest volume and sharpest insults. They may look vaguely like debates, but they are nothing of the sort. "Talk radio" is even worse, with made-up statistics, false allegations, the spread of rumor, and general name-calling taking the place of argument and evidence. (We've given this fallacy the nickname "the Rush Limbaugh fallacy," based on the fact that he has mastered it so thoroughly.) Most of these shows are designed solely to raise the heart rate of people who already believe the nonsense the host is talking about (no matter which side of the political spectrum he or she claims to represent).

It's worth pointing out that this "argument" almost always involves straw men (see the following entry) and very often involves scapegoating as well. The easiest way to deal with an issue is to identify an enemy, distort his real position, and blame everything on him amidst a flurry of name-calling.

Straw Man   One principal weapon of the indignation-mongers just described is the distortion and exaggeration of the views of others. This tactic is widespread in the talk media and in mainstream politics as well. In fact, the latter seem to be taking their cue from the former in recent years. (We recall the advice given by Newt Gingrich, former Speaker of the House of Representatives, to Republican candidates in 1994. When discussing Democratic candidates and proposals, he said, you should use terms such as —, —, and "traitor" as frequently as possible.) Nobody, it seems, trusts the American people to make political choices based on straightforward information. And, judging from the number of Americans who make no effort to obtain such information, there may be some basis for such an attitude.

Post Hoc   We usually explain post hoc reasoning in terms of simple-minded examples of cause and effect. But the real bamboozling takes place at more complicated levels. For example, while Jimmy Carter was president, interest rates went through the roof; while George Bush (the first such) was president, the economy went into a recession. Both presidents were blamed for these occurrences, but were the policies of either the cause of these effects? Probably not. At least most people did not stop to ask whether it was anything the president did or refused to do that might have caused them. It is our tendency to seize on easy, simple answers that helps give this fallacy, and most of the others, such a high profile.

Red Herring/Smokescreen   One might think of this as the "attention span" fallacy, since it seems to work best on listeners and readers who are unable to stay focused on an issue when they are tempted by distractions. These days, when politicians and other public figures dodge hard questions, they are generally allowed to get away with it. How long has it been since you've heard a reporter say, "But sir, you didn't answer the question!" Probably even longer than it's been since you heard a politician give a direct answer to a hard question. We've all heard it said that the media and the people they interview are interdependent—that is, they each depend on the other and have fundamentally the same interests (at the highest government and corporate levels), and that accounts for the easy treatment officials often get from interviewers. But we think it's also true that reporters themselves are prone to fall for the fallacy in question here. They are too likely to move on to the next question on their list when the public would be better served by a pointed follow-up question on an issue that has just been ducked. We think this is a serious failure and damaging to the public good.

Group Think Fallacy   This fallacy has undergone a major revival since the terrorist attacks of September 11, 2001. An understandable emotional shock followed those attacks, but even before the shock began to wear off, the motto for the country became "United We Stand." There's nothing unreasonable about a united stand, of course, but this motto soon began to stand for an intolerance of any position that ran counter to the official view of the United States government (as voiced by the White House). The prevailing view in many quarters, including many places in the government itself, was that all "good" Americans agreed with this official position. Considerable force was brought to bear in enforcing this group thinking, including describing critics as "giving aid and comfort" and so forth.

   Of course, it isn't just national policy that can cause this phenomenon to occur. At what may be the other end of the spectrum, notice how the referees in a basketball game call way too many fouls on your team and not nearly enough on the other team. Our loyalty to our group can affect our judgments in ways that range from the amusing to the dangerous.

Scare Tactics   Reasoning that uses scare tactics is like rain in Seattle: It happens all the time. The scare tactics fallacy ranks up there with the "argument" from outrage as a staple of talk radio hosts and other demagogues, which means it is easy to find examples. What's wrong with raising fuel-efficiency standards? Well, how would you like to drive around in an elfmobile?—Because that's what you're going to be driving if the car companies are forced to make cars more efficient. What's wrong with the proposed big tax cut? Nothing—if you'd just as soon eliminate Social Security and Medicare.

The fallacy of scare tactics is an appeal to fear, and fear can often provide a perfectly reasonable motivation: Evidence that some frightening thing will result from X is certainly a good reason for avoiding X. But mere *mention* of the frightening thing is not, nor is a vivid portrayal or depiction of the ominous event. You don't prove we should overthrow a dictator merely by describing what would happen if he set off a nuclear bomb in New York City—or by showing gruesome photos of what he did to someone else. When the danger depicted is not shown to be relevant, the thinking is fallacious.

The use of scare tactics is not uncommon in advertising, either. But getting consumers to worry about having dandruff or halitosis or odors in their carpets is no argument for purchasing some particular brand of shampoo or mouthwash or carpet cleaner. People are often motivated to buy a house or car because they fear someone else will make an offer ahead of them and they'll lose the opportunity. This is unreasonable when it results in a purchase they would not otherwise have made. We wonder how many people live in houses they decided they liked just because they were afraid they'd lose them if they didn't make their offer *right now*.

Appendix 3

The Scrapbook of Unusual Issues

*T*his section includes a number of items from here and there, mainly from newspapers, that struck us as amusing, out-of-the-ordinary, or just plain weird. All of them involve issues that can make for interesting discussions or subjects for writing assignments. (There's no reason critical thinking subjects have to be dull.) Like the essays in Appendix 1, these present opportunities to exercise your critical thinking skills.

Strange Stuff: News Out of the Ordinary

Golf-ball retriever's jail term tees off public

London — For 10 years John Collinson made a modest living diving for lost golf balls and selling them for 20 cents each. But after police caught him on a midnight expedition, a court frowned on his unusual job and jailed him for six months for theft.

The sentence provoked a public outcry, made the 36-year-old father of two a cause célèbre and prompted lawmakers, celebrities and the British media to campaign for this release.

Police arrested Collinson in August at Whetstone Golf Course in Leicester, central England. He and a colleague had fished 1,158 balls from Lily Pond, the bane of hundreds of golfers playing the difficult par 3 fifth hole.

Collinson, who made roughly $21,500 a year collecting balls at courses throughout the country, claimed in his defense they didn't belong to anyone. He told a jury at Leicester Crown Court last week he even filled out tax returns on his earnings. But the judge jailed him, saying, "It is obvious you show no remorse and no intention of quitting."

Gavin Dunnett, managing director of UK Lake-balls—a firm that buys balls from hundreds of divers and sells more than a million worldwide every year via the Internet—said Thursday that recovered balls are not stolen, but are abandoned property. He said more than 2,000 people had signed his online petition to "Free the Whetstone One."

Doodle crosses the line

MOUNT LEBANON, Pa. — A school suspended an 11-year-old girl for drawing two teachers with arrows through their heads, saying the stick figures were more death threat than doodle.

Becca Johnson, an honor-roll sixth grader at Mellon Middle School, drew the picture on the back of a vocabulary test on which she had gotten a D.

"That's my way of saying I'm angry," Becca said, adding she meant no harm to the teachers.

The stick figures, on a crudely drawn gallows with arrows in their heads, had the names of Becca's teacher and a substitute teacher written underneath. Another teacher spotted the doodle in the girl's binder Tuesday and reported it, prompting the three-day suspension.

Becca's parents, Philip and Barbara Johnson, denied the school's contention the drawings were "terrorist threats."

"She had done poorly on a test that was handed back to her. We've always told her that you can't take your feelings out on your teacher, so write about it or draw it, as a catharsis," Barbara Johnson said.

Brief lapse in judgment?

Poway — A high school vice principal was placed on leave Wednesday after she allegedly lifted girls' skirts—in front of male students and adults—to make sure they weren't wearing thong underwear at a dance.

"Everyone saw everything," said Kim Teal, whose 15-year-old daughter attended the dance but was not checked. "It was a big peep show."

Rita Wilson was placed on administrative leave Wednesday while the school district investigates the allegations concerning the dance last Friday for students at Rancho Bernardo High School.

Girls said they were told to line up outside the gym before entering the dance so Wilson could check their underwear. Those wearing thongs were turned away.

Cities Give Psychics License to Entertain, Not Exorcise

Believers in the occult and thrill-seekers are the bread and butter of psychic parlors.

For a few dollars, psychics foretell a client's future by gazing into a crystal ball or reading a palm.

Such transactions are legal entertainment, said Detective Jan Cater of the Sacramento County Sheriff's Department.

What is illegal, she said, is when clients are led to believe that they are cursed and must pay large sums of money to purge the evil.

"So-called psychics terrify people into believing that awful things will happen to them . . . . unless they pay to have the curses removed, Cater said.

Sacramento and other cities require that psychics and others in the "seer" trades undergo background checks before receiving a license issued by the police department.

But other communities, including unincorporated sections of Sacramento County, have no requirements—a situation that, according to Cater, can lead to big-time swindles.

"Psychic fraud isn't a major problem in the unincorporated areas (of the county), but it has the potential to be," Cater said.

In the city of Sacramento, the safeguards in place for several years are working, officials said. . . .

In San Francisco and other cities without license laws, psychic swindles are on the rise, authorities said.

One of Cater's biggest cases involved Ingrid, a Sonoma County woman who said she paid more than $265,000 over five years to "psychics" Louie Stevens and Nancy Uwnawich. The couple convinced Ingrid, 66, that she had a curse that had to be removed by them—or she would suffer, Ingrid said.

After wiping out her savings, Ingrid told the pair she had no more cash—except for $2,000 in her son's college trust fund.

"What's more important—your health or your son?" Uwnawich shouted, according to Ingrid.

Ingrid said she gave them the $2,000. . . .

An arrest warrant has been issued for Uwnawich, who remains at large.

By Edgar Sanchez
BEE STAFF WRITER

Monogamy? Don't Cheat Yourself

DEAR ANN: Why do you come down so hard on married men who cheat? I don't understand why you believe monogamy is the only "right" way when it comes to marriage. If monogamy works so well, how come so many men cheat and so many women want divorces?

Many other cultures openly accept polygamy. Even the Bible says a man can have more than one wife. And in many countries, adultery is accepted and shrugged off as nothing to get excited about. The wife gets the financial support and social position, and the mistress gets the sex. This sounds like a fair exchange to me.

The truth is, there is not a woman on the planet who can fully satisfy the needs of a powerful male. When women quit asking men to make them the center of their universe and learn to accept a strong man's desire for more than one female companion, families will live together longer, more happily and with less rancor.

–Truth Hurts In Texas

DEAR AUSTIN: Men in biblical times had multiple wives in order to ensure an abundance of offspring because so many women died in childbirth. It was not a license to cheat.

I am sure your approach appeals to a lot of men, but I doubt that the women in your life would go for it. And without their cooperation, you're not going to get very far. Of course, if you would like to live in one of those foreign countries that condones adultery, be my guest. Most women would be delighted to see you go. A few might even be willing to buy you a ticket.

Ann Landers (By permission of Esther P. Lederer and Creators Syndicate, Inc.)

Writer to 'Dear Abby' Faces Child-Porn Counts

MILWAUKEE — A man who wrote to "Dear Abby" for advice on how to handle his fantasies about having sex with young girls was charged Wednesday with possessing child pornography after the columnist turned him in, authorities say.

Paul Weiser, 28, was charged with three counts of possession of child pornography. He was ordered released on $10,000 bail on condition he avoid computers and contact with anyone under 18.

Police said 40 pornographic photographs of children were found in his computer after his arrest Monday.

"He acknowledges he needs help and denies ever acting upon any desires," said prosecutor Paul Tiffin.

"Dear Abby" columnist Jeanne Phillips, daughter of column founder Pauline Phillips, called police after receiving the letter.

Jeanne Phillips, who shares her mother's pen name, Abigail Van Buren, told the Milwaukee Journal Sentinel she agonized over whether to report Weiser, since the column's credibility is based on anonymity given those seeking advice.

"I lost sleep. Didn't sleep for days, because I really believe this man wrote to me genuinely seeking help," she said. "I was torn, because my readers do turn to me for help, yet there was the priority of the safety of those young girls."

She was said to be traveling on Wednesday and did not return a call seeking comment.

Weiser could get up to five years in prison and a $10,000 fine on each count, if convicted.

He did not speak during Wednesday's court hearing except to answer "yes" when asked if he understood the proceedings.

A preliminary hearing was set for March 25.

Associated Press

Strange Stuff: News Out of the Ordinary

'Whites' Send a Message

GREELEY, Colo — Unable to persuade a local school to change a mascot name that offends them, some students at the University of Northern Colorado have named their intramural basketball team "The Fighting Whites."

The students are upset with Eaton High School for using an American Indian caricature on the team logo. The team is called the Reds.

The university team said it chose a white man as its mascot to try to raise awareness of stereotypes that some cultures endure.

"The message is 'Let's do something that will let people see the other side of what it's like to be a mascot,'" said Solomon Little Owl, a team member and director of Native American Student Services at the university.

The team, made up of American Indians, Latinos and Anglos, wears jerseys that say, "Every thang's going to be all white."

"It's not meant to be vicious. It is meant to be humorous," said Ray White, a Mohawk American Indian on the team.

No 'ATHEISTS' Allowed

ST. PETERSBURG, Fla — Steven Miles has tooled around Gainesville, Fla., for 16 years with a license plate that says "ATHEIST."

To Miles, it is a form of self-expression, one he is happy to spend a few extra dollars every year to keep.

But to the state of Florida now, the tag is "obscene or objectionable," according to a letter Miles received last month from the Department of Highway Safety and Motor Vehicles.

"The plate must be canceled," the department ordered.

Miles said he is incensed and that giving up his tag is out of the question.

The vice president of Atheists of Florida said he intends to fight and is in touch with the American Civil Liberties Union.

Dummy is no woman

RENTON, Wash. — A woman with a full-size mannequin buckled into the front seat of her minivan tried to sneak into the car pool lane on Interstate 405 and became involved in a chain of crashes that backed up traffic for hours Tuesday morning, according to the Washington State Patrol.

Susan Aeschliman-Hill, 59, of Kent, Wash., acknowledged using the dummy—complete with a woman's sweater, makeup and wig—to drive illegally in the car pool lane. "When traffic gets real bad, I sometimes use (the mannequin)," she said.

State Patrol Trooper Monica Hunter said the woman likely will be cited for driving in the high-occupancy vehicle lane and making an unsafe lane change.

"Her passenger wasn't breathing, and that's one of our requirements," Hunter said.

By Rick Nelson, compiled from
the Associated Press

Christian School Expels Nude Dancer's Daughter

A Sacramento private school has expelled a kindergarten student three weeks before the end of the school year, saying her mother's work as a nude dancer clashes with its Christian philosophy.

Christina Silvas, 24, of Rancho Cordova said one reason she took the job as a dancer at Gold Club Centerfolds off Highway 50 was so she could afford the $400 monthly tuition at Capital Christian School.

"If you choose to do the wrong thing willfully, then God's word instructs me as to what my responsibility is," said Rick Cole, head pastor of Capital Christian Center. "I need to be faithful to my calling."

Silvas, who previously worked at the church as a Sunday school teacher, has a different view.

"I thought the church was supposed to accept everybody," she said. "That's my understanding of what God is about. My daughter is the one who goes to school there, not me, and they're turning her away."

Silvas, who is single, said school administrators telephoned her last week and told her that in response to persistent rumors, a parent went to the strip club's Web site, downloaded pictures of Silvas and brought them to school staff. Silvas told them she does dance at the all-nude bar, which doesn't serve alcohol, and subsequently met with Cole.

As head pastor of Capital Christian, which at 4,000 members is one of the largest Assemblies of God churches in the country, Cole had final say on the matter.

Silvas said Cole told her not only will her 5-year-old daughter be expelled, but as long as she keeps her job at the club, neither she nor her daughter can attend church there.

Silvas said her daughter enjoys the school's daily worship sessions and was looking forward to the end-of-the-year pool party and graduation ceremony. She hasn't told the girl why she won't be able to go to school next week.

"I'm still trying to figure out what I'm going to tell her," she said.

Silvas said that when she enrolled her daughter, she signed a statement that stipulated she would abide by the school's Christian commitment/philosophy and that "weekly church attendance is necessary for continued enrollment at CCS."

The statement also reads, in part, "CCS is interested in maintaining a partnership with our parents regarding the standards and criteria of a Christian learning structure that involves the entire family."

By working as an exotic dancer and refusing to change her vocation, Silvas violated the school's philosophy, Cole said.

"She was not in compliance with what she agreed to," he said. "There's a commitment form that parents sign. They agree to our Christian commitment and standard of living."

Seeking a resolution, Silvas and Cole met privately Tuesday. "I talked to her for over an hour, letting her know how much God cares about her and loves her and that he has a much better plan for her than what she is doing with her life right now," Cole said.

He promised that if Silvas quit her job, he and the church would forgive her, help her and even waive tuition for the month of June.

"My understanding was she would come back to me after thinking about it and let me know her decision," Cole said. "It's very stunning to me to see it on the news. We've been thrust into this media craze, but not by our desire."

Silvas said the decision is not simple and couldn't be made that quickly.

"I have other expenses besides my daughter's tuition," she said. "I am also concerned with providing a comfortable life for my daughter."

Silvas said she feels she is being demonized.

"I'm trying to let them know we're not evil because of our work, and we do have an awareness of God. My job is legal, it's not illegal."

Though Silvas is considering legal action, experts in education law say that may not be a good option.

"In a private school, it's hard to make a breach of contract action because they have the right to kick a kid out at any time for any reason," said Michael Sorgen, an education lawyer in San Francisco.

Even though the school has the legal right to expel the child, that doesn't make it right, Sorgen said.

By Erika Chavez
BEE STAFF WRITER

Ill Boy's New Hurdle: School Drug Rules

Life just got more complicated for an 8-year-old boy and his mother who's had great success battling his mental disorders with a doctor-approved marijuana therapy.

The youngster's medical condition has improved so dramatically that he can now attend public school, but school officials won't permit a school nurse to administer his cannabis capsules and won't let him take the pills himself on campus, the child's mother said Monday.

"Other kids get their medication," she complained. But the drug her son needs daily at 1 p.m. must be delivered by her personally, off the school grounds, she said.

"It makes him feel he's not normal, that he's being treated differently. He wonders why he's being targeted. He just wants to be normal," she said.

She hopes to persuade school officials to change their minds and allow the capsules to be given on campus.

The woman, whose name is being withheld by The Bee to protect the boy's identity, has been treating her son with medical cannabis for the past year, at home and at the private school he had been attending.

But in April, they moved from Rocklin to El Dorado County. She presented her son's new school with the required permission slip for students who need medication at school, a form she and the boy's doctor signed.

The day before the boy was to report to his new school, however, a message left on the family answering machine informed the mother that her son's recommended medication could not be administered on campus.

So, she says, she's been forced to drive a round trip of 26 miles each noontime to remove him from the school grounds, give him his capsules, and return him to class.

Vicki L. Barber, superintendent of the El Dorado County Office of Education, said she could not comment on any specific case. But she said state law permits schools to dispense drugs only when they are formally "prescribed" by a physician. The boy's doctor made a "recommendation," and there is a difference, Barber added, between a "prescription" and a doctor's "recommendation."

Proposition 215, the Compassionate Use Act of 1996, permits the use of medical marijuana and the possession of the drug by the patient or a primary caregiver.

A school district cannot be legally defined as a "primary caregiver," Barber said.

Because the district has a zero-tolerance policy, students are not permitted to have in their possession or to self-administer drugs of any kind, she said.

The boy's mother said the school district is relying on a technicality to dodge responsibility.

"There is no 'prescription' for 'oral cannabis,'" the capsule she prepares in a five-hour cooking and drying process at home, she said.

But it is a part of her son's "individual education plan" or IEP, the state's "prescription" for helping children with special needs, the mother said.

School district officials would not comment on the boy's specific IEP.

By Wayne Wilson
BEE STAFF WRITER

A letter to the editor of the local paper by one of your authors.

5 Million Teen-agers Perfect

You recently ran an Associated Press story that first appeared in the New York Times about a Port Orchard, Wash., Eagle Scout who was given a week to abandon his atheism or be kicked out of Boy Scouts of America. Boy Scout law requires scouts to be trustworthy, loyal, helpful, friendly, courteous, kind, obedient, cheerful, thrifty, brave, clean and reverent. An atheist, of course, finds it difficult to be reverent in the intended sense of the term.

Unfortunately, you ended the article with a paraphrase from Gregg Shields, a Boy Scout spokesman: "Mr. Shields said for the Boy Scouts to insist on anything less would be unfair to the 5 million members."

But there were two more sentences in the New York Times article and you missed the best point of the piece by leaving them out. Shields said: "It would be a disservice to all the other members to allow someone to selectively obey or ignore our rules."

The Times piece then added, "As for the other 11 points of the Scout Law, Mr. Shields could not say whether anyone had been ejected for being untrustworthy, disloyal, unhelpful, unfriendly, discourteous, unkind, disobedient, cheerless, unthrifty, cowardly or sloppy."

I for one believe it is a credit to scouting that none of those 5 million teen-age boys has ever been found guilty of any of those other 11 defects.

—**Richard Parker, Chico**

Strange Stuff: News Out of the Ordinary

As if the goings-on of government weren't scary enough, the state of North Carolina is calling in a Ghostbusters-like group to do a paranormal screening of the old state Capitol.

Although there have been no sightings of a huge marshmallow man, staffers at the Capitol say they have heard floorboards creak with invisible footsteps, keys jangle, and doors squeak open and shut.

"To be honest with you, I've always made it a rule to be out of the building at quitting time," said Raymond Beck, the Capitol historian. "I've had enough of those strange vibes here that I don't like sticking around after it gets dark."

Researchers from the Ghost Research Foundation will give the 162-year-old Raleigh landmark where the governor has his offices a "spectral inspection," using infrared cameras, electromagnetic field detectors and audio recorders.

The Capitol has gone through a number of night watchmen who begged off the duty after one night of creepy noises, Beck said.

But Owen J. Jackson, 84, managed the job for 12 years before retiring in 1990. He apparently never was slimed, and strains of gospel hymns, the thump-thump-thumps that followed him down stairs and the angry slams of doors never bothered him, Jackson said.

"You get used to something like that," Jackson said. "I think there's a couple (of) million dollars buried somewhere there, and they're just trying to tell us where it was."

It's hormonal

A Harvard research team has found that married men, whether fathers or not, have significantly less testosterone than single men, regardless of age or overall health status.

Anthropology graduate student Peter Gray and his colleagues also found that men who spent lots of time with their wives had even lower testosterone levels than other married men. The team tested 58 men in the Boston area, according to an article in a recent Harvard University Gazette.

Gray suggests that married men don't produce as much testosterone after they shift from dating to parenting roles.

"Married men, particularly fathers, are less likely to engage in dominance interaction and aggression," he said. "That means less risk taking, less conflicts or other behaviors that could lead, for example, to death by homicide.

And couldn't it be Mother Nature's way of keeping men from straying? After all, other studies have found that men with high levels of testosterone were more likely to commit adultery than those with less of the stuff.

"That's an interesting question," Gray said. "That's a topic that will be harder to get at."

Is skydiving dog cruelty?

Animal lovers are howling over a skydiving dog.

The parachuting dachshund, known as Brutus the Skydiving Dog, is set to perform at this weekend's Air and Space show at Vandenberg Air Force Base.

"What we feel is this is cruelty to animals," said Shirley Cram, shelter director and treasurer for the Volunteers for Inter-valley Animals. "It's exploiting the dog. It certainly isn't fun for that dog to jump out of the plane."

Brutus' skydiving partner disagrees.

"He gets all excited when I'm getting my gear ready," said Ron Sirull of Delray Beach, Fla., contending Brutus enjoys his aerial activities. He added, "He's totally up for it."

Sirull said his dog's veterinarian and the Arizona Humane Society have signed off the activity being safe for man's best friend.

Brutus is tucked into a special pouch affixed to his owner's chest for the jump and dons custom-made goggles for what Sirull calls his "fleafall." While Sirull has 1,000 jumps, Brutus has logged 100.

"That's equal to 700 jumps in dog years," his owner joked.

—Compiled by Caroline Liss from the Associated Press and Washington Post. In SAC BEE, 1 Nov. 2002.

10 Commandments Monument Must Go

MONTGOMERY, Ala. — A Ten Commandments monument in the rotunda of Alabama's judicial building violates the Constitution's ban on government promotion of religion, a federal judge ruled Monday.

U.S. District Judge Myron Thompson gave Alabama Chief Justice Roy Moore, who had the 5,300-pound granite monument installed in the state building, 30 days to remove it.

Thompson said previous court rulings have allowed displays on government property if they have a secular purpose and do not foster "excessive government entanglement with religion." He said the Ten Commandments monument fails this test.

"His fundamental, if not sole, purpose in displaying the monument was non-secular; and the monument's primary effect advances religion," Thompson said.

Moore testified during the trial that the commandments are the moral foundation of American law. He said the monument acknowledges God, but does not force anyone to follow the justice's conservative Christian religious beliefs.

A lawsuit seeking removal of the monument argued that it promoted the judge's faith in violation of the Constitution.

Moore installed the monument after the building closed on the night of July 31, 2001, without telling any other justices.

"This monument was snuck in during the middle of the night, and they can sneak it out just as easily. It's a gross violation of the rights of the citizens of Alabama," said Morris Dees, lead counsel and co-founder of the Southern Poverty Law Center. He urged Moore to remove the monument immediately.

The monument, which features the King James Bible version of the Ten Commandments sitting on top of a granite block, is one of the first things visitors see upon entering the building.

"Its sloping top and the religious air of the tablets unequivocally call to mind an open Bible resting on a podium," Thompson said.

In his ruling, Thompson said he found the monument to be more than just a display of the Ten Commandments.

"The court is impressed that the monument and its immediate surroundings are, in essence, a consecrated place, a religious sanctuary, within the walls of the courthouse," Thompson wrote.

An appeal is expected. Neither Moore nor his lead attorney, Stephen Melchior, had any immediate comment. An assistant to Melchior said they were reserving comment until they had read the opinion.

Moore fought to display a wooden plaque of the commandments on his courtroom wall in Etowah County before he won election as chief justice in November 2000.

"The basic issue is whether we will still be able to acknowledge God under the First Amendment, or whether we will not be able to acknowledge God," Moore testified.

The Rev. Barry Lynn, executive director of Americans United for Separation of Church and State, call the ruling a setback for "Moore's religious crusade."

"It's high time Moore learned that the source of U.S. law is the Constitution and not the Bible," Lynn said.

One of Moore's supporters, Alabama Christian Coalition President John Giles, said he believes there may be a backlash against the ruling in Alabama.

"I am afraid the judge's order putting a 30-day limit on removal of the monument will lead to an uprising of citizens protesting removal of that monument," Giles said.

Associated Press

Teen Claims Bias after School Bars Her Bid to Be Prom King

SACRAMENTO — An 18-year-old Encina High School senior is not being allowed to run for prom king because . . . she is a female.

Kristine Lester said Thursday that school officials told her that her name would not be on the ballot because only males can run for king and only females can run for queen.

"I just wanted to do something different," said Lester, who is openly gay and plans to wear a tuxedo at Saturday's prom. "I'm not the feminine type to run for queen."

Lester said she believes the school is discriminating against her because of her sexual orientation.

Officials with the San Juan Unified School District back Encina Principal Myrtle Berry's decision and denied that there was any discrimination involved.

"We don't discriminate," said district spokeswoman Deidra Powell.

—Sandy Louey

Stop Barring Men, Feminist Professor Told

Boston College gives her an ultimatum to allow males in class— or quit teaching

BOSTON — A radical feminist professor at Boston College has been given an ultimatum from the school: admit men to her classes or stop teaching.

Theologian Mary Daly lets only women take her courses.

Daly, whose seven major books, including "Outercourse," have made her a pioneer in feminist circles, has said she won't back down. Opening her classes to men would compromise her belief that women tend to defer to a man whenever one is in the room, she said.

Daly took a leave of absence from the Jesuit college this semester rather than bow to demands that she admit senior Duane Naquin into her class in feminist ethics.

Naquin, who claimed discrimination, has the backing of the Center for Individual Rights, a conservative law firm in Washington whose lawsuit ended affirmative action at the University of Texas. The firm sent a letter to BC in the fall threatening legal action if Daly did not relent.

Daly has argued Naquin did not have the prerequisite of another feminist studies course.

College officials said a second male student also complained of discrimination.

Daly has rejected a retirement offer from the college, the Boston Globe reported.

Daly, who is 70, taught only men when she first arrived at the Newton campus in 1966. The college of arts and science did not begin admitting women until 1970. In the early '70s, she said, she observed problems in her coed classes.

"Even if there were only one or two men with 20 women, the young women would be constantly on an overt or a subliminal level giving their attention to the men because they've been socialized to nurse men," she said.

Boston College officials said Daly's ground rules violate federal civil rights laws and school policy.

If a male professor tried to bar women from his classes, college spokesman Jack Dunn said, "we'd be run out of town."

Daly, who abandoned her Roman Catholic faith in the early 1970s, describes herself as a radical feminist, which she interprets as "going to the roots" of societal problems.

Her books include "The Church and the Second Sex," "Gyn/Ecology: The Metaethics of Radical Feminism" and "Outercourse," a theological autobiography.

She said she views the controversy as an attack on academic freedom and an assault on feminism by "an extreme right-wing organization" trying to "assert white male supremacy."

Daly's students are rallying around her, and 14 of them wrote a letter to college administrators.

"I think there comes a point where women need to claim their own space," said Kate Heekin, a Greenwich, Conn., senior. "If that needs to be a classroom, so be it."

By Robin Estrin
Associated Press

In Short . . .

She is Barbie's oldest friend, happily married and visibly pregnant with her second child—and some parents think she's a little too real for children. The pregnant version of Midge, which pops out a curled-up baby when her belly is opened, has been pulled from Wal-Mart shelves across the nation following complaints from customers, a company spokeswoman said.

Associated Press; from *The Sacramento Bee*, December 26, 2002.

Glossary

ad hominem Attempting to rebut a source's argument or claim or position, etc., on the basis of considerations that logically apply to the source rather than to the argument or claim or position.

affirmative claim A claim that includes one class or part of one class within another: A- and I-claims.

affirming the antecedent *See* modus ponens.

affirming the consequent An argument consisting of a conditional claim as one premise, a claim that affirms the consequent of the conditional as a second premise, and a claim that affirms the antecedent of the conditional as the conclusion.

ambiguous claim A claim that could be interpreted in more than one way and whose meaning is not made clear by the context.

analogical argument An argument in which something that is said to hold true of a sample of a certain class is claimed also to hold true of another member of the class.

analogy A comparison of two or more objects, events, or other phenomena.

analytic claim A claim that is true or false by virtue of the meanings of the words that compose it. *Contrast with* synthetic claim.

analytical definition A definition that specifies (1) the type of thing the defined term applies to and (2) the difference between that thing and other things of the same type.

antecedent *See* conditional claim.

appeal to anecdotal evidence, fallacy of A form of hasty generalization presented in the form of an anecdote or story. Also the fallacy of trying to prove (or disprove) that x is a causal factor for y by citing an example or two of an x that did (or didn't) cause y.

appeal to ignorance The view that an absence of evidence *against* a claim counts as evidence *for* that claim.

appeal to indignation *See* outrage, "argument" from.

appeal to pity *See* pity, "argument" from.

appeal to precedent The claim (in law) that a current case is sufficiently similar to a previous case that it should be settled in the same way.

apple polishing A pattern of fallacious reasoning in which flattery is disguised as a reason for accepting a claim.

argument An attempt to support a claim or an assertion by providing a reason or reasons for accepting it. The claim that is supported is called the conclusion of the argument, and the claim or claims that provide the support are called the premises.

argument from analogy *See* analogical argument.

argument pattern The structure of an argument. This structure is independent of the argument's content. Several arguments can have the same pattern (e.g., modus ponens) yet be about quite different subjects. Variables are used to stand for classes or claims in the display of an argument's pattern.

background information The body of justified beliefs that consists of facts we learn from our own direct observations and facts we learn from others.

bandwagon *See* peer pressure.

begging the question *See* question-begging argument.

biased generalization, fallacy of A generalization about an entire class based on a biased sample.

biased sample A sample that is not representative.

burden of proof, misplacing A form of fallacious reasoning in which the burden of proving a point is placed on the wrong side. One version occurs when a lack of evidence on one side is taken as evidence for the other side, in cases where the burden of proving the point rests on the latter side.

categorical claim   Any standard-form categorical claim or any claim that means the same as some standard-form categorical claim. *See* standard-form categorical claim.

categorical imperative   Kant's term for an absolute moral rule that is justified because of its logic: If you can wish that your maxim were a universal law, your maxim qualifies as a categorical imperative.

categorical logic   A system of logic based on the relations of inclusion and exclusion among classes ("categories"). This branch of logic specifies the logical relationships among claims that can be expressed in the forms "All Xs are Ys," "No Xs are Ys," "Some Xs are Ys," and "Some Xs are not Ys." Developed by Aristotle in the fourth century B.C.E., categorical logic is also known as Aristotelian or traditional logic.

categorical syllogism   A two-premise deductive argument in which every claim is categorical and each of three terms appears in two of the claims—for example, all soldiers are martinets and no martinets are diplomats, so no soldiers are diplomats.

causal claim   A statement that says or implies that one thing caused or causes another.

causal factor   A causal factor for some specific effect is something that contributes to the effect. More precisely, in a given population, a thing is a causal factor for some specified effect if there would be more occurrences of the effect if every member of the population were exposed to the thing than if none were exposed to the thing. To say that C is a causal factor for E in population P, then, is to say that there would be more cases of E in population P if every member of P were exposed to C than if no member of P were exposed to C.

causal hypothesis   A statement put forth to explain the cause or effect of something, when the cause or effect has not been conclusively established.

cause-and-effect claim   *See* causal claim.

chain argument   An argument consisting of three conditional claims, in which the antecedents of one premise and the conclusion are the same, the consequents of the other premise and the conclusion are the same, and the consequent of the first premise and the antecedent of the second premise are the same.

circularity   The property of a "causal" claim where the "cause" merely restates the effect.

circumstantial ad hominem   Attempting to discredit a person's claim by referring to the person's circumstances.

claim variable   A letter that stands for a claim.

common practice, "argument" from   Attempts to justify or defend an action or a practice on the grounds that it is common—that "everybody," or at least lots of people, do the same thing.

common thread   In common-thread reasoning, multiple occurrences of a feature are said to be united by a single relevant common thread.

complementary term   A term is complementary to another term if and only if it refers to everything that the first term does not refer to.

composition, fallacy of   To think that what holds true of a group of things taken individually necessarily holds true of the same things taken collectively.

conclusion   In an argument, the claim that is argued for.

conclusion indicator   A word or phrase (e.g., "therefore") that ordinarily indicates the presence of the conclusion of an argument.

conditional claim   A claim that state-of-affairs A cannot hold without state-of-affairs B holding as well—e.g., "If A then B." The A-part of the claim is called the *antecedent*; the B-part is called the *consequent*.

conditional proof   A deduction for a conditional claim "If P then Q" that proceeds by assuming that P is true and then proving that, on that assumption, Q must also be true.

confidence level   *See* statistical significance.

conflicting claims   Two claims that cannot both be correct.

confusing explanations and excuses, fallacy of   Mistaking an explanation of something for an attempt to excuse it.

conjunction   A compound claim made from two simpler claims. A conjunction is true if and only if both of the simpler claims that compose it are true.

consequent   *See* conditional claim.

contradictory claims   Two claims that are exact opposites—that is, they could not both be true at the same time and could not both be false at the same time.

contrapositive   The claim that results from switching the places of the subject and predicate terms in a claim and replacing both terms with complementary terms.

contrary claims   Two claims that could not both be true at the same time but could both be false at the same time.

control group   *See* controlled cause-to-effect experiment.

controlled cause-to-effect experiment   An experiment designed to test whether something is a causal factor for a given effect. Basically, in such an experiment two groups are essentially alike, except that the members of one group, the *experimental group*, are exposed to the suspected causal factor, and the members of the other group, the *control group*, are not. If the effect is then found to occur with significantly more frequency in the experimental group, the suspected causal agent is considered a causal factor for the effect.

converse   The converse of a categorical claim is the claim that results from switching the places of the subject and predicate terms.

deduction (proof)   A numbered sequence of truth-functional symbolizations, each member of which validly follows from earlier members by one of the truth-functional rules.

deductive argument An argument that is either valid or intended by its author to be so.

definition by example Defining a term by pointing to, naming, or describing one or more examples of something to which the term applies.

definition by synonym Defining a term by giving a word or phrase that means the same thing.

denying the antecedent An argument consisting of a conditional claim as one premise, a claim that denies the antecedent of the conditional as a second premise, and a claim that denies the consequent of the conditional as the conclusion.

denying the consequent *See* modus tollens.

deontologism *See* duty theory.

dependent premises Premises that depend on one another as support for their conclusion. If the assumption that a premise is false cancels the support another provides for a conclusion, the premises are dependent.

descriptive claim A claim that states facts or alleged facts. Descriptive claims tell how things are, or how they were, or how they might be. *Contrast with* prescriptive claims.

difference in question In relevant-difference reasoning, one item is said to have a feature ("the feature in question") that other similar items lack, and there is said to be only one other relevant difference ("the difference in question") between the item that has the feature in question and the other items that don't have the feature in question.

disjunction A compound claim made up of two simpler claims. A disjunction is false only if both of the simpler claims that make it up are false.

divine command theory The view that our moral duty (what's right and wrong) is dictated by God.

division, fallacy of To think that what holds true of a group of things taken collectively necessarily holds true of the same things taken individually.

downplayer An expression used to play down or diminish the importance of a claim.

duty theory The view that a person should perform an action because it is his or her moral duty to perform it, not because of any consequences that might follow from it.

dysphemism A word or phrase used to produce a negative effect on a reader's or listener's attitude about something or to tone down the positive associations the thing may have.

emotive force The feelings, attitudes, or emotions a word or an expression expresses or elicits.

envy, "argument" from Trying to induce acceptance of a claim by arousing feelings of envy.

equivalent claims Two claims are equivalent if and only if they would be true in all and exactly the same circumstances.

error margin A range of possibilities; specifically, a range of percentage points within which the conclusion of a statistical inductive generalization

falls, usually given as "plus or minus" a certain number of points.

euphemism An agreeable or inoffensive expression that is substituted for an expression that may offend the hearer or suggest something unpleasant.

experimental group *See* controlled cause-to-effect experiment.

expert A person who, through training, education, or experience, has special knowledge or ability in a subject.

explanation A claim or set of claims intended to make another claim, object, event, or state of affairs intelligible.

explanatory comparison A comparison that is used to explain.

explanatory definition A definition used to explain, illustrate, or disclose important aspects of a difficult concept.

extension The set of things to which a term applies.

factual claim A claim about a factual issue.

factual issue/question An issue that there are generally accepted methods for settling.

fallacy An argument in which the reasons advanced for a claim fail to warrant acceptance of that claim.

false dilemma This pattern of fallacious reasoning: "X is true because either X is true or Y is true, and Y isn't," said when X and Y could both be false.

feature in question *See* difference in question.

force, "argument" by Using a threat rather than legitimate argument to "support" some "conclusion."

functional explanation An explanation of an object or occurrence in terms of its function or purpose.

gambler's fallacy The belief that recent past events in a series can influence the outcome of the next event in the series. This reasoning is fallacious when the events have a predictable ratio of results, as is the case in flipping a coin, where the predictable ratio of heads to tails is 50–50.

generalization An argument offered in support of a general claim.

genetic fallacy Rejecting a claim on the basis of its origin or history.

good argument An argument that provides grounds for accepting its conclusion.

grouping ambiguity A kind of semantic ambiguity in which it is unclear whether a claim refers to a group of things taken individually or collectively.

group think fallacy Fallacy that occurs when someone lets identification with a group take the place of reason and deliberation when arriving at a position on an issue.

guilt trip Trying to get someone to accept a claim by making him or her feel guilty for not accepting it.

harm principle The claim that the only way to justify a restriction on a person's freedom is to show that the restriction prevents harm to other people.

hasty conclusion, fallacy of   A fallacy of inductive arguments that occurs when conclusions are drawn from a sample that is too small.

hasty generalization, fallacy of   A generalization based on a sample too small to be representative.

horse laugh   A pattern of fallacious reasoning in which ridicule is disguised as a reason for rejecting a claim.

hyperbole   Extravagant overstatement.

hypothesis   A supposition offered as a starting point for further investigation.

hypothetical imperative   Kant's term for a command that is binding only if one is interested in a certain result; an "if-then" situation.

implied target class   In an analogical argument, the class to which the sample items and the target item belong.

inconsistency (form of ad hominem)   A pattern of fallacious reasoning of the sort, "I reject your claim because you act inconsistently with it yourself," or "You can't make that claim now because you have in the past rejected it."

independent premises   Premises that do not depend on one another as support for the conclusion. If the assumption that a premise is false does not cancel the support another premise provides for a conclusion, the premises are independent.

indirect proof   Proof of a claim by demonstrating that its negation is false, absurd, or self-contradictory.

inductive analogical argument   *See* analogical argument.

inductive argument   An invalid argument whose premises are intended to provide some support, but less than conclusive support, for the conclusion.

inductive generalization   *See* generalization.

innuendo   An insinuation of something deprecatory.

intension   The set of characteristics a thing must have for a term correctly to apply to it.

invalid argument   An argument whose conclusion does not necessarily follow from the premises.

issue   A point that is or might be disputed, debated, or wondered about. Issues are often introduced by the word "whether," as in the example "whether this train goes to Chattanooga."

law of large numbers   A rule stating that the larger the number of chance-determined, repetitious events considered, the closer the alternatives will approach predictable ratios. Example: The more times you flip a coin, the closer the results will approach 50 percent heads and 50 percent tails.

legal moralism   The theory that, if an activity is immoral, it should also be illegal.

legal paternalism   The theory that a restriction on a person's freedom can sometimes be justified by showing that it is for that person's own benefit.

leveling   The process of omitting or de-emphasizing features in a description of a person, thing, or event, when the person doing the describing does not think those features are important. The result can be a distorted description.

line-drawing fallacy   The fallacy of insisting that a line must be drawn at some precise point when in fact it is not necessary that such a line be drawn.

loaded question   A question that rests on one or more unwarranted or unjustified assumptions.

logic   The branch of philosophy concerned with whether the reasons presented for a claim, if those reasons were true, would justify accepting the claim.

matter of fact   *See* factual matter.

matter of pure opinion   *See* nonfactual issue.

mean   A type of average. The arithmetic mean of a group of numbers is the number that results when their sum is divided by the number of members in the group.

median   A type of average. In a group of numbers, as many numbers of the group are larger than the median as are smaller.

mode   A type of average. In a group of numbers, the mode is the number occurring most frequently.

modus ponens   An argument consisting of a conditional claim as one premise, a claim that affirms the antecedent of the conditional as a second premise, and a claim that affirms the consequent of the conditional as the conclusion.

modus tollens   An argument consisting of a conditional claim as one premise, a claim that denies the consequent of the conditional as a second premise, and a claim that denies the antecedent of the conditional as the conclusion.

moral relativism   The view that what is morally right and wrong depends on and is determined by one's group or culture.

nationalism   A powerful and often fierce emotional attachment to one's country that can lead a person to blind endorsement of any policy or practice of that country. ("My country, right or wrong!") It is a subdivision of the group think fallacy.

naturalistic fallacy   The assumption that one can conclude directly from a fact (what "is") what a rule or a policy should be (an "ought") without a value-premise.

negation   The contradictory of a particular claim.

negative claim   A claim that excludes one class or part of one class from another: E- and O-claims.

nonexperimental cause-to-effect study   A study designed to test whether something is a causal factor for a given effect. Such studies are similar to controlled cause-to-effect experiments, except that the members of the experimental group are not exposed to the suspected causal agent by the investigators; instead, exposure has resulted from the actions or circumstances of the individuals themselves.

nonexperimental effect-to-cause study   A study designed to test whether something is a causal factor for a given effect. Such studies are similar to non-experimental cause-to-effect studies, except that the members of the experimental group display *the effect*, as compared with a control group whose members do not display the effect. Finding that the suspected cause is significantly more frequent in the experimental group is reason for saying that the suspected causal agent is a causal factor in the population involved.

nonfactual claim   A claim about a nonfactual issue.

nonfactual issue/question   An issue concerning which neither of two disagreeing parties is required to be mistaken or concerning which there is no generally accepted method of resolving.

non sequitur   The fallacy of irrelevant conclusion; an inference that does not follow from the premises.

objective claim   A claim about a factual matter. Objective claims are true or false regardless of our personal experiences, tastes, biases, and so on.

obverse   The obverse of a categorical claim is that claim that is directly across from it in the square of opposition, with the predicate term changed to its complementary term.

offense principle   The claim that an action or activity can justifiably be made illegal if it is sufficiently offensive.

opinion   A claim that somebody believes to be true.

outrage, "argument" from   An attempt to persuade others by provoking anger in them, usually by inflammatory words, followed by a "conclusion" of some sort.

peer pressure "argument"   A fallacious pattern of reasoning in which you are in effect threatened with rejection by your friends, relatives, etc., if you don't accept a certain claim.

perfectionist fallacy   Concluding that a policy or proposal is bad simply because it does not accomplish its goal to perfection.

personal attack ad hominem   A pattern of fallacious reasoning in which we refuse to accept another's argument because there is something about the person we don't like or of which we disapprove. A form of ad hominem.

pity, "argument" from   Supporting a claim by arousing pity rather than offering legitimate argument.

poisoning the well   Attempting to discredit in advance what a person might claim by relating unfavorable information about the person.

popularity, "argument" from   Accepting or urging others to accept a claim simply because all or most or some substantial number of people believe it—to do this is to commit a fallacy.

***post hoc, ergo propter hoc*, fallacy of**   Reasoning that X caused Y simply because Y occurred after X.

precising definition   A definition that limits the applicability of a term whose usual meaning is too vague for the use in question.

predicate term   The noun or noun phrase that refers to the second class mentioned in a standard-form categorical claim.

predictable ratio   The ratio that results of a series of events can be expected to have given the antecedent conditions of the series. Examples: The predictable ratio of a fair coin flip is 50 percent heads and 50 percent tails; the predictable ratio of sevens coming up when a pair of dice is rolled is 1 in 6, or just under 17 percent.

premise   The claim or claims in an argument that provide the reasons for believing the conclusion.

premise indicator   A word or phrase (e.g., "because") that ordinarily indicates the presence of the premise of an argument.

prescriptive claim   A claim that states how things ought to be. Prescriptive claims impute values to actions, things, or situations. *Contrast with* descriptive claims.

principle of utility   The basic principle of utilitarianism, to create as much overall happiness and/or to limit unhappiness for as many as possible.

proof surrogate   An expression used to suggest that there is evidence or authority for a claim without actually saying that there is.

property in question   In inductive generalizations and analogical arguments, the members of a sample are said to have a property. This property is the "property in question."

pseudoreason   A consideration offered in support of a position that is not relevant to the truth or falsity of the issue in question.

question-begging argument   An argument whose conclusion restates a point made in the premises or clearly assumed by the premises. Although such an argument is technically valid, anyone who doubts the conclusion of a question-begging argument would have to doubt the premises, too.

random sample   *See* random selection process.

random selection process   Method of drawing a sample from a target population so that each member of the target population has an equal chance of being selected.

rationalizing   Using a false pretext in order to satisfy our desires or interests.

red herring   *See* smokescreen.

reductio ad absurdum   An attempt to show that a claim is false by demonstrating that it has false or absurd logical consequences; literally, "reducing to an absurdity."

refutation via hasty generalization   When we ask someone to reject a general claim on the basis of an example or two that run counter to the claim, we commit a fallacy known as "refutation via hasty generalization."

relativism   The view that two different cultures can be correct in their differing opinions on the same factual issue.

relevant/relevance   A consideration is relevant to an issue if it is not unreasonable to suppose that its truth has some bearing on the truth or falsity of the issue. *See also* relevant difference

relevant difference   A relevant difference is one that is not unreasonable to suppose caused the feature in question.

representative sample   A sample that possesses all relevant features of a target population and possesses them in proportions that are similar to those of the target population.

rhetoric   In our usage, "rhetoric" is language used primarily to persuade or influence beliefs or attitudes rather than to prove logically.

rhetorical comparison   A comparison used to express or influence attitudes or affect behavior; such comparisons often make use of images with positive or negative emotional associations.

rhetorical definition   A definition used to convey or evoke an attitude about the defined term and its denotation; such definitions often make use of images with positive or negative emotional associations.

rhetorical devices   Rhetorical devices are used to influence beliefs or attitudes through the associations, connotations, and implications of words, sentences, or more extended passages. Rhetorical devices include slanters and fallacies. While rhetorical devices may be used to enhance the persuasive force of arguments, they do not add to the logical force of arguments.

rhetorical explanation   An explanation intended to influence attitudes or affect behavior; such explanations often make use of images with positive or negative emotional associations.

rhetorical force   *See* emotive force.

sample   That part of a class referred to in the premises of a generalizing argument.

sample size   One of the variables that can affect the size of the error margin or the confidence level of certain inductive arguments.

scapegoating   Placing the blame for some bad effect on a person or group of people who are not really responsible for it, but who provide an easy target for animosity.

scare tactics   Trying to scare someone into accepting or rejecting a claim. A common form includes merely describing a frightening scenario rather than offering evidence that some activity will cause it.

self-contradictory claim   A claim that is analytically false.

semantically ambiguous claim   An ambiguous claim whose ambiguity is due to the ambiguity of a word or phrase in the claim.

sharpening   The process of exaggerating those points that a speaker thinks are important when he or she is describing some person, thing, or event. The result can be a distorted description.

slanter   A linguistic device used to affect opinions, attitudes, or behavior without argumentation. Slanters rely heavily on the suggestive power of words and phrases to convey and evoke favorable and unfavorable images.

slippery slope   A form of fallacious reasoning in which it is assumed that some event must inevitably follow from some other, but in which no argument is made for the inevitability.

smokescreen   An irrelevant topic or consideration introduced into a discussion to divert attention from the original issue.

social utility   A focus on what is good for society (usually in terms of overall happiness) when deciding on a course of action. *See also* principle of utility.

sound argument   A valid argument whose premises are true.

spin   A type of rhetorical device, often in the form of a red herring or complicated euphemism to disguise a politician's statement or action that might otherwise be perceived in an unfavorable light.

square of opposition   A table of the logical relationships between two categorical claims that have the same subject and predicate terms.

standard-form categorical claim   Any claim that results from putting words or phrases that name classes in the blanks of one of the following structures: "All _____ are _____"; "No _____ are _____"; "Some _____ are _____"; and "Some _____ are not _____."

stare decisis   "Letting the decision stand." Going by precedent.

statistical significance   To say that some finding is statistically significant at a given confidence level—say, .05—is essentially to say that the finding could have arisen by chance in only about five cases out of one hundred.

stereotype   An oversimplified generalization about the members of a class.

stipulative definition   A definition used to introduce an unfamiliar term or to assign a new meaning to a familiar term.

straw man   A type of fallacious reasoning in which someone ignores an opponent's actual position and presents in its place a distorted, exaggerated, or misrepresented version of that position.

strong argument   An argument that has this characteristic: On the assumption that the premises are true, the conclusion is unlikely to be false.

subcontrary claims   Two claims that can both be true at the same time but cannot both be false at the same time.

subject term   The noun or noun phrase that refers to the first class mentioned in a standard-form categorical claim.

subjective claim   A claim expressing a person's subjective state of mind. *See* nonfactual claim.

subjectivism   The assumption that what is true for one person is not necessarily true for another.

subjectivist fallacy   This pattern of fallacious reasoning: "Well, X may be true for you, but it isn't true for me," said with the intent of dismissing or rejecting X.

syllogism   A deductive argument with two premises.

syntactically ambiguous claim   An ambiguous claim whose ambiguity is due to the structure of the claim.

synthetic claim   A claim whose truth value cannot be determined simply by understanding the claim—an observation of some sort is also required. *Contrast with* analytic claim.

target   In the conclusion of an inductive generalization, the members of an entire class of things is said to have a property or feature. This class is the "target" or "target class." In the conclusion of an analogical argument, one or more individual things is said to have a property or feature. The thing or things is the "target" or "target item."

target class   The population, or class, referred to in the conclusion of a generalizing argument.

target item   *See* target.

term   A word or an expression that refers to or denotes something.

tradition, "argument" from   "Arguing" that a claim is true on the grounds that it is traditional to believe it is true.

truth-functional equivalence   Two claims are truth-functionally equivalent if and only if they have exactly the same truth table.

truth-functional logic   A system of logic that specifies the logical relationships among truth-functional claims—claims whose truth values depend solely upon the truth values of their simplest component parts. In particular, truth-functional logic deals with the logical functions of the terms "not," "and," "or," "if . . . then," and so on.

truth table   A table that lists all possible combinations of truth values for the claim variables in a symbolized claim or argument and then specifies the truth value of the claim or claims for each of those possible combinations.

two wrongs make a right   This pattern of fallacious reasoning: "It's acceptable for A to do X to B because B would do X to A," said where A's doing X to B is not necessary to prevent B's doing X to A.

utilitarianism   The moral position unified around the basic idea that we should promote happiness as much as possible and weigh actions or derivative principles in terms of their utility in achieving this goal.

vague claim   A claim that lacks sufficient precision to convey the information appropriate to its use.

valid argument   An argument that has this characteristic: On the assumption that the premises are true, it is impossible for the conclusion to be false.

Venn diagram   A graphic means of representing a categorical claim or categorical syllogism by assigning classes to overlapping circles. Invented by English mathematician John Venn (1834–1923).

virtue ethics   The moral position unified around the basic idea that each of us should try to perfect a virtuous character that we exhibit in all actions.

weaseler   An expression used to protect a claim from criticism by weakening it.

wishful thinking   Accepting a claim because you want it to be true, or rejecting it because you don't want it to be true.

Answers, Suggestions, and Tips for Exercises Marked with a Triangle

Chapter 1: Thinking Critically: It Matters

Exercise 1-1

1. An argument is an attempt to support a claim or an assertion by providing a reason or reasons for accepting it.

4. Yes

7. No

10. It can be implied.

13. No

16. False

19. True

20. True

Exercise 1-3

1. Argument

4. No argument

7. Argument

10. Argument

Exercise 1-4

1. No argument

4. Argument

7. Argument

10. No argument

13. No argument (Warren says that there are reasons for her conclusion, but she doesn't tell us what they are.)

16. No argument

19. No argument

Exercise 1-5

1. a. The other three claims in the paragraph are offered as *reasons* for the claim that Hank ought not to take the math course.

3. d. The other two claims are given as reasons for believing claim d; they are premises of an argument and claim d is the conclusion.

4. c. The remainder of the passage provides examples of what is claimed in c. The claims in which these examples appear function as premises for c.

13. b. There is a lot of information in this passage, but answer (b) is certainly the *main* issue of the selection. The easiest way to see this is to notice that almost all of the claims made in the passage support this one. We'd put answer (c) in second place.

14. c. Answers (a) and (b) don't capture the futility of the prison policy expressed in the passage; answer (d) goes beyond what is expressed in the passage.

15. c. Answer (b) is in the running, but it is clear from the passage that the author isn't interested so much in whether the permit holders are individuals or corporations as in whether they are big-time operators or small-time operators.

16. b

20. c

Exercise 1-6 _____

1. Whether police brutality happens very often

4. Whether there exists a world that is essentially independent of our minds

7. Whether a person who buys a computer should take some lessons

10. Whether Native Americans, as true conservationists, have something to teach readers about our relationship to the earth. There are other points made in the passage, but they are subsidiary to this one.

Exercise 1-7 _____

1. There are two issues: whether they're going on Standard Time the next weekend and whether they'll need to set the clocks forward or back. Both speakers address both issues.

4. The issue is whether complaints about American intervention abroad are good or bad. Both speakers address this issue.

Exercise 1-8 _____

1. Suburbanite misses Urbanite's point. Urbanite addresses the effects of the requirement; Suburbanite addresses the issue of whether he and his neighbors can afford to comply with it.

3. On the surface, it may seem that both Hands address the issue of whether a person such as One Hand can feel safe in her own home. But it's clear that One Hand's real issue is whether the large number of handguns makes one unsafe in one's own home. Other Hand ignores this issue completely.

5. The issue for both parties is whether Fed-Up will be happier if he retires to Arkansas.

Exercise 1-9 _____

The distinction used is between factual claims and nonfactual claims.

1. Factual

4. Nonfactual

7. Factual

10. Factual

Exercise 1-10 _____

1. Factual

4. Factual

7. Factual. Although this is not possible to resolve as a practical matter, we can at least imagine circumstances under which we could test for life on any given planet.

10. Nonfactual

13. Nonfactual. This one is very controversial, of course, but if there were an agreed-upon method of settling the issue, it would have long since ceased to be so controversial. This is an obvious case where the claim's being nonfactual does not in the least prevent its being very important.

Exercise 1-11 _____

The factual claims are 2, 4, 6, 8.

Exercise 1-12 _____

1. The house, a two-story colonial-style building, burned to the ground.

4. The Coors Brewing Company began offering gay partners the same benefits as spouses in 1995.

7. McCovey was able to finish the assignment on time.

10. The Reverend Jesse Jackson's visit to Pakistan has been delayed due to lack of support from the Bush administration.

13. For two years the rapidly expanding global computer matrix had concerned Gates.

Exercise 1-13 _____

1. No nonfactual elements present

4. No nonfactual elements present

7. The second sentence is arguably nonfactual, since the phrase "on the face of it" is something about which disagreements might be difficult to settle. On the other hand, the phrase "might be" is such a strong weaseler (see Chapter 4), one might say that this sentence commits to very little at all.

10. One might change the second sentence to read, "Those who felt character was important went on to elect one who some think has the feeblest intellect of any president in history."

Exercise 1-14

1. b
4. b
7. b
10. a

Exercise 1-15

1. Argument
4. Argument
7. Explanation
10. Explanation

Chapter 2: Critical Thinking and Clear Writing

Exercise 2-2

7, 6, 4, 1, 3, 2, 5

Exercise 2-3

1. "Piano" is defined analytically.
4. "Red planet" is defined by synonym. (This one is tricky because it looks like a definition by example. But there is only *one* red planet, so the phrase refers to exactly the same object as the word "Mars.")
8. "Chiaroscuro" is defined by synonym.
11. "Significant other" is defined by example— several of them.

Exercise 2-4

1. The Raider tackle blocked the Giants linebacker.
4. How Therapy Can Help Victims of Torture
7. Susan's nose resembles Hillary Clinton's.
10. 6 Coyotes That Maul Girl Are Killed by Police
13. Second sentence: More than one disease can be carried and passed along to humans by a single tick.
16. We give to life good things.
19. Dunkelbrau—for those who crave the best-tasting real German beer
22. Jordan could write additional profound essays.
25. When she lay down to nap, she was disturbed by a noisy cow.
28. When Queen Elizabeth appeared before her troops, they all shouted "harrah."
32. AT&T, for as long as your business lasts.
33. This class might have had a member of the opposite sex for a teacher.
34. Married 10 times before, woman gets 9 years in prison for killing her husband.

Exercise 2-5

1. As a group
4. As a group
7. It's more likely that the claim refers to the Giants as a group, but it's possible that it refers to the play of individuals.
10. As individuals
12. Probably as individuals
15. Ambiguous. If the claim means that people are living longer than they used to, the reference is to people as individuals. If the claim means that the human race is getting older, then the reference is to people as a group. If the claim expresses the truism that to live is to age, then the reference is to people as individuals.

Exercise 2-6

In order of decreasing vagueness:

1. (d), (e), (b), (c), (f), and (a). Compare (e) and (b). If Eli and Sarah made plans for the future, then they certainly discussed it. But just discussing it is more vague—they could do that with or without making plans.
4. (c), (d), (e), (a), (b)

Exercise 2-7

1. a

4. b

7. a. But it's close.

10. b

15. a

Exercise 2-8

1. Too vague. Sure, you can't say exactly how much longer you want it cooked, but you can provide guidelines; for example, "Cook it until it isn't pink."

4. Not too vague.

7. Not too vague.

10. If this is the first time you are making frosting or if you are an inexperienced cook, this phrase is too vague.

Exercise 2-10

"Feeding" simply means "fertilizing" and is not too vague. "Frequently" is too vague. "No more than half" is not too vague. "Label-recommended amounts" is not too vague. "New year's growth begins" and "each bloom period ends" are pretty vague for a novice gardener, but because pinpoint timing apparently isn't crucial, the vagueness here is acceptable. "Similar" is too vague for a novice gardener. "Immediately after bloom" suggests that precise timing is important here, and we find the phrase too vague, at least for novices. "When the nights begin cooling off" is too vague even if precision in timing isn't terribly important.

Exercise 2-11

1. Twenty percent more than what? (You might wonder what "real dairy butter" is, but it's probably safe to assume that it's just plain old butter.)

4. This is not too bad, but the word "desert" covers a lot of territory—not all deserts are like the Sahara.

7. The comparison is okay, but don't jump to the conclusion that today's seniors are better students. Maybe the teachers are easier graders.

10. In the absence of absolute figures, this claim does not provide any information about how good attendance was (or about how brilliant the season was).

Exercise 2-12

1. Superior? In what way? More realistic character portrayal? Better expression of emotion? Probably the claim means only "I like Paltrow more than I like Blanchett."

4. Fine, but don't infer that they both grade the same. Maybe Smith gives 10 percent A's and 10 percent F's, 20 percent B's and 20 percent D's, and 40 percent C's, whereas Jones gives everyone a C. Who do you think is the more discriminating grader, given this breakdown?

7. Well, first of all, what is "long-distance"? Second, and more important, how is endurance measured? People do debate such issues, but the best way to begin a debate on this point would be by spelling out what you mean by "requires more endurance."

10. This is like a comparison of apples and oranges. How can the popularity of a movie be compared with the popularity of a song?

Exercise 2-13

1. The price-earnings ratio is a traditional (and reasonable) measure of a stock, and the figure is precise enough. Whether this is good enough reason to worry about the stock market is another matter; such a conclusion may not be supported by the price-earnings figure.

4. "Attend church regularly" is a bit vague; a person who goes to church each and every Christmas and Easter is a regular, although infrequent, attender. We don't find "majority" too vague in this usage.

7. "Contained more insights" is much too vague. The student needs to know more specifically what was the matter with his or her paper, or at least what was better about the roommate's paper.

10. These two sorts of things are much too different to be compared in this way. If you're starving, the chicken looks better; if you need to get from here to there, it's the Volkswagen. (This is the kind of question Moore likes to ask people. Nobody can figure out why.)

Exercise 2-15

1. Students should choose majors with considerable care.

4. If a nurse can find nothing wrong with you in a preliminary examination, a physician will be recommended to you. However, in this city physicians wish to protect themselves by having you sign a waiver.

7. Soldiers should be prepared to sacrifice their lives for their comrades.

10. Petitioners over sixty should have completed form E-7. ["He(she)" is awkward and retains sexist implications.]

13. Language is nature's greatest gift to humanity.

16. The proof must be acceptable to the rational individual.

17. The country's founders believed in the equality of all.

20. Athletes who want to play for the National Football League should have a good work ethic.

24. Most U.S. senators are men.

27. Mr. Macleod doesn't know it, but Ms. Macleod is a feminist.

30. To be a good politician, you have to be a good salesperson.

Exercise 2-16

In case you couldn't figure it out, the friend is a woman.

Chapter 3: Credibility

Exercise 3-5

Something like number 9 is probably true, given the huge, almost unimaginable difference in wealth between the richest and the poorest people on the planet, but we have no idea what the actual numbers are. We've seen number 12 going around the Web, but we don't know whether there's anything to it and we're not interested in conducting the appropriate experiments. We think the rest of these don't have much of a chance (although there are conspiracy theorists who seem to believe number 10.)

Exercise 3-8

1. In terms of expertise, we'd list (d), (c), and (b) first. Given what we've got to go on, we wouldn't assign expert status to either (a) or (e). We'd list all entries as likely to be fairly unbiased except for (a), which we would expect to be very biased.

3. Expertise: (b) first, then (a), then (c) and (d) about equal, and (e) last. We'd figure that (b) is most likely to be unbiased, with (c), (d), and (e) close behind; Choker would be a distant last on this scale. Her bad showing on the bias scale more than makes up for her high showing on the expertise scale.

Exercise 3-9

1. The most credible choices are either the FDA or *Consumer Reports*, both of which investigate health claims of the sort in question with reasonable objectivity. The company that makes the product is the least credible source because it is the most likely to be biased. The owner of the health food store would not qualify in the area of drugs, even if she is very knowledgeable regarding nutrition. Your local pharmacist can reasonably be regarded as credible, but he or she may not have access to as much information as the FDA or *CR*.

2. It would probably be a mistake to consider any of the individuals on this list more expert than the others, although different kinds and different levels of bias are fairly predictable on the parts of the victim's father, the NRA representative, and possibly the police chief. The senator might be expected to have access to more data that are relevant to the issue, but that would not in itself make his or her credibility much greater than that of the others. The problem here is that we are dealing with a value judgment that depends very heavily upon an individual's point of view rather than his or her expertise. What is important to this question is less the credibility of the person who gives us an answer than the strength of the supporting argument, if any, that he or she provides.

3. Although problem 2 hinges on a value judgment, this one calls for an interpretation of the original intent of a constitutional amendment. Here our choices would be either the Supreme Court justice or the constitutional historian, with a slight preference for the latter because Supreme Court justices are concerned more with constitutional issues as they have been interpreted by other courts than with original intent. The NRA representative is paid to speak for a certain point of view and would be the least credible in our view. The senator and the U.S. President would fall somewhere in between: Both might reasonably be expected to be knowledgeable about constitutional issues, but much less so than our first two choices.

Exercise 3-10

1. Professor Hilgert would possess the greatest degree of credibility and authority on (d), (f), and (h), and, compared with someone who had not lived in both places, on (i).

Exercise 3-12

1. We'd accept this as probably true—but probably only *approximately* true. It's difficult to be precise about such matters; Campbell will most likely lay off *about* 650 workers, including *about* 175 at its headquarters.

8. We'd accept this as likely.

12. No doubt cats that live indoors do tend to live longer than cats that are subject to the perils of outdoor life. If statistics on how much longer indoor cats live on the average were available, we'd expect the manufacturer to know them. But we suspect that such statistics would be difficult to establish (and probably not worth the effort), and we therefore have little confidence in the statistic cited here.

20. We'd reject this.

Chapter 4: Persuasion Through Rhetoric

Exercise 4-1

1. c

4. e

7. a

10. c

12. c

15. T

Exercise 4-2

(1) hyperbole (in Chapter 6 we'll call this "straw man"), (2) dysphemism, (3) not a rhetorical device, (4) dysphemism, (5) not a rhetorical device, (6) dysphemism

Exercise 4-3

(1) dysphemism, (2) dysphemism, (3) hyperbole, (4) weaseler, (5) proof surrogate, (6) not a downplayer in this context, (7) loaded question

Exercise 4-8

1. The quotation marks downplay the quality of the school.

4. Persuasive definition

6. No rhetorical device present

8. "Gaming" is a euphemism for "gambling."

11. "Clearly" is a proof surrogate; the final phrase is hyperbole.

14. "Adjusted" is a euphemism.

Exercise 4-9

1. "Japan, Inc." is a dysphemism.

4. "Getting access" is a euphemism, and, in this context, so is "constituents." We'll bet it isn't just *any* old constituent who gets the same kind of "access" as big campaign contributors.

7. The last sentence is hyperbolic.

10. (We really like this one.) "Even," in the first sentence, is innuendo, insinuating that members of Congress are more difficult to embarrass than others. The remainder is another case of innuendo with a dash of downplaying. Although it's a first-class example, it's different from the usual ones. Mellinkoff makes you think that Congress *merely* passes a law in response to the situation. But stop and think for a moment: Aside from the odd impeachment trial or congressional hearing, *all that Congress can do is pass laws!* So Mellinkoff's charge really should not be seen as belittling Congress at all.

13. "As you know" is a variety of proof surrogate. The remainder is a persuasive comparison.

18. Lots of them here! To begin, "orgy" is a dysphemism; "self-appointed" is a downplayer. The references to yurts and teepees is ridicule, and "grant-maintained" is a downplayer. The rest of it employs a heavy dose of sarcasm.

Chapter 5: More Rhetorical Devices

Exercise 5-2

1. "Argument" from popularity

4. "Argument" from pity

7. Subjectivism

10. "Argument" from outrage. There is also an example of straw man in the last sentence—we'll meet straw man in Chapter 6.

13. Rationalism (almost certainly)

Exercise 5-3

1. Not very.

3. Relevant. A popular automobile may have continued support from its maker, and this can be advantageous to the owner of such a car.

7. Not relevant. Notice, though, that our likes and dislikes seem to be influenced by the opinions of others, whether we want them to be or not.

10. It can be. Advertising a product as best-selling may create a feeling on the part of consumers that they will be out of step with the rest of society if they don't purchase the advertised product. (But within limits almost any product can be *said* to be popular or a best-seller, so the fact that such a claim is made is no reason for one to feel out of step by not purchasing the product.) Usually, however, the "best-seller" tag is intended to make us think that the product must be good because so many people cannot be wrong. In other words, such ads in effect are appeals to the "authority of the masses" or the "wisdom of society." However, unless you have some reason to believe (a) that the claims made in the ad about *unusual* popularity are *true*, and either (b) that the buyers of the product have themselves bought the product for some reason that applies in your case as well or (c) that you could indirectly benefit from the popularity of the item (popular cars, for instance, hold their resale value), then to buy a product on the basis of such advertising would be falling prey to a fallacy.

Exercise 5-5

1. Scare tactics

4. Apple polishing, with a touch of peer pressure

7. No fallacy

10. Smokescreen/red herring

Exercise 5-6

1. No fallacy

4. Peer pressure

7. Apple polishing

10. "Argument" from outrage

Exercise 5-7

1. Scare tactics

4. *Issue:* Whether this is fallacious depends largely on one's assessment of how likely he or she is to be among the 250 who die from accidents on a given day. In any case, it is not an argument for buying *this company's* accident insurance.

7. Two wrongs make a right

10. Ridicule

14. Common practice

17. We find ridicule in the first paragraph, a red herring in the second, and a loaded question in the third.

Chapter 6: More Fallacies

Exercise 6-2

1. Begging the question

4. Straw man

7. Straw man

10. Line-drawing fallacy (false dilemma)

Exercise 6-3

1. Inconsistency ad hominem

4. Inconsistency ad hominem

7. Circumstantial ad hominem

11. Personal attack ad hominem

Exercise 6-5

1. d
4. b
7. a
10. b

Exercise 6-6

1. c
4. c
7. b
10. c

Exercise 6-7

1. b
4. b
7. e
10. a

Exercise 6-8

1. Straw man, smokescreen/red herring
4. No fallacy. Notice that the passage is designed to attack the company, not the company's product. The wages it pays are relevant to the point at issue.
7. No fallacy
10. False dilemma
13. Genetic fallacy
16. Line-drawing fallacy (false dilemma)
19. Inconsistency ad hominem

Exercise 6-9

1. Circumstantial ad hominem
4. Straw man (Jeanne responds as if Carlos wanted to sleep until noon). Can also be analyzed as false dilemma ("Either we get up right now, at 4:00 A.M., or we sleep until noon.")
7. This begs the question. The conclusion merely restates the premise.
10. False dilemma
13. Misplaced burden of proof

Exercise 6-10

1. This is an example of burden of proof. Yes, it is indeed slightly different from the varieties explained in the text, and here's what's going on. The speaker is requiring proof of a sort that *cannot be obtained*—actually *seeing* smoke cause a cancer. So he or she is guilty of one type of "inappropriate burden of proof."
4. This is false dilemma because Sugarman's alternatives are certainly not the only ones. Notice that he is giving *no argument* against the Chicago study; he is simply using the false dilemma to deny the study's conclusion.
7. Inconsistency ad hominem
10. This is a case of misplaced burden of proof. The speaker maintains that the government is violating the law. The burden of proof therefore falls on the speaker to justify his or her opinion. Instead of doing that, he or she acts as if the fact that officials haven't disproved the claim is proof that the claim is true.

Exercise 6-12

1. Assuming that the sheriff's department has more than two officers, the speaker is misrepresenting her opponent's position. Straw man.
4. Misplaced burden of proof
7. Perfectionist fallacy (false dilemma)
10. This is an ad hominem. It rides the border between personal attack and the circumstantial variety.

Exercise 6-13

1. Ad hominem: inconsistency. You hear this kind of thing a lot.
4. Ad hominem: personal attack
7. Slippery slope
10. Ad hominem: personal attack

Exercise 6-16

1. Perfectionist fallacy (false dilemma)
5. Apple polishing
9. "Argument" from pity and "argument" from outrage
13. Two wrongs; a case can easily be made for common practice as well.
16. Straw man, technically, but this is also ridicule.

Exercise 6-17

1. This is an example of misplaced burden of proof. The fact that the airplane builders *might* be cutting corners is not evidence that they are *in fact* cutting corners. The speaker's contention that the manufacturers may be tempted to cut corners may be good grounds for scrutinizing their operations, but it's not good grounds for the conclusion that they really are cutting corners.

4. Yes—this is clearly fallacious. Bush's remark is irrelevant to the Democrats' claim. This case does not fit one of our regular categories. It's a smokescreen.

5. The quoted remark from Harris is not relevant to the conclusion drawn in this passage. This passage doesn't fit neatly into any of our categories, although ad hominem would not be a bad choice. Notice a possible ambiguity that may come into play: "Having an impact" might mean simply that Harris wants his work to be noticed by "movers and shakers"—or it could mean that he wishes to sway people toward a certain political view. It's likely that he intended his remark the first way, but it's being taken in the second way in this passage.

9. This is a borderline circumstantial ad hominem. It certainly does not follow that Seltzer and Sterling are making false claims from the fact that they are being paid by an interested party. But remember the cautions from Chapter 3: Expertise can be bought, and we should be very cautious about accepting claims made by experts who are paid by someone who has a vested interest in the outcome of a controversy.

Chapter 7: The Anatomy and Varieties of Arguments

Exercise 7-1

1. a. Premise
   b. Premise
   c. Conclusion

2. a. Premise
   b. Premise
   c. Conclusion

3. a. Conclusion
   b. Premise

4. a. Premise
   b. Premise
   c. Conclusion

5. a. Premise
   b. Conclusion
   c. Premise
   d. Premise

Exercise 7-2

1. Premise: All Communists are Marxists.
   Conclusion: All Marxists are Communists.

4. Premise: That cat is used to dogs.
   Conclusion: Probably she won't be upset if you bring home a new dog for a pet.

7. Premise: Presbyterians are not fundamentalists.
   Premise: All born-again Christians are fundamentalists.
   Conclusion: No born-again Christians are Presbyterians.

10. Premise: If we've got juice at the distributor, the coil isn't defective.
    Premise: If the coil isn't defective, then the problem is in the ignition switch.
    [Unstated premise: We've got juice at the distributor.]
    Conclusion: The problem is in the ignition switch.

Exercise 7-3

1. Conclusion: There is a difference in the octane ratings between the two grades of gasoline.

4. Conclusion: Scrub jays can be expected to be aggressive when they're breeding.

7. Conclusion: Dogs are smarter than cats.

10. Unstated conclusion: She is not still interested in me.

Exercise 7-4

1. Independent

3. Independent

6. Independent

9. Independent

12. Independent

15. Dependent

Exercise 7-5

1. Dependent
4. Dependent; one premise is unstated: What's true for rats is probably true for humans.
8. Independent
10. Independent

Exercise 7-6

1. To explain
4. To explain
7. To explain
9. To argue

Exercise 7-7

3. Valid; true
6. False
9. False

Exercise 7-8

(Refer to Exercise 7-2)

1. Invalid
4. Invalid
7. Valid
10. Valid

(Refer to Exercise 7-3)

1. Invalid
4. Invalid
7. The unstated premise "Being more easily trained is a *sure* sign of greater intelligence" would make the argument valid. An unstated premise such as "Being more easily trained is a *good* sign of greater intelligence" would make the argument fairly strong but invalid.
10. Valid

Exercise 7-9

1. Probably true; had "out of order" been written in pencil on the meter, we'd have a different opinion, since most of the meters in our town have those words scrawled on them.

5. Probably true; a restaurant that does a good job on these three different kinds of entrees will probably do a good job on the rest.
9. Probably true; it's possible that the killer cleaned up very thoroughly, but it's more likely that the body was brought from somewhere else.
12. True beyond a reasonable doubt; it may be that consumption will drop in the future or that discovery of new reserves will increase, but as long as consumption at some level continues, *eventually* all the oil will be used up.

Exercise 7-10

1. Assumed premise: All well-mannered people had a good upbringing.
4. Assumed conclusion: He will not drive recklessly.
7. Assumed premise: All dogs that scratch a lot have fleas or dry skin.
10. Assumed premise: Every poet whose work appears in many Sierra Club publications is one of America's outstanding poets.

Exercise 7-11

1. Assumed premise: Most people who are well-mannered had a good upbringing.
4. Assumed conclusion: He will drive safely.
7. Assumed premise: Most dogs that scratch a lot have fleas or dry skin. (Or: When this dog scratches a lot, he usually has either fleas or dry skin.)
10. Assumed premise: Most poets whose work appears in many Sierra Club publications are among America's outstanding poets.

Exercise 7-12

1. Assumed premise: All stores that sell only genuine leather goods have high prices.
4. Assumed premise: No ornamental fruit trees bear edible fruit.
7. Assumed premise: No former professional wrestler could be a very effective governor.
10. Assumed premise: If population studies show that smoking causes lung cancer, then all smokers will get lung cancer.

Exercise 7-13

1. Assumed premise: Most stores that sell only genuine leather goods have high prices.

4. Assumed premise: Few ornamental fruit trees bear edible fruit.

7. Assumed premise: Few people who were professional wrestlers could be very effective governors.

10. Assumed premise: If population studies show that smoking causes lung cancer, then most smokers will get lung cancer.

Exercise 7-14

1.
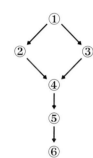

4.

Exercise 7-15

(See Exercise 7-2)

1. ① All Communists are Marxists.
② All Marxists are Communists.

4. ① That cat is used to dogs.
② She won't be upset if you bring home a new dog for a pet.

7. ① Presbyterians are not fundamentalists.
② All born-again Christians are fundamentalists.

③ No born-again Christians are Presbyterians.

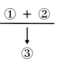

10. ① If we've got juice at the distributor, the coil isn't defective.
② If the coil isn't defective, then the problem is in the ignition switch.
③ The problem is in the ignition switch.

(See Exercise 7-3)

1. ① The engine pings every time we use the regular unleaded gasoline.
② The engine doesn't ping when we use super.
③ There is a difference in octane ratings between the two.

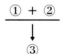

4. ① When blue jays are breeding, they become very aggressive.
② Scrub jays are very similar to blue jays.
③ Scrub jays can be expected to be aggressive when breeding.

7. ① It's easier to train dogs than cats.
② Dogs are smarter than cats.

10. ① If she were still interested in me, she would have called.
② She didn't call.
③ [Unstated] She's not still interested in me.

(See Exercise 7-4)

6. ① You're overwatering your lawn.
② There are mushrooms growing around the base of the tree.
③ Mushrooms are a sure sign of overwatering.
④ There are worms on the ground.
⑤ Worms come up when the earth is oversaturated.

9. ① If you drive too fast, you're more likely to get a ticket.
② (If you drive too fast,) you're also more likely to get into an accident.
③ You shouldn't drive too fast.

12. ① You should consider installing a solarium.
② Installing a solarium can get you a tax credit.
③ Installing a solarium can reduce your heating bill.
④ Installing a solarium correctly can help you cool your house in the summer.

15. ① We must paint the house now.
② If we don't, we'll have to paint it next summer.
③ If we have to paint it next summer, we'll have to cancel our trip.
④ It's too late to cancel our trip.

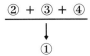

(See Exercise 7-5)

1. ① All mammals are warm-blooded creatures.
② All whales are mammals.
③ All whales are warm-blooded creatures.

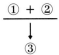

4. ① Rats that have been raised . . . have brains that weigh more. . . .
② The brains of humans will weigh more if humans are placed in intellectually stimulating environments.

8. ① The mayor now supports the initiative for the Glen Royale subdivision.
② Last year the mayor proclaimed strong opposition to further development in the river basin.
③ Glen Royale will add to congestion.
④ Glen Royale will add to pollution.
⑤ Glen Royale will make the lines longer at the grocery.
⑥ [Unstated] The mayor should not support the Glen Royale subdivision.

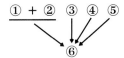

10. ① Jesse Brown is a good person for your opening in Accounting.
② He's as sharp as they come.
③ He has a solid background in bookkeeping.
④ He's good with computers.
⑤ He's reliable.
⑥ He'll project the right image.
⑦ He's a terrific golfer.
⑧ I know him personally.

Exercise 7-16

1. ① Your distributor is the problem.
② There's no current at the spark plugs.
③ If there's no current at the plugs, then either your alternator is shot or your distributor is defective.
④ [Unstated] Either your alternator is shot or your distributor is defective.
⑤ If the problem were in the alternator, then your dash warning light would be on.

⑥ The light isn't on.

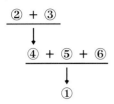

4. ① They really ought to build a new airport.
② It [a new airport] would attract more business to the area.
③ The old airport is overcrowded and dangerous.

Note: Claim number ③ could be divided into two separate claims, one about overcrowding and one about danger. This would be important if the overcrowding were clearly offered as a reason for the danger.

Exercise 7-17

1. ① Cottage cheese will help you to be slender.
② Cottage cheese will help you to be youthful.
③ Cottage cheese will help you to be more beautiful.
④ Enjoy cottage cheese often.

4. ① The idea of a free press in America is a joke.
② The nation's advertisers control the media.
③ Advertisers, through fear of boycott, can dictate programming.
④ Politicians and editors shiver at the thought of a boycott.
⑤ The situation is intolerable.
⑥ I suggest we all listen to NPR and public television.

Note: The writer may see claim ① as the final conclusion and claim ⑤ as his comment upon it. Claim ⑥ is probably a comment on the results of the argument, although it too could be listed as a further conclusion.

7. ① Consumers ought to be concerned about the FTC's dropping the rule requiring markets to stock advertised items.
② Shoppers don't like being lured to stores and not finding advertised products.
③ The rule costs at least $200 million and produces no more than $125 million in benefits.
④ The figures boil down to a few cents per shopper over time.
⑤ The rule requires advertised sale items to be on hand in reasonable numbers.

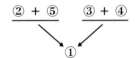

10. ① Well-located, sound real estate is the safest investment in the world.
② Real estate is not going to disappear as can dollars in savings accounts.
③ Real estate values are not lost because of inflation.
④ Property values tend to increase at a pace at least equal to the rate of inflation.
⑤ Most homes have appreciated at a rate greater than the inflation rate. . . .

13. ① About 100 million Americans are producing data on the Internet. . . . .
② Each user is tracked so private information is available in electronic form.
③ One Web site . . . promises, for seven dollars, to scan . . . etc.
④ The combination of capitalism and technology poses a threat to our privacy.

16. ① Measure A is consistent with the City's General Plan and city policies. . . .
② A "yes" vote will affirm the wisdom of well-planned, orderly growth. . . .
③ Measure A substantially reduces the amount of housing previously approved for Rancho Arroyo.
④ Measure A increases the number of parks and amount of open space.
⑤ Measure A significantly enlarges and enhances Bidwell Park.
⑥ Approval of Measure A will require dedication of 130.8 acres to Bidwell Park.
⑦ Approval of Measure A will require the developer to dedicate seven park sites.
⑧ Approval of Measure A will create 53 acres of landscaped corridors and greenways.
⑨ Approval of Measure A will preserve existing arroyos and protect sensitive plant habitats. . . .
⑩ Approval of Measure A will create junior high school and church sites.
⑪ Approval of Measure A will plan villages with 2,927 dwellings.
⑫ Approval of Measure A will provide onsite job opportunities and retail services.
⑬ [Unstated conclusion:] You should vote for Measure A.

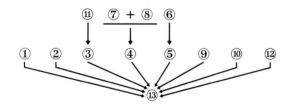

19. ① In regard to your editorial, "Crime bill wastes billions," let me set you straight. [Your position is mistaken.]
② Your paper opposes mandatory life sentences for criminals convicted of three violent crimes, and you whine about how criminals' rights might be violated.
③ Yet you also want to infringe on a citizen's rights to keep and bear arms.
④ You say you oppose life sentences for three-time losers because judges couldn't show any leniency toward the criminals no matter how trivial the crime.

⑤ What is your definition of trivial, busting an innocent child's skull with a hammer?

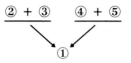

20. ① Freedom means choice.
② This is a truth antiporn activists always forget when they argue for censorship.
③ In their fervor to impose their morality, groups like Enough Is Enough cite extreme examples of pornography, such as child porn, suggesting that they are available in video stores.
④ This is not the way it is.
⑤ Most of this material portrays, not actions such as this, but consensual sex between adults.
⑥ The logic used by Enough Is Enough is that if something can somehow hurt someone, it must be banned.
⑦ They don't apply this logic to more harmful substances, such as alcohol or tobacco.
⑧ Women and children are more adversely affected by drunken driving and secondhand smoke than by pornography.
⑨ Few Americans would want to ban alcohol or tobacco even though they kill hundreds of thousands of people each year.
⑩ [Unstated conclusion] Enough Is Enough is inconsistent.
⑪ [Unstated conclusion] Enough Is Enough's antiporn position is incorrect.

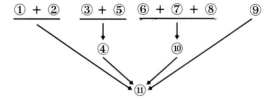

Box: Beer Makes You Smarter

1 = A herd of buffalo can only move as fast as the slowest buffalo.
2 = When the herd is hunted, it is the slowest and weakest ones at the back that are killed first.
3 = This natural selection is good for the herd as a whole.
4 = The general speed and health of the whole group keeps improving by the regular attrition of the weakest members.
5 = The human brain can only operate as fast as the slowest brain cells.

6 = Excessive intake of alcohol kills brain cells.
7 = Alcohol attacks the slowest and weakest brain cells first.
8 = Regular consumption of beer eliminates the weaker brain cells.
9 = The brain is made a faster and more efficient machine.
10 = You always are smarter after a few beers.

Note: 1–4 are offered as an analogy, not as an argument that 10 is true.

Chapter 8: Deductive Arguments I: Categorical Logic

Exercise 8-1

1. All salamanders are lizards.

4. All members of the suborder Ophidia are snakes.

7. All alligators are reptiles.

10. All places there are snakes are places there are frogs.

13. All people who got raises are vice presidents.

16. All people identical with Socrates are Greeks.

19. All examples of salt are things that preserve meat.

Exercise 8-2

1. No students who wrote poor exams are students who were admitted to the program.

4. Some first basemen are right-handed people.

7. All passers are people who made at least 50 percent.

10. Some prior days are days like this day.

13. Some holidays are holidays that fall on Saturday.

16. All people who pass the course are people who pass this test. Or: No people who fail this test are people who pass the course.

19. All times they will let you enroll are times when you've paid the fee.

Exercise 8-3

1. Translation: Some anniversaries are not happy occasions. (True)
Corresponding A-claim: All anniversaries are happy occasions. (False)
Corresponding E-claim: No anniversaries are happy occasions. (Undetermined)

Corresponding I-claim: Some anniversaries are happy occasions. (Undetermined)

4. Translation: Some allergies are things that can kill you. (True)
Corresponding A-claim: All allergies are things that can kill you. (Undetermined)
E-claim: No allergies are things that can kill you. (False)
Corresponding O-claim: Some allergies are not things that can kill you. (Undetermined)

Exercise 8-4

1. No non-Christians are non-Sunnis. (Not equivalent)

4. Some Christians are not Kurds. (Not equivalent)

7. All Muslims are Shiites. (Not equivalent)

10. All Muslims are non-Christians. (Equivalent)

Exercise 8-5

1. Some students who scored well on the exam are not students who didn't write poor essays. (Equivalent)

4. No students who were not admitted to the program are students who scored well on the exam. (Not equivalent)

7. All people whose automobile ownership is not restricted are people who don't live in the dorms. (Equivalent)

10. All first basemen are people who aren't right-handed. (Equivalent)

Exercise 8-6

2. All encyclopedias are nondefinitive works.

4. No sailboats are sloops.

Exercise 8-7

Translations of lettered claims:

a. Some people who have been tested are not people who can give blood.

b. Some people who can give blood are not people who have been tested.

c. All people who can give blood are people who have been tested.

d. Some people who have been tested are not people who can give blood.

e. No people who have been tested are people who can give blood.

2. Equivalent to (c).

4. Equivalent to (c).

Exercise 8-8

1. Obvert (a) to get "Some Slavs are not Europeans."

4. Obvert the conversion of (b) to get "Some members of the club are not people who took the exam."

7. Contrapose (a) to get "All people who will not be allowed to perform are people who did not arrive late." Convert (b) to get "Some people who will not be allowed to perform are people who did not arrive late."

10. Convert the obverse of (b) to get "No decks that will play digital tape are devices that are equipped for radical oversampling."

Exercise 8-9

1. Invalid (this would require the conversion of an A-claim).

4. Valid (this requires the conversion of an I-claim, which is valid).

7. Valid (the premise is the obverse of the conclusion).

10. Invalid (this conclusion does not follow, although its subcontrary, "Some people not allowed to play are people in uniform," does follow).

Exercise 8-10

1. The converse of (a) is the contradictory of (b), so (b) is false.

3. The contrapositive of (a) is a true O-claim that corresponds to (b); and that means that (b), its contradictory, is false.

5. Contrapose (a) to get "Some unproductive factories are not plants not for automobiles." Then obvert (b) to get "No unproductive factories are plants not for automobiles." Because (a) is true, (b) is undetermined.

9. The translation of (a) is "Some people enrolled in the class are not people who will get a grade." The obverse of the converse of (b) is "Some people enrolled in the class are not people who will get a grade." Wow! They're identical! So (b), too, is true.

Exercise 9-11

1. Valid:
   All P are G.
   No G are S.
   No S are P.

4. Invalid:
   All T are E.
   All T-T are E.   (T = times Louis is tired, etc.)
   All T-T are T.   (T-T = times identical with today)

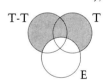

7. Valid:
   All H are S.
   No P are S.
   No P are H.

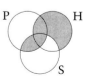

10. Invalid:
    All C are R.
    All V are C.
    No R are V.

(Note: There is more than one way to turn this into standard form. Instead of turning nonresidents into residents, you can do the opposite.)

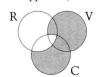

Exercise 8-12

1. No blank disks are disks that contain data.
   Some blank disks are formatted disks.
   Some formatted disks are not disks that contain data.
   Valid:

Formatted disks — Disks that contain data — Blank disks

4. All tobacco products are substances damaging to people's health.
   Some tobacco products are addictive substances.
   Some addictive substances are substances damaging to people's health.

   Valid:

   Addictive substances — Substances damaging to people's health — Tobacco products

7. All people who may vote are stockholders in the company.
   Mr. Hansen is not a person who may vote.
   Mr. Hansen is not a stockholder in the company.

   Invalid:

   Mr. Hansen — Stockholders in the company — People who may vote

Note: Remember that claims with individuals as subject terms are treated as A- or E-claims.

10. After converting, then obverting the conclusion:
    No arguments with false premises are sound arguments.
    Some arguments with false premises are valid arguments.
    Some valid arguments are not sound arguments.

    Valid:

    Valid arguments — Sound arguments — Arguments with false premises

Exercise 8-13

1. A
4. B

Exercise 8-14

1. a
4. b

Exercise 8-15

1. 0
4. 1

Exercise 8-16

1. c
4. c
7. b
10. e

Exercise 8-17

1. All T are F.
   Some F are Z.
   Some Z are T.

   Invalid; breaks rule 2

4. There are two versions of this item, depending on whether you take the first premise to say *no* weightlifters use motor skills or only some don't. We'll do it both ways:

   All A are M.
   No W are M.
   No W are A.

   Valid

   All A are M.
   Some W are not M.
   No W are A.

   Invalid; breaks rule 3

7. Using I = people who lift papers from the Internet
   C = people who are cheating themselves
   L = people who lose in the long run

   All I are C.
   All C are L.
   All I are C.

   Valid

10. D = people who dance the whole night
W = people who waste time
G = people whose grades will suffer

All D are W.
All W are G.
All D are G.

Valid

Exercise 8-18

(Refer to Exercise 8-11 for these first four items.)

2. (Given in standard form in the text)
Invalid: breaks rule 2

5. All voters are citizens.
Some citizens are not residents.
Some voters are not residents.
Invalid: breaks rule 2

7. All halyards are lines that attach to sails.
No painters are lines that attach to sails.
No painters are halyards.
Valid

8. All systems that can give unlimited storage . . . are
systems with removable disks.
No standard hard disks are systems with removable disks.
No standard hard disks are systems that can give
unlimited storage. . . .
Valid

(Refer to Exercise 8-12 for the next four items.)

2. After obverting both premises, we get:
No ears with white tassels are ripe ears.
Some ripe ears are not ears with full-sized kernels.
Some ears with full-sized kernels are not ears with
white tassels.
Invalid: breaks rule 1

5. After obverting the second premise:
Some compact disc players are machines with 24x
sampling.
All machines with 24x sampling are machines that
cost at least $100.
Some compact disc players are machines that cost
at least $100.
Valid

7. All people who may vote are people with stock.
No [people identical with Mr. Hansen] are people
who may vote.
No [people identical with Mr. Hansen] are people
with stock.
Invalid: breaks rule 3 (major term)

8. No off-road vehicles are vehicles allowed in the
unimproved portion of the park.
Some off-road vehicles are not four-wheel-drive
vehicles.

Some four-wheel-drive vehicles are allowed in the
unimproved portion of the park.
Invalid: breaks rule 1

Exercise 8-19

1. A = athletes; B = baseball players;
C = basketball players
Some A are not B.
Some B are not C.
Some A are not C.
Invalid: breaks rule 1

3. T = worlds identical to this one; B = the best of all
possible worlds; M = mosquito-containing worlds
No B are M.
All T are M.
No T are B.
Valid

6. P = plastic furniture; C = cheap furniture;
L = their new lawn furniture
All L are P.
All P are C.
All L are C.
Valid

9. D = people on the district tax roll; C = citizens;
E = eligible voters
All D are C.
All E are C.
All D are E.
Invalid: breaks rule 2

12. C = people identical to Cobweb; L = liberals;
T = officials who like to raise taxes
All C are L.
All L are T.
All C are T.
Valid

17. P = poll results; U = unnewsworthy items;
I = items receiving considerable attention from
the networks
All P are I.
Some P are U.
Some I are U.
Valid

18. E = people who understand that the Earth goes
around the Sun; W = people who understand what
causes winter and summer; A = American adults
All W are E.
Some A are not E.
Some A are not W.
Valid

20. N = the pornographic novels of "Madame
Toulouse"; W = works with sexual depictions
patently offensive to community standards and
with no serious literary, artistic, political, or

scientific value; O = works that can be banned as obscene since 1973

All O are W.
All N are W.
All N are O.
Invalid: breaks rule 2

Exercise 8-20

1. True. A syllogism with neither an A- nor an E-premise would have (I) two I-premises, which would violate rule 2; or (II) two O-premises, which would violate rule 1; or (III) an I-premise and an O-premise. Alternative (III) would require a negative conclusion by rule 1, and a negative conclusion would require premises that distribute at least two terms, the middle term and (by rule 3) at least one other. Because an I-premise and an O-premise collectively distribute only one term, alternative (III) won't work either.

4. True. An AIE syllogism whose middle term is the subject of the A-premise breaks exactly two rules. If the middle term is the predicate of the A-premise, this syllogism breaks three rules.

Exercise 8-23

1. L = ladybugs; A = aphid-eaters; G = good things to have in your garden

   All L are A.
   [All A are G.]
   All L are G.

   Valid

4. S = self-tapping screws; B = boons to the construction industry; P = things that allow screws to be inserted without pilot holes
   All S are P.
   [All P are B.]
   All S are B.

   Valid

Chapter 9: Deductive Arguments II: Truth-Functional Logic

Exercise 9-1

1. Q → P
2. Q → P
3. P → Q
4. Q → P
5. (P → Q) & (Q → P)

Exercise 9-2

1. (P → Q) & R
2. P → (Q & R)

   Notice that the only difference between (1) and (2) is the location of the comma. But the symbolizations have two different truth tables, so moving the comma actually changes the meaning of the claim. And we'll bet you thought that commas were there only to tell you when to breathe when you read aloud.

5. P → (Q → R). Compare (5) with (3).

11. ~C → S

12. ~(C → S)

16. S → ~C. Ordinarily, the word *but* indicates a conjunction, but in this case it is present only for

emphasis—*only if* is the crucial truth-functional phrase.

20. ~(F ∨ S) or (~F & ~S). Notice that when you "move the negation sign in," you have to change the wedge to an ampersand (or vice versa). Don't treat the negation sign as you would treat a minus sign in algebra class, or you'll wind up in trouble.

Box: Sports Logic Symbolizations

(1) B → (C & (J ∨ L))

(2) ((D & J) → B) & ((F & A) → (B → N))

(3) ((W & L) & D) → B

Exercise 9-3

1.

P	Q	R	(P → Q)	(P → Q) & R
T	T	T	T	T
T	T	F	T	F
T	F	T	F	F
T	F	F	F	F
F	T	T	T	T
F	T	F	T	F
F	F	T	T	T
F	F	F	T	F

5.

P	Q	R	Q → R	P → (Q → R)
T	T	T	T	T
T	T	F	F	F
T	F	T	T	T
T	F	F	T	T
F	T	T	T	T
F	T	F	F	T
F	F	T	T	T
F	F	F	T	T

12.

C	S	C → S	~(C → S)
T	T	T	F
T	F	F	T
F	T	T	F
F	F	T	F

Exercise 9-4

1. Invalid:

		(Premise)	(Premise)	(Conclusion)
P	Q	~Q	P ∨ ~Q	~P
T	T	F	T	F
T	F	T	T	F
F	T	F	F	T
F	F	T	T	T

(Row 2)

4. Invalid:

			(Conclusion)	(Premise)		(Premise)
P	Q	R	(P → Q)	~(P → Q)	(Q → R)	P→(Q→R)
T	T	T	T	F	T	T
T	T	F	T	F	F	F
T	F	T	F	T	T	T
T	F	F	F	T	T	T
F	T	T	T	F	T	T
F	T	F	T	F	F	T
F	F	T	T	F	T	T
F	F	F	T	F	T	T

(Row 4)

7. Invalid:

			(Premise)		(Premise)	(Conclusion)
P	Q	R	~Q	P & R	(P & R) → Q	~P
T	T	T	F	T	T	F
T	T	F	F	F	T	F
T	F	T	T	T	F	F
T	F	F	T	F	T	F
F	T	T	F	F	T	T
F	T	F	F	F	T	T
F	F	T	T	F	T	T
F	F	F	T	F	T	T

(Row 4)

Exercise 9-5

We've used the short truth-table method to demonstrate invalidity.

1. Valid. There is no row in the argument's table that makes the premises all T and the conclusion F.

2. Invalid. There are two rows that make the premises T and the conclusion F. (Such rows are sometimes called "counterexamples" to the argument.) Here they are:

L	W	S	P
T	F	F	F
T	T	F	F

(Remember: You need to come up with only *one* of these rows to prove the argument invalid.)

3. Invalid. There are two rows that make the premises T and the conclusion F:

M	P	R	F	G
T	T	F	F	T
T	T	F	T	F

4. Invalid. There are three rows that make the premises true and the conclusion F:

D	G	H	P	M
F	T	T	T	T
F	T	F	T	T
F	T	F	F	T

5. Invalid. There are two rows that make the premises T and the conclusion F:

R	S	B	T	E
T	T	F	F	F
F	F	T	F	F

Exercise 9-6

1. Chain argument

2. Disjunctive argument

3. Constructive dilemma

4. Modus tollens

5. Destructive dilemma

Exercise 9-7

1. 1. R → P   (Premise)
    2. Q → R   (Premise) /∴ Q → P
    3. Q → P   1, 2, CA

4. 1. P → Q   (Premise)
    2. ~P → S   (Premise)
    3. ~Q   (premise) / ∴ S
    4. ~P   1, 3, MT
    5. S   2, 4, MP

7. 1. ~S   (Premise)
    2. (P & Q) → R   (Premise)
    3. R → S   (Premise) / ∴ ~(P & Q)
    4. ~R   1, 3, MT
    5. ~(P & Q)   4, 2, MT

10. 1. (T ∨ M) → ~Q   (Premise)
    2. (P → Q) & (R → S)   (Premise)
    3. T   (Premise) /∴ ~P
    4. T ∨ M   3,   ADD
    5. ~Q   1, 4, MP
    6. P → Q   2,   SIM
    7. ~P   5, 6, MT

Exercise 9-8

1. 4. 1,3, CA
    5. 2,   CONTR
    6. 4,5, CA

4. 4. 3,   CONTR
    5. 2,4, MP
    6. 2,5, CONJ
    7. 1,6, MP

Exercise 9-9

There is usually more than one way to do these.

1. 1. P & Q   (Premise)
    2. P → R   (Premise) /∴ R
    3. P   1,   SIM
    4. R   2, 3, MP

2. 1. R → S   (Premise)
    2. ~P ∨ R   (Premise) /∴ P → S
    3. P → R   2,   IMPL
    4. P → S   1, 3, CA

4. 1. ~P ∨ (~Q ∨ R)   (Premise)
    2. P   (Premise) /∴ Q → R
    3. P → (~Q ∨ R)   1,   IMPL
    4. ~Q ∨ R   2, 3, MP
    5. Q → R   4,   IMPL

8. 1. ~Q & (~S & ~T)   (Premise)
    2. P → (Q ∨ S)   (Premise) /∴ ~P
    3. (~Q & ~S) & ~T   1,   ASSOC
    4. ~Q & ~S   3,   SIM
    5. ~(Q ∨ S)   4,   DEM
    6. ~P   2,5, MT

Exercise 9-10

1. 1. P → R   (Premise)
    2. R → Q   (Premise) /∴ ~P ∨ Q
    3. P → Q   1, 2, CA
    4. ~P ∨ Q   3,   IMPL

4. 1. P ∨ (Q & R)   (Premise)
    2. (P ∨ Q) → S   (Premise) /∴ S
    3. (P ∨ Q) & (P ∨ R)   1,   DIST
    4. P ∨ Q   3,   SIM
    5. S   2,4, MP

7. 1. (M ∨ R) & P   (Premise)
    2. ~S → ~P   (Premise)
    3. S → ~M   (Premise) /∴ R
    4. P → S   2,   CONTR
    5. P   1,   SIM
    6. S   4,5, MP
    7. ~M   3,6, MP
    8. M ∨ R   1,   SIM
    9. R   7,8, DA

10. 1. P ∨ (R & Q)   (Premise)
    2. R → ~P   (Premise)
    3. Q → T   (Premise) /∴ R → T
    4. (P ∨ R) & (P ∨ Q)   1,   DIST
    5. P ∨ Q   4,   SIM
    6. ~P → Q   5,   DN/IMPL
    7. R → Q   2,6, CA
    8. R → T   3,7, CA

Exercise 9-11

1. D → ~B

4. B → ~D

7. C → (B & ~D)

Exercise 9-12

1. Equivalent to (b)

4. Equivalent to (c)

7. Equivalent to (c)

Exercise 9-13

1. 1. P   (Premise)
   2. Q & R   (Premise)
   3. (Q & P) → S   (Premise) /∴ S
   4. Q   2,   SIM
   5. Q & P   1,4, CONJ
   6. S   3,5, MP

4. 1. P ∨ Q   (Premise)
   2. (Q ∨ U) → (P → T)   (Premise)
   3. ~P   (Premise)
   4. (~P ∨ R) → (Q → S)   (Premise) /∴ T ∨ S
   5. Q   1,3, DA
   6. Q ∨ U   5,   ADD
   7. P → T   2,6, MP
   8. ~P ∨ R   3,   ADD
   9. Q → S   4,8, MP
   10. T ∨ S   1,7,9, CD

7. 1. P → Q   (Premise) /∴ P → (Q ∨ R)
   2. ~P ∨ Q   1,   IMPL
   3. (~P ∨ Q) ∨ R   2,   ADD
   4. ~P ∨ (Q ∨ R)   3,   ASSOC
   5. P → (Q ∨ R)   4,   IMPL

10. 1. (S → Q) → ~R   (Premise)
    2. (P → Q) → R   (Premise) /∴ ~ Q
    3. ~R → ~(P → Q)   2,   CONTR
    4. (S → Q) → ~(P → Q)   1,3, CA
    5. ~(S → Q) ∨ ~(P → Q)   4,   IMPL
    6. ~(~S ∨ Q) ∨ ~(~P ∨ Q)   5,   IMPL (twice)
    7. (S & ~Q) ∨ (P & ~Q)   6,   DEM/DN (twice)
    8. ((S & ~Q) ∨ P) &
       ((S & ~Q) ∨ ~Q)   7,   DIST
    9. (S & ~Q) ∨ ~Q   8,   SIM
    10. ~Q ∨ (S & ~Q)   9,   COM
    11. (~Q ∨ S) & (~Q ∨ ~Q)   10,   DIST
    12. ~Q ∨ ~Q   11,   SIM
    13. ~Q   12,   TAUT

Exercise 9-14

1. 1. P → Q   (Premise)
   2. P → R   (Premise) /∴ P → (Q & R)
   ③. P   CP Premise
   4. Q   1,3, MP
   5. R   2,3, MP
   6. Q & R   4,5, CONJ
   7. P → (Q & R)   3–6, CP

4. 1. P → (Q ∨ R)   (Premise)
   2. T → (S & ~R)   (Premise) /∴ (P & T) → Q
   ③. P & T   CP Premise
   4. P   3,   SIM
   5. T   3,   SIM
   6. Q ∨ R   1,4, MP
   7. S & ~R   2,5, MP
   8. ~R   7,   SIM
   9. Q   6,8, DA
   10. (P & T) → Q   3–9, CP

7. 1. P ∨ (Q & R)   (Premise)
   2. T → ~(P ∨ U)   (Premise)
   3. S → (Q → ~R)   (Premise) /∴ ~S ∨ ~T
   ④. S   CP Premise
   5. Q → ~R   3,4, MP
   6. ~Q ∨ ~R   5,   IMPL
   7. ~(Q & R)   6,   DEM
   8. P   1,7, DA
   9. P ∨ U   8,   ADD
   10. ~~(P ∨ U)   9,   DN
   11. ~T   2,10, MT
   12. S → ~T   4–11, CP
   13. ~S ∨ ~T   12,   IMPL

10. 1. (P & Q) ∨ R   (Premise)
    2. ~R ∨ Q   (Premise) /∴ P → Q
    ③. P   CP Premise
    ④. ~Q   CP Premise
    5. ~R   2,4, DA
    6. P & Q   1,5, DA
    7. Q   6,   SIM
    8. ~Q → Q   4–7, CP
    9. Q ∨ Q   8,   IMPL
    10. Q   9,   TAUT
    11. P → Q   3–10, CP

Exercise 9-15

1. C → ~S
   ~L → S
   ‾‾‾‾‾
   C → L
   Valid

4. ~M ∨ C
   ~M → ~K
   C ∨ H
   T → ~ H
   ‾‾‾‾‾
   T → K
   Invalid

7. C ∨ S
   S → E
   C → R
   ‾‾‾‾‾
   R ∨ E
   Valid

10. C → ~L
    (E → (~C → ~T)) & E
    ‾‾‾‾‾
    L → ~T
    Valid

13. S → ~F
    ~S → ~T
    T
    ‾‾‾‾‾
    ~F
    Valid

Chapter 10: Inductive Arguments

Exercise 10-1

1. a
4. b
7. a
10. b
13. b
16. b
19. a

Exercise 10-2

1. b
4. a
7. a
10. b

Exercise 10-3

1. a
4. a
7. a
10. a

Exercise 10-5

1. "Tests in this class" is perfectly clear, "hard" (the property in question) is a little bit vague.
4. "Tolerant of stress" (the property in question) is vague.
7. Weather in Iowa is pretty vague, and so is "weather that sucks."
10. Everything in this one is way too vague.
13. "Suspicious people" is pretty vague, and "quite unhappy" is too.

Exercise 10-6

1. a
4. a
7. b

9. d
12. c

Exercise 10-7

1. In order of increasing cautiousness, we'd say d, f, b, e, a

Exercise 10-8

1. Insufficiently cautious
4. Overly cautious

Exercise 10-9

1. This argument is fairly strong; the conclusion exhibits a reasonable amount of caution.
4. This makes the argument weaker; a relevant difference between the sample and the target.
8. This makes the argument stronger. Since we don't know the terrain of the target ride, a variety within the sample strengthens the argument.
10. If you considered the fact that bicycling is generally easier on flat land than on hilly land, you went beyond the criteria for inductive arguments in general. This is "specialized" knowledge and is part of a different argument: "This year's ride will be on flat land, while previous rides were in hilly terrain. Bicycling is easier on flat land. Therefore, this year's ride will be easier."

Exercise 10-10

1. More cautious
4. More cautious
7. Neither more nor less cautious; the fact of the eclipse is not significant to the property in question.
10. More cautious

Exercise 10-11

1. More cautious
4. Less cautious

Exercise 10-12

1. The six students who turned in written evaluations

4. Generalization

6. No

8. It's not very strong. The sample is small, given that it's not random, and it's very likely to be unrepresentative: The students who bothered to write have relatively strong feelings about Ludlum one way or the other, and there is no reason to think that the spread of their opinions reflects the spread among Ludlum's students in general.

Exercise 10-13

1. No. If he bet that exactly 60 percent held the belief, he would be allowing for no error margin whatsoever. If he makes that bet, take him up on it.

4. 66 percent.

7. With a sample of 100, he can safely bet that no more than 70 percent share that belief, because the error margin is now ± 10 percent.

Exercise 10-14

1. The terms of the analogy are Tiger Woods and the speaker's child. The analogy is strong only if the speaker's child has other features in common with Tiger Woods, such as great powers of concentration, great physical ability, and a proper temperament for golf. It's unlikely that early lessons are as important as these traits.

4. The terms of the analogy are Senator Clinton's performance as a senator and her potential performance as president. There is a great deal more exposure as president and a greater number of constituencies to serve. Still, the similarities are significant. This conclusion gets more support from its premise than many in this exercise.

7. The terms of the analogy are Bush's ratings in Georgia and his ratings in Massachusetts. Since the political scene in these two states is very different, and since they have voted very differently in recent elections, this is not a very good argument.

10. The terms of the analogy are Warren's personal appearance and his care of the Barnes's house. These terms are sufficiently dissimilar—especially as regards their motivations—as to make for a weak argument. It *may* be that Warren's personal grooming will carry over to taking care of the house, but we suspect that many neat-appearing people live in messy abodes.

Exercise 10-15

1. Biased generalization

4. Hasty generalization; quite likely biased, too

8. Hasty generalization; biased, too

10. Biased generalization

13. Refutation by hasty generalization

Chapter 11: Causal Arguments

Exercise 11-1

1. Causal claim

4. Causal claim

7. Causal claim, although a very vague one

10. Not a causal claim

13. Not a causal claim

16. Not a causal claim

Exercise 11-2

1. Effect: cat is not eating; cause: cat is eating mice

4. Effect: the little guy's not dehydrating; cause: giving him water

7. Effect: that people cannot detect their own bad breath; cause: becoming used to the odor

10. Effect: a savings to the state in court expenses; cause: judges' failure to process shoplifting, trespassing, and small-claims charges

Exercise 11-3

1. a

4. b

7. a

10. b

13. a

16. b

19. a

Exercise 11-4

1. C; mowing the grass results in both fumes and grass dust.

4. C; shorter days contribute to both.

7. C; getting older can result in both conditions.

10. B; maybe smarter people eat more fish.

13. B; if there is more violence, there is likely to be more on TV.

16. A

19. A; C is also possible, since good health may have contributed both to Uncle Ted's attitude and to his longevity.

22. A; yes it could.

25. B; top executives can easily afford expensive clothes and nice cars.

Exercise 11-5

1. a

4. c

7. a

10. b, but the claim is vague

14. a

17. b

20. a

Exercise 11-9

1. There are are three causal hypotheses mentioned: One is that drinking wine weekly or monthly may cause dementia; a second is that drinking wine daily probably does *not* prevent dementia; and the third is that regular beer drinking is probably a cause of dementia.

   The study is cause-to-effect, but the study is largely nonexperimental because of the self-selection of the experimental group(s)—i.e., the drinkers—and the control group—the nondrinkers. Nothing is mentioned of the nature or size of

either group. The description of the study is quite vague. Although the source of the study appears to be a legitimate authority, the account given here would lead us to want more details of the study before we'd give more than a very tentative acceptance of the results.

4. Causal claim: Sleeping in a room with a light until age two is a cause of nearsightedness in later years. The study is nonexperimental, cause to effect. No differences between the experimental groups (children who slept with lights on) and the control group (children who slept in darkness). The differences in effect were 24 percent between night light and darkness, and 45 percent between a lamp and darkness. From what is reported, no problems can be identified.

   Although the study is fairly small, the results indicate it is likely that there is a causal connection between the described cause and effect—a d of about 11 percent would be necessary in an experimental study; the higher numbers here help compensate for the nonexperimental nature of the study.

7. Causal claim: Exercise prevents colds. The study is a controlled cause-to-effect experiment, with one experimental group and two control groups. The first control group consists of the ten non-exercising volunteers; the second consists of the experimental group prior to the jogging program.

   The experimental group had 25 percent fewer colds than the first control group and some non-indicated percent fewer than the second control group. We don't know enough about the groups and how they were chosen to tell if there are significant differences. Given the small size of the groups, a d of 40 percent is necessary to have statistical significance. The 25 percent figure is substantial and may indicate a causal connection, but it isn't enough to convince us to take up jogging.

Exercise 11-11

Our evaluations:

1. A, A, A

4. F, C, B

7. A, B, F

Exercise 11-12

1. This explanation is full of problems. It is untestable; its relevance is questionable (we couldn't have predicted blue eyes from a previous incarnation

unless we knew more about the incarnation, but the explanation is too vague to enable us to do that); it contains unnecessary assumptions; and it conflicts with well-established theory about how we get our eye color.

4. Reasonable explanation

7. Poor explanation; circular

10. Poor explanation; untestable (given the fact that subconscious desires are allowed); excessively vague; questionable relevance; conflicts with well-established theory

13. Reasonable explanation

17. Before we accepted this explanation of violence we'd want to consider alternatives: poverty, hopelessness, and discrimination, to name a few. Rap music and TV/movie violence may be reflections of violence rather than causes.

20. This poor explanation is untestable, unreliable, and extremely vague. The nondevout might add that it requires unnecessary assumptions.

Exercise 11-15

1. Explanation

4. Explanation

7. Explanation

10. Explanation

Exercise 11-16

1. Explanation

4. Explanation

5. Explanation used to excuse

Exercise 11-17

Of the first three items, numbers 2 and 3 use explanations to help justify an action (or omission, in the case of 3). Item 1 does not justify any behavior.

Exercise 11-19

1. This is just an explanation of how the garage got this cluttered.

4. This is an argument that Parker is giving a test today.

8. Host gives an explanation of why he can't shave. The explanation is intended to serve as a justification.

10. The speaker is explaining why this is a great movie, and in doing so is arguing that it is a great movie.

12. This is an explanation of why the contamination is getting worse and worse, and it might be used to argue that we should change what we allow people to do.

15. This is an explanation of why you are unable to sleep.

18. The speaker explains how touching the pins can fry the logic circuits and in doing so argues that if you touch the pins, you can expect this to be the result.

21. The author is explaining why women are worse off than men economically and in doing so is arguing that women are worse off. Don't be discouraged by the subtlety of real-life specimens.

25. The writer is explaining what the purpose of the Humane Society is and by doing so is arguing that the Humane Society is not an animal rights organization.

26. This is an explanation used as a justification.

Exercise 11-20

1. There is no argument present.

4. This is an explanation that *might* be used to justify the Rotary's behavior, but given the behavior in question, there is certainly no need to justify it.

7. Explanation used in an argument to justify making the 445 pages of report public.

10. This is an explanation that could easily *and mistakenly* be taken as an attempt to justify a molester's behavior.

Chapter 12: Moral, Legal, and Aesthetic Reasoning

Exercise 12-1

1. Nonfactual
4. Nonfactual
7. Nonfactual
10. Factual

Exercise 12-2

1. Not a value judgment, although it surely hints at one.
4. Value judgment
7. Not a value judgment in the ordinary sense, but since rides are often evaluated by degree of scariness, this may imply such a judgment.

Exercise 12-3

1. Not a moral value judgment
4. Moral value judgment
7. Not a moral value judgment
10. Moral value judgment

Exercise 12-4

2. People ought to keep their promises.
5. A mayor who takes bribes should resign.
7. Anyone who commits a third felony should automatically go to prison for twenty-five years.
8. Whatever is unnatural is wrong and should be avoided.

Exercise 12-5

1. Tory is being consistent in that what he is proposing for *both* sexes is that members of both should have the right to marry members of the *other* sex.
2. To avoid inconsistency, Shelley must be able to identify characteristics of art students, athletes, and children of alumni—for whom she believes special admissions programs are acceptable—and show that, unless they are also in one of the listed categories, these characteristics are not true of affirmative action students: women and members of minorities. Furthermore, the characteristics she identifies must be relevant to the issue of whether an individual should be admitted into the university. It may well be possible to identify the characteristics called for. (Remember that consistency is a necessary condition for a correct position, but it is not a sufficient one.)

3. Marin could be consistent only if he could show that the process of abortion involves killing and capital punishment does not. Because this is impossible—capital punishment clearly does involve killing—he is inconsistent. However, Marin's inconsistency is the result of his blanket claim that *all* killing is wrong. He could make a consistent case if he were to maintain only that the killing of *innocent* people is wrong, and that abortion involves killing innocent people but capital punishment does not. (Each of these last claims would require strong arguments.)

8. To avoid inconsistency, Harold would have to identify a relevant difference between the discrimination law and the marijuana law. In fact, there is one fairly obvious one to which he can appeal: The former has been declared contrary to the state constitution; the latter has not been alleged to be contrary to any constitution. So Harold may object to the failure to implement the latter on grounds that it, unlike the discrimination law, is unconstitutional. (It is a separate matter, of course, whether he can build a strong argument in the case of the marijuana law.)

Exercise 12-9

1. The harm principle: Shoplifting harms those from whom one steals.
2. The harm principle: Forgery tends to harm others.
4. We think the offense principle is the most relevant, because the practice in question is found highly offensive by most people (at least we believe—and hope—so). But one might also include the harm principle, because spitting in public can spread disease-causing organisms.
6. Legal moralism, because many people find adultery immoral; and, to a lesser extent, both the harm principle and legal paternalism, because adultery can increase the spread of sexually transmitted diseases.
10. The offense principle.

Exercise 12-12

1. a. Principle 4
   b. Principle 2
   Compatible

4. a. Principle 5
   b. Principle 2
   Compatible

Exercise 12-13

1. Relevant on Principle 7

4. Relevant on Principle 1

7. Relevant on Principle 3

Exercise 12-14

Principle 1: June's picture does not teach us anything, for no chimp can distinguish between truth and falsity; it is a curiosity rather than a work of art.

Principle 2: By looking at June's very symbolic paintings, we are compelled to accept her vision of a world in which discourse is by sight rather than by sound.

Principle 3: Perhaps the most far-reaching impact of June's art is its revelation of the horrors of encaging chimps; surely beings who can reach these heights of sublimely abstract expression should not see the world through iron bars.

Principle 4: Dear Zookeeper: Please encourage June to keep painting, as the vibrant colors and intense brushstrokes of her canvases fill all of us with delight.

Principle 5: I never thought I would wish to feel like a monkey, but June's art made me appreciate how chimps enjoy perceiving us humans as chumps.

Principle 6: This is not art, for no monkey's product can convey the highest, most valuable, human states of mind.

Principle 7: Whether by the hand of monkey or man, that the canvases attributed to June show lovely shapes and colors is indisputable.

Principle 8: What is art is simply what pleases a person's taste, and June obviously finds painting tasty, as she tends to eat the paint.

Exercise 12-15

1. a

4. b

7. b

Credits

TEXT

43 From Jaime O'Neill, "Who Said What?" *San Francisco Chronicle*, September 2, 2001. Reprinted by permission of the author. **60** "Watch for Weasel Numbers." Reprinted from the June 17, 2002, issue of *Business Week* magazine by permission. Copyright © 2002 by The McGraw-Hill Companies, Inc. **66** Edward Guthmann, "Potter's Take May Be Overhyped." Republished with permission of San Francisco Chronicle, from Edward Guthmann, "Potter's Take May Be Overhyped," *San Francisco Chronicle*, December 4, 2001; permission conveyed through Copyright Clearance Center, Inc. **79** Richard Lederer. "Check Your Chart" by Richard Lederer. Originally published in *Journal of Court Reporting*. Reprinted by permission of the author. **86** Bob Young. "Lovable Trickster Created a Monster with Bigfoot Hoax" by Bob Young, *Seattle Times*, December 5, 2002. Copyright © 2002 Seattle Times Company. Used with permission. **94** Dana Milbank, from "Bush on Iraq: Is He Stretching the Facts?" Copyright © 2002 The Washington Post Writers Group. Reprinted with permission. **99** Caroline Liss.

"Blonds Have Last Laugh," *Sacramento Bee*, October 4, 2002. Compiled by the *Sacramento Bee* from the Associated Press. **108** David Ho, "FTC: No Miracles in Weight Loss." Reprinted with permission of The Associated Press. **110** From Derrick Z. Jackson, "With Teens, 'Truth' Wins," *Boston Globe*, June 5, 2002. Copyright © 2002 by Globe Newspaper Co. (MA). Reproduced with permission of Globe Newspaper Co. (MA) in the format textbook via Copyright Clearance Center. **127** Diane White. "Your Cheatin' Heart," column in the *Boston Globe*, February 3, 1997. Reprinted courtesy of the *Boston Globe*. **145** From a column by Molly Ivins. Copyright © 1999 Molly Ivins. Reprinted with permission from Creators Syndicate. **159** "Positive Outlook Won't Delay Cancer Death, Study Says." Reprinted with permission of The Associated Press. **169** Mitchell Rosenthal, M.D. Letter to the editor published in *Time*, November 25, 2002. Reprinted by permission of the author. **208** Letter to editor of *Freethought Today*, quoted in *Free Inquiry*, Summer 2002. *Free*

Inquiry Magazine, published by the Council for Secular Humanism. Reprinted with permission; Richard Dawkins. Quotation from *Free Inquiry*, Summer 2002. *Free Inquiry Magazine*, published by the Council for Secular Humanism. Reprinted with permission. **214** Marianne Means. Excerpt. Hearst Newspapers. Used with permission. **267** Marilyn vos Savant. "English's Most Versatile Word." Copyright © Parade 1994, 1996. Reprinted with permission from Parade and Marilyn vos Savant. **323** From Marilyn vos Savant, *Ask Marilyn, Parade*, June 13, 1999. Copyright © 1999 Parade. Reprinted with permission from Parade. **374** USA Today. "Students Select Priorities," *USA Today*, September 13–15, 2002. Copyright © 2002 USA Today. Reprinted with permission. **408** "Television's Effect on Kids" from AP/Wide World Photos. Used with permission. **411** Gene Koretz, "E-Commerce: The Buyer Wins." Reprinted from the January 8, 2001, issue of *Business Week* magazine by permission. Copyright © 2001 by The McGraw-Hill Companies, Inc. **415** "HPV Vaccine

of the author.   **A47** Caroline Liss. "Strange Stuff: News Out of the Ordinary," *Sacramento Bee*, November 1, 2002. Compiled by the *Sacramento Bee* from the Associated Press and The Washington Post; "10 Commandments Monument Must Go." Reprinted with permission of The Associated Press. **A48** Sandy Louey. "Regional Digest: Teen Claims Bias After School Bars Her Bid to Be Prom King," *Sacramento Bee,* May 3, 2002. Copyright © 2002 *The Sacramento Bee.* Reprinted with permission. **A49** Robin Estrin. "Stop Barring Men, Feminist Professor Told." Reprinted with permission of The Associated Press. "In Short." Reprinted with permission of The Associated Press.

PHOTOS

xxi © Bettmann/Corbis.   **2** © Bettmann/Corbis.   **7** Sun Herald Staff Photo.   **9** Sacramento Bee Staff Photo.   **43** AP Photo/Eric Draper. **51** Getty Images.   **67** The Everett Collection.   **90** AP Photo/Rob Ostermaier.   **93** Getty Images.   **94** AP Photo/Dan Loh.   **133** AP Photo/ David J. Phillip.   **150** AP Photo/ David Duprey.   **155** © Reuters New Media Inc./Corbis.   **163** Getty Images.   **168** Associated Press AP. **170** Getty Images.   **203** David Haymore; courtesy of April Wells-Hayes.   **292** Marianne Larson **323** Marilyn vos Savant/Parade Magazine.   **326** © Snyder/Archive Photos/Getty Images.   **367** © Bettmann/Corbis.   **396** AP/Wide World Photos.   **403** The Everett Collec-tion.   **445** © Norbert Schafer/ Corbis.   **477** © Erich Lessing/Art Resource, NY. © 2000 Estate of Pablo Picasso/Artists Rights Society (ARS), New York.   **479** (both photos) Discover Magazine.   **483** Tilted Arc, 1981. Weatherproof steel, 12' × 120' × 2-1/2'. Collection: General Services Administration, Washington, D.C. Installed: Federal Plaza, New York. Destroyed by the Federal Government 1989. © 2003 Richard Serra/Artists Rights Society (ARS), New York. Photo courtesy Richard Serra. **484** © Scala/Art Resource, NY.

Index

About the Authors

Both Moore and Parker have taught philosophy at California State University, Chico, for more years than they care to count. Aside from courses in logic and critical thinking, Moore also tries to teach epistemology and analytic philosophy. He is also chair of the department and once was selected as the university's Outstanding Professor. Parker's other teaching duties include courses in the history of modern philosophy and philosophy of law; he has chaired the academic senate and once upon a time was dean of undergraduate education.

Moore majored in music at Antioch College; his Ph.D. is from the University of Cincinnati. For a time he held the position of the world's most serious amateur volleyball player. He and Marianne currently share their house with three large dogs. Moore has never sold an automobile.

Parker's undergraduate career was committed at the University of Arkansas; his doctorate is from the University of Washington. Single now, he has been married to three wonderful women (not at the same time), is a serious amateur flamenco guitarist, drives two British automobiles and a motorcycle (also not at the same time), and goes to Spain when he gets the chance.

Moore and Parker have been steadfast friends through it all.

Brooke Noel Moore and Richard Parker, not necessarily in the order pictured above.